SOCIAL PSYCHOLOGY READINGS

A CENTURY OF RESEARCH

SOCIAL PSYCHOLOGY READINGS

A CENTURY OF RESEARCH

EDITED BY

Amy G. Halberstadt

North Carolina State University

and

Steve L. Ellyson

Youngstown State University

McGRAW-HILL PUBLISHING COMPANY

New York   St. Louis   San Francisco   Auckland   Bogotá
Caracas   Hamburg   Lisbon   London   Madrid   Mexico
Milan   Montreal   New Delhi   Oklahoma City   Paris
San Juan   São Paulo   Singapore   Sydney   Tokyo   Toronto

SOCIAL PSYCHOLOGY READINGS
A Century of Research

1 2 3 4 5 6 7 8 9 0   HAL   HAL   8 9 4 3 2 1 0 9

ISBN 0-07-025543-1

This book was set in Times Roman by the College Composition Unit
in cooperation with Ruttle Shaw & Wetherill, Inc.
The editors were James D. Anker, Maria Chiappetta, and David Dunham;
the production supervisor was Leroy A. Young.
The cover was designed by Jo Jones.
Arcata Graphics/Halliday was printer and binder.

Library of Congress Cataloging-in-Publication Data

Social psychology readings: a century of research / edited by Amy G.
  Halberstadt and Steve L. Ellyson.
      p.   cm.
    Bibliography: p.
    Includes index
    ISBN 0-07-025543-1
    1. Social psychology.   I. Halberstadt, Amy G.   II. Ellyson, Steve L.
  HM251.S6754   1990
  302—dc20   89–12436

ABOUT THE EDITORS

AMY G. HALBERSTADT, a 1981 Ph.D. from The Johns Hopkins University, is presently in the Department of Psychology at North Carolina State University. STEVE L. ELLYSON, a 1974 Ph.D. from the University of Delaware, is presently in the Department of Psychology at Youngstown State University in Ohio where he received the 1989 Distinguished Professor Award for his teaching. Both are members of the American Psychological Association, the American Psychological Society, and the Society of Experimental Social Psychology.

Both have experience teaching in a variety of institutions; Professor Halberstadt taught at Vassar College and Professor Ellyson was previously on the psychology faculty at Beaver College, Linfield College, and the University of California, Davis. Dr. Halberstadt's research interests include nonverbal communication, socialization processes, gender and gender roles, and emotion. She is on the editorial board of the *Personality and Social Psychology Bulletin*, the *Journal of Nonverbal Behavior,* and the *Review of Personality and Social Psychology*. Dr. Ellyson's research interests include human nonverbal behavior, gender issues, altruism, person perception, and attitudes. He is on the editorial board of *Social Psychology Quarterly*.

Dr. Halberstadt has also coached women's fencing at the intercollegiate level and is a nationally ranked foil fencer, while Dr. Ellyson referees college and high school basketball during the winter and plays softball in the summer.

To All Our
Social Psychology Students—
Past, Present, and Future

CONTENTS

LIST OF AUTHORS

Antonia Abbey
Gordon W. Allport
Craig A. Anderson
Solomon E. Asch
James R. Averill
Albert Bandura
Ellen Berscheid
John T. Cacioppo
Hadley Cantril
Charles H. Cooley
Joel Cooper
Christian S. Crandall
John M. Darley
Kay Deaux
M. Robin DiMatteo
Karen K. Dion
John F. Dovidio
Leslie L. Downing
Steve L. Ellyson
Russell H. Fazio
Beverley Fehr
Sigmund Freud
Samuel L. Gaertner
George Gerbner
Lois Gould
David Greene
Larry Gross
Amy G. Halberstadt
Stephen G. Harkins
Albert H. Hastorf
Dianne Herman

Leta S. Hollingsworth
Pamela House
William James
Robert D. Johnson
Ellen Langer
Bibb Latané
Kurt Lewin
Hazel Markus
Stanley Milgram
Michael Morgan
Lee S. Newman
Richard E. Petty
Judith Rodin
Dorothea Ross
Lee Ross
Sheila A. Ross
Stanley Schachter
David Schumann
Jerome E. Singer
Nancy Signorielli
Mark L. Snyder
Elizabeth Decker Tanke
Norman Triplett
Colin M. Turnbull
James S. Uleman
G. William Walster
Elaine Walster (Hatfield)
Russell H. Weigel
Laraine Winter
Elissa Wurf
Mark P. Zanna

PREFACE

The field of social psychology did not exist a hundred years ago. The first attempt to apply experimental methods to social behavior was made by Norman Triplett, in an Indiana University lab in 1898. Since then social psychology has evolved into a dynamic and eclectic discipline probing the hows and whys of human social behavior.

Those of us who teach undergraduate social psychology are continually challenged with the task of presenting a meaningful picture of this field in the ten- to fifteen-week format of most introductory social psychology courses. Moreover, we want our students to be more incisive and careful thinkers. We, the editors of this book, have struggled with these problems for some time. Over a number of years of teaching social psychology, we have developed a set of readings that aims to achieve these goals. We now hope that other instructors and students will find this book of readings helpful in understanding this exciting and impressive field.

A fair question might be, "Why didn't you write a textbook on social psychology, instead of a readings book?" One answer is that there are a number of very good textbooks already on the market. Another important answer is that only through first-hand experience with the research literature can a student come to genuinely appreciate what social psychology is about. This "behind the scenes" vantage point encourages critical thinking more than does reading through the hundreds of quick references in a textbook. We believe that teachers can teach more effectively when using original readings from the literature in conjunction with the broader overview provided by a text. More importantly, students become more actively involved with the research questions because they are able to experience and appreciate the progression from hypotheses to conclusions, from questions to answers, and ultimately to more questions. As a result, students are more insightful, more critical, more curious. With original readings, they learn to *summarize* the goals of the research and what has actually been done. They learn to *analyze* whether the methods test the hypothesis and if the conclusions are supported by the results. They then become able to *integrate* the studies with one another and with their knowledge derived from their text and daily life. And finally, they begin to *generate* new propositions as to the next logical research step or question. This process makes social psychology come alive. And that makes our teaching and students' learning more effective, and, yes, more fun.

Providing a comprehensive and cogent overview of nearly 100 years of research has been a stimulating and rewarding enterprise. As we read and reread, and finally chose the specific readings for this book, we found ourselves organizing the ideas and research in somewhat new ways. This process often challenged our earlier conceptualizations of the field. The result is our own structuring of social psychology in this reader. We have found our organization to be logical in theory as well as effective in practice with any of the major texts.

Each reading is preceded by a short introduction. We wrote these to facilitate integration of the work of so many talented authors, and to provide what we view as common threads in the fabric that is social psychology.

The book is organized into five sections: an introductory section, "Frameworks," followed by "Social Knowledge," "Social Feelings," "Social Values," and "Social Control." The last four sections are constructed around a central issue in human social behavior, and each of these sections is further divided into subsections which reflect that area's major issues. Instead of relegating a separate section on applied social psychology to the back of the book, we have integrated political, health-related, business-related, and developmental applications within the major sections. Additionally, issues raised in one area are often important in other areas as well, thus we have tried to highlight the interrelationships across the area sections.

Section 1, Frameworks, provides an explanatory structure for the remainder of this book. It includes readings which help orient students to the materials that follow. An introductory chapter for students begins the section and is followed by the first formal modern social psychological study and an article by perhaps the most influential social psychologist of the twentieth century, Kurt Lewin.

Section 2, Social Knowledge, begins by examining attitude formation, attitude change, and the attitude-behavior consistency question. "Knowing ourselves" and "knowing others" are subsections that examine the perspective of self, person perception, attribution theory, and social cognition.

Section 3, Social Feelings, explores different accounts of emotion which can then be applied to two subsections. The subsections, "attraction and love" and "aggression and violence," include theory and research specific to those affective behaviors.

Section 4, Social Values, investigates cultural values and how they shape a wide range of social beliefs and behaviors. Included in this section are the subtopics of "stereotyping and prejudice" and "gender issues."

Section 5, "Social Control," focuses on subtle influences that affect our social behaviors as well as the more obvious and classic issues of conformity,
obedience, and persuasion. This section also incorporates considerations of
how groups affect individual behavior. Topics include deindividuation, group
polarization, social facilitation, and social loafing.

These thirty-nine readings from the social psychology literature span nearly
100 years. But this book should not be mistaken for a history reader. Nearly
half of the readings have appeared in the last ten years. Although we do not
claim to have exhaustively covered all possible areas in social psychology, we
have tried to provide a representative sampling of the field.

Readings were chosen in the following way. First, an initial pool of readings
was compiled on the basis of their observed or predicted importance to the
field, and usually their known replicability. Second, readings were evaluated
for their readability and appropriateness for a student audience. From the large
set remaining, readings were selected to create a balance between "basic" and
"applied" issues; between specific, focused studies and more comprehensive
integrative overviews; and among the four major areas of social psychology.
We tried to create a vital dialogue, balancing different attempts to understand
human social behavior.

The selection process was lengthy. Not a few minor and major disputes
arose between the editors during this process. It would have been far easier to
produce a readings book with four times this number of readings, and we have
not been able to include many excellent readings. Also, several of the longer
articles we did include are excerpted, and other articles are edited slightly. We
do not expect that all readings will be assigned to every class, but we do anticipate that students will want to explore some of these topics on their own.
Our aim has been to create a reader with many enticing choices for both the
social psychology instructor and the social psychology student. In short, we
hope that this will be a reader that is *read*.

Special Note about Editing

Some of the readings contained in this book are excerpted and abridged
from their original published forms. As researchers, as well as editors, we
were quite hesitant to alter the work of others. However, in attempting to
cover as many issues in social psychology as possible and to be responsive to
the needs of our audience, cuts were sometimes necessary. When faced with
the dilemma of either judicious trimming of long selections or total omission,
we often chose the former option. While we have attempted to keep such alterations at a minimum, all decisions made in this process are fully our responsibility.

The designation "abridged from" means that deletions are made. For the
most part, these deletions are minor, involving author notes, lengthy or less
essential footnotes, or somewhat redundant information. The designation "excerpted from" means that only a portion of a larger work, such as a book or

book chapter, has been selected for inclusion, and that fairly major editing may have been necessary.

Readers are directed to the copyright acknowledgments (pages 466-467) for information about the editing status of an individual work. In the case of abridged or excerpted works, readers seeking expansion of certain points or related information are strongly encouraged to consult the original publication.

Readers wishing to contact authors are directed to the *American Psychological Association Membership Register* for their current addresses. This book is available in most college and university libraries or departments of psychology and contains information for the majority of the living authors.

Acknowledgments

We are first and foremost grateful to the authors of the selections included in this volume for their permission to reprint their work.

We would also like to thank the fine people at McGraw-Hill, specifically Jim Anker, Maria Chiappetta, David Dunham, and Ann Nevius, for their patience and expertise throughout all phases of the production of this book.

We are also indebted to a number of our students who aided us in our selection and editing process. Their hard work and insight were invaluable. They are Holly Ballengee, Rebecca DenHartog, David A. DeSteno, Tessa L. Edeburn, Jennifer D. Hanson, Gina C. Marinucci, Tom A. Melio, Diane Mikolay, Nancy A. Morrison, and Rachel Wolfe.

Additionally, we express our appreciation to our colleagues and to the reviewers of this book. They are Peter A. Beckett, Youngstown State University; Ellen Berscheid, University of Minnesota; Sandra Carpenter, University of Alabama, Huntsville; Steven Ceci, Cornell University; John F. Dovidio, Colgate University; Ralph V. Exline, University of Delaware; Wm. Rick Fry, Youngstown State University; William G. Graziano, University of Georgia; Albert A. Harrison, University of California, Davis; Mark Masaki, Youngstown State University; Bernard Mausner, Beaver College; William McGuire, Yale University; Susan Mickler, Seton Hall University; James C. Morrison, Youngstown State University; David G. Myers, Hope University; Carol A. Olson, University of Akron School of Law; Kelly Shaver, College of William and Mary; Christopher J. Sweeney, Youngstown State University; Anthony Weston, State University of New York, Stony Brook; and Midge Wilson, DePaul University. Their contributions, in many ways, allowed this project to reach completion.

Finally, we would like to thank our families for their tolerance, encouragement, and grace under pressure. We promise to clean up as soon as this is done.

Amy G. Halberstadt

Steve L. Ellyson

SOCIAL PSYCHOLOGY READINGS

A CENTURY
OF RESEARCH

Frameworks

On Reading the Research Literature

Steve L. Ellyson and Amy G. Halberstadt

Why should you study original journal articles about social psychology? Good question. After all, many of the works reported in this reader will be summarized in your text. Why read further?

First, reading actual articles allows you to get a better understanding of the complexity and richness of the questions social psychologists ask and the answers that they obtain. Textbook authors must provide comprehensive coverage of many topics, so they can only briefly summarize the numerous studies that they describe. This strategy necessarily precludes an in-depth analysis of any one idea or of examples of how research studies investigate a particular topic or theory. This reader, by contrast, includes both in-depth reviews, theoretical discussions, and research studies that explore a variety of important and interesting topics. Also, the historical perspective of this reader highlights how social psychology has developed over the last 100 years.

Second, by reading the original sources you experience the research as directly as anyone can without actually being a participant in that particular study. We think that first-hand encounters with the actual foundations of social psychology enhances one's understanding of the field. Instead of reading someone else's very brief summaries, you can explore the research on your own, without anyone else mediating your analysis of the research questions or how the studies address them.

Third, because no one has predigested the material, you will find yourself organizing the material for yourself. This is an advantage! You may remember from your introductory psychology course that learning is promoted by active processing and organizing of material. You will certainly be doing this as you read and reread these classic and contemporary articles.

A word of caution: These readings are not designed to provide you with final answers. Rather, they are intended to further engage your curiosity about social phenomena. Coming to understand social psychology is a process. It involves questioning assumptions, developing tentative ideas, analyzing those ideas and their underlying assumptions, reworking new tentative hypotheses in association with close examination of data and theory, and analyzing them all over again. Thus, these readings are designed to stimulate further questioning, to help clarify your own assumptions, and to assist you in developing careful, thoughtful models of social behavior.

We encourage you to be an active participant as you encounter the articles in this book. As you read and reread these articles, try to imagine yourself as one of the subjects who took part in the study. What do you think you would have done in this study as a subject, or even as an experimenter? Ask yourself questions. Are the results intuitively plausible? Do they fit your social reality? If so, do the authors' explanations also make sense? What other explanations are possible? If the results don't fit your social experience, can you think of reasons why both the author's results and your own experience might be right (or wrong)? Could your social reality be influenced by idiosyncratic factors or by your own hidden assumptions? Or could the population sample studied be sufficiently different to account for different results? Or are these results counter-intuitive, yet reasonable in retrospect?

Because each of the following articles addresses human social behavior, apply your own knowledge and add to it. Natural curiosity about yourself and other people makes the material intrinsically interesting. Original research reports reveal what lies behind those one- or two-sentence references found throughout your textbooks. Reading the primary research literature takes you backstage at the play, to the sidelines for the sporting event, to a more revealing angle from which to observe the magician. Reading the original report allows a much greater appreciation of exactly what a study did and what the study found. Even though the vocabulary in an article may send you to your dictionary or to your instructor, and the statistics may seem like they are part of some obscure foreign language, don't be dismayed. Tenacity on your part will pay off with an appreciation of the way social psychologists attempt to find meaningful answers to meaningful questions.

One other point is important. It is often difficult to recognize our own perspective as we try to understand the perspectives of other people. Bem and Bem (1970) suggest that some of our assumptions (what they refer to as "nonconscious ideologies") are so entrenched in our culture that we are completely unaware of them. Referring to how an individual comes to have such hidden ground rules, the Bems ask:

> What happens when all [our] reference groups agree, when [our] religion, [our] family, [our] peers, [our] teachers, and the mass media all disseminate the same message? The consequence is a nonconscious ideology, a set of beliefs and attitudes which [we] accept implicitly but which remains outside [our] awareness because alternative conceptions of the world remain unimagined. As we noted earlier, only a very unparochial and intellectual fish is aware that [its] environment is wet. After all, what else could it be? Such is the nature of a nonconscious ideology (p. 89).

We all have underlying perspectives that influence how we come to understand new material. When you read about different cultures or even our own culture at an earlier time in history (for instance, Readings 13, 22, 28), you will become more aware than usual about others' underlying assumptions. As you explore these readings, try to apply this heightened awareness to your own assumptions and basic belief structures.

WHAT YOU WILL ENCOUNTER IN JOURNAL ARTICLES

Most of the readings that follow originally appeared in journals that report social psychology research. Journal studies are, however, written in a different style than the traditional textbook. The goal of the authors who write these articles is to present information clearly, and sometimes to persuade. This kind of writing requires a bit of getting accustomed to and the following should help you to get the most out of these readings.

The American Psychological Association has issued a Publication Manual (1983) with writing guidelines that most journal articles follow. Familiarity with this standardized format helps both beginners and veterans to understand an article's content.

What should you expect to find in a scientific research report? Reports of empirical studies typically include an *abstract*, an *introduction, methods, results, discussion* or *conclusions,* and a listing of *references,* although theoretical and review articles often vary somewhat from this format. It is appropriate at this point to give you a preview of what you are likely to find in each section of a typical journal article.

The Title

The title is usually a brief summary of the main idea of the article. It should, on its own, convey the fundamental issues addressed in the study.

The Abstract

The abstract is a brief overview of the entire article. Its purpose is to present the research in a nutshell. It includes the research goal, the subjects and method, the results and the conclusions, all in about 150 words or less. Since many readers skim the abstract to decide whether or not to read the full article, abstracts are usually well-written and informative, although they can also be intimidating by virtue of having packed so much information into such a small space. If you find yourself bogging down in a particular article, a quick review of the abstract is sometimes an effective way to get back on track.

The Introduction

In the introduction the author describes the reasons for doing the research, what has been done before, and how this is a new question or a novel and/or useful way to address the problem at hand. By carefully positioning the research in a historical context and selectively discussing work that has been done previously, a continuity is established between the research effort and the existing body of literature. Broad theoretical issues are often discussed early in the introduction, followed by an increasingly more specific focus.

Consider the following analogy. Your best friend has moved across the country and you embark on a motor trip to visit her. You will probably first consult regional maps, then a state map, and then a city map, and finally a neighborhood map as you try to locate your friend. The author of an article is also providing maps to readers. The directions become increasingly detailed, the research area more clearly focused. The single house you are looking for is much like the research question addressed by the report. A well-written introduction will allow you to make the trip from general questions to specific hypotheses without too much difficulty.

One thing you are sure to notice in most articles is that there are many references or citations to previously published research. Do not be intimidated by the presence of so many names and dates. Prior research provides much of the rationale for the current study. These citations are evidence that the author has been diligent in surveying the existing literature. The author's collecting and making sense of these citations can also be a time saver if you decide to continue exploring the topic on your own.

In addition to stating the general problem, the introduction describes the particular research strategy that the author uses and the specific hypotheses that will be tested. These hypotheses typically link "independent" variables, i.e., variables that the experimenter believes will affect subject behavior, with "dependent" variables, i.e., the specific subject behaviors, which hopefully are influenced by or "depend" on the independent variable (see the following Statistical Primer). You should search for these statements of what is expected to be found, and be clear in your mind as to exactly how the hypotheses will be tested.

Remember that it is the author's purpose in this section to plead a case for the importance of the research contained in the article. You should be able to follow the logic of the study and understand precisely what the author is examining. Just as your cross-country trip to your friend's house brought you closer and closer to your final destination, so too should the introduction section of a research article guide you to the author's destination, the hypotheses proposed. These are often summarized at the end of the introduction. Thus, the final paragraphs of the introduction are often another good summary to return to if you get bogged down in an article. Now that the author has identified why the research is important and what the research questions are, the next logical step is to find out how those questions will be answered. That is the function of the method section.

The Method Section

The method section is simply a detailed description of the way the study was conducted. Sometimes complex studies will begin with an *overview,* which summarizes the method. Detailed sections about the subjects and procedure then follow.

Subjects   This section is usually a factual account of who the subjects were and how many of them there were. Additional demographic data such as age, sex, race, institutional affiliation, etc., is often included as well. This information allows you to determine the generalizability of the sample, i.e., how applicable the results may be for other populations. The way the subjects were selected is often included as well as any inducements or payments they received to take part in the study. Look for and identify any specific differences between groups, or subdivisions of subjects. Do the subjects bring any differences to the study, such as their sex or personality differences, that might influence their behavior?

Materials If original questionnaires are used or a particular apparatus is employed, the author may provide a full description of these. The specific questions asked of the subjects are sometimes included in the text, or they may be appended at the very end of the article.

Procedure This section should describe what happened to subjects and what was asked of them. Through a step-by-step account of the exact procedures, along with specific instructions given subjects, you should have sufficient detail so that, given the resources, you could come very close to replicating (repeating) the study. The procedure section is also important in that it allows the reader to get the feel of what it would be like to be a subject in the study.

Pay particular attention to the author's attempts to isolate or rule out alternative explanations or reasons (other than the hypothesized ones) for the behavior tested. These attempts at keeping other variables from affecting the behavior of subjects and contaminating the study are as important in a research effort as the need for a sterile environment in the surgery room.

We might consider the analogy of fine-tuning a radio so that the signal you get is static free. There are many stations out there each sending different signals but you are interested in receiving just the one that is your favorite. The better your radio is at signal detection, channel separation, and noise suppression, the better the chances are that you can receive and enjoy any

particular station's output. Social psychologists are trying to receive a signal (in this case the explanation for a social behavior) in an environment that is potentially cluttered by a multitude of extraneous signals (unknown causes or explanations for that social behavior). The quality of research methodology is analogous to the quality of your radio in this example.

Continue to be an active reader and seek answers to questions. What are the independent variables or predictor variables to be tested? And what dependent behaviors will be used to test the hypotheses? How does the author try to prevent or minimize other variables from providing explanations for subject behavior that are confounded with the independent variables? You should be able to answer these questions after having read this section of the report.

Finally, you will want to compare the procedure with the stated intentions in the introduction. Given the questions identified in the introduction, and the rationale for the study, is the author appropriately measuring the variables of interest? That is, does the procedure allow for meaningful answers to the questions posed in the introduction?

While experimental research may sometimes seem overly complicated, the logic behind it is remarkably simple. Experimenters manipulate and record variables (quite literally, things that can vary between or among people, such as what happens to them and how they respond) to determine if the manipulated variables are in any way responsible for variation in subject behavior. Just as you might prepare a sauce once with butter and once with margarine, and then note differences in taste, smell, or appearance, or change brands of cat food and note differences in your cat's eating behavior, so too do experimenters look for differences. Hence, a typical experiment may entail something happening to one group of subjects that does not happen to another group. If that "something" (the independent variable) is important enough, then the behavior of the two groups (the dependent variable) should differ, assuming that the two groups were comparable to begin with. For example, in preparing the sauce above, you'd make sure that all other ingredients were the same and that the two sauces differed only by the butter/margarine variable. So the presence or absence of that "something" is the focus of an experiment. In a very real sense, the question asked is "does the difference make a difference?" The sauce made with butter may be superior in taste to the one made with margarine. And then again, it may not be. Your cat may be particularly enamored with one particular type of cat food (S. L. E.'s cat, Carmen Miranda, will only eat Friskies Buffet's Turkey and Giblets) or it may make absolutely no difference as your cat will eat anything put before it (like A. G. H.'s cat, Ananda, the epitome of an omnivore). Differences exist or can be created. You can't know whether there really is a difference until you meaningfully test the question. And that, in brief, is the logic behind experimentation.

The Results Section

This is the "how it turned out" section, in which experimenters quantitatively test their hypotheses based on the behavior of the subjects. The author should describe the results in such a way that unexpected as well as expected findings are shown. Not all hypotheses are supported; when the unexpected happens, it may be as important a finding as when the expected occurs. The numbers generated by measuring the subjects' behavior are summarized and analyzed in this section. Tables and figures often are employed to organize these numbers and the statistics generated from them, making the data easier to understand. Carefully examine all tables and figures. Read the titles of the tables or figures. Pay close attention to the column and row titles and the labels presented on figures. If you are unclear about what you are looking at, refer back to the text of the results section and determine where the reference to the table or figure is made

(such as "See Table 1." or "As shown in Figure 2,..."). Even though you may not understand the intricacies of specific statistics, you should be able to spot the patterns that emerge from the numbers and figures reported. A rudimentary understanding of statistics will enhance your understanding and ability to evaluate the results, but a good results section will be understandable even to the reader without any statistical knowledge.

An Aside about Statistics

Many students are unnerved by the statistics employed in research; students of social psychology are no exception. There is an impressive arsenal of statistical techniques and shorthand symbols that you will encounter if you spend any time reading the primary literature. Do not let these techniques and symbols deter you. The basic purpose of statistics is twofold. First, statistics are used to summarize large amounts of data in concise, manageable terms. Second, statistical techniques allow authors to determine, within certain parameters, if the results they obtained are sufficiently unlikely to have occurred by chance alone. Statistical techniques never allow us to completely rule out the possibility that a finding is merely due to chance. We can only say how unlikely it is that we have found a difference that does not, in reality, exist.

Your introductory psychology book may be a good source for the logic and meaning of statistics. If your introductory text does not have a chapter on experimental design and statistics, look for an appendix at the end of the book. Also, a brief statistical primer at the end of this chapter will help you make sense of the most frequently used terms and shorthand. In any case, no matter how exotic or mind boggling the "number crunching" you encounter, remember that statistics are used for the two basic purposes we discussed in the last paragraph: (1) to distill a quantity of numbers into more manageable and understandable form, and (2) to assess how likely it is that chance, or something other than what is hypothesized, can account for any differences obtained.

The Discussion or Conclusions Section

This is the "what this all means" section in which the results are interpreted by the author and the research is placed in perspective in light of previous findings. This section usually begins with a brief restatement of the hypotheses and the results that either support or do not support them. Be aware that the same data can be interpreted in different ways. Be skeptical. Authors usually, although not always, consider reasonable alternative explanations for their results. Even if they do not, you should.

Whereas the procedure and results sections are usually straightforward and compactly written, the discussion section typically allows a bit more expansiveness on the part of the writer. Now that the data are collected and the specific research questions have been answered to some degree, you, as a reader, are also less restrained. Don't be afraid to consider alternatives that the author has neglected. Critical thinking may also lead you to the conclusion that the author has overstated the significance of the findings. You are free to agree or disagree with the author's suggestions of "what this all means"; just be clear about your reasons and be prepared to support your own claims.

Many research reports conclude with the authors' suggestions for further research or implications for theoretical positions. Examine these and determine whether they make sense to you. If you were the author, what would be your next research question?

References

The final section of most articles is composed of complete reference information for all the cited work contained in the article. It provides easy access to any of the articles the authors have used, and is very helpful if you would like to know more about a specific study mentioned in the article.

When psychologists discuss research, they usually refer to articles by the author(s) and year published. This convention allows credit to be given where it is due and functions as a "shorthand" way to readily convey information.

In an effort to make this book of readings more useful, we have listed each article's citations in one master reference section at the end of the book. Each reference appears in its entirety followed by cross-referencing to all the articles within the reader that cite it.

A READING STRATEGY

There is no one strategy for reading research reports that will work for everyone. Some people read an article straight through while others skip around the sections. We suggest that until you become familiar with an approach that works best for you, consider the following strategy.

First, read the title and abstract carefully. Try to identify the general questions raised. Second, skim the entire article rapidly to get an overview of what the researcher did and what the findings are. Third, read the introduction and discussion sections to understand the starting and ending points of the author's reasoning as well as the conclusions. Underline the hypotheses presented in the introduction and locate them again in the discussion section. Fourth, read the method and results sections to determine how well the procedure allows for testing of the hypotheses and whether the hypotheses were confirmed or not. Underline or make marginal notes that highlight the major points made in the article. Fifth, reread the discussion, keeping in mind the original hypotheses and the reported results. Sixth, put the article aside for a few minutes and take a break. This will allow you to clear your mind of details and focus on the issues raised by this research. Seventh, return to carefully read the article from start to finish, paying attention to your underlining and marginal notes.

Finally, when you are finished reading an article, jot down a few notes about it. Try to summarize the article briefly and assess the logic of the author's thinking from introduction to discussion. You may even write your own abstract, adding your personal questions and comments. Now that you have the complete story, does it all make sense? You still may not be totally convinced by the data and arguments of the study. You have that right, especially now that you have been an intelligent consumer of the research and collected and considered all the facts. Being skeptical and entertaining alternative explanations for behavior is very much a part of being a good social psychologist.

Hopefully, this strategy will help you read research reports. Each author has presented us with challenging and exciting ideas about the ways we operate as social beings. We trust you will find these studies to be a catalyst for your own thinking about and understanding of human social behavior.

A NOTE ABOUT NONSEXIST LANGUAGE

In 1977, the American Psychological Association added guidelines encouraging the use of nonsexist language in the journals it publishes. In 1982, those guidelines became a requirement. Compliance with these guidelines requires authors to designate people in less ambiguous, less stereotypical, and less evaluative ways. For instance, the word *man* may be generic and refer to all humans, or it may refer only to males and not to females. A statement such as "Man threatens his own environment" is better posed as "Humans threaten their own environment" or "People threaten their own environment." This is not a trivial issue. Words are powerful messengers of not only who or what they describe; they also may contain evaluative meaning. Consider the phrase "man and wife." It is not only semantically unbalanced, but it also makes a

value judgment. A more precise and nonsexist phrase is either "man and woman" or "husband and wife." You will find few, if any, examples of sexist language in the more recent articles, although many of the older articles reflect the ideology of their times. And, hopefully, *you* will not fall into the trap of using sexist language in the psychology papers you write.

A BRIEF STATISTICAL PRIMER

Analysis of variance (ANOVA) is a statistical technique that allows comparison between two or more group means (see **Mean**) to determine if there are significant differences between or among the groups. The outcome of an analysis of variance is the "F ratio" (usually shortened to "F") which is a ratio of explained to unexplained variance. Explained variance is attributable to the investigator's intended manipulations (independent variables) while unexplained variance results from all other reasons for subjects' behavior, including chance. F may be tested for statistical significance (see **Statistical significance**). With an analysis of variance, one can examine both main effects and interaction effects (see **Main effects** and **Interaction effects**).

Chi square (X^2) is a statistical technique that assesses the degree to which two categorical or nominal variables are related. Although you could measure a person's attractiveness on a scale of one to ten, a person's eye color can only fall into one category. Most people are brown-eyed, or blue-eyed, or black-eyed, etc. For example, a chi square analysis might determine whether males or females systematically differ in their political party affiliation. Gender and party affiliation are categories; they do not lend themselves to an analysis dependent on interval or ratio scales.

Correlation (r) is a statistical technique that measures the degree of the relationship between two or more variables. The magnitude of the correlation ranges from 0 (no relationship) to 1 (perfect relationship) while the sign of the correlation (+ or −) indicates the direction (positive or negative) of the relationship. A positive correlation indicates that the variables change in the same direction. As one variable increases, the other variable also increases. Or, as one variable decreases, the other variable also decreases. For example, the number of years of formal education is positively correlated with income. A negative correlation implies that as one variable increases, the other decreases. For example, an individual's credit hours earned and his or her remaining time to graduation are negatively correlated. An important point to remember is that correlation does not necessarily imply causation but rather measures degree of relatedness.

df is an abbreviation for *degrees of freedom*. Degrees of freedom reflect the number of observations that are free to vary and are important in determining statistical significance (see **Statistical significance**). For most statistical techniques, the larger the sample, the smaller the magnitude of a difference needs to be for statistical significance to be obtained.

Dependent variables refer to the particular behaviors of the subjects that will be measured in the study. The investigator is predicting that the subjects' behavior will be dependent upon the independent variable. For example, suppose an investigator wants to test whether the frequency of novel answers to a creativity task is influenced by the presence of an audience. The frequency of novel answers is the dependent variable, while the presence or absence of an audience is the independent variable.

F (see **Analysis of variance**).

Independent variables refer to the differences that are hypothesized to distinguish between or to alter the behavior of subjects. They may be "subject variables," that is, dissimilarities that the subjects bring to the study (for example, age or degree of self-awareness) or they may be the result of manipulations introduced by the investigator (for example, type of persuasive appeal made or whether or not one observes someone acting aggressively).

Interaction effects are possible when two or more variables are studied at the same time. They occur when one variable has a different effect based on the level of another variable. For example, suppose a hypothetical study examines the influence of two factors, subject sex and the personality variable "need for approval," on how much time is spent playing with a baby (the dependent variable). If females play with the baby more than males do, regardless of their need for approval, then there is a main effect for sex (see **Main effects**). And if those high in need for approval play with the baby more than those low in need for approval, regardless of sex, then there is a main effect for the personality trait of need for approval. However, if males who are low in need for approval and females who are high in need for approval play frequently with the baby, but males high in need for approval and females low in need for approval *do not* play much with the baby, then an interaction exists. Thus, in this example, subject behavior would be "dependent on" both sex (male or female) and need for approval (high or low). Neither variable alone is sufficient to predict behavior; each is dependent on the other.

Main effects occur when the mean for one level of an independent variable is significantly different from the mean for another level. For example, suppose we have an independent variable labeled "type of classroom." If children in the "cooperative learning" classroom display less racial prejudice than do children in the conventional classroom, there is a main effect for classroom type.

Mean (abbreviated *M*) is the average of a group of scores, i.e., all scores are added and then divided by the total number of scores. An example of a mean is a student's grade point average.

N or *n* is an abbreviation for the "number of subjects."

Not significant (abbreviated *ns*) indicates that a statistical technique has determined that we cannot rule out chance as the reason for the effects obtained. This can occur when the means of two groups are not sufficiently dissimilar from one another.

Null hypothesis is the assumption that no difference exists between two or more groups in a study. It is usually the negation of the experimental hypothesis. If the investigator hypothesizes that variable X will have a significant effect on the dependent variable (subject behavior), then the null hypothesis is that variable X will have no effect on the dependent variable.

p is the abbreviation for **Probability.** It refers to the odds that a particular finding is due to chance (also known as "significance level"). The conventional standard for an acceptable level of significance is p <.05. Thus, if the study was conducted 100 times, the results obtained would be attributable to chance no more than 5 times. The smaller the level (e.g., p <.01 or p <.001), the less likely it is that the effect occurred by chance and the more confidence we have that the finding is actually a true difference.

SD is the abbreviation for standard deviation.

Standard deviation (see **Variance**).

Statistical significance refers to the degree to which a finding is likely to have occurred by chance. By convention, most researchers will not consider a result statistically significant unless a statistical procedure determines that the result has a probability of chance occurrence that is less than 5 percent (p <.05). A statistically significant difference is not guaranteed to be a true difference but has a greater likelihood of being a true one compared to a nonsignificant finding (see **Probability**).

t-test and *t* refer to a statistical technique that results from testing the statistical significance of the difference between the means of two groups. It takes into account how much diversity or variability there is within each group as well as how far the two means are from each other. For example, suppose we want to test the hypothesis that females smile more frequently than do males. We will find that there are some males who smile often and others who seldom smile, and that the same is true for females. A t-test will take into account the variability within the separate groups of males and females while it determines whether, overall, males and females differ in smiling frequency.

Validity is the degree to which a measurement evaluates what it is intended to evaluate. An honest bathroom scale furnishes a valid measurement of weight but has low validity as a measure of height.

Variance is a measure of how spread out or variable the scores are, that is, the degree to which a group of scores deviate from their mean. For example, consider the following two sets of scores: scores in Set A are 73, 74, 75, 76, and 77; scores in Set B are 55, 65, 75, 85, and 95. Although both sets have the same mean (75), Set B has a greater variability (scores are more spread out from the mean). The square root of the variance is the standard deviation, which represents the average deviation (i.e., distance) from the mean in a particular group of scores.

The Dynamogenic Factors in Pacemaking and Competition

Norman Triplett (1898)

This study on social facilitation (called dynamogenic factors in 1898) was the first social psychological experiment to be published. While others had theorized about social psychology (including Plato, Aristotle, and many other early philosophers), Triplett was the first to use scientific methods to test his hypotheses. We have included only the barest of details of Triplett's discussion of turn-of-the-century bicycle racers, but enough remains to understand how Triplett arrived at his hypothesis and developed it into a laboratory experiment with a repeated-measures design and counterbalanced testing. This article is rich with both physiological and motivational hypotheses, which are posited as possible explanations for changes in performance due to the presence of others. Many of these hypotheses have not stood the test of time (for example, theories about "brain worry" and "hypnotic suggestion"). While they amuse us now, they should also make us consider whether any of our contemporary theories will be cause for laughter 100 years hence.

The statistics in this article are not sophisticated by modern standards. Triplett's claims rest almost entirely upon descriptions of individual cases and what one might call "eyeball analyses" that is, finding differences that are readily apparent to any observer without the help of statistical analyses. Although all researchers desire group differences that are this obvious, they are rare indeed, especially given the complexity of the questions that researchers now address. Fortunately, advances in computer hardware and software and in statistical design allow investigators to ask and test many questions that could not be evaluated earlier, and to test these questions in precise and complex ways.

Thus, Triplett's article is interesting because of its historical import; it becomes doubly interesting when combined with a recent treatment of the same issue. The last article in this book (Reading 39—Harkins, 1987) is a more recent contribution to the understanding of social facilitation. Comparison of these two articles, separated by nearly 100 years, illustrates the rapid development of social psychological science.

A copy of the official bicycle records made up to the close of the season of 1897 was obtained from the Racing Board of the League of American Wheelmen. The definition of these races may be given as follows: The unpaced race against time is an effort by a single individual to lower the established record. No pacemaker is used; the only stimulation of the rider being the idea of reducing his own or some other man's former time. The paced race against time is also a single effort to make a record. It differs only in the fact

that a swift multicycle, such as a tandem or "quod," "makes the pace" for the rider. If he has well trained pacers and is skillful in changing crews as they come on, so as to avoid losing speed, the paced man may reduce the mark for the distance ridden. The two kinds of efforts described are not really races but are called so for convenience. Both are run with a flying start.

The third or paced competition race is a real race. Here, besides keeping up with the pacemaker, is the added element of beating the other contestants. It is often called a "loafing" race from the fact that the riders hang back and try to make pacemakers of each other, well knowing that a contestant starting out to make the pace can not win.

VALUE TO BE GIVEN THESE RECORDS

There are, it is computed, over 2,000 racing wheelmen, all ambitious to make records. The figures as they stand to-day have been evolved from numberless contests, a few men making records which soon fall to some of the host who are pressing closely behind. Reductions now made, however, are in general small in amount. Were all the men engaged in racing to make an effort to reduce the time in the kinds of races named, it is probable that the records already made would stand or be but very little reduced while the present leaders and their closest competitors would again assert their superiority, each in his own style of race. Regarding the faster time of the paced races, as derived from the records, it may be asked whether the difference is due to pacing or to the kind of men who take part; and whether the argument ascribing the difference noted to pacing or competition should have less validity from the fact that different men hold the records in the different races. Men fast at one kind of racing are found to be comparatively slow at another. It is for this reason, perhaps, that Michael refuses to meet any one in an unpaced contest. The racer finds by experience that race in which he is best fitted to excel and specializes in that. The difference in time, therefore, between the paced and unpaced race, as shown by the records, is a measure of the difference between the experts in the two classes of racers. It seems probable that the same amount of difference exists relatively between the averages of the classes they represent. A striking practical proof that the difference between the paced and unpaced trials, noted in the records, is due to pacing is found in the paced and unpaced time of some individual racers, in which the difference in time corresponds closely to that of the records. The fact may be mentioned, too, that wheelmen themselves generally regard the value of a pace to be from 20 to 30 seconds in the mile.

THEORIES ACCOUNTING FOR THE FASTER TIME OF PACED AND COMPETITION RACES

Of the seven or eight not wholly distinct theories which have been advanced to account for the faster time made in paced as compared with unpaced competitive races and paced races against time as against unpaced races against time, a number need only be stated very briefly. They are grouped according to their nature and first are given two mechanical theories.

Suction Theory

Those holding to this as the explanation assert that the vacuum left behind the pacing machine draws the rider following along with it. Anderson's ride of a mile a minute at Roodhouse, Ill., with the locomotive as pacemaker, is the strongest argument in its favor. Those maintaining this theory believe that the racer paced by a tandem is at a disadvantage as compared with the racer paced by a quod or a larger machine, as the suction exerted is not so powerful.

The Shelter Theory

This is closely related to the foregoing. Dr. Turner accepts it as a partial explanation of the aid to be gained from a pace, holding that the pacemaker or the leading competitor serves as a shelter from the wind, and that "a much greater amount of exertion, purely muscular, is required from a man to drive a machine when he is leading than when he is following, on account of the resistance of the air, and the greater the amount of wind blowing the greater the exertion, and conversely, the greater the shelter obtained the less the exertion."

This is the theory held, in general, by racers themselves. One of the champion riders of the country recently expressed this common view in a letter, as follows: "It is true that some very strong unpaced riders do not have any sort of success in paced racing. The only reason I can give for this is just simply that they have not studied the way to follow pace so as to be shielded from the wind. No matter which way it blows there is always a place where the man following pace can be out of the wind."

Encouragement Theory

The presence of a friend on the pacing machine to encourage and keep up the spirits of the rider is claimed to be of great help. The mental disposition has been long known to be of importance in racing as in other cases where energy is expended. It is still as true as in Virgil's time that the winners "can because they think they can."

The Brain Worry Theory

This theory shows why it is difficult for the leader in an unpaced competition race to win. For "a much greater amount of brain worry is incurred by making the pace than by waiting" (following). The man leading "is in a fidget the whole time whether he is going fast enough to exhaust his adversary; he is full of worry as to when that adversary means to commence his spurt; his nervous system is generally strung up, and at concert pitch, and his muscular and nervous efforts act and react on each other, producing an ever-increasing exhaustion, which both dulls the impulse-giving power of the brain and the impulse-receiving or contractile power of the muscles.''

Theory of Hypnotic Suggestions

A curious theory, lately advanced, suggests the possibility that the strained attention given to the revolving wheel of the pacing machine in front produces a sort of hypnotism and that the accompanying muscular exaltation is the secret of the endurance shown by some long distance riders in paced races.

The Automatic Theory

This is also a factor which favors the waiting rider, and gives him a marked advantage. The leader, as has been noted, must use his brain to direct every movement of his muscles. As he becomes more distressed it requires a more intense exertion of will power to force his machine through the resisting air. On the other hand, the "waiter" rides automatically. He has nothing to do but hang on. "His brain having inaugurated the movement leaves it to the spinal cord to continue it and only resumes its functions when a change of direction or speed is necessary.''—(Lagrange.) When he comes to the final spurt, his brain, assuming control again, imparts to the muscles a winning stimulus, while the continued brain work of the leader has brought great fatigue.

These facts seem to have a large foundation in truth. The lesser amount of fatigue incurred in paced trials is a matter of general knowledge. It is a common experience with wheelmen, and within that of the writer, that when following a lead on a long ride the feeling of automatic action becomes very pronounced, giving the sensation of a strong force pushing from behind. Of course the greater the distance ridden the more apparent becomes the saving in energy from automatic riding, as time is required to establish the movement. It may be remembered, in this connection, that while the average gain of the paced over the unpaced record is 34.4 seconds, the difference between them for the first mile is only 23.8 seconds.

As between the pacer and the paced, every advantage seems to rest with the latter. The two mechanical factors of suction and shelter, so far as they are involved, assist the rider who follows. So the psychological theories, the stimulation from encouragement, the peculiar power induced by hypnotism, and the staying qualities of automatic action, if of help at all, directly benefit the paced rider. The element of disadvantage induced by brain action, on the contrary, belongs more especially to the rider who leads.

The Dynamogenic Factors

The remaining factors to be discussed are those which the experiments on competition, detailed in the second part hereof, attempt to explain. No effort is made to weaken the force of the foregoing factors in accounting for the better time of paced races in comparison with unpaced races of the same type, but the facts of this study are given to throw whatever additional light they may.

This theory of competition holds that the bodily presence of another rider is a stimulus to the racer in arousing the competitive instinct; that another can thus be the means of releasing or freeing nervous energy for him that he cannot of himself release; and, further, that the sight of movement in that other, by perhaps suggesting a higher rate of speed, is also an inspiration to greater effort. These are the factors that had their counterpart in the experimental study following; and it is along these lines that the facts determined are to find their interpretation.

PART II

From the laboratory competitions to be described, abstraction was made of nearly all the forces above outlined. In the 40 seconds the average trial lasted, no shelter from the wind was required, nor was any suction exerted, the only brain worry incident was that of maintaining a sufficiently high rate of speed to defeat the competitors. From the shortness of the time and nature of the case, generally, it is doubtful if any automatic movements could be established. On the other hand, the effort was intensely voluntary. It may be likened to the 100 yard dash—a sprint from beginning to end.

Description of Apparatus

The apparatus for this study consisted of two fishing reels whose cranks turned in circles of one and three-fourths inches diameter. These were arranged on a Y shaped framework clamped to the top of a heavy table. The sides of this framework were spread sufficiently far apart to permit two persons turning side by side. Bands of twisted silk cord ran over the well lacquered axes of the reels and were supported at C and D, two meters distant, by two small pulleys. The records were taken from the course A D. The other course B C being used merely for pacing or competition purposes. The wheel on the side from which the records were taken communicated the movement made to a recorder, the stylus of which traced a curve on the drum of a kymograph. The direction of this curve corresponded to the rate of turning, as the greater the speed the shorter and straighter the resulting line.

Method of Conducting the Experiment

A subject taking the experiment was required to practice turning the reel until he had become accustomed to the machine. After a short period of rest the different trials were made with five-minute intervals between to obviate the possible effects of fatigue.

A trial consisted in turning the reel at the highest rate of speed until a small flag sewed to the silk band had made four circuits of the four-meter course. The time of the trial was taken by means of a stop-watch. The direction of the curves made on the drum likewise furnished graphic indications of the difference in time made between trials.

In the tables, A represents a trial alone, C a trial in competition.

STATEMENT OF RESULTS

In the course of the work the records of nearly 225 persons of all ages were taken. However, all the tables given below, and all statements made, unless otherwise specified, are based on the records of 40 children taken in the following manner: After the usual preliminaries of practice, six trials were made by each of 20 subjects in this order: first a trial alone, followed by a trial in competition, then another alone, and thus alternating through the six efforts, giving three trials alone and three in competition. Six trials were taken by 20 other children of about the same age, the order of trials in this case being the first trial alone, second alone, third a competition trial, fourth alone, fifth a competition, and sixth alone.

By this scheme, a trial of either sort, after the first one, by either of the two groups, always corresponds to a different trial by the opposite group. Further, when the subjects of the two groups come to their fourth and sixth trials, an equal amount of practice has been gained by an equal number of trials of the same kind. This fact should be remembered in any observation of the time made in trials by any group.

During the taking of the records, and afterwards in working them over, it was seen that all cases would fall into two classes:

First. Those stimulated—

1. to make faster time in competition trials,

2. in such a way as to inhibit motion.

Second. The small number who seemed little affected by the race.

The three tables which follow are made up from the records of the 40 subjects mentioned. The classification was in general determined by the time record as taken by the watch.

The first table gives the records of 20 subjects who, on the whole, were stimulated positively. The second table contains 10 records of subjects who were overstimulated. The third table shows the time of 10 subjects who give slight evidence of being stimulated. In the tables, A represents a trial alone, C a trial in competition. The 20 subjects given in Group A and Group B, of Ta-

TABLE I

SUBJECTS STIMULATED POSITIVELY

Group A

	Age.	A.	C.	A.	C.	A.	C.
Violet F.	10	54.4	42.6	45.2	41.0	42.0	46.0
Anna P.	9	67.0	57.o	55.4	50.4	49.0	44.8
Willie H.	12	37.8	38.8	43.0	39.0	37.2	33.4
Bessie V.	11	46.2	41.0	39.0	30.2	33.6	32.4
Howard C.	11	42.0	36.4	39.0	41.0	37.8	34.0
Mary M.	11	48.0	44.8	52.0	44.6	43.8	40.0
Lois P.	11	53.0	45.6	44.0	40.0	40.6	35.8
Inez K.	13	37.0	35.0	35.8	34.0	34.0	32.6
Harvey L.	9	49.0	42.6	39.6	37.6	36.0	35.0
Lora F.	11	40.4	35.0	33.0	35.0	30.2	29.0
Average	11	47.48	41.88	42.6	39.28	38.42	36.3
P.E.		6.18	4.45	4.68	3.83	3.74	3.74
Gains		5.6	.72	3.32	.86	2.12

Group B

	Age.	A.	A.	C.	A.	C.	A.
Stephen M.	13	51.2	50.0	43.0	41.8	39.8	41.2*
Mary W.	13	56.0	53.0	45.8	49.4	45.0	43.0*
Bertha A.	10	56.2	49.0	48.0	46.8	41.4	44.4
Clara L.	8	52.0	44.0	46.0	45.6	44.0	45.2
Helen M.	10	45.0	45.6	35.8	46.2	40.0	40.0
Gracie W.	12	56.6	50.0	42.0	39.0	40.2	41.4
Dona R.	15	34.0	37.2	36.0	41.4	37.0	32.8
Pearl C.	13	43.0	43.0	40.0	40.6	33.8	35.0
Clyde G.	13	36.0	35.0	32.4	33.0	31.0	35.0
Lucile W.	10	52.0	50.0	43.0	44.0	38.2	40.2
Average	11.7	48.2	45.68	41.2	42.78	39.0	39.82
P.E.		5.60	4.00	3.42	3.17	2.89	2.84
Gains		2.52	4.48	1.58	3.78	.82

*Left-handed.

TABLE II

SUBJECTS STIMULATED ADVERSELY

Group A

	Age.	A.	C.	A.	C.	A.	C.
Jack R.	9	44.2	44.0	41.8	48.0	44.2	41.0
Helen F.	9	44.0	51.0	43.8	44.0	43.0	41.2
Emma P.	11	38.4	42.0	37.0	39.6	36.6	32.0
Warner J.	11	41.6	43.6	43.4	43.0	40.0	38.0
Genevieve M.	12	36.0	36.0	32.6	32.8	31.2	34.8
Average	10.4	40.84	43.32	39.72	41.48	39.00	37.40
P.E.		2.41	3.57	3.25	3.85	3.55	2.52

GROUP B

	Age.	A.	A.	C.	A.	C.	A.
Hazel M.	11	38.0	35.8	38.2	37.2	35.0	42.0
George B.	12	39.2	36.0	37.6	34.2	36.0	33.8
Mary B.	11	50.0	46.0	43.4	42.0	48.0	36.8
Carlisle B.	14	37.0	35.4	35.0	33.4	36.4	31.4
Eddie H.	11	31.2	29.2	27.6	27.0	26.8	28.8
Average	11.8	39.08	36.48	36.36	34.76	34.40	34.56
P.E.		4.61	4.07	3.89	3.71	5.33	3.45

ble I, in nearly all cases make marked reductions in the competition trials. The averages show large gains in these trials and small gains or even losses for the succeeding trials alone. The second trial for Group A is a competition, for Group B a trial alone. The gain between the first and second trials of the first group is 5.6 seconds, between the first and second trials of the second group, 2.52 seconds. The latter represents the practice effect—always greatest in the first trials, the former the element of competition plus the practice. The third trial in Group A—a trial alone—is .72 seconds slower than the preceding race trial. The third trial in Group B—a competition—is 4.48 seconds faster than the preceding trial alone. The fourth trials in these two groups are on an equality, as regards practice, from an equal number of trials of the same kind. In the first case the gain over the preceding trial is 3.32 seconds. In the latter there is a loss of 1.58 seconds from the time of the preceding competition trial. In like manner there is an equality of conditions in regard to the sixth trial of these groups, and again the effect of competition plainly appears, the competition trial gaining 2.12 seconds, and the trial alone losing .82 seconds with respect to the preceding trial. These are decided differences.

The 10 subjects whose records are given in Table II are of interest. With them stimulation brought a loss of control. In one or more of the competition trials of each subject in this group the time is very much slower than that made in the preceding trial alone. Most frequently this is true of the first trial in competition, but with some was characteristic of every race. In all, 14 of the 25 races run by this group were equal or slower than the preceding trial alone. This seems to be brought about in large measure by the mental attitude of the subject. An intense desire to win, for instance, often resulting in over-stimulation.

TABLE III

SUBJECTS LITTLE AFFECTED BY COMPETITION

Group A

	Age.	A.	C.	A.	C.	A.	C.
Albert P.	13	29.0	28.0	27.0	29.0	27.0	28.6
Milfred V.	17	36.4	29.0	29.4	30.2	30.2	32.2
Harry V.	12	32.0	32.0	32.6	32.6	32.6	31.6
Robt. H.	12	31.4	31.4	32.2	35.4	35.0	32.4
John T.	11	30.2	30.8	32.8	30.6	32.8	31.8
Average	13	31.80	30.24	30.80	31.56	31.50	31.30
P.E.		1.90	1.13	1.71	1.7	2.06	1.05

Group B

	Age.	A.	A.	C.	A.	C.	A.
Lela T.	10	45.0	37.4	36.8	36.0	37.2	38.0
Lura L.	11	42.0	39.0	38.0	37.0	37.0	38.0
Mollie A.	13	38.0	30.0	28.0	30.0	30.2	29.6
Anna F.	11	35.0	31.8	32.4	30.0	32.0	30.4
Ora R.	14	37.2	30.0	29.0	27.8	28.4	26.8
Average	11.8	39.44	33.64	32.84	32.16	32.96	32.16
P.E.		3.11	2.88	3.03	2.75	2.69	3.71

Accompanying phenomena were labored breathing, flushed faces and a stiffening or contraction of the muscles of the arm. A number of young children of from 5 to 9 years, not included in our group of 40, exhibited the phenomena most strikingly, the rigidity of the arm preventing free movement and in some cases resulting in an almost total inhibition of movement. The effort to continue turning in these cases was by a swaying of the whole body.

This seems a most interesting fact and confirmatory of the probable order of development of the muscles as given by Dr. Hall and others. In the case of those sufficiently developed to have the fast forearm movement, fatigue or overstimulation seemed to bring a recurrence to the whole arm and shoulder movement of early childhood, and if the fatigue or excitement was sufficiently intense, to the whole body movement, while younger children easily fell into the swaying movement when affected by either of the causes named.

It reminds one of the way in which fatigue of a small muscle used in ergographic work will cause the subject to attempt to draw on his larger muscles, or, of the man who moves to the city and acquires the upright carriage and springing step of the city-bred man, who, when greatly fatigued, insensibly falls into the old "clodhopper" gait. This tendency to revert to earlier movements and also old manners of speech, as Höpfner has shown in his "Fatigue of School Children," is common, when, for any reason, the centers of control are interfered with. It may be said, therefore, that in the work under consideration the chief difference between this group and the large group in Table I was a difference in control; the stimulation inhibiting the proper function of the motor centers in the one case, and reinforcing it in the other. This, at least, seemed apparent from the characteristics exhibited by the two classes. Observation of the subjects of this class under trial, and careful scrutiny of their graphic records, show how decided gains were sometimes lost by the subject "going to pieces" at the critical point of the race, not being able to endure the nervous strain. Yet there exists no sharp line of division between subjects stimulated to make faster time and those affected in the opposite way. In some instances the nervous excitement acted adversely in every race trial, while in others, a gain in control, enabled the subject to make a material reduction in the last competition. A. B., one of three adults affected adversely, is an athletic young man, a fine tennis and hand-ball player, and known to be stimulated in contests of these kinds. It was noticed that in his competition trials time was lost because of his attempt to take advantage of the larger muscles of the arm and shoulder. After many trials and injunctions to avoid the movement he gained sufficient control to enable him to reduce the time in the competitions.

A. V., an adult of nervous organization, went half through his race with a great gain over his trial alone, but seeing his antagonist pushing him closely, broke down and lost the most of the gain made in the first half. The time of the trial alone was 38.6 seconds, that of the competition was 37.2 seconds.

It was found that A. V. made the first 75 turns in his competition trial in 15 seconds, the second half in 22.2 seconds. By the same means, each half of the preceding trial alone was 19.3 seconds—an exception to the rule that the last half is slower because of fatigue.

Other curves when worked out in this way gave similar results. The time record, therefore, it must be seen, is not always a true index to the amount of stimulation present. Had the trials consisted of but half as many turns the effect of competition as it appears in the tables would have been shown much more constantly. Table II would have been a smaller group if indeed any necessity existed for retaining it.

A comparison of the time made by the different groups shows that the subjects of Table I are much slower than those of Table II, and that a still greater difference exists between this group and the subjects found in Table III. It may be said that they are slower because of greater sluggishness of disposition, and that the reductions made are largely a result of the subjects warming up. This, indeed, may be a part of the cause for it, but as the larger reductions coincide with the competition trials this cannot be held to completely account for it. A glance over the individual records discovers some facts which furnish a plausible partial explanation, when taken in connection with the following fact. The age at which children acquire control of the wrist movements, a large factor in turning the reel with speed, was found to be about 11 years in general, although a few of 9 and 10 years had this power. Now, of the 20 subjects composing Table I, 7 are 10 years of age or younger, while two others, age 13, are left-handed and being compelled to use the right hand are slow in consequence. So, here are 9 subjects, a number nearly equal to the group in Table II or Table III, who had a reason for being slow. Were these omitted from the count, the time of the initial trial would be found not to vary materially from that of Table II.

Besides the lack of muscular development of the younger subjects mentioned above, many of the subjects of Table I seemed not to have proper ideals of speed. The desire to beat, if it did nothing else, brought them to a sense of what was possible for them. The arousal of their competitive instincts and the idea of a faster movement, perhaps, in the contestant, induced greater concentration of energy.

The subjects in Table III, are a small group who seemed very little affected by competition. They made very fast time, but they are older than the average; their muscular control was good, and they had the forearm movements. Practice gains while somewhat apparent at first in some cases are, on the whole, less in amount. Their drum records show fewer fluctuations and irregularities, and less pronounced fatigue curves at the end.

There seems to be a striking analogy between these subjects and those racing men who are fast without a pace, but can do little or no better in a paced or competition race.

CONCLUDING STATEMENT

From the above facts regarding the laboratory races we infer that the bodily presence of another contestant participating simultaneously in the race serves to liberate latent energy not ordinarily available. This inference is further justified by the difference in time between the paced competition races and the paced races against time, amounting to an average of 5.15 seconds per mile up to 25 miles. The factors of shelter from the wind, encouragement, brain worry, hypnotic suggestion, and automatic movement, are common to both, while the competitors participate simultaneously in person only in the first.

In the next place the sight of the movements of the pacemakers or leading competitors, and the idea of higher speed, furnished by this or some other means, are probably in themselves dynamogenic factors of some consequence.

READING 3

Behavior and Development as a Function of the Total Situation

Kurt Lewin (1946)

Kurt Lewin was one of the most influential theorists in the first hundred years of social psychology. The research investigations of his colleagues and students (particularly while he was at M.I.T.'s Research Center for Group Dynamics)

produced an exceptional array of social psychological concepts and studies. Lewin's interests encompassed a broad range of topics, such as attitude and attitude change research, group dynamics, and leadership, to name a few. He was also a strong proponent of action research, research aimed not only at the scientific analysis of social phenomena but, and perhaps more importantly, at bringing this knowledge to bear on contemporary societal problems and issues.

Lewin's most lasting theoretical contribution to social psychology is his emphasis on the psychological field, the "life space" comprised of the person and his or her environment. According to Lewin, behavior must be viewed as a function of the interaction of these two entities, the person and the environment. We present one of Lewin's later works, a classic reading that discusses his "field theory" and presents his notions of force, needs, and the impact of one's environment, past, present, and future. Although field theory as constituted by Lewin no longer attracts direct research attention, its impact on the entire field of social psychology is very much evident.

Morton Deutsch (1968), another well-known social psychologist, summarized some of the most important social psychological values, methods, and goals in one succinct statement by recognizing how much of social psychology was shaped by Lewin. He wrote that Lewin

believed that psychological events must be explained in psychological terms;...that psychological events must be studied in their interrelations with one another;...that the attempt to bring about change in a process is the most fruitful way to investigate it;...that the scientist should have a social conscience and should be active in making a world a better place to live in; and that a good theory is valuable for social action as well as for science (p. 478).

The Psychological Field

Stimulus and Situation: The Basic Formula For Behavior Scientific procedure is analytical in that it tries to determine or to "isolate" the effect of the various factors. It studies, for instance, the effect on the child of different intensities of light, of different degrees of hunger (Irwin, 1930; Pratt, 1933), of failure or praise. It is widely agreed, however, that the effect of a given stimulus depends upon the stimulus constellation and upon the state of the particular person at that time. The perceived form, size, and color of a visual object corresponding to the same retinal stimulus vary widely according to the visual background and the nature of the rest of the visual field (Gelb, 1938). The toys and other objects in a room may lead to very different reactions of the year-old child when the mother is present and when she is not (MacDonald, 1940). In general terms, behavior (B) is a function (F) of the person (P) and of his environment (E), $B = F(P,E)$. This statement is correct for emotional outbreaks as well as for "purposive" directed activities; for dreaming, wishing, and thinking, as well as for talking and acting.

Person and Psychological Environment In this formula for behavior, the state of the person (P) and that of his environment (E) are not independent of each other. How a child sees a given physical setting—for instance, whether the frozen pond looks dangerous to him or not—depends upon the developmental state and the character of that child (Murray, 1938) and upon his ideology (Mead, 1928). The worlds in which the newborn, the one-year-old child, and the ten-year-old child live are different even in identical physical or social surroundings. This holds also for the same child when it is hungry or satiated, full of energy or fatigued. In other words, $E = F(P)$. The reverse is also true: The state of the person depends upon his environment, $P = F(E)$. The state of the person after encouragement is different from that after discouragement (Fajans, 1933), that in an area of sympathy or security from that in an area of tension (Murphy, 1937), that in a democratic group atmosphere from that in an autocratic atmosphere (Lewin, Lippitt, and White, 1939). The momentary intellectual ability of a child as measured by

an intelligence test (MA) is different in an atmosphere of good rapport with the examiner from what it is in one of poor rapport. In regard to the effect of the environment upon development there is a consensus that environment may change intelligence, although opinion differs in regard to how much intelligence can be changed by environment (Terman, 1919; Wellman, 1932–1933; Stoddard and Wellman, 1934; Burks, 1940; Goodenough, 1940). Certainly the ideology, values, and attitudes of the growing individual depend greatly upon the culture in which he is reared (Mead, 1937; L. K. Frank, 1938) and upon his belonging to a privileged or underprivileged group (Dollard, 1937; Lewin, 1940b).

In summary, one can say that behavior and development depend upon the state of the person and his environment, $B = F(P,E)$. In this equation the person P and his environment E have to be viewed as variables which are mutually dependent upon each other. In other words, to understand or to predict behavior, the person and his environment have to be considered as *one* constellation of interdependent factors. We call the totality of these factors the life space (LSp) of that individual, and write $B = F(P,E) = F(LSp)$. The life space, therefore, includes both the person and his psychological environment. The task of explaining behavior then becomes identical with (1) finding a scientific representation of the life space (LSp) and (2) determining the function (F) which links the behavior to the life space. This function F is what one usually calls a *law*.

General Characteristics of a Psychological Field The novelist who tells the story behind the behavior and development of an individual gives us detailed data about his parents, his siblings, his character, his intelligence, his occupation, his friends, his status. He gives us these data in their specific interrelation, that is, as part of a total situation. Psychology has to fulfill the same task with scientific instead of poetic means. The method should be analytical in that the different factors which influence behavior have to be specifically distinguished. In science, these data have also to be represented in their particular setting within the specific situation. A totality of coexisting facts which are conceived of as mutually interdependent is called a *field* (Einstein, 1933). Psychology has to view the life space, including the person and his environment, as one field.

What means are most appropriate for analyzing and representing scientifically a psychological field have to be judged on the basis of their fruitfulness for explaining behavior. In this respect, the following general points should be remembered:

(1). A prerequisite for properly guiding a child or for the theoretical understanding of his behavior is the distinction between that situation which the teacher, the parents, or the experimenter sees and that situation which exists for the child as his life space. *Objectivity* in psychology demands representing the field correctly as it exists for the individual in question at that particular time. For this field the child's friendships, conscious and "unconscious" goals, dreams, ideals, and fears are at least as essential as any physical setting. Since this field is different for every age and for every individual, the situation as characterized by physics or sociology, which is the same for everybody, cannot be substituted for it. It is important, however, to know the physical and social conditions because they limit the variety of possible life spaces—probably as *boundary conditions* (Lewin, 1936a) of the psychological field.

(2). The social aspect of the psychological situation is at least as important as the physical. This holds even for the very young child.

(3). To characterize properly the psychological field, one has to take into account such *specific* items as particular goals, stimuli, needs, social relations, as well as such more *general* characteristics of the field as the *atmosphere* (for instance, the friendly, tense, or hostile atmosphere) or the amount of freedom. These characteristics of the *field as a whole* are as important in psychology as, for instance, the field of gravity for the explanation of events in classical physics. Psychological atmospheres are empirical realities and are scientifically describable facts (Lewin, Lippitt, and White, 1939).

(4). The concept of the psychological field as a determinant of behavior implies that everything which affects behavior at a given time should be represented in the field existing at that time, and that only those facts can affect behavior which are part of the present field (Lewin, 1936a).

(5). To avoid unnecessary assumptions, one can represent the psychological field scientifically by the interrelation of its parts in mathematical terms without asking what the "essence behind" this field is. Such a mathematical representation of the psychological field and the equations expressing the psychological laws are all that have to be known for predicting behavior.

Theories and Constructs: Law and the Individual Case

Theories Are Unavoidable Without theories it is impossible in psychology, as in any other science, to proceed beyond the mere collection and description of facts which have no predictive value. It is impossible to handle problems of conditions or effects without characterizing the *dynamic* properties behind the surface of the directly observable *phenotypical* properties.

The terms *need, association, conditioned reflex, excitatory tendency, gestalt, libido,* and *super-ego* are examples of theoretical constructs with which various psychological schools have attempted to characterize certain underlying dynamical or genotypical facts. It is important to distinguish those facts which are essential for prediction and explanation from their various symptoms. For instance, an emotional state such as anger can lead to a variety of very different symptoms (noisiness, as well as extreme politeness [Dembo, 1931]); tension can lead to aggressiveness as well as apathy (Lewin, Lippitt, and White, 1939). The same personality may manifest itself in practically opposite actions. In other words, a given state of a person corresponds to a variety of behavior and can, therefore, be inferred only from a combined determination of overt behavior and the situation. This is only another way of saying that behavior (B) is determined by the person and the environment $[B = F(P,E)]$ and not by the person or the environment alone.

Psychology has never avoided, nor can it avoid, theory (Reichenbach, 1928; Hull, 1930; Tolman, 1935; J. F. Brown, 1936; Lewin, 1938), but it can try to eliminate those speculative theories which are frequently introduced without clear intent or in a hidden way, and try instead to make use of openly stated empirical theories. The main desiderata for an efficient empirical theory are: (1) constructs which (a) are linked to observable facts (symptoms) by a so-called operational definition or by a number of operational definitions corresponding to the possibilities of observation under different circumstances; and constructs which (b) have clearly defined conceptual properties. (2) The laws should be verified by experiment. A law should be accepted as valid only if it is not contradicted by data in any branch of psychology. In this sense, a law should always be general.

Constructs Basic for Representing the Psychological Field

It seems to be possible to represent the essential properties of the life space with the help of relatively few (perhaps a dozen) related constructs. To some degree it is a matter of convenience which of a group of interrelated constructs are to be considered the basic ones (Reichenbach, 1928). For the purpose of this representation we shall use mainly the following constructs: psychological force, psychological position, and potency of a situation.

(1). The concept of force in psychology refers to phenomena which have been called *drive, excitatory tendency,* or by any other name expressing "tendency to act in a certain direction." The term *force* intends to express this directed element, attributing to it, in addition, a magnitude (strength of force) and a point of application, without assuming any additional implications (Lewin, 1938).

(2). The position of the person within the total psychological field and the position of the other parts of the field in relation to one another are of prime importance. This holds for the relative position of various areas of activities the child might enter, the relative position of social groups to which the child belongs, or would like to belong, and of areas of security and insecurity. Although it is not possible today to measure psychological distance or direction quantitatively, it is possible to treat some problems of position by means of the qualitative geometry called topology.

(3). Potency refers to the weight which a certain area of the life space has for a child relative to other areas. This concept is particularly valuable in case of "overlapping situations," that is, when the belongingness to two groups or the involvement in two or more activities at the same time is pertinent.

Cognitive Structure of the Life Space

The Life Space as a Whole During Development
An outstanding characteristic of the change of the life space during development is an increasing differentiation.

The life space of the newborn child may be described as a field which has relatively few and only vaguely distinguishable areas (Koffka, 1928). The situation probably corresponds to a general state of greater or less comfort. No definite objects or persons seem to be distinguished. No area called "my own body" exists. Future events or expectations do not exist; the child is ruled by the situation immediately at hand.

Some of the first areas which get a definite character seem to be connected with food and elimination. As early as three to six days the child reacts to being prepared for nursing (Marquis, 1931). A similar increase in size and differentiation of the life space occurs in other respects. The child studies his own body (Bühler, 1939) and his immediate physical surroundings. Within the first few months, certain social relations develop.

The increase of the life space in regard to the psychological time dimension continues into adulthood. Plans extend farther into the future, and activities of increasingly longer duration are organized as one unit. For instance, between two and six years of age the duration of play units increases (Barker, Dembo, and Lewin, 1941).

The differentiation of the life space also increases in the dimension of reality-irreality. The different degrees of irreality correspond to different degrees of fantasy. They include both the positive wishes and the fears. Dynamically, the level of irreality corresponds to a more fluid medium (J. F. Brown, 1933; Erikson, 1940) and is more closely related to the central layers of the person. This fact is particularly important for the psychology of dreams (Freud, 1916; T. French, 1939). Play can be understood as an action on the level of reality closely related to the irreal level (Sliosberg, 1934). The play technique (Homburger, 1937), in the study of personality, makes use of the fact that the irreal level is closely related to the central layers of the person.

The level of irreality in the psychological future corresponds to the wishes or fears for the future; the level of reality, to what is expected. The discrepancy between the structure of the life space on the levels of irreality and of reality is important for planning and for the productivity of the child (Barker, Dembo, and Lewin, 1941). Hope corresponds to a sufficient similarity between reality and irreality somewhere in the psychological future; guilt to a certain discrepancy

between reality and irreality in the psychological past. In the young child, truth and lying, perception and imagination are less clearly distinguished than in an older child (Piaget, 1932; Sliosberg, 1934; L. K. Frank, 1935). This is partly due to the fact that the younger child has not yet developed that degree of differentiation of the life space into levels of reality and irreality which is characteristic of the adult.

The speed with which the life space increases in scope and degree of differentiation during development varies greatly. A close relation seems to exist between intelligence or, more specifically, between mental age and the degree of differentiation of the person and the psychological environment (Lewin, 1935; Kounin, 1939). If this is correct, differences in IQ should be considered as different rates of increasing differentiation of the life space. Similar considerations apply to motor development (McGraw, 1935) and to social development.

The growth of the life space has a different rate at different times. Such differences are particularly important for the so-called developmental crises, as in adolescence (Dimock, 1937; Lewin, 1939).

Figure 1a and b represents schematically the scope and degree of differentiation of the life space as a whole at two developmental stages. The differentiation concerns the psychological environment as well as the person. The increasing differentiation of needs, for instance, can be represented as an increase in the differentiation of certain intrapersonal regions. The main differences between these developmental stages are: (1) an increase in the *scope* of the life space in regard to (a) what is part of the psychological present; (b) the time perspective in the direction of the psychological past and the psychological future; (c) the reality-irreality dimension; (2) an increasing *differentiation* of every level of the life space into a multitude of social relations and areas of activities; (3) an increasing *organization;* (4) a change in the general *fluidity* or *rigidity* of the life space.

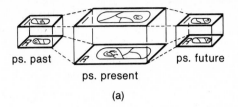

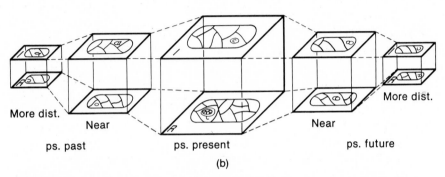

FIGURE 1 The life space at two developmental stages. Figure 1*a* represents the life space of a younger child. Figure 1*b* represents the higher degree of differentiation of the life space of the older child in regard to the present situation, the reality-irreality dimension, and the time perspective. *C*, child; *R*, level of reality; *I*, level of irreality; *Ps Past*, psychological past; *Ps Present*, psychological present; *Ps Future*, psychological future.

Not all the areas of this life space are accessible to the child. He sees older children engaged in certain activities, which he would like to do himself, but into which he finds he cannot enter because he is not strong or clever enough. Additional limitations of his space of free movements are established by the prohibitions of the adult or by other social taboos.

The relation between accessible and inaccessible regions in the life space, the size of the space of free movement, and the precision of boundary between accessible and inaccessible areas are of great importance for behavior and development of the normal and abnormal child (Lewin, 1936*a*).

The Position of the Person: Being Inside and Outside a Region

Position, Neighboringness, and Locomotion
The determination of the position of the person

within the life space is the first prerequisite for understanding behavior. His social position within or outside of various groups should be known; his position in regard to various activities, in regard to his goal regions, and in regard to physical areas should be determined. This is fundamental because the region in which the person is located determines (1) the quality of his immediate surroundings, (2) what kinds of regions are adjacent to the present region—that is, what possibilities the individual has for his next step—and (3) what step has the meaning of an action toward his goal and what step corresponds to an action away from his goal.

Most behavior can be conceived of as a change of position—in other words, as a locomotion of the person. (The other cases of behavior are changes of structure.) In turn, every behavior changes the situation. We shall mention only a few examples of the effect of the region in which the person is located.

"Adaptation" to a Situation A common phenomenon is what is usually called adaptation in the sense of "getting tuned to the present atmosphere." H. Anderson (1939) found that children of preschool age reacted to an aggressive approach with aggression, to a friendly approach in a friendly manner. Ronald Lippitt's (1940) study on democratic and autocratic atmospheres found similar adaptation of the children to the cultural atmosphere produced by the leader. J. R. P. French, Jr. (1944) found adaptation to group atmospheres in experiments with college freshmen.

Group Belongingness Most social goals can be characterized as a wish to belong or not to belong to a certain group. This group may be a group of friends, an athletic organization, or a favorite subgroup within a larger group. It may be a group of only two persons, as with the friendship between mother and child. Belonging or not belonging to the group is equivalent to having a position inside or outside this group. This position determines the rights and duties of the individual and is decisive for the ideology of the individual.

The Effect of the Group on the Individual The effect of group belongingness on the behavior of an individual can be viewed as the result of an overlapping situation: One situation corresponds to the child's own needs and goals; the other, to the goals, rules, and values which exist for him as a group member. Adaptation of an individual to the group depends upon the avoidance of too great a conflict between the two sets of forces (Lewin, 1938).

A child usually belongs to a great number of groups, such as his family, the school, the church, friends. Within the family he may belong to a subgroup containing him and his closest sibling. The effect of the various groups, particularly whether or not the child is ruled by the ideology and values of the one or the other, depends on the relative potency of these groups at that time. Schanck (1932) has found that the influence of public or private morale is different at home and in the church. In school children, the tendency to cheat changes with the social setting (Hartshorne and May, 1929).

Many conflicts in childhood are due to forces corresponding to the various groups to which the child belongs. Such conflicts are particularly important for children in marginal positions, that is, for children who are standing on the boundary between two groups. One example is the adolescent who no longer wants to belong to the children's group but who is not yet fully accepted by the adults. Uncertainty of the ground on which the child stands leads to an alternation between the values of the one and of the other group, to a state of emotional tension, and to a frequent fluctuation between overaggressiveness and overtimidity (Lewin, 1939). The degree to which such adolescent behavior is shown depends upon the degree to which children and adolescents are treated as separate groups in that culture (Benedict, 1934; Reuter, 1937).

Induced Needs: Group Goals and Individual Goals
The needs of the individual are, to a very high degree, determined by social factors. The needs of the growing child are changed and new needs induced as a result of the many small and large social groups to which he belongs. His needs are much affected, also, by the ideology and conduct of those groups to which he would like to belong or from which he would like to be set apart. The effects of the advice of the mother, of the demand of a fellow child, or of what the psychoanalyst calls *superego,* all are closely interwoven with socially induced needs. We have seen that the level of aspiration is related to social facts. We may state more generally that the culture in which a child grows affects practically every need and all his behavior and that the problem of acculturation is one of the foremost in child psychology.

One can distinguish three types of cases where needs pertain to social relations: (1) the action of the individual may be performed for the benefit of someone else (in the manner of an altruistic act); (2) needs may be induced by the power field of another person or group (as a weaker person's obedience of a more powerful one); (3) needs may be created by belonging to a group and adhering to its goals. Actually, these three types are closely interwoven.

Egoism and Altruism B. Wright (1941, 1942*a*, 1942*b*) studied children in a situation where they had a choice of keeping a preferred toy or giving it to someone else. The other child (who was not present) was either someone unknown or a best friend. The five-year-old child was practically always egoistic; the eight-year-old child showed considerable altruism, and more so toward the stranger (58 per cent generous choices) than to the friend (23 per cent generous choices). When acting as an umpire between a friend and a strange child in distributing the toys, the five-year-old child favored the friend more frequently than the stranger. The eight-year-old favored the stranger more frequently than the friend.

The greater altruism toward the stranger than toward the friend seems to be due partly to the fact that the child sees himself in the position of a host toward the stranger, but not toward the friend, and that his ideology requires that he be hospitable. The children judged other people to be altruistic or egoistic to the same degree as they themselves were. A preliminary study seems to indicate that adults in a similar setting are more egoistic than the eight-year-old child.

Obedience and Social Pressure In discussing problems of conflicts we have seen that the force acting on a person in the direction of a goal might be counteracted by induced forces corresponding to the will of another person. In view of the relation between psychological forces and psychological needs we can also speak of *induced needs*. The relation between two persons might be that of friends or that of enemies; the need of

each would depend greatly on the power field of the other.

Wiehe (Lewin, 1935) observed children between two and four years of age when a stranger entered the child's room. He found the strength of the power field of the stranger at a given moment to be influenced by the physical position of both persons. The effect of the power field on the child increases with decreasing distance. It is very high if the child is placed on the adult's lap. The power field is weaker back of the stranger, or where the child cannot be seen, than in front of the stranger. In other words, the strength of the power field of one person on another differs for different areas. J. D. Frank (1944), in experiments with students, and Waring, Dwyer, and Junkin (1939) in experiments with nursery school children at the dinner table, also found the effectiveness of the power field for creating induced forces to be greater if the distance between the persons is smaller.

Lippitt and White (1943), in experiments with ten-year-old children, tested the effect of induced needs during the presence and the absence of the inducing power field. They found that the amount of work output in an autocratic group atmosphere dropped very decisively within a few minutes when the leader left the room. This was in contrast to a democratic group atmosphere, where the work had been chosen and planned by the group itself, and where the work output was unchanged when the leader left.

Taking Over Foreign Goals An induced need may slowly change its character in the direction of an own need. In other words, the person not only will follow orders but also "accept" them (in the meaning of taking them over).

Horowitz (1936) found no prejudices against Negroes in white children under three years. The prejudices increased between four and six years. This increase was as great in New York as in the South. It was independent of the degree of acquaintance of the children with Negro children, and of the actual status of the Negro child in the class which the white child attended. The prejudices are, however, related to the attitude of the parents of the white child. This indicates that the prejudices against the Negroes are due to an induction and gradual taking-over of the culture of the parents by the child.

Individual Differences

We have seen that it is not possible to determine the specific characteristics of individuals by classifying them according to their overt behavior. Instead, one has to look for factors which can be inserted as constant values into the variables of the equations which represent psychological laws. In this way also the variability of behavior, that is, the difference in behavior of the same individual in different situations, becomes susceptible to treatment. This variability does not mean merely that the absolute frequency or intensity of a certain type of behavior depends upon the situation. Actually, the rank-order of individuals in regard to a certain trait may also be different in different situations. For instance,

Lewin, Lippitt, and White (1939) found in clubs of ten-year-old boys that, in regard to some "traits," such as "demanding attention from other club members" and "out-of-field conversation," the rank-order of the individual in different atmospheres remains rather constant ($r = .85$ and $r = .78$). In other traits, such as "dependence upon leader," there is scarcely any consistency of rank-order ($r = .02$). There are more extreme changes in the rank-order in "work-mindedness" than in "aggressiveness." The changes seem to be linked to the differences of meaning of the particular atmospheres to the particular children.

The attempts to link positively problems of individual differences and of general laws are relatively new in psychology. It can be expected that all problems of individual differences will be linked more and more with the general psychological laws of behavior and development and that in this way a deeper understanding of both the individual differences and the general laws will be possible.

Social Knowledge

Attitudes and Behavior

Attitudes

Gordon W. Allport (1935)

This section on social knowledge (Readings 4–12) begins by examining attitudes and their role in the behavior of the person holding the attitude. The concept of attitude was so central to social psychology that in the first few decades of this century, this field was described as "the scientific study of attitudes" (Allport, 1935). Today, attitudes and the attitude-behavior relationship continue to be at the very heart of social psychological thought.

Allport's comprehensive chapter on attitudes in the very first *Handbook of Social Psychology* (1935) summarizes and integrates all the work from the beginning of the scientific inquiry into attitudes. This chapter became required reading for all attitude researchers during the next few decades. In fact, portions of Allport's chapter are still reprinted in the most recent edition of the *Handbook* some 50 years later (the only original chapter so honored.)

The following excerpt begins with Allport's collection of the many definitions of attitude. Notice that an essential feature of these definitions is the concept of attitude as preparation or readiness to respond. Our views about attitudes have changed somewhat over the last half century, and a more recent conceptual definition is: "...an attitude is a mediating process grouping a set of objects of thought in a conceptual category that evokes a significant pattern of response...." (McGuire, 1985, p. 239). This is a thorough but complex definition, so McGuire also proposes a simpler working definition of attitudes as: "responses that locate 'objects of thought' on 'dimensions of judgment'" (p. 239). These definitions suggest that response readiness has developed into an evaluative and categorizing process.

Allport also summarizes our understanding of how attitudes develop and affect everyday life (for a more specific and detailed analysis of his work on attitudes and prejudice, see Reading 25). Allport identifies four conditions for forming attitudes. Three invoke socialization processes while a fourth (trauma) is suggestive of single-trial learning. (Another interesting early analysis of how attitudes are developed and maintained can be found in Reading 28—Hollingsworth, 1916.) Finally, this excerpt includes Allport's analysis of attitudes in everyday life. While his specific examples may seem dated, the chapter is rich in hypotheses and relates to continuing research today (see Reading 20—Bandura, Ross, & Ross, 1961 and Reading 24—Gould, 1972).

The concept of attitude is probably the most distinctive and indispensable concept in contemporary American social psychology. No other term appears more frequently in experimental and theoretical literature. Its popularity is not difficult to explain. It has come into favor, first of all, because it is not the property of any one psychological school of thought, and therefore serves admirably the purposes of eclectic writers. Furthermore, it is a concept which escapes the ancient controversy concerning the relative influence of heredity and environment. Since an attitude may combine both instinct and habit in any proportion, it avoids the extreme commitments of both the instinct-theory and environmentalism. The term likewise is elastic enough to apply either to the dispositions of single, isolated individuals or to broad patterns of culture. Psychologists and sociologists therefore find in it a meeting point for discussion and research. This useful, one might almost say peaceful, concept has been so widely adopted that it has virtually established itself as the keystone in the edifice of American social psychology. In fact several writers (cf. Bogardus, 1931; Thomas and Znaniecki, 1918; Folsom, 1931) *define* social psychology as the scientific study of attitudes.

As might be expected of so abstract and serviceable a term, it has come to signify many things to many writers, with the inevitable result that its meaning is somewhat indefinite and its scientific status called into question. Among the critics (e.g., Bain, 1927–28; McDougall, 1933; Symonds, 1927), McDougall has been the most severe:

> American social psychologists and sociologists have recently produced a voluminous literature concerning what they call "social attitudes"; the term is used to cover a multitude of facts of many kinds including almost every variety of opinion and belief and all the abstract qualities of personality, such as courage, obstinacy, generosity and humility, as well as the units of affective organization which are here called "sentiments." I cannot see how progress in social psychology can be made without a more discriminating terminology (1933, p. 219).

It is undeniable that the concept of 'attitude' has become something of a factotum for both psychologists and sociologists. But, in spite of all the animadversions of critics, the term is now in nearly universal use and plays a central role in most of the recent systematic studies in social psychology. It is therefore a concept which students must examine with unusual care.

ATTITUDES AS A FORM OF READINESS

Let us now consider a representative selection of definitions and characterizations of attitude.

> [An attitude is] readiness for attention or action of a definite sort (Baldwin, 1901–05).

> Attitudes are literally mental postures, guides for conduct to which each new experience is referred before a response is made (Morgan, 1934, p. 47).

> Attitude = the specific mental disposition toward an incoming (or arising) experience, whereby that experience is modified, or, a condition of readiness for a certain type of activity (*Dictionary of Psychology*, Warren, 1934).

> An attitude is a complex of feelings, desires, fears, convictions, prejudices or other tendencies

that have given *a set or readiness to act* to a person because of varied experiences (Chave, 1928).

> ...a more or less permanently enduring state of readiness of mental organization which predisposes an individual to react in a characteristic way to any object or situation with which it is related (Cantril, 1934*a*).

> From the point of view of Gestalt psychology a change of attitude involves a definite physiological stress exerted upon a sensory field by processes originating in other parts of the nervous system (Köhler, 1929, p. 184).

> An attitude is a tendency to act toward or against something in the environment which becomes thereby a positive or negative value (Bogardus, 1931, p. 62).

> By attitude we understand a process of individual consciousness which determines real or possible activity of the individual counterpart of the social value; activity, in whatever form, is the bond between them (Thomas and Znaniecki, 1918, p. 27).

> The attitude, or preparation in advance of the actual response, constitutes an important determinant of the ensuing social behavior. Such neural settings, with their accompanying consciousness, are numerous and significant in social life (F. H. Allport, 1924, p. 320).

> An attitude is a mental disposition of the human individual to act for or against a definite object (Droba, 1933).

> [An attitude] denotes the general set of the organism as a whole toward an object or situation which calls for adjustment (Lundberg, 1929).

> [Attitudes] are modes of emotional regard for objects, and motor "sets" or slight, tentative reactions toward them (Ewer, 1929, p. 136).

> An attitude, roughly, is a residuum of experience, by which further activity is conditioned and controlled.... We may think of attitudes as acquired tendencies to act in specific ways toward objects (Krueger and Reckless, 1931, p. 238).

> When a certain type of experience is constantly repeated, a change of set is brought about which affects many central neurons and tends to spread over other parts of the central nervous system. These changes in the general set of the central nervous system temper the process of reception.... In terms of the subjective mental

life these general sets are called attitudes (Warren, 1922, pp. 360 f.).

An attitude is a disposition to act which is built up by the integration of numerous specific responses of a similar type, but which exists as a general neural "set," and when activated by a specific stimulus results in behavior that is more obviously a function of the disposition than of the activating stimulus. The important thing to note about this definition is that it considers attitudes as broad, generic (not simple and specific) determinants of behavior (G. W. Allport, 1929).

We shall regard attitudes here as verbalized or verbalizable tendencies, dispositions, adjustments toward certain acts. They relate not to the past nor even primarily to the present, but as a rule, to the future. Sometimes, of course, it is a hypothetical future.... The "attitude" is primarily a way of being "set" toward or against things (Murphy and Murphy, 1931, p. 615).

It is not difficult to trace the common thread running through these diverse definitions. In one way or another each regards the essential feature of attitude as a *preparation or readiness for response*. The attitude is incipient and preparatory rather than overt and consummatory. It is not behavior, but the precondition of behavior. It may exist in all degrees of readiness from the most latent, dormant traces of forgotten habits to the tension or motion which is actively determining a course of conduct that is under way.

Some writers prefer to characterize attitudes in neurological and physiological terms. They regard attitudes as neural sets which in some cases may be as definite as a physical posture or muscular contraction, and in some cases diffuse and non-identifiable. Bernard (see Young, 1931, pp. 48 ff.) calls the identifiable bodily sets "neuromuscular attitudes" and the more diffuse mental sets, "neuropsychic attitudes." The former are fully prepared to issue into action, their final common path is determined. The neuropsychic attitudes on the other hand involve primarily the complex mechanisms of the cortex, which make delay and substitute forms of action pos-

sible. In principle, both mental and motor attitudes are alike. Both are expressions of a preparedness for adjustive behavior, and both ultimately are related to the neural substrata. What these neural substrata are, however, is a problem which remains almost wholly in the sphere of speculation. Only in the simplest instances can the direct involvement of definable regions of the body be determined. For the most part attitudes are diffuse and pervasive. That they involve skeletal, visceral, cortical, and subcortical activity probably no psychologist would deny, but what these correlates are none can tell.

Time and again the phenomena of perception, judgment, memory, learning, and thought have been reduced largely to the operation of attitudes (cf. e.g., Ach, 1905; Bartlett, 1932; Chapman, 1932; Pyle, 1928). Without guiding attitudes the individual is confused and baffled. Some kind of preparation is essential before he can make a satisfactory observation, pass suitable judgment, or make any but the most primitive reflex type of response. Attitudes determine for each individual what he will see and hear, what he will think and what he will do. To borrow a phrase from William James, they "engender meaning upon the world"; they draw lines about and segregate an otherwise chaotic environment; they are our methods for finding our way about in an ambiguous universe. It is especially when the stimulus is not of great intensity nor closely bound with some reflex or automatic response that attitudes play a decisive role in the determination of meaning and of behavior.

Since reflex and automatic response have little place in social psychology, it is with attitudes that social psychology must be concerned. The whims of fashion, the success and the failure of propaganda, the swing of public opinion, the depredations of a mob, and a change in moral standards are all alike unintelligible excepting in terms of the attitudes of individual men and women. It is knowledge of our associates' attitudes which enables each of us innumerable times every day to anticipate their behavior, and to insult, console, persuade, flatter, or amuse them, as we choose.

GENESIS OF ATTITUDES

Four Common Conditions for the Formation of Attitudes   One of the chief ways in which attitudes are built up is through the accretion of experience, that is to say, through the *integration* of numerous specific responses of a similar type. It is not, as a rule, the discrete and isolated experience which engenders an attitude; for in itself the single experience lacks organization in memory, meaning, and emotion. An attitude is characteristically a fusion, or, in Burnham's terms (1924, p. 285), a "residuum of many repeated processes of sensation, perception, and feeling."

It is a favorite doctrine of mental hygiene that *wholesome* attitudes are those which are the product of *all* experience that is relevant to a certain issue, without repressions or dissociations to mar their inclusiveness. Thus Morgan writes:

> A hasty generalization based on a very few incidents should be viewed with suspicion, [whereas if the attitude] grew from actual experiences, and is a correct abstract formulation of the lessons learned from a large number of these experiences, it should be rated high. (1934, p. 49)

Important as the mechanism of integration unquestionably is in the formation of attitudes, it has in recent years been criticized for its one-sided emphasis. The motto of integration is *e pluribus unum*. It inevitably implies that the infant is totally specific and fragmentary in his responses, and that in childhood his attitudes become gradually "pieced together," and that in adulthood he becomes still more thoroughly unified.

Certain recent developments in psychology have brought a quite contrary emphasis in their train. Integration, it is said, is not the only mechanism of development. It is supplemented by an equally important mechanism which has been variously called *individuation, differentiation,* or *segregation* (Holt, 1931; Lewin, 1935; Ogden, 1926; Pratt, Nelson, and Sun, 1930). According to this doctrine the original matrix of all attitudes is coarse, diffuse, and non-specific; it is the mass-action found in infancy, which tends only to have a general positive (adient) or negative (abient) orientation. From this point of view it might be said that in the beginning the infant has two primordial, non-specific attitudes, namely, approaching and avoiding. From this matrix, he must segregate action-patterns and conceptual systems which will supply him with adequate attitudes for the direction of his adaptive conduct.

A third important source of attitudes is the dramatic experience, or *trauma*. It is well known that a permanent attitude may be formed as the result of a compulsive organization in the mental field following a single intense emotional experience. Probably everyone can trace certain of his fears, dislikes, prejudices, and predilections to dramatic incidents of childhood. Sometimes, as Freudians have shown, the source of these early fixations are suppressed and forgotten, and the resulting attitude, though strong, seems to be of mysterious origin. But sometimes the whole process of traumatic fixation is accessible to memory. The recovery of the traumatic origins to consciousness does not necessarily weaken the attitude. The autobiography of W. E. Leonard (1927) illustrates the tenacity of early attitudes of fear in spite of the insight acquired into their origin. Although the traumatic experiences of childhood seem to be especially important, there is all through life a susceptibility to the influence of emotional shock. In *Days without End* Eugene O'Neill traces the genesis of a young man's atheistic attitude to the death of his parents, and the restoration of his religious attitude to the critical illness of his wife many years later. Even in old age radical changes of attitude through circumstances of dramatic moment are not unknown.

There is a fourth common condition under which attitudes are formed. Through the imitation of parents, teachers, or playmates, they are sometimes adopted *ready-made*. Even before he has an adequate background of appropriate experience a child may form many intense and lasting attitudes toward races and professions, toward religion and marriage, toward foreigners and servants, and toward morality and sin. A parent's tone of voice in disapproving of the ragamuffins who live along the railroad track is enough to produce an uncritical attitude in the child who has no basis in his experience for the rational adoption of the parent's point of view. It frequently happens that *subsequent* experience is fitted into the attitude thus uncritically adopted, not—as the mental hygienist advocates—made the basis for the attitude. In such cases every contact is prejudged, contradictory evidence is not admitted, and the attitude which was borrowed second-hand is triumphant. Few men have actually encountered "tricky Japanese" or "cruel Turks," few have known tragedy to follow a dinner party of thirteen, or the lighting of three cigarettes from the same match. And yet thousands of such attitudes and beliefs are adopted ready-made and tenaciously held against all evidence to the contrary.

PREJUDGMENT AND PREJUDICE

Whenever a pre-existing attitude is so strong and inflexible that it seriously distorts perception and judgment, rendering them inappropriate to the demands of the objective situation, the social psychologist usually designates this tenacious attitude as a *stereotype, a prejudice,* or sometimes, more loosely, as a *logic-tight compartment.* These three concepts, which are more or less interchangeable, are of great value in the explanation of social phenomena.* They explain why the skillful propagandist chooses solidified emotional attitudes to play upon. They tell why human beings persevere in ancient ruts of thought and action, and why "facts" are of relatively little importance in shaping public opinion, and why the dead hand of the past is permitted to fashion the social policies of the present day. They explain why the banal remarks of a famous man or woman are widely circulated and reverently quoted, and why the cleverer epigrams and shrewder pronouncements of an unknown sage are ignored or discounted. They help one to understand the characteristic conservatism and the "cultural lag" of society.

Experimental Studies of Prejudgment. In a simple way, Zillig (1928) demonstrated the effect of personal likes and dislikes upon observation and report. She had secretly instructed some children who were very popular with their schoolmates to make a certain error during a classroom demonstration of physical drill (for example, to raise their left arms instead of their right). Unpopular children in the same demonstration performed the exercise correctly. When the class was asked to report the names of the children who made mistakes during the exercise, the faultless but unpopular pupils received the blame! Working with the older students, Lund (1925) discovered an agreement between *desire* and *belief.* It is not knowledge, he found, which determines the strength of a conviction but rather the desirability of this conviction from the point of view of the individual holding it. Sargent (cited in Murphy and Murphy, 1931, pp. 681–683) discovered that the more intensely emotional an attitude the less flexible is the meaning or definition of the object of that attitude. For example, if one has a marked attitude toward socialism, the meaning of the concept is more stereotyped and less susceptible of change than if one pos-

Editors' note: Prejudice now often refers to evaluative or affective responses (feelings) toward an individual based on his/her group membership, whereas *stereotype* now refers to a belief or set of beliefs (cognitions) about that person based on his/her group membership.

sesses no strong feelings concerning the matter. Probably the best-known work in this field is that of Rice (1926–27). He demonstrated by the use of photographs the existence of visual stereotypes concerning vocational and racial types (e.g., the senator, the bootlegger, and the Bolshevik), as well as the effect of these stereotypes upon judgments concerning the intelligence and craftiness of the men whose pictures were employed.

A demonstration of aesthetic stereotypes has been made by Sherif (1935). This investigator secured, as a first step in his study, the rank-order preferences of his subjects for sixteen English and American authors (such as Barrie, Conrad, Cooper, Dickens, Poe, Scott, Stevenson, and Wilder). After an interval of several weeks he submitted sixteen literary passages, all from Stevenson, but each passage ascribed to one of the authors included in the first list. The subjects were then required to rank these passages in order of their literary merit. In no case did any subject suspect the deception.

A few judges reported that in ranking the passages they ignored altogether the names of the "authors" which appeared underneath each passage. In these cases, as might be expected, the correlation between the original preference for the authors and the rating for the merit of the passage was zero. But for the remaining subjects, nearly two hundred in number, the average correlation was +.46. Work attributed to a favorite author is considered good, and work attributed to an uncongenial author is considered bad. Since the passages are in fact from a single author, and since the same results are secured whatever author's name is appended to a passage, it is clear that the correlations obtained can only be a measure of prejudice.

ATTITUDES AND EVERYDAY LIFE

Social psychology, by its very nature, must be concerned with the problems of everyday life (cf. Cantril, 1934b). This chapter has already indicated the importance of attitudes in the study of racial relations, esthetic and moral prejudice, public opinion, the psychology of rural and student populations, and in other practical fields. One could extend very greatly this list of problems.

Changing Social Attitudes   Hart (1933) has surveyed in broad perspective the decline of public interest in religion and the growth of interest in science; he has studied also the growth and decline of sentiment favorable to prohibition, the increasing opposition in America to the interests of big business, and the increasing sentiment for disarmament. His method was indirect and consisted in the study of the circulation and contents of widely read magazines where one finds "precipitated layers of evidence about the intellectual and emotional life of past years."

It should be noted that in proportion as *common* attitudes are changed in the same direction social stability is essentially preserved, for all individuals alter their opinions together. The phenomenon in this case would be one merely of "social change." But in proportion as the common attitudes are disrupted and replaced by all manner of diverse and discordant *individual* attitudes there results inevitably a "social disintegration." The present century has witnessed the breaking-down of many common social attitudes, and the growth of very few new common attitudes to take their place. It must, therefore, be regarded as a period of social disintegration.

Criminality   The almost complete failure of both traditional and "enlightened" penology has intensified interest in the case-histories of individual delinquents (Glueck and Glueck, 1930, 1934). These histories reveal first and foremost the importance of attitudes. As a group, prisoners have intense attitudes of self-justification, loyalty, and belief in luck, as well as a tendency to exaggerate the defects of society and of their enemies (Field, 1931). Some reformers rest their efforts upon a policy of habit-training, assuming that re-education and rehabilitation are to be achieved only through a slow process of reconditioning each separate habit. Contrary to this policy, others insist that the best way to reform is to change an individual's point of view as a whole. If a new orientation can be acquired, the old and socially unsatisfactory habits will be dropped out and new ones will be automatically acquired. This point of view assumes that general attitudes exert a control over specific and subordinate attitudes (cf. pp. 820–824), an assumption which derives much support from Dunlap's discovery (1932) that the breaking of habits does not depend on the slow and painful process of reconditioning so much as upon the formation of a new controlling attitude.

The Influence of Moving Pictures upon Children
Using "rational scales" of the type described in the preceding section, Peterson and Thurstone (1933) studied the effect of films that treat controversial subjects in a partisan way. After seeing *The Birth of a Nation* a group of over four hundred children who had previously had little or no acquaintance with Negroes showed a pronounced shift of attitude in a direction unfavorable to the Negro, and after an interval of five months a large part of the prejudice remained. *The Son of the Gods* caused a shift of attitude in a direction definitely favorable to the Chinese; *Four Sons* made children more friendly toward the Germans; *The Criminal Code* caused a greater leniency toward criminals; *All Quiet on the Western Front* increased pacifism; *The Street of Chance* made children more severe in their judgment of gambling. Only one or two films failed to show some significant influence upon children's attitudes. It was clearly shown that the effects lasted over an interval of many months. In many cases they were undoubtedly permanent.

Vocational Psychology Tests for attitudes seem destined to become an established supple-

ment to tests for intelligence and skill. In the vocational field, interests (Fryer, 1931; Stone, 1933; Strong, 1927) are of great importance, likewise attitudes toward the occupation, the employer (Bogardus, 1927; Uhrbrock, 1933), and fellow workers. Although this type of study is still to a large extent experimental, it is supported by urgent demands from vocational counselors and from those engaged in personnel work.

Radicalism and Conservatism One of the problems which has aroused considerable interest is the nature of radical and conservative attitudes. The varieties of human activity to which the designations of "conservative" and "radical" may be applied are so numerous that attitudes wholly and consistently generalized will be rarely, if ever, encountered. Not every act of a radical is uniformly rebellious, and no conservative is steadfast in his loyalties to every established custom and code. Several investigators (G. W. Allport, 1929; Droba, 1934b; Likert, 1932–33; Vetter, 1930a, 1930b), however, find so many instances where radical (or conservative) opinion pertaining to diverse issues are consistently combined in the same individuals that they favor the view that to a considerable extent these attitudes may be generalized. The fact, for example, that certain justices of the United States Supreme Court can be relied upon to give "dissenting" liberal opinions and that the others are safely on the side of tradition is proof of the point at issue. Kolstad (1933) found that members of conservative religious bodies were more nationalistic in their sentiments than members of the free and non-conformist sects; also students attending private, non-sectarian colleges were more radical in their outlook than students attending public or sectarian colleges. Finally, many investigators agree that the more radical students on the whole have higher intelligence than the conservative students (G. W. Allport, 1929; Kolstad, 1933; Moore, 1925; Vetter, 1930b).

Influencing Attitudes Are attitudes influenced to a greater extent by the prestige of experts or by the prestige of the majority? This question has considerable practical significance. Moore (1921) found that in matters pertaining to speech and to morality college students more frequently change their own opinions to conform to those of the majority, but that in matters of esthetic judgment the expert is more influential. Boldyreff and Sorokin (1932) likewise found marked suggestibility to the esthetic opinions of experts. Following the false suggestion that musical critics preferred one of two *identical* Victrola records, the great majority of students actually "heard" these records as different and agreed that the one designated was preferable. Marple (1933) found that people are influenced greatly by both majority and expert opinion on social and political issues, and that the influence of the majority seems to be more marked than that of the expert. Considered psychologically, *propaganda* is altogether a matter of influencing attitudes. Among the writers who have treated propaganda from this point of view are Doob (1934), Biddle (1931, 1932), Dodge (1920), and Chen (1933).

RÉSUMÉ

Within the past fifteen years the doctrine of attitudes has almost completely captured and refashioned the science of social psychology. The nature of attitudes, however, is still in dispute, and it may correctly be questioned whether a science reared upon so amorphous a foundation can be strong. What is most urgently needed is a clarification of the doctrine of attitudes, and to this task the present chapter has been addressed.

Because of historical considerations it is necessary to include a wide range of subjective determining tendencies under the general rubric of Attitude. Yet it is both possible and desirable to distinguish between attitudes and many correlative forms of readiness-for-response. Attitudes proper may be *driving* or *directive, specific* or *general, common* or *individual*. They characteristically have a material or conceptual object of reference, and are "pointed" in some direction with respect to this object. If they are so generalized that the object and the direction are not identifiable, they then merge into what may be called the "traits" of personality. Common attitudes can be roughly classified and measured, and when abstracted from the personalities which contain them they constitute the "socius" which is that portion of the unique personality of special interest to social science.

Attitudes are never directly observed, but, unless they are admitted, through inference, as real and substantial ingredients in human nature, it becomes impossible to account satisfactorily either for the consistency of any individual's behavior, or for the stability of any society.

READING 5

Increasing Attitude-Behavior Correspondence by Broadening the Scope of the Behavioral Measure

Russell H. Weigel and Lee S. Newman (1976)

Weigel and Newman address an old but continuing controversy that is fundamental in social psychology, namely, the relationship between the attitudes one holds and how one behaves. In a classic study of attitudes and behavior toward Chinese in the depression era, LaPiére (1934) challenged notions about the correspondence between attitudes and behavior. Since LaPiére, the debate has continued, fueled by an important review of the research by Wicker (1969) who reported that attitudes did not predict behavior well at all.

Many studies have attempted to demonstrate the ability of attitudes to predict behavior. After examining 109 studies, Ajzen and Fishbein (1977) conclude that attitudes predict behavior when the measures of both the attitude and the behavior have similar degrees of specificity. Thus, if the attitude survey is general, the measurements of behavior must tap a similarly general domain in order for the attitude survey to be predictive of behavior. And, measuring specific attitudes corresponding to specific behaviors is much more likely to predict those behaviors than very general measures of attitudes. Also, both measures should assess both the behavior *and* the target (person or thing) at which the behavior is directed. Finally, multiple measures of an attitude are more likely to correlate with the attitude than will only a single measure of that attitude.

Weigel and Newman summarize Ajzen and Fishbein's arguments (from an earlier 1973 review), and then test attitude-behavior correspondence in a study that resolves many of the problems noted by Ajzen and Fishbein. In this study, Weigel and Newman investigate attitudes about a variety of environmental issues. Several months later they examine three types of behavior directly relevant to the attitudes measured. They collect both the attitude and behavior measures from the *same* person (unlike LaPiére, 1934, and a surprising number of other researchers). They also use an attitude scale that they know is reliable, and they measure the targeted behaviors several times to increase the stability of their behavior indices.

Abstract

Concerns about the adequacy of both the methodology and behavioral criteria employed in much of the past research on attitude-behavior consistency prompted this field experiment. The environmental attitudes of 44 subjects were assessed using a measure whose reliability and validity had been previously established. During the next 8 months each subject was offered opportunities to engage in a variety of distinct ecologically oriented behaviors. As hypothesized, the attitude measure exhibited only modest capacity to predict performance or nonperformance of the actions associated with each of these single behavioral criteria (mean r = .29, p < .10). However, when these single criteria were combined into a more comprehensive behavioral index intended to map out an action domain of comparable breadth to the attitude domain assessed, the correlation between scores on this index and scores on the attitude measure was much more pronounced (r = .62, p < .001). The implications of these findings for attitude-behavior research are discussed.

The frequent reports of low or nonsignificant correlations between attitude measures and behavioral criteria (e.g., Wicker, 1969) clearly challenge the proposition that attitudes are precursors of action (i.e., predispositions to respond to an object in a consistently favorable or unfavorable manner). It is a challenge that has provoked a variety of reactions ranging from profound disenchantment with the utility of attitudes for understanding human activity (Deutscher, 1966; Wicker, 1969) to phenomenologically oriented defenses of the attitude concept (Brandt, 1970; Kelman, 1974). Other authors have responded to the accumulated evidence of attitude-behavior inconsistency by suggesting conceptual and methodological refinements intended to increase the likelihood of correspondence between attitude and action. These refinements represent a shift in the focus of research efforts; a shift from examining whether or not attitudes are related to behavior to examining the conditions under which attitudes and behavior covary. In particular, more recent research has displayed recurring interest in both the effects of other personal and situational variables which, when operative, could counteract and obscure the impact of attitude on behavior (Bowers, 1968; Ehrlich, 1969; Frideres, Warner, & Albrecht, 1971; Insko & Schopler, 1967; Schofield, 1975; Warner & DeFleur, 1969; Weigel & Amsterdam, 1976) and the degree to which the attitude measure specified the behavioral criterion employed (Crespi, 1971; Davidson & Jaccard, 1975; Fishbein, 1966; Heberlein & Black, 1976; Weigel, Vernon, & Tognacci, 1974; Weinstein, 1972; Wicker & Pomazal, 1971).

Fishbein and Ajzen (Ajzen & Fishbein, 1970, 1972, 1973; Fishbein, 1967, 1973) have presented a carefully articulated conceptual model which simultaneously addresses both the "other variables" and specificity issues. First, they suggest that attitude measures should focus on the respondent's beliefs and feelings about engaging in particular behaviors (i.e., attitude toward the act) rather than on the respondent's beliefs and feelings about particular objects. That is, instead of asking about respondents' general attitudes toward black people as a group, researchers should assess their attitudes toward the act of working with blacks, living in a desegregated neighborhood, participating in a civil rights demonstration, and so on. Consistent with the specificity notion, the likelihood of engaging in a particular action should be better predicted by one's attitude toward the act itself than by one's attitude toward an associated object or class of objects. The second suggestion advanced by Fishbein and Ajzen represents an attempt to specify the other variables which should be measured along with attitude toward the act to facilitate behavioral prediction. At various times in its development the nonattitudinal variables incorporated into this model included the personal and social norms pertinent to the behavior in question and the person's motivation to comply with these norms. Variables not incorporated into the model, then, are assumed to influence behavior only if they affect attitude toward the act or one of these nonattitudinal predictor variables.

Although a number of studies have provided empirical support for Fishbein and Ajzen's conceptual model (see Ajzen & Fishbein, 1973), some concerns also have been expressed. Schwartz and Tessler (1972), for example, pointed out that since a wide array of extraneous variables could affect the attitude-behavior relationship (e.g., competing attitudes and motives, activity level, expressive style, demographic characteristics), the model's selective focus is not sufficient to eliminate the necessity for sampling further from these other potential antecedents of behavior. Indeed, because the number of potentially important other variables is essentially infinite, the logic of this approach confronts attitude researchers concerned with the behavioral implications of their measures with the formidable task of attempting to anticipate and independently assess the full range of variables that might disrupt attitude-behavior correspondence.

Schwartz and Tessler also noted the limitations of reliance on attitude toward the act. While their research indicated that attitude-toward-act measures improved prediction of a given behavior, the authors caution that attitude toward the act is limited to the prediction of only very specific behaviors in particular situations, "while researchers often wish to use attitudes to predict a range of presumably related behavior across a variety of situations" (Schwartz & Tessler, 1972, p. 235). Indeed, when evaluating the wisdom of employing attitude-toward-act measures, it seems reasonable to ask whether or not the attitude concept has become somewhat sterile in evolving from a concept representing a relatively stable underlying disposition capable of mediating a variety of object-related behaviors to a concept which seems to equate attitudes and behaviors under specified situational circumstances. Certainly as Cook and Selltiz (1964) have pointed out, "if validly distinguished, a dispositional concept has, by its very nature, a wider range of situational relevance—including projectability into relatively novel situations" (p. 36). Without contesting the power of attitude-toward-act measures for predicting a specific behavioral response, then, we feel that the proposition that traditional attitude-toward-object measures can capture broad, enduring dispositions with strong and diverse behavioral implications merits further investigation. While this view stands in marked contrast to the bulk of the currently available findings revealing nonsignificant correlations between attitude-toward-object measures and overt behavior, two lines of argument raising questions about the adequacy of the methodology and behavioral criteria employed in these studies can be developed which suggest the wisdom of renewed inquiry.

The Methodology Problem

Although Wicker's influential review of the attitude-behavior literature (Wicker, 1969) indicates that traditional attitude-toward-object measures rarely have been able to account for as much as 10% of the variance on overt behavioral measures, serious methodological problems cast doubt on the quality of much of the research cited. Indeed, when Dillehay (1973) critically re-examined the most frequently referenced investigations reporting low correspondence between attitudes and actions, he concluded that these studies (Kutner, Wilkins, & Yarrow, 1952; LaPiére, 1934; Minard, 1952) were irrelevant to the attitude-behavior issue for a variety of reasons. For example, Dillehay points out that in both LaPiére's (1934) widely cited study and a similar investigation conducted by Kutner et al. (1952), it was quite likely that the subjects who provided the behavioral data were *not* the same people from whom the attitude data were obtained.

A pervasive problem which prompts further suspicions about the credibility of much of the past attitude-behavior research is the widespread lack of concern with establishing the reliability and validity of the attitude measures employed. The point is simple, important, and frequently overlooked: One reason why a low correlation between attitude and behavior might obtain in a given study is that a poor quality attitude measure was used. In hopes of examining this possibility further, we managed to recover 42 of the 47 original papers cited in Wicker's (1969) tabular summary of the attitude-behavior literature. Our purpose was to determine the effect of variation in the quality of the attitude measure (i.e., whether or not data documenting the reliability and validity of a measure had been collected) on the magnitude of the attitude-behavior correlations observed. This effort was abandoned be-

cause in the vast majority of the cases the attitude measures employed were not described in sufficient detail to permit such an appraisal. The absence of this information in these published studies is revealing in itself, however. That is, it seems reasonable to demand that investigations purporting to examine the relationship between attitudes and actions should explicitly provide evidence of the internal consistency of the attitude measure for the current sample as well as some evidence of the measure's validity derived from an independent sample. Without these data the question of how frequently poor quality attitude measures have been responsible for low attitude-behavior correlations remains unanswered but provocative.

The Behavioral Criterion Problem

Attitude measures should be expected to predict only behaviors that are appropriate to the attitude under consideration. It would follow, then, that measures assessing attitudes toward a highly specific object or behavior should predict behavioral responsiveness to that particular object or the likelihood that the individual will engage in the behavior specified. As previously noted, this specificity hypothesis has received empirical support in a number of studies. On the other hand, when the attitude object is a general or comprehensive one (e.g., black people, the environment, the government), then the behavioral criterion should be equally general or comprehensive. An adequate test of attitude-behavior consistency under these circumstances would demand the use of several independent measures of behavior designed to adequately sample the universe of action implications engaged by the attitude measure.[1]

---

[1]Despite the logic of this argument, 85% of the 42 studies we recovered from Wicker's tabular list utilized behavioral criterion measures which could be characterized as a single or repeated observation of only one type of action. By contrast, those investigators who included a number of distinct

This latter point has been articulated repeatedly (Calder & Ross, 1973; Doob, 1947; Fishbein, 1973; Thurstone, 1931; Tittle & Hill, 1967a) but largely ignored in past empirical research. In elaborating these arguments, Fishbein (1973) has emphasized that while two people may hold equally favorable attitudes toward a given object, their specific actions with respect to that object may vary considerably. Taken together, however, their behaviors will be similar in revealing the same degree of favorableness toward the object. Hence, Fishbein concludes that scores on traditional attitude-toward-object measures should not be expected to predict an isolated single act, but should predict "multiple-act criteria" (single or multiple observations of *different* behaviors reflecting the overall pattern of the person's actions with respect to the attitude-object).

The only empirical evidence related to this claim has been generated quite recently. Fishbein and Ajzen (1974) had 62 undergraduates check which of 100 religious behaviors they had performed as well as complete five traditional attitude measures assessing beliefs and feelings about religion. Results indicated that scores on all five attitude scales were highly correlated with the total number of different behaviors performed (mean $r = .66$), whereas the correlations between the attitude scales and single behavioral self-report items were low and nonsignificant (mean $r = .14$). Although these findings support the proposition that attitude-toward-object measures can predict multiple-act criteria, the data remain vulnerable to criticism on two grounds. First, the authors rely on retrospective behavioral reports rather than on direct observation of behaviors in constructing their multiple-act measure. In view of the evidence that self-reports often contain substantial error (Brislin & Olmstead, 1973; Tittle & Hill, 1967b), this reliance remains disconcerting despite the counterarguments noted by Fishbein and Ajzen. Second, not only were many of the activities part of the regular experience of the subjects but the attitude measures apparently were taken immediately after the behavioral self-report measures were completed. Given this state of affairs, the high correlations may have resulted from a tendency for subjects to infer their attitudes from the frequency with which their past behavioral choices—choices made salient by the data-gathering procedure—implied a given attitude (Bem, 1967).[2] Insofar as these difficulties tend to limit the confidence which can be placed in Fishbein and Ajzen's findings, they serve to underscore the need for further inquiry with respect to the capacity of attitude-toward-object measures for predicting broad configurations of object-relevant behaviors.

The hypothesis of the present study was tested under the following conditions. The study utilized an attitude scale measuring concern about environmental quality. The scale's content ranged broadly across conservation, and pollution issues and evidence of the measure's reliability and validity had been previously established. Because of the broad focus of the attitude measure, a fair test of attitude-behavior relationships demanded that subjects be presented with a diverse array of opportunities to manifest in their overt behavior variation in their concern about environmental protection. Consequently, a variety of behavioral measures was employed, and scores on the attitude scale were compared with scores on these measures. These separate

---

object-relevant behaviors in their criterion measures all found evidence that attitude scores were significantly related to at least some of the behavioral criteria employed in each study (Bernberg, 1952; Carr & Roberts, 1965; Fendrich, 1967; Goodmonson & Glaudin, 1971; Heron, 1954; Potter & Klein, 1957; Tittle & Hill, 1967a).

---

[2]Schwartz and Tessler (1972) raise a similar objection with respect to two other studies conducted by Ajzen and Fishbein (1969, 1970). They argue that relatively novel behavioral criteria should be utilized to preclude the possibility that past performance is the primary determinant of both attitude scores and behavioral reports.

measures also were combined to form a more comprehensive behavioral index intended to encompass a behavioral domain of comparable breadth to the attitude domain assessed. Under these conditions, we hypothesized that attitude scores reflecting broadly focused concerns about environmental quality will be highly correlated with scores on the comprehensive behavioral index but not with performance or nonperformance of each of the separate behaviors from which the index was derived.

METHOD

Subjects

A survey of attitudes toward a variety of social problems (about 20% of the items focused on environmental issues) was administered to 91 residents of a medium-sized New England town. These 91 respondents represented 87% of the total number of subjects designated by the original random sample. In order to reduce the number of subjects to a manageable size with respect to our capacities for behavioral follow-up, a subsample of 50 individuals was selected on a random basis. The 3-month interval between the administration of the initial attitude survey and the first follow-up contact generated some attrition: Four persons could not be contacted because they had moved away from the area during the interim, one person could not be contacted because she was on vacation for the entire summer, and one other was dropped from further consideration because he was in the process of moving during the summer, which precluded the possibility of obtaining the full range of behavioral data from him. The final subject pool, then, consisted of 44 persons including 25 males and 19 females.

Procedures

Beginning 3 months after the survey data had been collected, the subjects were contacted three times during the ensuring 5-month period and of-

fered opportunities to participate in a variety of organized ecology projects. First, a confederate solicited signatures on the three petitions described below in the Behavioral Criteria section. The confederate had previously participated in an intensive training program which included the learning of a standardized script specifying how to approach the subjects, role-playing procedures designed to anticipate potential questions and develop a standard set of responses, and 10 practice interviews with persons in a neighboring town not included in the present study. The confederate was given a randomized list of names and addresses. He was not given any information as to how the subjects had responded to the initial survey and was instructed not to probe for the general level of interest in environmental issues. Instead, the importance of approaching each individual on the list in the same manner was emphasized repeatedly. Approximately 6 weeks later, a second confederate contacted the subjects soliciting their help in a series of roadside litter pick-ups. After another 8-week interval, a third confederate contacted the subjects soliciting their participation in a recycling program. Both of these latter activities are described more fully in the Behavioral Criteria section. The order in which subjects were to be contacted was varied for each confederate to ensure that a given subject would not be uniformly contacted early or late with respect to all three activities. The same types of training and blinding procedures were employed for the second and third confederates as for the first.

Each of the three confederates claimed to be a member of an environmental protection organization comprised of local citizens. This pretext was necessary to provide a credible cover story which would minimize the likelihood of suspicion about being contacted repeatedly with respect to the petition, litter pick-up, and recycling enterprises. None of the subjects expressed any suspicions about the legitimacy of the organization nor did any subjects question whether the confederates were associated with the survey that they had taken previously. With respect to the ethical implications of these deceptions, it should be noted that the organization did in fact fulfill all promises made to the subjects: Signed petitions were forwarded to the specified congressman, roadside litter pick-ups were conducted as scheduled, and bottles and papers were collected on a weekly basis and delivered to the local recycling center. When the recycling project was concluded, each participating subject was contacted personally. It was explained that because of time commitments and financial considerations, the recycling program could not be continued. In general, subjects indicated that they regretted the termination of the recycling program but were appreciative of the time and effort required making the program difficult to manage on a volunteer basis. Thus, while subjects were never informed about the full nature of the experiment for fear of undermining their future responsiveness to environmental organizations, pains were taken to ensure that all subjects were treated with dignity and that all our obligations to provide environmental programs in which they could participate were honored.

The Attitude Measure

The environmental concern scale, a measure focusing on the level of attitudinal concern about a variety of conservation and pollution issues, was embedded in the initial survey. The measure was composed of 16 items, 9 of which were negatively stated and 7 of which were positively stated. Subjects rated each item along a 5-point Likert dimension ranging from strongly agree to strongly disagree. Each item was scored from 0 to 4, allowing the summed score across items for a given respondent to range from 0 to 64, with high scores indicating greater concern about protecting environmental quality. The environmental concern scale exhibited excellent internal consistency with respect to the responses of the 44 subjects included in the present study: Cronbach's (1951) alpha = .88 and Scott's (1968)

Homogeneity Ratio (H.R.) = .33. The highly satisfactory level of interitem consistency was not surprising because preliminary evidence of the reliability and validity of the environmental concern scale had been established previously. The items comprising this scale were selected from a pool of 31 items used by Weigel et al. (1974) in the prediction of subjects' responsiveness to requests for help in Sierra Club activities by members of that organization. The 16 items chosen were those which were the best predictors of the behavioral criterion employed in the Weigel et al. investigation (mean item-criterion correlation = .28, $p < .05$). Taken together, the 16 items exhibited a very satisfactory level of internal consistency for this previous sample ($\alpha = .83$, H.R. = .25).

The items included in the environmental concern scale employed in the present investigation, then, were employed on the basis of previously collected data suggesting their utility in terms of both forming a homogeneous attitude scale and demonstrated ability to predict behavioral variation. With respect to the considerations about attitude-behavior relationships raised in the introduction, the present investigation employed an attitude measure which had evinced both internal consistency and validity on a separate sample. What remained was to use this promising instrument to put the present hypotheses regarding attitude-behavioral relationships to an appropriate test. Such a test required the establishment of a set of behavioral criteria that specified a configuration of behaviors of sufficient breadth that they corresponded to the broad attitudinal focus of the environmental concern scale.

The Behavioral Criteria

Behavioral measures were employed which (a) were relatively novel with respect to the subjects' past experience, (b) were clearly related to environmental issues, and (c) would provide a number of independent opportunities to display the intensity of one's behavioral commitment to protecting environmental quality. Three general types of behavior, each involving a set of distinct actions, were assessed.

Petitioning   Three petitions were brought door-to-door by the first of the trained confederates. All three petitions were presented in a single trip and always in the following order: (a) a petition opposing oil drilling off the New England coast, (b) a petition opposing construction of nuclear power plants, and (c) a petition proposing more stringent regulation and punishment of those who remove air pollution devices from their automobile exhaust systems. Each petition had places for four signatures, but no names appeared on the petitions when presented to any given subject. This procedure was intended to standardize the presentation of petitions and to control for any differential sensitivity to conformity pressures resulting from previous accumulation of names. Each subject received a rehearsed explanation of the rationale for each petition and was told at the outset that the petitions would be sent to the congressman for the district. All subjects, regardless of whether or not they signed petitions, were asked if they would circulate the petitions to family or friends who might be interested in signing them. Subjects who accepted the blank petitions to circulate to friends and family were also given a preaddressed, stamped envelope in which to mail back signed sheets. An innocuous number in the upper right-hand corner of the "circulation" petitions enabled subject identification when the petitions were returned. Although 16 subjects refused to sign any petitions, and only 17 signed all three petitions, all but 2 subjects agreed to circulate extra copies to friends and family. Thus, while not all of the subjects who agreed followed through on their promise, nearly all of them were exposed to the opportunity to circulate not just at the door but by actually having blank petitions in hand. Petitioning behavior, then, was com-

prised of four separate acts: signing or not signing each of the three petitions and returning or not returning circulated petitions with at least one signature. Performance of a given act was scored 1 and nonperformance was scored 0.

Roadside litter pick-ups   Six weeks after the initial follow-up contact, a second confederate solicited the subjects' aid in a roadside litter pick-up program being conducted in nearby areas in the town. Subjects who agreed to participate gave the confederate their home phone number, specified whether they would prefer to work on weekday evenings or weekends, and were asked to recruit a friend or family member to participate as well. In a subsequent phone call, each subject was given a choice of three separate times to participate in the pick-up program. Subjects who indicated that they could participate at one of the three scheduled times were reminded of their promise in a second phone call the night before the scheduled date. Behavioral participation in the roadside litter pick-up program, then, involved two separate acts: participating or not participating on one of the three dates and recruiting or not recruiting at least one other person as the confederate had explicitly encouraged each subject to do. Performance of a given act was scored 1 and nonperformance was scored 0.

Recycling   Approximately 8 weeks later, subjects were contacted again by a third confederate. They were asked if they were willing to take part in a recycling program in which they would bundle their papers, remove metal rings from their bottles and put the recyclables outside where these materials could be picked up on a regular weekly route. Papers and bottles were then picked up every week for 8 weeks and delivered to a local recycling facility. In this instance a similar action (placing recyclable materials in the appropriate place at the time agreed upon) could be either performed or not performed on eight different occasions. Performance on a given occasion was scored 1 and non-performance was scored 0.

Comprehensive Behavioral Index It should be obvious that these 14 distinct behaviors were not selected capriciously. Rather, they were chosen because they provided a means of operationalizing the intensity of subjects' responses to the petitioning, litter pick-up, and recycling projects. For example, summing across the separate actions associated with the petition drive yielded a behavioral commitment scale with scores ranging from 0 to 4: one point for each petition signed and one point for returning circulated petitions. Similarly, summing across the separate actions associated with the litter pick-up and recycling projects yielded scales scored 0-2 and 0-8, respectively. These three scales, then, represented organized sets of actions—relatively independent avenues through which the attitude under consideration might seek behavioral expression.[3] All three scales were incorporated into a more comprehensive behavioral index in order to further articulate the contours of a behavioral domain comparable in breadth to the attitude domain assessed. In order to give the petitioning, litter pick-up and recycling scales equal weight in this index, subjects' z scores on each component scale were computed and summed.

RESULTS

Consistent with the arguments presented in the introduction, it was hypothesized that scores on the environmental concern scale would be highly correlated with scores on the comprehensive be-

havioral index but not with performance or non-performance of each of the separate behaviors from which the index was derived. The attitude-behavior correlations pertinent to this hypothesis are presented in Table 1.

These data support the hypothesis of the present study; attitude-behavior correspondence increases as the scope of the behavioral measure is broadened. Although the attitude scores made good predictions of a few of the single act criteria, and two thirds of these correlation coefficients were significant at the .05 level of confidence or better, the magnitude of the average correlation with the 14 single behaviors was quite modest (mean $r = .29$, $p < .10$). Combining single behaviors into three general categories yielded behavioral scales reflecting the intensity of the subject's responsiveness to the petitioning, litter pick-up, and recycling projects. The average correlation between attitude scores and scores on these three behavioral scales was considerably stronger (mean $r = .42$, $p < .01$). As hypothesized, the correlation between scores on the comprehensive behavioral index and scores on the environmental concern scale (.62, $p < .001$) was higher than the correlations between attitude scores and scores on any of the component behaviors. The meaning of these differences is underscored when one notes that while attitudinal variation, on the average, can account for less than 10% of the variance on the single behavioral measures, the amount of shared variance between attitudinal concern and the overall pattern of environmentally oriented actions is 38%.

DISCUSSION

The present study was designed to minimize the methodological and behavioral criterion problems which compromise the value of much of the past research on the relationship of attitudes and actions. The results indicate that a substantial attitude-behavior correlation can obtain when an attitude measure of established quality is em-

---

[3]The intercorrelations among these three behavioral scales were .29, $p < .10$ for the petitioning and litter pick-up measures, .07, $p > .10$ for the petitioning and recycling measures, and .25, $p < .10$ for the litter pick-up and recycling measures. The mean intercorrelation of .20 is sufficiently small to indicate the relative independence of the three behavioral scales—a finding which weakens the argument that subjects who opted to participate in the first environmental project would, by virtue of that response, be predisposed toward participation in later related activities.

TABLE 1						

CORRELATIONS BETWEEN SUBJECTS' ENVIRONMENTAL ATTITUDES AND BEHAVIORAL CRITERIA

Single behaviors	r^a	Categories of behavior	r^b	Behavioral index	r^b
Offshore oil	.41**				
Nuclear power	.36*	Petitioning behavior	.50**		
Auto exhaust	.39**	scale (0–4)			
Circulate petitions	.27				
Individual participation	.34*	Litter pick-up scale	.36*		
Recruit friend	.22	(0–2)		Comprehensive behavioral index	.62***
Week 1	.34*				
Week 2	.57***				
Week 3	.34*				
Week 4	.33*	Recycling behavior	.39**		
Week 5	.12	scale (0–8)			
Week 6	.20				
Week 7	.20				
Week 8	.34*				

Note. $N = 44$.
[a]Point-biserial correlations are reported in this column.
[b]Pearson product-moment correlations are reported in this column.
  *$p < .05$.
 **$p < .01$.
***$p < .001$.

ployed in conjunction with behavioral measures that map out an action domain of comparable breadth to the attitude domain assessed. Attitude scores representing broadly focused concerns about environmental quality made only modest predictions of performance or nonperformance of the 14 separate actions observed in this study. However, the correlation between scores on the attitude measure and scores on the comprehensive index combining these separate actions was much more pronounced.

These data seem compelling for a variety of reasons. First, the behavioral criteria utilized in this study were all overt behaviors, thereby eliminating the problems associated with using self-reports of past activities.[4] Second, the field setting and noncollege sample avoids the heavy-

---

[4]The scoring procedures used were unusually restrictive. For example, subjects receiving a score of 0 for the litter pick-up program not only included individuals who initially refused to participate in the project but also those subjects who gave the confederate their home phone numbers and agreed to participate but could not make one of the three alternative dates subsequently specified. Insofar as giving one's phone number to a representative of an environmental organization and expressing a willingness to work represent an increment in behavioral commitment over outright refusal, we might have justified the use of a 0–3 scoring system for the litter pick-up scale, in which 0 = refusal, 1 = agree to participate and give phone number but cannot make one of the three specified dates, 2 = participate alone, and 3 = participate and recruit others as well. When this scoring procedure is employed, the correlation between environmen-

reliance on undergraduate subjects that is characteristic of past research. Third, since the behavioral data were collected several months after the attitude measure was administered, the magnitude of the correlation observed suggests both the enduring character of attitudes and their continuing relevance for understanding actions with respect to the attitude object. Finally, the correlation characterizing the relationship between scores on the attitude scale and scores on the comprehensive behavioral index (.62) is much stronger than has generally been reported in previous research. As Wicker (1969) pointed out, attitude-behavior correlations "are rarely above .30 and often near zero. Only rarely can as much as 10% of the variance in overt behavioral measures be accounted for by the attitudinal data" (p. 65). By contrast, variation in environmental attitudes accounted for 38% of the variance in the overall behavioral configuration in the present study. Aside from documenting strong attitude-behavior correspondence in this instance, these findings suggest that future research examining the behavioral implications of attitude-toward-object measures should employ several independent measures of behavior designed to adequately sample the universe of object-relevant actions.

The strong attitude-behavior relationship observed in the present study is particularly impressive in that it emerged even in the absence of any attempt to take systematic cognizance of the effects of intervening personal and situational variables operating to attenuate the relationship. This outcome seems especially encouraging for attitude research because of the practical impossibility of anticipating all of the variables which

might disrupt attitude-behavior correspondence for a given subject in a given situation. A single example from the present study illustrates this point. A subject who scored high on the environmental concern scale initially agreed to participate in the litter pick-up project but later reversed her decision. In reneging on her offer, she told the confederate that she would have liked to participate, but her husband had asked her not to do so. She explained that her husband opposed her participation because he had hopes of organizing the Boy Scouts in a similar project and felt that the current project could undermine the realization of those hopes. In this case, pressure from the husband represented a situational variable which prevented the subject's participation in the litter pick-up program despite her proenvironment attitude. The effect of this idiosyncratic situational variable in disrupting attitude-behavior consistency was neutralized, in part, by assessing other environmentally oriented behaviors in which this situational pressure was not operative. Although the accuracy of such anecdotal information cannot be evaluated with precision, its implication remains provocative: The inordinate difficulty involved in attempting to anticipate and measure the effects of a potentially large number of extraneous variables may be circumvented by using multiple behavioral criteria.

In sum, the present data indicate that a high-quality attitude measure focusing on a general or comprehensive attitude-object can make strong predictions of behavioral variation when that behavioral variation is sought in the context of patterned sets of actions rather than in a single act. These findings stand in marked contrast to the predominantly pessimistic assessment of the utility of the attitude concept apparent in much contemporary social psychology literature. While this previous literature has been useful in inhibiting cavalier inferences about the meaning of attitude data, it also seems to have generated some unnecessary and unfortunate overkill. In the past when inconsistency occurred between

---

tal concern scores and litter pick-up scores jumps from .36 to .52 ($p < .01$). This, in turn, increases the correlation between environmental attitudes and scores on the comprehensive behavioral index to .68 ($p < .001$), raising the amount of shared variance to 47%. The more restrictive scoring procedure has been emphasized here, however, to avoid the possibility of confounding intentions and overt actions in this behavioral scale.

attitudes and behavior, the tendency was to question the wisdom of conceptualizing attitudes as underlying dispositions mediating a variety of behaviors rather than to question either the quality of the particular attitude measure or the appropriateness of the behavioral criteria employed. When these latter considerations are taken into account, the present data suggest that attitudes will exhibit a robust capacity to influence the direction that behavior will take. These data do not obviate the need for caution in claiming that a given study of attitudes is socially significant merely because the attitude-object is socially significant (Wicker, 1969). However, they do suggest that carefully developed attitude-toward-object measures will continue to be valuable tools in psychological research—tools capable of complementing both direct behavioral observation and highly specific, behaviorally focused attitude measures by assessing dispositions with enduring action implications across a variety of situational contexts.

Cognitive dissonance was theorized to occur when an individual perceives an inconsistency between two attitudes that he or she holds, or between an attitude and a behavior. This perception of inconsistency leads to a state of arousal that the individual seeks to reduce. Recent work indicates that more important than mere inconsistency is the perception that one has brought about an aversive event that could have been avoided but is now irrevocable (Cooper & Fazio, 1984).

Self-perception is a more parsimonious (simpler) proposal for describing how we come to know attitudes and beliefs. The theory predicts: "To the extent that internal cues are weak, ambiguous, or uninterpretable, the individual . . . must . . . rely on . . . external cues to infer the individual's inner states" (p. 25, Bem, 1972).

At first, researchers tried to develop a critical study that would incontrovertibly decide between the two competing theories. However, as Fazio, Zanna, and Cooper (1977) show in Reading 6, both theories are successful in explaining attitude change, but under different conditions. Thus the two theories serve as complementary formulations that enhance our understanding of attitude change.

READING 6

Dissonance and Self-Perception: An Integrative View of Each Theory's Proper Domain of Application

Russell H. Fazio, Mark P. Zanna, and Joel Cooper (1977)

In the late 1950s and 1960s, two major theories emerged to try to predict how we come to know our attitudes and beliefs and how we form attitudes that are consistent with our behaviors and other attitudes. Both theories reverse our common sense view that attitudes guide behavior, and suggest, instead, that our behavior directs our attitudes.

Abstract

The literature concerning the controversy between self-perception theories is reviewed. It is proposed that the two theories be regarded not as "competing" formulations but as complementary ones and, furthermore, that each theory is applicable only to its own specialized domain. Self-perception theory, it is suggested, accurately characterizes attitude change phenomena in the context of attitude-congruent behavior and dissonance theory attitude change in the context of attitude-discrepant behavior. Attitude-congruent is defined as any position within an individual's latitude of acceptance; attitude-discrepant as any position in the latitude of rejection. An experimental test of these notions produced confirming evidence. Subjects who were given an opportunity to misattribute any potential dissonance arousal to an external stimulus did not change their attitudes, relative to low choice subjects, if they were committed to endorsing a position in their latitude of rejection. If the commitment concerned a position in the latitude of acceptance, how-ever, these subjects did exhibit attitude change relative to low choice subjects.

If an individual freely chooses to perform a behavior which is discrepant from his attitude, he tends later to realign his attitude toward that behavior. For example, a subject who complies with an experimenter's request to write an attitude-discrepant essay against the legalization of marijuana is typically found to favor such legalization to a lesser degree than previously. This now classic attitude change effect is readily explained by both Festinger's theory of cognitive dissonance (1957) and Bem's self-perception theory (1972). Dissonance theory, in general, concerns the relationship between various cognitions. The theory posits the existence of a drivelike motivation to maintain consistency among relevant cognitions. Self-perception theory, on the other hand, concerns the passive inference of attitudinal dispositions from behavior. According to Bem (1972), "Individuals come to 'know' their own attitudes, emotions, and other internal states partially by inferring them from observations of their own overt behavior and/or the circumstances in which this behavior occurs" (p. 2). Social psychologists vary in which theory they endorse.

Although the underlying processes posited by each theory differ, the predictions drawn from each are very similar. According to both, individuals closely examine the behavior in question and the external environment. Both theories stress the importance of various situational cues, e.g., freedom of choice and level of monetary inducement, as possible external justifications (or, in the "language" of self-perception theory, external causal attributions) for the performance of attitude-discrepant behavior. In addition, both theories possess rare predictive and explanatory power in the sense that they can account for a great deal of attitude change data.

Given the similarity of dissonance and self-perception theories and the historical dominance of attitude research in social psychology, it is understandable that a controversy as to the relative superiority of one theory over the other emerged soon after Bem's (1965, 1967) proposal of self-perception theory as an alternative to cognitive dissonance theory. Social psychologists have largely conceptualized the two as "competing" theories and have expended much effort to disconfirm their nonpreferred theory. The details of the controversy need not be reviewed here. It will suffice to remark that the issue is far from settled. Neither theory has been convincingly demonstrated to be relatively superior (cf. Greenwald, 1975), despite a plethora of so-called "crucial experiments" (e.g., Snyder & Ebbesen, 1972; Ross & Shulman, 1973; Green, 1974; Schaffer, 1975; Swann & Pittman, 1975).

It shall be the aim of this paper to provide an integrated framework for the operation of both dissonance and self-perception processes. We hope to refocus the manner in which the two theories are viewed and to suggest an integration. More specifically, we propose that they not be regarded as "competing" theories. Our basic tenet is that dissonance and self-perception are actually complementary and that, within its proper domain of application, each theory is correct. Together the two theories provide a more complete conceptual framework for explaining the manner in which, and the conditions under which, the examination of one's behavior will lead to attitude change.

DISSONANCE THEORY AND ATTITUDE-DISCREPANT BEHAVIOR

A major difference between cognitive dissonance theory and self-perception theory concerns the matter of aversive tension. A motivation to reduce cognitive discrepancies is a central part of dissonance theory but, "in the self-perception explanation, there is no aversive motivational pressure postulated" (Bem, 1972, p. 17). This difference provides the characteristic by which dissonance and self-perception processes must ultimately be distinguished.

The recent development by Zanna and Cooper (1974) of an attributional framework in which the possible occurrence of dissonance arousal can be investigated has led to research on the question of dissonance as an aversive arousal state. Given the extensive review of this research by Zanna and Cooper (1976), only two relevant studies will be summarized here. We will emphasize the relevance of these findings to our view that dissonance and self-perception theories are complementary.

Following Schachter and Singer's (1962) theory that an emotion is a combination of arousal and a cognitive label, Zanna and Cooper (1974) reasoned that the arousal which is postulated to occur when one freely chooses to write a counterattitudinal essay is also amenable to cognitive labeling. As long as an individual in an induced-compliance setting attributes this presumed arousal to his performance of a counterattitudinal behavior, he will experience dissonance and attempt to reduce it, possibly via attitude change (cf. Worchel & Arnold, 1974). However, if the situational cues provide a reasonable alternative to which he can "misattribute" this arousal, then no dissonance and no subsequent attitude change will occur.

Zanna and Cooper (1974) varied potential cognitive labels by giving subjects a placebo which ostensibly produced a side effect of relaxation or tension or no side effect. Subjects were then placed in an induced-compliance situation where they wrote a counterattitudinal essay under conditions of high or low choice. The no side effects condition demonstrated the typical effect in which high choice subjects changed their attitudes more than low choice subjects. Of particular importance is the fact that this effect failed to occur in the conditions where subjects could attribute their arousal to the pill which supposedly made them feel tense. In the relaxation conditions, the attitude change effect was accentuated—presumably because the high choice subjects experienced arousal, despite believing that they had taken a relaxing drug.

From the data of Zanna and Cooper's experiment (1974), and other studies using the "misattribution" approach (e.g., Zanna, Higgins, & Taves, 1976), it is possible to infer that aversive arousal does result when one performs a counterattitudinal behavior. Cooper, Zanna, & Taves (1975) went further by demonstrating that arousal is a necessary condition for attitude-discrepant behavior to lead to attitude change. In their study, counterattitudinal advocacy did not affect subjects' attitudes when they had taken a drug (phenolbarbitol) which inhibited their becoming aroused. However, when subjects had taken an arousing drug (amphetamine), they did change their attitudes. This result constitutes further evidence that arousal is associated with attitude change in counterattitudinal, induced compliance situations.

Taken together, these studies confirm the dissonance theory proposition that freely choosing to perform an attitude-discrepant behavior leads to a state of aversive arousal (cf. Kiesler & Pallak, 1976). The findings cast serious doubt on the self-perception view that people infer their attitudes from counterattitudinal behavior without experiencing aversive motivational pressure. Self-perception theory obviously remains a powerful and useful predictive tool in the domain of attitude-discrepant behaviors. It well predicts the occurrence of attitude change and, furthermore, suggests the attributional process involved in the identification of arousal as dissonance. However, the theory cannot be considered to accurately capture and depict the process by which a person who behaves counterattitudinally is led to make a change of cognition. The research described demonstrates that cognitive inconsistency is accompanied by aversive arousal.

SELF-PERCEPTION THEORY AND ATTITUDE-CONGRUENT BEHAVIOR

An additional major difference between dissonance and self-perception theories concerns the theories' implications for attitude-congruent behavior. Self-perception theory predicts that a new attitude will emerge if an individual performs a behavior which is more extreme than is implied by his attitude. It is not necessary for the behavior to be attitude-discrepant. That is, self-perception theory leads to the expectation that attitude change will occur if the behavioral advocacy lies anywhere along the attitudinal continuum other than the person's preferred position.

Dissonance theory, on the other hand, predicts attitude change only if the behavior performed is discrepant with the attitude. The theory is not applicable to situations in which pro-attitudinal advocacy occurs. In fact, one might argue that the theory leads to a prediction of no attitude change in such situations on the basis that the two cognitions—attitude and the behavioral advocacy—form a consonant relationship.

There now exists much independent evidence supporting the basic self-perception notion concerning the inference of attitude from behavior (e.g., Bandler, Madaras, & Bem, 1968; Salancik, 1974). Also, in what has become a research area of increasing interest, it has been reliably demonstrated that an individual's interest in an activity can actually be undermined if he is provided with oversufficient external justification for the performance of a behavior he would normally freely engage in (e.g., Deci, 1971; Lepper, Greene, & Nisbett, 1973; Benware & Deci, 1975; Ross, 1976). Such "overjustification effects" are easily interpretable from a self-perception analysis, but are outside the realm of dissonance theory.

Most relevant to our concerns is the fact that Kiesler, Nisbett, and Zanna (1969) demonstrated attitude change in the direction of *more* favorability to the position advocated. Subjects committed themselves to argue against air pollution (a behavior generally consistent with their attitudes) to passers-by in the street. In addition, some of the subjects were led to believe that the performance of this behavior had implications for belief, while other subjects were led to believe that there was no such link between beliefs and behavior. Brief-relevant subjects were found to be more favorable to the position they were to advocate than were belief-irrelevant subjects or control subjects who were not committed to the behavior.

In the Kiesler et al. study (1969; cf. also Zanna & Kiesler, 1971), it is important to note the extremity of the behavior relative to the attitude. Although subjects committed themselves to perform a behavior which was generally consistent with their attitudes, proselytizing against pollution to passers-by on a street corner is probably a more extreme behavior than was implied by the subjects' attitudes. That is, while the subjects did hold antipollution attitudes, their attitudes were unlikely to have been of such an extreme nature that they would typically, and without request, proselytize against pollution. Any action which appears as ordinary behavior in relation to an individual's attitude should not lead to attitude change. The act implies nothing new about attitude and will not result in a self-attribution of a new, more extreme attitude. Only if the overt action is more extreme than implied by an individual's attitude will a self-attribution result in a shift to a more extreme position (cf. Pallak & Kleinhesselink, 1976).

LATITUDES OF ACCEPTANCE AND REJECTION

Thus far, we have argued that dissonance theory is appropriately applied to attitude-discrepant behaviors and self-perception theory to attitude-congruent behaviors. In conjunction, we suggest, the two theories can account for attitude change effects which result from the full range of behaviors. However, each theory has its proper and specialized domain of application.

In order to define each theory's domain, we have used such terms as attitude-congruent vs. attitude-discrepant, proattitudinal vs. counter-attitudinal, and consistent vs. inconsistent. In fact, such vague terms permeate the entire literature in this area. How are these terms to be defined? Operationally, at least, social psychologists have defined them by dichotomizing the attitudinal continuum. Any position on the same side of the midpoint as the subject's expressed attitude is typically considered congruent and any position on the opposite side is considered discrepant. Such an operational definition obscures some important distinctions. After all, is it not basically attitude-congruent for someone who is only slightly in favor of a given proposal to write an essay pointing out a few of the disadvantages of the proposal? Similarly, would it not be just as attitude-discrepant for this person to write an essay favoring an extreme version of the proposal as to write an essay arguing against the adoption of the proposal?

Festinger's (1957) original statement merely proposed that two cognitions are dissonant or discrepant with one another when one does not "follow from" the other. An endorsement of an extreme radical position does not follow from a slightly liberal attitude any more so than an endorsement of a conservative position does. That is, it may be just as counterattitudinal for a person who views himself as occupying a center-left position to favor a radical proposal as it is to favor a conservative one.

A more precise and psychologically meaningful definition than the typical midpoint dichotomy seems necessary. Such a definition may be garnered from the work of Sherif and his colleagues (Sherif, Sherif, & Nebergall, 1965; Sherif & Hovland, 1961; Hovland, Harvey, & Sherif, 1957) who developed a useful and relevant technique of attitude measurement. In their research, the investigators had subjects indicate which one of a continuum of extreme pro- to extreme con-attitudinal statements they found most acceptable, which additional positions they found

acceptable, and which they found objectionable. The range of acceptable positions, including the most acceptable position, was termed the latitude of acceptance; the range of objectionable positions, the latitude of rejection.

We propose that attitude-congruent behavior be defined as the endorsement of any position within an individual's latitude of acceptance. This procedure avoids the arbitrariness of a midpoint dichotomy and permits each individual to define for him or herself those positions deemed to be attitude-congruent. It is within the latitude of acceptance, we suggest, that self-perception theory applies. The endorsement of a position, other than the most acceptable position, within this latitude may lead to a self-attributional inference that one holds that newly-endorsed position as his attitude. Correspondingly, attitude-discrepant behavior is defined as the endorsement of any position within an individual's latitude of rejection—regardless of whether this region is on the same side of the midpoint as the individual's most acceptable position, on the opposite side, or on both sides. We propose that this latitude of rejection defines the domain to which dissonance theory is applicable. Writing an essay in support of a statement within one's latitude of rejection may lead to dissonance arousal and subsequent attitude change.

The following experiment was designed and conducted to test the above theoretical notions. After completing a latitudes measure, and provided his latitudes met certain a priori criteria necessitated by the experimental procedure, each subject was committed to write an essay supporting either the most extreme position within his latitude of acceptance (Accept conditions) or the least extreme position within his latitude of rejection (Reject conditions). These two positions were always adjacent ones (see Fig. 1). In addition, subjects were committed under conditions of low choice or high choice. Within the Reject condition, high choice subjects should change their attitudes more than low choice subjects via a dissonance reduction process. Within the Accept conditions, high choice subjects should infer more extreme attitudes than low choice subjects via a self-perception process.

In order to examine the crucial question of arousal and to identify the attitude change process as dissonance or self-perception, one further variable, the presence of a stimulus to which dissonance could potentially be misattributed, was included. Because dissonance is not aroused in low choice settings, this misattribution stimulus was paired only with high choice Accept and Reject conditions. Within the Reject conditions, we have argued that dissonance theory is applicable. Thus, subjects in the high choice–misattribution condition should experience dissonance arousal, misattribute that arousal, and exhibit no attitude change (cf. Zanna & Cooper, 1974). The prediction for the Reject conditions, then, is that final attitudes in the high choice–no misattribution condition should be more extreme than both those in the low choice condition and those in the high choice–misattribution condition. Within the Accept conditions, we have argued that self-perception theory is applicable. Since no arousal is expected to occur, the opportunity to misattribute arousal should not obviate attitude change. Thus, the prediction in the Accept conditions is that the final attitudes of

both the high choice–misattribution subjects and the high choice–no misattribution subjects should be more extreme than the attitudes of the low choice subjects.

METHOD

Subjects

Seventy-five male and female freshmen at Princeton University were recruited for a survey of people's political attitudes, for which they were promised $1.50. Of these subjects, 48 met the a priori criteria that had been established concerning the latitudes measure (see below) and were included in the experiment. Subjects were randomly assigned to condition with the restriction that there be an equal number (n = 8) in each condition. They were run in individual booths in groups of two to five.

Procedure

After all subjects for a given experimental period arrived, the experimenter began by explaining the alleged purpose of the experiment. He indicated that he and a professor in the department were beginning a research program in or-

FIGURE 1 A hypothetical latitudes measure depicting the position that individual would have been assigned to support in either the Accept or Reject Conditions.

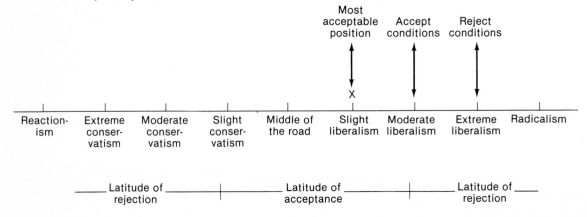

der to study voting behavior in the '76 presidential election and that the present study was concerned with political attitudes. After these introductory remarks, each subject was told to enter a 4 ft 4 in × 3 ft 4 in × 6 ft 4 in (133 cm × 103 cm × 195 cm) soundproof booth where the subject completed the latitudes measure.

Latitudes The measure consisted of nine statements, each of which began with the phrase "The socio-political philosophy of this nation should be one of..." and concluded with one of the following nine terms: radicalism, extreme liberalism, moderate liberalism, slight liberalism, middle of the road, slight conservatism, moderate conservatism, extreme conservatism, reactionism. The subject was instructed to place a symbol by the one statement he found most acceptable, another symbol by any other statements he found acceptable, and yet another symbol by any he found objectionable. The instructions asked him to judge each and every statement.

In order to be included as a subject the individual's latitudes were required to meet certain criteria. Since the majority of Princeton students held liberal positions, we chose to have all subjects argue in the liberal direction so as to compare the endorsement of statements on the same side of the midpoint as the subject's preferred position. The following criteria were necessary: (1) The most acceptable position had to be no more conservative than middle of the road. (2) At least one statement more liberal than the most acceptable positions had to be checked as acceptable. (3) At least one statement more liberal than any acceptable positions had to be checked as objectionable. Employing these criteria insured that each subject would be capable of assignment to any experimental condition.

At this point, the experimenter explained that the purpose of the study, the first in a program of research which was to culminate in our investigation of voting behavior, was to ascertain what dis-

tinctions people made between various political philosophies and what arguments they perceived to support those positions. The subjects were told that in past research of this sort concerning such issues as the legalization of marijuana and the military draft, we had discovered that one of the best ways to find out what the relevant arguments were was to have people write short, forceful essays supporting a given position. Subjects were told that the same procedure was to be employed in this study.

The experimenter continued by remarking that the essays would be content analyzed in order to discover what the relevant arguments in support of a position were. In order to associate the essay with a foreseeable and possibly undesired consequence (cf. Cooper & Worchel, 1970; Nel, Helmreich, & Aronson, 1969), one further use to which the essay would be put was detailed. A local high school teacher who had four or five classes of sophomores had supposedly heard about the study and asked that we help him in a class project. The teacher intended to have a few members of his class engage in a debate concerning political philosophies before an assembly of all his classes. The essays the subjects wrote were ostensibly to be sent to the debaters who would use those arguments in the debate. Thus, the subjects were led to believe that their arguments might possibly convince some high school sophomores to adopt that position.

Subjects were also told that "in order to avoid any systematic bias," they would be randomly assigned to a position to write about. The experimenter commented that such random assignment was one of the few methods of control a social scientist could employ in a study of this sort.

After randomly assigning each subject to experimental condition and preparing the necessary materials, the experimenter handed each subject a booklet, entitled "1975 Princeton University Political Survey." The first page of the booklet asked for the subject's name and class. The second page informed the subject of the position he was to support in his essay. Printed on this page was either the most extreme liberal position within the subject's latitude of acceptance (Accept conditions) or the least extreme liberal position within his latitude of rejection (Reject conditions). The instructions on this page told the subject to complete the questions on the following pages and to then "write a short, forceful and persuasive essay" supporting the position he had been assigned on the blank sheet at the end of the booklet.

Choice Manipulation   The presence or absence of a "Subject Consent Form" as the next page constituted the choice manipulation. This form began with the following paragraph.

> I understand the nature of the study in which I am being asked to participate. I am aware that my essay will be used in a high school government class. I further understand that I will be paid $1.50 for simply appearing here today, regardless of whether or not I actually decide to participate in the entire study. In addition, I understand that I can leave at any time, if I so desire.

The form then asked the subject to check whether he chose to participate and to allow the release of his essay to the high school class or whether he chose not to participate, and to sign his name and fill in the date. The form concluded with two sentences thanking the subject, if he chose to participate, "for your voluntary agreement to write an essay supporting the position assigned to you" or, if he chose not to participate, "for taking the time to come here today." Also printed in large letters on the bottom of this page, as a reminder to the subject of what he was agreeing to write, was the position the subject had been assigned. All subjects, in fact, chose to participate. This form appeared in the high choice booklets, but was absent in the low choice booklets.

Misattribution Stimulus   In the two high choice misattribution conditions, a one page question-

naire entitled "Departmental Equipment Inquiry" followed the subject consent forms. The booth each subject was seated in was to serve as the stimulus to which dissonance arousal might be misattributed. The page began by explaining that the booths had been recently purchased and installed by the psychology department and that this was, in fact, the first time the booths were being used. The department was supposedly interested in people's assessments of the new booths. The inquiry was supposedly "unrelated to the actual study" and "had been placed in a random position in each booklet in order to assess the effect of duration of time spent in the booth on evaluations of the booth."

The questionnaire began with an item labeled "general measure" which asked subjects to rate on a 31-point scale "To what degree do the booths make you feel tense or uncomfortable?" The endpoints of the scale were labeled "Not tense or uncomfortable at all" and "Very tense or uncomfortable." Three specific measures, each a 31-point scale with endpoints labeled "Not at all adequate" and "Perfectly adequate" followed. These items asked the subject to rate the lighting, air ventilation, and size of the booth. Thus, this questionnaire provided subjects in the booth conditions with an opportunity to "blame" any aversive arousal they might be feeling on the booths, rather than on their decision to write the essay.

Dependent Variable   The next page of the booklet contained the dependent variable. In the low choice conditions, this page followed the notification of the position the subject was to support. In the high choice–no booth conditions, it followed the subject consent form. In the high choice–booth conditions, it appeared immediately after the booth questionnaire. The measure was a 31-point scale with endpoints labeled "Extremely Conservative" and "Extremely Liberal." The question asked, "To what degree do you perceive yourself to be politically conservative or liberal?"

The last page of the booklet was a blank sheet of paper on which the subject was to write the essay. Since the critical behavior was the commitment to write the essay (Wicklund, Cooper, & Linder, 1967), no subject was required to actually complete the essay. As soon as all the subjects in a group had completed the measures and had begun to write, the experimenter interrupted, informed the subjects that the experiment had ended, and carefully debriefed them.

RESULTS

Preliminary examination of the data indicated that, on the average, subjects held a slight to moderate liberal position as their most acceptable position. The initial position mean was 6.44 on a scale where reactionism was scored as 1 and radicalism as 9. Subjects assigned to the Accept conditions endorsed either a moderate or extreme liberal position. Those assigned to the Reject conditions endorsed either an extreme liberal or radical position.

Because the initial and final attitude scales differed markedly, it was not possible to compute a change score. Hence, the data were analyzed in a 2 × 3 analysis of covariance, with the subject's most acceptable position in the latitudes scale serving as the covariate. The adjusted means are presented in Table 1.[1] Attitudes were more extreme in the Accept than in the Reject conditions (Accept $M = 21.77$, Reject $M = 19.60$; $F(1,41) = 13.22, p < .001$). This main effect indicates that Accept subjects were more willing to agree with the position they committed themselves to endorsing than were Reject subjects. In addition, the analysis revealed a main effect for the conditions under which subjects committed themselves to writing the essay ($F(2,41) = 5.61, p < .01$). Overall, high choice–no booth subjects ($M = 21.92$) tended to express more extreme attitudes than high choice–booth

---
[1]All significant levels reported in this paper are based on two-tailed comparisons.

subjects ($M = 20.59$) who, in turn, expressed more extreme attitudes than low choice subjects ($M = 19.55$). The interaction effect was not statistically significant ($F(2,41) = 1.10$).

Within the Reject conditions, the mean in the high choice–no booth condition was significantly greater than both the mean in the low choice condition ($t(41) = 2.35, p < .05$) and the mean in the high choice–booth condition ($t(41) = 2.23, p < .05$). Thus, in the case of objectionable positions, the opportunity to attribute one's arousal to the booth obviated attitude change—a finding that is indicative of a dissonance process.

Also informative is the fact that a weighted contrast revealed the mean in the high choice–booth–Reject condition to be significantly different from the average of the means of the other three high choice conditions ($t(41) = 3.12, p < .01$). Thus, as expected, final attitudes were less extreme in the one condition where subjects were both experiencing dissonance and given an opportunity to misattribute that arousal.

Within the two high choice–booth conditions, subjects' assessments of the booth were also examined. The prediction, of course, is that the Reject subjects, since they are the ones who are misattributing dissonance arousal, should evaluate the booths more negatively than the Accept subjects. Because the data were highly skewed, they were analyzed by a nonparametric arcsine transformation of the proportion of subjects in each condition who fell below the overall median (Langer & Abelson, 1972). The only dimension on which the booths were judged differently by Accept and Reject subjects was that concerning the adequacy of the air ventilation. Apparently, air ventilation was the most salient dimension on which the booths could plausibly be considered inadequate. Six of the eight Reject subjects, compared to two of the eight Accept subjects, rated the air ventilation below the overall median ($z = 2.09, p < .04$). Thus, it was those subjects whom we suggested were experiencing dissonance arousal who found the booths relatively inadequate. This judgment served to

TABLE 1			
ADJUSTED MEANS			
Latitude	Low choice	High choice–No booth	High choice–Booth
Accept	20.33ab	22.70c	22.29c
Reject	18.77a	21.14bc	18.89a

Note. The higher the mean, the more liberal subjects perceived themselves to be. Cell means not sharing a common subscript differ beyond the 5% significance level (except the low choice–Accept vs. high choice–booth–Accept comparison which is at $p = .06$).

"explain" the cause of their discomfort and to obviate what would otherwise have been motivational pressure to change their attitudes.

DISCUSSION

The results of the experiment provide support for the conceptual framework that was developed earlier in this paper. Subjects who endorsed an acceptable position more extreme than their most acceptable position shifted their attitudes towards that endorsement when they had decision freedom. This effect occurred even when subjects were provided with an arousal misattribution cue. Since the cue did not attenuate attitude change, it is reasonable to assume that dissonance arousal did not occur. Instead, the attitude change occurred via a self-perception process. In addition, subjects who freely chose to endorse a position within their latitude of rejection subsequently expressed more extreme attitudes. In the context of objectionable positions, the misattribution cue was employed and served to attenuate attitude change, indicating that dissonance arousal occurred. By "blaming" the booths for their discomfort, subjects were able to avoid the need to adjust their attitudes to justify their behavior (cf. Zanna & Cooper, 1974, 1976).

Can either self-perception or dissonance theory explain the data in both the Accept and the Reject conditions? We doubt that either theory is capable of that. Self-perception theory has difficulty with the attenuation of attitude change which was found to occur in the Reject conditions. Dissonance theory, on the other hand, finds the lack of attenuation of attitude change in the Accept conditions difficult to explain. However, dissonance theory might maintain that endorsing any position along the continuum, other than the most acceptable one, does not "follow from" one's attitude. The more extreme this endorsement, relative to one's most acceptable position, the greater the arousal which is experienced. Such an explanation would be forced to assume that the likelihood of misattribution to some external stimulus changes as a function of level of arousal. At lower levels of arousal, as in the Accept conditions, an individual is more likely to attribute that arousal to his own behavior rather than to some external stimulus. Thus, no misattribution nor the subsequent attenuation of attitude change occurred in the Accept conditions. At higher levels of arousal, as in the Reject conditions, misattribution to some external cue is more likely than attribution to the agreement to write the essay. Thus, attitude change was attenuated in the Reject conditions.

Such an explanation cannot be rejected completely by the data since we are concerned in the Accept conditions with the lack of a difference between the high choice–no booth and the high choice–booth conditions. However, there seems to be no compelling reason to assume that the likelihood of misattribution to some external stimulus changes as a function of level of arousal. Also, this explanation, since it asserts that there is more arousal in the Reject condition than in the Accept condition, leads to the prediction of greater attitude change in the high choice–Reject condition than in the high choice–Accept condition. The fact that the data tend in the opposite direction casts serious doubt upon this explanation.

Thus, the findings provide evidence for the notion that both dissonance and self-perception processes occur. However, each theory can be appropriately applied only to its own specialized domain. Self-perception theory convincingly explains attitudinal shifts within an individual's latitude of acceptance. Correspondingly, dissonance theory provides an accurate account for attitude change effects within the latitude of rejection.

Unfortunately, in order to maintain random assignment, our procedure could not differentiate the amount of discrepancy between the most acceptable position and the endorsed position from the latitudes of acceptance and rejection. In order to argue within their randomly assigned latitude, subjects in the Reject conditions tended to endorse a position about one step more extreme than those in the Accept conditions. We are not, however, suggesting that a certain, specifiable amount of discrepancy is necessary to arouse dissonance processes. Large or small discrepancies could arouse dissonance, if the endorsed position were to fall within the latitude of rejection. It is our position that these individually defined latitudes delineate whether dissonance or self-perception processes will occur. In fact, when one examines only those subjects in the high choice–booth conditions who endorsed a position two units from their most acceptable positions, one finds that the final adjusted attitude scores of the two subjects in the Accept condition are higher than any of the scores of the seven subjects from the Reject condition. Equalizing for discrepancy, then, there still seems to be a difference between the conditions—more change in the Accept-booth condition than in the Reject-booth condition. Although necessarily based upon a small number of cases, this internal analysis suggests that

even if discrepancy were equalized, one would find latitudinal position to serve as an indicator of the attitudinal process occurring.

What periods during the history of an attitude favor the likelihood of self-perception or dissonance processes operating? Latitudes of acceptance and rejection provide the key through which some meaningful implications can be drawn. A wide latitude of acceptance will increase the likelihood of a self-perception process occurring, while a wide latitude of rejection will make a dissonance process more likely. We might speculate that the period during which attitudes are formed is characterized by a broad latitude of acceptance. After all, when an individual has little information about, or experience with, an attitude object, he is likely to endorse a number of positions as acceptable ones. On the other hand, firmly established attitudes regarding attitude objects toward which an individual has had much relevant experience are likely to be characterized by the acceptability of relatively few positions and, hence, by a wide latitude of rejection. In short, while self-perception seems applicable to the early stages of attitude development, dissonance theory may be most relevant to later stages when an individual is more certain of his feelings toward an attitude object.

It should be noted that our experimental procedure involved what we considered to be the simplest method of operationalizing acceptable vs. objectionable behaviors. Subjects were committed to endorsing attitudinal positions within or beyond their latitudes of acceptance. The behavior itself, and the consequences of that behavior, were held constant. That is, all subjects were to write an essay which they were led to believe might convince some high school students to adopt the position advocated.

However, it is reasonable to assume that the same pattern of data would accrue if the position endorsed where held constant and the extremity of the behavior and/or consequences varied. One can imagine a behavioral latitudes measure on which individuals could indicate which behaviors they found acceptable and which objectionable. Performance of a behavior more extreme than implied by one's attitude yet within the behavioral latitude of acceptance may lead to the self-perception of a new attitude. Performance of a behavior within the behavioral latitude of rejection may lead to dissonance-induced attitude change. For example, for an individual who favors the legalization of marijuana, signing a petition to that effect may be within the latitude of acceptance, and, therefore, evoke a self-perception process. On the other hand, marching on the state capital may fall within the latitude of rejection, and, therefore, produce dissonance. These different processes may occur even though the position endorsed is identical for the two behaviors. Further research is necessary to examine the extent of the similarity between a methodology employing behavioral latitudes and the methodology used in this study.

Hopefully, our conceptualization and the data that accompany it will serve to call a truce between dissonance and self-perception theorists. Within its proper domain of application, each theory is superior to the other, but, in general, no such relative superiority exists. Alone neither theory can explain all the data. Together, they provide social psychology with provocative and convincing explanations of the effects of overt behavior on attitudes.

Knowing Ourselves

excerpt from *Human Nature and the Social Order*

Charles H. Cooley (1902)

Attitudes are only one piece of the puzzle making up self-knowledge. Although one might initially question inclusion of a discussion of the self under *Social Knowledge,* social psychologists recognize that the self is, at least in part, socially constructed. Thus, we begin this subsection with an excerpt from Cooley who, in 1902, was one of the first theorists to discuss the social construction of the self. Written six years before the first textbooks that coined the term "social psychology," Cooley's ideas have continued to be influential. To understand Cooley, however, it helps to turn to William James's (1890) description of the self. "In its widest possible sense," James wrote, "a man's Self is the sum total of all he *can* call his, not only his body and his psychic powers, but his clothes and his house, his wife and his children, his ancestors and his friends, his reputation and his works, his lands and horses and yacht and bank-account" (p. 291).*

It is this description of the self as body or possessions that Cooley rejects, although he expands upon the idea that the self strives to act upon the world in a potent manner. The self also comes to be known through the looking-glass of others' images of that self. This is by no means a negative view. Cooley recognizes the importance of an equilibrium between social sensitivity and responsiveness to the feelings and beliefs of others, on one hand, and a directness and simplicity of action that allows us to maintain our own individuality and mental clarity on the other.

Cooley's ideas about the sense of self evolving only in relation to a social world provided a foundation for George Herbert Mead and the symbolic interactionists, for whom the mutual influence between a person and his or her social world is a basic tenet. Cooley has a more passive perception of this process, believing that our social selves are formed through the reflected appraisals of others. Later theorists developed models that invoke more active processing of others' evaluations. They suggest that we must mutually negotiate our respective identities before interactions can proceed smoothly, and that we continue to reinforce and regenerate our identities as we engage in an interaction.

Note that Cooley also begins with the notion of an instinct of self-feeling, but he defines it more as a *predisposition* to develop a sense of self, much like present beliefs about a predisposition to learn language. He also recognizes that the concept of instinct has very little meaning outside of its interaction with experience in the world; thus, in the nature-nurture issue, Cooley is clearly an interactionist.

This reading is also interesting in comparison with that of Hollingsworth (Reading 28) published 14 years later. The perceptions of sex differences and the proposed causes are quite different and may well reflect hidden assumptions on the part of both authors. When reading both of these articles, it is important to remember how much we now know about sex differences and similarities. You may wish to compare Cooley's beliefs about sex differences in the self structure with the present-day social psychological literature reported in your text.

Other hidden assumptions that we hold become apparent when we compare present-day assumptions about the self with historical viewpoints about the self. For example, we tend to think that issues of self-knowledge or self-fulfillment are the consequences of simply having a self. Baumeister (1987), however, argues that these issues did not always exist, and that they are a function of historical developments regarding the self.

---

* *Editors' note:* James's reference to wives and children as possessions equivalent to homes and yachts was standard for his day and age. Much has changed since 1890, not the least of which is the legal status of and psychological concern for women, children, and others who were previously afforded much less than full standing.

THE SOCIAL SELF—1.
THE MEANING OF "I"

It is well to say at the outset that by the word "self" in this discussion is meant simply that which is designated in common speech by the pronouns of the first person singular, "I," "me," "my," "mine," and "myself." "Self" and "ego" are used by metaphysicians and moralists in many other senses, more or less remote from the "I" of daily speech and thought, and with these I wish to have as little to do as possible. What is here discussed is what psychologists call the empirical self, the self that can be apprehended or verified by ordinary observation. I qualify it by the word social not as implying the existence of a self that is not social—for I think that the "I" of common language always has more or less distinct reference to other people as well as the speaker—but because I wish to emphasize and dwell upon the social aspect of it.

The emotion or feeling of self may be regarded as instinctive, and was doubtless evolved in connection with its important function in stimulating and unifying the special activities of individuals.* It is thus very profoundly rooted in the history of the human race and apparently indispensable to any plan of life at all similar to ours. It seems to exist in a vague though vigorous form at the birth of each individual, and, like other instinctive ideas or germs of ideas, to be defined and developed by experience, becoming associated, or rather incorporated, with muscular, visual, and other sensations; with perceptions, apperceptions, and conceptions of every degree of complexity and of infinite variety of content; and, especially, with personal ideas. Meantime the feeling itself does not remain unaltered, but undergoes differentiation and refinement just as does any other sort of crude innate feeling. Thus, while retaining under every phase its characteristic tone or flavor, it breaks up into innumerable self-sentiments. And concrete self-feeling, as it exists in mature persons, is a whole made up of these various sentiments, along with a good deal of primitive emotion not thus broken up. It partakes fully of the general development of the mind, but never loses that peculiar gusto of appropriation that causes us to name a thought with a first-personal pronoun. The other contents of the self-idea are of little use, apparently, in defining it, because they are so extremely various. It would be no more futile, it seems to me, to attempt to define fear by enumerating the things that people are afraid of, than to attempt to define "I" by enumerating the objects with which the word is associated. Very much as fear means primarily a state of feeling, or its expression, and not darkness, fire, lions, snakes, or other things that excite it, so "I" means primarily self-feeling, or its expression, and not body, clothes, treasures, ambition, honors, and the like, with which this feeling may be connected. In either case it is possible and useful to go behind the feeling and inquire what ideas arouse it and why they do so, but this is in a sense a secondary investigation.

But perhaps the best way to realize the naïve meaning of "I" is to listen to the talk of children playing together, especially if they do not agree very well. They use the first person with none of the conventional self-repression of their elders, but with much emphasis and variety of inflection, so that its emotional animus is unmistakable.

As many people have the impression that the verifiable self, the object that we name with "I," is usually the material body, it may be well to say that this impression is an illusion, easily dispelled by any one who will undertake a simple examination of facts. It is true that when we philosophize a little about "I" and look around for a tangible object to which to attach it, we soon fix upon the material body as the most available *locus;* but when we use the word naïvely, as in ordinary speech, it is not very common to think

---

*It is, perhaps, to be thought of as a more general instinct, of which anger, etc., are differentiated forms, rather than as standing by itself.

of the body in connection with it; not nearly so common as it is to think of other things. There is no difficulty in testing this statement, since the word "I" is one of the commonest in conversation and literature, so that nothing is more practicable than to study its meaning at any length that may be desired. One need only listen to ordinary speech until the word has occurred, say, a hundred times, noting its connections, or observe its use in a similar number of cases by the characters in a novel. Ordinarily it will be found that in not more than ten cases in a hundred does "I" have reference to the body of the person speaking. It refers chiefly to opinions, purposes, desires, claims, and the like, concerning matters that involve no thought of the body.

That the "I" of common speech has a meaning which includes some sort of reference to other persons is involved in the very fact that the word and the ideas it stands for are phenomena of language and the communicative life. It is doubtful whether it is possible to use language at all without thinking more or less distinctly of some one else, and certainly the things to which we give names and which have a large place in reflective thought are almost always those which are impressed upon us by our contact with other people. Where there is no communication there can be no nomenclature and no developed thought. What we call "me," "mine," or "myself" is, then, not something separate from the general life, but the most interesting part of it, a part whose interest arises from the very fact that it is both general and individual. That is, we care for it just because it is that phase of the mind that is living and striving in the common life, trying to impress itself upon the minds of others. "I" is a militant social tendency, working to hold and enlarge its place in the general current of tendencies.

The reference to other persons involved in the sense of self may be distinct and particular, as when a boy is ashamed to have his mother catch him at something she has forbidden, or it may be vague and general, as when one is ashamed to do something which only his conscience, expressing his sense of social responsibility, detects and disapproves; but it is always there. There is no sense of "I," as in pride or shame, without its correlative sense of you, or he, or they. Even the miser gloating over his hidden gold can feel the "mine" only as he is aware of the world of men over whom he has secret power; and the case is very similar with all kinds of hid treasure. Many painters, sculptors, and writers have loved to withhold their work from the world, fondling it in seclusion until they were quite done with it; but the delight in this, as in all secrets, depends upon a sense of the value of what is concealed.

In a very large and interesting class of cases the social reference takes the form of a somewhat definite imagination of how one's self—that is any idea he appropriates—appears in a particular mind, and the kind of self-feeling one has is determined by the attitude toward this attributed to that other mind. A social self of this sort might be called the reflected or looking-glass self:

"Each to each a looking-glass
Reflects the other that doth pass."

As we see our face, figure, and dress in the glass, and are interested in them because they are ours, and pleased or otherwise with them according as they do or do not answer to what we should like them to be; so in imagination we perceive in another's mind some thought of our appearance, manners, aims, deeds, character, friends, and so on, and are variously affected by it.

A self-idea of this sort seems to have three principal elements: the imagination of our appearance to the other person; the imagination of his judgment of that appearance, and some sort of self-feeling, such as pride or mortification. The comparision with a looking-glass hardly suggests the second element, the imagined judgment, which is quite essential. The thing that moves us to pride or shame is not the mere mechanical reflection of ourselves, but an imputed sentiment, the imagined effect of this reflection upon another's mind. This is evident from the fact that the character and weight of that other, in whose mind we see ourselves, makes all the difference with our feeling. We are ashamed to seem evasive in the presence of a straightforward man, cowardly in the presence of a brave one, gross in the eyes of a refined one, and so on. We always imagine, and in imagining share, the judgments of the other mind. A man will boast to one person of an action—say some sharp transaction in trade—which he would be ashamed to own to another.

As already suggested, instinctive self-feeling is doubtless connected in evolution with its important function in stimulating and unifying the special activities of individuals. It appears to be associated chiefly with ideas of the exercise of power, of being a cause, ideas that emphasize the antithesis between the mind and the rest of the world. The first definite thoughts that a child associates with self-feeling are probably those of his earliest endeavors to control visible objects—his limbs, his playthings, his bottle, and the like. Then he attempts to control the actions of the persons about him, and so his circle of power and of self-feeling widens without interruption to the most complex objects of mature ambition. Although he does not say "I" or "my" during the first year or two, yet he expresses so clearly by his actions the feeling that adults associate with these words that we cannot deny him a self even in the first weeks.

The process by which self-feeling of the looking-glass sort develops in children may be followed without much difficulty. Studying the movements of others as closely as they do they soon see a connection between their own acts and changes in those movements; that is, they perceive their own influence or power over persons. The child appropriates the visible actions of his parent or nurse, over which he finds he has some control, in quite the same way as he appropriates one of his own members or a plaything, and he will try to do things with this new possession, just as he will with his hand or his rattle. A girl six months old will attempt in the most evident and deliberate manner to attract attention to herself, to set going by her actions some of those movements of other persons that she has appropriated. She has tasted the joy of being a cause, of exerting social power, and wishes more of it. She will tug at her mother's skirts, wriggle, gurgle, stretch out her arms, etc., all the time watching for the hoped-for effect. These performances often give the child, even at this age, an appearance of what is called affectation, that is, she seems to be unduly preoccupied with what other people think of her. Affectation, at any age, exists when the passion to influence others seems to overbalance the established character and give it an obvious twist or pose.

Strong joy and grief depend upon the treatment this rudimentary social self receives. In the case of M. I noticed as early as the fourth month a "hurt" way of crying which seemed to indicate a sense of personal slight. It was quite different from the cry of pain or that of anger, but seemed about the same as the cry of fright. The slightest tone of reproof would produce it. On the other hand, if people took notice and laughed and encouraged, she was hilarious. At about fifteen months old she had become "a perfect little actress," seeming to live largely in imaginations of her effect upon other people. She constantly and obviously laid traps for attention, and looked abashed or wept at any signs of disapproval or indifference. At times it would seem as if she could not get over these repulses, but would cry long in a grieved way, refusing to be comforted. If she hit upon any little trick that made people laugh she would be sure to repeat it, laughing loudly and affectedly in imitation. She had quite a repertory of these small performances, which she would display to a sympathetic audience, or even try upon strangers. I have seen her at sixteen months, when R. refused to give her the scissors, sit down and make-believe cry, putting up her under lip and snuffling, meanwhile looking up now and then to see what effect she was producing.

In such phenomena we have plainly enough, it seems to me, the germ of personal ambition of every sort. Imagination co-operating with instinctive self-feeling has already created a social "I," and this has become a principal object of interest and endeavor.

Progress from this point is chiefly in the way of a greater definiteness, fullness, and inwardness in the imagination of the other's state of mind. A little child thinks of and tries to elicit certain visible or audible phenomena, and does not go back of them; but what a grown-up person desires to produce in others is an internal, invisible condition which his own richer experience enables him to imagine, and of which expression is only the sign. Even adults, however, make no separation between what other people think and the visible expression of that thought. They imagine the whole thing at once, and their idea differs from that of a child chiefly in the comparative richness and complexity of the elements that accompany and interpret the visible or audible sign. There is also a progress from the naïve to the subtle in socially self-assertive action. A child obviously and simply, at first, does things for effect. Later there is an endeavor to suppress the appearance of doing so; affection, indifference, contempt, etc., are simulated to hide the real wish to affect the self-image. It is perceived that an obvious seeking after good opinion is weak and disagreeable.

I doubt whether there are any regular stages in the development of social self-feeling and expression common to the majority of children. The sentiments of self develop by imperceptible gradations out of the crude appropriative instinct of new-born babes, and their manifestations vary indefinitely in different cases. Many children show "self-consciousness" conspicuously from the first half-year; others have little appearance of it at any age. Still others pass through periods of affectation whose length and time of occurrence would probably be found to be exceedingly various. In childhood, as at all times of life, absorption in some idea other than that of the social self tends to drive "self-consciousness" out.

Sex-difference in the development of the social self is apparent from the first. Girls have, as a rule, a more impressible social sensibility; they care more obviously for the social image, study it, reflect upon it more, and so have even during the first year an appearance of subtlety, *finesse,* often of affectation, in which boys are comparatively lacking. Boys are more taken up with muscular activity for its own sake and with construction, their imaginations are occupied somewhat less with persons and more with things. In a girl *das ewig Weibliche,* not easy to describe but quite unmistakable, appears as soon as she begins to take notice of people, and one phase of it is certainly an ego less simple and stable, a stronger impulse to go over to the other person's point of view and to stake joy and grief on the image in his mind. There can be no doubt that women are as a rule more dependent upon immediate personal support and corroboration than are men. The thought of the woman needs to fix itself upon some person in whose mind she can find a stable and compelling image of herself by which to live. If such an image is found, either in a visible or an ideal person, the power of devotion to it becomes a source of strength. But it is a sort of strength dependent upon this personal complement, without which the womanly character is somewhat apt to become a derelict and drifting vessel. Men, being built more for aggression, have, relatively, a greater power of standing alone. But no one can really stand alone, and the appearance of it is due simply to a greater momentum and continuity of character which stores up the past and resists immediate influences. Directly or indirectly the imagination of how we appear to others is a controlling force in all normal minds.

The vague but potent phases of the self associated with the instinct of sex may be regarded, like other phases, as expressive of a need to exert power and as having reference to personal function. The youth, I take it, is bashful precisely because he is conscious of the vague stirring of an aggressive instinct which he does not know how either to effectuate or to ignore.

And it is perhaps much the same with the other sex: the bashful are always aggressive at heart; they are conscious of an interest in the other person, of a need to be something to him. And the more developed sexual passion, in both sexes, is very largely an emotion of power, domination, or appropriation. There is no state of feeling that says "mine, mine," more fiercely. The need to be appropriated or dominated which, in women at least, is equally powerful, is of the same nature at bottom, having for its object the attracting to itself of a masterful passion. "The desire of the man is for the woman, but the desire of the woman is for the desire of the man."*

Although boys have generally a less impressionable social self than girls, there is great difference among them in this regard. Some of them have a marked tendency of *finesse* and posing, while others have almost none. The latter have a less vivid personal imagination; they are unaffected chiefly, perhaps, because they have no vivid idea of how they seem to others, and so are not moved to seem rather than to be; they are unresentful of slights because they do not feel them, not ashamed or jealous or vain or proud or remorseful, because all these imply imagination of another's mind. I have known children who showed no tendency whatever to lie; in fact, could not understand the nature or object of lying or of any sort of concealment, as in such games as hide-and-coop. This excessively simple way of looking at things may come from unusual absorption in the observation and analysis of the impersonal, as appeared to be the case with R., whose interest in other facts and their relations so much preponderated over his interest in personal attitudes that there was no temptation to sacrifice the former to the latter. A child of this sort gives the impression of being non-

moral; he neither sins nor repents, and has not the knowledge of good and evil. We eat of the tree of this knowledge when we begin to imagine the minds of others, and so become aware of that conflict of personal impulses which conscience aims to allay.

Possibly some will think that I exaggerate the importance of social self-feeling by taking persons and periods of life that are abnormally sensitive. But I believe that with all normal and human people it remains, in one form or another, the mainspring of endeavor and a chief interest of the imagination throughout life. As is the case with other feelings, we do not think much of it so long as it is moderately and regularly gratified. Many people of balanced mind and congenial activity scarcely know that they care what others think of them, and will deny, perhaps with indignation, that such care is an important factor in what they are and do. But this is illusion. If failure or disgrace arrives, if one suddenly finds that the faces of men show coldness or contempt instead of the kindliness and deference that he is used to, he will perceive from the shock, the fear, the sense of being outcast and helpless, that he was living in the minds of others without knowing it, just as we daily walk the solid ground without thinking how it bears us up. This fact is so familiar in literature, especially in modern novels, that it ought to be obvious enough. The works of George Eliot are particularly strong in the exposition of it. In most of her novels there is some character like Mr. Bulstrode in "Middlemarch" or Mr. Jermyn in "Felix Holt," whose respectable and long-established social image of himself is shattered by the coming to light of hidden truth.

It is true, however, that the attempt to describe the social self and to analyze the mental processes that enter into it almost unavoidably makes it appear more reflective and "self-conscious" than it usually is. Thus while some readers will be able to discover in themselves a quite definite and deliberate contemplation of the reflected self, others will perhaps find nothing but a sympathetic impulse,

---

*Attributed to Mme. de Staël.

so simple that it can hardly be made the object of distinct thought. Many people whose behavior shows that their idea of themselves is largely caught from the persons they are with, are yet quite innocent of any intentional posing; it is a matter of subconscious impulse or mere suggestion. The self of very sensitive but non-reflective minds is of this character.

variants of it have been used in hundreds of studies (see Snyder & Gangestad, 1986, for a recent analysis of the scale's psychometric properties along with a shortened 18-item scale). An excellent example of questionnaire development, with measures of several types of reliability and validity, this paper successfully launched self-monitoring research.

Self-Monitoring of Expressive Behavior

Mark L. Snyder (1974)

As Cooley (1902) points out in Reading 7, there are differences in the degree to which individuals are aware of and care about other people's perceptions of and judgments about them. One area of research that emerges from this perspective investigates *self-presentation*: the subtle techniques we use to convey impressions and/or information about ourselves to others (Goffman, 1959). Baumeister (1982) suggests that our primary motives in self-presentation are (a) to gain rewards, which we do by pleasing the individuals with whom we are interacting, and (b) to increase our own self-fulfillment, which we do by constructing a public image that corresponds to our ideal self.

A second area of research to emerge investigates *self-monitoring*: the degree to which an individual looks to and uses external, situational information to guide personal behavior. A very exciting aspect of self-monitoring research is its integration of social and personality psychology. On the basis of individuals' degree of self-monitoring, researchers have successfully predicted different behavior in different situations, and when and for whom attitude-behavior consistency will be greatest.

The empirical work in this area began in 1974, when Snyder published the self-monitoring scale included in this reading. Since then, this scale and

Abstract

A social psychological construct of self-monitoring (self-observation and self-control guided by situational cues to social appropriateness) of expressive behavior and self-presentation was proposed. An internally consistent, temporally stable self-report measure of individual differences in self-monitoring was constructed. Four converging laboratory and field studies of peer perception ratings, criterion group membership, self-control of facial and vocal emotional expressive behavior, and attention to normative social comparison information were conducted to demonstrate the convergent and discriminant validity of the Self-Monitoring Scale (SM). The use of SM to investigate hypotheses concerning consistency in expression across situations and between channels of expressive behavior was discussed.

A common observation in literature and cultural folklore has been that certain non-language behaviors, such as voice quality, body motion, touch, and the use of personal space appear to play a prominent role in communication. Furthermore, laboratory and field research clearly indicates that much information about a person's affective states, status and attitude, cooperative and competitive nature of social interaction, and interpersonal intimacy is expressed and accurately communicated to others in nonverbal expressive behavior (e.g., Ekman, 1971; Hall, 1966; Mehrabian, 1969; Sommer, 1969).

Much interest in nonverbal expressive behavior stems from a belief that it may not be under voluntary control and might function as a pipeline or radarscope to one's true inner "self" (e.g., Freud, 1959). Although nonverbal behavior may often escape voluntary attempts at censorship (Ekman & Friesen, 1969), there have been numerous demonstrations that individuals can voluntarily express various emotions with their vocal and/or facial expressive behavior in such a way that their expressive behavior can be accurately interpreted by observers (e.g., Davitz, 1964). In fact, some social observers have proposed that the ability to manage and control expressive presentation is a prerequisite to effective social and interpersonal functioning. Thus Goffman (1955) has likened social interaction to a theatrical performance or "line" of verbal and nonverbal self-expressive acts which are managed to keep one's line appropriate to the current situation. Such self-management requires a repertoire of face-saving devices, an awareness of the interpretations which others place on one's acts, a desire to maintain social approval, and the willingness to use this repertoire of impression management tactics. Within the more restricted domain of facial expressions of emotional affect, Ekman (1971) has suggested that individuals typically exercise control over their facial expressions to intensify, deintensify, neutralize, or mask the expression of a felt affect, according to various norms of social performance.

There are, however, striking and important individual differences in the extent to which individuals can and do monitor their self-presentation, expressive behavior, and nonverbal affective display. Clearly, professional stage actors can do what I cannot. Politicians have long known how important it is to wear the right face for the right constituency. LaGuardia learned the expressive repertoires of several different cultures in New York and became "chameleon-like" the son of whatever people he was facing. Yet little research has directly concerned such individual differences in the self-control of expressive behavior. At best, some dispositional correlates of spontaneous and natural expression

of emotion have been reported (e.g., Buck, Savin, Miller, & Caul, 1972; Davitz, 1964).

A CONCEPT OF SELF-MONITORING OF EXPRESSIVE BEHAVIOR

How might individual differences in the self-control of expressive behavior arise? What might be the developmental, historical, and current motivational origins of self-control ability and performance? Perhaps some individuals have learned that their affective experience and expression are either socially inappropriate or lacking. Such people may *monitor* (observe and control) their self-presentation and expressive behavior. The goals of self-monitoring may be (a) to communicate accurately one's true emotional state by means of an intensified expressive presentation; (b) to communicate accurately an arbitrary emotional state which need not be congruent with actual emotional experience; (c) to conceal adaptively an inappropriate emotional state and appear unresponsive and unexpressive; (d) to conceal adaptively an inappropriate emotional state and appear to be experiencing an appropriate one; (e) to appear to be experiencing some emotion when one experiences nothing and a nonresponse is inappropriate.

An acute sensitivity to the cues in a situation which indicate what expression or self-presentation is appropriate and what is not is a corollary ability to self-monitoring. One such set of cues for guiding self-monitoring is the emotional expressive behavior of other similar comparison persons in the same situation.

There is some evidence of an acute version of this process. When persons are made uncertain of their emotional reactions, they look to the behavior of others for cues to define their emotional states and model the emotional expressive behavior of others in the same situation who appear to be behaving appropriately (Schachter & Singer, 1962).

On the other hand, persons who have not learned a concern for appropriateness of their self-presentation would not have such well-developed self-monitoring skills and would not be so vigilant to social comparison information about appropriate patterns of expression and experience. This is not to say that they are not emotionally expressive or even that they are less so than those who monitor their presentation. Rather, their self-presentation and expressive behavior seem, in a functional sense, to be controlled from within by their affective states (they express it as they feel it) rather than monitored, controlled, and molded to fit the situation.

SELF-MONITORING AND CONSISTENCY IN EXPRESSION: BETWEEN MODALITIES AND ACROSS SITUATIONS

Do people, as Freud (1959) believed, say one thing with their lips and another with their fingertips? More specifically, what governs the consistency between expression in different channels of expression, such as vocal and facial, and the consistency between nonverbal and verbal expression? The self-monitoring approach provides one perspective on differences and consistencies across channels of expression, including verbal self-presentation.

It is likely that when one is monitoring, various channels are monitored differentially, and perhaps some forgotten. Thus, what may be communicated by one channel may differ from what is communicated by another. For example, I may cover my sadness by putting on a happy face but forget to use a happy voice.

Ekman and Friesen (1969, 1972) have demonstrated with psychiatric patients and student nurses that in deception situations people are more likely to monitor their facial than body presentation, with the result that the deception is more likely to be detected from an examination of body cues than facial cues. Thus, the information encoded in monitored channels should differ from that encoded in nonmonitored channels. However, it is likely that great consistency characterizes that set of channels

of expressive (verbal or nonverbal) behaviors which are simultaneously monitored according to the same criteria. Furthermore, self-monitored expressive behavior should vary more from situation to situation than nonmonitored expressive behavior. Self-monitoring individuals should be most likely to monitor and control their expression in situations which contain reliable cues to social appropriateness. Thus, such a person would be more likely to laugh at a comedy when watching it with amused peers than when watching it alone. The laughing behavior of the non-self-monitoring person should be more invariant across those two situations and more related to how affectively amused he himself actually is. The expressive behavior of self-monitoring individuals should be more reflective of an internal affect state when it is generated in a situation with minimal incentives for, and cues to, self-monitoring.

The cross-situational variability of the self-monitoring versus the consistency of the non-self-monitoring individuals is similar to the "traits versus situations" issue: Is behavior controlled by situational factors and hence predictable from characteristics of the surrounding situation, or is it controlled by internal states and dispositions which produce cross-situational consistency and facilitate prediction from characteristics of the person, measures of internal states, or dispositions (Mischel, 1968; Moos, 1968, 1969)? Bem (1972) has proposed that the issue be redirected from an "either traits or situations for all behavior of all people" debate to a search for moderating variables which would allow the specification for an individual of equivalence classes of situations and responses across which he monitors his behavior with respect to a particularly central self-concept. In these areas he would show trait-like cross-situational and inter-response mode consistency; in others he would not. In the domain of expressive behavior, individual differences in self-monitoring are a moderating variable which identifies individuals who demonstrate or fail to demonstrate consistency across channels of expression and between situations differing in monitoring properties.

IN SEARCH OF A MEASURE OF INDIVIDUAL DIFFERENCES IN SELF-MONITORING

How can we capture individual differences in self-monitoring? A review of the literature suggests at least one currently available measure which might serve to identify individuals who differ in self-monitoring.

The self-monitoring individual is one who, out of a concern for social appropriateness, is particularly sensitive to the expression and self-presentation of others in social situations and uses these cues as guidelines for monitoring his own self-presentation. Is there then any difference between this person and the individual with a high "need for approval" as measured by the Marlowe-Crowne Social Desirability Scale (Crowne & Marlowe, 1964)? In a wide variety of situations, individuals who have a high need for approval give socially desirable responses. They conform more than low-need-for-approval individuals in an Asch situation; they verbally condition better; they do not show overt hostility toward one who has insulted and double-crossed them; and they are less likely to report dirty words in a perceptual defense task (Crowne & Marlowe, 1964). All of this would suggest that the high-need-for-approval person is one who modifies his behavior from situation to situation. However, other evidence suggests that this ability to alter behavior may be severely limited to contingencies of social approval (Bem, 1972).

In addition, it may be only the social approval of adult experimenters which is reinforcing and sought after. In a sociometric study, fraternity members with a high need for approval were described by their peers as individuals who spend most of their time alone rather than with other people, do not go out of their way to make friends, are not very conversational, and do not act friendly toward other fraternity members (study by Stephen C. Bank, reported in Crowne & Marlowe, 1964, pp. 162–163).

In another study on verbal conditioning, high- and low-need-for-approval subjects did not differ in the extent to which they modeled the behavior of a peer (actually a confederate) they had previously observed perform the experimental task appropriately (Crowne & Marlowe, 1964, pp. 61–72). Furthermore, and particularly relevant to the self-monitoring of expressive behavior, this self-control ability may not extend into the domain of expressive behavior. Zaidel and Mehrabian (1969) reported that individuals who scored high on the Need for Approval Scale were actually less able to communicate either positive or negative affect facially or vocally than were low-need-for-approval subjects. In this experimental situation, the socially desirable response and the one which would gain the approval of the experimenter would clearly be the accurate expression and communication of affect. Thus, although high-need-for-approval individuals may be motivated to modify their expressive self-presentation in order to gain approval, they may lack the necessary self-control abilities and skills.

Self-monitoring would probably best be measured by an instrument specifically designed to discriminate individual differences in concern for social appropriateness, sensitivity to the expression and self-presentation of others in social situations as cues to social appropriateness of self-expression, and use of these cues as guidelines for monitoring and managing self-presentation and expressive behavior. Accordingly, an attempt was made to transpose the self-monitoring concept into a self-report scale which reliably and validly measures it.

The convergence between diverse methods of measuring of self-monitoring was examined according to the strategy of construct valida-tion (Cronbach & Meehl, 1955). To demon-strate discriminant validity (Campbell & Fiske, 1959), comparisons were made between self-monitoring and need for approval in the pre-diction of each external criterion in the vali-dation strategy. Need for approval was chosen for these critical comparisons for two reasons. Its conceptual relationship to self-monitoring has already been discussed. Naturally, this pro-cedure also further individuates the type of per-son identified by the Need for Approval Scale. In addition, Campbell (1960) has recommended that in view of the general response tendency of some individuals to describe themselves in a favorable manner, and the close relationship between probability of endorsement of person-ality statements and their social desirability, all tests of the voluntary self-descriptive sort should be demonstrated to predict their crite-rion measures better than a measure of the gen-eral social desirability factor.

CONSTRUCTION OF THE SELF-MONITORING SCALE

Forty-one true-false self-descriptive statements were administered to 192 Stanford University un-dergraduates. The set included items which de-scribe (a) concern with the social appropriate-ness of one's self-presentation (e.g., "At parties and social gatherings, I do not attempt to do or say things that others will like"); (b) attention to social comparison information as cues to appro-priate self-expression (e.g., "When I am uncer-tain how to act in social situations, I look to the behavior of others for cues"); (c) the ability to control and modify one's self-presentation and expressive behavior (e.g., "I can look anyone in the eye and tell a lie with a straight face [if for a right end]"); (d) the use of this ability in partic-ular situations (e.g., "I may deceive people by being friendly when I really dislike them"); and (e) the extent to which the respondent's expres-sive behavior and self-presentation is cross-situationally consistent or variable (e.g., "In dif-ferent situations and with different people, I often act like very different persons").

The individual items were scored in the di-rection of high self-monitoring. For approxi-mately half the items, agreement was keyed as high SM; for the remainder, disagreement was keyed as high SM.

An item analysis was performed to select items to maximize internal consistency. In this procedure, the top and bottom thirds in total test scores of persons were found. Then the percentages of persons in each group who re-sponded in the manner keyed as high SM were determined. Finally, the percentage in the bot-tom group was subtracted from the percentage in the top group. This difference (D) served as an index of item validity to discriminate total test scores (Anastasi, 1968). D is directly pro-portional to the difference between the num-ber of "correct" and "incorrect" total score discriminations made by an item. D values are not independent of item difficulty and are bi-ased in favor of items of intermediate difficulty level. D is, then, an appropriate criterion for selecting items according to both discrimina-tive power and intermediate difficulty level (Nunnally, 1967).

Items were discarded on the basis of low D scores until a set of 25 items remained which maximized the internal consistency of the scale (Nunnally, 1967, pp. 263–265). The Self-Monitoring Scale has a Kuder-Richardson 20 re-liability of .70, and a test-retest reliability of .83 ($df = 51$, $p < .001$, one-month time interval). Cross-validation on an independent sample of 146 University of Minnesota undergraduates yielded a Kuder-Richardson 20 reliability coef-ficient of .63.

The 25 items of the SM, proportions of re-spondents answering the item in the low-SM-scored direction, their D values, and item-total point-biserial correlations calculated for the University of Minnesota sample are presented in Table 1.

TABLE 1

INSTRUCTIONS, ITEMS, SCORING KEY, DIFFICULTY, AND DISCRIMINATION INDEXES FOR THE SELF-MONITORING SCALE[a]

Item and scoring key[b]	Difficulty[c]	Discrimination			
		D[d]	x^{2e}	p	r_{pb}[f]
1. I find it hard to imitate the behavior of other people. (F)	.63	.50	32.07	.0005	.33
2. My behavior is usually an expression of my true inner feelings, attitudes, and beliefs. (F)	.67	.23	7.26	.01	.13
3. At parties and social gatherings, I do not attempt to do or say things that others will like. (F)	.17	.21	8.29	.005	.34
4. I can only argue for ideas which I already believe. (F)	.43	.29	8.91	.005	.22
5. I can make impromptu speeches even on topics about which I have almost no information. (T)	.69	.21	6.41	.025	.32
6. I guess I put on a show to impress or entertain people. (T)	.65	.44	26.5	.0005	.45
7. When I am uncertain how to act in a social situation, I look to the behavior of others for cues. (T)	.20	.19	6.55	.025	.24
8. I would probably make a good actor. (T)	.69	.36	17.8	.0005	.43
9. I rarely need the advice of my friends to choose movies, books, or music. (F)	.64	.24	6.78	.01	.15
10. I sometimes appear to others to be experiencing deeper emotions than I actually am. (T)	.57	.20	4.78	.05	.39
11. I laugh more when I watch a comedy with others than when alone. (T)	.33	.23	6.51	.025	.29
12. In a group of people I am rarely the center of attention. (F)	.64	.32	13.09	.0005	.40
13. In different situations and with different people, I often act like very different persons. (T)	.40	.22	5.54	.025	.40
14. I am not particularly good at making other people like me. (F)	.30	.27	10.12	.005	.22
15. Even if I am not enjoying myself, I often pretend to be having a good time. (T)	.61	.21	5.67	.025	.24
16. I'm not always the person I appear to be. (T)	.26	.23	7.17	.01	.33
17. I would not change my opinions (or the way I do things) in order to please someone else or win their favor. (F)	.61	.34	15.5	.0005	.34
18. I have considered being an entertainer. (T)	.79	.28	12.64	.0005	.46
19. In order to get along and be liked, I tend to be what people expect me to be rather than anything else. (T)	.79	.25	9.96	.005	.29
20. I have never been good at games like charades or improvisational acting. (F)	.52	.45	25.96	.0005	.31
21. I have trouble changing my behavior to suit different people and different situations. (F)	.36	.38	19.35	.0005	.45
22. At a party I let others keep the jokes and stories going. (F)	.65	.24	6.80	.01	.36
23. I feel a bit awkward in company and do not show up quite so well as I should. (F)	.54	.21	11.05	.001	.32
24. I can look anyone in the eye and tell a lie with a straight face (if for a right end). (T)	.58	.38	19.25	.0005	.33
25. I may deceive people by being friendly when I really dislike them. (T)	.46	.35	15.07	.0005	.32

Note: T = true; F = false; SM = Self-Monitoring Scale.
[a]Directions for Personal Reaction Inventory were: The statements on the following pages concern your personal reactions to a number of different situations. No two statements are exactly alike, so consider each statement carefully before answering. If a statement is *TRUE* or *MOSTLY TRUE* as applied to you, blacken the space marked *T* on the answer sheet. If a statement is *FALSE* or *NOT USUALLY TRUE* as applied to you, blacken the space marked *F*. Do not put your answers on this test booklet itself.
It is important that you answer as frankly and as honestly as you can. Your answers will be kept in the strictest confidence.
[b]Items keyed in the direction of high SM.
[c]Difficulty = proportion of individuals not responding in SM-keyed direction.
[d]Discrimination = difference between proportions of individuals in upper and lower thirds of total scores responding in high-SM direction.
[e]x^2 calculated from the contingency table relating frequencies of T, F for each item and upper third, lower third for *total* SM score (including that item).
[f]Point-biserial correlations between individual items and total scores with that item excluded.

Correlations with Other Scales

Correlations between the SM and related but conceptually distinct individual differences measures provide some evidence for its discriminant validity. There is a slight negative relationship ($r = -.1874$, $df = 190$, $p < .01$) between the SM and the Marlowe-Crowne Social Desirability Scale (M-C SDS, Crowne & Marlowe, 1964). Individuals who report that they observe, monitor, and manage their self-presentation are unlikely to report that they engage in rare but socially desirable behaviors.

There is a similarly low negative relationship ($r = -.2002$, $df = 190$, $p < .01$) between the SM and the Minnesota Multiphasic Personality Inventory Psychopathic Deviate scale. High-SM subjects are unlikely to report deviant psychopathological behaviors or histories of maladjustment.

There is a small and nonsignificant negative relationship ($r = -.25$, $df = 24$, ns) between the SM and the c scale of the Performance Style Test, (e.g., Ring & Wallston, 1968). The c scale was designed to identify a person who is knowledgeable about the kind of social performance required in a wide range of situations and who seeks social approval by becoming whatever kind of person the situation requires. He is literally a chameleon. Clearly the SM and c do not identify the same individuals.

The SM was also found to be unrelated to Christie and Geis's (1970) Machiavellianism ($r = -.0931$, $df = 51$, ns), Alpert-Haber (1960) Achievement Anxiety Test ($r = +.1437$, $df = 51$, ns), and Kassarjian's (1962) inner-other directedness ($r = -.1944$, $df = 54$, ns).

It thus appears that SM is relatively independent of the other variables measured.

VALIDATION: SELF-MONITORING AND PEER RATINGS

As a first source of validity evidence for the SM, a sociometric study of peer ratings was conducted. In choosing this method, it was assumed that a person who has good control of his self-presentation and expressive behavior and who is sensitive to social appropriateness cues should be seen as such a person by others who have had the opportunity for repeated observation of his self-presentation in a wide variety of social situations.

Method

Subjects The subjects in this study were 16 members of a male fraternity living group at Stanford University who agreed to participate in an investigation of person perception.

Procedure Each subject completed the SM and the M-C SDS and then participated in a sociometric person perception task.

Each subject indicated for each of six other members of the fraternity specified for him by the experimenter whether the following self-monitoring attributes were very true, mostly true, somewhat true, or not at all true:

(1) Concerned about acting appropriately in social situations;
(2) Openly expresses his true inner feelings, attitudes, and beliefs;
(3) Has good self-control of his behavior. Can play many roles;
(4) Is good at learning what is socially appropriate in new situations;
(5) Often appears to lack deep emotions; and
(6) Has good self-control of his emotional expression. Can use it to create the impression he wants.

In addition, two other judgments were required: "Is ingratiating. Attempts to do or say things designed to make others like him more" (same 4-point scale as above) and "How much do you like this person?" (very much, moderately, somewhat, not at all).

Results and Discussion

Each subject in the experiment served as a judge of six others and was in turn judged by six other members of his living group. For each person as a stimulus, ratings of him were summed across his six judges to form a single score on each dimension which could range from 0 (six ratings of not at all true) to 18 (six ratings of very true). For each person, a single "peer rating of self-monitoring" score was computed by summing across the six self-monitoring dimensions.

The group of 16 subjects was then dichotomized at the median to form a high-SM group ($n = 8$) and a low-SM group ($n = 8$).

Self-monitoring characteristics were seen as more true of high-SM ($M = 50.5$) than of low-SM ($M = 40.2$) individuals ($t = 2.69$, $df = 14$, $p < .02$, two-tailed test). No differences were observed between high-SM and low-SM individuals on ingratiation or liking ($t = .49$ and $.20$, respectively, $df = 14$, ns).

Mean peer ratings of self-monitoring, ingratiation, and liking for high M-C SDS (above the median, $n = 8$) and low M-C SDS (below the median, $n = 8$) were also calculated. In contrast to SM scores, M-C SDS scores were unrelated to peer rating of self-monitoring (high M-C SDS $M = 54.0$, low M-C SDS $M = 56.7$, $t = .59$, $df = 14$, ns).

The relationship between the SM, M-C SDS, and peer rating of self-monitoring may be examined in terms of product-moment correlations. There is a significant relationship between the SM and peer rating of self-monitoring ($r = .45$, $df = 14$, $p < .05$). The higher an individual's score on the SM, the more frequently self-monitoring characteristics were attributed to him. The M-C SDS and peer rating of self-monitoring are not related ($r = -.14$, $df = 14$, ns).

An image emerges of the high-SM individual as perceived by his peers. He is a person who, out of a concern for acting appropriately in social situations, has become particularly skilled at controlling and modifying his social behavior and emotional expression to suit his surroundings on the basis of cues in the situation which indicate what attitudes and emotions are appropriate. The low-SM individual, as perceived by his peers, is less able and/or less likely to control and modify his self-presentation and expressive behavior to keep it in line with situational specifications of appropriateness. He is also less vigilant to such cues.

High and low scorers on the M-C SDS, by contrast, do not differ in these characteristics. In fact, the evidence suggests that if in fact the M-C SDS is a measure of need for approval, this need is not related to the ability (as perceived by one's peers) to control and monitor one's self-presentation and emotional expressive behavior on the basis of situation-to-situation variation in contingencies of social appropriateness.

VALIDATION: SELF-MONITORING, STAGE ACTORS, AND PSYCHIATRIC WARD PATIENTS

Another means of establishing the validity of an instrument is by predicting how pre-determined groups of individuals would score when the instrument is administered to them. According to this strategy, SM scores of criterion groups chosen to represent extremes in self-monitoring were compared with the unselected sample of Stanford University undergraduates.

Professional Stage Actors

Groups of individuals known to be particularly skilled at controlling their expressive behavior (e.g., actors, mime artists, and politicians) should score higher on the SM than an unselected sample. The SM was administered to a group of 24 male and female dramatic actors who were appearing in professional productions at Stanford and in San Francisco.

Their average score on the SM was 18.41 with a standard deviation of 3.38. This is significantly higher than the mean SM score for the Stanford sample ($t = 8.27$, $df = 555$, $p < .001$).

Thus, stage actors do score higher than non-actors on the SM. Actors probably do have particularly good self-control of their expressive behavior and self-presentation while on stage. It is not clear that actors are any more concerned about monitoring their expressive presentation in other situations.

Hospitalized Psychiatric Ward Patients

The behavior of hospitalized psychiatric patients is less variable across situations than that of "normals." Moos (1968) investigated the reactions of patients and staff in a representative sample of daily settings in a psychiatric inpatient ward in order to assess the relative amount of variance accounted for by settings and individual differences. The results indicated that for patients, individual differences accounted for more variance than setting differences; whereas for staff, individual differences generally accounted for less variance than setting differences. One interpretation of this finding is that psychiatric ward patients are unable or unwilling to monitor their social behavior and self-presentation to conform to variations in contingencies of social appropriateness between situations. In fact, diagnoses of "normal" and "psychopathological" may be closely related to cross-situational plasticity or rigidity (Cameron, 1950). Moos (1969) has reported that situational factors play an increasingly potent role in the behavior of institutionalized individuals as therapy progresses.

Accordingly, it was expected that a sample of hospitalized psychiatric ward patients should score lower on the SM than nonhospitalized normals.

The SM was administered to 31 male hospitalized psychiatric patients at the Menlo Park Veterans Administration Hospital. Their psychiatric diagnoses varied, and most had been previously institutionalized. Each patient's cumulative length of hospitalization varied from several months to several years.

The average SM score for this group was 10.19 with a standard deviation of 3.63. This is signif-

icantly lower than the mean SM score for the Stanford sample ($t = 3.44, df = 562, p < .001$).

VALIDATION: SELF-MONITORING AND THE EXPRESSION OF EMOTION

If the SM discriminates individual differences in the self-control of expressive behavior, this should be reflected behaviorally. In a situation in which individuals are given the opportunity to communicate an arbitrary affective state by means of nonverbal expressive behavior, a high-SM individual should be able to perform this task more accurately, easily, and fluently than a low SM.

Method

Subjects: Expression of Emotion Male and female students whose SM scores were above the 75th percentile (SM > 15) or below the 25th percentile (SM < 9) were recruited by telephone from the pool of pretested introductory psychology students. In all, 30 high-SM and 23 low-SM subjects participated in the study and received either course credit or $1.50.

Procedure: Expression of Emotion Each subject was instructed to read aloud an emotionally neutral three-sentence paragraphs (e.g., "I am going out now. I won't be back all afternoon. If anyone calls, just tell him I'm not here.") in such a way as to express each of the seven emotions anger, happiness, sadness, surprise, disgust, fear, and guilt or remorse using their vocal and facial expressive behavior. The order of expression was determined randomly for each subject. The subject's facial and upper-body expressive behavior was filmed and his voice tape-recorded. It was suggested that he imagine he was trying out for a part in a play and wanted to give an accurate, convincing, natural, and sincere expression of each emotion—one that someone listening to the tape or watching the film would be able to understand as the emotion the subject had been instructed to express. The procedure is similar to one used by Levitt (1964).

These filmed and taped samples of expressive behavior were scored by judges who indicated which of the seven emotions the stimulus person was expressing. Accuracy of the judges was used as a measure of the expressive self-control ability of the stimulus subjects.

Judgments of Expressive Behavior: Subjects The films and tapes of expressive behavior were scored by a group of 20 high-SM (SM > 15, or top 25%) and 13 low-SM (SM < 9, or bottom 25%) naive judges who were paid $2.00 an hour.

Judgments of Emotional Expressive Behavior: Procedure Judges participated in small groups of both high- and low-SM judges who watched films for approximately one fourth of the subjects in the expression experiment and listened to the tapes of approximately another one fourth of the subjects. For each stimulus segment, judges indicated which of the seven emotions had been expressed.

Results and Discussion

Accuracy of Expression and SM Scores Accuracy of the judges in decoding the filmed and taped expressive behavior for each stimulus person was used as a measure of his self-control of expressive behavior ability. For each of the 53 subjects in the expression task, the average accuracy of his judges was computed separately for films and tapes and high- and low-SM judges. Table 2 represents these accuracy scores as a function of stimulus (expresser) SM scores, facial or vocal channel of expression, and judge SM score for naive judges. Each stimulus person expressed seven emotions. Therefore, mean accuracy scores can range from 0 to 7.

The average accuracy scores for each stimulus person's facial and vocal expressive behavior, as judged by high-SM and low-SM judges, were entered into an analysis of variance. Expresser SM score (high SM or low SM) was a between-stimulus-persons factor; chan-

TABLE 2

SM AND ACCURACY OF EXPRESSION OF EMOTION: NAIVE JUDGES

Stimulus	High-SM judge		Low-SM judge	
	Face	Voice	Face	Voice
High SM (*n* = 30)				
M[a]	3.353	4.047	3.196	3.564
Variance	.718	.636	1.117	1.769
Low SM (*n* = 23)				
M	2.518	2.957	2.493	3.094
Variance	1.348	.982	1.479	2.102

Note: SM = Self-Monitoring Scale.
[a]Average accuracy computed for each stimulus across all judges who rated him and then averaged across *n* stimulus persons; range = 0–7.

nel of expression (face or voice) and judge SM score (high SM or low SM) were within-stimulus-persons factors.

The following pattern of results emerges. Individuals who scored high on the SM were better able to communicate accurately an arbitrarily chosen emotion to naive judges than were individuals who scored low on the SM. That is, judges were more often accurate in judging both the facial and vocal expressive behavior generated in this emotion communication task by high-SM stimuli than by low-SM stimuli ($F = 11.72$, $df = 1/51$, $p < .01$). For both high- and low-SM stimuli, accuracy was greater in the vocal than the facial channel ($F = 19.12$, $df = 1/153$, $p < .001$). Finally, there was a tendency for high-SM judges to be better judges of emotion than low-SM judges ($F = 1.69$, $df = 1/153$, $p < .25$). In addition, high-SM judges may have been more differentially sensitive to the expressive behavior of high- and low-SM stimuli. That is, the difference in accuracy for judging high-SM and low-SM stimuli for high-SM judges was greater than the corresponding difference for low-SM judges. However, once again the differences are not significant ($F = 2.41$, $df = 1/153$, $p < .25$).

Discriminant Validation: SM versus M-C SDS

In the sample of 192 from which the subjects for the expression task were selected, scores on the SM and M-C SDS were very slightly correlated ($r = -.1874$). However, in the sample of 53 subjects chosen for this experiment, the correlation was $-.3876$ ($df = 51, p < .01$). Furthermore, individuals who scored below the median on the M-C SDS were better able than those who scored above the median to voluntarily communicate emotion in this experimental task ($F = 4.462, df = 1/51, p < .05$). These differences present a rival explanation of the differences observed in self-control of expressive behavior between high-SM and low-SM groups.

To discriminate between the SM and M-C SDS as predictors of self-control of expression ability, two analyses of covariance were performed. In the first, accuracy scores for naive judges collapsed across judge SM score and channel were examined as a function of stimulus SM scores as the independent variable and stimulus M-C SDS scores as the covariate. After removing the effects of the covariate (M-C SDS), there is still a highly significant treatment (SM) effect ($F = 7.13, df = 1/50, p < .01$). That is, individuals who scored high on the SM were better able than low-SM scorers to accurately express and communicate arbitrary emotions independent of their M-C SDS scores.

In the second analysis of covariance, accuracy scores for naive judges collapsed across judge SM score and channel were examined as a function of stimulus M-C SDS as the independent variable and stimulus SM scores as the covariate. The results of this analysis are quite conclusive. After removing the effects of the covariate (SM), there is no remaining relationship between the independent variable (M-C SDS) and expression accuracy ($F = .75, df = 1/50, ns$). That is, whatever relationship exists between M-C SDS scores and self-control of expression ability is entirely accounted for by the slight negative correlation between the M-C SDS and SM.

Thus, the results of this experiment clearly indicate that scores on the SM are related to the self-control of expressive behavior. High-SM individuals were better able than low-SM individuals to express arbitrary emotional states in facial and vocal behavior.

VALIDATION: SELF-MONITORING AND ATTENTION TO SOCIAL COMPARISON INFORMATION

It has been proposed that out of a concern for social appropriateness of his behavior, a high-SM individual is particularly attentive to social comparison information and uses this information as guidelines to monitor and manage his self-presentation and expressive behavior.

Consistent with this formulation, high-SM individuals are seen by their peers as better able to learn what is socially appropriate in new situations than are low-SM. Two SM items which best predict performance in the emotion expression task are: "When I am uncertain how to act in a social situation, I look to the behavior of others for cues," and "I laugh more when I watch a comedy with others than when alone."

All of this suggests that, given the opportunity in a self-presentation situation, a high-SM individual should be more likely to seek out relevant social comparison information.

Method

Subjects Subjects were recruited from the pretested introductory psychology subject pool on the basis of high-SM scores (SM > 15) or low-SM scores (SM < 9). A total of 14 high-SM and 13 low-SM subjects participated in the experiment and were paid $1.00.

Procedure Each subject performed a self-presentation task in a situation designed to facilitate self-monitoring. He was asked to respond to a series of true-false self-descriptive personality test items in preparation for a discussion of how test-takers decide how to respond to ambiguously worded questionnaire items. During the task he was given the opportunity to consult a "majority response sheet" which listed the modal response of his introductory psychology class for each item in order to consider possible alternative interpretations of the items in preparation for the discussion.

Pretesting had indicated that the task was interpreted as neither social pressure to consult the information nor a test of resistance to temptation to cheat. Rather it appears that a situation was created in which the subjects knew that normative social comparison information was available to them and they could consult it or not as they wished in preparation for a later discussion of their self-descriptions on the questionnaire items.

Unknown to the subject who performed this task alone, an observer in the next room recorded the frequency with which the subject consulted the majority response sheet and timed each look. The sheet had been left by the experimenter at the far corner of the subject's table so that consulting it required observable but not effortful behavior by the subject. It was expected that a high-SM subject would look more often, as measured by frequency and duration of looking, at this social comparison information than would a low-SM subject.

Results and Discussion

Results on the dependent measures of seeking out of social comparison information were analyzed as a function of both SM and M-C SDS scores ($r_{SM.M-C SDS} = -.067$, $df = 25$, ns) in a 2×2 (High SM, Low SM $\times$ High M-C SDS, Low M-C SDS) unweighted means analysis of variance.

There were three measures of seeking out social comparison information during the self-presentation task: (a) frequency of looking at the majority response sheet as recorded by the ob-server; (b) frequency of looking at the majority response sheet as measured by the subject's retrospective self-report; and (c) total duration of looking at the majority response sheet as timed by the observer. These three measures are highly intercorrelated ($r_{12} = .92$, $r_{13} = .90$, $r_{23} = .83$, $df = 25$, $p < .001$). The means for each of these measures are presented in Table 3.

For frequency of looking as recorded by an observer, a high-SM subject looked more frequently than a low-SM at the majority response sheet ($F = 4.70$, $df = 1/23$, $p < .05$). Given the opportunity to consult social comparison information in a self-presentation situation in which they expected to justify their self-descriptions, high self-monitors did so more frequently than did low self-monitors. There was no systematic relationship between M-C SDS and looking behavior ($F = .122$, $df = 1/23$, ns), nor was there any interaction between SM and M-C SDS scores ($F = .011$, $df = 1/23$, ns). Thus, there was no relationship between the tendency to describe one-self in socially desirable fashion and consulting social comparison information in this self-presentation situation.

TABLE 3

THREE MEASURES OF LOOKING AT SOCIAL COMPARISON INFORMATION

Measure	n	Frequency of looking[a]	Frequency of looking[b]	Total duration of looking (in seconds)
High SM, low M-C SDS	6	14.67	15.83	20.83
High SM, high M-C SDS	8	12.25	12.25	19.38
Low SM, low M-C SDS	7	5.14	5.83	5.43
Low SM, high M-C SDS	6	4.83	4.13	4.83

Note: SM = Self-Monitoring Scale; M-C SDS = Marlowe-Crowne Social Desirability Scale.
[a]Recorded by observer.
[b]Subject's self-report.

Analyses of subjects' self-report of looking behavior and total time looking measured by the observer result in identical conclusions. For either measure, high-SM subjects were more likely than low-SM to seek out social comparison information.

CONCLUSIONS

Individuals differ in the extent to which they monitor (observe and control) their expressive behavior and self-presentation. Out of a concern for social appropriateness, the self-monitoring individual is particularly sensitive to the expression and self-presentation of others in social situations and uses these cues as guidelines for monitoring and managing his own self-presentation and expressive behavior. In contrast, the non-self-monitoring person has little concern for the appropriateness of his presentation and expression, pays less attention to the expression of others, and monitors and controls his presentation to a lesser extent. His presentation and expression appear to be controlled from within by his experience rather than by situational and interpersonal specifications of appropriateness.

A self-report measure of individual differences in self-monitoring was constructed. The Self-Monitoring Scale is internally consistent, temporally stable, and uncorrelated with self-report measure of related concepts.

Four studies were conducted to validate the Self-Monitoring Scale. According to their peers, individuals with high SM scores are good at learning what is socially appropriate in new situations, have good self-control of their emotional expression, and can effectively use this ability to create the impressions they want. Theater actors scored higher and hospitalized psychiatric ward patients scored lower than university students. Individuals with high SM scores were better able than those with low SM scores to intentionally express and communicate emotion in both the vocal and facial channels of expressive behav-

ior. In a self-presentation task, individuals with high SM scores were more likely than those with low scores to seek out and consult social comparison information about their peers. Self-monitoring and need for approval were compared as predictors of each external criterion to demonstrate the discriminant validity of the SM.

<hr>

READING 9

The Dynamic Self-Concept: A Social Psychological Perspective

Hazel Markus and Elissa Wurf (1987)

Markus and Wurf organize the burgeoning literature on the self-concept in this reading. Presenting a dynamic view of the self-concept, they suggest that the self-concept (a) has many different facets with different degrees of centrality, (b) serves many motivations, and (c) is responsive to social surroundings. Whereas researchers once investigated the self-concept as a single, unitary construct, we now understand that it includes the ideal or desired self (Higgins, Klein, & Strauman, 1985; Horney, 1950; Rogers, 1954), the undesired self (Ogilvie, 1987; Sullivan, 1953), the possible selves (Markus & Nurius, 1986), and other peripheral to central self-respects that can be accessed via the working self-concept.

This is a very exciting time for research on self-concept, especially when taking a social psychological stance. Actually, two social psychological stances are possible. As seen in Reading 7, Cooley and the symbolic interactionists stress how the self is influenced and at least partially created through social interaction; in this reading Markus and Wurf discuss how the self mediates and directly influences social interaction. Thus, by focusing on the self-concept and its mediation of interpersonal as well as intrapersonal processes, Markus and Wurf provide a nice contrast to the symbolic interactionist approach of Cooley and the more recent approaches of self-presentation and self-monitoring. From their review, we can see that the self-concept partially constructs as well as is constructed from our social reality.

The unifying premise of the last decade's research on the self is that the self-concept does not just reflect on-going behavior but instead mediates and regulates this behavior. In this sense the self-concept has been viewed as dynamic—as active, forceful, and capable of change. It interprets and organizes self-relevant actions and experiences; it has motivational consequences, providing the incentives, standards, plans, rules, and scripts for behavior; and it adjusts in response to challenges from the social environment. Virtually all of the early theoretical statements on the self-concept accord it this dynamic role (see Gordon & Gergen 1968), yet until very recently the empirical work lagged far behind these sophisticated conceptions of how the self-system functions. Indeed, the majority of self-concept research could best be described as an attempt to relate very complex global behavior, such as delinquency, marital satisfaction, or school achievement, to a single aspect of the self-concept, typically self-esteem.

In 1974, Wylie reviewed the literature and concluded that the self-concept simply could not be powerfully implicated in directing behavior. In the last decade, however, researchers have redoubled their efforts to understand the self-concept as one of the most significant regulators of behavior (see Suls 1982, Suls & Greenwald 1983, Schlenker 1985a). They have been sustained by their faith in the importance of the self-concept, by a number of compelling theoretical accounts of self-concept functioning, and by the poor showing of those approaches that ignore the self (e.g., theories that focus solely on life events or social structural features of the environment). In this review, we focus primarily on research that views the self-concept as a dynamic interpretive structure that mediates most signif-

icant *intrapersonal* processes (including information processing, affect, and motivation) and a wide variety of *interpersonal* processes (including social perception; choice of situation, partner, and interaction strategy; and reaction to feedback).

Progress in research on the self-concept came as a result of three advances. The first was the realization that the self-concept can no longer be explored as if it were a unitary, monolithic entity. The second was the understanding that the functioning of the self-concept depends on both the self-motives being served (e.g., self-enhancement, consistency maintenance, or self-actualization) and on the configuration of the immediate social situation. The third advance was a consequence of observing more fine-grained behavior. Overt, complex actions may not always be the appropriate dependent variables. An individual's behavior is constrained by many factors other than the self-concept. As a consequence, the influence of the self-concept will not always be directly revealed in one's overt actions. Instead, its impact will often be manifest more subtly, in mood changes, in variations in what aspects of the self-concept are accessible and dominant, in shifts in self-esteem, in social comparison choices, in the nature of self-presentation, in choice of social setting, and in the construction or definition of one's situation.

CONTENT AND STRUCTURE

The Multifaceted Self-Concept

The most dramatic change in the last decade of research on the self-concept can be found in work on its structure and content. One of the formidable stumbling blocks to linking the self-concept to behavioral regulation has been the view of the self-concept as a stable, generalized, or average view of the self. How could this crude, undifferentiated structure sensitively mediate and reflect the diversity of behavior to which it was supposedly related? The solution has been to view the self-concept as a multifaceted phenomenon, as a set or collection of images, schemas, conceptions, prototypes, theories, goals, or tasks (Epstein 1980, Schlenker 1980, Carver & Scheier 1981, Rogers 1981, Greenwald 1982, Markus & Sentis 1982, Markus 1983, Greenwald & Pratkanis 1984, Kihlstrom & Cantor 1984).

Whether researchers define the self-concept in terms of hierarchies, prototypes, networks, spaces, or schemas, they generally agree that the self-structure is an active one. What began as an apparently singular, static, lump-like entity has become a multidimensional, multifaceted dynamic structure that is systematically implicated in all aspects of social information processing. Among sociologists there has been a similar movement, and it is now commonplace to refer to the multiplicity of identity (Burke 1980, Martindale 1980, Stryker 1980, Rowan 1983, Weigert 1983, Lester 1984). Identity is described as including personal characteristics, feelings, and images (e.g., Burke 1980, Stryker 1980, Schlenker 1985b), as well as roles and social status. With this development, psychologists and sociologists are achieving a complete convergence in how they think about the self.

Types of Self-Representations

Not all of the self-representations that comprise the self-concept are alike. Some are more important and more elaborated with behavioral evidence than others. Some are positive, some negative; some refer to the individual's here-and-now experience, while others refer to past or future experiences. Moreover, some are representations of what the self actually is, while others are of what the self would like to be, could be, ought to be, or is afraid of being. Self-representations that can be the subject of conscious reflection are usually termed self-conceptions.

The most apparent difference among self-representations is in their centrality or importance. Some self-conceptions are core conceptions (Gergen 1968) or salient identities (Stryker 1980, 1986), while others are more peripheral. Central conceptions of the self are generally the most well elaborated and are presumed to affect information processing and behavior most powerfully. Yet, more peripheral or less well-elaborated conceptions may still wield behavioral influence.

Self-representations also differ in whether or not they have actually been achieved. Some selves are not actual, but are possible for the person; other selves are hoped-for ideals. Markus & Nurius (1986) theorize that among one's set of self-conceptions are possible selves—the selves one would like to be or is afraid of becoming. These selves function as incentives for behavior, providing images of the future self in desired or undesired end-states. They also function to provide an evaluative and interpretive context for the current view of self. Representations of potential have also been explored by Schlenker (1985b) and Levinson (1978).

Building on earlier notions of the ego ideal (Freud 1925, Horney 1950, Rogers 1951), Rosenberg (1979) discusses ideal self-conceptions, distinguishing those ideal self-conceptions that are likely to be realized from those that are glorified images of the self. Higgins (1983) extends this work and hypothesizes that there are at least three classes of self-conceptions: those that reflect the "actual" self, those that represent the "ideal" self or the attributes the person would like to possess, and those that represent the "ought" self, which are representations of characteristics that someone, self or other, believes the person should possess. A discrepancy between any two of these self-concepts can induce a state of discomfort; and different kinds of discrepancy produce different types of discomfort. For example, Higgins et al. (1985, 1986) find that a discrepancy between actual and ideal selves is associated with depression, while a discrepancy between actual and ought selves is related to anxiety.

A third difference in self-representations is whether they refer to past, present, or future views of the self—what Schutz (1964) calls the tense of the self-conception and what Nuttin (1984) refers to as its temporal sign. Images of the self in the past or future may be as significant as the here-and-now aspects of self (Markus & Nurius 1986, Nuttin & Lens 1986).

A final difference among self-representations is in their positivity or negativity. Most work focuses on positive self-conceptions, but there has been some focus on what Sullivan (1953) called the "bad me," or the individual's negative self-conceptions. The majority of this work attempts to understand the "I'm no good, I'm useless or worthless" thinking that seems to predominate in the selves of many depressed individuals. Beck (1967) has postulated that depressives carry with them a depressive self-schema that continually distorts self-relevant thoughts. A large variety of studies now demonstrate that depressed individuals do indeed think more negatively about themselves than about others, and that this negativity pervades all aspects of their information processing (Derry & Kuiper 1981, Kuiper & Derry 1981, Kuiper & MacDonald 1982, Ingram et al., 1983, Kuiper & Higgins 1985, Pietromonaco 1985). Currently, investigators disagree as to whether this negativity is a function of a fixed schema that distorts thinking, or whether the thinking of depressives is a fairly accurate reflection and integration of their life experiences.

There has been little attention to negativity in the self-concepts of people who are not depressed. Rosenberg & Gara (1985), following Erikson (1950), talk about the importance of negative identities, but little empirical work focuses on peoples' negative self-views. Indeed, many self-concept theorists (e.g., Tesser & Campbell 1984) give the impression that individuals do virtually everything within their power to avoid forming negative self-conceptions; yet work by Wurf & Markus (1983) suggests that even nondepressed, high self-esteem individuals can have negative self-conceptions that may be elaborated into self-schemas. Thus they find, for example, individuals who describe themselves as shy, lazy,

or fat; who feel bad about these characteristics; who feel these are important aspects of their self-definition; yet who maintain overall high self-esteem. They suggest that negative self-conceptions are critical in initiating the process of self-concept change. Moreover, Wurf (1986) hypothesizes that these negative self-schemas may function to help individuals cope with the negativity in their lives, ensuring that negative experiences do not swamp the entire self-concept.

In the work on self-representations, several important concerns remain untouched. First, there has been relatively little attention paid to the representation of affect in the self-concept, beyond the assumption that self-conceptions vary in their valence. Some (Guntrip 1971; Kernberg 1977) assume that each self-representation contains both an affective and a cognitive component. Greenwald & Pratkanis (1984) suggest that affect functions as a heuristic that guides how various self-relevant experiences are organized, assigning them either to a positive class or a negative class. Similarly, Fast (1985) argues that affect plays a major role in determining the connections among our experiences; it defines the similarity of our actions and thus provides the basis of the initial organization of the self-concept. Still others (e.g., Salovey & Rodin 1985) view affect as a consequence of the set of self-conceptions that are currently active.

A second missing element is speculation about how representations of the self differ in form and function depending on when, how, and why they were formed. Some representations may be derived from straighforward perception and organization of one's own behavior. These representations may be directly accessible to conscious awareness; or, they may not be accessible because they are so well rehearsed they have become automatic. Self-representations can assume a variety of forms—neutral, motor, and sensory as well as verbal. Nonverbal representations may be inaccessible to conscious awareness. Finally, some self-representations may be actively repressed and kept from consciousness because they are based in certain defenses or desires (Singer & Salovey 1985, Silverman & Weinberger 1985). Representations of the self that derive from wishes or needs may have a very different form and function than representations that derive from straightforward organization of one's behavior.

A third important issue has to do with the structure and organization of self-representations. What happens when two self-conceptions are incompatible? Higgins (1983; Higgins et al., 1985, 1986) has attempted to relate different types of self-concept discrepancy to emotional disorders, and Linville (1982) suggests that a complex self-structure can protect the individual from emotional turmoil. Similarly, a variety of studies from a sociological perspective suggest that the more identities individuals have, the better their mental health (Kessler & McRae 1982, Coleman & Antonucci 1983). However, this may only be true if the identities can be successfully integrated with each other (Thoits 1983, Pietromonaco et al., 1986). In general, the relationship between variation in the configuration of the self-structure and differential behavior is largely unexplored.

Sources of Self-Representations

Self-representations differ in their origins. Some self-representations result from inferences that people make about their attitudes and dispositions while watching their own actions. People also make inferences from their internal physiological (arousal) reactions (Bandura 1977), and their cognitions, emotions, and motivations (Harter 1983, Anderson 1984, Anderson & Ross 1984). Anderson finds that people's thoughts and feelings have even greater weight in determining self-perceptions than do behaviors. In fact, when observers are given information about the actor's thoughts and feelings, they come to see the actor very much as that person views him- or herself; whereas when they are given information about the actor's behaviors, they may see him or her quite differently (Anderson 1984).

Representations of the self also derive from direct attempts at self-assessment. Trope (1983, 1986) presents a formal model of self-assessment that describes the diagnosticity of a task, based on the person's uncertainty about his or her ability level and the probabilities of success and failure. In research drawing on this model, Trope and his associates find that people prefer to do tasks that are maximally diagnostic of their abilities, particularly when they are uncertain about those abilities (Trope 1983). People may differ in their willingness to seek out potentially threatening information about the self (Sorrentino & Short 1986). In certain situations they may be more willing to seek out or accept potentially threatening information—for example, during life transitions (Cantor et al., 1985) or when making decisions with long-term consequences (Trope 1986).

People also learn about themselves from others, both through social comparisons and direct interactions. McGuire and his colleagues (McGuire 1984, McGuire & McGuire 1982) find that one of the most powerful determinants of currently available self-conceptions is the configuration of the immediate social environment. Individuals will focus on whatever aspects of themselves are most distinctive in a particular social setting: for example, short children will notice their height when in classroom of taller children. Social comparison can be a potent source of self-knowledge (Suls & Miller 1977, Schoeneman 1981). Children learn how to use social comparison to evaluate themselves and become progressively more skilled at doing this during their school years (Frey & Ruble 1985). People compare with superior others to evaluate themselves and with inferior others to make themselves feel good; the comparison others may be chosen to satisfy one or both motives (Brickman & Janoff-Bulman 1977, Gruder 1977, Taylor et al., 1983). Finally, direct interaction with others also provides information about the self (see the section below on interpersonal processes). Symbolic interactionists in fact suggest that all self-knowledge derives from social interaction (Baldwin 1897, Cooley 1902, Mead 1934; for a historical review, see Scheibe 1985; for a review of symbolic interactionism, see Stryker 1980).

The growth of self-structures is determined by both the information the person receives about the self (through self-perception, social comparison, and reflected appraisals) and by the individual's ability to cognitively process self-conceptions. Harter's (1983) model of the development of self-conceptions posits a tendency for self-descriptions to become increasingly abstract, incorporating first behaviors (e.g., "good at doing sums"), then traits ("smart"), then single abstractions ("scientific"), then higher order abstractions ("intellectual"). Within each of the phases, there is an alternating sequence of first overgeneralizing self-conceptions and then differentiating and reintegrating them (e.g., first the child thinks of herself as "all smart," and then later as "smart in English, but dumb in math"). Thus, conceptions of the self within different domains may be at different developmental stages.

The Working Self-Concept

Among both psychologists and sociologists, an emphasis on the multiplicity or multidimensionality of the self-concept or identity has led to the realization that it is no longer feasible to refer to *the* self-concept. Instead it is necessary to refer to the working, on-line, or accessible self-concept (Schlenker 1985b, Cantor & Kihlstrom 1986, Markus & Nurius 1986, Rhodewalt 1986, Rhodewalte & Agustsdottir 1986). The idea is simply that not all self-representations or identities that are part of the complete self-concept will be accessible at any one time. The working self-concept, or the self-concept of the moment, is best viewed as a continually active, shifting array of accessible self-knowledge.

This approach to the self-concept is welcomed now for several reasons. First, it flows naturally

out of an increasingly large volume of research indicating that individuals are heavily influenced in all aspects of judgment, memory, and overt behavior by their currently accessible pool of thoughts, attitudes, and beliefs (Nisbett & Ross 1980, Higgins & King 1981, Sherman et al. 1981, Snyder 1982). Second, this view of the self-concept moves much closer to that implied by the symbolic interactionists (Mead 1934, Stryker 1980). There is not a fixed or static self, but only a current self-concept constructed from one's social experiences. Third, this formulation allows for a self-concept that can be at once both stable and malleable. Core aspects of self (one's self-schemas) may be relatively unresponsive to changes in one's social circumstances. Because of their importance in defining the self and their extensive elaboration, they may be chronically accessible (Higgins et al. 1982). Many other self-conceptions in the individual's system, however, will vary in accessibility depending on the individual's motivational state or on the prevailing social conditions. The working self-concept thus consists of the core self-conceptions embedded in a context of more tentative self-conceptions that are tied to the prevailing circumstances.

Results that are taken to reveal the malleability of the self (Gergen 1965, 1968, Morse & Gergen 1970, Fazio et al. 1981, Jones et al. 1981, McGuire & McGuire 1982) can be explained by assuming that the contents of working self-concept have changed. That is, the circumstances surrounding the experimental manipulation make certain self-conceptions, and not others, accessible in thought and memory. For example, if after responding to questions about extroversion, subjects appear to view themselves as more extroverted than do subjects who have responded to questions about introversion (see Fazio et al. 1981), it is because most individuals can be assumed to have conceptions of themselves as both introverts and extroverts. The extrovert manipulation makes salient one's extrovert self-representations and the individual is likely to see the self at that moment as relatively more extroverted. Temporary change that occurs in the self-concept when one set of self-conceptions is activated and accessible in working memory rather than another is only one type of self-concept malleability. It is to be distinguished from change of a more enduring nature, the type that occurs when new self-conceptions are added to the set, when self-conceptions change in meaning, or when the relationship among self-components changes.

Self-concept and identity theorists appear to be converging on a notion of the self-concept as containing a *variety* of representations—representations that are not just verbal propositions or depictions of traits and demographic characteristics. Rather, representations of self may be cognitive and/or affective; they may be in verbal, image, neural, or sensorimotor form; they represent the self in the past and future as well as the here-and-now; and they are of the actual self and of the possible self. Some are organized into structures that contain both a well-elaborated knowledge base and production rules for how to behave when certain conditions are met. Other self-conceptions may be more tentative, constructed on the spot for a particular social interaction. At any one time, only some subset of these various representations is accessed and invoked to regulate or accompany the individual's behavior. The important remaining task is systematically to implicate these diverse representations of the self and the various organizations they can assume in the regulation of behavior; and conversely, to delineate how actions in turn influence these various self-representations.

SELF-REGULATION

While some self theorists grapple with the content and structure of the self-concept, others focus on the problem of self-regulatory processes: how individuals control and direct their own actions. Research on self-structure and on self-regulation would appear to have direct relevance

for each other, but they are pursued in two virtually nonoverlapping literatures. Self-regulation theorists are concerned with the very general problem of the individual's involvement in controlling his or her own behavior. By self-regulation, some theorists mean how the person, as opposed to the environment, controls behavior, but they do not focus specifically on representations of the self as regulators (e.g., Kanfer 1970). In this section, we review those approaches to self-regulation that at least implicitly involve the self-concept.

The self-concept, of course, is only one of numerous factors, including culture, the social environment, individual need or tension states, and non-self-relevant cognitions, that may directly influence behavior. Although behavior is not exclusively controlled by self representations, it has become increasingly apparent that the representations of what individuals think, feel, or believe about themselves are among the most powerful regulators of many important behaviors.

Self-regulation operates with varying degrees of efficiency. Sometimes the person attempts to regulate her behavior, and she is able to do so effectively: all phases of self-regulation flow naturally one after another. Other times, however, the person attempts to regulate her behavior, but cannot do so. She cannot decide between which of multiple salient goals to pursue; she ends up mulling over her goals, rather than acting to achieve them; she lacks the appropriate procedural knowledge and doesn't know what to do; or she tries but repeatedly fails. There are any number of ways in which the self-regulatory process can go wrong. The involvement of the self-concept has been suggested as a critical variable in how smoothly self-regulatory processes function. The nature and effects of this involvement, however, are unclear.

Some authors suggest that self-regulation will operate most efficiently when the person is self-focused. Carver & Scheier (1981) are the primary proponents of this position. Their theory claims that when a behavioral standard is salient and the person is focused on the self, attention to the self will lead to a comparison between the current state and the standard. The discrepancy between where the person is and where he wants to be is presumed to motivate attempts at behavior (provided the person expects that he can reach the standard; if he expects not to be able to reach it, then he is predicted to withdraw, physically or mentally, from attempts at change). Carver & Scheier use a variety of manipulations (mirrors, audiences, cameras, or dispositional differences in self-consciousness) to demonstrate that self-focused individuals regulate themselves more effectively (i.e., more in line with standards) than do non-self-focused individuals (see Carver & Scheier 1981 for a summary of this research). Greenwald (1982, Breckler & Greenwald 1986) suggests that what is really being affected by self-awareness manipulations is the person's ego involvement; if the manipulation calls up one of the person's "ego tasks," then the person will be ego-involved and will regulate behavior more effectively.

In opposition to these formulations, other authors seem to imply that focusing on the self (implicating the self-concept) can interfere with the smooth operation of self-regulation. Kuhl (1985), for example, suggests that focusing on "states" (internal states or external goals), rather than on actions, impairs effective self-regulation. Similarly, Wicklund (1986) suggests that people who are dynamically oriented (attending to the environment), rather than statically oriented (attending to personal characteristics), will best regulate themselves. Further, the dynamically oriented person is focused on his or her relationship to the environment and, while behaving, experiences a loss of self (cf. Csikszentimihayli 1975). The role of the self in such theories is unclear, because there are circumstances under which these authors claim that self-involvement aids self-regulation. Kuhl (1984), for example, suggests that "the *full* repertoire of volitional strategies is provided only if the current intention is a self-related one" (p.127). And Wick-

lund (1986) suggests that a focus on one's own standards for performance may aid dynamically oriented functioning.

Clearly, there is a need for further theorizing to reconcile these approaches. The existence of such disparate theories suggests that there are ways in which the self-concept can both facilitate and interfere with self-regulation. For example, all the theories seem to agree that a focus on discrepancies between where the self is and where it wants to be may effectively motivate behavior (provided the discrepancy is not too large). In contrast, a focus either solely on where the self is or on where it wants to be, without any attention to the discrepancy between the two, is unlikely to motivate behavior change. Consistent with this, research on "self-regulatory failure" (Tomarken & Kirschenbaum 1982) demonstrates that monitoring one's successes (on well-learned behaviors) leads to decreased performance, while monitoring one's failures (i.e., discrepancies) leads to increased performance. For new behaviors (which are characterized by a discrepancy between where one is and where one wants to be), monitoring successes is either superior to or equal to monitoring failure in increasing performance.

A further reconciliation might involve distinguishing between the self as "me" and the self as "I." While theories of self-structure focus on the content of the self, on the "me," theories of self-regulation implicitly focus on dynamic, process-oriented aspects of self—the "I." The subjective experience of loss of self during peak experiences (Privette 1983) or effective self-regulation may reflect a lack of attention to the "me." This does not mean, however, that the self is not involved. The person may experience a subjective loss of self when performing behaviors that are "ego syntonic," that is, congruent with the ego ideal. Instead of expressing a loss of self, these behaviors may reflect the fullest involvement of self, experienced as a merging of the "I" with the behavior it enacts.

THE DYNAMIC SELF-CONCEPT

In the developing model of the dynamic self-concept, the self-concept is viewed as a collection of self-representations, and the working self-concept is that subset of representations which is accessible at a given moment. These representations vary in their structure and function and have been given a variety of labels. They are activated depending on the prevailing social circumstances and on the individual's motivational state. Some self-representations are more or less automatically activated as a result of salient situational stimuli. Many others, however, are willfully recruited or invoked in response to whatever motives the individual is striving to fulfill. The person may, as we discuss below, seek to develop or maintain a positive affective state about the self—a motive frequently referred to as self-enhancement. Alternatively, or simultaneously, the person may seek to maintain a sense of coherence and continuity, fulfilling a self-consistency motive. Yet another important motive is what Maslow (1954) referred to as self-actualization, the desire to improve or change the self, to develop, grow, and fulfill one's potential. These various self-motives, in conjunction with social circumstance, determine the contents of the working self-concept.

The structures active in the working self-concept are the basis on which the individual initiates actions and also the basis for the observation, judgment, and evaluation of these actions. The influence of the working self-concept in the shaping and controlling of behavior can be seen in two broad classes of behaviors: *intrapersonal processes,* which include self-relevant information processing, affect regulation, and motivational processes; and *interpersonal processes,* which include social perception, social comparison, and seeking out and shaping interaction with others. The outcomes of one's intrapersonal and interpersonal behavior determine the current motivational state and the salient social conditions for the next cycle of self-regulation.

INTRAPERSONAL PROCESSES MEDIATED BY THE SELF-CONCEPT

In defending the importance of the self-system, early self theorists devoted a significant amount of their theorizing to identifying the crucial functions that the self performed (Allport 1955, Erikson 1950). Several major functions were specified. These included providing the individual with a sense of continuity in time and space, providing an integrating and organizing function for the individual's self-relevant experiences, regulating the individual's affective state, and providing a source of incentive or motivation for the individual.

The first general function, providing a sense of continuity, has received little empirical attention and has been accepted largely as a matter of faith. Recently, however, some theorists have focused specifically on the related question of how individuals weave together various self-conceptions. Most people appear to construct a current autobiography or narrative (Bruner 1986; Dennett 1982; Gergen & Gergen 1983)—a story that makes the most coherent or harmonious integration of one's various experiences. This narrative is a superstructure to which individuals attach their current set of life experiences. This personal narrative is a particularly intriguing type of self-representation because it is very often revised. The flexibility and malleability of self-structure organization is further supported by research suggesting that individuals often rewrite their personal histories to support a current self-view (Ross & Conway 1986, Greenwald 1980).

The other intrapersonal functions of the self have been the source of a burgeoning experimental literature. With the self-concept operationalized as a set of cognitive structures, it became obvious that the self-concept can influence every aspect of the processing of self-relevant information. Individuals appear to be differentially sensitive to stimuli that are self-relevant and to privilege the processing of these stimuli. Such selective processing seems to occur even outside of the subject's awareness.

INTERPERSONAL PROCESSES MEDIATED BY THE SELF-CONCEPT

As the person strives to carry out such personally motivated behavior, he or she is inevitably swept up in social interaction. Other people often serve as the means for achieving one's goals, requiring the person to have skills for successful negotiation. Further, these interactions—a cup of coffee with a friend or an intimate moment with a lover— are very often ends in themselves. Because of these dependencies on others, people both shape and are shaped by their social interactions. The self-concept provides a framework that guides the interpretation of one's social experiences but that also regulates one's participation in these experiences. A great deal of social behavior, sometimes quite consciously and sometimes unwittingly, is in the service of various self-concept requirements. The relevant research questions include how the self-concept influences social perception, how the self-concept guides the selection of situations and interaction partners, what strategies the individual uses to shape and interpret interactions with others, and how the person reacts to feedback from others that is incongruent with the self-concept.

Recent research and theorizing promises further progress in research on the role of the self-concept in interpersonal interaction. Advances include, first, the suggestion that the nature of the relationship may critically influence the strategies the self will use in social interaction (Jussim 1986; Tedeschi & Norman 1985); and second, the demonstration that the person's interaction goals influence his or her behavior toward others (Darley et al. 1986). A third ad-

vance in the literature is the attention to reactions of "targets" as well as of perceivers (Hilton & Darley 1985; Swann & Ely 1984). Fourth, several theorists suggest that in order to study self-presentation effectively, the process will have to be studied over time. While there is theorizing about how the self acts in interaction over time (e.g., Darley & Fazio 1980), little research actually undertakes such a process analysis. A fifth promising direction is the examination of how self-conceptions, desired or possible as well as actual, impact on and are affected by the process (e.g., see Wicklund & Gollwitzer 1982, Schlenker 1985b).

CONCLUSION

In this chapter we have reviewed the recent research in social psychology that emphasizes the dynamic nature of the self-concept.

The research summarized here has focused primarily on how the self-concept may guide and control behavior. The reciprocal relation is assumed, but it is much less often addressed. How is the self-concept adjusted and calibrated as a consequence of one's actions? What happens to the self-concept of the individual who keeps changing what is personally relevant to maintain self-esteem? And finally, what is the relationship between momentary variations in which self-conceptions are active and more long-term, enduring changes in the self-concept? It should be possible to develop a model of the self-concept that reveals its relatively continuous and stable nature but at the same time reflects the fact that the self-concept is dynamic and capable of change, as it reflects and mediates the actions of individuals who are negotiating a variety of social circumstances.

Knowing Others

They Saw a Game: A Case Study

Albert H. Hastorf and Hadley Cantril (1954)

The final set of readings in this section examines the process by which we make sense of the behavior of others. Hastorf and Cantril address more than just the social events in a football game; this study examines not only how others are perceived, but also how that perception may be faulty, biased, and not entirely reliable. At stake in this study is our understanding of reality. Hastorf and Cantril suggest that our experiences of the same thing are not shared, and that, in fact, "the 'thing' simply is *not* the same for different people" (p. 133). The world we see may at times be more a reflection of what lies behind our eyes rather than what lies in front of them. Almost 30 years later, Loy and Andrews (1981) successfully replicated this study using the very same film with Dartmouth and Princeton students and alumni.

Although the transactionist viewpoint advocated by Hastorf and Cantril has not been integrated into mainstream social psychology, the point is extremely important, especially in regard to our evaluation of scientific "facts." Our perceptions of others and our perception of data are influenced by what we already believe that we know about the individuals or about scientific theories. How much does loyalty to people, colleges, causes, and nations influence our perceptions of events that indicate possible wrongdoings or shortcomings? To what degree are our perceptions influenced by what we already "know" to be true? Bem and Bem (1970) coined the phrase "nonconscious ideologies" to describe beliefs that are so basic to our world views that we may not even be aware that we have them. We are not often aware of how much our allegiances or world views (Unger, Draper, & Pendergrass, 1986) influence our social knowledge.

When obviously compelling evidence is disregarded, it makes one wonder what is needed to evoke a change in a belief. Are humans always so set in their convictions that there are no data or circumstances sufficient to disconfirm these beliefs? We hope that you, as budding social psychologists, will consider what it takes to establish an "objective" stance, and, in fact, whether such a stance is possible.

On a brisk Saturday afternoon, November 23, 1951, the Dartmouth football team played Princeton in Princeton's Palmer Stadium. It was the last game of the season for both teams and of rather special significance because the Princeton team had won all its games so far and one of its players, Kazmaier, was receiving All-American mention and had just appeared as the cover man on *Time* magazine, and was playing his last game.

A few minutes after the opening kick-off, it became apparent that the game was going to be a rough one. The referees were kept busy blowing their whistles and penalizing both sides. In the second quarter, Princeton's star left the game with a broken nose. In the third quarter, a Dartmouth player was taken off the field with a broken leg. Tempers flared both during and after the game. The official statistics of the game, which Princeton won, showed that Dartmouth was penalized 70 yards, Princeton 25, not counting more than a few plays in which both sides were penalized.

Needless to say, accusations soon began to fly. The game immediately became a matter of concern to players, students, coaches, and the administrative officials of the two institutions, as well as to alumni and the general public who had not seen the game but had become sensitive to the problem of big-time football through the recent exposures of subsidized players, commercialism, etc. Discussion of the game continued for several weeks.

One of the contributing factors to the extended discussion of the game was the extensive space given to it by both campus and metropolitan newspapers. An indication of the fervor with which the discussions were carried on is shown by a few excerpts from the campus dailies.

For example, on November 27 (four days after the game), the *Daily Princetonian* (Princeton's student newspaper) said:

> This observer has never seen quite such a disgusting exhibition of so-called "sport." Both teams were guilty but the blame must be laid primarily on Dartmouth's doorstep. Princeton, obviously the better team, had no reason to rough up Dartmouth. Looking at the situation rationally, we don't see why the Indians should make a deliberate attempt to cripple Dick Kazmaier or any other Princeton player. The Dartmouth psychology, however, is not rational itself.

The November 30th edition of the *Princeton Alumni Weekly* said:

> But certain memories of what occurred will not be easily erased. Into the record books will go in indelible fashion the fact that the last game of Dick Kazmaier's career was cut short by more than half when he was forced out with a broken nose and a mild concussion, sustained from a tackle that came well after he had thrown a pass.
>
> This second-period development was followed by a third quarter outbreak of roughness that was climaxed when a Dartmouth player deliberately kicked Brad Glass in the ribs while the latter was on his back. Throughout the often unpleasant afternoon, there was undeniable evidence that the losers' tactics were the result of an actual style of play, and reports on other games they have played this season substantiate this.

Dartmouth students were "seeing" an entirely different version of the game through the editorial eyes of the *Dartmouth* (Dartmouth's undergraduate newspaper). For example, on November 27 the *Dartmouth* said:

> However, the Dartmouth-Princeton game set the stage for the other type of dirty football. A type which may be termed as an unjustifiable accusation.
>
> Dick Kazmaier was injured early in the game. Kazmaier was the star, an All-American. Other stars have been injured before, but Kazmaier had been built to represent a Princeton idol. When an idol is hurt there is only one recourse—the tag of dirty football. So what did the Tiger Coach Charley Caldwell do? He announced to the world that the Big Green had been out to extinguish the Princeton star. His purpose was achieved.
>
> After this incident, Caldwell instilled the old see-what-they-did-go-get-them attitude into his players. His talk got results. Gene Howard and Jim Miller were both injured. Both had dropped back to pass, had passed, and were standing unprotected in the backfield. Result: one bad leg and one leg broken.
>
> The game was rough and did get a bit out of hand in the third quarter. Yet most of the roughing penalties were called against Princeton while Dartmouth received more of the illegal-use-of-the-hands variety.

On November 28 the *Dartmouth* said:

> Dick Kazmaier of Princeton admittedly is an unusually able football player. Many Dartmouth men traveled to Princeton, not expecting to win—only hoping to see an All-American in action. Dick Kazmaier was hurt in the second period, and played only a token part in the remainder of the game. For this, spectators were sorry.
>
> But there were no such feelings for Dick Kazmaier's health. Medical authorities have confirmed that as a relatively unprotected passing and running star in a contact sport, he is quite liable to injury. Also, his particular injuries—a broken nose and slight concussion—were no more serious than is experienced almost any day in any football practice, where there is no more serious stake than playing the following Saturday. Up to the Princeton game, Dartmouth players suffered about 10 known nose fractures and face injuries, not to mention several slight concussions.
>
> Did Princeton players feel so badly about losing their star? They shouldn't have. During the past undefeated campaign they stopped several individual stars by a concentrated effort, including such mainstays as Frank Hauff of Navy, Glenn Adams of Pennsylvania and Rocco Calvo of Cornell.

In other words, the same brand of football con-demned by the *Prince*—that of stopping the big man—is practiced quite successfully by the Tigers.

Basically, then, there was disagreement as to what had happened during the "game." Hence we took the opportunity presented by the occasion to make a "real life" study of a perceptual problem.[1]

PROCEDURE

Two steps were involved in gathering data. The first consisted of answers to a questionnaire designed to get reactions to the game and to learn something of the climate of opinion in each institution. This questionnaire was admin-istered a week after the game to both Dart-mouth and Princeton undergraduates who were taking introductory and intermediate psychol-ogy courses.

The second step consisted of showing the same motion picture of the game to a sample of undergraduates in each school and having them check on another questionnaire, as they watched the film, any infraction of the rules they saw and whether these infractions were "mild" or "flagrant."[2] At Dartmouth, mem-bers of two fraternities were asked to view the film on December 7; at Princeton, members of two undergraduate clubs saw the film early in January.

The answers to both questionnaires were care-fully coded and transferred to punch cards.

---

[1]We are not concerned here with the problem of guilt or responsibility for infractions, and nothing here implies any judgment as to who was to blame.

[2]The film shown was kindly loaned for the purpose of the experiment by the Dartmouth College Athletic Council. It should be pointed out that a movie of a football game follows the ball, is thus selective, and omits a good deal of the total action on the field. Also, of course, in viewing only a film of a game, the possibilities of participation as spectator are greatly limited.

RESULTS

Table 1 shows the questions which received dif-ferent replies from the two student populations on the first questionnaire.

Questions asking if the students had friends on the team, if they had ever played football themselves, if they felt they knew the rules of the game well, etc. showed no differences in ei-ther school and no relation to answers given to other questions. This is not surprising since the students in both schools come from essentially the same type of educational, economic, and eth-nic background.

Summarizing the data of Tables 1 and 2, we find a marked contrast between the two student groups.

Nearly all *Princeton* students judged the game as "rough and dirty"—not one of them thought it "clean and fair." And almost nine-tenths of them thought the other side started the rough play. By and large they felt that the charges they understood were being made were true; most of them felt the charges were made in order to avoid similar situations in the future.

When Princeton students looked at the movie of the game, they saw the Dartmouth team make over twice as many infractions as their own team made. And they saw the Dartmouth team make over twice as many infractions as were seen by Dartmouth students. When Princeton students judged these infractions as "flagrant" or "mild," the ratio was about two "flagrant" to one "mild" on the Dartmouth team, and about one "fla-grant" to three "mild" on the Princeton team.

As for the *Dartmouth* students, while the plu-rality of answers fell in the "rough and dirty" category, over one-tenth thought the game was "clean and fair" and over a third introduced their own category of "rough and fair" to describe the action. Although a third of the Dartmouth students felt that Dartmouth was to blame for starting the rough play, the majority of Dart-mouth students thought both sides were to blame. By and large, Dartmouth men felt that

TABLE 1

DATA FROM FIRST QUESTIONNAIRE

Question	Dartmouth students (N = 163) %	Princeton students (N = 161) %
1. Did you happen to see the actual game between Dartmouth and Princeton in Palmer Stadium this year?		
Yes	33	71
No	67	29
2. Have you seen a movie of the game or seen it on television?		
Yes, movie	33	2
Yes, television	0	1
No, neither	67	97
3. (Asked of those who answered "yes" to either or both of above questions.) From your observations of what went on at the game, do you believe the game was clean and fairly played, or that it was unnecessarily rough and dirty?		
Clean and fair	6	0
Rough and dirty	24	69
Rough and fair*	25	2
No answer	45	29
4. (Asked of those who answered "no" on both of the first questions.) From what you have heard and read about the game, do you feel it was clean and fairly played, or that it was unnecessarily rough and dirty?		
Clean and fair	7	0
Rough and dirty	18	24
Rough and fair*	14	1
Don't know	6	4
No answer	55	71
(Combined answers to questions 3 and 4 above)		
Clean and fair	13	0
Rough and dirty	42	93
Rough and fair*	39	3
Don't know	6	4
5. From what you saw in the game or the movies, or from what you have read, which team do you feel started the rough play?		
Dartmouth started it	36	86
Princeton started it	2	0
Both started it	53	11
Neither	6	1
No answer	3	2
6. What is your understanding of the charges being made?**		
Dartmouth tried to get Kazmaier	71	47
Dartmouth intentionally dirty	52	44
Dartmouth unnecessarily rough	8	35
7. Do you feel there is any truth to these charges?		
Yes	10	55
No	57	4
Partly	29	35
Don't know	4	6
8. Why do you think the charges were made?		
Injury to Princeton star	70	23
To prevent repetition	2	46
No answer	28	31

*This answer was not included on the checklist but was written in by the percentage of students indicated.
**Replies do not add to 100% since more than one charge could be given.

		Total number of infractions checked against			
		Dartmouth team		Princeton team	
Group	N	Mean	SD	Mean	SD
Dartmouth students	48	4.3*	2.7	4.4	2.8
Princeton students	49	9.8*	5.7	4.2	3.5

TABLE 2

DATA FROM SECOND QUESTIONNAIRE CHECKED WHILE SEEING FILM

*Significant at the .01 level.

the charges they understood were being made were not true, and most of them thought the reason for the charges was Princeton's concern for its football star.

When Dartmouth students looked at the movie of the game they saw both teams make about the same number of infractions. And they saw their own team make only half the number of infractions the Princeton students saw them make. The ratio of "flagrant" to "mild" infractions was about one to one when Dartmouth students judged the Dartmouth team, and about one "flagrant" to two "mild" when Dartmouth students judged infractions made by the Princeton team.

It should be noted that Dartmouth and Princeton students were thinking of different charges in judging their validity and in assigning reasons as to why the charges were made. It should also be noted that whether or not students were spectators of the game in the stadium made little difference in their responses.

INTERPRETATION: THE NATURE OF A SOCIAL EVENT

It seems clear that the "game" actually was many different games and that each version of the events that transpired was just as "real" to a particular person as other versions were to other people. A consideration of the experien-

tial phenomena that constitute a "football game" for the spectator may help us both to account for the results obtained and illustrate something of the nature of any social event.

Like any other complex social occurrence, a "football game" consists of a whole host of happenings. Many different events are occurring simultaneously. Furthermore, each happening is a link in a chain of happenings, so that one follows another in sequence. The "football game," as well as other complex social situations, consists of a whole matrix of events. In the game situation, this matrix of events consists of the actions of all the players, together with the behavior of the referees and linesmen, the action on the sidelines, in the grandstands, over the loud-speaker, etc.

Of crucial importance is the fact that an "occurrence" on the football field or in any other social situation does not become an experiential "event" unless and until some significance is given to it: an "occurrence" becomes an "*event*" only when the happening has significance. And a happening generally has significance only if it reactivates learned significances already registered in what we have called a person's assumptive form-world.

Hence the particular occurrences that different people experienced in the football game were a limited series of events from the total matrix of events *potentially* available to them. People experienced those occurrences that reactivated significances they brought to the occasion; they failed to experience those occurrences which did not reactivate past significances. We do not need to introduce "attention" as an "intervening third" (to paraphrase James on memory) to account for the selectivity of the experiential process.

In this particular study, one of the most interesting examples of this phenomenon was a telegram sent to an officer of Dartmouth College by a member of a Dartmouth alumni group in the Midwest. He had viewed the film which had been shipped to his alumni group from Princeton after its use with Princeton students, who saw, as we noted, an average of over nine infractions by Dartmouth players during the game. The alumnus, who couldn't see the infractions he had heard publicized, wired:

> Preview of Princeton movies indicates considerable cutting of important part please wire explanation and possibly air mail missing part before showing scheduled for January 25 we have splicing equipment.

The "same" sensory impingements emanating from the football field, transmitted through the visual mechanism to the brain, also obviously gave rise to different experiences in different people. The significances assumed by different happenings for different people depend in large part on the purposes people bring to the occasion and the assumptions they have of the purposes and probable behavior of other people involved. This was amusingly pointed out by the New York *Herald Tribune's* sports columnist, Red Smith, in describing a prize fight between Chico Vejar and Carmine Fiore in his column of December 21, 1951. Among other things, he wrote:

> You see, Steve Ellis is the proprietor of Chico Vejar, who is a highly desirable tract of Stamford, Conn., welterweight. Steve is also a radio announcer. Ordinarily there is no conflict between Ellis the Brain and Ellis the Voice because Steve is an uncommonly substantial lump of meat who can support both halves of a split personality and give away weight on each end without missing it.
>
> This time, though, the two Ellises met head-on, with a sickening, rending crash. Steve the Manager sat at ringside in the guise of Steve the Announcer broadcasting a dispassionate, unbiased, objective report of Chico's adventures in the ring....
>
> Clear as mountain water, his words came through, winning big for Chico. Winning? Hell, Steve was slaughtering poor Fiore.
>
> Watching and listening, you could see what a valiant effort the reporter was making to remain cool and detached. At the same time you had an illustration of the old, established truth that when anybody with a preference watches a fight, he sees only what he prefers to see.
>
> That is always so. That is why, after any fight that doesn't end in a clean knockout, there always are at least a few hoots when the decision is announced. A guy from, say, Billy Graham's neighborhood goes to see Billy fight and he watches Graham all the time. He sees all the punches Billy throws, and hardly any of the punches Billy catches. So it was with Steve.
>
> "Fiore feints with a left," he would say, honestly believing that Fiore hadn't caught Chico full on the chops. "Fiore's knees buckle," he said, "and Chico backs away." Steve didn't see the hook that had driven Chico back....

In brief, the data here indicate that there is no such "thing" as a "game" existing "out there" in its own right which people merely "observe." The "game" "exists" for a person and is experienced by him only in so far as certain happenings have significances in terms of his purpose. Out of all the occurrences going on in the environment, a person selects those that have some significance for him from his own egocentric position in the total matrix.

Obviously in the case of a football game, the value of the experience of watching the game is enhanced if the purpose of "your" team is accomplished, that is, if the happening of the desired consequence is experienced—i.e., if your team wins. But the value attribute of the experience can, of course, be spoiled if the desire to win crowds out behavior we value and have come to call sportsmanlike.

The sharing of significances provides the links except for which a "social" event would not be experienced and would not exist for anyone.

A "football game" would be impossible except for the rules of the game which we bring to the situation and which enable us to share with others the significances of various happenings. These rules make possible a certain repeatability of events such as first downs, touchdowns, etc. If a person is unfamiliar with the rules of the game, the behavior he sees lacks repeatability and consistent significance and hence "doesn't make sense."

And only because there is the possibility of repetition is there the possibility that a happening has a significance. For example, the balls used in games are designed to give a high degree of repeatability. While a football is about the only ball used in games which is not a sphere, the shape of the modern football has apparently evolved in order to achieve a higher degree of accuracy and speed in forward passing than would be obtained with a spherical ball, thus increasing the repeatability of an important phase of the game.

The rules of a football game, like laws, rituals, customs, and mores, are registered and preserved forms of sequential significances enabling people to share the significances of occurrences. The sharing of sequential significances which have value for us provides the links that operationally make social events possible. They are analogous to the forces of attraction that hold parts of an atom together, keeping each part from following its individual, independent course.

From this point of view it is inaccurate and misleading to say that different people have different "attitudes" concerning the same "thing." For the "thing" simply is *not* the same for different people whether the "thing" is a football game, a presidential candidate, Communism, or spinach. We do not simply "react to" a happening or to some impingement from the environment in a determined way (except in behavior that has become reflexive or habitual). We behave according to what we bring to the occasion, and what each of us brings to the occasion is more or less unique. And except for these significances which we bring to the occasion, the happenings around us would be meaningless occurrences, would be "inconsequential."

From the transactional view, an attitude is not a predisposition to react in a certain way to an occurrence or stimulus "out there" that exists in its own right with certain fixed characteristics which we "color" according to our predisposition (2). That is, a subject does not simply "react to" an "object." An attitude would rather seem to be a complex of registered significances reactivated by some stimulus which assumes its own particular significance for us in terms of our purposes. That is, the object as experienced would not exist for us except for the reactivated aspects of the form-world which provide particular significance to the hieroglyphics of sensory impingements.

READING 11

The "False Consensus Effect": An Egocentric Bias in Social Perception and Attribution Processes

Lee Ross, David Greene, and Pamela House (1977)

Attribution theory was first developed by Fritz Heider (1944, 1958), who recognized that we are all intuitive social psychologists, with our own implicit theories of human behavior that help guide our behavior. Heider believed that a major goal for individuals is to organize and understand the social world around them. Basic to Heider's beliefs about human beings is that people are motivated to make their social experiences understandable, controllable, and predictable. To do so, we occasionally impose structure where none exists, and we ignore information that does not fit into our cognitive structures.

Heider began a sophisticated description of the kinds of attributions the "common-sense psychologist" makes, including internal (personal) versus external (situational) explanations for causes. Both of these factors can be broken down into more specific constituent parts. Since the publication of Heider's *The Psychology of*

Interpersonal Relations in 1958, attribution theory and research have greatly expanded upon these ideas. Early work began with more detailed descriptions of the attribution process itself (e.g., Jones and Davis's theory of correspondent inferences, 1965; Kelley's model of causal attribution, 1967; and McArthur's analysis of that model, 1972). Research identifying different attribution biases then followed (e.g., "behavior engulfing the field," Jones & Harris, 1967; "fundamental attribution error," Ross, 1977; "illusory correlation," Chapman & Chapman, 1969; "self-serving bias," Miller & Ross, 1975; and "false consensus bias," Ross, Greene, and House, 1977.) The following article by Ross, Greene, and House on false consensus bias spawned a mini-literature devoted solely to investigations of this bias. A meta-analysis of 115 false consensus studies conducted only eight years after the original Ross et al. report suggests that the phenomenon is broadly based and persistent although, as expected, the strength of the effect varies somewhat across different behavioral domains (Mullen, Atkins, Champion, Edwards, Hardy, Story, & Vanderklok, 1985).

Abstract

Evidence from four studies demonstrates that social observers tend to perceive a "false consensus" with respect to the relative commonness of their own responses. A related bias was shown to exist in the observers' social inferences. Thus, raters estimated particular responses to be relatively common and relatively unrevealing concerning the actors' distinguishing personal dispositions when the responses in question were similar to the raters' own responses; responses differing from those of the rater, by contrast, were perceived to be relatively uncommon and revealing of the actor. These results were obtained both in questionnaire studies presenting subjects with hypothetical situations and choices and in authentic conflict situations. The implications of these findings for our understanding of social perception phenomena and for our analysis of the divergent perceptions of actors and observers are discussed. Finally, cognitive and perceptual mechanisms are proposed which might account for distortions in perceived consensus and for corresponding biases in social inference and attributional processes.

In a sense, every social observer is an intuitive psychologist who is forced by everyday experience to judge the causes and implications of behavior.

Many researchers and theorists have expressed a general interest in naive epistemology and implicit psychological theories. However, it has been the attribution theorists (Heider, 1958; Jones & Davis, 1965; Jones, Kanouse, Kelley, Nisbett, Valins, & Weiner, 1972; Kelley, 1967, 1973) who have pursued this topic most vigorously and most systematically. The primary focus of formal attribution theory (following Kelley, 1967, 1973) has been the logical rules or "schemata" that the layman employs in making causal inferences and extracting social meaning from particular configurations of data. In the typical attribution study it has thus been the *experimenter* who has supplied the relevant data and, in so doing, has manipulated the degree of apparent response consistency, distinctiveness, and consensus presented to the social observer. This research strategy (e.g., McArthur, 1972) has obvious and undeniable advantages if the experimenter's primary concern is the attributor's rules for data analysis and data interpretation. But such a strategy also has serious costs, for it necessarily demands that one overlook those potentially crucial phases in the attribution process, preceding data analysis, during which the data must first be acquired, coded, and recalled from memory.

The professional psychologist relies upon well-defined sampling techniques and statistical procedures for estimating the commonness of particular responses. Where such estimates are relevant to subsequent interpretations and inferences, he can proceed with confidence in his data. Intuitive psychologists, by contrast, are rarely blessed either with adequate "baseline" data or with the means of acquiring such data. To the extent that their systems for interpreting social responses depend upon estimates of commonness or oddity they must, accordingly, rely largely upon subjective impressions and intuitions.

The source of attributional bias that we shall consider in the present paper directly involves the probability estimates made by intuitive psychologists. Specifically, we shall report research demonstrating that laymen tend to perceive a "false consensus"—to see their own behavioral choices and judgments as relatively common and appropriate to existing circumstances while viewing alternative responses as uncommon, deviant, or inappropriate. Evidence shall also be reported for an obvious corollary to the false consensus proposition: The intuitive psychologist judges those responses that differ from his own to be more revealing of the actor's stable dispositions than those responses which are similar to his own. Thus, we contend that the person who feeds squirrels, votes Republican, or drinks Drambuie for breakfast will see such behaviors or choices by an actor as relatively common and relatively devoid of information about his personal characteristics. By contrast, another person who ignores hungry squirrels, votes Democrat, or abstains at breakfast will see the former actor's responses as relatively odd and rich with implications about the actor's personality.

The term *relative* is critical in this formulation of the false consensus bias and it requires some clarification. Obviously, the man who would walk a tightrope between two skyscrapers, launch a revolution, or choose a life of clerical celibacy recognizes that his choices would be shared by few of his peers and are revealing of personal dispositions. It is contended, however, that he would see his personal choices as less deviant and revealing than would those of us who do not walk tightropes, launch revolutions, or become celibate clerics. Furthermore, the present thesis does not deny that "pluralistic ignorance" could lead to erroneous esti-

mates by minority and majority alike. The incidence of infant abuse, for instance, might be underestimated by abusing and nonabusing parents alike. The relative terms of the false consensus thesis demand only that abusing parents estimate child abuse to be more common and less indicative of personal dispositions than do nonabusing parents.

References to "egocentric attribution" (Heider, 1958; Jones & Nisbett, 1972) to "attributive projection" (Holmes, 1968; Murstein & Pryer, 1959) and to a host of related projection phenomena (e.g., Cameron & Magaret, 1951; Cattell, 1944; Murray, 1933) have appeared sporadically in the literature. Perhaps most directly relevant to present concerns are empirical demonstrations of correlations between subjects' own behavior and their estimates about their peers. For instance, Katz and Allport (1931) demonstrated that the admitted frequency of cheating by a student was positively related to his estimate of the number of other students who have cheated. Holmes (1968) summarized several other related demonstrations dealing with political beliefs and judgments of personal attributes and, more recently, Kelley and Stahelski (1970) have stressed the role of egocentric perceptions in the prisoner's dilemma situation.

In the present paper we shall demonstrate the generality of the false consensus or egocentric attribution bias. More importantly, we shall explore its implications for our understanding of social perception phenomena and the often divergent perceptions of actors and observers. Finally, we shall discuss more basic shortcomings of the intuitive psychologist which may underlie such phenomena.

STUDY 1

Method

Study 1 presented subjects with questionnaires containing one of four brief stories composed specifically for our purposes. A total of 320 Stanford undergraduates (80 for each of the four stories) participated. Each story asked the readers to place themselves in a particular setting in which a series of events culminated in a clear behavioral choice. The subjects were not immediately required to state their own choice but were asked to estimate the percentage of their peers who would choose each of the two possible courses of action suggested. The four stories and the consensus questions are reproduced below:

Supermarket Story

As you are leaving your neighborhood supermarket a man in a business suit asks you whether you like shopping in that store. You reply quite honestly that you do like shopping there and indicate that in addition to being close to your home the supermarket seems to have very good meats and produce at reasonably low prices. The man then reveals that a videotape crew has filmed your comments and asks you to sign a release allowing them to use the unedited film for a TV commercial that the supermarket chain is preparing.

What % of your peers do you estimate would sign the release? ____ %
What % would refuse to sign it? ____ % (Total % should be 100%)

Term Paper Story

You arrive for the first day of class in a course in your major area of study. The professor says that the grade in your course will depend on a paper due the final day of the course. He gives the class the option of two alternatives upon which they must vote. They can either do papers individually in the normal way or they can work in teams of three persons who will submit a single paper between them. You are informed that he will still give out the same number of A's, B's, and C's, etc., but that in the first case every student will be graded in-

dividually while in the second case all three students who work together get the same grade.

What % of your peers do you estimate would vote for group papers? ____ %
What % would vote for individual papers? ____ % (Total % should be 100%)

Traffic Ticket Story

While driving through a rural area near your home you are stopped by a county police officer who informs you that you have been clocked (with radar) at 38 miles per hour in a 25-mph zone. You believe this information to be accurate. After the policeman leaves, you inspect your citation and find that the details on the summons regarding weather, visibility, time, and location of violation are highly inaccurate. The citation informs you that you may either pay a $20 fine by mail without appearing in court or you must appear in municipal court within the next two weeks to contest the charge.

What % of your peers do you estimate would pay the $20 fine by mail? ____ %
What % would go to court to contest the charge? ____ % (Total should be 100%)

Space Program Referendum Story

It is proposed in Congress that the space program be revived and that large sums be allocated for the manned and unmanned exploration of the moon and planets nearest Earth. Supporters of the proposal argue that it will provide jobs, spur technology, and promote national pride and unity. Opponents argue that a space program will either necessitate higher taxes, or else drain money from important domestic priorities. Furthermore, they deny that it will accomplish the desirable effects claimed by the program's supporters. Both sides, of course, refute each other's claims and ultimately a public referendum is held.

What % of your peers do you estimate would vote for the proposed allocation of funds for space exploration? ____ %

What % would vote against it? ____ % (Total should be 100%)

After completing the relevant percentage estimates, subjects were required to fill out a three-page questionnaire. On one page, they were first asked to indicate which of the two behavioral options they personally would choose and then asked to rate themselves on a series of Likert-type personality scales. This self description page of the questionnaire was either followed or preceded by two pages on which the reader was required to rate the personal traits of the "typical person" of the reader's own age and sex who would choose each of the two specific options presented in the story. For example, subjects who read the Supermarket Story were required on one page to rate the traits of "the typical person...who *would* sign the commercial release" and, on another page, to rate "the typical person...who *would not* sign the commercial release." The order of these three rating sheets was systematically varied.[1]

The nature of the rating scales merits some emphasis. For each story, the actors were rated with respect to a different set of four personal characteristics that might influence or be reflected by the behavioral choice described in the story. (In the Supermarket Story, for example, the traits considered were *shyness, cooperativeness, trust,* and *adventurousness*.) For each trait a 100-point rating scale was used. The midpoint and two extremes of this scale were labeled to specify both the *extremity* of the dispositional inference made and the rater's *confidence* concerning the relevant actors' dispositions. Thus,

for the disposition of "cooperativeness," the scale was anchored as follows:

+ 50 *Certainly more* cooperative than the average person of my age and sex, *probably very much more* cooperative.

   0 Probably average with respect to cooperativeness. I have no reason to assume that the actor differs from the average person of my age and sex with respect to this characteristic.

− 50 *Certainly less* cooperative than the average person of my age and sex, *probably very much less* cooperative.

Summary of Hypotheses The consensus estimates and trait ratings for each story provided a test of two principal hypotheses:

1. Subjects who "choose" a particular hypothetical response will rate that response as more probable for "people in general" than will subjects who "choose" the alternative response.
2. Subjects who "choose" a specified response will use less extreme and less confident trait ratings in characterizing a "typical" person making that response than will subjects who "choose" the alternative response.

Results

Perceptions of Consensus The data presented in Table 1 offer strong support for the first of the experimental hypotheses. For each of the stories, those subjects who claimed that they personally would follow a given behavioral alternative also tended to rate that alternative as relatively probable for "people in general"; those subjects who claimed that they would reject the alternative tended to rate it as relatively improbable for "people in general."

The effect of subjects' own behavior choice upon their estimates of commonness was statistically significant for each story individually. When Story was treated as a "fixed" variable in

---

[1]In the interests of brevity and clarity, neither self-ratings nor the "order of presentation" variable receives detailed consideration in this report. It should be noted only that self-ratings were irrelevant to our present hypotheses and, similarly, that the order variable produced no significant main effects or interaction effects of immediate theoretical relevance.

TABLE   1

PERCEIVED CONSENSUS: ESTIMATED COMMONNESS OF OWN AND ALTERNATIVE
BEHAVIORAL CHOICES (STUDY 1)

Story	Rater's own choice in hypothetically described situation	n(%)	Estimates of consensus: Estimated percentage of raters who would choose		F
			Option 1	Option 2	
Supermarket story	Sign release	53(66%)	75.6	24.4	17.7
	Not sign release	27(34%)	57.3	42.7	
Term paper story	Choose individual paper	64(80%)	67.4	32.6	16.5
	Choose group paper	16(20%)	45.9	54.1	
Traffic ticket story	Pay speeding fine	37(46%)	71.8	28.2	12.8
	Contest charge	43(54%)	51.7	48.3	
Space program story	Vote for cutback	32(40%)	47.9	52.1	4.9
	Vote against cutback	48(60%)	39.0	61.0	
Summary of four stories[a]	Choose option 1	186(58%)	65.7	34.3	49.1
	Choose option 2	134(42%)	48.5	51.5	

[a]Unweighted average of means for four stories.

an analysis of variance combining the data for all four stories, the main effect of Rater's Choice was highly significant, $F(1,312) = 49.1$, $p < .001$, while the Story × Rater's Choice interaction was trivial, $F(1,312) = 1.37$, $p > .10$. It is clear that the Rater's reported behavioral choices were associated with, and presumably exerted a large and consistent effect upon, their perceptions of behavioral consensus.

Trait Ratings   To test the second experimental hypothesis, individual trait ratings were measured as absolute discrepancies from the midpoint of the 100-point Likert-type scale. Ratings for the four traits for each story were then combined to provide an overall measure of the rater's inferences about the "typical" actor who might choose each of the behavioral alternatives specified. The results are summarized in Table 2.

The pattern of trait ratings for each story is in accord with the research hypothesis. That is, relatively strong inferences about the typical person

who might choose a given response are made by those raters who personally would choose the *alternative* response. The difference scores in Table 2 are the critical indices; in each case this difference score is more positive (or less negative) for the rater who would choose the second alternative over the first. For two of the stories (Supermarket Story and Term Paper Story), the effect of Rater's Own Choice upon the difference in ratings for the two behavioral alternatives was clearly significant, $F(1,78) = 17.27$, $p < .001$ and $F = 21.83$, $p < .001$, respectively. For one story (Traffic Ticket Story) the effect was marginally significant, $F = 3.18$, $p < .10$, and for one story (Space Program Story) the effect was relatively trivial.

The four stories again may be considered within a single analysis of variance. When Story is treated as a fixed variable, the main effect of the subject's own behavioral choice upon the difference in trait ratings is highly significant, $F(1,312) = 37.40$, $p < .001$. The Story × Subject's Choice Interaction, however, is also sig-

TABLE 2

TRAIT RATINGS: RATERS' INFERENCES ABOUT PERSONAL DISPOSITIONS OF "TYPICAL ACTORS" BEHAVING LIKE OR UNLIKE THE RATER (STUDY 1)

Story	Traits	Rater's own choice	Trait ratings:[a] Rater's assessment of person who would choose		Difference	F
			Option 1	Option 2		
Supermarket story	Shyness Cooperativeness	Sign release (n = 53)	60.4	89.5	−29.1	17.27
	Trust Adventurousness	Not sign release (n = 27)	90.0	65.3	+24.7	
Term paper story	Gregariousness Laziness	Choose individual grade (n = 64)	66.4	66.6	−0.2	21.83
	Competitiveness Generosity	Choose group grades (n = 16)	100.9	46.8	+54.1	
Traffic ticket story	Self-confidence Legal knowledge	Pay speeding fine (n = 37)	35.8	77.4	−41.6	3.18
	Argumentativeness Miserliness	Contest charge (n = 43)	59.4	79.2	−19.2	
Space program story	Rationality Social concern	Vote for cutback (n = 32)	56.8	67.9	−11.1	1.81
	Idealism Selfishness	Vote against cutback (n = 48)	68.9	68.9	0	
Summary of four stories[b]		Choose option 1	54.9	75.4	−20.5	37.40
		Choose option 2	79.8	65.1	+14.7	

[a]Larger numbers reflect stronger trait inferences and greater willingness to assert that the person would prove deviant or discrepant from average with respect to the four specified traits.
[b]Unweighted average of means for four stories.

nificant, $F(3,312) = 3.71$, $p < .05$. Thus, like perceptions of behavioral consensus, trait inferences are systematically influenced by the rater's own behavioral choices, although the effect is less consistent for the latter measure than the former.

An obvious question arises concerning the relationship between the two effects that have been demonstrated. However, consideration of this question, and other questions concerning alternative interpretations and underlying mechanisms, shall be postponed until the procedures and principal results for the remaining three studies have been reported.

STUDY 2

Rationale and Method

Study 2 attempted to extend the domain of the false consensus effect. Whereas Study 1 had demonstrated that subjects tend to overestimate the degree of consensus enjoyed by their own behavioral choices in a hypothetical conflict situation, Study 2 was designed to explore a more general tendency for subjects to overestimate the extent to which others share their habits, preferences, fears, daily activities, expectations, and other personal characteristics.

The procedure was simple. A total of 80 Stanford undergraduates completed a questionnaire dealing with 35 person description items (see Table 3). Each item presented a pair of mutually exclusive and exhaustive categories. Half of the subjects first categorized themselves with respect to the 35 variables and then proceeded to estimate the percentage of "college students in general" who fit into each category; the remainder answered these questions in reverse order. (The "order variable" produced no relevant main effects or interaction effects and, accordingly, receives no further consideration in this report.)

The hypothesis in Study 2 was simply that subjects who placed themselves in a given personal description category would estimate the percentage of "college students in general" in that category to be greater than would subjects who placed themselves in the alternative category.

Results

The personal description items (listed in the same order presented to subjects) and the relevant percentage estimates made by subjects are summarized in Table 3. One of the 35 items, a Political Expectation item concerning the impeachment of President Nixon, became unusable in the midst of the study. Each of the remaining 34 items separately tested the false consensus hypothesis (although the tests were not "independent" since the same group of subjects responded to all items). A quick inspection of the results presented in the table reveals considerable, although less than universal, support for the hypothesis. Overall, the difference in percentage estimates was in the predicted direction for 32 of the 34 items, and the magnitude of the two reversals was trivial. That is, subjects who placed themselves in a given descriptive category consistently estimated the percentage of "college students in general" in that category to be greater than did subjects who placed themselves in the alternative category. Of the items showing the predicted effect, 17 produced differences significant beyond the .10 level while 11 differences were significant beyond the .01 level.

Further examination of the data reveals that three of the seven categories provided fairly strong and consistent support for the false consensus hypothesis. Most dramatic were the items pertaining to Political Expectations: Subjects who expected women soon to be appointed to the Supreme Court, poverty to abate, nuclear weapons to be used, or extraterrestrial life to be discovered, perceived these views to be relatively widespread among their peers; subjects with the opposite expectations similarly thought that their own expectations were characteristic of "college students in general." Less dramatic but reasonably consistent support was also provided by these items dealing with Personal Traits and Views and those probing Personal Problems. For example, subjects who categorized themselves as shy, optimistic, or supporters of the Women's Liberation Movement and subjects who reported that they often thought about dying, had difficulty in controlling their temper, frequently experienced depression, or felt their emotional needs to be unsatisfied, were relatively inclined to think that their peers shared these traits and views or problems. Similarly, subjects who reported opposite traits and views or felt themselves to be free of the personal problems specified tended to perceive relatively high consensus for their particular characteristics.

Sporadic support for the false consensus hypothesis was provided by items dealing with three descriptive categories: Personal Preferences, Personal Characteristics, and Personal Expectations. The only items providing no significant differences supporting the hypothesis were those dealing with everyday Personal Activities (e.g., television watching, tennis playing, etc.).

In summary, it is evident that the false consensus effect applies to many types of personal behaviors, feelings, opinions, and characteristics, although there is some ambiguity about the specific domain and the limits of the phenome-

TABLE 3

RATERS' SELF-CATEGORIZATIONS AND THEIR CATEGORIZATIONS OF "COLLEGE STUDENTS IN GENERAL" (STUDY 2)

Questionnaire item: Category 1 (category 2)	Raters' estimates of percentage of college students in category 1		Direction of difference (+ predicted: − opposite to predicted)	t
	Mean estimates by raters placing themselves in category 1	Mean estimates by raters placing themselves in category 2		
Personal traits and views				
Shy (not shy)	45.9	35.9	+	2.66‡
Optimistic (not)	61.9	50.4	+	2.58†
Competitive (not)	75.1	69.9	+	1.35
Politically left of center (not)	59.7	58.0	+	< 1
Supporter of women's lib (not)	57.3	33.4	+	3.96§
Unweighted mean of five items	60.0	49.5		
Personal preferences				
Brown (white) bread	52.5	37.4	+	3.26‡
To be alone (with others)	36.0	30.7	+	1.18
Italian (French) movies	51.6	43.4	+	2.00†
City (country) life	51.4	49.8	+	< 1
Basketball (football)	36.7	37.7	−	< 1
Unweighted mean of five items	45.6	39.8		
Personal characteristics				
Male (female)	58.7	57.1	+	1.01
Brown (blue) eyes	58.3	54.5	+	1.63
Subscribe (don't) to magazines on list provided	56.9	42.7	+	2.76‡
First-born (laterborn) child	42.2	37.1	+	1.57
Hometown more (less) than 200,000	58.2	51.9	+	1.68*
Unweighted mean of five items	54.9	48.7		
Personal problems				
Think about dying? yes (no)	44.0	25.6	+	2.87‡
Hard to make friends? yes (no)	38.7	35.1	+	< 1
Difficulty controlling temper? yes (no)	42.1	27.9	+	3.26‡
Frequently depressed? yes (no)	55.1	39.2	+	3.25‡
Emotional needs satisfied? yes (no)	52.9	42.2	+	2.29†
Unweighted mean of five items	46.6	34.0		
Personal activities				
Watch TV 30 hours/month? yes (no)	49.2	40.9	+	< 1
Play tennis once a week? yes (no)	33.0	30.3	+	< 1
Attend religious service once a month? yes (no)	26.5	27.5	−	< 1
Donate blood once a year? yes (no)	22.6	21.2	+	< 1
Long distance phone call once a week? yes (no)	50.7	45.0	+	1.06
Unweighted mean of five items	36.4	33.0		
Personal expectations				
Marriage by age 30? yes (no)	74.5	71.9	+	< 1
Better financial status than parent? yes (no)	68.3	61.8	+	1.86*
Live outside U.S. for one year in next 20? yes (no)	37.4	36.9	+	< 1
Great satisfaction from job or career? yes (no)	53.5	43.3	+	< 1
Death before 70th birthday? yes (no)	57.6	43.9	+	2.81‡
Unweighted mean of five items	58.3	51.6		

TABLE 3

RATERS' SELF-CATEGORIZATIONS AND THEIR CATEGORIZATIONS OF
"COLLEGE STUDENTS IN GENERAL" (STUDY 2) (Continued)

Questionnaire item: Category 1 (category 2)	Raters' estimates of percentage of college students in category 1		Direction of difference (+ predicted: – opposite to predicted)	t
	Mean estimates by raters placing themselves in category 1	Mean estimates by raters placing themselves in category 2		
Political expectations				
Removal of Nixon from office? yes (no)	Deleted			
Woman in Supreme Court within decade? yes (no)	63.3	34.6	+	6.19§
Poverty problem reduced in next 20 years? yes (no)	61.8	43.1	+	3.81§
Nuclear weapon used in warfare in next 20 years? yes (no)	58.8	31.2	+	3.21‡
Discovery of extraterrestrial life by year 2000? yes (no)	56.6	29.3	+	5.48§
Unweighted mean of four items	60.1	34.6		

$^*p < .10.$
$†p < .05.$
$‡p < .01.$
$§p < .001.$

non. It is premature to attempt any post hoc generalizations in this regard, although such generalizations should be facilitated by an appreciation of possible experiential, perceptual, and cognitive mechanisms that may be responsible for the false consensus effect.

DISCUSSION*

Considered together, Studies 1, 3, and 4 offer strong support for the hypothesis that raters' perceptions of social consensus and their social inferences about actors reflect the raters' own behavioral choices. The relevant research hypotheses were confirmed both in questionnaire studies presenting situations, choices, and judgments that were hypothetical and in an actual conflict situation demanding personally relevant behavioral choices and social judgments about specific actors. Study 2, furthermore, extended the potential do-

main of the false consensus phenomenon to include perceptions of commonness or oddity regarding a wide variety of personal problems, expectations, preferences, and characteristics. The implications of these four studies for our conception of the "intuitive psychologist" should be clear. His intuitive estimates of deviance and normalcy, and the host of social inferences and interpersonal responses that accompany such estimates, are systematically and egocentrically biased in accord with his own behavioral choices. More generally, it is apparent that attributional analyses may be distorted not only by biases in the intuitive psychologist's eventual analysis of social data but also by biases in the earlier processes through which relevant data are estimated, sampled, or inferred.

False Consensus Mechanisms

Motivational Factors Investigators who have discussed false consensus phenomena or egocentric attributional biases have typically empha-

---

*Editors' note: Studies 3 and 4 have been omitted.

sized their motivational status or function for the individual. Such biases, it is contended, both foster and justify the actor's feelings that his own behavioral choices are appropriate and rational responses to the demands of the environment, rather than reflections of his distinguishing personal dispositions. More dynamic interpretations (e.g., Bramel, 1962, 1963; Edlow & Kiesler, 1966; Lemann & Solomon, 1952; Smith, 1960) have stressed the ego-defensive or dissonance-reducing function of attributive projection, particularly as a response to failure or negative information about one's personal characteristics.

It is worth noting that the desire to forestall trait inferences about oneself could lead to three distinct types of influence or distortion. First, one might distort one's private perception and/or one's public estimate of the degree of consensus for one's own responses. Second, when the response to be reported is merely hypothetical or otherwise unverifiable, one could distort one's response report; that is, report a response that is more common, and presumably more normative, than one's probable or real response. Finally, one could distort one's actual behavior in the relevant situation; that is, actually conform to the response of one's peers to the extent that it enjoys high consensus, even if one's personal preferences, perceptions, or proclivities dictate an alternative response.

The present research cannot speak to the first of these potential sources of distortion. With regard to the other alternatives, there is some relevant evidence at hand. It is apparent at least that the false consensus phenomenon was not restricted to circumstances where response reports were hypothetical or otherwise free from verification. Indeed, the false consensus hypotheses were as strongly confirmed for Study 4 in which the raters' own choices were real and consequential as they were for Study 3 in which the conflict situation described was merely hypothetical. It is possible, of course, that subjects' actual decisions in Study 4 about whether or not to wear the sandwich board were influenced by

their assumptions about the modal response of their peers. If so, it is worth emphasizing the costs of such conformity, for example, facing an uncomfortable stroll on campus wearing the sandwich board or, alternatively, confronting a disappointed experimenter, were far from inconsequential for the subject.

Selective Exposure and Availability Factors Several nonmotivational factors that create the impression that one's own judgments and responses enjoy a high degree of consensus can be grouped together under the heading of "selective exposure" effects. Obviously, we tend to know and associate with people who share our background, experiences, interests, values, and outlook. Such people *do*, in disproportionate numbers, respond as we would in a wide variety of circumstances. Indeed, our close association is determined, in part, by feelings of general consensus and we may be inclined to exclude those whom we believe do not share our judgments and responses. This exposure to a biased sample of people and behavior does not demand that we err in our estimates concerning the relevant populations, but it does make such errors likely. More subtle, and more cognitive in flavor, are the factors which increase our ability to recall, visualize, or imagine paradigmatic instances of behavior. In a given situation the specific behaviors that we have chosen, or would choose, are likely to be more readily retrievable from memory and more easily imagined than opposite behaviors. In Kahneman and Tversky's (1973) terms, the behavioral choices we favor may be more "available," and we are apt to be misled by this ease or difficulty of access in estimating the likelihood of relevant behavioral options.

Ambiguity Resolution Factors A second nonmotivational source of the false consensus effect arises from the intuitive psychologist's response to ambiguity in the nature and magnitude of situational forces and in the meaning and implications of various response alternatives. Attempts to resolve such ambiguity involve interpretation, estimation, and guesswork, all of which can exert a parallel effect on the attributer's own behavior choices and upon his predictions and inferences about the choices of others.

The biasing effect of ambiguity resolution perhaps is most obvious when the attributer's knowledge of a response or situation is second-hand and lacking in important specific details. Consider, for example, the subject who must decide on the precise meaning of such modifiers as *often* or *typically* or of any other potentially ambiguous descriptors encountered in the context of questionnaire items (for example, in Study 2). It is obvious that both the response category to which that subject assigns himself and his categorizations of his peers will be similarly influenced by these decisions about the precise meaning of terms.

Similarly, the subject who read about the impromptu television commercial dilemma in Study 1 was forced to imagine the interviewer, the physical setting, and a host of other situational details which might encourage or inhibit the relevant behavioral options. If these imagined details seemingly would encourage one to sign the release then the subject was more likely to assume that he personally would sign, that a similar decision would be a common response among his peers, and that signing the release would reflect little about the distinguishing dispositions of any particular actor. By contrast, if the details imagined by the subject would inhibit signing of the release, the subject was more apt to assume that he personally would refuse, that his peers typically would do likewise, and that signing of the release would reveal much about the personal dispositions of the relevant actor.

In questionnaire studies this resolution of ambiguities in descriptions of situations and behaviors may seem a troublesome artifact. However, the same factor becomes an important source of bias in everyday social judgments and inferences where attributers may often respond to accounts of situations or actions that are vague and frequently second-hand. The intuitive psychologist constantly is confronted with statements like "Sally hardly ever dates short men" or "John refused to pay the painter's bill when he saw the paint job." In such circumstances he is forced to resolve ambiguities or uncertainties in the statement, and such resolutions will exert parallel effects upon his assumptions about his own behavior, his impressions about consensus, and his inferences about the dispositions of those whose behavior has been loosely categorized or described.

The false consensus bias, in summary, both reflects and creates distortions in the attribution process. It results from nonrandom sampling and retrieval of evidence and from idiosyncratic interpretation of situational factors and forces. In turn, it biases judgments about deviance and deviates, helps lead actors and observers to divergent perceptions of behavior, and, more generally, promotes variance and error in the interpretation of social phenomena.

When Are Social Judgments Made? Evidence for the Spontaneousness of Trait Inferences

Laraine Winter and James S. Uleman (1984)

This reading concludes our section on social knowledge and how we come to know others. As social observers, we often think we can gather "the facts, and just the facts," and that we keep these "objective" observations of others separate from our forming of deliberate impressions and judgments of others. But are the facts and the judgments we draw from the facts this distinct in our information processing? Winter and Uleman show that we may form impressions of others without intending to, and without even realizing that we have jumped to a conclusion.

Winter and Uleman's research raises the general question of how much control we usually exercise over our own cognitive processes (and the behavior that follows from them), and, indeed, how much control we can have over these processes. Their results suggest that the trait attributions we make about others are spontaneous and nonconscious as opposed to deliberate and intentional. Finally, if people jump to conclusions of others, must they accept these conclusions uncritically and act on them?

Abstract

Do people make trait inferences, even without intentions or instructions, at the encoding stage of processing behavioral information? Tulving's encoding specificity paradigm (Tulving & Thomson, 1973) was adapted for two recall experiments. Under memory instructions only, subjects read sentences describing people performing actions that implied traits. Later, subjects recalled each sentence under one of three cuing conditions: (a) a dispositional cue (e.g., generous), (b) a strong, nondispositional semantic associate to an important sentence word, or (c) no cue. Recall was best when cued by the disposition words. Subjects were unaware of having made trait inferences. Interpreted in terms of encoding specificity, these results indicate that subjects unintentionally made trait inferences at encoding. This suggests that attributions may be made spontaneously, as part of the routine comprehension of social events.

Although research on social inferences has dominated social psychology for well over a decade, the lion's share of scientific attention has centered on inferences made in response to explicit instructions. But as several researchers have recently pointed out (Berscheid, Graziano, Monson, & Dermer, 1976; Pyszczynski & Greenberg, 1981; Wong & Weiner, 1981), there is little research on whether and when such inferences occur spontaneously. This issue of whether and when social inferences are initiated in the absence of investigators' instructions is important in its own right and has se-

rious import for research in social cognition. The spontaneousness of these inferences largely determines their frequency outside the laboratory and is therefore crucial to any claim regarding their psychological importance.

Early researchers in person perception and impression formation (e.g., Asch, 1946; Tagiuri, 1958) expressed complete confidence that the phenomena they studied were not only spontaneous but pervasive and central to everyday psychological functioning. For example, Asch wrote in 1946,

> We look at a person and immediately a certain impression of his character forms itself in us. A glance, a few spoken words are sufficient to tell us a story about a highly complex matter. We know that such impressions form with remarkable rapidity and great ease. Subsequent observations may enrich or upset our first view, but we can no more prevent its rapid growth than we can avoid perceiving a given visual object or hearing a melody (Asch, 1946, p. 258).

In a marked contrast, more recent person perception research has at least implicitly characterized social judgments as deliberate, even laborious mental operations, performed under particular and unusual conditions. These conditions include having a mental set induced by experimental instruction (e.g., Enzle & Schopflocher, 1978) or a need to feel in control (e.g., Berscheid et al., 1976). Underlying this research is the assumption that making attributions is always a discrete mental operation, easily separable from other stages in the information-processing sequence, and that it is an optional stage that is engaged only under special circumstances (e.g., Pryor & Kriss, 1977, with regard to causal attributions). Indeed, authors who discuss person perception in terms of an explicit processing sequence (e.g., Schneider, Hastorf, & Ellsworth, 1979, chap. 1) commonly identify trait attributions as a relatively late stage, dependent on the outcome of several earlier operations performed on the behavioral information.

A few recent researchers, working in the conceptual framework of information processing, have discussed the possibility that attributions are as spontaneous as early theorists like Asch posited. The notion that attributional phenomena are an integral part of the process of encoding information, rather than a separate mental operation occurring at retrieval, was raised by Smith and Miller (1979), who proposed that attributional processing is "intrinsically involved in the initial comprehension of sentences and therefore that it goes on all the time, not just when a subject is asked an attributional question" (1979, p. 2247). Similarly, Carlston (1980) considered the effects of spontaneous inference making on subsequent memories for behavior and impressions.

The present research was a direct test of the possibility that inferences about personality can be part and parcel of the encoding of behavioral information, carried out without instructions or other unusual motivating conditions (i.e., spontaneously). Although this does not imply that trait inferences must always be spontaneous, or that they must always occur at encoding, a demonstration that trait inferences may also occur spontaneously at encoding would strongly suggest that they are ordinarily an integral part of the process of observing behavior and not essentially discrete operations motivated by particular purposes and dependent on information retrieval. Our basic proposal is that people sometimes make spontaneous social inferences as part of their initial comprehension of social information. Even without explicit questions or goals, they do not simply store some representation of the information as it is presented. Instead, they make inferences and store both the information and their inferences in memory.

To test the notion that trait inferences ordinarily are made at encoding, we adapted the encoding specificity paradigm developed by Tulving and his associates (Thomson & Tulving, 1970; Tulving & Osler, 1968; Tulving & Pearlstone, 1966; Tulving & Thomson, 1973).

In encoding specificity experiments, target words like *chair* are paired with weak semantic associates, such as *glue*. Subjects study lists of such pairs with the expectation that their memory for the target words will be tested. They are then asked to recall the target words in the presence of either the input cue (*glue*), a strong semantic associate of the target (e.g., *table*), or no cue. Tulving's results (e.g., Thomson & Tulving, 1970) showed that recall was best when the input cue was present, whereas recall cued by the strong semantic associate was in fact no better than noncued recall.

If people make trait inferences when they observe behavior and encode the information, those inferred traits should be stored in memory along with the information on which they were based. Therefore, as part of the encoding context of the behavioral information, the attributed trait itself should serve as a self-generated covert input cue and thus as an effective retrieval cue for the behavioral information. It should be possible, then, to show that people make trait inferences at encoding by demonstrating the retrieval effectiveness for the behavioral information of subjects' most likely trait inference. For instance, if reading "The librarian carries the old woman's groceries across the street," subjects infer that the librarian is helpful, then the word *helpful* ought to be a good retrieval cue for the sentence.

Disposition cues were selected that were related to the sentences primarily by the subjects' inferences.

The retrieval effectiveness of the disposition cues was defined by comparison with noncued recall and was also compared with the effectiveness of strong semantic associates to important sentence parts (e.g., books, a strong associate to librarian, and bags, a strong associate to carries the groceries). The retrieval effectiveness of such semantic associations has been established in verbal-learning research. This "extralist cuing effect" has been explained from a variety of conceptual frameworks (e.g., Bilodeau & Blick, 1965; Bahrick, 1969, 1970; Tulving & Thomson, 1973). These semantic associates were included as a control for the possibility that the retrieval effectiveness of the disposition words might be due to a priori semantic associations to sentence words rather than to dispositional inferences. Sets of strong associates to actors or predicates were derived in free-association tests. Our purpose was to pit the disposition cues against another set of cues that empirically had strong semantic associations with the sentences. If the disposition cues facilitate sentence recall merely because of associative contiguity with sentences, one would expect the semantic cues to produce stronger recall, because those a priori relations are empirically very strong, whereas the a priori associations between disposition words and sentences are extremely weak. But if the disposition cues were as effective as, or more effective than the strong semantic associates, this strength must be due to the episodic link between sentence and cue, that is, to their temporal co-occurrence and consequent proximity in episodic memory organization.

We can thus posit that the strongest link between the sentences and the disposition words is provided by an inference made by the subject at encoding, rather than by a priori semantic associations between the dispositions and sentences. The association between the sentence words and the disposition words is provided by episodic memory. Whatever link exists in semantic memory between disposition cues and sentences must be weaker than that between the sentences and semantic cues, because the disposition cues do not show up in the free-association pretests, whereas the semantic cues do.

Hence, the semantic and disposition cues are hypothesized to facilitate recall for different reasons. The semantic cues are closely associated with the semantic representations of the words that constitute the sentences. Presenting subjects with the semantic associate during the recall phase should facilitate retrieval of the target sentence parts on the basis of the extralist cuing effect (cf. Tulving & Thomson, 1973). The encoding-specific cue (the inferred disposition), by contrast, is hypothesized

to facilitate retrieval primarily because of the inferred trait's close episodic relation to the target information. Therefore, presenting subjects with the encoding-specific cue should provide access to the whole target sentence even though there is little or no semantic association between cues and sentence parts. The sentences and their corresponding semantic and disposition cues are presented in Table 1.

This research comprised two phases, construction of the stimuli and the recall experiments. Each experiment presented subjects with behavior descriptions that were to be recalled later in the presence either of (a) a personality attribute of the actor implied by the described action, (b) a semantic associate to one of the words of the sentence, or (c) no cue. Stimuli with the appropriate specifications were established through six pretests. Short declarative sentences were written that described simple actions in behavioral, non-evaluative terms, avoiding implications about actors' intentions, traits, attitudes, or feelings. Accordingly, verbs like *helps* were avoided in favor of phrases that described only the behavior (e.g., "...carried the groceries across the street"). No inferences were provided explicitly for the subject (see Table 1).

EXPERIMENT 1

Method

Subjects Ninety male and female undergraduates enrolled in the introductory psychology course at NYU participated in the experiment in partial fulfillment of a course requirement. They were tested in groups of 2 to 12, and sessions lasted about 30 min.

Materials The 18 sentences were presented one at a time by a Kodak Carousel Slide Projector. In addition, there were three slides containing a distractor task, with instructions on one slide and three anagrams on each of the other two slides. After the slide presentation, each subject re-

---

TABLE 1

SENTENCE STIMULI, THEIR CUES, AND CHARACTERISTICS

Sentences[a]	Semantic cues[b]		Disposition cues[b]
	Actor	Verb	
The accountant *takes* the orphans *to the circus.*	numbers (16)	fun (16)	kindhearted (25)
The secretary *solves the mystery* half-way through the book.	typewriter (19)	detective (22)	clever (23)
The barber *loses 20 lbs.* in 6 weeks on a new diet.	hair (45)	fat (21)	willpower (25)
The reporter *steps on* his girlfriend's *feet* as they foxtrot.	newspaper (21)	ouch (15)	clumsy (43)

[a]The italicized portion served as stimuli in the pretest for Experiment 2, obtaining semantic associations to verbs.
[b]Semantic cues, actor; semantic cues, verb; and disposition cues came from Pretests. Numbers in parentheses indicate the percentage of subjects who gave the response.

---

ceived a recall sheet containing the recall cues, on which responses were to be written. There were three kinds of cues on each sheet, counterbalanced across sentence blocks. Thus, one-third of the subjects had a particular six-sentence block cued by semantic cues, another block cued by disposition cues, and the last by no cue. There were three groups of subjects that differed only in the type of cue they received for each block of sentences. A postrecall questionnaire followed the recall sheets, for the last 60 subjects tested.

Procedure Following Tulving's procedure (e.g., Tulving & Thomson, 1973), written instructions informed subjects that they were participating in a memory experiment. They were asked to study the sentences carefully because they would be tested on them later. Subjects viewed each of the 18 sentence slides for 5 s. We randomly determined the order of the slides for each group of subjects.

The distractor task (included to allow short-term memory to dissipate) followed the presentation of the sentences. Immediately after the last sentence was presented, a slide with instructions to unscramble the six anagrams that followed was shown for 5 s. The anagrams were shown on two slides, three anagrams on each. Subjects were allowed 1 min for each slide. The recall sheets were then distributed. Subjects were allowed 10 min to recall as many sentences and as much of each as they could.

After the recall sheets were collected, the first 30 subjects were informally questioned about their recollection of the mental operations they had used (a) as they read the sentences and (b) later as they tried to recall them. Their responses helped to clarify which questions could profitably be asked and the best wording to use. On the basis of this, a postrecall questionnaire was constructed, and these questionnaires were given to the last 60 subjects tested. The first question was open-ended, asking whether they had used any method or strategy to remember the sentences and if so to describe it briefly. The second question presented them with four plausible strategies for committing the sentences to memory (visual imagery, judgments about causality, judgments about personality, and word-meaning associations) and asked them to estimate the percentage of the time they had used each. The third question explained the three cuing conditions and asked them to rate how heavily they had relied on each type of cue (word-meaning or personality trait) or had applied cues of their own, by using 11-point scales to indicate their answers.

Results and Discussion

Each sentence had a similar four-part structure, generally consisting of actor (A), verb (V), direct or indirect object (O), and a prepositional phrase or second object (P). One point was given for recall of each of the four parts. Thus the maximum score for one sentence was four points. Because there were 18 sentences, the highest possible score a subject could receive was 72. We used lenient scoring. No consideration was given for verbatim recall or spelling. Credit was given for appropriate recall of consistent sentence parts: That is, when subjects responded to the cue *bag* with "The farmer carries the old woman's groceries," they received credit for recall of verb and object but not for actor recall (because the appropriate actor was the librarian). We also used this scoring practice for noncued recall when occasional words were erroneously recalled as parts of the wrong sentence. The first five recall protocols in each condition were scored by two independent coders. The interrater agreement was 96.4%.

We assessed the hypothesis that recall cued by dispositions would be at least as strong as semantic-cued recall and superior to noncued recall by using a split-plot factorial analysis of variance (ANOVA). On the recall sheets, three blocks of sentences had been rotated through the three cuing conditions in a Latin square. Hence, block-cue pairing was a 3-level between-subjects factor. Type of cue was a 3-level within-subjects factor, as all subjects received all three types of cues. The other within-subjects factor was the sentence part recalled, a 4-level factor (A, V, O, and P). This yielded a $3 \times 3 \times 4$ (Pairing $\times$ Cue Type $\times$ Sentence Part) ANOVA.

The analysis revealed significant main effects for cue type, $F(2, 168) = 23.00, p < .001$ and for sentence part, $F(3, 252) = 12.40, p < .001$.

The interaction between cue type and sentence part was also significant, $F(6,504 = 67.65, p < .001$.

The mean recall rates of the three types of cues were ordered as predicted. Mean recall with the disposition cue was strongest (2.42), followed by recall with the semantic cue (2.14) and by noncued recall (1.36). The significance of these differences was assessed by using Newman-Keuls multiple comparison tests (Kirk, 1968), which use a stairstep approach to the error rate, according to which the critical value for differences between means varies with the number of means in a set. This test showed that recall cued with disposition words was significantly stronger than noncued recall, $W(.01) = .97$, and nonsignificantly stronger than recall with the semantic cues. Semantic-cued recall was also significantly stronger than noncued recall, $W(.01) = .644$.

The main effect for sentence part was revealed by a Newman-Keuls test to be due to the superiority of actor recall (2.12) to that of preposition (1.88) and Verb (1.90) recall, $W(.01) = .23$ and .21.

The significant Cue $\times$ Sentence Part interaction is depicted in Figure 1. Analyses of simple main effects within each cue type showed that sentence parts were differentially recalled for the semantic cue, $F(3, 258) = 74.05, p < .001$, and for the disposition cue, $F(3,258) = 22.91, p < .001$, but not for noncued recall.

We computed another set of simple main effects and protected t tests in order to compare recall of each sentence part in the three cuing conditions. Actors were recalled differentially by cue type, $F(2, 172) = 41.52, p < .001$. Semantic cues were more effective for actors than disposition cues, $t(86) = 4.90, p < .001$, which were in turn more effective than no cues, $t(86) = 4.92, p < .001$. As Figure 1 suggests, this is a different ordering than that for the other three sentence parts across cue conditions. The simple main effects for verbs, objects and prepositions were also significant, $Fs(2,172) > 20.35, ps < .001$; and for each sentence part, disposition-

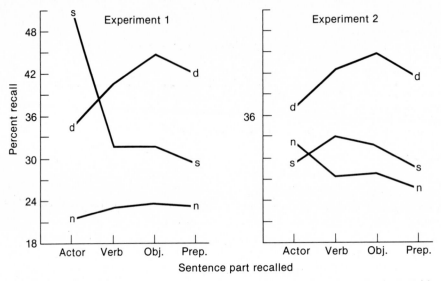

FIGURE 1 Percentage recall of sentence parts, for disposition cues (d), semantic cues (s) and no cue (n). Percentage recall = mean recall divided by .06 for Experiment 1, and .04 for Experiment 2.

cued recall was greater than semantic-cued recall, $ts(86) > 3.46$, ps .001, which was in turn greater than noncued recall, $ts(86) > 1.99$, $ps < .05$.

In summary, as Figure 1 suggests, both disposition-and semantic-cued recall were superior to noncued recall but not different from each other overall. The disposition cues' effectiveness was greatest for sentence verbs, objects, and prepositions, whereas the semantic cues' effectiveness was greatest for sentence actors.

We also tallied the combination of sentence parts that were recalled primarily to examine differences in the kinds of sentence information each type of cue had retrieved best. We tabulated the recall for each of the 15 possible combinations of parts (e.g., actor, actor + verb). Inspection of this table reveals, first, that sentence recall overall was primarily due to recall of total sentences rather than sentence parts, and secondarily to recall of predicates. These observations were confirmed by the results of a $3 \times 3 \times 15$ (Block-Cue Pairing $\times$ Cue Type $\times$

Combination of Parts) split-plot ANOVA. It showed significant main effects for cue type, $F(2, 168) = 22.92$, $p < .001$; for combination, $F(14, 1176) = 188.17$, $p < .001$; and for the interaction between these two within-subject factors, $F(28, 2352) = 13.34$, $p < .001$. Newman-Keuls tests were computed between all pairs of means involved in the main effect for combination of parts. They showed that this main effect occurred because the recall of the total sentence (AVOP) was stronger than that of any other sentence-part combination, $W(.01)$ from .389 to .583; and the recall of the VOP combination (i.e., the predicate) was stronger than any other combination except AVOP, $W(.01)$ from .40 to .60.

In summary, the most frequently recalled combination of sentence parts was the whole sentence, for which both the disposition and the semantic cues were more effective than no cue. The entire predicate (VOP) was also frequently recalled, most often with disposition cues. And actors alone were most frequently cued by semantic cues.

The question of subjects' awareness of making social judgments was assessed in several ways. The first 30 subjects were questioned informally about their recollections of having made personality-related or cause-related inferences as they read the sentences. Although demand characteristics would predict that subjects in such situations would strive to be agreeable and confirm the experimenter's suggestions, most subjects regretfully reported having made no such judgments at all. Even after the debriefing, some did not believe they had made trait inferences and were greatly surprised by evidence supplied by their own recall sheets that trait cues had actually been effective in promoting their recall.

For the remaining 60 subjects, the formal post-recall questionnaire was employed to assess introspective awareness. Alternative memory and recall strategies were described equally plausibly, since Nisbett and Wilson (1977) have pointed out that the a priori causal theories people use to explain events are preeminently those that seem plausible. The four strategies were (a) visual imagery, (b) association to word meanings. (c) judgments about causality, and (d) judgments about personality. Subjects were asked to estimate the percentage of time they had used each.

To the open-ended question, virtually no subjects reported having made causal- or personality-related judgments, and only 10 mentioned anything at all about the persons in the sentences. The mean percentage of time subjects reported using each strategy were as follows: 36.5% for visual imagery, 18.3% for causality-related thoughts, 36.6% for personality-related thoughts, and 45.5% for word-meaning associations.

To assess the question of introspective awareness more precisely, Pearson product-moment correlations were computed between self-reports and actual recall scores. In addition to the scores, we calculated for each subject the ratio of the disposition-cued recall score to the total recall score. This was taken as an additional index of the retrieval effectiveness of the disposition cues. For example, if a subject had a total recall score of 20

and had recalled 10 items (i.e., parts of sentences) that were cued with the disposition cues, his or her ratio would be .5. Both the disposition-cued scores and the ratios were correlated with the self-reports.

EXPERIMENT 2

One criticism that may be leveled at Experiment 1 is that semantic-cued recall may have been unfairly matched against disposition-cued recall because the semantic cue was an associate of only the actor, and actors had been chosen specifically for their semantic independence from the rest of the sentence. Dispositions, although not strong semantic associates of any of the sentence parts, might still be preferentially relevant to the other major syntactic division of the sentence, the predicate. Because the predicates comprised three parts and the actors only one, disposition cues may have been superior in recall only because they were relevant to a large portion of each sentence. Indeed, there is evidence that semantic and disposition cues retrieved sentence parts differentially. Of the sentences recalled through semantic cues, 37% consisted of the actor alone, and 3% the predicate only. Disposition cues retrieved actors alone only 1% of the time, and predicate parts alone 26% of the time. Free recall fell between these two, with 12% actors alone and 24% predicates alone.

We conducted Experiment 2 to meet this criticism by pitting disposition-cued recall against recall cued by strong associates to the sentence verbs.[*]

GENERAL DISCUSSION

In both experiments, recall of sentences was at least as good with dispositional cues as with either type of strong semantic cue and clearly superior to noncued recall. Yet subjects had not

---

Editors' note: Results from Experiment 2 are reported in the General Discussion

been instructed to make dispositional inferences and seemed unaware of having done so. Thus, the results of the experiments provide evidence that personality inferences may occur in the absence of any particular purpose such as a prediction of a requirement to follow an experimenter's instructions.

How well do these results support the notion that personality inferences are made spontaneously from behavioral information as it is encoded? This question may be rephrased in terms of how well we have ruled out the possibility that a disposition cue like *helpful* may be effective in retrieval if it was not present at encoding. Two major alternatives to the encoding specificity hypothesis present themselves as explanations for the retrieval effectiveness of the disposition words. One is that the disposition cues were actually functioning as semantic associates to sentences, rather than representing outcomes of an encoding-specific inference. The second concerns the locus of the hypothesized inference in the information-processing sequence: Might an inference have occurred at some later stage?

First, are there undetected a priori semantic associations between the disposition cues and the sentences that are strong enough to retrieve the sentences better than the intended semantic associates did? We designed the extensive pretesting to reduce this possibility. Even though pretesting did not identify these disposition words as semantic associates, it is still possible that such associations existed and operated to help subjects retrieve sentences. But if the disposition words were operating as semantic associates, then their effectiveness should have been specific to sentence parts. For instance, had the entire recall advantage of the disposition words resided in the recall of predicates, then it could be argued that the disposition words were merely associated with kinds of behavior in subjects' implicit personality theories (e.g., motioning pedestrians to cross the street is an instance of considerateness). The superiority of the disposition-cued recall might then be accounted

for by rival theories of retrieval. For example, according to the generation-recognition theory (e.g., Bahrick, 1969), presentation of a disposition cue might allow subjects to generate a set of behaviors that exemplify the disposition and then to recognize the correct one. (We designed a Pretest to minimize this possibility). But in fact the disposition words had an advantage over other retrieval cues in the recall of the entire sentence and combinations of sentence parts that included the semantically unrelated actor. Most telling is the difference between disposition-cued and semantic-cued recall of these combinations in Experiment 2. In that study, both cues related in different ways to sentence verbs; the semantic cues were related by virtue of a priori associations, and the disposition words were related by virtue of inferences that subjects made on reading the sentences. Disposition cues retrieved the entire sentence 65 times as compared with 51 times for the verb associate, a significant superiority, as our a posteriori test revealed. In addition, the disposition words retrieved combinations that included the actor significantly more often than did the semantic-verb associates. These patterns of recall are more consistent with the encoding-specificity notion, which holds that the sentence is linked in the episodic memory system with the disposition word, which is a de facto input cue because it was inferred at encoding. Although the disposition cues may arguably have a semantic association with some of the sentence predicates (as the pretest for Experiment 2 showed clearly), the actors, which were randomly paired with predicates, certainly had no a priori associations with the disposition words (e.g., carpenter: considerate). Hence the superior recall of entire sentences, including the semantically unrelated actors, through disposition cuing suggests that those cues were operating on episodic memory of the sentences' representations more than on their semantic representations.

A second issue concerns the most likely locus of the inference in information processing, short-term or long-term store. Even if important a priori associations between disposition words and sentences were ruled out, the possibility would remain that a personality inference is made, not at encoding, but at a later processing stage, during retrieval perhaps (Postman, 1972). Even though this interesting possibility has not been absolutely eliminated in the present experiments, several circumstances make it less plausible than the encoding hypothesis. If inferences were made when the sentences were retrieved, one would expect noncued recall to be as strong as disposition-cued recall, or at any rate much higher than it was, because the sentences must have been retrieved from long-term store before inferences could be made on them. Because noncued recall is much lower than disposition-cued recall, a nonencoding hypothesis must hold that subjects made inferences from the sentences while they were available but not accessible (cf. Tulving & Pearlstone, 1966). In other words, sentences that had not been retrieved from long-term store would be the basis of personality inferences, in this scenario. This possibility seems much less parsimonious than the hypothesis that the inferences are made from the sentences while they are held in short-term store during encoding. Thus, the data suggest that such inferences may be an intrinsic part of the process of encoding information and do not always require a separate mental operation subsequent to information retrieval.

The fact that subjects made covert trait inferences without intentions to do so brings up the intriguing possibility that trait inferences may qualify as automatic processes. This issue has important implications for the question of how spontaneous such social inferences are, because automatic processes possess characteristics that would strongly argue for their spontaneousness (e.g., being difficult to suppress or change). In addition to the absence-of-intentionality characteristic, however, automatic processes may occur without awareness and without interference from other ongoing mental activity (Bargh, 1984;

Hasher & Zacks, 1979; Kahneman, 1973; Posner & Snyder, 1975; Schneider & Shiffrin, 1977; Shiffrin & Schneider, 1977). The present evidence for absence of awareness is problematic because the 10-min interval between encoding and reporting leaves open the possibility that subjects may have been momentarily aware of their mental processes but forgot them by the time they were asked to introspect. The criterion of absence-of-interference from simultaneous mental activity has not been addressed in the present experiments. This issue, as well as other criteria for automaticity, is being investigated in current research.

One limit to the generality of these findings must be pointed out. The sentences used in the experiments described actions that, in Jones and Davis' terminology, are correspondent to personality traits. Correspondence, in their theory, means the extent to which "the act and the underlying characteristic or attribute are similarly described by the inference" (Jones & Davis, 1965, p. 223). Our sentences were not only written to represent correspondent acts but were also selected from a set of 39, partly on the basis of pretest subjects' ability to make reliable and consensual correspondent inferences. Thus there were no sentences like, "The man walks down the street." We are not suggesting that people make personality inferences about every piece of behavior they observe. But it should also be remembered that sentences were pretested for vividness or extremeness. Thus it cannot be said that only extreme behaviors instigate trait inferences. Some commonplace behaviors do too.

What are the implications of the possibility that inferred dispositions are often stored in memory with behavioral information? There is a body of research that has explored the relation between the memory status of social information and consequent judgments (e.g., Carlston, 1980; Higgins & King, 1981; Taylor & Fiske, 1978; Reyes, Thompson, & Bower, 1980; Srull & Wyer, 1979). The import of this research is that the accessibility of information has an impact on the outcome of social judgments, such as decisions of guilt or innocence. Our results suggest that dispositional judgments may be made unintentionally at encoding and stored with the information on which they are based. That should increase their subsequent accessibility, and this may influence subsequent judgments. When the original unintended dispositional judgment is evaluative, it may prejudice subsequent judgments, perhaps without the judge's awareness.

A second implication is that the relative effectiveness of dispositional cues in recall of behavioral information may be one basis for the overestimation of behavioral consistency across situations or time. People frequently make this error in perceiving others (Mischel, 1968). There is recent evidence (Lenauer, Sameth, & Shaver, 1976; Moore, Sherrod, Liu, & Underwood, 1979) that people increasingly make this same error in self-perception as time passes.

A third implication is that if dispositions are stored in memory with supportive behavioral information, then memory searches using these dispositions as retrieval cues may be one basis for the occurrence of confirmatory hypothesis testing (Snyder, 1981) and perseverance effects (Ross & Anderson, 1982).

Perhaps the most basic issue concerns the early assumptions expressed by seminal person-perception researchers regarding the facile nature of these processes. The possibility that trait inferences are encoding specific and spontaneous would tend to support these notions and to suggest that such processes occur when behavior is being casually observed, in ordinary situations entirely lacking the character of laboratory experiments. The supposition that they are not occurring when not instructed is therefore gratuitous, and researchers who present subjects with descriptions of behavior, for any experimental purpose, should be mindful of this possibility.

Social Feelings

Accounts of Emotion

excerpt from *The Principles of Psychology*

William James (1890)

We begin this section (Readings 13–20) by asking one of the oldest questions in social psychology: ''How do we come to have emotions?'' James's work is distinctive for its functionalist approach. He believed that the many descriptions of what emotions are and when they occur do not advance our understanding of them. In contrast, James reframes the emotion question to consider the process whereby emotions evolve and what their purpose might be. In the excerpt that follows, James (1890) launched the debate with a surprising reversal of common-sense thought, which you might remember from your introductory psychology course. James, who many regard as the father of American psychology, suggests that in emotion-arousing circumstances (e.g., danger) our body responds physiologically to the event, and it is these bodily changes and our awareness of these changes that result in the emotion.

His theory has not been well-supported by actual research, as reported by Schachter and Singer (1962) in the next article (Reading 14). More recently, however, the Ekman, Levenson, and Friesen (1983) finding that slight heart rate and body temperature alterations are associated with different emotional experiences suggests that physiological arousal may actually differentiate between emotions, although this may be more a consequence of emotion than a cause. Thus, James's conceptualization of how we experience emotion is still debated, and the pendulum may swing back to reveal that there is a kernel of truth to James's argument.

THE EMOTIONS

In speaking of the instincts it has been impossible to keep them separate from the emotional excitements which go with them. Objects of rage, love, fear, etc., not only prompt a man to outward deeds, but provoke characteristic alterations in his attitude and visage, and affect his breathing, circulation, and other organic functions in specific ways. When the outward deeds are inhibited, these latter emotional expressions still remain, and we read the anger in the face, though the blow may not be struck, and the fear betrays itself in voice and color, though one may suppress all other sign. *Instinctive reactions and emotional expressions thus shade imperceptibly into each other. Every object that excites an instinct excites an emotion as well.* Emotions, however, fall short of instincts, in that the emotional reaction usually terminates in the subject's own body, whilst the instinctive reaction is apt to go farther and enter into practical relations with the exciting object.

Were we to go through the whole list of emotions which have been named by men, and study their organic manifestations, we should find that our descriptions had no absolute truth; that they only applied to the average man; that every one of us, almost, has some personal idiosyncrasy of expression, laughing or sobbing differently from his neighbor, or reddening or growing pale where others do not. We should find a like variation in the objects which excite emotion in different persons. Jokes at which one explodes with laughter nauseate another, and seem blasphemous to a third; and occasions which overwhelm me with fear of bashfulness are just what give you the full sense of ease and power. The internal shadings of emotional feeling, moreover, merge endlessly into each other. Language has discriminated some of them, as hatred, antipathy, animosity, dislike, aversion, malice, spite, vengefulness, abhorrence, etc., etc.; but in the dictionaries of synonyms we find these feelings distinguished more by their severally appropriate objective stimuli than by their conscious or subjective tone.

The result of all this flux is that the merely descriptive literature of the emotions is one of the most tedious parts of psychology. And not only is it tedious, but you feel that its subdivisions are to a great extent either fictitious or unimportant, and that its pretences to accuracy are a sham. But unfortunately there is little psychological writing about the emotions which is not merely descriptive. As emotions are described in novels, they interest us, for we are made to share them. We have grown acquainted with the concrete objects and emergencies which call them forth, and any knowing touch of introspection which may grace the page meets with a quick and feeling response. Confessedly literary works of aphoristic philosophy also flash lights into our emotional life, and give us a fitful delight. But as far as ''scientific psychology'' of the emotions goes, I may have been surfeited by too much reading of classic works on the subject, but I should as lief read verbal descriptions of the shapes of the rocks on a New Hampshire farm as toil through them again. They give one nowhere a central point of view, or a deductive or generative principle. They distinguish and refine and specify *in infinitum* without ever getting on to another logical level. Whereas the beauty of all truly scientific work is to get to ever deeper levels. Is there no way out from this level of individual description in the case of the emotions? I believe there is a way out, but I fear that few will take it.

The trouble with the emotions in psychology is that they are regarded too much as absolutely individual things. So long as they are set down as so many eternal and sacred psychic entities, like the old immutable species in natural history, so long all that *can* be done with them is reverently to catalogue their separate characters, points, and effects. But if we regard them as products of more general causes (as 'species' are now regarded as products of heredity and variation),

the mere distinguishing and cataloguing becomes of subsidiary importance. Having the goose which lays the golden eggs, the description of each egg already laid is a minor matter. Now the general causes of the emotions are indubitably physiological. Prof. C. Lange, of Copenhagen, in the pamphlet from which I have already quoted, published in 1885 a physiological theory of their constitution and conditioning, which I have already broached the previous year in an article in *Mind*. None of the criticisms which I have heard of it have made me doubt its essential truth. I will therefore devote the next few pages to explaining what it is. I shall limit myself in the first instance to what may be called the *coarser* emotions, grief, fear, rage, love, in which every one recognizes a strong organic reverberation, and afterwards speak of the *subtler* emotions, or of those whose organic reverberation is less obvious and strong.

EMOTION FOLLOWS UPON THE BODILY EXPRESSION IN THE COARSER EMOTIONS AT LEAST

Our natural way of thinking about these coarser emotions is that the mental perception of some fact excites the mental affection called the emotion, and that this latter state of mind gives rise to the bodily expression. My theory, on the contrary, is that *the bodily changes follow directly the perception of the exciting fact, and that our feeling of the same changes as they occur* IS *the emotion.* Common-sense says, we lose our fortune, are sorry and weep; we meet a bear, are frightened and run; we are insulted by a rival, are angry and strike. The hypothesis here to be defended says that this order of sequence is incorrect, that the one mental state is not immediately induced by the other, that the bodily manifestations must first be interposed between, and that the more rational statement is that we feel sorry because we cry, angry because we strike, afraid because we tremble, and not that we cry, strike, or tremble, because we are sorry, angry, or fearful, as the case may be. Without the bodily states following on the perception, the latter would be purely cognitive in form, pale, colorless, destitute of emotional warmth. We might then see the bear, and judge it best to run, receive the insult and deem it right to strike, but we should not actually *feel* afraid or angry.

Stated in this crude way, the hypothesis is pretty sure to meet with immediate disbelief. And yet neither many nor far-fetched considerations are required to mitigate its paradoxical character, and possibly to produce conviction of its truth.

To begin with, no reader of the last two chapters will be inclined to doubt the fact that *objects do excite bodily changes* by a preorganized mechanism, or the farther fact that *the changes are so indefinitely numerous and subtle that the entire organism may be called a sounding-board*, which every change of consciousness, however slight, may make reverberate. The various permutations and combinations of which these organic activities are susceptible make it abstractly possible that no shade of emotion, however slight, should be without a bodily reverberation as unique, when taken in its totality, as is the mental mood itself. The immense number of parts modified in each emotion is what makes it so difficult for us to reproduce in cold blood the total and integral expression of any one of them. We may catch the trick with the voluntary muscles, but fail with the skin, glands, heart, and other viscera. Just as an artificially imitated sneeze lacks something of the reality, so the attempt to imitate an emotion in the absence of its normal instigating cause is apt to be rather 'hollow.'

The next thing to be noticed is this, that *every one of the bodily changes, whatsoever it be, is* FELT, *acutely or obscurely, the moment it occurs*. If the reader has never paid attention to this matter, he will be both interested and astonished to learn how many different local bodily feelings he can detect in himself as characteristic of his various emotional moods. It would be

perhaps too much to expect him to arrest the tide of any strong gust of passion for the sake of any such curious analysis as this; but he can observe more tranquil states, and that may be assumed here to be true of the greater which is shown to be true of the less. Our whole cubic capacity is sensibly alive; and each morsel of it contributes its pulsations of feeling, dim or sharp, pleasant, painful, or dubious, to that sense of personality that every one of us unfailingly carries with him. It is surprising what little items give accent to these complexes of sensibility. When worried by any slight trouble, one may find that the focus of one's bodily consciousness is the contraction, often quite inconsiderable, of the eyes and brows. When momentarily embarrassed, it is something in the pharynx that compels either a swallow, a clearing of the throat, or a slight cough; and so on for as many more instances as might be named. Our concern here being with the general view rather than with the details, I will not linger to discuss these, but, assuming the point admitted that every change that occurs must be felt, I will pass on.

I now proceed to urge the vital point of my whole theory, which is this: *If we fancy some strong emotion, and then try to abstract from our consciousness of it all the feelings of its bodily symptoms, we find we have nothing left behind*, no 'mind-stuff' out of which the emotion can be constituted, and that a cold and neutral state of intellectual perception is all that remains. It is true that, although most people when asked say that their introspection verifies this statement, some persist in saying theirs does not. Many cannot be made to understand the question. When you beg them to imagine away every feeling of laughter and of tendency to laugh from their consciousness of the ludicrousness of an object, and then to tell you what the feeling of its ludicrousness would be like, whether it be anything more than the perception that the object belongs to the class 'funny,' they persist in replying that the thing proposed is a physical impossibility, and that they always *must* laugh if they see a funny object. Of course the task proposed is not the practical one of seeing a ludicrous object and annihilating one's tendency to laugh. It is the purely speculative one of subtracting certain elements of feeling from an emotional state supposed to exist in its fulness, and saying what the residual elements are. I cannot help thinking that all who rightly apprehend this problem will agree with the proposition above laid down. What kind of an emotion of fear would be left if the feeling neither of quickened heartbeats nor of shallow breathing, neither of trembling lips nor of weakened limbs, neither of goose-flesh nor of visceral stirrings, were present, it is quite impossible for me to think. Can one fancy the state of rage and picture no ebullition in the chest, no flushing of the face, no dilatation of the nostrils, no clenching of the teeth, no impulse to vigorous action, but in their stead limp muscles, calm breathing, and a placid face? The present writer, for one, certainly cannot. The rage is as completely evaporated as the sensation of its so-called manifestations, and the only thing that can possibly be supposed to take its place is some cold-blooded and dispassionate judicial sentence, confined entirely to the intellectual realm, to the effect that a certain person or persons merit chastisement for their sins. In like manner of grief: what would it be without its tears, its sobs, its suffocation of the heart, its pang in the breast-bone? A feelingless cognition that certain circumstances are deplorable, and nothing more. Every passion in turn tells the same story. A purely disembodied human emotion is a nonentity. I do not say that it is a contradiction in the nature of things, or that pure spirits are necessarily condemned to cold intellectual lives; but I say that for *us*, emotion dissociated from all bodily feeling is inconceivable. The more closely I scrutinize my states, the more persuaded I become that whatever moods, affections, and passions I have are in very truth constituted by, and made up of, those bodily changes which we ordinarily call their expression or consequence; and the more it seems to

me that if I were to become corporeally anaesthetic, I should be excluded from the life of the affections, harsh and tender alike, and drag out an existence of merely cognitive or intellectual form. Such an existence, although it seems to have been the ideal of ancient sages, is too apathetic to be keenly sought after by those born after the revival of the worship of sensibility, a few generations ago.

Let not this view be called materialistic. It is neither more nor less materialistic than any other view which says that our emotions are conditioned by nervous processes. No reader of this book is likely to rebel against such a saying so long as it is expressed in general terms; and if any one still finds materialism in the thesis now defended, that must be because of the special processes invoked. They are *sensational* processes, processes due to inward currents set up by physical happenings. Such processes have, it is true, always been regarded by the platonizers in psychology as having something peculiarly base about them. But our emotions must always be *inwardly* what they are, whatever be the physiological ground of their apparition. If they are deep, pure, worthy, spiritual facts on any conceivable theory of their physiological source, they remain no less deep, pure, spiritual, and worthy of regard on this present sensational theory. They carry their own inner measure of worth with them; and it is just as logical to use the present theory of the emotions for proving that sensational processes need not be vile and material, as to use their vileness and materiality as a proof that such a theory cannot be true.

If such a theory is true, then each emotion is the resultant of a sum of elements, and each element is caused by a physiological process of a sort already well known. The elements are all organic changes, and each of them is the reflex effect of the exciting object. Definite questions now immediately arise—questions very different from those which were the only possible ones without this view. Those were questions of classification: "Which are the proper genera of emotion, and which the species under each?" or of description: "By what expression is each emotion characterized?" The questions now are *causal*: "Just what changes does this object and what changes does that object excite?" and "How come they to excite these particular changes and not others?" We step from a superficial to a deep order of inquiry. Classification and description are the lowest stage of science. They sink into the background the moment questions of genesis are formulated, and remain important only so far as they facilitate our answering these. Now the moment the genesis of an emotion is accounted for, as the arousal by an object of a lot of reflex acts which are forthwith felt, *we immediately see why there is no limit to the number of possible different emotions which may exist, and why the emotions of different individuals may vary indefinitely,* both as to their constitution and as to objects which call them forth. For there is nothing sacramental or eternally fixed in reflex action. Any sort of reflex effect is possible, and reflexes actually vary indefinitely, as we know.

> "We have all seen men dumb, instead of talkative, with joy; we have seen fright drive the blood into the head of its victim, instead of making him pale; we have seen grief run restlessly about lamenting, instead of sitting bowed down and mute; etc., etc., and this naturally enough, for one and the same cause can work differently on different men's blood-vessels (since these do not always react alike), whilst moreover the impulse on its way through the brain to the vaso-motor centre is differently influenced by different earlier impressions in the form of recollections or associations of ideas." (Lange, 1887, p. 75).

In short, *any classification of the emotions is seen to be as true and as 'natural' as any other,* if it only serves some purpose; and such a question as "What is the 'real' or 'typical' expression of anger, or fear?" is seen to have no objective meaning at all. Instead of it we now have the question as to how any given 'expression' of anger or fear may have come to exist; and that is a real question of physiological mechanics on the one hand, and of history on the other, which (like all real questions) is in essence answerable, although the answer may be hard to find.

READING 14

Cognitive, Social, and Physiological Determinants of Emotional State

Stanley Schachter and Jerome E. Singer (1962)

Schachter and Singer agree with James (Reading 13) that the presence of physiological arousal is necessary for the experience of emotion, but they emphasize cognition as the second necessary factor for emotion. Arguing that we are motivated to seek adequate explanations for our physiological arousal, Schachter and Singer suggest that when explanations for our arousal are not apparent, we search for situational cues to derive emotion labels for our arousing experience. You will find (as did Schachter and Singer) that the subjects did not always act as predicted, and so the results section includes several kinds of analyses, as Schachter and Singer attempt to explore their data thoroughly. This makes the article more difficult to understand at face value, but it also allows you to see post hoc (after the fact) reasoning at its best.

Of the three concluding propositions in their article, only a modified version of the first one (that emotions will be experienced to the degree that arousal is attributed to emotion-eliciting situational cues) has received reliable support by other studies. The many studies generated from Schachter and Singer's theory of emotion now suggest that the role of physiological arousal has been overstated, but the role of cognition has not (Reisenzein, 1983). Thus, Schachter and Singer's study continues as a classic in the research on emotion for both beginning the emphasis on cognition in the emotion equation and for marking the beginning of the ongoing cognitive era in social psychology.

The problem of which cues, internal or external, permit a person to label and identify his own emotional state has been with us since the days that James (1890) first tendered his doctrine that "the bodily changes follow directly the perception of the exciting fact, and that our feeling of the same changes as they occur *is* the emotion" (p. 449). Since we are aware of a variety of feeling and emotion states, it should follow from James's proposition that the various emotions will be accompanied by a variety of differentiable bodily states. Following James's pronouncement, a formidable number of studies were undertaken in search of the physiological differentiators of the emotions. The results, in these early days, were almost uniformly negative. All of the emotional states experimentally manipulated were characterized by a general pattern of excitation of the sympathetic nervous system but there appeared to be no clear-cut physiological discriminators of the various emotions. This pattern of results was so consistent from experiment to experiment that Cannon (1929) offered, as one of the crucial criticisms of the James-Lange theory, the fact that "the same visceral changes occur in very different emotional states and in non-emotional states" (p. 351).

More recent work, however, has given some indication that there may be differentiators. Ax (1953) and Schachter (1957) studied fear and anger. On a large number of indices both of these states were characterized by a similarly high level of autonomic activation but on several indices they did differ in the degree of activation. Wolf and Wolff (1947) studied a subject with a gastric fistula and were able to distinguish two patterns in the physiological responses of the stomach wall. It should be noted, though, that for many months they studied their subject during and following a great variety of moods and emotions and were able to distinguish only two patterns.

Whether or not there are physiological distinctions among the various emotional states must be considered an open question. Recent work might be taken to indicate that such differences are at best rather subtle and that the variety of emotion, mood, and feeling states are by no means matched by an equal variety of visceral patterns.

This rather ambigious situation has led Ruckmick (1936), Hunt, Cole, and Reis (1958), Schachter (1959) and others to suggest that cognitive factors may be major determinants of emotional states. Granted a general pattern of sympathetic excitation as characteristic of emotional states, granted that there may be some differences in pattern from state to state, it is suggested that one labels, interprets, and identifies this stirred-up state in terms of the characteristics of the precipitating situation and one's apperceptive mass. This suggests, then, that an emotional state may be considered a function of a state of physiological arousal[1] and of a cognition appropriate to this state of arousal. The cognition, in a sense, exerts a steering function. Cognitions arising from the immediate situation as interpreted by past experience provide the framework within which one understands and labels his feelings. It is the cognition which determines whether the state of physiological arousal will be labeled as "anger," "joy," "fear," or whatever.

In order to examine the implications of this formulation let us consider the fashion in which these two elements, a state of physiological

---

[1] Though our experiments are concerned exclusively with the physiological changes produced by the injection of adrenalin, which appear to be primarily the result of sympathetic excitation, the term physiological arousal is used in preference to the more specific "excitation of the sympathetic nervous system" because there are indications, to be discussed later, that this formulation is applicable to a variety of bodily states.

arousal and cognitive factors, would interact in a variety of situations. In most emotion inducing situations, of course, the two factors are completely interrelated. Imagine a man walking alone down a dark alley, a figure with a gun suddenly appears. The perception-cognition "figure with a gun" in some fashion initiates a state of physiological arousal; this state of arousal is interpreted in terms of knowledge about dark alleys and guns and the state of arousal is labeled "fear." Similarly a student who unexpectedly learns that he has made Phi Beta Kappa may experience a state of arousal which he will label "joy."

Let us now consider circumstances in which these two elements, the physiological and the cognitive, are, to some extent, independent. First, is the state of physiological arousal alone sufficient to induce an emotion? Best evidence indicates that it is not. Marañon[2] (1924), in a fascinating study (which was replicated by Cantril & Hunt, 1932, and Landis & Hunt, 1932) injected 210 of his patients with the sympathomimetic agent adrenalin and then simply asked them to introspect. Seventy-one percent of his subjects simply reported their physical symptoms with no emotional overtones; 29% of the subjects responded in an apparently emotional fashion. Of these the great majority described their feelings in a fashion that Marañon labeled "cold" or "as if" emotions, that is, they made statements such as "I feel *as if* I were afraid" or "*as if* I were awaiting a great happiness." This is a sort of emotional "déjà vu" experience; these subjects are neither happy nor afraid, they feel "as if" they were. Finally a very few cases apparently reported a genuine emotional experience. However, in order to produce this reaction in most of these few cases, Marañon (1924) points out:

---

[2] Translated copies of Marañon's (1924) paper may be obtained by writing to the senior author.

One must suggest a memory with strong affective force but not so strong as to produce an emotion in the normal state. For example, in several cases we spoke to our patients before the injection of their sick children or dead parents and they responded calmly to this topic. The same topic presented later, during the adrenal commotion, was sufficient to trigger emotion. This adrenal commotion places the subject in a situation of 'affective imminence' (pp. 307–308).

Apparently, then, to produce a genuinely emotional reaction to adrenalin, Marañon was forced to provide such subjects with an appropriate cognition.

Though Marañon (1924) is not explicit on his procedure, it is clear that his subjects knew that they were receiving an injection and in all likelihood knew that they were receiving adrenalin and probably had some order of familiarity with its effects. In short, though they underwent the pattern of sympathetic discharge common to strong emotional states, at the same time they had a completely appropriate cognition or explanation as to why they felt this way. This, we would suggest, is the reason so few of Marañon's subjects reported any emotional experience.

Consider now a person in a state of physiological arousal for which no immediately explanatory or appropriate cognitions are available. Such a state could result were one covertly to inject a subject with adrenalin or, unknown to him, feed the subject a sympathomimetic drug such as ephedrine. Under such conditions a subject would be aware of palpitations, tremor, face flushing, and most of the battery of symptoms associated with a discharge of the sympathetic nervous system. In contrast to Marañon's (1924) subjects he would, at the same time, be utterly unaware of why he felt this way. What would be the consequence of such a state?

Schachter (1959) has suggested that precisely such a state would lead to the arousal of "evaluative needs" (Festinger, 1954), that is, pressures would act on an individual in such a state to understand and label his bodily feelings. His bodily state grossly resembles the condition in which it has been at times of emotional excitement. How would he label his present feelings? It is suggested, of course, that he will label his feelings in terms of his knowledge of the immediate situation.[3] Should he at the time be with a beautiful woman he might decide that he was wildly in love or sexually excited. Should he be at a gay party, he might, by comparing himself to others, decide that he was extremely happy and euphoric. Should he be arguing with his wife, he might explode in fury and hatred. Or, should the situation be completely inappropriate he could decide that he was excited about something that had recently happened to him or, simply, that he was sick. In any case, it is our basic assumption that emotional states are a function of the interaction of such cognitive factors with a state of physiological arousal.

This line of thought, then, leads to the following propositions:

1. Given a state of physiological arousal for which an individual has no immediate explanation, he will "label" this state and describe his feelings in terms of the cognitions available to him. To the extent that cognitive factors are potent determiners of emotional states, it could be anticipated that precisely the same state of physiological arousal could be labeled "joy" or "fury" or "jealousy" or any of a great diversity of emotional labels depending on the cognitive aspects of the situation.

2. Given a state of physiological arousal for which an individual has a completely appropriate explanation (e.g., "I feel this way because I have just received an injection of adrenalin") no eval-

uative needs will arise and the individual is unlikely to label his feelings in terms of the alternative cognitions available.

Finally, consider a condition in which emotion inducing cognitions are present but there is no state of physiological arousal. For example, an individual might be completely aware that he is in great danger but for some reason (drug or surgical) remain in a state of physiological quiescence. Does he experience the emotion "fear"? Our formulation of emotion as a joint function of a state of physiological arousal and an appropriate cognition, would, of course, suggest that he does not, which leads to our final proposition.

3. Given the same cognitive circumstances, the individual will react emotionally or describe his feelings as emotions only to the extent that he experiences a state of physiological arousal.[4]

PROCEDURE

The experimental test of these propositions requires (a) the experimental manipulation of a state of physiological arousal, (b) the manipulation of the extent to which the subject has an appropriate or proper explanation of his bodily state, and (c) the creation of situations from which explanatory cognitions may be derived.

In order to satisfy the first two experimental requirements, the experiment was cast in the framework of a study on the effects of vitamin supplements on vision. As soon as a subject arrived, he was taken to a private room and told by the experimenter:

In this experiment we would like to make various tests of your vision. We are particularly interested

---

[3] This suggestion is not new for several psychologists have suggested that situational factors should be considered the chief differentiators of the emotions. Hunt, Cole, and Reis (1958) probably make this point most explicitly in their study distinguishing among fear, anger, and sorrow in terms of situational characteristics.

[4] In his critique of the James-Lange theory of emotion, Cannon (1929) also makes the point that sympathectomized animals and patients do seem to manifest emotional behavior. This criticism is, of course, as applicable to the above proposition as it was to the James-Lange formulation. We shall discuss the issues involved in later papers.

in how certain vitamin compounds and vitamin supplements affect the visual skills. In particular, we want to find out how the vitamin compound called "Suproxin" affects your vision.

What we would like to do, then, if we can get your permission, is to give you a small injection of Suproxin. The injection itself is mild and harmless; however, since some people do object to being injected we don't want to talk you into anything. Would you mind receiving a Suproxin injection?

If the subject agrees to the injection (and all but 1 of 185 subjects did) the experimenter continues with instructions we shall describe shortly, then leaves the room. In a few minutes a physician enters the room, briefly repeats the experimenter's instructions, takes the subject's pulse and then injects him with Suproxin.

Depending upon condition, the subject receives one of two forms of Suproxin—epinephrine or a placebo.

Epinephrine or adrenalin is a sympathomimetic drug whose effects, with minor exceptions, are almost a perfect mimicery of a discharge of the sympathetic nervous system. Shortly after injection systolic blood pressure increases markedly, heart rate increases somewhat, cutaneous blood flow decreases, while muscle and cerebral blood flow increase, blood sugar and lactic acid concentration increase, and respiration rate increases slightly. As far as the subject is concerned the major subjective symptoms are palpitation, tremor, and sometimes a feeling of flushing and accelerated breathing. With a subcutaneous injection (in the dosage administered to our subjects), such effects usually begin within 3–5 minutes of injection and last anywhere from 10 minutes to an hour. For most subjects these effects are dissipated within 15–20 minutes after injection.

Subjects receiving epinephrine received a subcutaneous injection of ½ cubic centimeter of a 1:1000 solution of Winthrop Laboratory's Suprarenin, a saline solution of epinephrine bitartrate.

Subjects in the placebo condition received a subcutaneous injection of ½ cubic centimeter of saline solution. This is, of course, completely neutral material with no side effects at all.

Manipulating an Appropriate Explanation

By "appropriate" we refer to the extent to which the subject has an authoritative, unequivocal explanation of his bodily condition. Thus, a subject who had been informed by the physician that as a direct consequence of the injection he would feel palpitations, tremor, etc. would be considered to have a completely appropriate explanation. A subject who had been informed only that the injection would have no side effects would have no appropriate explanation of his state. This dimension of appropriateness was manipulated in three experimental conditions which shall be called: Epinephrine Informed (Epi Inf), Epinephrine Ignorant (Epi Ign), and Epinephrine Misinformed (Epi Mis).

Immediately after the subject had agreed to the injection and before the physician entered the room, the experimenter's spiel in each of these conditions went as follows:

Epinephrine Informed

I should also tell you that some of our subjects have experienced side effects from the Suproxin. These side effects are transitory, that is, they will only last for about 15 or 20 minutes. What will probably happen is that your hand will start to shake, your heart will start to pound, and your face may get warm and flushed. Again these are side effects lasting about 15 or 20 minutes.

While the physician was giving the injection, she told the subject that the injection was mild and harmless and repeated this description of the symptoms that the subject could expect as a consequence of the shot. In this condition, then, subjects have a completely appropriate explanation of their bodily state. They know precisely what they will feel and why.

Epinephrine Ignorant

In this condition, when the subject agreed to the injection, the experimenter said nothing more relevant to side effects and simply left the room. While the physician was giving the injection, she told the subject that the injection was mild and harmless and would have no side effects. In this condition, then, the subject has no experimentally provided explanation for his bodily state.

Epinephrine Misinformed

I should also tell you that some of our subjects have experienced side effects from the Suproxin. These side effects are transitory, that is, they will only last for about 15 or 20 minutes. What will probably happen is that your feet will feel numb, you will have an itching sensation over parts of your body, and you may get a slight headache. Again these are side effects lasting 15 or 20 minutes.

And again, the physician repeated these symptoms while injecting the subject.

None of these symptoms, of course, are consequences of an injection of epinephrine and, in effect, these instructions provide the subject with a completely inappropriate explanation of his bodily feelings. This condition was introduced as a control condition of sorts. It seemed possible that the description of side effects in the Epi Inf condition might turn the subject introspective, self-examining, possibly slightly troubled. Differences on the dependent variable between the Epi Inf and Epi Ign conditions might, then, be due to such factors rather than to differences in appropriateness. The false symptoms in the Epi Mis condition should similarly turn the subject introspective, etc., but the instructions in this condition do not provide an appropriate explanation of the subject's state.

Subjects in all of the above conditions were injected with epinephrine. Finally, there was a placebo condition in which subjects, who were injected with saline solution, were given precisely the same treatment as subjects in the Epi Ign condition.

Producing an Emotion Inducing Cognition

Our initial hypothesis has suggested that given a state of physiological arousal for which the individual has no adequate explanation, cognitive factors can lead the individual to describe his feelings with any of a diversity of emotional labels. In order to test this hypothesis, it was decided to manipulate emotional states which can be considered quite different—euphoria and anger.

There are, of course, many ways to induce such states. In our own program of research, we have concentrated on social determinants of emotional states and have been able to demonstrate in other studies that people do evaluate their own feelings by comparing themselves with others around them (Schachter, 1959; Wrightsman, 1960). In this experiment we have attempted again to manipulate emotional state by social means. In one set of conditions, the subject is placed together with a stooge who has been trained to act euphorically. In a second set of conditions the subject is with a stooge trained to act in an angry fashion.

Euphoria Immediately[5] after the subject had been injected, the physician left the room and the experimenter returned with a stooge whom he introduced as another subject, then said:

> Both of you have had the Suproxin shot and you'll both be taking the same tests of vision. What I ask you to do now is just wait for 20 minutes. The reason for this is simply that we have to allow 20 minutes for the Suproxin to get from the injection site into the bloodstream. At the end of 20 minutes when we are certain that most of the Suproxin has

---

[5] It was, of course, imperative that the sequence with the stooge begin before the subject felt his first symptoms for otherwise the subject would be virtually forced to interpret his feelings in terms of events preceding the stooge's entrance. Pretests had indicated that, for most subjects, epinephrine-caused symptoms began within 3–5 minutes after injection. A deliberate attempt was made then to bring in the stooge within 1 minute after the subject's injection.

been absorbed into the bloodstream, we'll begin the tests of vision.

The room in which this was said had been deliberately put into a state of mild disarray. As he was leaving, the experimenter apologetically added:

> The only other thing I should do is to apologize for the condition of the room. I just didn't have time to clean it up. So, if you need any scratch paper or rubberbands or pencils, help yourself. I'll be back in 20 minutes to begin the vision tests.

As soon as the experimenter had left, the stooge introduced himself again, made a series of standard icebreaker comments, and then launched his routine. For observation purposes, the stooge's act was broken into a series of standard units, demarcated by a change in activity or a standard comment. In sequence, the units of the stooge's routine were the following:

1. Stooge reaches for a piece of paper and starts doodling saying, "They said we could use this for scratch, didn't they?" He doodles a fish for some 30 seconds, then says:
2. "This scrap paper isn't even much good for doodling" and crumples paper and attempts to throw it into wastebasket in far corner of the room. He misses but this leads him into a "basketball game." He crumples up other sheets of paper, shoots a few baskets, says "Two points" occasionally. He gets up and does a jump shot saying, "The old jump shot is really on today."
3. If the subject has not joined in, the stooge throws a paper basketball to the subject saying, "Here, you try it."
4. Stooge continues his game saying, "The trouble with paper basketballs is that you don't really have any control."
5. Stooge continues basketball, then gives it up saying, "This is one of my good days. I feel like a kid again. I think I'll make a plane." He makes a paper airplane saying, "I guess I'll make one of the longer ones."

6. Stooge flies plane. Gets up and retrieves plane. Flies again, etc.
7. Stooge throws plane at subject.
8. Stooge, flying plane, says, "Even when I was a kid, I was never much good at this."
9. Stooge tears off part of plane saying, "Maybe this plane can't fly but at least it's good for something." He wads up paper and making a slingshot of a rubber band begins to shoot the paper.
10. Shooting, the stooge says, "They [paper ammunition] really go better if you make them long. They don't work right if you wad them up."
11. While shooting, stooge notices a sloppy pile of manila folders on a table. He builds a tower of these folders, then goes to the opposite end of the room to shoot at the tower.
12. He misses several times, then hits and cheers as the tower falls. He goes over to pick up the folders.
13. While picking up, he notices, behind a portable blackboard, a pair of hula hoops which have been covered with black tape with a few wires sticking out of the tape. He reaches for these, taking one for himself and putting the other aside but within reaching distance of the subject. The stooge tries the hula hoop, saying, "This isn't as easy as it looks."
14. Stooge twirls hoop wildly on arm, saying, "Hey, look at this—this is great."
15. Stooge replaces the hula hoop and sits down with his feet on the table. Shortly thereafter the experimenter returns to the room.

This routine was completely standard, though its pace, of course, varied depending upon the subject's reaction, the extent to which he entered into this bedlam and the extent to which he initiated activities of his own. The only variations from this standard routine were those forced by the subject. Should the subject originate some nonsense of his own and request the stooge to join in, he would do so. And, he would of course, respond to any comments initiated by the subject.

Subjects in each of the three "appropriateness" conditions and in the placebo condition were submitted to this setup. The stooge, of course, never knew in which condition any particular subject fell.

Anger Immediately after the injection, the experimenter brought a stooge into the subject's room, introduced the two and after explaining the necessity for a 20 minute delay for "the Suproxin to get from the injection site into the bloodstream" he continued, "We would like you to use these 20 minutes to answer these questionnaires." Then handing out the questionnaires, he concludes with, "I'll be back in 20 minutes to pick up the questionnaires and begin the tests of vision."

Before looking at the questionnaire, the stooge says to the subject,

I really wanted to come for an experiment today, but I think it's unfair for them to give you shots. At least, they should have told us about the shots when they called us; you hate to refuse, once you're here already.

The questionnaires, five pages long, start off innocently requesting face sheet information and then grow increasingly personal and insulting. The stooge, sitting directly opposite the subject, paces his own answers so that at all times subject and stooge are working on the same question. At regular points in the questionnaire, the stooge makes a series of standardized comments about the questions. His comments start off innocently enough, grow increasingly querulous, and finally he ends up in a rage. In sequence, he makes the following comments.

1. Before answering any items, he leafs quickly through the questionnaire saying, "Boy, this is a long one."

2. Question 7 on the questionnaire requests, "List the foods that you would eat in a typ-ical day." The stooge comments, "Oh for Pete's sake, what did I have for breakfast this morning?"

3. Question 9 asks, "Do you ever hear bells? _____ . How often? _____ ." The stooge remarks, "Look at Question 9. How ridiculous can you get? I hear bells every time I change classes."

4. Question 13 requests, "List the childhood diseases you have had and the age at which you had them" to which the stooge remarks, "I get annoyed at this childhood disease question. I can't remember what childhood diseases I had, and especially at what age. Can you?"

5. Question 17 asks "What is your father's average annual income?" and the stooge says, "This really irritates me. It's none of their business what my father makes. I'm leaving that blank."

6. Question 25 presents a long series of items such as "Does not bathe or wash regularly," "Seems to need psychiatric care," etc. and requests the respondent to write down for which member of his immediate family each item seems most applicable. The question specifically prohibits the answer "None" and each item must be answered. The stooge says, "I'll be damned if I'll fill out Number 25. 'Does not bathe or wash regularly'—that's a real insult." He then angrily crosses out the entire item.

7. Question 28 reads: "How many times each week do you have sexual intercourse?" 0–1 _____ 2–3 _____ 4–6 _____ 7 and over _____ . The stooge bites out, "The hell with it! I don't have to tell them all this."

8. The stooge sits sullenly for a few moments then he rips up his questionnaire, crumples the pieces and hurls them to the floor, saying, "I'm not wasting any more time. I'm getting my books and leaving" and he stamps out of the room.

9. The questionnaire continues for eight more questions ending with: "With how many men

(other than your father) has your mother had extramarital relationships?'' 4 and under _____ : 5–9 _____ : 10 and over _____ .

Subjects in the Epi Ign, Epi Inf and Placebo conditions were run through this ''anger'' inducing sequence. The stooge, again, did not know to which condition the subject had been assigned.

In summary, this is a seven condition experiment which, for two different emotional states, allows us (a) to evaluate the effects of ''appropriateness'' on emotional inducibility and (b) to begin to evaluate the effects of sympathetic activation on emotional inducibility. In schematic form the conditions are the following:

EUPHORIA	ANGER
Epi Inf	Epi Inf
Epi Ign	Epi Ign
Epi Mis	Placebo
Placebo	

The Epi Mis condition was not run in the Anger sequence. This was originally conceived as a control condition and it was felt that its inclusion in the Euphoria conditions alone would suffice as a means of evaluating the possible artifactual effect of the Epi Inf instructions.

Measurement

Two types of measures of emotional state were obtained. Standardized observation through a one-way mirror was the technique used to assess the subject's behavior. To what extent did he act euphoric or angry? Such behavior can be considered in a way as a ''semiprivate'' index of mood for as far as the subject was concerned, his emotional behavior could be known only to the other person in the room—presumably another student. The second type of measure was self-report in which, on a variety of scales, the subject indicated his mood of the moment. Such measures can be considered ''public'' indices of mood for they would, of course, be available to the experimenter and his associates.

Observation

Euphoria For each of the first 14 units of the stooge's standardized routine an observer kept a running chronicle of what the subject did and said. For each unit the observer coded the subject's behavior in one or more of the following categories:

Category 1: Joins in activity. If the subject entered into the stooge's activities, e.g., if he made or flew airplanes, threw paper basketballs, hula hooped, etc., his behavior was coded in this category.

Category 2: Initiates new activity. A subject was so coded if he gave indications of creative euphoria, that is, if, on his own, he initiated behavior outside of the stooge's routine. Instances of such behavior would be the subject who threw open the window and, laughing, hurled paper basketballs at passersby; or, the subject who jumped on a table and spun one hula hoop on his leg and the other on his neck.

Categories 3 and 4: Ignores or watches stooge. Subjects who paid flatly no attention to the stooge or who, with or without comment, simply watched the stooge without joining in his activity were coded in these categories.

For any particular unit of behavior, the subject's behavior was coded in one or more of these categories. To test reliability of coding two observers independently coded two experimental sessions. The observers agreed completely on the coding of 88% of the units.

Anger For each of the units of stooge behavior, an observer recorded the subject's responses and coded them according to the following category scheme:

Category 1: Agrees. In response to the stooge the subject makes a comment indicating that he agrees with the stooge's standardized comment or that he, too, is irked by a particular item on the questionnaire. For example, a subject who responded to the stooge's comment on the "father's income" question by saying, "I don't like that kind of personal question either" would be so coded (scored +2).

Category 2: Disagrees. In response to the stooge's comment, the subject makes a comment which indicates that he disagrees with the stooge's meaning or mood; e.g., in response to the stooge's comment on the "father's income" question, such a subject might say, "Take it easy, they probably have a good reason for wanting the information" (scored −2).

Category 3: Neutral. A noncommittal or irrelevant response to the stooge's remark (scored 0).

Category 4: Initiates agreement or disagreement. With no instigation by the stooge, a subject, so coded, would have volunteered a remark indicating that he felt the same way or, alternatively, quite differently than the stooge. Examples would be "Boy I hate this kind of thing" or "I'm enjoying this" (scored +2 or −2).

Category 5: Watches. The subject makes no verbal response to the stooge's comment but simply looks directly at him (scored 0).

Category 6: Ignores. The subject makes no verbal response to the stooge's comment nor does he look at him; the subject, paying no attention at all to the stooge, simply works at his own questionnaire (scored −1).

A subject was scored in one or more of these categories for each unit of stooge behavior. To test reliability, two observers independently coded three experimental sessions. In order to get a behavioral index of anger, observation protocol was scored according to the values presented in parentheses after each of the above definitions of categories. In a unit-by-unit comparison, the two observers agreed completely on the scoring of 71% of the units jointly observed. The scores of the two observers differed by a value of 1 or less for 88% of the units coded and in not a single case did the two observers differ in the direction of their scoring of a unit.

Self Report of Mood and Physical Condition

When the subject's session with the stooge was completed, the experimenter returned to the room, took pulses and said:

Before we proceed with the vision tests, there is one other kind of information which we must have. We have found, as you can probably imagine, that there are many things beside Suproxin that affect how well you see in our tests. How hungry you are, how tired you are, and even the mood you're in at the time—whether you feel happy or irritated at the time of testing will affect how well you see. To understand the data we collect on you, then, we must be able to figure out which effects are due to causes such as these and which are caused by Suproxin.

The only way we can get such information about your physical and emotional state is to have you tell us. I'll hand out these questionnaires and ask you to answer them as accurately as possible. Obviously, our data on the vision tests will only be as accurate as your description of your mental and physical state.

In keeping with this spiel, the questionnaire that the experimenter passed out contained a number of mock questions about hunger, fatigue, etc., as well as questions of more immediate relevance to the experiment. To measure mood or emotional state the following two were the crucial questions:

1. How irritated, angry or annoyed would you say you feel at present?

I don't feel at all irritated or angry (0)	I feel a little irritated and angry (1)	I feel quite irritated and angry (2)	I feel very irritated and angry (3)	I feel extremely irritated and angry (4)

2. How good or happy would you say you feel at present?

I don't feel at all happy or good (0)	I feel a little happy and good (1)	I feel quite happy and good (2)	I feel very happy and good (3)	I feel extremely happy and good (4)

To measure the physical effects of epinephrine and determine whether or not the injection had been successful in producing the necessary bodily state, the following questions were asked:

1. Have you experienced any palpitation (consciousness of your own heart beat)?

Not at all (0)	A slight amount (1)	A moderate amount (2)	An intense amount (3)

2. Did you feel any tremor (involuntary shaking of the hands, arms or legs)?

Not at all (0)	A slight amount (1)	A moderate amount (2)	An intense amount (3)

To measure possible effects of the instructions in the Epi Mis condition, the following questions were asked:

1. Did you feel any numbness in your feet?
2. Did you feel any itching sensation?
3. Did you experience any feeling of headache?

To all three of these questions was attached a four-point scale running from "Not at all" to "An intense amount."

In addition to these scales, the subjects were asked to answer two open-end questions on other physical or emotional sensations they may have experienced during the experimental session. A final measure of bodily state was pulse rate which was taken by the physician or the experimenter at two times—immediately before the injection and immediately after the session with the stooge.

When the subjects had completed these questionnaires, the experimenter announced that the experiment was over, explained the deception and its necessity in detail, answered any questions, and swore the subjects to secrecy. Finally, the subjects answered a brief questionnaire about their experiences, if any, with adrenalin and their previous knowledge or suspicion of the experimental setup. There was no indication that any of the subjects had known about the experiment beforehand but 11 subjects were so extremely suspicious of some crucial feature of the experiment that their data were automatically discarded.

Subjects

The subjects were all male, college students taking classes in introductory psychology at the University of Minnesota. Some 90% of the students in these classes volunteer for a subject pool for which they receive two extra points on their final exam for every hour that they serve as experimental subjects. For this study the records of all potential subjects were cleared with the Student Health Service in order to insure that no harmful effects would result from the injections.

Evaluation of the Experimental Design

The ideal test of our propositions would require circumstances which our experiment is far from realizing. First, the proposition that: "A state of physiological arousal for which an individual has no immediate explanation will lead him to label this state in terms of the cognitions available to him" obviously requires conditions under which the subject does not and cannot have a proper explanation of his bodily state. Though we toyed with such fantasies as ventilating the experimental room with vaporized adrenalin, reality forced us to rely on the disguised injection of Suproxin—

a technique which was far from ideal for no matter what the experimenter told them, some subjects would inevitably attribute their feelings to the injection. To the extent that subjects did so, differences between the several appropriateness conditions should be attenuated.

Second, the proposition that: "Given the same cognitive circumstances the individual will react emotionally only to the extent that he experiences a state of physiological arousal" requires for its ideal test the manipulation of states of physiological arousal and of physiological quiescence. Though there is no question that epinephrine effectively produces a state of arousal, there is also no question that a placebo does not prevent physiological arousal. To the extent that the experimental situation effectively produces sympathetic stimulation in placebo subjects, the proposition is difficult to test, for such a factor would attenuate differences between epinephrine and placebo subjects.

Both of these factors, then, can be expected to interfere with the test of our several propositions. In presenting the results of this study, we shall first present condition by condition results and then evaluate the effect of these two factors on experimental differences.

RESULTS

Effects of the Injections on Bodily State

Let us examine first the success of the injections at producing the bodily state required to examine the propositions at test. Does the injection of epinephrine produce symptoms of sympathetic discharge as compared with the placebo injection? Relevant data are presented in Table 1 where it can be immediately seen that on all items subjects who were in epinephrine conditions show considerably more evidence of sympathetic activation than do subjects in placebo conditions. In all epinephrine conditions pulse rate increases significantly when compared with the decrease characteristic of the placebo conditions. On the scales it is clear that epinephrine subjects experience considerably more palpitation and tremor than do placebo subjects. In all possible comparisons on these symptoms, the mean scores of subjects in any of the epinephrine conditions are greater than the corresponding scores in the placebo conditions at better than the .001 level of significance. Examination of the absolute values of these scores makes it quite clear that subjects in epinephrine conditions were, indeed, in a state

TABLE 1

THE EFFECTS OF THE INJECTIONS ON BODILY STATE

Condition	N	Pulse		Self-rating of				
		Pre	Post	Palpitation	Tremor	Numbness	Itching	Headache
Euphoria								
Epi Inf	27	85.7	88.6	1.20	1.43	0	0.16	0.32
Epi Ign	26	84.6	85.6	1.83	1.76	0.15	0	0.55
Epi Mis	26	82.9	86.0	1.27	2.00	0.06	0.08	0.23
Placebo	26	80.4	77.1	0.29	0.21	0.09	0	0.27
Anger								
Epi Inf	23	85.9	92.4	1.26	1.41	0.17	0	0.11
Epi Ign	23	85.0	96.8	1.44	1.78	0	0.06	0.21
Placebo	23	84.5	79.6	0.59	0.24	0.14	0.06	0.06

of physiological arousal, while most subjects in placebo conditions were in a relative state of physiological quiescence.

The epinephrine injection, of course, did not work with equal effectiveness for all subjects; indeed for a few subjects it did not work at all. Such subjects reported almost no palpitation or tremor, showed no increase in pulse and described no other relevant physical symptoms. Since for such subjects the necessary experimental conditions were not established, they were automatically excluded from the data and all further tabular presentations will not include such subjects. Table 1, however, does include the data of these subjects. There were four such subjects in euphoria conditions and one of them in anger conditions.

In order to evaluate further data on Epi Mis subjects it is necessary to note the results of the "numbness," "itching," and "headache" scales also presented in Table 1. Clearly the subjects in the Epi Mis condition do not differ on these scales from subjects in any of the other experimental conditions.

Effects of the Manipulations on Emotional State

Euphoria: Self-report The effects of the several manipulations on emotional state in the euphoria conditions are presented in Table 2. The

scores recorded in this table are derived, for each subject, by subtracting the value of the point he checks on the irritation scale from the value of the point he checks on the happiness scale. Thus, if a subject were to check the point "I feel a little irritated and angry" on the irritation scale and the point "I feel very happy and good" on the happiness scale, his score would be +2. The higher the positive value, the happier and better the subject reports himself as feeling. Though we employ an index for expositional simplicity, it should be noted that the two components of the index each yield results completely consistent with those obtained by use of this index.

Let us examine first the effects of the appropriateness instructions. Comparison of the scores for the Epi Mis and Epi Inf conditions makes it immediately clear that the experimental differences are not due to artifacts resulting from the informed instructions. In both conditions the subject was warned to expect a variety of symptoms as a consequence of the injection. In the Epi Mis condition, where the symptoms were inappropriate to the subject's bodily state the self-report score is almost twice that in the Epi Inf condition where the symptoms were completely appropriate to the subject's bodily state. It is reasonable, then, to attribute differences between informed subjects and those in other conditions to differences in manipulated appropriateness rather than to artifacts such as introspectiveness or self-examination.

It is clear that, consistent with expectations, subjects were more susceptible to the stooge's mood and consequently more euphoric when they had no explanation of their own bodily states than when they did. The means of both the Epi Ign and Epi Mis conditions are considerably greater than the mean of the Epi Inf condition.

It is of interest to note that Epi Mis subjects are somewhat more euphoric than are Epi Ign subjects. This pattern repeats itself in other data shortly to be presented. We would attribute this difference to differences in the appropriateness dimension. Though, as in the Epi Ign condition,

TABLE 2

SELF-REPORT OF EMOTIONAL STATE IN THE EUPHORIA CONDITIONS

Condition	N	Self Report scales	Comparison	p [a]
Epi Inf	25	0.98	Epi Inf vs. Epi Mis	< .01
Epi Ign	25	1.78	Epi Inf vs. Epi Ign	.02
Epi Mis	25	1.90	Placebo vs. Epi Mis,	ns
Placebo	26	1.61	Ign, or Inf	

[a] All p values reported throughout paper are two-tailed.

a subject is not provided with an explanation of his bodily state, it is, of course, possible that he will provide one for himself which is not derived from his interaction with the stooge. Most reasonably he could decide for himself that he feels this way because of the injection. To the extent that he does so he should be less susceptible to the stooge. It seems probable that he would be less likely to hit on such an explanation in the Epi Mis condition than in the Epi Ign condition for in the Epi Mis condition both the experimenter and the doctor have told him that the effects of the injection would be quite different from what he actually feels. The effect of such instructions is probably to make it more difficult for the subject himself to hit on the alternative explanation described above. There is some evidence to support this analysis. In open-end questions in which subjects described their own mood and state, 28% of the subjects in the Epi Ign condition made some connection between the injection and their bodily state compared with the 16% of subjects in the Epi Mis condition who did so. It could be considered, then, that these three conditions fall along a dimension of appropriateness, with Epi Inf condition at one extreme and the Epi Mis condition at the other.

Comparing the placebo to the epinephrine conditions, we note a pattern which will repeat itself throughout the data. Placebo subjects are less euphoric than either Epi Mis or Epi Ign subjects but somewhat more euphoric than Epi Inf subjects. These differences are not, however, statistically significant. We shall consider the epinephrine-placebo comparisons in detail in a later section of this paper following the presentation of additional relevant data. For the moment, it is clear that, by self-report, manipulating appropriateness has had a very strong effect on euphoria.

Behavior Let us next examine the extent to which the subject's behavior was affected by the experimental manipulations. To the extent that his mood has been affected, one should expect that the subject will join in the stooge's whirl of manic activity and initiate similar activities of his own. The relevant data are presented in Table 3. The column labeled "Activity index" presents summary figures on the extent to which the subject joined in the stooge's activity. This is a weighted index which reflects both the nature of the activities in which the subject engaged and the amount of time he was active. The index was devised by assigning the following weights to the subject's activities: 5—hula hooping; 1—shooting with slingshot; 3—paper airplanes; 2—paper basketballs; 1—doodling; 0—does nothing. Pretest scaling on 15 college students ordered these activities with respect to the degree of euphoria they represented. Arbitrary weights were assigned so that the wilder the activity, the heavier the weight. These weights are multiplied by an estimate of the amount of time the subject spent in each activity and the summed products make up the activity index for each subject. This index may be considered a measure of behavioral euphoria. It should be noted that the same between-condition relationships hold for the two components of this index as for the index itself.

TABLE 3

BEHAVIORAL INDICATIONS OF EMOTIONAL STATE IN THE EUPHORIA CONDITIONS

Condition	N	Activity index	Mean number of acts initiated
Epi Inf	25	12.72	.20
Epi Ign	25	18.28	.56
Epi Mis	25	22.56	.84
Placebo	26	16.00	.54

p value[a]		
Comparison	**Activity index**	**Initiates**
Epi Inf vs. Epi Mis	.05	.03
Epi Inf vs. Epi Ign	ns	.08
Plac vs. Epi Mis, Ign, or Inf	ns	ns

[a]Tested by X^2 comparison of the proportion of subjects in early condition initiating new acts.

The column labeled "Mean number of acts initiated" presents the data on the extent to which the subject deviates from the stooge's routine and initiates euphoric activities of his own.

On both behavioral indices, we find precisely the same pattern of relationships as those obtained with self-reports. Epi Mis subjects behave somewhat more euphorically than do Epi Ign subjects who in turn behave more euphorically than do Epi Inf subjects. On all measures, then, there is consistent evidence that a subject will take over the stooge's euphoric mood to the extent that he has no other explanation of his bodily state.

Again it should be noted that on these behavioral indices, Epi Ign and Epi Mis subjects are somewhat more euphoric than placebo subjects but not significantly so.

Anger: Self-report   Before presenting data for the anger conditions, one point must be made about the anger manipulation. In the situation devised, anger, if manifested, is most likely to be directed at the experimenter and his annoyingly personal questionnaire. As we subsequently discovered, this was rather unfortunate, for the subjects, who had volunteered for the experiment for extra points on their final exam, simply refused to endanger these points by publicly blowing up, admitting their irritation to the experimenter's face or spoiling the questionnaire. Though, as the reader will see, the subjects were quite willing to manifest anger when they were alone with the stooge, they hesitated to do so on material (self-ratings of mood and questionnaire) that the experimenter might see and only after the purposes of the experiment had been revealed were many of these subjects willing to admit to the experimenter that they had been irked or irritated.

This experimentally unfortunate situation pretty much forces us to rely on the behavioral indices derived from observation of the subject's presumably private interaction with the stooge. We do, however, present data on the self-report scales in Table 4. These figures are derived in

	TABLE	4		
SELF-REPORT OF EMOTIONAL STATE IN THE ANGER CONDITIONS				
Condition	N	Self Report scales	Comparison	p
Epi Inf	22	1.91	Epi Inf vs. Epi Ign	.08
Epi Ign	23	1.39	Placebo vs. Epi Ign or Inf	ns
Placebo	23	1.63		

the same way as the figures presented in Table 2 for the euphoria conditions, that is, the value checked on the irritation scale is subtracted from the value checked on the happiness scale. Though, for the reasons stated above, the absolute magnitude of these figures (all positive) is relatively meaningless, we can, of course, compare condition means within the set of anger conditions. With the happiness-irritation index employed, we should, of course, anticipate precisely the reverse results from those obtained in the euphoria conditions; that is, the Epi Inf subjects in the anger conditions should again be less susceptible to the stooge's mood and should, therefore, describe themselves as in a somewhat happier frame of mind than subjects in the Epi Ign condition. This is the case; the Epi Inf subjects average 1.91 on the self-report scales while the Epi Ign subjects average 1.39.

Evaluating the effects of the injections, we note again that, as anticipated, Epi Ign subjects are somewhat less happy than Placebo subjects but, once more, this is not a significant difference.

Behavior   The subject's responses to the stooge, during the period when both were filling out their questionnaires, were systematically coded to provide a behavioral index of anger. The coding scheme and the numerical values attached to each of the categories have been described in the methodology section. To arrive at an "Anger index" the numerical value assigned to a subject's responses to the stooge is summed together for the several units of stooge behavior. In the coding scheme used, a positive value to this index indicates that the subject agrees with the stooge's comment and is growing angry. A negative value indicates that the subject either disagrees with the stooge or ignores him.

The relevant data are presented in Table 5. For this analysis, the stooge's routine has been divided into two phases—the first two units of his behavior (the "long" questionnaire and "What did I have for breakfast?") are considered essentially neutral revealing nothing of the stooge's mood; all of the following units are considered "angry" units for they begin with an irritated remark about the "bells" question and end with the stooge's fury as he rips up his questionnaire and stomps out of the room. For the neutral units, agreement or disagreement with the stooge's remarks is, of course, meaningless as an index of mood and we should anticipate no difference between conditions. As can be seen in Table 5, this is the case.

For the angry units, we must, of course, anticipate that subjects in the Epi Ign condition will be angrier than subjects in the Epi Inf condition.

This is indeed the case. The Anger index for the Epi Ign condition is positive and large, indicating that these subjects have become angry, while in the Epi Inf condition the Anger index is slightly negative in value, indicating that these subjects have failed to catch the stooge's mood at all. It seems clear that providing the subject with an apppropriate explanation of his bodily state greatly reduces his tendency to interpret his state in terms of the cognitions provided by the stooge's angry behavior.

Finally, on this behavioral index, it can be seen that subjects in the Epi Ign condition are significantly angrier than subjects in the Placebo condition. Behaviorally, at least, the injection of epinephrine appears to have led subjects to an angrier state than comparable subjects who received placebo shots.

Conformation of Data to Theoretical Expectations

Now that the basic data of this study have been presented, let us examine closely the extent to which they conform to theoretical expectations. If our hypotheses are correct and if this experimental design provided a perfect test for these hypotheses, it should be anticipated that in the euphoria conditions the degree of experimentally produced euphoria should vary in the following fashion:

$$\text{Epi Mis} \geq \text{Epi Ign} > \text{Epi Inf} = \text{Placebo}$$

And in the anger conditions, anger should conform to the following pattern:

$$\text{Epi Ign} > \text{Epi Inf} = \text{Placebo}$$

In both sets of conditions, it is the case that emotional level in the Epi Mis and Epi Ign conditions is considerably greater than that achieved in the corresponding Epi Inf conditions. The results for the Placebo condition, however, are ambiguous for consistently the Placebo subjects fall between the Epi Ign and the Epi Inf subjects.

TABLE	5

BEHAVIORAL INDICATIONS OF EMOTIONAL STATE IN THE ANGER CONDITIONS

Condition	N	Neutral units	Anger units
Epi Inf	22	+ 0.07	−0.18
Epi Ign	23	+ 0.30	+ 2.28
Placebo	22[a]	−0.09	+ 0.79

Comparison for anger units	p
Epi Inf vs. Epi Ign	< .01
Epi Ign vs. Placebo	< .05
Placebo vs. Epi Inf	ns

[a]For one subject in this condition the sound system went dead and the observer could not, of course, code his reactions.

This is a particularly troubling pattern for it makes it impossible to evaluate unequivocally the effects of the state of physiological arousal and indeed raises serious questions about our entire theoretical structure. Though the emotional level is consistently greater in the Epi Mis and Epi Ign conditions than in the Placebo condition, this difference is significant at acceptable probability levels only in the anger conditions.

In order to explore the problem further, let us examine the experimental factors identified earlier, which might have acted to restrain the emotional level in the Epi Ign and Epi Mis conditions. As was pointed out earlier, the ideal test of our first two hypotheses requires an experimental setup in which the subject has flatly no way of evaluating his state of physiological arousal other than by means of the experimentally provided cognitions. Had it been possible to physiologically produce a state of sympathetic activation by means other than injection, one could have approached this experimental ideal more closely than in the present setup. As it stands, however, there is always a reasonable alternative cognition available to the aroused subject—he feels the way he does because of the injection. To the extent that the subject seizes on such an explanation of his bodily state, we should expect that he will be uninfluenced by the stooge. Evidence presented in Table 6 for the anger condition and in Table 7 for the euphoria conditions indicates that this is, indeed, the case.

TABLE 6

THE EFFECTS OF ATTRIBUTING BODILY STATE TO THE INJECTION ON ANGER IN THE ANGER EPI IGN CONDITION

Condition	N	Anger index	p
Self-informed subjects	3	− 1.67	ns
Others	20	+ 2.88	ns
Self-informed vs. Others			.05

TABLE 7

THE EFFECTS OF ATTRIBUTING BODILY STATE TO THE INJECTION ON EUPHORIA IN THE EUPHORIA EPI IGN AND EPI MIS CONDITIONS

Epi Ign			
	N	Activity index	p
Self-informed subjects	8	11.63	ns
Others	17	21.14	ns
Self-informed vs. Others			.05

Epi Mis			
	N	Activity Index	p
Self-informed subjects	5	12.40	ns
Others	20	25.10	ns
Self-informed vs. Others			.10

As mentioned earlier, some of the Epi Ign and Epi Mis subjects in their answers to the open-end questions clearly attributed their physical state to the injection, e.g., "the shot gave me the shivers." In Tables 6 and 7 such subjects are labeled "Self-informed." In Table 6 it can be seen that the self-informed subjects are considerably less angry than are the remaining subjects; indeed, they are not angry at all. With these self-informed subjects eliminated the difference between the Epi Ign and the Placebo conditions is significant at the .01 level of significance.

Precisely the same pattern is evident in Table 7 for the euphoria conditions. In both the Epi Mis and the Epi Ign conditions, the self-informed subjects have considerably lower activity indices than do the remaining subjects. Eliminating self-informed subjects, comparison of both of these conditions with the Placebo condition yields a difference significant at the .03 level of significance. It should be noted, too, that the self-informed subjects have much the same score on the activity index as do the experimental Epi Inf subjects (Table 3).

It would appear, then, that the experimental procedure of injecting the subjects, by providing an alternative cognition, has, to some extent, obscured the effects of epinephrine. When account is taken of this artifact, the evidence is good that the state of physiological arousal is a necessary component of an emotional experience for when self-informed subjects are removed, epinephrine subjects give consistent indications of greater emotionality than do placebo subjects.

Let us examine next the fact that consistently the emotional level, both reported and behavioral, in Placebo conditions is greater than that in the Epi Inf conditions. Theoretically, of course, it should be expected that the two conditions will be equally low, for by assuming that emotional state is a joint function of a state of physiological arousal and of the appropriateness of a cognition we are, in effect, assuming a multiplicative function, so that if either component is at zero, emotional level is at zero. As noted earlier this expectation should hold if we can be sure that there is no sympathetic activation in the Placebo conditions. This assumption, of course, is completely unrealistic for the injection of placebo does not prevent sympathetic activation. The experimental situations were fairly dramatic and certainly some of the placebo subjects gave indications of physiological arousal. If our general line of reasoning is correct, it should be anticipated that the emotional level of subjects who give indications of sympathetic activity will be greater than that of subjects who do not. The relevant evidence is presented in Tables 8 and 9.

As an index of sympathetic activation we shall use the most direct and unequivocal measure available—change in pulse rate. It can be seen in Table 1 that the predominant pattern in the Placebo condition is a decrease in pulse rate. We shall assume, therefore, that those subjects whose pulse increases or remains the same give indications of sympathetic activity while those subjects whose pulse decreases do not. In Table 8, for the euphoria condition, it is immediately

TABLE 8			
SYMPATHETIC ACTIVATION AND EUPHORIA IN THE EUPHORIA PLACEBO CONDITION			
Subjects whose:	*N*	Activity Index	*p*
Pulse decreased	14	10.67	*ns*
Pulse increased or remained same	12	23.17	*ns*
Pulse decrease vs. pulse increase or same			.02

clear that subjects who give indications of sympathetic activity are considerably more euphoric than are subjects who show no sympathetic activity. This relationship is, of course, confounded by the fact that euphoric subjects are considerably more active than noneuphoric subjects—a factor which independent of mood could elevate pulse rate. However, no such factor operates in the anger condition where angry subjects are neither more active nor talkative than calm subjects. It can be seen in Table 9 that Placebo subjects who show signs of sympathetic activation give indications of considerably more anger than do subjects who show no such signs. Conforming to expectations, sympathetic activation accompanies an increase in emotional level.

It should be noted, too, that the emotional levels of subjects showing no signs of sympathetic

TABLE 9			
SYMPATHETIC ACTIVATION AND ANGER IN ANGER PLACEBO CONDITION			
Subjects whose:	*N*[a]	Anger Index	*p*
Pulse decreased	13	+ 0.15	*ns*
Pulse increased or remained same	8	+ 1.69	*ns*
Pulse decrease vs. pulse increase or same			.01

[a]*N* reduced by two cases owing to failure of sound system in one case and experimenter's failure to take pulse in another.

activity are quite comparable to the emotional level of subjects in the parallel Epi Inf conditions (see Tables 3 and 5). The similarity of these sets of scores and their uniformly low level of indicated emotionality would certainly make it appear that both factors are essential to an emotional state. When either the level of sympathetic arousal is low or a completely appropriate cognition is available, the level of emotionality is low.

DISCUSSION

Let us summarize the major findings of this experiment and examine the extent to which they support the propositions offered in the introduction of this paper. It has been suggested, first, that given a state of physiological arousal for which an individual has no explanation, he will label this state in terms of the cognitions available to him. This implies, of course, that by manipulating the cognitions of an individual in such a state we can manipulate his feelings in diverse directions. Experimental results support this proposition for following the injection of epinephrine, those subjects who had no explanation for the bodily state thus produced, gave behavioral and self-report indications that they had been readily manipulable into the disparate feeling states of euphoria and anger.

From this first proposition, it must follow that given a state of physiological arousal for which the individual has a completely satisfactory explanation, he will not label this state in terms of the alternative cognitions available. Experimental evidence strongly supports this expectation. In those conditions in which subjects were injected with epinephrine and told precisely what they would feel and why, they proved relatively immune to any effects of the manipulated cognitions. In the anger condition, such subjects did not report or show anger; in the euphoria condition, such subjects reported themselves as far less happy than subjects with an identical bodily state but no adequate knowledge of why they felt the way they did.

Finally, it has been suggested that given constant cognitive circumstances, an individual will react emotionally only to the extent that he experiences a state of physiological arousal. Without taking account of experimental artifacts, the evidence in support of this proposition is consistent but tentative. When the effects of "self-informing" tendencies in epinephrine subjects and of "self-arousing" tendencies in placebo subjects are partialed out, the evidence strongly supports the proposition.

The pattern of data, then, falls neatly in line with theoretical expectations. However, the fact that we were forced, to some extent, to rely on internal analyses in order to partial out the effects of experimental artifacts inevitably makes our conclusions somewhat tentative. In order to further test these propositions on the interaction of cognitive and physiological determinants of emotional state, a series of additional experiments, published elsewhere, was designed to rule out or overcome the operation of these artifacts. In the first of these, Schachter and Wheeler (1962) extended the range of manipulated sympathetic activation by employing three experimental groups—epinephrine, placebo, and a group injected with the sympatholytic agent, chlorpromazine. Laughter at a slapstick movie was the dependent variable and the evidence is good that amusement is a direct function of manipulated sympathetic activation.

In order to make the epinephrine-placebo comparison under conditions which would rule out the operation of any self-informing tendency, two experiments were conducted on rats. In one of these, Singer (1961) demonstrated that under fear inducing conditions, manipulated by the simultaneous presentation of a loud bell, a buzzer, and a bright flashing light, rats injected with epinephrine were considerably more frightened than rats injected with a placebo. Epinephrine-injected rats defecated, urinated, and trembled more than did placebo-injected rats. In nonfear control conditions, there were no differences between epinephrine and placebo groups, neither group giving any indication of fear. In another study, Latané and Schachter (1962) demonstrated that rats injected with epinephrine were notably more capable of avoidance learning than were rats injected with a placebo. Using a modified Miller-Mowrer shuttlebox, these investigators found that during an experimental period involving 200 massed trials, 15 rats injected with epinephrine avoided shock an average of 101.2 trials while 15 placebo-injected rats averaged only 37.3 avoidances.

Taken together, this body of studies does give strong support to the propositions which generated these experimental tests. Given a state of sympathetic activation, for which no immediately appropriate explanation is available, human subjects can be readily manipulated into states of euphoria, anger, and amusement. Varying the intensity of sympathetic activation serves to vary the intensity of a variety of emotional states in both rats and human subjects.

Let us examine the implications of these findings and of this line of thought for problems in the general area of the physiology of the emotions. We have noted in the introduction that the numerous studies on physiological differentiators of emotional states have, viewed en masse, yielded quite inconclusive results. Most, though not all, of these studies have indicated no differences among the various emotional states. Since as human beings, rather than as scientists, we have no difficulty identifying, labeling, and distinguishing among our feelings, the results of these studies have long seemed rather puzzling and paradoxical. Perhaps because of this, there has been a persistent tendency to discount such results as due to ignorance or methodological inadequacy and to pay far more attention to the very few studies which demonstrate *some* sort of physiological differences among emotional states than to the very many studies which indicate no differences at all. It is conceivable, however, that these results should be taken at face value and that emotional states may, indeed, be generally characterized by a high level of sympathetic activation with few if any physiological distinguishers among the many emotional states. If this is correct, the findings of the present study may help to resolve the problem. Obviously this study does *not* rule out the possibility of physiological differences among the emotional states. It is the case, however, that given precisely the same state of epinephrine-induced sympathetic activation, we have, by means of cognitive manipulations, been able to produce in our subjects the very disparate states of euphoria and anger. It may indeed be the case that cognitive factors are major determiners of the emotional labels we apply to a common state of sympathetic arousal.

Let us ask next whether our results are specific to the state of sympathetic activation or if they are generalizable to other states of physiological arousal. It is clear that from our experiments proper, it is impossible to answer the question for our studies have been concerned largely with the effects of an epinephrine created state of sympathetic arousal. We would suggest, however, that our conclusions are generalizable to almost any pronounced internal state for which no appropriate explanation is available. This suggestion receives some support from the experiences of Nowlis and Nowlis (1956) in their program of research on the effects of drugs on mood. In their work the Nowlises typically administer a drug to groups of four subjects who are physically in one another's presence and free to interact. The Nowlises describe some of their results with these groups as follows:

> At first we used the same drug for all 4 men. In those sessions seconal, when compared with placebo, increased the checking of such words as expansive, forceful, courageous, daring, elated, and impulsive. In our first statistical analysis we were confronted with the stubborn fact that when the same drug is given to all 4 men in a group, the N that has to be entered into the analysis is 1, not 4. This increases the cost of an already expensive experiment by a considerable factor, but it cannot be denied that the effects of these drugs may be and often are quite contagious. Our first attempted solution was to run tests on groups in which each man had a different drug

during the same session, such as 1 on seconal, 1 on benzedrine, 1 on dramamine, and 1 on placebo. What does seconal do? Cooped up with, say, the egotistical benzedrine partner, the withdrawn, indifferent dramamine partner, and the slightly bored lactose man, the seconal subject reports that he is distractible, dizzy, drifting, glum, defiant, languid, sluggish, discouraged, dull, gloomy, lazy, and slow! This is not the report of mood that we got when all 4 men were on seconal. It thus appears that the moods of the partners do definitely influence the effect of seconal (p. 350).

It is not completely clear from this description whether this "contagion" of mood is more marked in drug than in placebo groups, but should this be the case, these results would certainly support the suggestion that our findings are generalizable to internal states other than that produced by an injection of epinephrine.

Finally, let us consider the implications of our formulation and data for alternative conceptualizations of emotion. Perhaps the most popular current conception of emotion is in terms of "activation theory" in the sense employed by Lindsley (1951) and Woodworth and Schlosberg (1958). As we understand this theory, it suggests that emotional states should be considered as at one end of a continuum of activation which is defined in terms of degree of autonomic arousal and of electro-encephalographic measures of activation. The results of the experiment described in this paper do, of course, suggest that such a formulation is not completely adequate. It is possible to have very high degrees of activation without a subject either appearing to be or describing himself as "emotional." Cognitive factors appear to be indispensable elements in any formulation of emotion.

SUMMARY

It is suggested that emotional states may be considered a function of a state of physiological arousal and of a cognition appropriate to this state of arousal. From this follows these propositions:

1. Given a state of physiological arousal for which an individual has no immediate explanation, he will label this state and describe his feelings in terms of the cognitions available to him. To the extent that cognitive factors are potent determiners of emotional states, it should be anticipated that precisely the same state of physiological arousal could be labeled "joy" or "fury" or "jealousy" or any of a great diversity of emotional labels depending on the cognitive aspects of the situation.

2. Given a state of physiological arousal for which an individual has a completely appropriate explanation, no evaluative needs will arise and the individual is unlikely to label his feelings in terms of the alternative cognitions available.

3. Given the same cognitive circumstances, the individual will react emotionally or describe his feelings as emotions only to the extent that he experiences a state of physiological arousal.

An experiment is described which, together with the results of other studies, supports these propositions.

READING   15

A Constructivist View of Emotion

James R. Averill (1980)

Emotions form an interesting subset of human behaviors; they are the basis of many of our most fundamental experiences. Attraction, caring, happiness, and love as well as vengefulness, sorrow, anger, conflict, and aggression are important markers of the human experience.

Mr. Spock, the half human, half Vulcan from the *Star Trek* series, is an interesting character for more than just his pointed ears. Taking after his Vulcan father, he is a nonemotional being. Spock views human emotions as weaknesses, believing that they are inherently irrational and that they cause us to override reason. Is he right? Do you agree or do you somehow feel sorry for Spock because he is unable to experience the broad range of human emotions?

A social constructivist account of emotion, the following reading by Averill focuses on how emotions are derived from our appraisals of the situation. Whereas Schachter and Singer (Reading 14) see both cognition and arousal as necessary and sufficient independent factors, Averill identifies emotions as social constructions that can only be fully understood by also including a social level of analysis. Also, you may see some similarities between Averill's identification of emotions as socially constituted and Cooley's (Reading 7) identification of the self-concept as socially created.

As you read this chapter, you will see that Averill invokes the concepts of "role" and "syndrome" to describe emotions, and he does this to try to create a new way of thinking about emotion. Instead of classifying emotional experience in the traditional way, i.e., by content (happy, sad, afraid), he classifies them by degree of involvement or control (low, medium, high). He also explores our social beliefs about emotions as passions, and as out of our control. A major claim in this chapter is that emotional experiences are a consequence of our *interpretation* of an event, and those interpretations are steeped in a sociocultural context as well as in the immediate situation.

This returns us to Mr. Spock. Is Spock right that emotions are out of our control and irrational? Do we have choices about what we feel or even *that* we feel? Averill's theory threatens some of our basic assumptions about emotion and may provide us with a rejoinder to the Vulcan perspective.

Abstract

Traditionally, the emotions have been viewed from a biological perspective; that is, the emotions have been seen as genetically determined and relatively invariable responses. The present chapter, by contrast, views the emotions as social constructions. More precisely, the emotions are here defined as socially constituted syndromes or transitory social roles. A role-conception does not deny the contribution of biological systems to emotional syndromes; it does, however, imply that the functional significance of emotional responses is to be found largely within the sociocultural system. With regard to subjective experience, a person interprets his own behavior as emotional in much the same way that an actor interprets a role "with feeling." This involves not only the monitoring of behavior (including feedback from physiological arousal, facial expressions, etc.), but also an understanding of how the emotional role fits into a larger "drama" written by society. Some of the biological, personal, and situational factors that influence emotional behavior are also discussed.

The term "constructivist" in the title of this chapter has a double meaning. First, it means that the emotions are social *constructions*, not biological givens. Second, it means that the emotions are *improvisations*, based on an individual's interpretation of the situation. These two meanings are not independent. Very briefly, the emotions are viewed here as transitory social roles, or socially constituted syndromes. The social norms that help constitute these syndromes are represented psychologically as cognitive structures or schemata. These structures—like the grammar of a language—provide the basis for the appraisal of stimuli, the organization of responses, and the monitoring of behavior, that is, for the improvisation of emotional roles.

THE DEFINITION OF EMOTION

The concept of emotion encompasses a wide range of phenomena, and this fact accounts for much of the controversy in the area. Ostensibly competing theories are often not incompatible; they simply address different phenomena, or different aspects of the same phenomenon. It is therefore important to specify at the outset the scope of the analysis in this chapter. Basically, I am concerned with the concept of emotion as it is used in everyday discourse and with the kinds of emotions recognized in ordinary language, for example, anger, grief, fear, hope, love, etc. This means that the chapter deals primarily with *human* emotions. For reasons that will become evident during the course of the discussion, I believe that the application of emotional concepts to animals is primarily metaphorical or derivative. A focus on human emotions is not, however, a limitation. On the contrary, present formulation will have to be broad enough to encompass a wide range of emotions such as love, courage, hope, anxiety, and jealousy, to mention but a few. These are as representative of human emotions as are fear and anger, the states most studied by psychologists.

At first, it might seem that, by taking commonly recognized human emotions as a starting point, the problem of analysis has been greatly compounded. Everyday behavior is, after all, highly variable, and the ordinary language of emotion often seems vague and confusing. However, any theory of emotion must eventually deal with the emotions as they are conceptualized and experienced in everyday affairs. By focusing on such phenomena from the outset, it may be hoped that our conclusions will be of direct relevance to our ultimate concerns. That is not the case with many current theories of emotion, which often represent little more than extrapolations to the area of emotion of constructs developed to account for other types of behavior. Most drive theories of emotion are, for example, offshoots of learning theory; and most physiological theories are based on animal studies and hence are only tangentially related to human emotions.

A focus on the emotions as ordinarily conceived does not, of course, obviate the need for precision. In this section, therefore, I will try to develop a definition of emotion that is precise and yet broad enough to cover the major categories of human emotions. In doing this, I will follow the classical method of *definition by ge-*

nus and difference. That is, I will first indicate the generic class of phenomena to which the emotions belong, and then I will indicate how the emotions can be differentiated from other members of that class.

The Generic Class of Phenomena to Which Emotions Belong

Depending on the aspect of emotional behavior that one wishes to emphasize, the emotions can be classed with a variety of different phenomena. In what follows, I will consider, first, the commonalities between emotions and other *behavioral syndromes* and, second, the commonalities between emotions and *transitory social roles*.

Emotions as Syndromes A syndrome may be defined as a *set* of responses that covary in a *systematic fashion*. The two key elements in this definition are "set" and "systematic." The notion of *set* implies that a syndrome consists of a variety of different elements; that is, a syndrome is not a unitary or invariant response. But not any set of elements can form a syndrome. The elements must also be related in such a manner that they form a coherent *system*. In this sense, syndromes could also be defined as systems of behavior, as opposed to specific reactions.

To illustrate the syndromic nature of emotional reactions, consider the case of anger. There are certain behaviors that are typical of anger (including the way the individual appraises the situation), but none of these is necessary for the attribution of anger. Thus, the person who is angry may lash out at his antagonist, or he may withdraw from the situation; he may experience a high degree of physiological arousal, or he may calmly retaliate; his subjective experience may vary from exhilaration to depression; in addition, under some conditions, he may not even realize that he is angry.

Of course, the individual must do or experience something, or else we would not classify his behavior as angry. This fact has led some theorists to postulate that the concept of anger must refer to events that lie "below the surface," so to speak. Depending on the theorist, the postulated event may be a neurological circuit, a subjective experience, or perhaps an intervening drive variable. But the basic idea is the same: There is some event that is common to all instances of anger, and to which the term "anger" ultimately refers.

A syndromic conception of emotion denies this last assumption. Emotional syndromes are "polythetic." This term was introduced by Sokal and Sneath (1963) to describe biological classes (e.g., species), but it has been extended by Jensen (1970) to behavioral classes as well. Polythetic classes or syndromes are not definable in terms of a limited number of common characteristics or "essences." It follows that what is true of one member of a polythetic class is not necessarily true of other members of the class. Moreover, the boundaries between polythetic classes are often indistinct, and members of different classes may share elements in common (e.g., a person may lash out in fear as well as anger).

The importance of the above considerations for an analysis of emotional behavior will become apparent in subsequent sections. For the moment, I only wish to emphasize the fact that an emotional syndrome may include many diverse elements, some of biological and some of social origin, but none of which is essential to the identification of the syndrome as a whole.

Emotions as Transitory Social Roles   The conception of emotions as syndromes can be misleading in several important respects. Diseases are also syndromes. And, although there are many close parallels between the notion of disease and the notion of emotion, I do not want to reinforce the hoary idea that emotions are diseases of the mind. But, even more important, because of its close association with medicine, the term "syndrome" has a strong biological or physiological connotation. By contrast, the view

I am presenting here is that emotions are social constructions, not biological givens. Therefore, it will be useful to point out some commonalities between the emotions and another broad class of phenomena, namely, social roles.

A role may be defined as a socially prescribed set of responses to be followed by a person in a given situation. This definition is similar in certain respects to that of a syndrome described earlier. However, the notion of a syndrome, by itself, does not indicate the nature of the mechanisms or "rules" that govern the selection of, and covariation among, various response elements. In the case of social roles, the nature of the relevant rules are stipulated; they are, namely, social norms or shared expectancies regarding appropriate behavior.

In the second section of this chapter I will examine in detail the conception of emotions as transitory social roles. At this point, let me simply note that a role-conception is perfectly compatible with the definition of emotions as complex syndromes. To illustrate this point, let me digress briefly. The concept of a syndrome is commonly applied to disease states. But the symptomatology that a patient displays when ill is determined, in part, by the "sick role" he adopts (Parsons, 1951; Segall, 1976). This is true even in cases where the source of the illness can be traced rather directly to some physiological source, such as injury or infection. In the case of brain damage and other organically based mental disorders, the role-expectations of the subject may actually outweigh physiological factors in determining the nature of the syndrome. And when we consider "functional" or neurotic disorders, such as hysterical reactions, organic factors are by definition absent or minimal. Syndromes of the latter type are constituted by the role being played; stated somewhat differently, the syndrome is a manifestation of the sick role as interpreted by the patient.

Extending the above line of reasoning to the emotions, it may be said that any given emotional syndrome represents the enactment of a transitory social role. This assertion does not deny the importance of biological factors in many, if not most, emotional syndromes. It does mean, however, that emotions are not just remnants of our phylogenetic past, nor can they be explained in strictly physiological terms. Rather, they are social constructions, and they can be *fully* understood only on a social level of analysis.

Differentiae

A definition of emotion in terms of syndromes and/or transitory social roles is incomplete, for other psychological phenomena could be similarly described. Some differentiae must therefore be added. The two most important of these have to do with the appraisal of emotional stimuli and the experience of passivity (being "overcome" by emotion).

The Appraisal of Emotional Stimuli In saying that emotions belong to the class of transitory social roles, they already have been differentiated from syndromes that are primarily organic in origin. Social roles require an active interpretation by the individual for their enactment. However, there is another sense in which the emotions are dependent on cognitive activity, and this helps to distinguish emotions not only from other organic syndromes but also from certain other social roles. I am referring to the fact that emotions have objects. A person cannot simply be angry, fearful, or proud. He must be angry *at* something, fearful *of* something, proud *of* something, and so forth.

The object of an emotion is dependent on an individual's appraisal of the situation. The notion of appraisal was introduced systematically into the study of emotion by Arnold (1960) and Lazarus (1966). Emotional appraisals differ from "cold" perceptual judgments in that the former are *evaluative*; that is, they represent judgments about what is desirable and undesirable as opposed to judgments about what is true or false.

Thus, if a certain picture disgusts me, it is because I consider it to be either aesthetically or morally in bad taste, regardless of whether or not I consider it to be an accurate portrayal of events. Of course, not all evaluative judgments are emotional. An art critic or a trial judge may strive to be impersonal and objective in making an evaluative judgment. Emotional appraisals, by contrast, are highly *personal*. For example, if I perceive another person to be in danger, I do not ordinarily become afraid (unless perhaps I have some personal interest in that other person). It is this feature that makes emotional appraisals so revealing of an individual's personality. If you know what makes an individual proud, angry, sad, joyful, fearful, etc., then you know what that person considers important about himself, even those aspects of his personality that he may not recognize or admit.

There has been much speculation about the mechanisms that help mediate emotional appraisals (see Leventhal, 1979; Mandler, 1975). This is not the place to review such speculations, for they are not particularly relevant to a definition of emotion. Our concern here is with the logical status of emotional appraisals, and not with explanatory mechanisms (which are, in any case, only poorly understood).

From a logical point of view, the process of appraisal is an aspect of an emotional syndrome, not something antecedent to it. That is, the appraised object is not something that exists out there, independent of the observer. Rather, it is a meaning imposed on the environment—a cognitive construction, so to speak. For example, I may be angry at John for insulting me, when in actuality John was only trying to be helpful by correctly pointing out a mistake I had made. John's insult is based on my appraisal of the situation; it is as much a part of my anger as is my feeling of hurt.

The fact that appraisals are part of emotional syndromes was pointed out quite forcefully by John Dewey (1894, 1895) in an attempt to resolve some inconsistencies in the James–Lange theory. More recently, a similar point has been made by Leeper (1970) and Solomon (1976), both of whom define emotions in terms of perceptual or evaluative judgments.

If appraisal is part of an emotional syndrome, then the appraised object becomes an important criterion for distinguishing one emotion from another and, ipso facto, emotional from nonemotional states. This can be illustrated easily by the following thought experiment. Try to distinguish between three closely related emotions, such as anger, envy, and jealousy. Exactly the same response (e.g., striking another person, rise in blood pressure, loathing, etc.) might be involved in each case. However, if the responding individual believes that another person has done him an injustice, then the response might be attributed to anger; if the individual believes that the other person has something (perhaps legitimately) that otherwise would be his, then the response might be classified as jealousy; and if the individual simply believes that the other person is in a more favorable position, though without any detriment to himself, then the response might be identified as envy.

At the risk of repetition, it must be emphasized that the relationship between an emotion and its object is logical as well as psychological. Revenge for wrongdoing is part of what we mean by anger; resentment over the good fortune of another is part of what we mean by envy, and so forth. In order to "discover" the object of an emotion, we therefore need to examine the meaning of the emotional concept. And the meaning of an emotional concept, like that of any concept, is primarily a matter of social convention.

The Experience of Passivity Although an important differentia, the appraised object is not by itself sufficient to distinguish emotional from nonemotional phenomena. Thus, I may appraise a situation as involving wrongdoing and seek to punish the wrongdoer, but without ever becoming angry. An additional criterion must therefore be added to our definition of emotion. This criterion is readily identifiable if we consider the

older and now somewhat archaic term for emotion, namely, passion. The term "passion" derives from the Latin, *pati,* which in turn is related to the Greek, *pathos.* Also derived from these same roots are such terms as "passivity," "patient," and "pathology." The root meaning of these concepts is that the individual is undergoing or suffering some change. An emotion, in other words, is not something we do (an action), but something that happens to us (a passion).

Colloquially, the passivity of emotion is expressed in many ways. We "fall" in love, are "consumed" by envy, "haunted" by guilt, "paralyzed" by fear, and so forth. Traditional theories have attempted to account for expressions such as these, and the experiences they ostensibly represent, in one or more of the following ways: (a) by relating the emotions to biologically primitive ("instinctive") reactions; (b) by emphasizing the role of the automatic ("involuntary") nervous system in the mediation of emotion; and/or (c) by assuming that the emotions are basically noncognitive ("irrational") responses. The present analysis, by contrast, assumes that the emotions are social constructions and that they require the same level of cognitive capacity as do other complex forms of social behavior. How is the passivity of emotion to be explained on the basis of such an assumption?

Much of the remainder of this chapter will be devoted to answering the above question. To adumbrate briefly, the classification of a response as either an action or a passion involves an *interpretation*: Actions are responses that are interpreted as self-initiated; passions are responses that are interpreted as beyond self-control. No one would probably object to this statement as it applies to the behavior of others. But what I shall be arguing below is that the feeling or subjective experience of emotion also involves an interpretation of one's own behavior. This is, of course, a somewhat unusual way of speaking, for it is common to distinguish interpretations from direct experiences. Nevertheless, most psychologists recognize that even simple sensory experiences involve some interpretive elements, and the same is certainly true of more complex emotional experiences.

The idea that the experience of emotion involves an interpretation of one's own behavior has recently received considerable impetus from attribution theory (e.g., Schachter, 1971; Nisbett & Valins, 1971). It is not, however, limited to any one theoretical framework. For example, Alfred Schutz (1968), a phenomenologist, has argued that the experience of behavior as deliberate or emotional is not inherent to the response, but is a meaning bestowed on spontaneous activity. Similarly, Bem (1972), a behaviorist, has suggested that emotional reactions, like other responses, are emitted spontaneously or unselfconsciously, only to be interpreted in the light of antecedent and consequent events. And Schafer (1976), a psychoanalyst, has suggested that emotions be viewed as "disclaimed actions," that is, as responses that an individual performs but for which he does not, or cannot, accept responsibility.

In short, the experience of passivity (of being "overcome" by emotion) is not intrinsic to the response, as most biologically oriented theories imply. Rather, it is an interpretation of behavior. A major problem for a constructivist view of emotions is to elucidate the source and functional significance of such an interpretation.

A Definition

To summarize the discussion thus far, the following definition of emotion may be offered: *An emotion is a transitory social role (a socially constituted syndrome) that includes an individual's appraisal of the situation and that is interpreted as a passion rather than as an action.* This definition does not cover all of the phenomena that in ordinary language are sometimes labeled "emotional." But no definition can be stretched to cover all borderline phenomena and still retain any precision. With certain qualifications that will be discussed more fully below, the present definition does cover most commonly recognized human emotions.

EMOTIONAL SYNDROMES AS TRANSITORY SOCIAL ROLES

The part of the above definition that is most likely to cause misunderstanding is the contention that emotions are transitory social roles. This section, therefore, will be devoted to an elaboration of that contention.

Not all aspects of a role-conception of emotion can be examined here. I will therefore limit discussion to four major issues: (a) understanding the meaning of emotional roles; (b) monitoring the performance; (c) involvement in emotional roles; and (d) factors that influence involvement in and/or performance of emotional roles. I will then consider briefly some of the limitations of an analysis of emotion in terms of social roles.

Understanding the Meaning of Emotional Roles

Before a role can be enacted, its meaning must be understood, and its requirements must be perceived. This observation might seem so blatantly obvious that it hardly needs mention. Yet, what is obvious can also be overlooked. I will illustrate this by considering briefly Stanley Schachter's (1971) influential theory of emotion. According to this theory, emotions are a joint product of two factors: physiological arousal and cognitive appraisals regarding the source of that arousal. More specifically, Schachter postulates that feedback from the physiological arousal provides a nondescript affective tone to experience, while the cognitive appraisal of situational cues determines which, if any, emotion will be experienced. This means that precisely the same state of arousal might be "labeled" as anger, love, joy, fear, guilt, etc., depending on the cues present in the situation.

I do not wish to review here the many ingenious experiments stimulated by Schachter's theory (see Schachter, 1971; Nisbett & Valins, 1971; Dienstbier, 1978; Zillmann, 1978). Basically, I agree with much of what Schachter has to say. Like most good theories, however, his raises more questions than it answers. Consider for a moment Schachter's use of the term "labeling" to refer to the way people describe their emotional experiences. This terminology implies that there is a highly contingent relationship between emotional concepts and underlying states—as though a person could pick an emotional label out of a box and pin it onto bodily reactions, following instructions provided by situational cues. But the person who says "that makes me angry" or "I love you" is not simply labeling an internal state; he is entering into a complex relationship with another person. Any comprehensive theory of emotion must include within its scope an analysis of the meaning of such relationships, and the latter kind of analysis goes far beyond a specification of the cues, physiological or situational, that help determine the use of emotional "labels."

The relationship between emotional concepts and emotional behavior has been examined in some detail elsewhere (Averill, 1980). Suffice it here to note that, from a constructivist point of view, when a person makes a self-attribution of emotion he enters into a transitory social role, the meaning of which is only symbolized by the emotional "label" he applies to his behavior. Stated somewhat differently, a person's emotional behavior and experiences are determined by the meaning of the emotional role as he interprets it. The "labeling" of behavior is often an important part of this process, but only a part (and not even a necessary part, at that).

What is involved in understanding the meaning of an emotional role, aside from knowing how to apply emotional concepts in a manner appropriate to the situation? Perhaps most important, the person must be able to view his own behavior from the perspective of others. Within the symbolic-interactionist tradition (see Hewett, 1976), this is called "role-taking" as opposed to "role-making." That is, by taking the role of others, a person learns how to respond (role-making) so that his behavior conforms to social expectations.

Taking the role of another can proceed on two levels. In any concrete interaction, the person must take into account specific others when improvising his own responses. (I will have more to say about this level of interaction in a subsequent section on the importance of social feedback for role-enactment.) On a broader level, the person must also take into account the expectations of the cultural group to which he belongs, or what Mead (1934) called the "generalized other." When a person responds in a manner that conforms to the expectations of the generalized other, that is, when he construes his own behavior as others might construe it, then he understands the meaning of the role he is making.

The above account is incomplete in an important respect, as an analogy with a drama may illustrate. A drama is not simply a set of individual roles intertwined in a certain fashion. The drama also has a plot, and a plot is different (but not more) than the sum of individual roles. In order to perform a role adequately, an actor must not only know his own part, and the parts of others, but he must also understand how the various roles relate to the plot (and subplots) of the play.

In the case of social roles, the plot is the cultural system. This means that the emotions can only be fully understood as part of the culture as a whole. Of course, such understanding is seldom conscious on the part of individuals. A person understands most social roles in much the same way that he understands linguistic rules—on an intuitive rather than an intellectual level. One task for theories of emotion is to make such intuitive understandings explicit.

Monitoring the Performance

Earlier I suggested that the experience of emotion is basically an interpretation of one's own behavior. Such an interpretation has two aspects: (a) understanding the meaning of the emotional role and (b) monitoring behavior in light of that understanding. The first aspect was discussed above, and we may now turn to the second.

Two orders or kinds of monitoring may be distinguished (see Harré & Secord, 1972). All behavior is controlled and corrected by innumerable feedback loops, or what may be called "first-order" monitoring. In lower animals, first-order monitoring provides the stuff of consciousness; among humans, the conscious aspects of first-order monitoring correspond roughly to what phenomenological psychologists have called "prereflective" or "lived" experience. However, as a result of the same cognitive capacities that are reflected in language, humans also are able to reflect upon and conceptualize their lived experiences. Such "reflective experience" (in phenomenological terminology) is the product of "second-order" monitoring.

The distinction between first-order monitoring (prereflective experience) and second-order monitoring (reflective experience) can be illustrated by the following example. Consider a music critic at a symphony. He may become completely absorbed in the experience. But subsequently, when writing about the experience, he must analyze the performance, relate it to other performances of the same work that he has heard before, etc. In the latter case, the critic is reflecting upon his original experience. The reflection in this example is retrospective, but that is not a necessary feature of reflective experience. Typically, a music critic analyzes a performance while listening to it; that is, he reflects upon his experience as it occurs.

Having drawn the distinction between prereflective and reflective experience for analytic purposes, an important qualification must immediately be added. Completely prereflective experience is a myth, at least on the human level. All experience is filtered, organized, and given meaning by the categories of reflective thought. Thus, continuing with the above illustration, a music critic listening to a new performance can never completely disregard his past learning and ways of thought, no matter how hard he tries to discard the role of critic and how engrossing he finds the experience to be. In fact, were it not for well-established categories of thought, he probably would not find the experience engrossing at all.

The emotions are often considered to be the epitome of prereflective or lived experience, as though they were the product of first-order monitoring only. But that is not the case. Emotional experiences are reflective, the product of second-order monitoring. Moreover, the categories of reflective thought that give an emotional experience its meaning are based on a person's understanding of the emotional role as discussed above.

Involvement in Emotional Roles

The emotions do not occur in an all-or-none fashion. Rather, emotional episodes can range along a continuum from relatively mild to highly intense. From a role-theoretical point of view, this continuum can be analyzed in terms of involvement (see Sarbin & Coe, 1972). As points of reference, I will describe briefly three levels of involvement in emotional roles. I will then examine some of the personal and situational factors that help determine such involvement.

Low Involvement   At the lowest level of involvement, enactment of an emotional role is largely a formality. An example is the philanderer who falls in love with nearly every woman he meets or the teacher who scolds a child for being naughty while inwardly laughing at the child's antics. The most common expression of emotion at this level is a simple verbal statement: "It's all right, I love you"; "Don't do it again, it makes me angry"; "I am sorry to hear of your misfortune"; and so forth. Such statements are not necessarily insincere just because they lack a great deal of personal involvement. They are generally appropriate to the situation and sufficient to achieve the desired end. In fact, if a person becomes too involved in an emotional role when the situation does not call for it, he is liable to be considered insincere or "affected."

Medium Involvement As involvement in an emotional role increases, physiological arousal, expressive reactions, etc., are called into play. Feedback from such organic responses adds greatly to the feeling tone of the experience. Indeed, following William James's (1890) famous formulation, many theorists have considered organic feedback as a necessary condition for the experience of emotion. It is therefore worth emphasizing that such feedback is subject to second-order monitoring as described above, and it is the monitoring that determines the quality of experience, not the feedback per se. In fact, the mere belief that one is physiologically aroused may greatly facilitate involvement in an emotional role (see Nisbett & Valins, 1971). The importance of organic involvement is thus due as much to its symbolic significance as to direct physiological feedback.[1] This perhaps explains why people often try to work themselves into a state of physiological arousal when emotional. For example, a lover may engage in a variety of behaviors in order to stoke the fires of his passion; an injured person may brood about the provocation until his anger is at just the right pitch for revenge; and the bereaved may seek attention by wallowing in his grief. It is as though, without organic involvement, the emotional response will not be experienced as convincing—either by oneself or by others.

High Involvement At the highest level of involvement, the person may become so engrossed

in the emotional role that he no longer seems in control of his own behavior. The dictates of the role are paramount. After the episode the person may claim that he did not know what he was doing, or that he was not himself. When evaluating responses at this level of involvement, it must be remembered that it is part of the meaning of emotion to be "overcome," "gripped," "seized," etc. This meaning helps determine not only the kind of behavior that will be exhibited, but also how the response will be experienced.

Low Involvement and the Passivity of Emotion
The definition of emotion offered earlier stipulated that emotional roles be interpreted as passions rather than as actions. It is easy to see how this definition applies to high levels of emotional involvement. But how can a response at a low level of involvement be interpreted as a passion? At this level the individual does not experience any loss of control, and hence the response would seem to belong to the category of actions, not passions.

There are two reasons why a response at a low level of involvement might be interpreted as a passion rather than as an action. First, the more extreme occurrences of a response often determine how more mild occurrences are interpreted. For example, a violent attack on one occasion helps determine how a mild threat will be interpreted on other occasions. In other words, the meaning of emotional responses at a low level of involvement is determined, in part, by the knowledge that, under different circumstances, involvement in the role might be much greater.

To illustrate a second reason why a response at a low level of involvement might be interpreted as a passion rather than as an action, consider the following example. If I tell my sweetheart that I love her, I may feel quite insulted if she interprets the remark as premeditated or deliberate, no matter how unpassionate I happen to be at the moment. The remark is meant to be interpreted as part of an emotional syndrome, which implies a degree of commitment and sin-

---

[1] The symbolism associated with physiological arousal—especially visceral reactions—not only influences the personal experience (interpretation) of emotional responses, but it also has had a profound influence on scientific theories of emotion. For a historical review of this issue, see Averill (1974).

cerity that is often lacking in more deliberate ("calculated") responses. Another example of the same principle: If I reprimand a friend for behavior I disapprove of, and if the reprimand turns out to be hurtful, I may attribute my remark to anger, thus abnegating responsibility; on the other hand, if the reprimand turns out to be helpful, I may interpret the response as an action, thus assuming credit for being so honest and forthright.

As these examples illustrate, the actual behavior exhibited (thoughts, remarks, etc.) represents only one factor contributing to the interpretation of a response as a passion. The other factor, as explained earlier, involves an understanding of the relevant emotional role. When a person interprets a perfunctory remark, say, as the manifestation of an emotion, he is asking that the remark be understood and judged by standards that apply to emotional reactions and not by standards that apply to deliberate, rational acts. These standards have to do with such matters as the degree of commitment and the assignment of responsibility, among other things.

There are a number of factors that influence how an emotional role will be enacted. Among these are such personal variables as the motivation, prior experience, and capacity of the actor, and such situational variables as the physical and social settings in which the response occurs.

Limitations of a Role-Theoretical Approach

I have tried to illustrate how the emotions might be analyzed in terms of social roles. Much more could be said along these lines, of course, but space does not allow a more detailed analysis. I will therefore conclude the section with a few observations on the limits of such an approach.

To begin with, the assertion that emotions are transitory social roles is a metaphorical way of speaking. The concept of a role has its primary application in stage productions. Shakespeare observed that "all the world's a stage," and role-theory is basically a working out of the implications of that metaphor. The role-metaphor is least strained when applied to professional occupations and other formalized behavior patterns. When applied to highly personal experiences, such as emotional reactions, it might seem that the role-metaphor is being stretched beyond meaningful limits. If the emotions can be conceptualized as social roles, is there any kind of behavior that cannot be so regarded? Probably not! As Goffman (1959) has equipped, "All the world is not of course, a stage, but the crucial ways in which it isn't are not easy to specify" (p. 72).

If one cannot specify the ways in which some behavior does *not* conform to a role, then the entire analysis becomes a mere play on words; it allows neither proof nor disproof. The issue, however, is not whether the emotions are *really* social roles; the issue is, rather, whether the emotions can be fruitfully viewed from this perspective. I believe they can be. At the very minimum, a role-analysis forces us to consider the meaning (or functional significance) of the emotions within a social context.

Another limitation of a role-analysis is that it does not deal directly with some of the major problems that must be addressed by a theory of emotion. This is particularly true with regard to mechanisms (cognitive and physiological) that help mediate emotional reactions. Social roles represent functional units within a social system; they do not refer to psychological states as such. To be of psychological interest, the social role must be enacted. How are norms represented cognitively? And by what mechanism does the interpretation of a social role as a passion lead to the experience of being "overcome" by emotion?

The point that I now wish to emphasize is that a role-analysis can never be sufficient *by itself* to account for emotional behavior. But this is true of any approach that is limited to a single level of analysis, whether biological, psychological, or social.

Finally, it must also be recognized that a role-analysis is more appropriate to some emotions than to others. Startle, for example, does not lend itself to an analysis as a social role. And, on a more complex level, it would be fatuous to claim that a person who becomes frightened upon meeting the proverbial bear in the woods is enacting a role. However, this limitation may not be as serious as it at first appears. Startle might better be considered a reflex than an emotion, and most "natural" fears (e.g., of falling, and even of bears in the woods) are not very representative of emotions in general. Costello (1976) has posed the issue as follows: "Clear-cut events in the environment may produce what look like emotional behaviors such as fear and rage. But are these emotions in the same sense that we usually use the term?" (p. 14). He answers in the negative, and I largely agree. To repeat what was stated earlier, emotions as we know them are the product of reflective experience. The person who meets a bear while alone in the woods must improvise and interpret his reactions according to categories of thought (cognitive systems) acquired during socialization; and it is such improvisation and interpretation that allows the response properly to be called fear.

In summary, a role-analysis capitalizes on metaphor and hence is difficult to prove or disprove; it is largely silent with regard to intervening psychological mechanisms; and it is more appropriate to some emotions than to others. Because of these limitations, I have defined emotions as syndromes as well as transitory social roles. Of course, the conception of emotions as syndromes is also somewhat metaphorical, since the notion of a syndrome has its primary application elsewhere (e.g., in medicine). The syndrome metaphor has the advantage of being somewhat more neutral and hence is less likely to lead to polemical argument than the role-metaphor. Nevertheless, I want to emphasize that these two metaphors are in no way incompatible. Emotional roles are socially constituted syndromes. Moreover, in spite of its limitations, the role-metaphor has a major advantage; namely, it serves as a constant reminder that emotions are social constructions and not just biological givens.

CONCLUDING OBSERVATIONS

I have defined emotions as "transitory social roles." I am not entirely satisfied with this definition, for it is based on metaphor. However, many psychologists may feel uncomfortable with the role-concept for another reason; namely, it implies that the emotions cannot be explained in strictly psychological or physiological terms. (Ironically, psychologists do not feel uncomfortable about the use of physiological metaphors— "conceptual nervous systems"—in the explanation of emotional behavior.) Concepts at the social level of analysis seem to carry a kind of "excess meaning" that is especially troublesome to psychologists. But is meaning "excessive" simply because it is not reducible to psychological or physiological terms? My answer to this question is, obviously, no. I would maintain that the meaning and significance of emotional syndromes can be fully understood only on the social level of analysis.

By this last statement, I am not suggesting that a social level of analysis is *sufficient* for an understanding of the emotions, only that it is *necessary*. But even this modest suggestion often meets with objection. Two of the reasons for objection deserve brief comment. First, the role-concept may make emotional reactions appear *too* meaningful or functionally significant. The parent who becomes angry at a child for spilling milk and the couple who fall romantically in love are not responding *in order to* fulfill some social obligation. Second, a role-concept, with its emphasis on the normative aspects of behavior, seems to ignore the abnormal and often harmful aspects of emotional behavior. The person who commits a crime of passion, the phobic who cannot leave the house, or the jealous husband who destroys his marriage—the behavior of such people is not explicable simply by reference to social norms.

With regard to the first objection, it is true that most persons do not become emotional in order to fulfill some social obligation. But a role-analysis is no more objectionable in this respect than is an analysis in terms of biologically based adaptive patterns. For example, two animals—or people—do not usually mate in order to produce offspring, and any particular act of mating may have no such effect. Nevertheless, the net result of mating by enough couples, a sufficient number of times, is reproduction of the species. Analogously, any specific episode of anger, love, fear, hope, pride, etc., may meet no social need. But if on the average, or over the long run, such emotional syndromes conform to social norms, then their net result will be functional within the social system.

With regard to the second objection, abnormal emotional reactions represent deviations from social norms. In general, three types of deviations may occur: (a) The emotion may be "flat," or fall short of social expectations; (b) the emotion may be exaggerated, or exceed social expectations; and (c) the emotion may be unsuited, as when a person laughs at a funeral, becomes angry at a favor, etc. The reasons for such deviation in emotional behavior are to be found in the motives, prior experience, and capacities of the individual, as well as in the immediate situation (e.g., conflicting demands and/or secondary gains). In this sense, the explanation of deviant emotional behavior is not fundamentally different from the explanation of normal emotional syndromes. The focus of attention is, however, different in each case. In the explanation of normal emotional syndromes, the focus is on commonalities (e.g., social norms), and the factors that contribute to individual differences are treated as background. In the explanation of emotional deviations, this figure-ground relationship must be reversed, and the factors that contribute to individual differences must become the focus of attention.

To summarize, then, emotional syndromes are among the roles societies create, and individuals enact, albeit with varying degrees of proficiency and fidelity. Often, an emotional role is built upon, or incorporates elements from, one or more biological systems of behavior. But the meaning of the emotion—its functional significance—is to be found primarily within the sociocultural system. The emotions are not remnants of previously serviceable habits, as Darwin maintained. Rather, they are presently serviceable, and one of the tasks of theory is to shed light on the functions that emotional syndromes now serve.

Attraction and Love

Physical Attractiveness and Dating Choice: A Test of the Matching Hypothesis

Ellen Berscheid, Karen K. Dion, Elaine Walster (Hatfield), and G. William Walster (1971)

Who do you like, and why? Who do you love, and why? These are questions that have concerned humans far beyond the relatively short history of social psychology. Songs, books, movies, even advice columns center on these affairs of the heart, which Averill (Reading 15) and others might term "affairs of the mind" or "affairs of the culture."

Many of our folk sayings display conflicting assumptions about attraction and love. Does absence make the heart grow fonder? Or is it out of sight, out of mind? Do birds of a feather flock together? Or do opposites attract? Can you love someone without commitment? Or do love and marriage go together like the proverbial horse and carriage? These are valid questions that require complex answers. The following articles provide a representative sample of the work done by social psychologists in the area of attraction and love.

This article is a classic paper exploring both the *matching hypothesis* for romantic affiliations and the importance of physical attractiveness in developing relationships. As part of a series of studies on the matching hypothesis, the two studies reported here attempt to make sense of previous results that were inconclusive. To do so, the researchers make some friendly amendments to their own theory that are more successful in predicting people's behavior. They continue to think through the issues, and you will see in the discussion section how theory evolves based on results. Although the character of dating has changed very much since the early 1970s, many of the social psychological principles derived by Berscheid and her colleagues still seem to hold for developing and continuing personal relationships.

Abstract

Previous studies have failed to find support for the hypothesis, derived from Level of Aspiration Theory, that individuals chose to date those whose "social desirability" level is similar to their own. In the present experiments, which were designed to test the matching hypothesis, the salience of possible rejection by the dating choice was varied. Both experiments found support for the principle of matching in social choice. This support was obtained, however, not just under conditions in which rejection was presumably salient but for all conditions of choice. This and additional findings were discussed.

Several investigators have speculated about the role that physical attractiveness may play in the process of romantic attraction (e.g., de Jong, 1952; Elder, 1969). Of particular interest has been whether or not people tend to "pair-off" with individuals of their own physical attractiveness level. That a positive relationship should exist between the physical attractiveness of the seeker and that of the sought-after was hypothesized by Walster, Aronson, Abrahams, and Rottman (1966). Deriving their hypotheses from Level of Aspiration Theory (see Lewin, Dembo, Festinger, and Sears, 1944), they predicted that an individual will choose a date of approximately his own level of social desirability when making a *realistic* social choice. Realistic social choices, according to LA Theory, are influenced not only by the objective desirability of the choice alternative, but by the individual's perception of the *probability* of attaining that goal. One's social desirability (which includes one's assessment of his own physical attractiveness) should influence one's perception of the probability of attaining any particular social object. When making realistic choices, then, one should choose romantic partners of approximately his own level of physical attractiveness.

The Walster et al. (1966) experiment, conducted in a computer dating setting, did not support the matching hypothesis. An individual's own level of physical attractiveness affected neither his liking for his or her date nor his tendency to ask out the date a second time. Everyone, regardless of his own degree of physical attractiveness, liked best and most often asked out the extremely attractive dates. Unattractive Ss were aware that the extremely attractive dates did not like them as much as did dates more similar in appearance, but this did not affect their preferences or behavior. Other experimenters have also reported failures to support the matching hypothesis (i.e., Brislin and Lewis, 1968; Walster, 1970). Support for the matching principle is available only in an unpublished study by Kiesler and Baral (1966).

The matching hypothesis seems reasonable, however, and several attempts have been made to reconcile its plausibility with the data which has failed to support it.

1. It has been proposed that individuals begin to pair up on the basis of social desirability only after extensive experience with a specific group of potential dates.[1] It has been argued that initially everyone will approach the most socially desirable dates possible. After a time, the most desirable couples select each other and thus eliminate themselves from the "dating market." Matching then occurs only when an individual realizes that time is running out and that he must settle for a person of moderate attractiveness. Thus, it has been argued that the matching hypothesis is more likely to be demonstrated with older Ss, and

with Ss who have known each other for some time, than with the 18-year old strangers used in the Walster et al. (1966) study.

2. Other attempts at reconciliation have focused upon the lack of salience of social *rejection* in the computer dance situation. According to LA Theory, goal-setting is influenced by the valence of possible failure to the individual. An individual who has little or no fear of failure should choose a much more difficult goal than an individual for whom the negative valence of failure is very great.

Fear of failure may arise from personality factors. Thus, it has been suggested that only certain personality types—namely, those with high rejection fears—will operate on the matching principle. Situational factors may also heighten or minimize fear of failure. If the probability of failure is zero in a situation, individuals would have no reason to operate on the matching principle. People placed in circumstances where the possibility of rejection is especially salient, embarrassing, or costly, however, should be especially prone to show evidence of matching.

It has been argued that the Walster et al. (1966) setting minimized the negative valence of possible failure. The subjects were incoming freshmen, the school year had just started, and a possible rejection by a date may not have been perceived to be as unpleasant as it would have been later in the year when social pressure to date and awareness of social restrictions would have increased. In addition, it may have been unusually difficult for incoming freshmen to assess their probability of failure. Although they undoubtedly had an excellent idea as to where they stood in a high school "dating market," the freshmen had virtually no information as to their ranking in the college dating market since they had only been at college 1 week. Both these factors may have minimized subjects' fear of rejection and caused everyone to set higher and

---

[1] Walster et al. defined "social desirability" as "The sum of an individual's social assets, weighted by *importance and salience* for others." Social assets such as physical attractiveness, popularity, personableness, and material resources were presumed to be important factors in determining one's social desirability level.

more undifferentiated levels of aspiration than they normally would.

3. Others have argued that individuals in the computer dance setting were choosing dates under *idealistic* rather than *realistic* choice conditions. According to LA Theory, idealistic choices are completely determined by the desirability of the choice alternative. They represent what the individual *wishes* he could get, while realistic choices represent what the individual *expects* to get and, therefore, what it is worthwhile to attempt to get. Because dates for the Walster et al. (1966) computer dance were assigned, individuals were not forced to consider their own attractiveness in initially deciding who to attempt to date. Thus, some individuals were probably able to obtain their ideal goal of a very attractive date even though such an attainment might have been impossible in their actual social life. Perhaps those who achieved their ideal goal showed more interest in *retaining* it than they would have shown in trying to *attain* it initially.

The following two experiments, independently conceived and conducted, tested the matching hypothesis under conditions designed to emphasize or de-emphasize the possibility of rejection by the object of dating choice. It was hypothesized that the matching hypothesis be supported under conditions of *realistic* choice, or when possible rejection by the object of choice was emphasized. Little support for the hypothesis was expected under conditions of *idealistic* choice, or conditions under which a date with the object of choice was guaranteed.

EXPERIMENT I: THE WALSTER-WALSTER EXPERIMENT (1969)

This experiment tested the hypothesis that the principle of matching would operate in a computer dance setting if the probability and penalties of rejection were increased. Thus, the original Walster et al. (1966) experiment was

repeated with slight modifications in which the probability of rejection was increased for some Ss and minimized for others.

As in the original experiment, the physical attractiveness and personality of each subject was assessed. In this experiment, however, Ss were asked to specify exactly the kind of date they would prefer. They could specify the level of physical attractiveness, personality, popularity, etc., of their prospective date. In one set of conditions the possibility of rejection by dating choice was made very salient and the negative consequences of the date's rejection of them were emphasized. In another set of conditions, the possibility of rejection was minimized. An attempt was made to make individuals confident that whichever date they chose would be happy to date them. It was predicted that the matching principle would operate most strongly in the conditions in which rejection was made salient and least strongly, or not at all, in the conditions in which the probability of rejection was minimized.

Method

Subjects* Advertisements were circulated on the University of Minnesota campus for a "Computer Matching Dance." From a large number of freshmen and sophomores purchasing tickets to the dance, a subsample of 177 males and 170 females were randomly selected to participate in the study.

Procedure At the time tickets were purchased, S's level of physical attractiveness was assessed. Four student accomplices rated S's physical attractiveness on a nine-point scale, ranging from 0 "Extremely Unattractive," to 8 "Extremely Attractive." These ratings served as our indicant of S's level of social desirability.

> After purchasing their tickets, Ss filled out a questionnaire designed to assess whether physical attractiveness was positively correlated with other

---

Editors' note: Subjects are abbreviated as Ss throughout this reading.

indicants of social desirability, as Walster et al. had shown it to be. Subjects were requested to give estimates of (1) their intelligence, (2) the degree of consideration they typically showed for others, (3) their level of physical attractiveness, (4) their popularity with the opposite sex, (5) the extent to which they had an outgoing personality, (6) the "goodness" of their personality as viewed by others of the same sex, (7) the "goodness" of personality as viewed by others of the opposite sex, (8) the degree of nervousness typically felt on dates, (9) their ease of obtaining exceptionally attractive dates, (10) the frequency of dates in the past year, and (11) the number of people they had dated. Each *S*'s answers to questions 1, 3, 4, 6, 7, 8, and 9 were summed to form an index of *S*'s Perceived Social Desirability.

After completing the above questionnaire, Rosenfeld's (1964) Fear of Rejection Scale was administered to permit later assessment of the *S*'s chronic fear of rejection level.

When the questionnaires had been completed, *S*s were directed to a nearby room where *E* explained that they had been randomly selected to participate in a special experimental program. It was in the presentation of this program that the possibility of rejection was made salient for High Probability of Rejection (High POR) *S*s and minimized Low Probability of Rejection (Low POR) *S*s.

High POR *S*s were told that a random sample of students (*O*s) who had agreed to participate in a study of computer matched dating had been obtained. These *O*s presumably had been told that, if they wished, they could change their minds about participating after meeting their tentatively assigned date. *E* said that a special meeting would be set up before the computer dance so that each *O* could meet the date assigned to him. After the brief get-together, *O* would decide whether or not he or she wished to date *S*. *S*s were told that, so far, approximately 50% of the *O*s had refused to date their computer matches after meeting them. *E* added that because of scheduling difficulties, if *O* decided that she did not wish to date *S*, it would be impossible to give *S* another se-

lection for the dance. An appointment the next day was then arranged so that *S* could meet the date assigned to him and she could decide whether or not to date him.

As in the High POR condition, Low POR *S*s were told that a random sample of *O*s had agreed to participate in the study. Low POR *S*s were told, however, that *O*s had been informed that results of the computer study would be of little value if everyone felt free to change his mind about participating after he had been matched with a partner. Therefore, as a condition of participating in the study, all *O*s had agreed to attend the computer dance with whichever partner was assigned to them. Again an appointment was then arranged with Low POR *S*s for the next day. These *S*s, however, were merely to pick up the name and address of their assigned date.

Interview data indicated that all *S*s understood the procedure.

After the high or low fear of rejection manipulation had been performed,

*S*s were requested to specify the characteristics that they desired in a date. All *S*s were told that *E* had a very large pool of *O*s and could, therefore, guarantee finding an *O* who possessed almost any combination of traits the *S* wished. Each *S* was then asked to specify on a questionnaire how intelligent, considerate, physically attractive, popular, and reserved or outgoing in personality he wished his date to be.

Choices were indicated on a nine-point scale ranging from 0 (indicating that it was unnecessary that *O* possess any of the quality in question) to 8 (indicating that it was necessary that *O* possess a high degree of the quality). Popularity and physical attractiveness specifications were summed to form an index of the level of social desirability each *S* requested in his date (SD Index).

Finally, *S*s were asked to rank according to importance, ten characteristics one could wish a date to have. These were age, height, race, religion, year in college, intelligence, considerateness, physical attractiveness, popularity, and personality.

Results

Test of Hypotheses   It will be recalled that we predicted that the matching principle would operate more strongly in the high POR condition than in the low POR condition. Thus, we expected to secure a Physical Attractiveness × Probability of Rejection interaction. This expectation was not confirmed (Interaction $F = .21$, $df = 3, 331$). Rather, it is evident that the more physically attractive the S, the more socially desirable a date he requested, regardless of whether or not the possibility of rejection had been minimized or heightened. Attractive Ss chose more physically attractive dates ($F = 6.02$, $p < .001$) and more popular dates ($F = 7.17$, $p < .001$), and thus dates higher on the Social Desirability Index ($F = 8.56$, $p < .001$) than did unattractive Ss. It appears that subjects in this experiment were operating on the matching principle, and operating on this principle to the same extent in both conditions.

Looking at some of the other requests made in dates, there is some evidence that physically attractive Ss requested more outgoing dates than did those who were physically unattractive ($F = 3.34, p < .05$). It is interesting, how-

ever, that there appeared to be no difference in preference in the level of intelligence attractive and unattractive Ss wished to have in their dates ($F = 1.06$, $p = .37$), nor a difference in the extent to which they wished their dates to be considerate ($F = .18$, $p = .91$).

The above results, then, while they show definite evidence of matching, show no evidence that the situational manipulation of heightening or minimizing fear of rejection had any effect upon the level of social desirability requested in a date.

One might expect the matching principle to operate more strongly with individuals who are typically concerned about the possibility of rejection than with individuals less concerned with rejection. It will be recalled that Ss completed Rosenfeld's (1964) Fear of Rejection Scale. Subjects were divided into three groups on the basis of their scores on this test. Subjects scoring from 1 to 29 were classified as low in fear of rejection. Those scoring from 30 to 40 were classified as medium in fear of rejection, and those scoring from 41 to 74 were classified as being high in fear of rejection.

An analysis of the effect of level of physical attractiveness and fear of rejection (as assessed

---

TABLE 1

EFFECT OF PROBABILITY OF REJECTION ON CHOICE OF ROMANTIC PARTNERS

		Requirements in Date	
Probability of rejection:	N	Physical attractiveness	Popularity
Low			
Very unattractive Ss	45	6.27	5.44
Fairly unattractive Ss	53	6.55	5.72
Fairly attractive Ss	55	6.58	5.95
Very attractive Ss	46	6.78	5.98
High			
Very unattractive Ss	46	6.24	5.37
Fairly unattractive Ss	29	6.59	5.79
Fairly attractive Ss	42	6.62	5.98
Very attractive Ss	31	6.90	6.16

by Rosenfeld's scale) upon dating choice indicates that attractiveness and fear of rejection do not interact in affecting the social desirability of S's dating choices (Interaction $F = 1.47$, $df = 6$, 323).

Additional Analyses

1. Although males and females did not differ on the Social Desirability (physical attractiveness plus popularity) they wish in a date ($F = 3.30$, $df = 1, 331$, $p = .07$), several sex differences in preferences are evident. Specifically, females request more intelligent dates ($F = 21.85$, $p < .001$), more considerate dates ($F = 28.38$, $p < .001$), and more outgoing dates ($F = 23.68$, $p < .001$) than do males. There is also a slight, but nonsignificant, tendency for females to request more popular dates than males ($F = 3.33$, $p = .07$). On the other hand, males request that their dates possess more physical attractiveness than do females ($F = 29.20$, $p < .001$).
2. It was expected that, as in the Walster et al. (1966) experiment, each S's level of physical attractiveness as judged by the student accomplices would correlate positively with the extent to which the S perceived that he possessed other social assets. This expectation was confirmed. The more physically attractive an individual was, the higher he rated himself on the Perceived Social Desirability index ($F = 9.64$, $p < .001$). When we examine the individual items making up the index, we find that physically attractive individuals judge themselves to be more physically attractive ($F = 11.15$, $p < .001$), more popular ($F = 13.24$, $p < .001$), as having a better personality, both when judged by the opposite sex ($F = 3.89$, $p < .001$) and when judged by the same sex ($F = 2.96$, $p < .05$), and more able to get dates ($F = 11.92$, $p < .001$) than do unattractive individuals. In addition, attractive Ss report themselves as having had more dates

($F = 18.62$, $p < .001$), with more individuals ($F = 7.94$, $p < .001$) than do unattractive Ss.

EXPERIMENT II: THE BERSCHEID-DION EXPERIMENT

Again, this experiment tested the hypothesis that the matching principle would operate more strongly under realistic conditions of dating choice, or conditions in which there was a possibility that S would be rejected by the person of his choice, than under idealistic choice conditions in which a date with the object of a choice was guaranteed.

To test this hypothesis the physical attractiveness of all Ss was assessed as part of a "study of undergraduate dating." Each S was later asked to choose from among six photographs of opposite-sex peers, also presumably participating in the study, the person with whom they would actually like to go out with on a date. The six photographs had previously been rated in attractiveness by undergraduate student judges and varied from attractive to unattractive. We expected that Ss making choices under realistic conditions would choose dates similar to themselves in attractiveness, while Ss making choices under idealistic conditions would uniformly choose attractive dates.

Several studies have suggested that physical attractiveness is a more important component of a woman's social desirability than it is of a man's (e.g., Coombs & Kenkel, 1966). To test the hypothesis that matching on the basis of physical attractiveness is more pronounced for female Ss than for male Ss, both male and female Ss were asked to participate in the study.

It was predicted, then, that our 2 × 2 × 2 design (Attractiveness of S × Condition of Choice × Sex of S) would yield a three-way interaction of the nature described above.

Subjects

One hundred thirteen University of Minnesota undergraduates who were neither married, engaged, nor going steady participated in the study. All agreed to take part in an "undergraduate dating study" said to involve participation in two separate laboratory sessions, in return for $2.00.

Procedure

Session 1   At this first session, Ss were asked to fill out two questionnaires. The first questionnaire was entitled "Undergraduate Activity/ Attitude Survey." It was designed to secure some information about each S's dating experiences and his self-perceptions. The questionnaire included items concerning S's dating history and current dating status, and also requested S to estimate the relative importance of his own personal appearance, his personality, and his intelligence in attracting people of the same sex and of the opposite sex. In addition, each S rated his satisfaction with a number of his physical characteristics (e.g., chest, face, waist) and his satisfaction with several other personal characteristics (e.g., personality, creativeness, intelligence level). These last "Body-Cathexis" and "Self-Cathexis" scales were adapted from scales constructed by Secord and Jourard (1953). Subjects were assured that their replies to the "Activity/ Attitude" questionnaire would be treated in a confidential manner.

> When Ss had completed the first questionnaire, they were reminded that they had agreed to participate in a second session. They were informed that the procedure of the second session would vary for those participating in the study. Some students would simply be asked to tell the experimenters more about their dating attitudes, while others would be randomly selected to take part in an actual computer dating situation.
>
> Each S was asked to fill out a second questionnaire, which ostensibly was used in the event S was selected to go out on a computer date. The second dating questionnaire had to do principally with dating preferences. Ss were asked to indicate, for example, which extracurricular activities interested them most, what kinds of activities they pre-

ferred on dates, and what personal characteristics they preferred in dates (e.g., religion, height, etc.). Ss had been requested to bring, if possible, a yearbook picture of themselves to session 1. Whether they brought pictures of themselves or not, they were informed that since many Ss did not have a recent yearbook picture available, a photographer had been hired to take Polaroid snapshots. (A yearbook picture was requested to make plausible the subsequent presentation to Ss of six facsimiles of yearbook photos of potential dates.) Ss were then ushered into a room, posed by the photographer in a standard position, and a full-length picture was taken.

Session 2   All Ss were informed that they had been randomly selected to take part in the computer dating study. The information contained in their dating preference questionnaires ostensibly had been fed into a computer, and had yielded six dating possibilities. Ss were instructed that they would have an opportunity to choose from among the six potential dates the one they would most like to meet and date.

If Ss had been randomly assigned to the *Realistic* condition, he was further instructed that a date would be arranged only if his dating choice had reciprocated his choice. Male Ss, for example, were told:

> These girls have all seen your pictures, along with the pictures of other boys with whom they have been matched on the basis of the dating questionnaire. To insure the greatest compatability between people, a choice must be made by mutual consent. . . . If they do, we will arrange the date. In fairness to the other boys in the study, we can only give each boy one choice.

If S had been assigned to the *Idealistic* condition, it was made clear that he was guaranteed a date with anyone he chose:

> Since we felt that it would be difficult to give everyone a choice, we decided to have the boys choose whom they wanted to meet. As a condition for being in this part of the study, the girls have therefore agreed to go out with whoever picks

them from among their computer matches. After you decide, we will arrange a date with the girl you have chosen. In fairness to the boys taking part, we can only give each boy one choice.

The experimenter then took a set of six pictures from an envelope marked with Ss name and asked him to decide which one of the girls (or boys) he would like to meet. The set included photographs of two members of the opposite sex who were very physically attractive, two of medium attractiveness, and two who were physically unattractive.[2]

After making their choice Ss were then given a questionnaire checking their understanding of the experimental procedure, were thanked for their participation, paid the $2.00 which had been agreed upon, and debriefed.

Results and Discussion

Realistic-Idealistic Choice Manipulation   Only one S failed to understand the experimental instructions. He was therefore discarded, leaving $N = 112$ (56 males, 56 females) who correctly responded on the questionnaire designed to check understanding of the condition of choice.

Physical Attractiveness Ratings of Subjects   A rating of each S's general physical attractiveness was made on the basis of the Polaroid snapshots taken at Session 1. Four undergraduate judges, two males and two females, placed all female Ss and then all male Ss into two equal-frequency categories, physically "attractive" and "unattractive." The degree of

---

[2] The physical attractiveness rating of each of the pictures was determined in a preliminary study. One hundred Minnesota undergraduates rated 50 yearbook pictures of persons of the opposite sex with respect to physical attractiveness. The criteria for choosing the 12 pictures to be used experimentally were: (a) High inter-rater agreement as to the physical attractiveness of the stimulus (the average inter-rater correlation for all of the pictures was .70); (b) Pictures chosen to represent the very attractive category and very unattractive category were not at the very extreme ends of attractiveness.

inter-judge agreement on category placement of each picture determined, for purpose of this study, whether S was classified as "attractive" or "unattractive."

Dependent Variable   An index of the degree of physical attractiveness Ss preferred in their dates was constructed by giving Ss who chose one of the two most attractive persons pictured in the photographs as his dating choice a score of 3; Ss who chose an average person were assigned a score of 2; and those who chose an unattractive person were given a score of 1.

Test of Hypotheses   It will be recalled that our $2 \times 2 \times 2$ design (Attractiveness of $S \times$ Condition of Choice $\times$ Sex of S) was expected to yield a three-way interaction such that Ss in the Realistic condition would choose dates similar to themselves in attractiveness while Ss in the Idealistic conditions would uniformly choose attractive dates, and that the matching effect would be more pronounced for female Ss than for male Ss. The mean level of physical attractiveness of dates chosen in each of the groups is reported in Table 2.

It is evident that the expected three-way interaction was not obtained ($F = .25$, $df = 1$, 104), nor were any significant two-way interactions apparent.

Rather, a main effect on the attractiveness of S dimension was secured ($F = 6.46$, $df = 1, 104$, $p < .01$). Attractive Ss chose more attractive dates than did unattractive Ss.

The variation of condition of choice did not appear to significantly influence the extent of matching which occurred, ($F = 1.41$, $df = 1$, 104). Ss in this experiment, as in the Walster - Walster experiment, appear to have operated on the matching principle even under conditions of choice in which a date was guaranteed.

With respect to the third variable of interest, Sex of S, the means for the various groups reveal that while females tended to choose slightly less attractive dates than males, the impact upon dating choice of this variable failed to reach an

TABLE 2					
PHYSICAL ATTRACTIVENESS OF CHOSEN DATES[a]					
	Male		Females		
	Attractive	Unattractive	Attractive	Unattractive	Mean
Realistic choice condition	2.71	2.71	2.71	2.36	2.63
Idealist choice condition	2.93	2.64	2.93	2.50	2.75
Mean	2.82	2.68	2.82	2.43	

[a]$N = 14$ each cell; a mean of 3.00 is the maximum score possible.

acceptable level of statistical significance ($F = 1.41$, $df = 1$, 104).

Additional Analyses The questionnaires completed by Ss contained several items designed to permit us to explore the relationship between a person's physical attractiveness and other variables. We were especially interested in the relationship between a S's physical attractiveness as determined from his Polaroid photo, and his actual dating history. If the physical attractiveness ratings of the Polaroid photos truly reflect a S's social desirability, there should be a relationship between these physical attractiveness ratings and frequency of dating.

The physical attractiveness of female Ss appears to be strongly related to their actual dating popularity. Attractive females had more dates within the past year ($r = .61$), the past month ($r = .50$), and the past week ($r = .44$) than unattractive females. (The Pearson r's on all three dating indices are different from O at $p < .01$.) While there also appears to be a positive correspondence between dating frequency and physical attractiveness for male subjects (past year $r = .25$; month $r = .21$; week $r = .13$), none of the coefficients representing the relationship are significantly different from O. There is a significant difference between male and female coefficients on the first variable, number of dates in past year ($Z = 2.13$). The male-female differences on the other two

indices of dating frequency do not reach an acceptable level of confidence. (In both cases $Z = 1.65$, $p = .10$.)

The finding that physical attractiveness is more strongly related to the woman's dating frequency than to a man's seems intuitively reasonable and is compatible with the results of several studies which have examined the factors college students report to be important in making dating choices (e.g., Coombs and Kenkel, 1966; Williamson, 1966). These studies consistently show that males place more importance on physical attractiveness in making dating and mating choices than do females. The finding is also similar to that of Walster et al. (1966) who reported an r of .31 between physical attractiveness and dating popularity for men and an r of .46 for women. The difference between these r's with a reported N of 327 men and 327 women is significant at the .02 level of confidence ($Z = 2.31$).

The data gathered concerning the number of close friends of the same and opposite sex reported by Ss of varying attractiveness levels, is somewhat perplexing. There appears to be a relationship between a male's physical attractiveness and the number of close friends he reports. Not only do more physically attractive males have more close friends of the opposite sex ($r = .51$, $p < .01$) but they appear to have more same-sex friends ($r = .29$, $p < .05$). No such relationship between physical attractiveness and number of friendships exists for girls (same-sex $r = -.10$; opposite-sex $r = .21$).

It appears, then, that physical attractiveness is not to be related to dating frequency for men, but rather to general friendship popularity. The reverse seems to be true for women.

With respect to S's perceptions of the relative importance of their own physical appearance, intelligence, and personality in attracting members of the opposite sex, there is evidence that the more physically attractive the woman, the more likely she is to rank physical attractiveness as an important personal asset in attracting members of the opposite sex ($r = .38$, $p < .01$). While men show no evidence of a significant relationship between physical attractiveness and the importance they place on their own physical attractiveness as an asset in attracting the opposite sex ($r = .17$), there appears to be evidence that the more physically attractive a man, the less importance he places upon intelligence as an asset ($r = -.36$, $p < .01$).

We were also interested in the relationship between physical attractiveness and degree of satisfaction with physical and nonphysical characteristics of the self. It will be recalled that Ss completed questionnaries adapted from scales devised by Secord and Jourard (1953) to assess satisfaction with various physical characteristics (Body-Cathexis) and also with nonphysical personal characteristics, such as personality, intelligence, and happiness (Self-Cathexis). Physical attractiveness of Ss as judged by the Polaroid photos was not related to body-cathexis for either males ($r = .07$) or for females ($r = -.05$). Nor was physical attractiveness related to self-cathexis for either sex (male $r = -.03$; female $r = .16$). Previous findings by Secord and Jourard had led us to expect that there would be a correspondence between the degree to which Ss felt satisfaction with their physical characteristics and their degree of satisfaction with nonphysical characteristics. This expectation was confirmed only with female Ss ($r = .48$, $p < .01$). Men

did not show evidence of a significant relationship between self- and body- cathexis ($r = .23$). The difference between the coefficients of males and that of females is not significant.

SUMMARY AND CONCLUSIONS

Previous studies have failed to find support for the hypothesis that people in dating situations tend to pair off in terms of social desirability. It was thought that perhaps these failures to support the matching hypothesis were due to the inadvertent minimization of possibility of rejection by the object of dating choice. Thus, in both of the investigations reported here an attempt was made to vary the salience of the possibility of rejection by the date chosen. Both of the present investigations found support for the principle of matching in social choice. This support, however, was obtained not just under conditions in which rejection was presumably salient, but for all conditions of choice within the two studies. Since the two attempts to maximize probability of rejection did not seem to affect the extent to which matching was evident in dating choice, it seems that we must look elsewhere for an explanation of why previous studies failed to find support for the hypothesis, and, now, why the present experiments did.

One explanation seems most plausible for the obtained differences. Perhaps timing is extremely important in detecting operation of the matching principle. In each of the present experiments Ss had to decide how desirable a date they wished to approach. In Walster et al. (1966) and Brislin and Lewis (1968), Ss were assigned to interact with dates of varying levels of social desirability. After extensive interaction they were asked how desirable their date was and how much they wished to continue dating her. Dating choice in these studies was one of *maintaining* a social contact rather than one of attempting to *achieve* contact. It may be that the matching principle is a more potent determinant of how desirable a person one will be willing to approach than it is of how much another will be liked and approached again after initial contact.

Some additional evidence supports this notion. On their initial questionnaires, Ss in the Walster et al. experiment (1966) were asked how socially desirable they expected a "suitable" or "acceptable" date to be. The more attractive the S was, the more attractive, personable, and considerate he *expected* his date to be. Subjects were then given a chance to interact with real dates. After this point the operation of the matching principle could no longer be detected.

While the results of the present studies support the matching hypothesis, our attempts to discover factors which may affect the extent to which it will determine social choice failed. We expected that it would be a stronger determinant of choice when the possibility of rejection by the chosen person was salient than when a date with the chosen person was guaranteed. Two different situational manipulations of salience of rejection failed to show an effect upon matching. It could, of course, be argued that rejection in our supposedly idealistic choice condition was as salient to Ss as it was in our realistic choice conditions. It may have been that although a date was guaranteed in the idealistic conditions, Ss anticipated the prospect of a disgruntled date who would show her displeasure throughout the evening and this prospect influenced dating choice. It is clear, however, that Ss in the idealistic conditions would have more of a chance to bowl their dates over with their personalities or an enjoyable evening which might overcome the date's initial displeasure than would realistic condition Ss who could expect to be rejected before getting a foot in the door. If so, idealistic condition Ss should have evidenced less matching than realistic condition Ss. Another possible explanation of the failure of the possibility of rejection manipulation may be simply that realistic considerations in social choice are so ingrained that even under a "no strings" choice one's own physical attractiveness is still a strong influencing factor.

Our expectation of finding a personality difference in matching along the fear of rejection dimension was unconfirmed, as was our expectation that females would show more matching than males. Thus, although previous experiments had led us to believe that the matching phenomenon was probably fragile and that evidence of its operation could be discerned only under limited conditions, the present data suggest that matching, at least with respect to physical attractiveness, might operate under a fairly wide variety of conditions.

In sum, the results of the present studies indicate that attempts to interact with those of opposite-sex will be more frequent among those of approximately the same level of attractiveness. That physical attractiveness acts as a "gatekeeper" for interactions with members of the opposite sex is evident not only from the matching tendencies observed in these experiments, but also from the observed relationship between physical attractiveness and dating frequency. This relationship, which was especially strong for women, raises a number of questions. Concerning marital choice and satisfaction, for example, it would be interesting to know if physically attractive women use their range of opportunities for interaction with a variety of men to choose a mate who will be compatible along such dimensions as similarity of interests, values, and background or any of the factors which appear to lead to marital stability. Given a wider range of choice and more experience in interacting with members of the opposite sex, it seems logical that a wiser choice could be made.

It also would be interesting to know the relationship, if any, between physical attractiveness and various personality characteristics. Given the correlation between attractiveness and frequency of interaction with the opposite sex, it would be surprising if attractiveness were not related to various personality characteristics, especially those having to do with self-confidence, etc. While no self-cathexis items bore a relationship to physical attractiveness for men, some relationships were observed for females. Physically attractive women, as one might expect, report more satisfaction with their general popularity ($r = .39$), their leadership ability ($r = .39$), and their degree of self-consciousness ($r = .32$). They also report, however, more dissatisfaction with their degree of self-understanding ($r = .31$) than unattractive women do. Perhaps more sensitive scales could better explore the possible relationship between physical attractiveness and other personality characteristics, especially those which are likely to facilitate rewarding interactions.

In any event, the precise nature of the role physical attractiveness plays in interpersonal attraction, whether it is limited to opposite-sex attraction, whether its importance is limited to the college age group, its importance relative to other known variables in attraction such as attitudinal similarity, both initially and over time, is a matter for future research.

Sex Differences in Attributions for Friendly Behavior: Do Males Misperceive Females' Friendliness?

Antonia Abbey (1982)

The following article by Abbey suggests that there are sex differences in simple perceptions about others' motives, in this case friendliness and seduction. In this study, college-aged men perceived their interactions with college-aged women in more sexual terms than did the women. It seems that the friendly actions of women may be misinterpreted by men as indications of sexual interest on the part of the women, and Abbey's research following this 1982 study further supports this hypothesis (see Abbey, 1987; Abbey & Melby, 1986; Abbey, Cozzarelli, McLaughlin, & Harnish,

1987). The result is a cross-sex misunderstanding of the sort that confuses both parties. This type of attribution error may be a contributing factor in date rape and sexual violence (see also Reading 29).

This study also indicates the value of attribution theory in understanding a wide range of human behavior. If Abbey is right that men apply more of a sexually oriented perspective than women in their attempts to understand and organize social behavior, then what other implicit belief differences might exist between males and females? This question highlights for us, once again, the notion of nonconscious ideologies (Bem and Bem, 1970; see Reading 1) and the effects that our hidden assumptions may have on our behavior.*

Abstract

This investigation tested the hypothesis that friendliness from a member of the opposite sex might be misperceived as a sign of sexual interest. Previous

---

Editors' note: At this point, we as editors want to report on another attribution study that may be relevant to your own academic experiences at present. Wilson and Linville (1982) apply attribution theory to the real-world problem of improving one's grades. Poor academic performance or even dropping out of school are often accompanied by the personal belief that one is not smart enough or hard-working enough to succeed academically. Either way, the attribution being made is about one's self and/or ability. Wilson and Linville's attributional "intervention" provides another interpretation for students who are worried about their academic performance. Specifically, Wilson and Linville suggested to freshman that they view their academic problems as temporary and within their control. Those freshmen who learned that college students generally improve academically from the freshman to upperclass years had significantly lower dropout rates, significantly higher grade point averages, and scored significantly better on sample items on the GRE compared to freshmen not receiving information about academic improvement over time. Thus, this simple attribution of causes for poor grades appears to mediate future academic performance as measured by a variety of short-term and longer-term variables. Recognizing several possible alternative explanations, Wilson and Linville retested their hypotheses in two additional studies (1985) and found similar results. Thus, our own academic performance can sometimes be positively influenced by our attributions of unstable and temporary causes. As budding social psychologists, you may wish to generate hypotheses as to why this attribution might be successful.

research in the area of acquaintance and date rape suggests that males frequently misunderstand females' intentions. A laboratory experiment was conducted in which a male and female participated in a 5-minute conversation while a hidden male and female observed this interaction. The results indicate that there were sex differences in subjects' rating of the actors. Male actors and observers rated the female actor as being more promiscuous and seductive than female actors and observers rated her. Males were also more sexually attracted to the opposite-sex actor than females were. Furthermore, males also rated the male actor in a more sexualized fashion than females did. These results were interpreted as indicating that men are more likely to perceive the world in sexual terms and to make sexual judgments than women are. Males do seem to perceive friendliness from females as seduction, but this appears to be merely one manifestation of a broader male sexual orientation.

The research described in this article grew out of the observation that females' friendly behavior is frequently misperceived by males as flirtation. Males tend to impute sexual interest to females when it is not intended. For example, one evening the author and a few of her female friends shared a table at a crowded campus bar with two male strangers. During one of the band's breaks, they struck up a friendly conversation with their male table companions. It was soon apparent that their friendliness had been misperceived by these men as a sexual invitation, and they finally had to excuse themselves from the table to avoid an awkward scene. What had been intended as platonic friendliness had been perceived as sexual interest.

After discussions with several other women verified that this experience was not unique, the author began to consider several related, researchable issues. Do women similarly misjudge men's intentions or is this bias limited to men only? How frequently do these opposite-sex misunderstandings occur? What causes them and what circumstances elicit them?

Research on other subcultural groups indicates that intergroup misperceptions may be common. For example, La France and Mayo (1976, 1978a, 1978b) have examined racial differences in the interpretations of various nonverbal cues. They have found that black and white Americans frequently interpret the same nonverbal cues, such as a direct gaze, quite differently. For example, white listeners gaze at the speaker more than black listeners do. Consequently, interracial encounters may be cumbersome because the participants' signals for yielding the floor or ending the conversation may differ. Because neither individual realizes that their nonverbal vocabularies conflict, they are likely to mistakenly attribute the awkwardness of the conversation to the other's dislike of them.

Although similar research has not been conducted concerning opposite-sex misunderstandings, a great deal has been written about date and acquaintance rape that may be applicable. Although a simple verbal misunderstanding is in no way comparable to rape in either magnitude or consequences, the underlying process that produces these two events may be related. Several authors have described how our cultural beliefs about the dating situation might lead to sexual misunderstandings and, in the extreme case, rape (Bernard, 1969; Brodyaga, Gates, Singer, Tucker, & White, 1975; Medea & Thompson, 1974; Russell, 1975; Weis & Borges, 1973; Hendrick, 1976; Goodchilds, 1977). These authors argue that women are socialized to flirt and play "hard to get." Even when sexually attracted to a man, a woman is expected to say "no" to his sexual advances, at least at first. And, in a complementary fashion, men are taught to initiate all sexual encounters and to believe that women prefer lovers who are aggressive, forceful, and dominant.

According to this argument these social mores may cause men to unwittingly force sexual relations on their dates, mistaking their true lack of sexual interest for mere coyness. Date and acquaintance rape are prevalent. Researchers estimate that 48—58% of all reported rapes are committed by someone the victim knows (Amir, 1971; Kanin, 1957, 1967; Katz & Mazur, 1979; Kirkpatrick and Kanin, 1957). Kanin and Parcell (1977) found that 50.7% of the 292 female undergraduates they polled had experienced some level of sexual aggression on a date during the previous year. Of these, 23.8% involved forced intercourse (see also Krikpatrick and Kanin, 1957, and Kanin, 1967). After interviewing college males who had engaged in sexual aggression toward their dates, Kanin (1969) argues that

> The typical male enters into heterosexual interaction as an eager recipient of any subtle signs of sexual receptivity broadcasted by his female companion. In some instances, however, these signs are innocently emitted by a female naive in erotic communication. He perceives erotic encouragement, eagerly solicits further erotic concessions, encounters rebuff, and experiences bewilderment (pp. 18–19).

Although many authors have speculated about the causes of date rape, little research has been conducted in this area. One notable exception is an experiment designed by Hendrick (1976) to examine sex differences in perceptions of the opposite sex. Male and female subjects viewed a videotape of a 12-minute interaction between a male and a female confederate. The tape ended with the male asking the female for a date and her acceptance. Subjects were also provided with a hypothetical scenario in which the couple went up to the woman's apartment and sexual intercourse occurred although she had said ''no.''

The results yielded several interesting findings. Male subjects rated the female actor as more physically attractive and sexually promiscuous than did female subjects. Surprisingly, males also rated the male actor as more physically attractive, sexually promiscuous, and provocative than females did. Males were less likely than females to believe that the fe-

male had really meant no. In fact, males were more likely than females to state that even if the female actor had meant no, the occurrence of sexual intercourse was her fault. The external validity of these findings is limited by the artificiality of the situation the observers rated and by the fact that they were passively watching rather than actively engaging in the interaction. Nonetheless, these results provide fairly strong preliminary support for the hypothesis that men and women perceive each others' sexual intentions differently.

In sum, the available literature on date and acquaintance rape suggests that males are unable to distinguish females' friendly behavior from their seductive behavior because of the differential meaning that the relevant cues have for the two sexes. Men may have been socialized to view any form of friendly behavior from a woman as an indication of sexual interest.

In order to test empirically the hypothesis that men misperceive women's intentions, an experiment was designed in which a male and a female would interact with each other while another male and female would observe this interaction. Hence, unlike Hendrick's (1976) experiment in which subjects reacted to the behavior of confederates on a videotape, in this case half of the subjects were participants in the interaction. This paradigm also permits examination of both actors' reactions to their partners. If the results do indicate that males misperceive females' intentions, such results would be difficult to interpret without knowing if females similarly misperceive males' intentions.

The observers were included in the design to provide greater insight into this phenomenon. Although it was hypothesized that males are unable to distinguish female's friendly behavior from their seductive behavior because of the differential meaning that the relevant cues have for the two sexes, other explanations of this effect are tenable. For instance, it could be argued that males mistakenly perceive sexual interest in females for ego-enhancing motives; it makes them feel good to think that a woman is sexually attracted to them. However, if male observers as well as male actors perceive the female as being sexually attracted to the male actor, then this lends support to the notion of a general male bias. By comparing the male actors' ratings of the female actor to the male observers' ratings of her, one can assess the extent to which these ratings are due to ego-enhancing motives as opposed to a more general masculine orientation toward female behavior.

The inclusion of female observers provides additional information about the boundaries of this effect. Again, because it was proposed that the hypothesized effect is due to differences in sex role socialization, one would expect the female observers' ratings to be similar to the female actors' ratings and unlike the males' ratings. However, alternatively, one could argue that this phenomenon is due to some kind of actor-observer difference. It may be that all outsiders, regardless of sex, misperceive the female actors' intentions. By comparing the female observers' ratings to the male observers' ratings, we can test these competing explanations.

Although it was predicted that male subjects would misperceive the female actor, it was less clear as to how female subjects would rate the male actor. The evidence in the nonverbal-cues literature, which indicates that women are better at interpreting nonverbal cues than men are (Buck, Miller, & Caul, 1974; Hall, 1978; Rosenthal, Hall, DiMatteo, Rogers, & Archer, 1979), suggests that women may be capable of correctly distinguishing men's friendly behavior from their seductive behavior. However, the pervasiveness of the cultural myth that men are primarily interested in women for sexual reasons may lead one to predict that women may also mistake a man's friendly behavior as a sign of sexual interest. Therefore, no predictions were made as to how the male actor would be judged by the female subjects.

METHOD

Subjects

Subjects were 144 white Northwestern University undergraduates who received credit toward a course requirement of research participation.[1] Subjects were scheduled in groups of four such that none of the students scheduled for the same session knew each other. In all, 36 complete sessions were run (72 males, 72 females).

Procedure

Subjects reported to a large anteroom with five connecting cubicles. Subjects were reminded by the experimenter that the study concerned the acquaintance process and were told that the purpose of the experiment was to determine the ways in which the topic of conversation affects the smoothness of initial interactions. Pairs of subjects would each be assigned a different topic, which they would discuss for 5 minutes. Then they would fill out a questionnaire that would assess their opinion of the conversation. Finally, they would engage in a second conversation about a different topic either with the same or a different partner and fill out a second questionnaire. Subjects were told that the experimenter wanted a male and a female in each pair, and they drew pieces of paper to determine who would interact with whom. (Unbeknown to the subjects, this random draw was also used to determine their role assignment.) Although subjects were told by the experimenter that each pair would have a slightly different task, they were led to believe that both pairs would be engaging in

---

[1]It seemed unlikely that subjects would rate friendly behavior from opposite-sex individuals of a different race in the same manner as they would rate similar behavior from a member of the same race. Therefore, because it was desirable to have all four participants in a session be of the same race (and because the great majority of the students in the subject pool were white), the subject population was limited to white students.

conversations. This was done to keep the actors from correctly guessing that they were being observed.

After the draw the experimenter asked the subjects to fill out a brief questionnaire "before the actual study begins." Subjects were placed in individual cubicles to complete this questionnaire. They were given this questionnaire solely to provide the experimenter with the opportunity to give the observers their instructions. After waiting 3 minutes, the experiment placed both observers in the same room and explained their task to them. Then they were asked to wait quietly and avoid talking while the actors were prepared.

The experimenter then escorted the actors into the "conversation" room in which the one-way mirror through which the observers were watching was hidden by sheer pastel curtains. The actors were seated in chairs facing each other about 4 ft. (1.2 m) apart. They were instructed to talk for 5 minutes about their experiences of that year at Northwestern.

The experimenter immediately joined the observers and turned on a microphone that allowed them to hear the conversation. The observers had a clear view of the actors' profiles. After 5 minutes the experimenter turned off the microphone, reminded the observers to remain silent, and returned to the actors' room to stop the conversation. The experimenter gave the actors questionnaires containing the dependent measures and asked them to fill them out in their individual cubicles. Then the experimenter gave the observers their questionnaires and asked them to return to their original rooms to complete them. When all four subjects were finished, they were brought together in the center room and thoroughly debriefed.

Dependent Measures

After the conversation, subjects completed a questionnaire that asked them to evaluate the quality of the conversation (this was included in order to make the cover story more convincing) and their reactions to the male and female actors. First, subjects were asked to describe one actor's personality in an open-ended question. Then they rated that actor on a variety of trait terms using a 7-point Likert-type scale. Then they answered the same questions about the other actor.[2] The subjects were asked to base their ratings on how they thought the actor was "trying to behave" because according to the experimental hypothesis it is the target person's intentions that are misjudged. The key trait terms were the adjectives *flirtaious, seductive,* and *promiscuous;* these words were selected because they were thought to measure the construct "sexuality." Additional trait terms such as *considerate, interesting, likeable,* and *intelligent* were included to avoid alerting subjects to the true focus of the study. Other important dependent variables were subjects' responses to questions asking them if they would like to get to know the actors, if they were sexually attracted to the opposite-sex actor, if they would like to date him or her, and why or why not. The observers were also asked if they thought each of the actors was sexually attracted to and would like to date his or her partner and why or why not. Finally, the actors were asked to respond "yes" or "no" to a question asking them if they would like to interact with the same partner in the second half of the experiment.[3]

---

[2]The order in which observers completed these questions was counterbalanced so half of them rated the female actor first, whereas the other half rated the male actor first. The actors, however, always answered the questions about themselves. This was done because during pilot testing actors asked to rate themselves first complained that it was too difficult to do, whereas actors who were asked to rate their partner first did not raise any objections.

[3]Subjects were led to believe that two conversations would take place so that this behavioroid measure could be included. However, no significant differences were found; virtually all the actors preferred to interact with the same partner.

RESULTS[4]

Sex of Experimenter

Two male and two female experimenters conducted the study. The results of a $2 \times 2 \times 2$ (Sex of Subject $\times$ Role of Subject $\times$ Sex of Experimenter) analysis of variance indicated that the sex of experimenter did not have an effect on subjects' responses. Therefore, all further analyses were conducted by summing across this variable.

Sex Differences

As expected, there were no sex differences in subjects' ratings of the female actor's friendliness and these ratings were quite high (female $M = 6.0$; male $M = 5.7$). A multivariate analysis of variance combining subjects' ratings of the female actor on the three sexual adjectives—*flirtatious, seductive,* and *promiscuous*—into a Sexuality Index (interitem correlations ranged from .39 to .62, $p < .001$) indicated that there was a significant sex of subject effect for this variable, $F(3, 138) = 3.09$, $p < .03$. An examination of the univariate findings indicated that, as predicted, male subjects rated the female actor as being significantly more promiscuous than female subjects did, $F(1, 140) = 7.67, p < .01$ (see Table 1). Similarly, there was a marginal effect, $F(1, 140) = 2.98$, $p < .09$, for males to rate the female actor as being more seductive than did females. However, there were no sex differences

TABLE 1

MEAN SCORES FOR RATINGS OF THE FEMALE ACTOR ON THE SEXUALITY ITEMS AS A FUNCTION OF SEX OF SUBJECT

Ratings of female actor	Sex of subject		$p <$
	Male	Female	
Promiscuous	2.2	1.7	.01
Seductive	2.3	1.9	.09
Flirtatious	2.9	2.8	ns

in subjects' ratings of the female actor's flirtatiousness.

A multivariate analysis of variance combining actors' responses to the questions "Would you like to get to know your partner better?"; "Would you be interested in becoming friends with your partner?"; "Are you sexually attracted to your partner?"; and "Would you be interested in dating your partner?" into a Future Interaction Index for actors (interitem correlations ranged from .56 to .88, $p < .001$) yielded a significant sex-of-subject effect, $F(4, 67) = 2.83$, $p < .03$. Responses to the question asking the actors if they were sexually attracted to their partner indicated that the male actors were more sexually attracted to their partners than the female actors were, $F(1, 70) = 7.17$, $p < .01$ (male $M = 3.5$, female $M = 2.4$). None of the other univariate results were significant.

Also, a multivariate analysis of variance combining observers' responses to questions asking them how sexually attracted they were to the opposite-sex actor and how interested they were in dating her or him into a Sexual Attraction Index for observers ($r = .85$, $p < .001$) showed a significant effect for sex of subject, $F(2, 69) = 4.83$, $p < .01$, again indicating greater male interest than female interest. Univariate analyses indicated that the male observers were more sexually attracted

[4]Because of a concern that the actors might not act particularly friendly during their interaction, two conditions were added to the design; one in which the female actor was instructed to act friendly and one in which the male was instructed to act friendly. There was also a control group in which neither actor received any instructions. A $2 \times 2 \times 3$ (Sex of Subject $\times$ Role of Subject $\times$ Instruction Condition) analysis of the data indicated that subjects from all three groups perceived the actors as being quite friendly. This manipulation did not affect subjects' responses to any of the key dependent variables, so subjects' scores were collapsed across this variable for all further analyses.

to, $F(1, 70) = 9.10$, $p < .004$, and eager to date, $F(1,70) = 8.87$, $p < .004$, the opposite-sex actor than were the female observers (sexually attracted: male $M = 3.3$, female $M = 2.1$; date: male $M = 3.3$, female $M = 2.2$). Similarly, the male observer thought that the female actor wanted to be friends with the male actor, $F(1,70) = 3.25$, $p < .08$, was sexually attracted to the male actor, $F(1,70) = 6.58$, $p < .01$, and wanted to date the male actor, $F(1, 70) = 6.80$, $p < .01$, more than the female observer did (friends: male $M = 4.1$, female $M = 3.5$; sexually attracted: male $M = 3.2$, female $M = 2.4$; date: male $M = 3.1$, female $M = 2.3$).

Analyses of subjects' ratings of the male actor exhibited some surprising sex-of-subject effects. A multivariate analysis of variance combining subjects' ratings of the male actor on the Sexuality Index (interitem corelations ranged from .40 to .72, $p < .001$)—flirtatious, seductive, and promiscuous—indicated that there was a significant sex-of-subject effect, $F(3, 138) = 2.99$, $p < .03$. The univariate analyses indicated that the male actors and observers rated the male actor as being significantly more flirtatious, $F(1, 140) = 4.21$, $p < .04$, and seductive, $F(1, 140) = 9.07$, $p < .003$, than the female subjects did. There was also a significant sex by role interaction for each of

these variables, $F(1,140) = 4.21$, $p < .04$, $F(1, 140) = 4.12$, $p < .04$, respectively. Tukey (b) tests indicated that the female actors' and the male actors' ratings were significantly different ($p < .05$) with the male actor rating himself as significantly more flirtatious and seductive than the female actor rated him (see Table 2).[6] There was a marginal trend for males to rate the male actor as being more promiscuous than females did, $F(1, 140) = 3.34$, $p < .07$. Male actors and observers also rated the male actor as being more attractive than females did, $F(1,140) = 7.94$, $p < .01$ (male $M = 4.4$; female $M = 3.8$).

Gender of Stimulus

Because of the intriguing similarity of the males' ratings of both the male and female actor, the data were reanalyzed as a repeated measures analysis of variance. Gender of the stimulus was conceptualized as a repeated measure with respondents' ratings of the female actor representing one level of the variable and respondents' ratings of the male actor repre-

---

[6]The Statistical Package for the Social Sciences (SPSS) Tukey (b) statistic averages the Tukey and Newman-Keuls range values at each step.

TABLE 2

MEAN SCORES FOR RATINGS OF THE MALE ACTOR ON THE SEXUALITY ITEMS AS A FUNCTION OF SEX OF SUBJECT AND ROLE OF SUBJECT

| | Rating of the male actor | | | | | | | | |
| | Flirtatious[a] | | | Seductive[b] | | | Promiscuous[c] | | |
Sex of subject	Actor	Observer	M	Actor	Observer	M	Actor	Observer	M
Female	2.1	2.4	2.3	1.5	1.9	1.7	1.8	1.8	1.8
Male	3.1	2.4	2.8	2.5	2.1	2.3	2.1	2.1	2.1

[a]Sex of Subject × Role interaction, $p < .04$. Sex-of-subject effect, $p < .04$.
[b]Sex of Subject × Role interaction, $p < .04$. Sex-of-subject effect, $p < .003$.
[c]Sex of Subject × Role interaction, ns. Sex-of-subject effect, $p < .07$.

senting the second level of the variable. This analysis permits testing of the hypothesis that there is an overall sex-of-subject effect (same-sex subjects rate both actors similarly) or, alternatively, a gender-of-stimulus effect (both sexes rate actors of the same gender similarly).

For the dependent variable flirtatious, this analysis indicated a significant gender-of-stimulus effect, $F(1, 140) = 5.76, p < .05$. Examination of the means indicates that the female actor was rated as more flirtatious than the male actor by all respondents (female actor $M = 2.8$; male actor $M = 2.5$). However, this finding was not replicated with the other two dependent variables, seductive and promiscuous. For both of these variables there was a significant sex-of-subject effect indicating that male subjects rated both actors higher than female subjects did, $F(1, 140) = 6.98, p < .01$; $F(1,140) = 6.52, p < .02$, respectively (seductive: male subjects $M = 2.2$, female subjects $M = 1.8$; promiscuous: male subjects $M = 2.2$, female subjects $M = 1.7$).

Role

There was a large and systematic role effect indicating that actors thought more highly of themselves and their partners than the observers did (see Table 3). The male actors and the female actors rated the female actor as being significantly more considerate, interesting, likeable, warm, intelligent, and sincere than did the male and female observers. Similarly, both actors rated the male actor as being significantly more cheerful, interesting, likeable, warm, intelligent, attractive, and sincere than the observers did. Actors also thought more highly of their conversation than the observers did. Compared to observers, actors rated the conversation as more interesting and educational and their ideas as more creative and were more likely to say there was not enough time to talk, $F(1, 140) = 3.99–36.57, .001 < p < .05$ for all significant role effects.

TABLE 3

MEAN SCORES FOR RATINGS OF THE MALE ACTOR, THE FEMALE ACTOR, AND THE CONVERSATION AS A FUNCTION OF ROLE OF SUBJECT

Rating	Actor	Observer
Female actor		
Considerate	5.6	5.2
Interesting	5.4	5.0
Likeable	5.8	5.4
Warm	5.6	5.0
Intelligent	5.4	5.0
Sincere	5.9	5.2
Male actor		
Cheerful	5.4	5.0
Interesting	5.3	4.7
Likeable	5.8	5.4
Warm	5.2	4.8
Intelligent	5.4	5.0
Attractive	4.4	3.9
Sincere	5.8	5.4
Conversation		
Interesting	5.1	4.1
Educational	4.0	3.4
Presence of creative ideas	3.7	3.2
Not enough time to talk	4.5	3.2

DISCUSSION

Sex Differences

The results of the experiment were generally consistent with our predictions. Males rated the female actor as being more promiscuous and seductive than females did. Male actors were more sexually attracted to their partners than their partners were to them. Similarly, the male observers were more sexually attracted to and eager to date the opposite-sex actor than the female observers were. Finally, the male observers rated the female actors as being more sexually attracted to and willing to date their partners than the female observers did.

It is noteworthy that most of the significant differences were found with the traits and behaviors most obviously sexual in nature. There were no sex differences in subjects' ratings of the female actor's flirtatiousness, the mildest trait term. In fact, the finding that both sexes rated the female actor as being more flirtatious than the male actor substantiates the interpretation that this term has a connotation that implies female gender. There were also no sex differences in actors' desire to get to know their partner better, to become friends, or to date their partner. This sex difference in perception of the opposite sex is only apparent when unmistakably sexual terms are used.

As mentioned earlier, if this effect was due to a self-serving bias on the male actors' part, then the male actors' ratings should have been significantly higher than the male observers' ratings. Similarly, if it was due to actor-observer differences, then the female actors' (the target persons') ratings should have been different from the other three participants' (her observers) ratings. Therefore, the absence of any significant sex by role interactions for these key dependent variables is consistent with the hypothesis that this effect is due to a general masculine style of viewing female behavior.[7]

In sum, the above results provide support for the hypothesis that men mistakenly interpret women's friendliness as an indication of sexual interest. According to the female actors' self-ratings, they intended to be friendly yet they were perceived as being seductive and promiscuous by the male subjects. Clearly, one has no way of judging if the women's behavior truly was seductive or not. What is important, however, is her own perception of her behavior. If she felt she was not being sexually provocative, then she would be offended if a man interpreted her behavior this way, regardless of how an unbiased observer would rate her behavior. In future research similar interactions can be videotaped and later rated by judges, thereby providing a clearer interpretation of these findings.

Although most of the predictions were substantiated by the results, an examination of the subjects' ratings of the male actor necessitated rethinking the initial hypothesis. Not only were males inclined to rate the female actor in sexual terms but they also rated the male actor in a similar manner. Male actors perceived themselves as being more flirtatious and seductive than the female actors rated them. Furthermore, male actors perceived themselves and male observers perceived the male actor as being more attractive and promiscuous than females did. The repeated measures analysis, which combined males' ratings of both actors and found a significant sex-of-subject effect for the variables seductive and promiscuous, corroborates this conclusion. These findings also replicate Hendrick's (1976) results; in his study, male subjects, who were observers, rated the male actor as being more physically attractive and sexually promiscuous than females did.

The results of this experiment indicate that men are more likely to perceive the world in sexual terms and to make sexual judgments than women are. The predicted effect that men misperceive friendliness from women as seduction, appears to be merely one manifestation of this broader male sexual orientation.

Alternatively, one could explain these findings by arguing that males and females in our experiment were equally likely to make sexual judgments but that males were simply more willing than females to admit them. Although this explanation is feasible, we consider it to be unlikely. Respondents' explanations as to why they were or were not interested in dating the opposite-sex actor were coded. Males and females were equally likely to mention sexual factors such as "I'm not physically attracted to her" or "The magnetism was not there" as influencing their decision (females = 22%, males = 25%; interrater reliability = .91). If fe-

---

[7]It is possible that the male observers thought they would have the opportunity to meet the female actor later. This could have caused them to rate her in a sexual manner for ego-enhancing motives also. Based on comments that respondents made during the debriefing, the author considers this to be unlikely. (Most observers reported that they thought it would be their turn to interact with each other next; they did not seem to think they would be asked to interact with either of the actors.)

males and males were equally willing to admit their sexual judgments in open-ended responses, then it is likely that they were both being equally honest about these feelings throughout the questionnaire. Also, an approximately equal number of males and females volunteered the information that they were currently dating (females = 19%; males = 17%). Therefore, differential levels of sexual availability do not explain the findings.

Further verification of our revised hypothesis—that males perceive more sexuality in their own and in others' behavior than females do—comes from the recent work of Zellman, Johnson, Giarrusso, and Goodchilds (1979). Zellman et al. (1979) asked adolescents, ranging in age from 14 to 18 years, whether they view various cues in the dating situation as indicators that their partner is interested in engaging in sexual relations. They found "a consistent tendency for female respondents to view the behaviors of both male and female actors as less expressive of an interest in sex than males did" (p. 11). Females were less likely than males to feel that the type of clothes either sex wore, the male's reputation, the setting in which the date occurred, or various dating behaviors (telling the date you love him or her, tickling, looking into the date's eyes, etc.) were signs of sexual interest. Not only do their findings provide independent support for the hypothesis that males view the world in a more sexualized manner than females do but they also extend it to a different age group.

A thorough explanation as to why males and females differ in their propensity to make sexual judgments is beyond the scope of this paper. An explanation based on differential socialization could probably be proposed. Certainly the stereotypes of our culture, as evidenced by the mass media's depiction of men and women, portray men as having a greater interest in sexual matters than do women. Once men develop this sexual orientation, it may act as a generalized expectancy, causing them to interpret ambiguous information, such as that presented in our study, as evidence in support of their beliefs. As Markus (1977) suggests, events that fit one's self-schemas have a greater impact than those that do not. Consequently, if the issue of sexuality is more central to men's concerns than those of women, then males may be more aware of the potential sexual meaning of others' behavior. Future research that delineates the extent of this phenomenon and the conditions under which it does and does not occur may help elucidate its origin.

Role Effects

The role effects, though unexpected, were both extensive and consistent. Actors had a higher opinion of themselves, their partner, and their conversation than observers did. This effect cannot be dismissed as a self-serving bias (Bradley, 1978; Miller & Ross, 1975; Snyder, Stephan, & Rosenfield, 1976), because it applies not only to the self and the conversation that one participated in but also to one's partner, a complete stranger, as well. Perhaps because the observers are not involved in the interaction they may remain more judgmental. Actors may be "caught up in" what is happening and, therefore, be unable to analyze it objectively. There may be a psychological reality to the situation for the actors that makes the experience more involving and pleasant, consequently inflating their ratings (Brickman, 1978). Observing, on the other hand, is a passive behavior that arouses only weak emotions and, therefore is likely to lead to lower ratings (Brickman, 1978).

Alternatively, one could argue that the role differentiation established a sense of "we versus them." This can cause the actors to inflate their "in-group" ratings and the observers to deflate their "out-group" ratings (Tajfel, 1974, 1978).

SUMMARY AND CONCLUSIONS

Although the initial hypothesis appears to be only partially correct, its implications remain the same. Men do in some circumstances mistake friendliness for seduction. In fact, the whole issue of sexual availability appears to be more salient for men than for women, as evidenced by men's greater tendency to make sexual judgments.

In conclusion, the results of this laboratory investigation corroborate the author's personal experience: Men do tend to read sexual intent into friendly behavior. However, this appears to occur because of a general male bias rather than an attitude about females only. Evidently, women are not subject to this bias (at least not under these circumstances) and are, therefore, unlikely to misjudge male intentions in the way that men misjudge those of women. It is for future researchers to determine the underlying causal factors that contribute to this male bias and the specific circumstances that elicit it.

READING 18

Prototype Analysis of the Concepts of Love and Commitment

Beverley Fehr (1988)

The research on interpersonal attraction initially focused on the early stages of loving (i.e., becoming attracted to another person). More recent work has begun to focus on more enduring love relationships and to explore individuals' perceptions of their love experiences, including the issue of commitment (e.g., Davis, 1985; Dion & Dion, 1985; Hendrick & Hendrick, 1986; Shaver & Hazan, 1988; Sternberg, 1986; and Sternberg & Barnes, 1988). This new orientation is reflected in the following studies by Fehr, who employs a prototype analysis approach.

Fehr first summarizes five views on the relation between love and commitment, and then sets out to examine the overlap as well as the differences between everyday perceptions of these two concepts. Her research is distinctive for her attitude that we know quite a lot about what

experts thinks, but we don't know much about what everyone else thinks about love and commitment. In keeping with her goal of assessing the general public's concepts, you may want to list the attributes that *you* see as comprising love and commitment before reading her review. You can then compare your list to the findings compiled from the 313 subjects in Fehr's Studies 1 and 2.

Abstract

I analyzed lay conceptions of love and commitment from a prototype perspective. In Study 1, subjects listed the features of love and/or commitment. In Study 2, centrality (prototypicality) ratings of these features were obtained. In Study 3, central features were found to be more salient in memory than were peripheral features. In Study 4, it was shown that it sounded peculiar to hedge central but not peripheral features. In Study 5, central features of love (commitment) were expected to be more applicable than peripheral features as relationships increased in love (commitment). In Study 6, violations of central features of love (commitment) were perceived as contributing to a greater decrease in love (commitment) than were violations of peripheral features. Concerning the relation between love and commitment, I concluded that the findings across several studies fit best with Kelley's (1983) description of these concepts as largely overlapping but partially independent.

PROTOTYPE ANALYSIS OF THE CONCEPTS OF LOVE AND COMMITMENT

"Love and marriage go together like a horse and carriage—you can't have one without the other." The words of this old song are relevant to the contemporary issue of how love and commitment are related. Although not everyone agrees that "you can't have one without the other," few would disagree that love and commitment are of crucial importance in people's lives. Kelley (1983) lists a number of reasons why the concepts of love and commitment deserve scientific attention. First, the kinds of questions people ask about their own relationships almost invariably involve love and commitment issues (e.g., "How can I be sure my partner loves me?" "How can I get my partner to make a commitment to our relationship?"). Second, the analysis of these concepts "takes us deeply into the personal and interpersonal processes involved in the formation and continuation of close heterosexual relationships" (p. 267). Finally, an analysis of love and commitment can serve to illustrate the problems that arise when complex phenomena with rich everyday associations are dismembered for scientific or conceptual analysis.

Indeed, the search for definitions of love and of commitment carried out in psychology and other related disciplines has been marked with conflict, confusion, and disagreement. Such a singular lack of success raises the question of whether definitions of love and commitment are even possible; that is, definitions in the classical sense whereby concepts are defined by a necessary and sufficient set of criterial attributes.

Social scientists have offered many definitions of love. Watson (1924) defined love as an innate emotion elicited by cutaneous stimulation of the erogenous zones. According to Freud (1922/ 1951), the desire for sexual union is at the core of emotion. When that desire is blocked, one compensates for the resultant frustration by idealizing the other person and falling in love with him or her. Fromm (1956) saw love as a device used to reduce one's sense of isolation and loneliness. More recently, Rubin (1970) defined love as an attitude held toward another, which predisposes one to think, feel, and act in certain ways toward that person. For Swenson (1972), love is behavior such as giving gifts, sharing activities, and disclosing intimate information. According to Centers (1975), love is a response evoked in people when their interaction with another is rewarding. Skolnick (1978) defined love as "a constructed experience built with feelings, ideas, and cultural symbols" (p. 104). Lasswell and Lasswell (1976) defined love in terms of affect (feeling, emotion), physiological arousal, and cognition. It is difficult to imagine what emotion

would not fit some of these definitions. They are so broad that they apply to virtually every concept in psychology (e.g., attitudes, motives).

Others have discussed types of love. Hatfield and Walster (1978) preferred to dichotomize the concept and define each type separately:

> Passionate love is a wildly emotional state, a confusion of feelings: tenderness and sexuality, elation and pain, anxiety and relief, altruism and jealousy. Companionate love...is a lower-key emotion. It's friendly affection and deep attachment to someone (p. 2).

Lee (1977) avoided defining the concept, but rather spoke of styles of loving. Berscheid and Walster (1978) observed that one would think it would be easy for scientists to devise a definition of love. Yet, even though everyone knows what it means, scientists have found it impossible to agree on a single definition.

Similarly, a potpourri of definitions have been offered for commitment. One dominant theme is the notion of engaging in (or pledging to engage in) a consistent line of activity (e.g., Becker, 1960; Brehm & Cohen, 1962; Kiesler, 1971). Hinde (1979) used the term to refer to situations in which one or both partners perceive their relationship as continuing indefinitely and/or direct their behavior towards its continuation. Leik and Leik (1977) defined interpersonal commitment as an unwillingness to consider any other exchange partner(s). Several writers have defined commitment as the avowal of an intent to maintain a relationship (e.g., Levinger, 1980; Rosenblatt, 1977). Dean and Spanier (1974) regarded commitment as "the strength of an individual's desire and determination to continue a particular marital relationship" (p. 113). Johnson (1982) differentiated between personal commitment, defined as "an individual's dedication to the maintenance of a line of action" (p. 53), and structural commitment, external constraints that make it difficult to disengage oneself should one's sense of personal commitment decline.

Is a classical definition of love and commitment possible? The fact that experts have been unable to agree on definitions of these terms suggests that laypeople may not base their use of the words *love* and *commitment* on a classical definition. The experts' arguments also suggest that they have assumed that such a classical definition can be found. This may be because concepts have traditionally been thought of as defined by a set of necessary and sufficient criterial attributes. Category membership is therefore an all-or-none phenomenon: Any instance that meets the criterion is a member; others are nonmembers. Boundaries between concepts are thus clearly defined. Because each member must possess the particular set of attributes that is the criterion for category inclusion, all members have a full and equal degree of membership, and therefore are equally representative of the category. The traditional, classical view of concepts fosters the assumption that a precise definition of love and commitment is both necessary and possible. This assumption about the nature of concepts seems to have been implicit in the search for a definition of love and commitment.

Within psychology, Eleanor Rosch has been mainly responsible for rekindling an interest in the nature of concepts through her articulation of prototype theory as an alternative to the classical view (e.g., Mervis & Rosch, 1981; Rosch, 1973). Rosch maintained that many natural language categories are internally structured into a prototype (clearest cases, best examples) of the category, surrounded by other members that can be ordered in terms of their degree of resemblance to the prototypical cases. Rosch delineated two criteria that must be met in order to make the case that a concept has internal structure (i.e., is prototypically organized). The first is: "Can subjects make meaningful judgments about internal structure—the degree to which instances are good or poor members of categories?" (Rosch, 1975a, p. 194). Second, "Can a reasonable case be made that internal structure affects cognition with respect to categories?" (p. 194). For example, Rosch (1973) demonstrated that

subjects found it meaningful to provide prototypicality ratings for types of fruit; apples were rated reliably as better examples of fruit than were olives. With regard to the second criterion, Rosch found that ratings of prototypicality were predictive of subjects' reaction time in a category verification task (i.e., subjects took longer to verify the statement "Olive is a fruit" than "Apple is a fruit"). The greater the convergence of such measures of internal structure, the greater the confidence with which one can make the case that a concept is prototypically organized.

The purpose of this research was to discover the kinds of features that are listed for the concepts of love and commitment; which features are considered prototypical of each concept and which are not; and how this prototype structure affects the way these concepts are thought about, remembered, used in language, and applied to interpersonal relationships.

Relation Between the Concepts of Love and Commitment

A prototype analysis of love and commitment can also serve to elucidate the relation between these concepts. There are five major views on the relation between love and commitment: (a) that they are identical; (b) that they are largely overlapping but partially independent; (c) that they are completely independent; (d) that commitment is a component of love; and (e) that love is a component of commitment. Money (1980) virtually equated the two when he defined love as "the personal experience of and manifest expression of being attached or bonded to another person" (p. 218). In a multidimensional scaling analysis of types of heterosexual relationships, Forgas and Dobosz (1980) found love and commitment to be one of three basic underlying dimensions. They consider love and commitment to be highly similar, if not identical concepts.

Kelley (1983) suggested that love and commitment are largely overlapping, but partially independent concepts. The roots of this position date back more than 25 years when Thibaut and Kelley (1959) argued for the partial independence of the concepts of attraction and dependence, stating that "a member's dependency on the group [dyad] is not necessarily highly correlated with his attraction to the group, his 'morale' or satisfaction from belonging to it" (p. 23).

Some see love and commitment as being orthogonal. Rosenblatt (1977) suggested that commitment is different from and maybe even independent of love. Solomon (1981) emphatically declared that "Love is not a 'commitment,' has nothing to do with commitment....Love is an emotion; a commitment is a promise...to do something—or to continue to do something—whatever one's feelings" (p. xxxiii).

Recently, Sternberg (1986) proposed a new theory of love in which commitment is a component of love, along with intimacy and passion. Sternberg's decision-commitment component includes the initial decision that one loves another, as well as the long-term commitment to maintain that love. The intimacy component consists of feelings (e.g., closeness, connectedness, bondedness) that engender the experience of warmth in a relationship. The passion component refers to drives that lead to romance, physical attraction, and sexual activity. These three components form the vertices of his triangular theory of love.

According to Rusbult's (1980) investment model, commitment is determined by three factors: satisfaction (or love), alternatives, and investments. Drawing on Thibaut and Kelley's (1959) interdependence theory, Rusbult asserted that individuals will be committed to a relationship to the extent that it is satisfying (the rewards outweigh the costs); it exceeds their comparison level for alternatives; and, they have invested inextricable resources (e.g., time, money, emotional energy) in the relationship. Thus in Rusbult's view, love (satisfaction) and commitment need not be strongly correlated because commitment may be produced by poor alternatives or large investments.

These five views of the relation between the concepts of love and commitment are depicted in Figure 1. A prototype approach, which is concerned with the everyday use of natural language concepts, can shed light on these hypotheses on the relation between the concepts of love and commitment. If the layperson sees love and commitment as virtually identical, they should share the same set of attributes. If these concepts are seen as completely independent of each other, they should have no attributes in common. For these concepts to be considered as largely overlapping, one would expect them to share a large number of features, but each concept would also possess some unique features. Further, if these concepts are considered partially independent, the shared features should be considered more central to each concept than the unique features. Finally, if com-

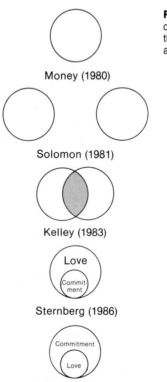

Money (1980)

Solomon (1981)

Kelley (1983)

Sternberg (1986)

Rusbult (1980)

FIGURE 1 Five views on the relation between the concepts of love and commitment.

mitment is seen as a component of love, then the features listed for commitment should be a subset of those listed for love. However, love should also possess other, additional features. Conversely, if love is a component of commitment, then the features listed for love should be a subset of those listed for commitment, and commitment should possess additional features.

I conducted six studies designed to elucidate the internal structure of love and commitment and the relation between these concepts. In all studies, subjects were students (mean age 22 years) enrolled in undergraduate classes at the University of British Columbia who volunteered their participation. According to Erikson (1963), the formation of intimate relationships is the central developmental task during this phase of the lifespan. Thus, the concepts of love and commitment were presumably salient for these students. Consistent with the Roschian tradition, they are referred to as *laypersons* in the sense that they are non-experts in the scientific study of love and commitment.

STUDY 1: FREE LISTING OF FEATURES OF LOVE AND COMMITMENT

The purpose of this study was to elicit the features or attributes of the concepts of love and commitment. Subjects were asked to generate the attributes of either love *or* commitment, or both love *and* commitment. The example provided was either a list of attributes or a script (i.e., the example told a story).

Method

Procedure Subjects (N = 141; 103 females and 37 males; (1 S did not indicate gender) completed one of the versions of the attribute generation questionnaire. The versions differed first in whether subjects were asked to list features of love or commitment only or of both concepts (in which case the order of love and commitment was counterbalanced). Second, the example provided was either a list of attributes or a script. For the attribute list subjects were told "If you were asked to list the characteristics of the concept *extraversion* you might write:". This was followed by a list of attributes such as liveliness, vivaciousness, sociability, and so on. The script example was taken from Fehr and Russell's (1984, Study 6) script- or story-like description of terror. Each version of the questionnaire was completed by 20–29 students, yielding a total of 185 protocols—96 for love and 89 for commitment.

Results and Discussion

Subjects generated an average of 6.81 features for love and 4.91 features for commitment. A panel of three judges (graduate students in psychology with extensive experience in this coding task) coded the features (see Fehr, 1986, for a detailed description of the coding procedure). Essentially, responses that were different grammatical forms of the same word were grouped together, as were words accompanied by modifiers (e.g., very, slightly, etc.). Finally, words/phrases that were judged as identical in meaning were combined.

The coding procedure yielded a total set of 183 love attributes. Of these, 115 responses were idiosyncratic (i.e., mentioned by only one subject). These were discarded, leaving a final list of sixty-eight love attributes. The attributes appear in Table 1, along with the frequency with which each was generated. No single feature was mentioned by all subjects. One attribute was mentioned by 44 percent of respondents, three by at least 20 percent of the respondents, and thirteen by at least 10 percent of the respondents.

The final commitment list consisted of 118 attributes, 78 of which were idiosyncratic. Table 1 shows the 40 nonidiosyncratic commitment attributes and the frequency with which each was generated. One attribute was mentioned by 35 percent of the respondents, three by 20 percent or more of the respondents, and thirteen by at least 10 percent of the respon-

TABLE 1

**FREQUENCY OF FREE LISTING AND MEAN CENTRALITY RATINGS OF
THE FEATURES OF LOVE AND COMMITMENT**

Love			Commitment		
Feature	Percentage of subjects	Mean rating	Feature	Percentage of subjects	Mean rating
*trust	14.58	7.500	*loyalty	12.36	6.724
*caring	43.75	7.284	*responsibility	28.09	6.605
*honesty	11.46	7.176	living up to your word	23.60	6.566
friendship	22.92	7.081	faithfulness	19.10	6.553
*respect	11.46	7.014	*trust	13.48	6.539
			"being there" for the other		
*concern for the other's well-being	8.33	7.000	in good and bad times	11.24	6.526
*loyalty	5.21	7.000	*devotion	21.35	6.421
commitment	13.54	6.919	reliable	6.74	6.342
accept other the way s/he is	15.63	6.824	give your best effort	10.11	6.276
*supportiveness	9.38	6.784	*supportiveness	4.49	6.263
want to be with the other	28.13	6.784	perseverance	34.83	6.118
			*concern for the other's		
interest in the other	5.21	6.689	well-being	6.74	6.066
*affection	4.17	6.676	*honesty	14.61	6.053
closeness	8.33	6.649	love	14.61	6.053
understanding	12.50	6.608	*respect	8.99	6.039
*sharing	13.54	6.581	*caring	10.11	6.013
want best for other	2.08	6.581	a high priority	3.37	5.908
forgiveness	7.29	6.554	*giving	6.74	5.882
intimacy	5.21	6.527	a promise	12.36	5.776
other is important	4.17	6.459	obligation	17.98	5.750
openness	3.13	6.392	*sacrifice	15.73	5.711
feel relaxed with other	6.25	6.365	*sharing	6.74	5.711
*liking	6.25	6.338	hard work	4.49	5.658
compassion	4.17	6.311	*helping	12.36	5.618
*devotion	3.13	6.284	working out problems	4.49	5.618
*giving	6.25	6.230	conscious decision	4.49	5.408
happiness	29.17	6.216	*attachment	7.87	5.382
feel free to talk about anything	19.79	6.189	*liking	3.37	5.382
do things for the other	4.17	6.135	giving and taking	4.49	5.355
feel good about self	7.29	6.068	maturity	2.25	5.289
*responsibility	4.17	6.041	*long-lasting	6.74	5.250
warm feelings	16.67	6.041	mutual agreement	11.24	5.237
patient	3.13	6.000	work toward common goals	5.62	5.224
*long-lasting	2.08	6.000	*affection	2.25	5.197
miss other when apart	7.29	5.986	*put other first	8.99	4.987
comfort	2.08	5.946	attention focused on other	6.74	4.961
*attachment	8.33	5.892	*contentment	2.25	4.645
sexual appeal	3.13	5.865	*security	3.37	4.592
touching	4.17	5.824	*think about other all the time	3.37	3.829
sexual passion	9.38	5.811	feel trapped	4.49	2.487
need each other	3.13	5.797			
mutual	3.13	5.784			
*contentment	10.42	5.770			
*put other first	9.38	5.703			

TABLE 1

FREQUENCY OF FREE LISTING AND MEAN CENTRALITY RATINGS OF THE FEATURES OF LOVE AND COMMITMENT *(Continued)*

	Love	
Feature	Percentage of subjects	Mean rating
unconditional	6.25	5.689
wonderful feelings	3.13	5.622
physical attraction	5.21	5.581
laughing	5.21	5.473
*sacrifice	13.54	5.432
*helping	8.33	5.419
empathy	8.33	5.351
admiration	2.08	5.311
positive outlook	4.17	5.284
kind	4.17	5.135
protectiveness	3.13	5.108
have a lot in common	7.29	5.108
excitement	4.17	5.027
*security	6.25	4.986
*think about the other all the time	13.54	4.446
energy	3.13	4.284
heart rate increases	8.33	4.257
euphoria	10.42	4.122
gazing at the other	3.13	4.095
see only the other's good qualities	4.17	3.446
butterflies in stomach	4.17	3.405
uncertainty	5.21	2.878
dependency	4.17	2.811
scary	3.13	2.284

*Features shared by love and commitment.

Note: Percentage of subjects who listed each feature is based on 96 protocols for love, 89 protocols for commitment. Centrality ratings made on a scale from 1 (extremely poor feature of love [commitment]) to 8 (extremely good feature of love [commitment]).

dents. Love and commitment share twenty-one features.

No single feature was mentioned by all subjects for either concept. Instead there was substantial variability in the extent to which certain features came to mind, ranging from 43.75 percent of the respondents who mentioned caring as a feature of love to only 2.08 percent who mentioned admiration. Similarly, for commitment, 34.83 percent of the subjects mentioned perseverance, whereas only 2.25 percent mentioned contentment.

Features of Love   For love, one large cluster consists of features that are positive in affective tone; subjects wrote about feelings of happiness, caring, contentment, affection, euphoria, and so on. Interestingly, there are also features in the love prototype that are negative in hedonic tone; more than one respondent mentioned features like scary and uncertainty. Social psychologists have touched upon this theme of a "dark side" of love when describing romantic or passionate love. For example, Berscheid and Fei (1977) found that feelings of dependency (also mentioned here) and insecurity were experienced by men and women involved in romantic relationships. Similarly, Hatfield and Walster (1978) observed that feelings of ambivalence, anxiety, and jealousy are a frequent concomitant of passionate love.

The prototype of love also includes behaviors (e.g., laughing, gazing at the other, doing things for the other, and helping), and a physiological component (e.g., butterflies in stomach, heartrate increases, sexual passion). Cognitive activities, like ruminating (e.g., think about the other all the time), and positive distortion (e.g., see only other's good qualities) are included along with a more rational component in which the other is respected and admired. There are also features suggesting an expectation that the relationship will endure (e.g., commitment, security, longlasting). Another theme in these features is a lack of inhibition when one is with the loved one (e.g., feel free to talk about anything, feel relaxed with the other, openness). This is reciprocal in that the item *accept the other as s/he is* was mentioned, as was *unconditional*. Finally, there are clusters of features that could be loosely described as social support (e.g., supportiveness, empathy, comfort) and altruism (e.g., sacrifice, put other first, concern for other's well-being).

Features of Commitment The features of commitment have a different flavor than those of love. Whereas in the love prototype the largest cluster refers to the experience of positive affect, the commitment prototype is characterized by the theme of making a decision, and following through on it. Features like perseverance, living up to your word, faithfulness, and reliability are consistent with this idea. The behavioral features of commitment also reflect this notion (e.g., give your best effort, hard work). As with love, there is a cognitive aspect to commitment that is irrational: think about the other all the time. However, for commitment, levelheadedness and rationality are predominant; the relationship is seen as a conscious decision, a prom-

ise, a mutual agreement, and so on. Again, there is the expectation that the relationship will endure (e.g., longlasting). The positively-toned affective features in commitment (e.g., contentment, affection, caring) are muted compared to the intensity of some of the emotions associated with love. A negatively valenced feature is feel trapped, (and possibly obligation). Like love, social support and altruism are part of the commitment prototype. Unlike love, this apparent selflessness is tempered by considerations of equity, namely, giving and taking.

Relation Between the Concepts of Love and Commitment A certain percentage of subjects (20.22 percent) mentioned love as a feature of commitment (and 14.58 percent mentioned commitment as a feature of love), and these concepts shared certain features. This suggests that love and commitment are not seen as completely independent. On the other hand, the fact that the majority of subjects did not spontaneously mention love for commitment, and commitment for love, and that some, but not all features are shared, suggests that the concepts are not synonymous. If commitment was considered a component of love, one would expect that fewer subjects would list commitment when asked to generate features of love than vice versa, and that the features of commitment would be a subset of those listed for love. Although commitment shares about half of its features with love (love shares just less than a third of its features with commitment), commitment still possesses nineteen unique features (see Figure 2). Love therefore subsumes a substantial proportion of commitment, but not the whole thing. If love was considered a component of commitment, one would expect that the features of love would be a subset of those listed for commitment. However, only twenty-one of the sixty-eight features listed for love were also listed for commitment. The findings obtained in this study seem most consistent with Kelley's (1983) description of love and commitment as overlapping concepts.

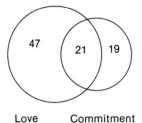

FIGURE 2 Number of features generated for love and commitment.

Love 68   Commitment 40

This study answers the question: "What attributes come to mind when laypeople are asked about the concepts of love and commitment?" It does not directly answer the question, "How central or important is each attribute to love or commitment?" Nor does it tell us the degree of interdependence laypeople perceive between these concepts. It is possible that although people use several of the same attributes to describe love and commitment, they could still see these concepts as being largely independent of each other. This would be the case if the unique features were considered most central to each concept, whereas the shared features were seen as peripheral. If the concepts are seen as moderately independent of each other, one would expect no difference between centrality ratings of shared and unique features. Finally, if people conceptualize love and commitment as only partially independent, then the unique features should be seen as less central to each concept than the overlapping features. These issues are addressed in Study 2.

STUDY 2: CENTRALITY RATINGS OF THE FEATURES OF LOVE AND COMMITMENT

The purpose of this study was to discover the prototype structure of the concepts of love and commitment. In other words, are some attributes considered central to each concept, whereas others are considered peripheral? The degree of interrelatedness perceived between these concepts was also investigated.

Method

Subjects ($N = 172$; 111 women and 56 men from two different psychology classes; 5 subjects did not indicate gender) received either the love or commitment features (taken from Study 1) and were asked to rate how central each feature was to the concept by using a scale ranging from 1 (extremely poor feature of love [commitment]) to 8 (extremely good feature of love [commitment]). The commitment attributes were rated for centrality by 76 subjects; 96 subjects rated love attributes.

Results

The mean centrality ratings for the features given by the two classes were highly correlated ($r = .93$ for the love attributes, $r = .92$ for the commitment attributes). The data sets were combined for further analyses. Table 1 shows the mean centrality rating for each love and commitment attribute.

Results from studies on gender differences in the experience of love (e.g., Dion & Dion, 1985) suggested the possibility that men and women might differ in terms of the features they considered most important to love. Thus, men's and women's centrality ratings were compared using a weighted means ANOVA. For love, there was no overall difference between men's and women's ratings, nor did differences emerge when analyses were performed separately for central features and for peripheral features (all $Fs < 1.75$, $ps > .10$). Similarly, for commitment, comparisons of men's and women's centrality ratings revealed no significant differences in terms of overall ratings, ratings of only central attributes, or ratings of only peripheral attributes (all $Fs < 1.69$, $ps > .10$). . Men's and women's centrality ratings were highly correlated (for love, $r = .93$; for commitment, $r = .89$). Thus, in the remaining studies, data from women and men were combined.

To test whether love and commitment are seen as partially independent concepts, a 2 × 2 mixed ANOVA was performed on the centrality ratings, with concept (love or commitment) as the between-subjects variable and type of attribute (shared or unique) as the within-subjects variable. If love and commitment are only partially independent, shared attributes should be considered more central to each concept than unique attributes. First, there was a main effect for concept, $F(1,148) = 5.15$, $p < .05$, such that overall, love attributes received higher mean ratings than commitment attributes (5.91 vs. 5.65). Second, there was a main effect for type of attribute, $F(1,148) = 86.07$, $p < .001$; shared attributes received higher centrality ratings than did unique attributes (5.96 vs. 5.59). This effect was tempered by a significant Concept × Attribute interaction, $F(1,148) = 74.81$, $p < .001$. Simple effects analyses revealed that for love, shared attributes received significantly higher mean ratings than unique attributes, $F(1,73) = 206.16$, $p < .001$ (6.26 vs. 5.55). For commitment, the difference between centrality ratings of shared and unique features (5.66 vs. 5.63) was nonsignificant ($F < 1$).

Finally, if love and commitment are largely overlapping but partially independent, one would expect that the centrality ratings of the shared features of love and commitment would be moderately to highly correlated. This correlation was quite high, $r = .75$.

Discussion

The first noteworthy feature of these data is that subjects considered some features to be more prototypical of each concept than others. Moreover, they agreed on these ratings; the ratings were stable across classes. The fact that subjects found this a meaningful task fulfills Rosch's first criterion for demonstrating internal structure, and hence lends credence to the hypothesis that love and commitment are prototypically organized.

It is interesting to note which attributes these college-age respondents thought were most central to love and commitment. For love, trust emerged as the most central attribute, followed by caring, honesty, and friendship. How does the layperson's view of love, as uncovered in this study, map onto theories of love proposed by psychologists? Rubin (1973) saw love as consisting of three components: caring, attachment, and intimacy. Caring and intimacy are central to the layperson's view, whereas attachment is seen as less central. Rubin also regarded liking as a construct distinct from love with two underlying dimensions: affection and respect. In this study, liking was considered a central feature of love, as were its proposed dimensions.

To what extent does the layperson's view of love correspond with the companionate-passionate distinction made by Hatfield and Walster (1978)? These data include features that appear to depict passionate love: miss other when apart, physical attraction, touching, sexual passion, think about other all the time, euphoria, heartrate increases, gazing at other, scary, and so on. These data also include features descriptive of companionate love: trust, caring, respect, friendship, loyalty, and the like. Interestingly, not one of the features that describe passionate love was considered central to love; in fact these features received the lowest centrality ratings. These data are inconsistent with the stereotype that college-age students see love only in romantic terms.

For commitment, features such as loyalty, responsibility, live up to your word, and faithfulness were considered most central. Features like contentment, security, think about the other all the time, and feel trapped were considered peripheral to the concept. In some ways definitions of commitment given by laypeople paralleled those given by social scientists. One of the main themes in the scientific literature is pledging oneself to a line of action. The central features—loyalty, live up to your word, and a promise—are consonant with this theme. However, definitions of commitment as an intent to maintain a relationship are not really represented in this feature list, nor are definitions which construe commitment as an unwillingness to consider an alternate exchange partner.

A comparison of the mean ratings of unique versus shared features revealed that shared attributes received significantly higher centrality ratings than unique attributes, particularly for the concept of love. This result suggests that the everyday conceptualization of love and commitment is consistent with Kelley's (1983) description of these concepts as partially independent.

A significant next step was to discover whether the prototype structure of these concepts influences the everyday view of the nature and dynamics of interpersonal relationships. This was the focus of Studies 5 and 6.*

STUDY 5: APPLICABILITY OF CENTRAL AND PERIPHERAL FEATURES TO LOVING AND COMMITTED RELATIONSHIPS

Kelley et al. (1983) suggest that a relationship has moved to a new stage or level when a marked change in any relationship property occurs. Social psychologists have written about the kinds of changes that take place as relationships become close (e.g., Perlman & Fehr, 1987). For instance, the partners interact more often and for longer periods of time, they gain more knowledge of one another, they increase their investment in the relationship, and so on.

Presumably, as a relationship becomes more loving or committed, people's perceptions of the features that are applicable to or characteristic of the relationship change. A question that arises is this: What is the nature of these changes? From a prototype perspective, one would expect that as a relationship becomes more loving or committed, the central features of love or commitment, respectively, would become systematically more applicable to or descriptive of the relationship. Peripheral features might be seen as moderately applicable to most relationships, or variations in

their applicability might be less closely tied to changes in the relationship. The rationale is that central features are closer to the core meaning of the concept, and therefore, changes in the level of love or commitment in a relationship should be most evident in changes in the applicability of those features. For example, greater caring in a relationship, a central feature of love, ought to be perceived as indicative of greater love. However, an increase in security, a peripheral feature, should not necessarily connote an increase in love. Another possibility is that as a relationship becomes more loving or committed, all the features of love or commitment, central and peripheral, are seen as more descriptive of the relationship. If this view is correct, then increases in both caring and security would be seen as indicative of greater love in a relationship.

Finally, it is also possible that while the concepts of love and commitment have a particular cognitive structure, people's actual experiences in relationships might override the effects of this structure. In other words, people's experiences might have such powerful effects that any absolute weighting of the features of love and commitment in cognitive representation becomes irrelevant when addressing the nature and dynamics of interpersonal relationships. Thus people's responses might be determined by their prior experiences in relationships. If someone felt cared for in a particular relationship, but nevertheless felt insecure, that person might emphasize the importance of a peripheral feature like security as an indicator of greater love. Another person might emphasize a completely different feature. These three possibilities were examined in Study 5.

Method

Subjects ($N = 30$) were presented with a type of relationship on the screen of a Radio Shack TRS 80 Model III or IV microcomputer. Below the relationship type appeared a randomly selected central or peripheral attribute, followed by the question "To what extent is this attribute (printed below

---

*Editors' Note: Studies 3 and 4 are omitted.

the relationship type) applicable to this relationship?'' Each subject rated the applicability of a randomly selected central attribute and a peripheral attribute to sixteen relationship types (on a scale ranging from 1 [not at all applicable] to 9 [extremely applicable], resulting in a total of thirty-two judgments. Four levels of love and four levels of commitment were selected from lists of types of relationships which had been prerated for degree of love and commitment: High, Medium high, Medium low, and Low. Within each level, four relationship types were selected randomly (see Table 2 for examples), yielding a total of sixteen types for each concept. Fifteen subjects rated the applicability of central and peripheral love attributes to love relationships; fifteen rated the applicability of commitment attributes to commitment relationships.

Results and Discussion

The data were analyzed in a 4 × 2 repeated measures ANOVA with type of relationship (High, Medium high, Medium low, or Low) and type of attribute (central or peripheral) as within-subject factors. The results were analyzed separately for love and commitment. On the basis of prototype approach, a significant Relationship × Attribute interaction was predicted for each concept, such that as a relationship increased in love (commitment), the central attributes of the concept would be seen as increasingly more applicable. For love, there was a significant main effect for type of relationship, $F(3,42) = 19.06$, $p < .001$, indicating that as the relationships became more loving, the mean applicability of all attributes increased. There was no main effect for attribute, $F(1,14) = 2.55$, $p < .10$. The predicted Relationship × Attribute interaction was obtained, $F(3,42) = 4.47$, $p < .01$ (see Figure 3). Mean applicability ratings for central features were, from high to low love relationships, 7.41, 6.80, 4.54, and 3.86. Mean ratings for peripheral features were, from high to low love re-

	TABLE 2	
TYPES OF RELATIONSHIPS		
	Love relationships	Commitment relationships
High	Husband and wife	Husband and wife
	A middle-aged child caring for his/her elderly parent because she/he wants to	Parent and young child
Medium high	Close friends	A long, involved "going steady" relationship at school
	Short, mutual first love	
		A permanent but nonsexual relationship between two young religious people
Medium low	A high school dating relationship that breaks up once the couple has gone away to college	A salesperson and a regular customer
		A "going steady" relationship maintained to impress peers
	A short, emotional holiday affair	
Low	Political opponents	A one-night sexual encounter
	A one-night sexual encounter	Interviewer and job applicant

lationships, 5.87, 6.19, 4.76, and 4.32. Simple effects analyses (using the error term from the interaction) revealed that although the applicability of both central and peripheral love features increased as the relationships became more loving, this effect was stronger for central features, $F(3,42) = 32.10$, $p < .001$, than for peripheral features, $F(3,42) = 8.56$, $p < .05$.

Similar results were obtained for commitment. There was a significant main effect for

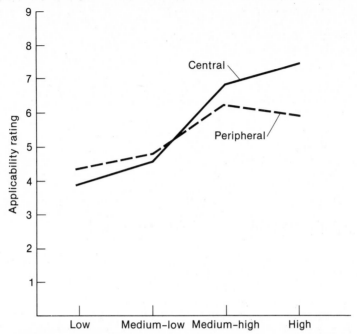

FIGURE 3 Applicability of central and peripheral features to types of loving relationships.

type of relationship, $F(3,42) = 64.84$, $p < .001$, such that as the relationships became more committed, all attributes were seen as more applicable. No main effect for type of attribute was obtained, $F(1,14) = 1.24$, $p < .10$. There was a significant Relationship × Attribute interaction, $F(3,42) = 3.17$, $p < .05$. Mean applicability ratings for central attributes were, from high to low commitment relationships, 7.33, 6.76, 4.49, and 2.38. Mean ratings for peripheral attributes were 6.55, 6.27, 3.97, and 3.27, respectively. Simple effects analyses showed that while the applicability of both central and peripheral commitment features increased as the relationships became more committed, this effect was stronger for central features, $F(3,42) = 56.87$, $p < .001$, than for peripheral features, $F(3,42) = 29.68$, $p < .001$.

I hypothesized that as relationships become more loving or committed, central features would be seen as increasingly more characteristic of the

relationship than would peripheral features. Although both central and peripheral features of love (commitment) were seen as more applicable as the relationships became more loving (committed), central and peripheral features assumed differential importance as a relationship increased in love (commitment). Figure 3 shows that the applicability of central attributes of love increased systematically as the relationships became more loving (similar results were obtained for commitment). Peripheral features did not exhibit the same regularity. For one, peripheral features more than central features tended to be moderately applicable to all relationship types. This was particularly striking for commitment, in which the range of mean applicability ratings on the 9-point scale only spanned 1.87 points compared to 3.55 for central features. (For love, these figures are 3.28 and 4.60, respectively). Thus, although both central and peripheral features become more descriptive of the relationship as it increases in love or commitment, it is the central features that act as true barometers of a move toward increased love or commitment.

STUDY 6: VIOLATIONS OF THE FEATURES OF LOVE AND COMMITMENT

What repercussions do violations of relationship attributes have for evaluations of the level of love or commitment perceived to exist in a relationship? Perhaps, violations of any of the features of love and commitment are seen as seriously harming the relationship. On the other hand, if central attributes of love and commitment have a more pronounced impact on relationship experiences than peripheral attributes, one might expect a violation or negation of a central feature to threaten more seriously the status of a relationship. Thus from a prototype perspective, a change in a peripheral feature might be expected to have only a minimal effect. Stated differently, violations of peripheral attributes might be considered forgivable, whereas violations of central attributes would be more likely to be seen as grounds for relationship dissolution. As in Study 5, the third possibility is that subjects' responses might be determined by their own experiences with the dissolution or deterioration of relationships.

I hypothesized that a violation of the central attributes of love (commitment) would be seen as having a greater effect on whether the relationship would continue to be loving (committed), whereas a violation of the peripheral attributes of love (commitment) would be seen as exerting a lesser influence. Further, violations of the central attributes of love were expected to have an effect relatively independent of violations of the attributes of commitment, and vice versa.

Method

Subjects ($N = 234$) received the following description of a loving and committed relationship:

Pat and Chris love each other and are committed to one another. They began dating toward the end of their first year at U.B.C. and they will both be graduating in the spring. Pat and Chris enjoy doing things together and frequently go to movies, sports events, out for dinner, and so on. They also spend many evenings together just watching TV or visiting with friends. Certain things could happen that would have little or no impact on their relationship. Other things could have a major impact.

Subjects were asked to rate the impact of each event using a scale ranging from 1 (not at all likely) to 9 (extremely likely that the event will decrease love [commitment]). The events consisted of love and commitment attributes worded in the negative (e.g., Pat no longer cares for Chris). Each version of the questionnaire contained eighteen commitment attributes and fifteen or sixteen love attributes (presented in a random order), and was rated by 27–30 subjects for impact on love and by 27–30 subjects for impact on commitment.

Results

Subjects' ratings were analyzed in the context of a $2 \times 2 \times 2$ mixed ANOVA with type of concept (love or commitment) and type of attribute (central or peripheral) as within-subjects variables and type of impact rating (love or commitment) as a between-subjects variable. A significant main effect for type of attribute was predicted such that violations of central attributes should have a greater impact than violations of peripheral attributes. Also, a three-factor interaction was expected between type of concept, type of attribute, and type of impact rating. The central attributes of love were expected to have a greater impact on ratings of love than on commitment, whereas the central attributes of commitment were expected to have a greater impact on ratings of commitment than on love; peripheral attributes were expected to have generally less impact.

First, there was no main effect for type of impact rating ($F < 1$). There was a main effect for type of concept, $F(1,232) = 4.33$, $p < .05$, such that overall, love attributes received higher mean impact ratings than did commitment attributes (6.29 vs. 6.21). The predicted main effect for type of attribute was obtained, $F(1,232) = 592.00$, $p < .001$; violations of central attributes were seen to have a greater impact than violations of peripheral attributes (6.90 vs. 5.60). A significant Concept × Attribute interaction was also obtained, $F(1,232) = 62.55$, $p < .001$. Simple effects analyses revealed that for love attributes, central features received higher mean impact ratings than peripheral features (7.09 vs. 5.48), $F(1,232) = 844.04$, $p < .001$. For commitment attributes this difference was less pronounced (6.61 vs. 5.71), although still statistically significant, $F(1,232) = 319.42$, $p < .001$.

Discussion

Effect of Violations of Central and Peripheral Features As expected, violations of central attributes had a larger impact than did violations of peripheral attributes. For the everyday person, a loss of sense of caring, trust, honesty, respect, or a feeling that friendship is no longer a part of the relationship are all considered to seriously threaten or undermine the extent to which a relationship is seen as loving. Whether or not one stops feeling euphoric, gazing at one's partner, seeing only the partner's good qualities or no longer feels dependent on the partner is not regarded as diagnostic of diminishing love in the relationship.

Commitment in a relationship is seriously endangered by disloyalty, failing to live up to one's word, unfaithfulness, no longer accepting the relationship as a responsibility, and so forth. Feeling discontent, insecure, not constantly thinking about one's partner, and so on are not perceived as directly threatening the level of commitment.

It was noted in Study 2 that the features of love that seem to match descriptions of companionate love (e.g., trust, caring, friendship) were rated as most central to love. Interestingly, in Study 6, it was these features, if violated, that were seen as causing a decrease in love. On the other hand, the more passionate-like features of love (which were seen as largely peripheral to love in Study 2) if violated, were not perceived as having a significant negative impact on love. When distinguishing between passionate and companionate love, Hatfield and Walster (1978) commented that, "Passionate love is a fragile flower—it wilts in time. Companionate love is a sturdy evergreen; it thrives with contact" (p. 125). Similarly, Cunningham and Antill (1981), when describing the development of love, stated that, "Acceptance of the differences which inevitably appear may dampen the flames of passionate or romantic love but leave a mature companionate love in its place" (p. 35). This view of passionate love as a transient aspect of the early stages of a loving relationship, which then becomes supplanted by a more enduring, companionate love seems consistent with the results obtained here. Violations of the passionate-like features of love were seen as relatively inconsequential, while violations of the companionate-like aspects of love were seen to seriously undermine the relationship.

Rating Impact of Love Versus Impact on Commitment It did not make any difference whether subjects were asked to rate the impact of violations of love attributes on love or on commitment, nor did it make a difference if subjects were asked to rate the impact of violations of commitment attributes on commitment or on love. A possible explanation for this finding is that seeing both love and commitment attributes activated both love and commitment prototypes, so that subjects rated violations of love attributes in terms of their impact on love and violations of commitment attributes in terms of their impact on commitment. In other words, seeing features may be so powerful in evoking the appropriate category label that the actual judgment the subject is asked to make becomes irrelevant.

Another plausible interpretation of this finding is that love and commitment are so similar that subjects were unable to distinguish between them.

In his chapter on love and commitment, Kelley (1983) commented that the display of ardent affection stimulated by passionate feelings, for example, can be mistaken as an avowal of obligation to adhere to the partner. In his words, "Expressions of love can be easily confused with expressions of commitment" (p. 314). Kelley's succinct statement is consistent with the results of this study: subjects failed to differentiate between the two concepts. His statement also captures the importance of the implications of the prototype structure of these concepts for close relationships.

Impact of Violations of Love Versus Commitment Attributes   There was a significant main effect for type of concept, such that overall, violations of love attributes were seen to have a greater impact than violations of commitment attributes. In Study 2, love attributes also received higher centrality ratings than did commitment attributes. One explanation for this finding suggested in Study 2 was that the larger number of love features may elicit more polarized or extreme ratings. This might apply to ratings of impact as well as to ratings of centrality. If, however, one takes this result at face value, it would seem that people are more willing to tolerate deviations in commitment, or at least perceive such violations as less devastating for the relationship than violations of love.

In conclusion, this study suggests that laypersons may pay particular attention to central attributes (and changes in these attributes) as a way of assessing the state of their relationships. The layperson's monitoring of what is and is not an important indicator of demise in love or commitment deserves our attention, both in terms of learning more about the dynamics of interpersonal relationships from the layperson's perspective and in terms of the clinical implications of these warning signs.

GENERAL DISCUSSION

The first major issue addressed in this research was what is the content and structure of the concepts of love and commitment? The second major question was to what extent, if at all, are these concepts associated in people's minds? The latter is addressed first.

Relation Between the Concepts of Love and Commitment

The pattern of findings across these studies seems inconsistent with the hypothesis that love and commitment are completely independent concepts. To give a few examples, if these concepts are independent they should not have shared any features; when asked to list features for one concept, the other concept should not have been mentioned; subjects should not have falsely recalled having seen the other concept in a memory experiment.

In Sternberg's (1986) theory of love, commitment is a component of love, along with intimacy and passion. If the layperson's view maps onto Sternberg's model, one would expect that commitment should share all of its features with love, although love would also possess unique features. However, in Study 1, nearly half of the features listed for commitment were unique; they were not subsumed by love. In Rusbult's (1980) model, love is a component of commitment, along with alternatives and investments. Here one would expect that love would share all of its features with commitment, although commitment would also possess unique features. However most of the features listed for love in Study 1 were unique; only twenty-one of sixty-eight features were shared with commitment. Several additional findings were incompatible with both the Sternberg and Rusbult models. For example, in Study 6, subjects should have discriminated between violations of features of love versus commitment *on* love versus commitment. In Rusbult's model, a violation of commitment attributes should not necessarily imply difficulties with love; it could just as easily imply better alternatives or few investments. Similarly for Sternberg, a violation of love should not necessarily imply a violation of commitment; it could just as easily suggest problems with intimacy or passion.

This leaves two models: The view that love and commitment are virtually the same, and the view that they are related but partially independent concepts. Certainly the notion of considerable overlap is well supported by these data. In fact, the high correlation between mean centrality ratings of the shared features of love and commitment ($r = .75$), lends support to the view that these concepts are synonymous. Also, in Study 6 it made no difference whether subjects were asked to rate the impact of violations of love or commitment attributes on love or commitment.

However, the notion of partial independence between these concepts can also be defended. For example, Study 1 showed that each concept possesses a set of unique features. Further, most of the respondents did not mention love when asked about commitment, and vice versa, suggesting that the concepts are somewhat independent. Also, in Study 3, most of the subjects did not erroneously think they had seen love when presented with the features of commitment, and vice versa. Thus, Kelley's view of the relation between the concepts of love and commitment as being largely overlapping but partially independent fits best with the data on the everyday view of the concepts of love and commitment obtained here.

Are Love and Commitment Prototype Concepts?

The internal structure of a concept is demonstrated through a convergence of operations. The triangulation of results across these studies suggests that the concepts of love and commitment are amenable to a prototype conceptualization. The predictions derived from Rosch's (1973) theory worked well when extrapolated to and tested in the domain of love and commitment in interpersonal relationships.

These studies have served to provide information that was largely absent from the literature on love and commitment, namely how everyday people view these concepts and the relation between them. Existing theoretical approaches seem not to capture the breadth of the lay conceptions of love and commitment as uncovered in these studies. Perhaps no single theory or definition ever could. For love, the theoretical position most akin to lay conceptions is Hatfield and Walster's (1978) conceptualization of companionate and passionate love. However, as discussed in Study 1, the prototype of love contains other features in addition to the companionate and passionate components (e.g., feeling uninhibited when with the loved one, altruism). The prototype approach also sheds light on the relative importance people place on each of these components. When comparing passionate and companionate love, Hatfield and Walster commented that "Probably in any relationship, we drift in and out between the two" (p. 10). Consistent with this conjecture, both companionate and passionate features of love were listed by laypeople. However, it was clearly the case that the companionate features were seen as most central to love and that changes in these features were considered most diagnostic of either increased or decreased love in a relationship. The results obtained here also suggest that it is the companionate component of love that is most closely related to commitment. The features of love that were shared with commitment were almost exclusively companionate in nature. Also, it was found in Study 6 that violations of central features of love had a more negative impact on commitment than did violations of peripheral features.

The prototype of commitment bears only limited resemblance to the definitions that appear in the literature. As was the case with love, there are so many features listed for commitment that it would be difficult to capture them in a single definition. This implies, however, that experts' definitions are overlooking many aspects considered important by ordinary people. Most of the existing theoretical approaches emphasize pledging oneself to the continuation of a relationship. When asked "What is commitment?"

experts are likely to reply "staying in a relation-ship," whereas laypersons give rich, descriptive information on the kinds of features that char-acterize such a relationship. Experts also appear not to consider the potentially negative aspects of commitment that are mentioned by ordinary people, such as feelings of obligation or feeling trapped. Finally, the prototype of commitment, as uncovered in these studies, included an af-fective component (e.g., contentment, affection), whereas existing approaches tend to conceptu-alize commitment in behavioral (e.g., staying in a relationship) or cognitive (e.g., the decision to stay in a relationship) terms.

In conclusion, the importance of love and commitment in people's lives warrants the in-vestigation of what people mean by these terms. Informal, everyday appraisals of love and com-mitment in personal relationships are based on such conceptualizations. These implicit theories suggest aspects of love and commitment that are important to ordinary people but are often over-looked in existing explicit theories of these concepts.

Aggression and Violence

READING 19

excerpt from *Civilization and Its Discontents*

Sigmund Freud (1930)

Humans are able to be loving and caring, but can also be remarkably violent and aggressive. Much debate has focused on the origins of violence in humans. This debate crosses broad disciplinary lines involving biologists, ethologists, anthropologists, sociologists, philosophers, theologians, as well as social psychologists. The debate also affects public policy and is incorporated into our legal system's attempt to control crime and violence.

And yet, our responses to violence as a culture appear to be somewhat inconsistent; while we value peace and tranquility, we are fascinated by the darker side of human social behaviors. Graphically violent movies do well at the box office. We have penalties in our sporting events for unnecessary roughness, implying that certain levels of roughness are tolerable (or even desirable). We worry over whether this or that political leader is a "wimp." The debates over gun control and the death penalty often evoke images and statements about revenge and violence. Eldridge Cleaver is credited with stating that "Violence is as American as apple pie." Is he right? If he is, is it inevitable?

Although most social psychologists now give only a passing reference to Freud, his writings have been extremely influential in twentieth-century thought, and are rich in social psychological hypotheses. In this excerpt, Freud develops his ideas on aggression. For Freud, aggression is an instinctive response, but a response that can nevertheless be held under control by civilization's persistent efforts. The integrative nature of Freud's work makes it delightful to read even for those who do not accept the thrust of psychoanalysis. Freud builds a case from not wanting to love his neighbor to the meaning of the evolution of civilization. Whereas hypotheses about the origins of civilization are inherently untestable, there is much heuristic value even in this brief segment, including hypotheses regarding attitudes towards strangers, ingroup and outgroup processes, and whether happiness is related to the freedom to be aggressive.

[Freud begins his discussion of civilization and aggression by examining the well-known imperative:] 'Thou shalt love thy neighbour as thyself.' It is known throughout the world and is undoubtedly older than Christianity, which puts it forward as its proudest claim. Yet it is certainly not very old; even in historical times it was still strange to mankind. Let us adopt a naive attitude towards it, as though we were hearing it for the first time; we shall be unable then to suppress a feeling of surprise and bewilderment. Why should we do it? What good will it do us? But, above all, how shall we achieve it? How can it be possible? My love is something valuable to me which I ought not to throw away without reflection. It imposes duties on me for whose fulfilment I must be ready to make sacrifices. If I love someone, he must deserve it in some way. He deserves it if he is so like me in important ways that I can love myself in him; and he deserves it if he is so much more perfect than myself that I can love my ideal of my own self in him. Again, I have to love him if he is my friend's son, since the pain my friend would feel if any harm came to him would be my pain too—I should have to share it. But if he is a stranger to me and if he cannot attract me by any worth of his own or any significance that he may already have acquired for my emotional life, it will be hard for me to love him. Indeed, I should be wrong to do so, for my love is valued by all my own people as a sign of my preferring them, and it is an injustice to them if I put a stranger on a par with them. But if I am to love him (with this universal love) merely because he, too, is an inhabitant of this earth, like an insect, an earthworm or a grass-snake, then I fear that only a small modicum of my love will fall to his share—not by any possibility as much as, by the judgement of my reason, I am entitled to retain for myself. What is the point of a precept enunciated with so much solemnity if its fulfilment cannot be recommended as reasonable?

On closer inspection, I find still further difficulties. Not merely is this stranger in general unworthy of my love; I must honestly confess that he has more claim to my hostility and even my hatred. He seems not to have the least trace of love for me and shows me not the slightest consideration. If it will do him any good he has no hesitation in injuring me, nor does he ask himself whether the amount of advantage he gains bears any proportion to the extent of the harm he does to me. Indeed, he need not even obtain an advantage; if he can satisfy any sort of desire by it, he thinks nothing of jeering at me, insulting me, slandering me and showing his superior power; and the more secure he feels and the more helpless I am, the more certainly I can expect him to behave like this to me. If he behaves differently, if he shows me consideration and forbearance as a stranger, I am ready to treat him in the same way, in any case and quite apart from any precept. Indeed, if this grandiose commandment had run 'Love thy neighbour as thy neighbour loves thee', I should not take exception to it. And there is a second commandment, which seems to me even more incomprehensible and arouses still stronger opposition in me. It is 'Love thine enemies'. If I think it over, however, I see that I am wrong in treating it as a greater imposition. At bottom it is the same thing.[1]

I think I can now hear a dignified voice admonishing me: 'It is precisely because your neighbour is not worthy of love, and is on the contrary your enemy, that you should love him as yourself.'

Now it is very probable that my neighbour, when he is enjoined to love me as himself, will answer exactly as I have done and will repel me for the same reasons. I hope he will not have the same objective grounds for doing so, but he will have the same idea as I have. Even so, the behaviour of human beings shows differences, which ethics, disregarding the fact that such differences are determined, classifies as 'good' or 'bad'. So long as these undeniable differences have not been removed, obedience to high ethical demands entails damage to the aims of civilization, for it puts a positive premium on being bad.

The element of truth behind all this, which people are so ready to disavow, is that men are not gentle creatures who want to be loved, and who at the most can defend themselves if they are attacked; they are, on the contrary, creatures among whose instinctual endowments is to be reckoned a powerful share of aggressiveness. As a result, their neighbour is for them not only a potential helper or sexual object, but also someone who tempts them to satisfy their aggressiveness on him, to exploit his capacity for work without compensation, to use him sexually without his consent, to seize his possessions, to humiliate him, to cause him pain, to torture and to kill him. Who, in the face of all of his experience of life and of history, will have the courage to dispute this assertion? As a rule this cruel aggressiveness waits for some provocation or puts itself at the service of some other purpose, whose goal might also have been reached by milder measures. In circumstances that are favourable to it, when the mental counter-forces which or-

---

[1] A great imaginative writer may permit himself to give expression—jokingly, at all events—to psychological truths that are severely proscribed. Thus Heine confesses: 'Mine is a most peaceable disposition. My wishes are: a humble cottage with a thatched roof, but a good bed, good food, the freshest milk and butter, flowers before my window, and a few fine trees before my door; and if God wants to make my happiness complete, he will grant me the joy of seeing some six or seven of my enemies hanging from those trees. Before their death I shall, moved in my heart, forgive them all the wrong they did me in their lifetime. One must, it is true,

---

forgive one's enemies—but not before they have been hanged.' (*Gedanken und Einfälle* [section I].)

dinarily inhibit it are out of action, it also manifests itself spontaneously and reveals man as a savage beast to whom consideration towards his own kind is something alien. Anyone who calls to mind the atrocities committed during [human recorded history] will have to bow humbly before the truth of this view.

The existence of this inclination to aggression, which we can detect in ourselves and justly assume to be present in others, is the factor which disturbs our relations with our neighbour and which forces civilization into such a high expenditure [of energy]. In consequence of this primary mutual hostility of human beings, civilized society is perpetually threatened with disintegration. The interest of work in common would not hold it together; instinctual passions are stronger than reasonable interests. Civilization has to use its utmost efforts in order to set limits to man's aggressive instincts and to hold the manifestations of them in check by psychical reaction-formations. Hence, therefore, the use of methods to incite people into identifications and aim-inhibited relationships of love, hence the restriction upon sexual life, and hence too the ideal's commandment to love one's neighbour as oneself—a commandment which is really justified by the fact that nothing else runs so strongly counter to the original nature of man. In spite of every effort, these endeavours of civilization have not so far achieved very much. It hopes to prevent the crudest excesses of brutal violence by itself assuming the right to use violence against criminals, but the law is not able to lay hold of the more cautious and refined manifestations of human aggressiveness. The time comes when each one of us has to give up as illusions the expectations which, in his youth, he pinned upon his fellowmen, and when he may learn how much difficulty and pain has been added to his life by their ill-will. At the same time, it would be unfair to reproach civilization with trying to eliminate strife and competition from human activity. These things are undoubtedly indispensable. But opposition is not necessarily enmity; it is merely misused and made an *occasion* for enmity.

The communists believe that they have found the path to deliverance from our evils. According to them, man is wholly good and is well-disposed to his neighbour; but the institution of private property has corrupted his nature. The ownership of private wealth gives the individual power, and with it the temptation to ill-treat his neighbour; while the man who is excluded from possession is bound to rebel in hostility against his oppressor. If private property were abolished, all wealth held in common, and everyone allowed to share in the enjoyment of it, ill-will and hostility would disappear among men. Since everyone's needs would be satisfied, no one would have any reason to regard another as his enemy; all would willingly undertake the work that was necessary. I have no concern with any economic criticisms of the communist system; I cannot enquire into whether the abolition of private property is expedient or advantageous. But I am able to recognize that the psychological premises on which the system is based are an untenable illusion. In abolishing private property we deprive the human love of aggression of one of its instruments, certainly a strong one, though certainly not the strongest; but we have in no way altered the differences in power and influence which are misused by aggressiveness, nor have we altered anything in its nature. Aggressiveness was not created by property. It reigned almost without limit in primitive times, when property was still very scanty, and it already shows itself in the nursery almost before property has given up its primal, anal form; it forms the basis of every relation of affection and love among people (with the single exception, perhaps, of the mother's relation to her male child). If we do away with personal rights over material wealth, there still remains prerogative in the field of sexual relationships, which is bound to become the source of the strongest dislike and the most violent hostility among men who in other respects are on an equal footing. If we were to remove this factor, too, by allowing complete freedom of sexual life and thus abolishing the family, the germ-cell of civilization, we cannot, it is true, easily foresee what new paths the development of civilization could take; but one thing we can expect, and that is that this indestructible feature of human nature will follow it there.

It is clearly not easy for men to give up the satisfaction of this inclination to aggression. They do not feel comfortable without it. It is always possible to bind together a considerable number of people in love, so long as there are other people left over to receive the manifestation of their aggressiveness. I once discussed the phenomenon that it is precisely communities with adjoining territories, and related to each other in other ways as well, who are engaged in constant feuds and in ridiculing each other. In this respect the Jewish people, scattered everywhere, have rendered most useful services to the civilizations of the countries that have been their hosts; but unfortunately all the massacres of the Jews in the Middle Ages did not suffice to make that period more peaceful and secure for their Christian fellows. When once the Apostle Paul had posited universal love between men as the foundation of his Christian community, extreme intolerance on the part of Christendom towards those who remained outside it became the inevitable consequence. [Also,] the dream of a Germanic world-dominion called for antisemitism as its complement; and it is intelligible that the attempt to establish a new, communist civilization in Russia should find its psychological support in the persecution of the bourgeois. One only wonders, with concern, what the Soviets will do after they have wiped out their bourgeois.

In all that follows I adopt the standpoint, therefore, that the inclination to aggression is an original, self-subsisting instinctual disposition in man, and I return to my view that it constitutes the greatest impediment to civilization. At one point in the course of this enquiry, I was led to the idea that civilization was a special process which mankind undergoes, and I am still under the influence of that idea. I may now add that civilization is a process in the service of Eros, whose purpose is to combine single human individuals, and after that families, then races, peoples and nations, into one great unity, the unity of mankind. Why this has to happen, we do not know; the work of Eros is precisely this. These collections of men are to be libidinally bound to one another. Necessity alone, the advantages of work in common, will not hold them together. But man's natural aggressive instinct, the hostility of each against all and all against each, opposes this programme of civilization. This aggressive instinct is the derivative and the main representative of the death instinct which we have found alongside of Eros and which shares world-dominion with it. And now, I think, the meaning of the evolution of civilization is no longer obscure to us. It must present the struggle between Eros and Death, between the instinct of life and the instinct of destruction, as it works itself out in the human species. This struggle is what all life essentially consists of, and the evolution of civilization may therefore be simply described as the struggle for life of the human species.

READING 20

Transmission of Aggression Through Imitation of Aggressive

Albert Bandura, Dorothea Ross, and Sheila A. Ross (1961)

In social psychology, four basic theories for aggression have been posited. McDougall (1908), Freud (Reading 19), and others found instinct to be the culprit in aggressive behavior. In frustration-aggression theory, Dollard, Doob, Miller, Mowrer Sears (1939) claimed that "aggression is always a consequence of frustration" and "frustration" always leads to some form of aggression." Berkowitz (1969) later revised this theory to include aversive stimuli as mediating variables between frustration and aggression. A third theory, traditional behaviorism, invokes reinforcement principles of learning; aggression becomes the strategy of choice based on its ability to pay off, or reward, the aggressor. The fourth theory, social learning, suggests that aggression can be learned simply by observing others, without any reinforcement associated with it.

One of the earliest social learning studies is Bandura, Ross, and Ross. This study and others by Bandura and his colleagues (e.g., Bandura & Huston, 1961) generated hundreds of other studies replicating, modifying, and extending social learning principles. Much work has been conducted on when behavior is learned although not necessarily performed, what characteristics of the model are important (e.g., the model's gender, and/or relative power, or similarity to the learner), and how distant the modeling can be (e.g., in the same room, on television, in the movies).

The Bandura experiments are classics for describing a new type of learning previously unidentified. Additionally, this study stands as a landmark in its movement away from traditional behaviorism for (a) noting children's perceptions of sex roles and the importance of these perceptions to their subsequent behavior, and (b) looking inward to motivational and cognitive aspects of behavior. Finally, most psychologists believe that the ramifications of social learning theory are clear: Expression and support for violence in our culture will perpetuate a cycle of violence.

A previous study, designed to account for the phenomenon of identification in terms of incidental learning, demonstrated that children readily imitated behavior exhibited by an adult model in the presence of the model (Bandura & Huston, 1961). A series of experiments by Blake (1958) and others (Grosser, Polansky, & Lippitt, 1951; Rosenblith, 1959; Schachter & Hall, 1952) have likewise shown that mere observation of responses of a model has a facilitating effect on subjects' reactions in the immediate social influence setting.

While these studies provide convincing evidence for the influence and control exerted on others by the behavior of a model, a more crucial test of imitative learning involves the generalization of imitative response patterns to new settings in which the model is absent.

In the experiment reported in this paper children were exposed to aggressive and nonaggressive adult models and were then tested for amount of imitative learning in a new situation in the absence of the model. According to the prediction, subjects exposed to aggressive models would reproduce aggressive acts resembling those of their models and would differ in this respect both from subjects who observed nonagressive models and from those who had no prior exposure to any models. This hypothesis assumed that subjects had learned imitative habits as a result of prior reinforcement, and these tendencies would generalize to some extent to adult experimenters (Miller & Dollard, 1941).

It was further predicted that observation of subdued nonaggressive models would have a generalized inhibiting effect on the subjects' subsequent behavior, and this effect would be reflected in a difference between the nonaggressive and the control groups, with subjects in the latter group displaying significantly more aggression.

Hypotheses were also advanced concerning the influence of the sex of model and sex of subjects on imitation. Fauls and Smith (1956) have shown that preschool children perceive their parents as having distinct preferences regarding sex appropriate modes of behavior for their children. Their findings, as well as informal observation, suggest that parents reward imitation of sex appropriate behavior and discourage or punish sex inappropriate imitative responses, e.g., a male child is unlikely to receive much reward for performing female appropriate activities, such as cooking, or for adopting other aspects of the maternal role, but these same behaviors are typically welcomed if performed by females. As a result of differing reinforcement histories, tendencies to imitate male and female models thus acquire differential habit strength. One would expect, on this basis, subjects to imitate the behavior of a same-sex model to a greater degree than a model of the opposite sex.

Since aggression, however, is a highly masculine-typed behavior, boys should be more predisposed than girls toward imitating aggression, the difference being the most marked for subjects exposed to the male aggressive model.

METHOD

Subjects

The subjects were 36 boys and 36 girls enrolled in the Stanford University Nursery School. They ranged in age from 37 to 69 months, with a mean age of 52 months.

Two adults, a male and a female, served in the role of model, and one female experimenter conducted the study for all 72 children.

Experimental Design

Subjects were divided into eight experimental groups of six subjects each and a control group consisting of 24 subjects. Half the experimental subjects were exposed to aggressive models and half were exposed to models that were subdued and nonaggressive in their behavior. These groups were further subdivided into male and female subjects. Half the subjects in the aggressive and nonaggressive conditions observed same-sex models, while the remaining subjects in each group viewed models of the opposite sex. The control group had no prior exposure to the adult models and was tested only in the generalization situation.

It seemed reasonable to expect that the subjects' level of aggressiveness would be positively related to the readiness with which they imitated aggressive modes of behavior. Therefore, in order to increase the precision of treatment comparisons, subjects in the experimental and control groups were matched individually on the basis of ratings of their aggressive behavior in social interactions in the nursery school.

The subjects were rated on four five-point rating scales by the experimenter and a nursery school teacher, both of whom were well acquainted with the children. These scales measured the extent to which subjects displayed physical aggression, verbal aggression, aggression toward inanimate objects, and aggressive inhibition. The latter scale, which dealt with the subjects' tendency to inhibit aggressive reactions in the face of high instigation, provided a measure of aggression anxiety.

Fifty-one subjects were rated independently by both judges so as to permit an assessment of interrater agreement. The reliability of the composite aggression score, estimated by means of the Pearson product-moment correlation, was .89.

The composite score was obtained by summing the ratings on the four aggression scales; on the basis of these scores, subjects were arranged in triplets and assigned at random to one of two treatment conditions or to the control group.

Experimental Conditions

In the first step in the procedure subjects were brought individually by the experimenter to the experimental room and the model who was in the hallway outside the room, was invited by the experimenter to come and join in the game. The experimenter then escorted the subject to one corner of the room, which was structured as the subject's play area. After seating the child at a small table, the experimenter demonstrated how the subject could design pictures with potato prints and picture stickers provided. The potato prints included a variety of geometrical forms; the stickers were attractive multicolor pictures of animals, flowers, and western figures to be pasted on a pastoral scene. These activities were selected since they had been established, by previous studies in the nursery school, as having high interest value for the children.

After having settled the subject in his corner, the experimenter escorted the model to the opposite corner of the room which contained a small table and chair, a tinker toy set, a mallet, and a 5-foot inflated Bobo doll. The experimenter explained that these were the materials provided for the model to play with and, after the model was seated, the experimenter left the experimental room.

With subjects in the *nonaggressive condition,* the model assembled the tinker toys in a quiet subdued manner totally ignoring the Bobo doll.

In contrast, with subjects in the *aggressive condition,* the model began by assembling the tinker toys but after approximately a minute had elapsed, the model turned to the Bobo doll and spent the remainder of the period aggressing toward it.

Imitative learning can be clearly demonstrated if a model performs sufficiently novel patterns of responses which are unlikely to occur independently of the observation of the behavior of a model and if a subject reproduces these behaviors in substantially identical form. For this reason, in addition to punching the Bobo doll, a response that is likely to be performed by children independently of a demonstration, the model exhibited distinctive aggressive acts which were to be scored as imitative responses. The model laid Bobo on its side, sat on it and punched it repeatedly in the nose. The model then raised the Bobo doll, picked up the mallet and struck the doll on the head. Following the mallet aggression, the model tossed the doll up in the air aggressively and kicked it about the room. This sequence of physically aggressive acts was repeated approximately three times, interspersed with verbally aggressive responses such as, "Sock him in the nose...," "Hit him down...," "Throw him in the air...," "Kick him...," "Pow...," and two nonaggressive comments, "He keeps coming back for more" and "He sure is a tough fella."

Thus in the exposure situation, subjects were provided with a diverting task which occupied their attention while at the same time insured observation of the model's behavior in the absence of any instructions to observe or to learn the responses in question. Since subjects could not perform the model's aggressive behavior, any learning that occurred was purely on an observational or covert basis.

At the end of 10 minutes, the experimenter entered the room, informed the subject that he would now go to another game room, and bid the model goodbye.

Aggression Arousal

Subjects were tested for the amount of imitative learning in a different experimental room that was set off from the main nursery school building. The two experimental situations were thus clearly differentiated; in fact, many subjects were under the impression that they were no longer on nursery school grounds.

Prior to the test for imitation, however, all subjects, experimental and control, were subjected to mild aggression arousal to insure that they were under some degree of instigation to aggression. The arousal experience was included for two main reasons. In the first place, observation of aggressive behavior exhibited by others tends to reduce the probability of aggression on the part of the observer (Rosenbaum & deCharms, 1960). Consequently, subjects in the aggressive condition, in relation both to the nonaggressive and control groups, would be under weaker instigation following exposure to the models. Second, if subjects in the nonaggressive condition expressed little aggression in the face of appropriate instigation, the presence of an inhibitory process would seem to be indicated.

Following the exposure experience, therefore, the experimenter brought the subject to an anteroom that contained these relatively attractive toys: a fire engine, a locomotive, a jet fighter plane, a cable car, a colorful spinning top, and a doll set complete with wardrobe, doll carriage, and baby crib. The experimenter explained that the toys were for the subject to play with but, as soon as the subject became sufficiently involved with the play material (usually in about 2 minutes), the experimenter remarked that these were her very best toys, that she did not let just anyone play with them, and that she had decided to reserve these toys for the other children. However, the subject could play with any of the toys that were in the next room. The experimenter and the subject then entered the adjoining experimental room.

It was necessary for the experimenter to remain in the room during the experimental session; otherwise a number of the children would either refuse to remain alone or would leave before the termination of the session. However, in order to minimize any influence her presence might have on the subject's behavior, the experimenter remained as inconspicuous as possible by busying herself with paper work at a desk in the far corner of the room and avoiding any interactions with the child.

Test for Delayed Imitation

The experimental room contained a variety of toys including some that could be used in imitative or nonimitative aggression, and others that tended to elicit predominantly nonaggressive forms of behavior. The aggressive toys included a 3-foot Bobo doll, a mallet and peg board, two dart guns, and a tether ball with a face painted on it which hung from the ceiling. The nonaggressive toys, on the other hand, included a tea set, crayons and coloring paper, a ball, two dolls, three bears, cars and trucks, and plastic farm animals.

In order to eliminate any variation in behavior due to mere placement of the toys in the room, the play material was arranged in a fixed order for each of the sessions.

The subject spent 20 minutes in this experimental room during which time his behavior was rated in terms of predetermined response categories by judges who observed the session through a one-way mirror in an adjoining observation room. The 20-minute session was divided

into 5-second intervals by means of an electric interval timer, thus yielding a total number of 240 response units for each subject.

The male model scored the experimental sessions for all 72 children. Except for the cases in which he served as model, he did not have knowledge of the subjects' group assignments. In order to provide an estimate of interscorer agreement, the performances of half the subjects were also scored independently by a second observer. Thus one or the other of the two observers usually had no knowledge of the conditions to which the subjects were assigned. Since, however, all but two of the subjects in the aggressive condition performed the models' novel aggressive responses while subjects in the other conditions only rarely exhibited such reactions, subjects who were exposed to the aggressive models could be readily identified through their distinctive behavior.

The responses scored involved highly specific concrete classes of behavior and yielded high interscorer reliabilities, the product-moment coefficients being in the .90s.

Response Measures

Three measures of imitation were obtained:

> *Imitation of physical aggression:* This category included acts of striking the Bobo doll with the mallet, sitting on the doll and punching it in the nose, kicking the doll, and tossing it in the air.
>
> *Imitative verbal aggression:* Subject repeats the phrases, "Sock him," "Hit him down," "Kick him," "Throw him in the air," or "Pow."
>
> *Imitative nonaggressive verbal responses:* Subject repeats, "He keeps coming back for more," or "He sure is a tough fella."

During the pretest, a number of the subjects imitated the essential components of the model's behavior but did not perform the complete act, or they directed the imitative aggressive response to some object other than the Bobo doll.

Two responses of this type were therefore scored and were interpreted as partially imitative behavior.

Mallet aggression: Subject strikes objects other than the Bobo doll aggressively with the mallet.

Sits on Bobo doll: Subject lays the Bobo doll on its side and sits on it, but does not aggress toward it.

The following additional nonimitative aggressive responses were scored:

Punches Bobo doll: Subject strikes, slaps, or pushes the doll aggressively.

Nonimitative physical and verbal aggression: This category included physically aggressive acts directed toward objects other than the Bobo doll and any hostile remarks except for those in the verbal imitation category; e.g., "Shoot the Bobo," "Cut him," "Stupid ball," "Knock over people," "Horses fighting, biting."

Aggressive gun play: Subject shoots darts or aims the guns and fires imaginary shots at objects in the room.

Ratings were also made of the number of behavior units in which subjects played nonaggressively or sat quietly and did not play with any of the material at all.

RESULTS

Complete Imitation of Models' Behavior

Subjects in the aggression condition reproduced a good deal of physical and verbal aggressive behavior resembling that of the models, and their mean scores differed markedly from those of subjects in the nonaggressive and control groups who exhibited virtually no imitative aggression (see Table 1).

Since there were only a few scores for subjects in the nonaggressive and control conditions (approximately 70% of the subjects had zero scores), and the assumption of homogeneity of variance could not be made, the Friedman two-way analysis of variance by ranks was employed to test the significance of the obtained differences.

The prediction that exposure of subjects to aggressive models increases the probability of aggressive behavior is clearly confirmed (see Table 2). The main effect of treatment conditions is highly significant both for physical and verbal imitative aggression. Comparison of pairs of scores by the sign test shows that the obtained overall differences were due almost entirely to the aggression displayed by subjects who had been exposed to the aggressive models. Their scores were significantly higher than those of either the nonaggressive or control groups, which did not differ from each other (Table 2).

Imitation was not confined to the model's aggressive responses. Approximately one-third of the subjects in the aggressive condition also repeated the model's nonaggressive verbal responses while none of the subjects in either the nonaggressive or control groups made such remarks. This difference, tested by means of the Cochran Q test, was significant well beyond the .001 level (Table 2).

Partial Imitation of Models' Behavior

Differences in the predicted direction were also obtained on the two measures of partial imitation.

Analysis of variance of scores based on the subjects' use of the mallet aggressively toward objects other than the Bobo doll reveals that treatment conditions are a statistically significant source of variation (Table 2). In addition, individual sign tests show that both the aggressive and the control groups, relative to subjects in the nonaggressive condition, produced significantly more mallet aggression, the difference being particularly marked with regard to female subjects. Girls who observed nonaggressive models performed a mean number of 0.5 mallet aggression responses as compared to mean values of

	TABLE 1				

MEAN AGGRESSION SCORES FOR EXPERIMENTAL AND CONTROL SUBJECTS

	Experimental Groups				Control groups
	Aggressive		Nonaggressive		
Response category	F Model	M Model	F Model	M Model	
Imitative physical aggression					
Female subjects	5.5	7.2	2.5	0.0	1.2
Male subjects	12.4	25.8	0.2	1.5	2.0
Imitative verbal aggression					
Female subjects	13.7	2.0	0.3	0.0	0.7
Male subjects	4.3	12.7	1.1	0.0	1.7
Mallet aggression					
Female subjects	17.2	18.7	0.5	0.5	13.1
Male subjects	15.5	28.8	18.7	6.7	13.5
Punches Bobo doll					
Female subjects	6.3	16.5	5.8	4.3	11.7
Male subjects	18.9	11.9	15.6	14.8	15.7
Nonimitative aggression					
Female subjects	21.3	8.4	7.2	1.4	6.1
Male subjects	16.2	36.7	26.1	22.3	24.6
Aggressive gun play					
Female subjects	1.8	4.5	2.6	2.5	3.7
Male subjects	7.3	15.9	8.9	16.7	14.3

18.0 and 13.1 for girls in the aggressive and control groups, respectively.

Although subjects who observed aggressive models performed more mallet aggression ($M = 20.0$) than their controls ($M = 13.3$), the difference was not statistically significant.

With respect to the partially imitative response of sitting on the Bobo doll, the overall group differences were significant beyond the .01 level (Table 2). Comparison of pairs of scores by the sign test procedure reveals that subjects in the aggressive group reproduced this aspect of the models' behavior to a greater extent than did the nonaggressive ($p = .018$) or the control ($p = .059$) subjects. The latter two groups, on the other hand, did not differ from each other.

Nonimitative Aggression

Analyses of variance of the remaining aggression measures (Table 2) show that treatment conditions did not influence the extent to which subjects engaged in aggressive gun play or punched the Bobo doll. The effect of conditions is highly significant ($X^2_r = 8.96$, $p < .02$), however, in the case of the subjects' nonimitative physical and verbal aggression. Further comparison of treatment pairs reveals that the main source of the overall difference was the aggressive and nonaggressive groups which differed significantly from each other (Table 2), with subjects exposed to the aggressive models displaying the greater amount of aggression.

TABLE 2

SIGNIFICANCE OF THE DIFFERENCE BETWEEN EXPERIMENTAL AND CONTROL GROUPS IN THE EXPRESSION OF AGGRESSION

Response category	X^2r	Q	p	Comparison of pairs of treatment conditions		
				Aggressive vs. nonaggressive p	Aggressive vs. control p	Nonaggressive vs. control p
Imitative responses						
Physical aggression	27.17		< .001	< .001	< .001	.09
Verbal aggression	9.17		< .02	.004	.048	.09
Nonaggressive verbal responses		17.50	< .001	.004	.004	ns
Partial imitation						
Mallet aggression	11.06		< .01	.026	ns	.005
Sits on Bobo		13.44	< .01	.018	.059	ns
Nonimitative aggression						
Punches Bobo doll	2.87		ns			
Physical and verbal	8.96		< .02	.026	ns	ns
Aggressive gun play	2.75		ns			

Influence of Sex of Model and Sex of Subjects on Imitation

The hypothesis that boys are more prone than girls to imitate aggression exhibited by a model was only partially confirmed. The t tests computed for subjects in the aggressive condition reveal that boys reproduced more imitative physical aggression than girls ($t = 2.50$, $p < .01$). The groups do not differ, however, in their imitation of verbal aggression.

The use of nonparametric tests, necessitated by the extremely skewed distributions of scores for subjects in the nonaggressive and control conditions, preclude an overall test of the influence of sex of model per se, and of the various interactions between the main effects. Inspection of the means presented in Table 1 for subjects in the aggression condition, however, clearly suggests the possibility of a Sex x Model interaction. This interaction effect is much more consistent and pronounced for the male model than for the female model. Male subjects, for example, exhibited more physical ($t = 2.07, p < .05$) and verbal imitative aggression ($t = 2.51, p < .05$), more nonimitative aggression ($t = 3.15, p < .025$), and engaged in significantly

more aggressive gun play ($t = 2.12, p < .05$) following exposure to the aggressive male model than the female subjects. In contrast, girls exposed to the female model performed considerably more imitative verbal aggression and more nonimitative aggression than did the boys (Table 1). The variances, however, were equally large and with only a small N in each cell the mean differences did not reach statistical significance.

Data for the nonaggressive and control subjects provide additional suggestive evidence that the behavior of the male model exerted a greater influence than the female model on the subjects' behavior in the generalization situation.

It will be recalled that, except for the greater amount of mallet aggression exhibited by the control subjects, no significant differences were obtained between the nonaggressive and control groups. The data indicate, however, that the absence of significant differences between these two groups was due primarily to the fact that subjects exposed to the nonaggressive female model did not differ from the controls on any of the measures of aggression.

With respect to the male model, on the other hand, the differences between the groups are striking. Comparison of the sets of scores by means of the sign test reveals that, in relation to the control group, subjects exposed to the nonaggressive male model performed significantly less imitative physical aggression ($p = .06$), less mallet aggression ($p = .003$), less nonimitative physical and verbal aggression ($p = .03$), and they were less inclined to punch the Bobo doll $p = .07$).

While the comparison of subgroups, when some of the overall tests do not reach statistical significance, is likely to capitalize on chance differences, nevertheless the consistency of the findings adds support to the interpretation in terms of influence by the model.

Nonaggressive Behavior

With the exception of expected sex differences, Lindquist (1956) Type III analyses of variance of the nonaggressive response scores yielded few significant differences.

Female subjects spent more time than boys playing with dolls ($p < .001$), with the tea set ($p < .001$), and coloring ($p < .05$). The boys, on the other hand, devoted significantly more time than the girls to exploratory play with the guns ($p < .01$). No sex differences were found in respect to the subjects use of the other stimulus objects, i.e., farm animals, cars, or tether ball.

Treatment conditions did produce significant differences on two measures of nonaggressive behavior that are worth mentioning. Subjects in the nonaggressive condition engaged in significantly more nonaggressive play with dolls than either subjects in the aggressive groups ($t = 2.67$, $p < .02$), or in the control group ($t = 2.57$, $p < .02$).

Even more noteworthy is the finding that subjects who observed nonaggressive models spent more than twice as much time as subjects in aggressive condition ($t = 3.07$, $p < .01$) in simply sitting quietly without handling any of the play material.

DISCUSSION

Much current research on social learning is focused on the shaping of new behavior through rewarding and punishing consequences. Unless responses are emitted, however, they cannot be influenced. The results of this study provide strong evidence that observation of cues produced by the behavior of others is one effective means of eliciting certain forms of responses for which the original probability is very low or zero. Indeed, social imitation may hasten or short-cut the acquisition of new behaviors without the necessity of reinforcing successive approximations as suggested by Skinner (1953).

Thus subjects given an opportunity to observe aggressive models later reproduced a good deal of physical and verbal aggression (as well as nonaggressive responses) substantially identical with that of the model. In contrast, subjects who were exposed to nonaggressive models and those who had no previous exposure to any models only rarely performed such responses.

To the extent that observation of adult models displaying aggression communicates permissiveness for aggressive behavior, such exposure may serve to weaken inhibitory responses and thereby to increase the probability of aggressive reactions to subsequent frustrations. The fact, however, that subjects expressed their aggression in ways that clearly resembled the novel patterns exhibited by the models provides striking evidence for the occurrence of learning by imitation.

In the procedure employed by Miller and Dollard (1941) for establishing imitative behavior, adult or peer models performed discrimination responses following which they were consistently rewarded, and the subjects were similarly reinforced whenever they matched the leaders' choice responses. While these experiments have been widely accepted as demonstrations of learning by means of imitation, in fact, they simply involve a special case of discrimination learning in which the behavior of others serves as discrimination stimuli for responses that are already part of the subject's repertoire. Auditory or visual environmental cues could easily have been substituted for the social stimuli to facilitate the discrimination learning. In contrast, the process of imitation studied in the present experiment differed in several important respects from the one investigated by Miller and Dollard in that subjects learned to combine fractional responses into relatively complex novel patterns solely by observing the performance of social models' behavior in the exposure setting, and without any reinforcers delivered either to the models or to the observers.

An adequate theory of the mechanisms underlying imitative learning is lacking. The explanations that have been offered (Logan, Olmsted, Rosner, Schwartz, & Stevens, 1955; Maccoby, 1959) assume that the imitator performs the model's responses covertly. If it can be assumed additionally that rewards and punishments are self-administered in conjunction with the covert responses, the process of imitative learning could be accounted for in terms of the same principles that govern instrumental trial-and-error learning. In the early stages of the developmental process, however, the range of component responses in the organism's repertoire is probably increased through a process of classical conditioning (Bandura & Huston, 1961; Mowrer, 1950).

The data provide some evidence that the male model influenced the subjects' behavior outside the exposure setting to a greater extent than was true for the female model. In the analyses of the Sex X Model interactions, for example, only the comparisons involving the male model yielded significant differences. Similarly, subjects exposed to the nonaggressive male model performed less aggressive behavior than the controls, whereas comparisons involving the female model were consistently nonsignificant.

In a study of learning by imitation, Rosenblith (1959) has likewise found male experimenters more effective than females in influencing childrens' behavior. Rosenblith advanced the tentative explanation that the school setting may involve some social deprivation in respect to adult males which, in turn, enhances the male's reward value.

The trends in the data yielded by the present study suggest an alternative explanation. In the case of a highly masculine-typed behavior such as physical aggression, there is a tendency for both male and female subjects to imitate the male model to a greater degree than the female model. On the other hand, in the case of verbal aggression, which is less clearly sex linked, the greatest amount of imitation occurs in relation to the same-sex model. These trends together with the finding that boys in relation to girls are in general more imitative of physical aggression but do not differ in imitation of verbal aggression, suggest that subjects may be differentially affected by the sex of the model but that predictions must take into account the degree to which the behavior in question is sex-typed.

The preceding discussion has assumed that maleness-femaleness rather than some other personal characteristics of the particular models involved, is the significant variable—an assumption that cannot be tested directly with the data at hand. It was clearly evident, however, particularly from boys' spontaneous remarks about the display of aggression by the female model, that some subjects at least were responding in terms of a sex discrimination and their prior learning about what is sex appropriate behavior (e.g., "Who is that lady. That's not the way for a lady to behave. Ladies are supposed to act like ladies..." "You should have seen what that girl did in there. She was just acting like a man. I never saw a girl act like that before. She was punching and fighting but not swearing"). Aggression by the male model, on the other hand, was more likely to be seen as appropriate and approved by both the boys ("Al's a good socker, he beat up Bobo. I want to sock like Al.") and the girls ("That man is a strong fighter, he punched and punched and he could hit Bobo right down to the floor and if Bobo got up he said, 'Punch your nose.' He's a good fighter like Daddy'') .

The finding that subjects exposed to the quiet models were more inhibited and unresponsive than subjects in the aggressive condition, together with the obtained difference on the aggression measures, suggests that exposure to inhibited models not only decreases the probability of occurrence of aggressive behavior but also generally restricts the range of behavior emitted by the subjects.

"Identification with aggressor" (Freud, 1946) or "defensive identification" (Mowrer, 1950), whereby a person presumably transforms himself from object to agent of aggression by adopting the attributes of an aggressive threatening model so as to allay anxiety, is widely accepted as an explanation of the imitative learning of aggression.

The development of aggressive modes of response by children of aggressively punitive adults, however, may simply reflect object displacement without involving any such mechanism of defensive identification. In studies of child training antecedents of aggressively antisocial adolescents (Bandura & Walters, 1959) and of young hyper-aggressive boys (Bandura, 1960), the parents were found to be nonpermissive and punitive of aggression directed toward themselves. On the other hand, they actively encouraged and reinforced their sons' aggression toward persons outside the home. This pattern of differential reinforcement of aggressive behavior served to inhibit the boys' aggression toward the original instigators and fostered the displacement of aggression toward objects and situations eliciting much weaker inhibitory responses.

Moreover, the findings from an earlier study (Bandura & Huston, 1961), in which children imitated to an equal degree aggression exhibited by a nurturant and a non-nurturant model, together with the results of the present experiment in which subjects readily imitated aggressive models who were more or less neutral figures suggest that mere observation of aggression, regardless of the qual-

ity of the model-subject relationship, is a sufficient condition for producing imitative aggression in children. A comparative study of the subjects' imitation of aggressive models who are feared, who are liked and esteemed, or who are essentially neutral figures would throw some light on whether or not a more parsimonious theory than the one involved in "identification with the aggressor" can explain the modeling process.

SUMMARY

Twenty-four preschool children were assigned to each of three conditions. One experimental group observed aggressive adult models; a second observed inhibited nonaggressive models; while subjects in a control group had no prior exposure to the models. Half the subjects in the experimental conditions observed same-sex models and half viewed models of the opposite sex. Subjects were then tested for the amount of imitative as well as nonimitative aggression performed in a new situation in the absence of the models.

Comparison of the subjects' behavior in the generalization situation revealed that subjects exposed to aggressive models reproduced a good deal of aggression resembling that of the models, and that their mean scores differed markedly from those of subjects in the nonaggressive and control groups. Subjects in the aggressive condition also exhibited significantly more partially imitative and nonimitative aggressive behavior and were generally less inhibited in their behavior than subjects in the nonaggressive condition.

Imitation was found to be differentially influenced by the sex of the model with boys showing more aggression than girls following exposure to the male model, the difference being particularly marked on highly masculine-typed behavior.

Subjects who observed the nonaggressive models, especially the subdued male model, were generally less aggressive than their controls.

The implications of the findings based on this experiment and related studies for the psychoanalytic theory of identification with the aggressor were discussed.

READING 21

Temperature and Aggression: Effects on Quarterly, Yearly, and City Rates of Violent and Nonviolent Crime

Craig A. Anderson (1987)

At times, the mediators of human behavior may stem from purely environmental factors. Working frantically during the hottest months of the year to meet our deadline for this book, we wondered why our conversations were becoming increasingly fragmented and irritated. Was it the hectic nature of our schedules? Was it that we were finally realizing unresolvable intellectual differences between us?

These are good hypotheses, but the next reading reminded us of another, which turned out to be the most probable one.

Anderson's article confirms the heat-violence relationship first studied by Baron in 1972. Building on both field and experimental research, Anderson's work suggests a linear relationship between heat and violent crime. He also notes that the reasons for this relationship are as yet unclear. Future research might attempt to identify the underlying processes, as well as indicating inexpensive, practical solutions for attenuating or eliminating the effect. We found the second to last paragraph in the Anderson article particularly useful, in light of our own personal experience described above. We realized that after so many years of working under demanding conditions, and also after years of good intellectual engagement with each other, that the culprit was most likely the hot summer weather. A particularly hot summer and particularly high levels of ozone do not provide a good combination for collegiality. Violence was

fortunately not a possibility because one of us was in Ohio and the other in New York; instead, moving to cooler quarters allowed us to regain our good humor and our ability to engage in intellectual debate.

Abstract

The hypothesized relation between uncomfortably hot temperatures and aggressive behavior was examined in two studies of violent and nonviolent crime. Data on rates of murder, rape, assault, robbery, burglary, larceny-theft, and motor vehicle theft were gathered from archival sources. The first three crimes listed are violent; the latter four are less violent (labeled nonviolent). On the basis of previous research and theory (Anderson & Anderson, 1984), it was predicted that violent crimes would be more prevalent in the hotter quarters of the year and in hotter years. Furthermore, it was predicted that this temperature-crime relation would be stronger for violent than for nonviolent crime. Study 1 confirmed both predictions. Also, differences among cities in violent crime were predicted to be related to the hotness of cities; this effect was expected to be stronger for violent than for nonviolent crimes. Study 2 confirmed both predictions, even when effects of a variety of social, demographic, and economic variables were statistically removed. Theoretical and practical implications are discussed.

Environmental factors affect a wide variety of aggression-related phenomena. For example, negative affect and interpersonal disliking are related to uncomfortably hot temperatures and to crowding (e.g., Bell, Garnand, & Heath, 1984; Griffitt, 1970; Griffitt & Veitch, 1971). Unpleasant odors influence physical aggression against others (Rotton, Frey, Barry, Milligan, & Fitzpatrick, 1979). The concentration of negative and positive ions in the air affects aggression and moods (Baron, Russell, & Arms, 1985; Charry & Hawkinshire, 1981). High ozone levels have been associated with increased family violence and assaults (Rotton & Frey, 1985). In sum, considerable evidence suggests that naturally occurring variations in our immediate environments exert powerful influences on social and antisocial affects and behaviors.

The most intensively studied relation, though, is that between temperature and aggressive behavior. Early theoretical thinking, as well as the prevailing folklore, postulated a positive linear (or at least monotonic) relation, with increasingly hot temperatures leading to increased aggressive behavior. Laboratory studies yielded mixed results, with the hot temperatures sometimes producing increased aggression and sometimes decreased aggression (e.g., Baron, 1972; Baron & Lawton, 1972). Subsequent laboratory studies suggested that negative affect mediated the temperature-aggression relation and that the relation was curvilinearly shaped in the form of an inverted U (Baron & Bell, 1976). (See Baron, 1979, for a review of this literature; see also Palamarek & Rule, 1979.) Up to moderate levels of negative affect, increases in negative affect (resulting from increasingly uncomfortable temperatures, for example) would produce increased aggression. At high levels of negative affect, though, further increases in negative affect (or hot temperatures) would increase attempts to escape from the situation. To the extent that such escape behaviors are incompatible with aggressive behaviors, the result would be decreased aggression at the highest levels of negative affect. For instance, the best way to reduce the negative affect produced by an argument with a neighbor in hot weather is to stop arguing and go inside your air-conditioned house.

There are, however, several interpretational and methodological problems with the curvilinear model and associated data (see Anderson & Anderson, 1984). Most revolve around the obviousness of temperature manipulations in the laboratory and possible subject reactions or strategies deriving from awareness of what is being tested. Field studies in which subjects do not know they are participating in a study avoid these problems.

Data from a variety of field studies examining the temperature-aggression relation have yielded primarily linear effects, with high temperatures producing the highest levels of aggression. For example, Carlsmith and Anderson (1979) found that between 1967 and 1971 the probability of a riot in the United States increased monotonically with ambient temperature. Anderson and Anderson (1984) examined daily frequencies of crimes in two major cities. In both cities, the frequency of violent crimes was positively linearly related to temperature; in neither case was there a quadratic (curvilinear) relation. Furthermore, when they adjusted for the level of nonviolent crimes, the predicted linear trend was still highly significant. In addition, the adjustments yielded a significant quadratic effect, but one that was precisely opposite in form to that predicted by the negative affect model derived from the laboratory studies discussed earlier. That is, increases in temperature at the high temperature range were associated with larger increases in violent crime than were corresponding increases in temperature at the moderate temperature range. Recently, Harries and Stadler (1983; Harries, Stadler, & Zdorkowski, 1984) showed similar linear effects on assaults in another major U.S. city.

Thus the field studies clearly show that even at very high temperatures (and presumably high negative affect) aggressive behavior increases with further increases in temperature. Two explanations for this contradiction of the laboratory studies seem particularly plausible. First, as suggested earlier (and in Anderson & Anderson, 1984), a variety of artifactual processes in the labs may result from subject awareness of temperature manipulations. That is, the inverted U model may be wrong, and the supportive data may be artifactual. Second, it may be that in those field settings that potentiate violent crimes, the perpetrators cannot readily escape the circumstances inducing the negative affect, whereas subjects in the lab can do so. That is, the inverted U model may be correct only in those limited circumstances where the person can escape the conditions that are producing the negative affect and where escape involves performing only nonaggressive behaviors. In the real world, of course, negative affect is often produced by circumstances we cannot control or avoid. Indeed, we sometimes cannot even identify the sources of our discontent.

Regardless of which explanation is true, it would appear that one should expect essentially linear relations between temperature and aggression in most real-world settings. The theoretical rationale for this prediction is as follows. Uncomfortably hot temperatures produce a generally negative level of arousal and negative affect. This negative affect is then transferred (cf. Zillmann, 1978) to a salient object in the person's immediate attention, an object that can be seen by the person as a reasonable source of the negative arousal. It may be, for instance, a spouse with whom one is arguing. In this way, negative arousal from a variety of sources (including temperature, ozone, ions, and lack of sleep) may be attributed to or focused on a ready target. If the negative arousal is sufficient, and if escape from the negative circumstances is not possible, aggressive behavior will be directed at the target. The exact process through which negative affect produces aggression has been the subject of much debate for many years (e.g., the frustration-aggression hypothesis, Miller, 1941). One may attack a perceived source of negative arousal as punishment for having created the arousal. At a less conscious level, negative arousal may automatically prime aggressive interpretational and behavioral schemata because of their semantic or associationistic similarity (cf. Berkowitz, 1984). Regardless of how one gets from negative affect to aggression, this model suggests that in most settings, increases in temperature will be associated with increases in aggressive behaviors even at very hot temperature levels.

Before accepting this pronouncement as true, though, note the interpretational problems with the field studies to date. The major problem is that they all are based on correlational data. Thus, causal statements are risky at best. For example, temperatures are highly related to sea-sonal events such as vacation time, students being out of school, and alcohol consumption, events that might influence crime rates.

One can control for this confounding to some extent in several ways. In the Anderson and the Harries studies, temperature effects were assessed after the effects of various time cycles (e.g., months, days of week) were partialed out. Anderson and Anderson (1984) also reasoned that violent and nonviolent crimes are probably related to many of the same confounded factors and that one should therefore correct for nonviolent crime rates when examining temperature effects on violent crime rates.

The best control for necessarily confounded (i.e., correlational) data is replication of hypothesized conceptual relations with the use of different measures in different contexts. This triangulation procedure works because the hidden or uncontrolled confounds present in a particular study will typically be absent in different studies of the same relation. If the hypothesized relation is obtained in such different studies, one can be more confident that postulated confounds do not account for the relation. To the extent that studies using a variety of measures of aggression in a variety of contexts all yield the same temperature-aggression relation, we can be confident that the relation is due to actual temperature effects rather than to uncontrolled artifacts.

OVERVIEW

The present pair of studies follows this triangulation rationale in extending previous work on the relation between temperature and aggression. Both studies examine variations in violent and nonviolent crime indexes as a function of temperature-related variables. Violent crimes were expected to be positively related to temperature. Nonviolent crimes may also be positively related to temperature, either because of confounds with variables related to temperature (e.g., alcohol consumption) or because of the aggressive component inherent in nonviolent crimes. In either case, violent crimes were expected to be more highly related to temperature than were nonviolent crimes because the behaviors involved are considerably more aggressive in nature. The first study examined crime rates in the United States over a 10-year period as a function of quarter of year (first, second, third, and fourth) and year (1971–1980). The second study examined crime rates in different cities as a function of a variety of social, economic, demographic, and environmental variables.

STUDY 1

In the United States, quarters of the year are closely related to temperature. In particular, the second and third quarters (April through September) have considerably more hot days than the first and fourth quarters. Therefore, one might expect violent crimes to be particularly prevalent in the second and third quarters. In addition, some years are notably hotter than others. Thus, one might also expect year effects that are related to temperature differences among years.

Method

Data were taken from the Federal Bureau of Investigation's (FBI's) *Uniform Crime Reports for the United States* (U.S. Department of Justice, 1981, 1982). For each quarter of the 10-year period of 1971 through 1980, a crime index was reported for each of seven crimes: murder, rape, aggravated assault, robbery, burglary, larceny-theft, and motor vehicle theft. The FBI crime index for each crime was created by setting the number of crimes reported in the first quarter of 1971 at 100. Changes in the number of crimes reported in subsequent quarters were reflected in proportional changes in the index. For instance, a murder index score of 200 meant that twice as many murders were reported in that quarter as were reported in the first quarter of 1971. A separate set of z scores was computed

for each crime on the basis of the 40 data points for that crime. These seven crimes were then combined (z-score averages) into a violent crime index and a nonviolent crime index for each quarter of the 10-year period. The former consisted of murder, rape, and aggravated assault; the latter, of the remaining four crimes.[1]

The temperature-aggression model predicts a greater incidence of violent crime in the second and third quarters because those quarters are the hottest in the United States. The prediction for effect of years is less straightforward. First, an estimate of how hot in general the various years must be created. To do this, data from the 1971 through 1980 issues of *Climatological Data* (U.S. Department of Commerce, 1983a) were examined. Specifically, for each of 240 reporting stations throughout the United States, the number of hot days that occurred in each year was recorded and averaged across stations. The 240 stations selected were all those stations that had reported this data for each of the 10 years. The definition of a hot day was that the maximum temperature recorded was $\geq 32.2°C$ (90°F). The yearly averages derived by this procedure were used to assess temperature effects on crime across years.

Results

Violent Crime   Quarter of year proved to be a highly significant predictor of level of violent crime, $F(3,27) = 87.43$, $p < .0001$. More important, the contrast testing the temperature-aggression hypothesis was also highly significant, $F(1,27) = 137.28$, $p < .0001$. Violent crime was considerably higher in the second and third quarters ($M = 147.0$) than in the first and fourth ($M = 129.2$). The residual from this contrast was also highly significant,

---

[1]Note that the nonviolent crimes contain some aggression or violence. They are, however, considerably less violent than those summarized by the violent crime index. The label *nonviolent* is simply easier to use and think about than *violent-but-less-so-than-the-others*.

$F(2,27) = 62.51, p < .0001$, apparently because violent crime was considerably higher in the third quarter ($M = 156.0$) than in the second ($M = 138.1$). This latter difference also was quite significant, $t(27) = 8.30$, $p < .0001$, and may be due to the fact that the third quarter (July, August, and September) is the hottest of all.

Year effects, in general, were very strong, $F(9,27) = 40.20$, $p < .0001$. Temperature differences among years accounted for a highly significant portion of violent crime differences, $F(1, 27) = 105.16$, $p < .0001$. More violent crimes occurred in the hotter years than in the cooler years. The residual year effect (after accounting for temperature differences) was also very strong, $F(8,27) = 32.09$, $p < .0001$. Inspection of the year means suggested that part of the residual year effect might have resulted from a general increase in violent crime over time. Further analysis revealed that this linear year effect was quite significant, $F(1,27) = 210.03$, $p < .0001$. The new residual year effect (after accounting for both temperature differences and the linear year effect) was still significant, $F(7,27) = 6.67$, $p < .0005$.

Nonviolent Crime   Quarter of year also yielded a significant effect on the level of nonviolent crime, $F(3,27) = 10.18, p < .0001$. The contrast testing the difference between the average of the second and third quarters ($M = 113.6$) against the first and fourth quarters ($M = 110.7$) was also significant, although considerably less so than the corresponding contrast effect for violent crime, $F(1,27) = 6.57$, $p < .02$. The residual from this contrast also was significant, $F(2,27) = 59.86, p < .0001$. Apparently this resulted because the fourth quarter mean was higher than the temperature-based contrast would have it ($M = 117.4$) and because the second quarter mean was lower ($M = 108.15$). These results suggest that nonviolent crime is related to temperature somewhat, but not to the same extent as violent crime. As expected, the difference between violent and nonviolent crime rates was greater in the hottest quarters of the year, as shown in Figure 1.

The year effect on nonviolent crime was significant, $F(9,27) = 22.84, p < .0001$. As in the violent crime analysis, a regression (contrast) analysis revealed that the temperature differences among years accounted for a significant portion of the year effect, $F(1,27) = 15.08$, $p < .001$. Note that this is again considerably smaller than the comparable effect on violent crime. That is, the "hotness" of years seemed to have more impact on violent than on nonviolent crime, as shown in Figure 2.

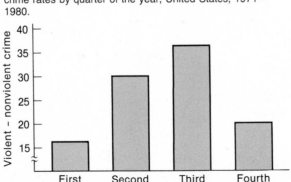

FIGURE 1   The difference between violent and nonviolent crime rates by quarter of the year, United States, 1971–1980.

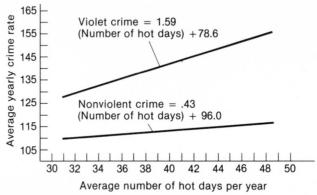

FIGURE 2 Effects of yearly differences in temperature on violent and nonviolent crime rates, United States, 1971–1980.

The residual year effect on nonviolent crime was highly significant, $F(8,27) = 23.81$, $p < .0001$. Nonviolent crime appeared to increase over the 10-year period. This linear year effect accounted for much of the residual year effect, $F(1,27) = 76.89$, $p < .0001$. However, the new residual year effect (after accounting for temperature differences and linear year effects) was still significant, $F(7,27) = 16.23$, $p < .0001$.

In sum, the analyses of violent and nonviolent crime showed both to be related to quarterly and yearly temperature differences. Also, as expected, the temperature effects appeared stronger for violent crime than for nonviolent crime.

Violent-Nonviolent Crime The aforementioned analyses do not directly test the most precise version of the temperature-aggression hypothesis. Specifically, they do not show that temperature affects violent crime rates significantly more than it affects nonviolent crime rates, although Figures 1 and 2 suggest that this interaction exists. The simplest and most direct way to test this hypothesis is to subtract nonviolent crime rates from the corresponding violent crime rates to see if the predicted temperature effects still obtain. Note that a repeated measure ANOVA, with type of crime as the repeated measure, yields essentially the same tests of the Type of Crime × Temperature (quarter and year) interactions.

The results of this analysis confirmed the reliability of the interactions suggested by Figures 1 and 2. First, the quarter effect was highly significant, indicating that the quarter effects differed as a function of type of crime. More important, the predicted contrast was highly significant, $F(1,27) = 119.80$, $p < .0001$. That is, the violent crime rates were considerably larger than nonviolent crime rates in the hotter second and third quarters ($M = 33.46$), but only moderately so in the cooler first and fourth quarters ($M = 18.48$).

The residual from the contrast was also significant, $F(2,27) = 7.60$, $p < .01$. It resulted from the fact that violent crime was most elevated in the third quarter, relative to nonviolent crime, possibly because that is the hottest quarter. Indeed, the violent-nonviolent crime difference was significantly greater in the third quarter ($M = 36.97$) than in the second ($M = 29.95$), $F(1,27) = 13.14$, $p < .0001$. The residual quarter effect, after removing the variance explained by these two contrasts, was not significant, $F(1,27) = 2.06$.

As expected from the previous analyses and from Figure 2, the year effect was also significant, $F(9,27) = 23.41$, $p < .0001$, indicating that the year effects differed for violent and nonviolent crime. The specific test of whether temperature differences among years were differentially related to violent and nonviolent crime rates was also significant, $F(1,27) = 68.04$, $p < .0001$. In essence, this confirms that the slopes in Figure 2 are significantly different from each other; temperature differences among years were more strongly related to violent crime rates than to nonviolent crime rates.

The residual year effect was significant, $F(8,27) = 17.83$, $p < .0001$. Inspection of the means by year suggested that violent crime increased more rapidly over years than did nonviolent crime. This linear year effect was highly significant, $F(1,27) = 80.88$, $p < .0001$. However, the residual year effect was still significant even after removing both the temperature year and the linear year effects, $F(7,27) = 8.82$, $p < .0001$.

Adjusted Violent Crime Recall that the reason for comparing the temperature effects on violent and nonviolent crime is to control for confounded factors that correlate with temperature and crime (e.g., economic conditions). The difference analysis already described provides one way to do this. An alternative is to remove the effects of nonviolent crime (and presumably the confounded effects) from violent crime rates statistically and examine temperature effects (via quarter and year analyses) on the adjusted violent crime rates.

As previously reported, nonviolent crime was highly correlated with violent crime ($r = .77$), indicating that many of the same variables influence the different types of crime. The effect of nonviolent crime as a covariate in the ANOVA on violent crime was highly significant, $F(1,26) = 354.64$, $p < .0001$. The effects of nonviolent crime were removed statistically, and the ANOVA was computed on the adjusted violent crime rates (with the loss of 1 degree of freedom).

The quarter effect on adjusted violent crime was still quite strong, $F(3,26) = 26.38$, $p < .0001$. The

crucial contrast between the hot second and third quarters ($Ms = 143.7$ and 146.3, respectively) and the cool first and fourth quarters ($Ms = 132.6$ and 129.9) was highly significant, $F(1,26) = 76.43$, $p < .0001$. The residual from this contrast was not significant, (p > .25).

Once again, the year effect was significant, $F(9,26) = 16.00$, $p < .0001$. More important, the temperature differences among years accounted for a significant portion of the adjusted violent crime differences, $F(1,26) = 36.28$, $p < .0001$. The residual year effect was also significant, $F(8,26) = 13.46$, $p < .0001$. Inspection of the adjusted violent crime means revealed that violent crime increased more with time than did nonviolent crime. This linear year effect was highly significant, $F(1,26) = 27.66$, $p < .0001$. The new residual year effect (after accounting for temperature differences and the linear year effect) was still significant, $F(7,26) = 11.43$, $p < .0001$.

Discussion

Study 1 provides strong support for the temperature-aggression hypothesis. Specifically, periods in which more hot days occurred were associated with increased violent crime. This occurred both within years, as shown by the quarter effects, and between years, as shown by the temperature-year effects. This occurred to a significantly greater extent for violent than for nonviolent crime. This occurred even when violent crime rates were statistically adjusted for level of concomitant nonviolent crime.

Although the statistical results clearly confirm the temperature-aggression hypothesis, they do not give us a good feel for the magnitude of the effect. To assess this, I used the regression results of the temperature-year analysis of adjusted violent crime to estimate the proportional change in violent crime to be expected from a 10-day change in the number of hot days experienced in a year. The result was that a year with 10 more hot days than normal produced about 7% more murders, rapes, and assaults. Thus, the effect of temperature seems both reliable and of a fairly large magnitude.

The importance of getting both quarter and year temperature effects should not be overlooked. Had only a quarter effect been observed, alternative explanations relying on a variety of seasonal differences would have been plausible. For instance, the second and third quarters have longer daylight hours, contain the traditional vacation times, are filled with more outdoor activities, are the focus of youth vacations from school and youth unemployment, and may be associated with increases in alcohol consumption. Thus, increases in violent crime rates may be due to increased opportunity, increased frustration, decreased inhibitions, and other seasonal effects rather than to temperature.

However, most such alternative explanations, for either quarter or year effects, cannot account for both. For instance, although the increased free time of youths out of school may be a plausible explanation for increased violence in the second and third quarters, it cannot explain the temperature effects of different years. Youths are out of school in the summer regardless of whether it is a hot or cool year. This is an example of triangulation within the same study. The same reasoning rules out a variety of alternative explanations, such as the seasonal unemployment rates of youths and amount of daylight hours.

Similarly, one should not overlook the importance of two additional findings: (a) quarter and year temperature effects were larger on violent crime than on nonviolent crime, and (b) even when nonviolent crime effects were partialed out, the quarter and year temperature variables were still related to violent crime. The high correlation between these two types of crimes ($r = .77$) suggests that they are influenced by many similar variables. But the temperature-aggression hypothesis states that hot temperatures should influence violent crimes the most. Thus, partialing out the effects of nonviolent crime should have removed most extraneous confounds with quarter and year temperature differences and left the

pure temperature effects on violent crime relatively untouched. Similarly, the difference score analysis directly compared the size of temperature effects on violent and nonviolent crime. In sum, these results provide further internal triangulation evidence against many alternative explanations. Increases in free time and alcohol consumption, for instance, would be expected to influence both violent and nonviolent crimes. Yet the second and third quarters (associated with increased free time and alcohol consumption) showed increases primarily in violent crime.

Obviously, such internal triangulation and statistical procedures are not perfect solutions to the causality question in correlation data. But each additional data set supporting the basic temperature-aggression model should increase confidence in it. The case for the temperature-aggression hypothesis would be strengthened considerably if predictions derived from it were supported in a very different context (external triangulation). One such prediction concerns the crime rates in different cities. If hot temperatures do produce increases in violent crime, we should expect cities located in hot climates to have higher violent crime rates than cities in cooler climates. This should hold when the effects of correlated variables such as nonviolent crime, economic, conditions, and social characteristics have been statistically removed. Study 2 examines this prediction.

STUDY 2

The basic unit of analysis in Study 2 was the Standard Metropolitan Statistical Area (SMSA) established by the Census Bureau. (These areas will be called cities throughout the rest of this article.) The goal of this study was to test the temperature-aggression hypothesis by seeing whether cities in hot climates had higher violent crime rates than cities in cooler climates. Although the basic idea is simple, testing it is complex. The most difficult problem concerns differences between cities that are confounded with temperature. Cities differ in many ways that are correlated with geographic location (hence, temperature) and with crime. These social variables include the economic characteristics, racial composition, age, and education of the residents, to mention just a few. Thus, any reasonable test of the temperature-aggression hypothesis requires that the effects of these social variables be controlled statistically.

Method

Data for this study were obtained from four archival sources. Crime rates for each of 260 cities were obtained from the 1980 FBI *Uniform Crime Reports of the United States*. (Several other SMSAs had incomplete crime data.) The reported crimes were the same as in Study 1. A violent crime index based on *z*-score averages of murder, rape, and aggravated assault rates was computed for each city. A similar nonviolent crime index, based on robbery, burglary, larceny-theft, and motor vehicle theft, was also computed.

Several climate variables were obtained from the 1980 volume of *Climatological Data: National Summary*. For each city, the following measures were obtained: number of hot days ($\geq$ 32.2°C, 90°F, cooling degree days (amount of cooling needed to maintain a comfortable base temperature of 18.3°C, 65°F), average humidity, number of cloudy days (80 to 100% cloud cover), number of rainy days ($\geq$ .25 mm), number of cold days $\leq$ 0°C, 32°F), heating degree days (amount of heating needed to maintain a comfortable base temperature of 18.3°C, 56°F), and number of snowy days ($\geq$ 25.4 mm). Preliminary analyses indicated that the snow, rain, and humidity variables did not contribute significant unique increments to the prediction of crime; they were dropped from all reported analyses.[2]

Social variables were obtained from two volumes of the 1980 census report: the *Census of the Population: General Population Characteristics* (U.S. Department of Commerce, 1983b), and the *Census of the Population: General Social and Economic Characteristics* (U.S. Department of Commerce, 1983c). The following variables were obtained: unemployment, per capita income, poverty rate, mobility (percentage living in a different home in 1975), high school education (percentage of the $\geq$ 25-year-old population that had graduated), college education (percentage of the $\geq$ 25-year-old population that had attended 4 or more years), population size, percentage Black, percentage Spanish,[3] percentage less than 18 years old, percentage 18 to 64 years old, percentage 65 and over, median age, number of law enforcement employees.

A derived variable, police, was computed by dividing the number of law enforcement employees by the population. Note that the law enforcement employee estimates were not reported by SMSA, but by city. To estimate these for each SMSA, the totals for cities falling in a given SMSA were computed. Data for several cities were missing, so the derived variable, police, also had several missing data points.

Several other variables had a few missing data points. Therefore, the degrees of freedom in the subsequent analyses vary as a function of which variables were used.

A second derived variable was computed by subtracting nonviolent crime rates from the corresponding violent crime rates. The reason for doing so was the same as in Study 1: to control for unmeasured correlated variables that influence crime rates in general and simultaneously to allow a test of the critical hypothesis that temperature influences violent crime more so than

---

[2]Because humidity contributes to perceptions of comfort, one might expect humidity effects. In naturally occurring variations in temperature and humidity, however, temperature variations contribute more to comfort than do humid-

ity variations. Thus humidity typically fails to contribute significant unique increments (Kenrick & MacFarlane, 1984).

[3]This refers to people of Spanish-speaking origins (e.g., Hispanics or Mexican Americans). *Spanish* is the designation used by the Census Bureau.

nonviolent crime. In essence, this difference variable provides tests of interactions involving type of crime (violent vs. nonviolent).

Also as in Study 1, the relation between violent and nonviolent crime rates was quite strong ($r = .72$), suggesting that many of the same extraneous variables influenced both types of crime in a similar way. Thus an adjusted violent crime index was computed in which the relation between violent and nonviolent crime was statistically removed via regression procedures. Again, the reason for doing so was to eliminate, as far as possible, confounding influences on the temperature-aggression relation under investigation. In sum, the analyses that follow were conducted on four crime variables: violent crime, nonviolent crime, violent crime minus nonviolent crime, and adjusted violent crime.

Results and Discussion

Data analysis consisted of two major steps. First, a social model of crime was derived for each of the four crime variables. To do this, I performed a number of regression analyses to test the various social variables (economic, demographic, etc.) listed earlier. The goal of this preliminary step was to identify those variables that contributed most to the prediction of crime so that their effects could be partialed out before the climate variables were tested. Fourteen social variables were measured. Thus, it was impossible to test a social model complete with all interactions. Such a model would contain 91 two-way, 364 three-way, 1001 4-way interactions, and so on, but there were only 216 data points without missing values. Therefore, two simplifying assumptions were made. First, I assumed that three-way and higher order interactions would be negligible, uninterpretable, and most likely the product of Type I errors. Second, I assumed that there would be no true crossover two-way interactions. The implication of this is that one need examine only the two-way interactions involving variables that have yielded some evidence of main effects.

On the basis of this reasoning, I performed regression analyses to identify social variables with significant main effects for each of the four crime variables. I then examined two-way interactions involving variables with significant main effects. For both sets of analyses (main effects and two-ways), the least significant predictor was dropped in successive runs until all variables kept in the model were significant at an alpha of .05. Note that all significance tests were conducted on the unique (unconfounded) variance.

Once the social model of each type of crime was established, I performed the second major step in the analysis. This was to see to what extent the climate variables added significant unique increments to the prediction of crime.

Social Models

Violent Crime Differences among cities in violent crime rates were well predicted by 9 variables and 8 of their interactions. This does not mean that the 17 retained predictors (9 main effects, 8 interactions) should be interpreted as causal agents in violent crime, nor should one assume that deleted predictors are all causally unrelated to violent crime. Such inferences, which would require much more evidence than is available from one study (i.e., the need for triangulation), are beyond the scope of this article. However, the retained variables do account for an amazingly large portion of the violent crime variance ($R^2 = .75$). Thus, the model provides an excellent (albeit conservative) base for examining climate effects.[4]

The social model for violent crime is presented in Table 1. Included are the F values, the raw

---

[4]The tests are conservative in that the variance shared by the social model variables and the temperature variables is removed completely from the temperature variables. Note also that the cautions about interpreting the social models made earlier, and the claims for the use of these models as bases for testing the climate effects, hold for the nonviolent crime, the violent-nonviolent crime differences, and adjusted violent crime analyses to be reported later.

TABLE 1

SOCIAL MODEL OF VIOLENT CRIME

Variable	Main effects F(1,243)	r(251)	Regression slope	Variable	Two-way interactions F(1,235)	Regression slope
Black	109.68	.57	+	Black×High School	30.64	+
Moved	47.70	.36	+	Spanish×High School	25.26	+
College	42.79		−	Moved×Income	21.52	+
Spanish	23.13	.21	+	Income×College	15.79	−
Income	16.64		+	Black×College	13.92	−
Young	9.52		−	Black×Spanish	9.49	+
High school	4.96		+	Spanish×College	8.31	−
Poverty	4.57	.35	+	Black×Young	3.88	−
Population	4.53	.27	+			

Note: Black = percentage of Blacks in population; moved = percentage living in a different home in 1975; college = percentage of adults with a college education; Spanish = percentage of population of Spanish-speaking origin; income = per capita income; young = percentage under 18; high school = percentage of adults with a high school education; poverty = percentage living below poverty level; population = population size in thousands. Only effects significant at .05 are listed.

correlation with violent crime (where significant), and the direction of the slope estimate associated with the predictor. Note that the variables are listed in order of effect size and that each effect (reported by the F) is the unique increment of that predictor, controlling for all of the other variables listed in the table. (Of course, main effects are not tested with interactions in the model; Cohen & Cohen, 1975.) Although interpretation of these results is beyond the scope of this article, a description of several of the results may make it easier to understand the results in the table.

The largest main effect was for percentage of Blacks, $F(1,243) = 109.68$, $p < .0001$. The simple correlation between violent crime and percentage of Blacks was .57 ($p < .0001$). The sign of the slope from the regression model was positive, as in the simple correlation, indicating that the larger the proportion of a city's population that was Black, the more violent crimes were reported.

The largest interaction was Black × High School, $F(1,235) = 30.64$, $p < .0001$. The sign of the slope (positive) indicates that the relation between percentage of Blacks and violent crime

became more positive as the percentage of adults in the city who were high school graduates increased.

The Income × College interaction had a negative slope. This indicates that the negative relation between the percentage of college graduates in a city and violent crime rate (the main effect of college) became more negative as average income level increased.

Climate Effects

Violent Crime Each of the climate variables was added separately to the social model, and the unique contribution was assessed. For violent crime, each temperature variable added significantly, whereas the remaining climate variables did not. As expected, the number of hot days and the cooling degree-days measures were positively related to violent crime, whereas the number of cold days and the heating degree-days measures were negatively related to violent crime, $Fs(1,234) \geq 7.21$, $ps < .01$. That is, even after accounting for and removing the effects of a variety of social variables, temperature was still strongly related to violent crime rates. Cities that had more hot days, required more cooling, had fewer cold days, and required less heating had significantly elevated rates of violent crime. In subsequent analyses, the temperature measures were pitted against one another by including two at a time in the model and testing unique increments. Because these measures were highly intercorrelated, the unique increments of each decreased, as expected. For instance, when the number of hot days and the number of cold days were both in the model, the unique variance of cold days was not significant, but the unique variance of hot days was, $F(1,233) = 5.43$, $p < .03$. The only finding of interest from these analyses was that number of cold days consistently contributed the least unique variance.

Nonviolent Crime The results of the climate variable analyses of nonviolent crime contrasted sharply with the violent crime results. Briefly, none of the climate variables contributed significant unique variance in predicting nonviolent crime, $Fs(1,213) \leq 2.46$, $ps > .12$. This result, in combination with the violent crime results already reported, strongly supports the hypothesized temperature-aggression relation. However, it does not directly test the hypothesis that temperature will have a significantly greater impact on violent than on nonviolent crime rates. The violent-nonviolent difference score analysis tests this interaction prediction.

Violent-Nonviolent Crime Only one of the temperature measures was reliably related to differences between violent and nonviolent crime rates. The number of hot days experienced in the cities was positively related to the preponderance of violent crime, $F(1,211) = 4.15$, $p < .05$. That is, number of hot days was more strongly related to violent crime than to nonviolent crime to a significant degree. None of the other climate variables was significant by itself.

One variable, however, did become significant when added to the model along with number of hot days. Specifically, the amount of

cooling required to maintain a comfortable temperature became significantly (and positively) related to the difference between violent and nonviolent crime, $F(1,210) = 5.38$, $p < .01$. In this model, number of hot days became somewhat more significant as well, $F(1,210) = 9.48$, $p < .001$.

These results directly test and provide strong support for the temperature-aggression hypothesis. Even after controlling for a wide range of social variables, the hotness of a city was positively related to violent crime rates, but not to nonviolent crime rates. Furthermore, the difference in the temperature relations with these two types of crimes was statistically reliable.

Adjusted Violent Crime Although all the temperature variables produced effects in the expected direction, once again only number of hot days yielded a significant unique increment in predicting violent crime adjusted for nonviolent crime. The number of hot days was strongly and positively related to adjusted violent crime, $F(1,216) = 11.28$, $p < .001$. In addition, number of hot days remained highly significant ($p < .005$) regardless of which other climate variables were entered in the model with it. Thus it is clear that the temperature of a city, in particular the number of truly hot days, is strongly related to the rate of violent crime in that city.

None of the nontemperature climate variables was significant when added to the social model by itself. Interestingly, one variable became highly significant when added to the social model along with number of hot days. Number of cloudy days became a significant predictor of adjusted violent crime, $F(1,198) = 12.07$, $p < .001$. The relation was positive, with more violent crime in cities with more cloudy days. This relation appeared only when number of hot days was in the model, probably because these two variables are themselves negatively related. That is, the positive relation between hot days and violent crime obscured the cloudy-day-violent-crime relation. This finding is consistent with previous work linking amount of sunshine (lack of cloud cover) to mood and helping behavior (Cunningham, 1979). It is important to note that number of hot days remained a highly significant predictor of violent crime even when number of cloudy days was in the model, $F(1,198) = 22.55$, $p < .0001$.

These regression results were also used to estimate the magnitude of the temperature effects. Consider two hypothetical cities of moderate size (600,000), identical in all respects except climate. Assume that City A is 1 standard deviation hotter than City B (i.e., it has 42 more hot days per year). The present results suggest that City A will experience about 7% more violent crimes than City B. That is, City A will have (in each year) about 140 more murders, rapes, and assaults.

Finally, note that the same basic temperature-crime relations reported in the regression analyses also appear in the simple correlations. All of the significant climate and social variable correlations with crime, based on those cities having complete data, are reported in Table 2.

TABLE 2

SIMPLE CORRELATIONS BETWEEN THE CRIME VARIABLES AND THE CLIMATE AND SOCIAL VARIABLES

Variable	Crime variable			
	Violent crime	Nonviolent crime	Violent-nonviolent crime	Adjusted violent crime
Climate				
No. hot days	.52***	.20*	.46***	.55***
No. cold days	−.60***	−.36***	−.36***	−.49***
Heating degree days	−.65***	−.40***	−.38***	−.53***
Cooling degree days	.53***	.28***	.37***	.48***
Humidity				
Cloudy	−.36***	−.34***		−.18*
No. rainy days	−.37***	−.33***		−.20*
No. snowy days	−.48***	−.35***	−.22*	−.34***
Social				
% Black	.57***	.26**	.46***	.56***
% recently moved	.39***	.35***		.21*
% college		.28***	−.20*	
Police ratio	.23**	.33***		
% Spanish	.37***	.35***		
% unemployed				
Per capita income		.33***	−.36***	−.27**
Poverty rate	.48***		.44***	.52***
% high school graduates		.19*	−.34***	−.30***
Population	.29***	.40***		
% young (< 18 years)			.29***	.25**
% adult (18 to 64 years)				
% elderly (≥ 65 years)				
Median age				

Note: $N = 206$. Only correlations significant at .01 are listed.
*$p < .01$.
**$p < .001$.
***$p < .0001$.

GENERAL DISCUSSION

Temperature-Aggression Relation

The results of these two studies provide powerful support for the temperature-aggression hypothesis. Considering all the published field studies on temperature and aggression, it becomes clear that increases in temperature lead to increases in aggression. The relation has been shown in a variety of ways with a variety of measures of aggression at a variety of levels of analysis. Carlsmith and Anderson (1979) showed that the conditional probability of a riot is linearly (or monotonically) related to temperature. Anderson and Anderson (1984) found that the number of daily violent crimes increased directly as a function of temperature, in two different cities. They also showed that this effect did not occur for nonviolent crimes and that adjusting for nonviolent crimes did not eliminate the violent crime-temperature relation. Study 1 of the present article revealed temperature effects on overall U.S. violent crime as a function of quarter of the year and among years. Finally, Study 2 showed that temperature differences could account for a significant portion of differences in violent crime rates between U.S. cities.

A common reaction to data of this type is to attempt to discover potential confounds that may explain the results. This is scientifically healthy, as correlational data are risky bases for causal analysis, thus the need for the process I have labeled *triangulation*. A brief look at the most obvious possible confounds is warranted, for if they cannot be dismissed, the present results become much less important.

The major problem in these data is that temperature is correlated with time of year and with various social and behavioral factors. A variety of seasonal effects, including adults' vacations, school vacations, hours of daylight, youth unemployment, and free time, may be dismissed for a variety of reasons. Specifically, temperature-related year effects (Study 1) as well as temperature-related city effects (Study 2) occurred despite the irrelevance of the seasonal variables just listed. And as previously mentioned, in the earlier Anderson and Harries studies the effects of various time cycles (months, days of week) were partialed out, yet temperature-aggression effects were still obtained. Thus the obtained effects cannot be accounted for by the seasonal variables.

More potential alternative explanations can be created, of course. Space limitations preclude a listing (and rebuttal) of all that I have created or encountered. Thus I leave it to the reader to consider additional ones and to test their applicability across the wide range of studies on the temperature-aggression relation. Barring some new, robust alternative, it seems safe to conclude that temperature effects on aggression are real, fairly strong, and certainly important.

A quadratic temperature term (number of hot days squared) was included to see if it contributed significantly (beyond the linear effect) to the prediction of violent crime, violent-nonviolent crime rate differences, and adjusted violent crime. Basically, this term tests the curvilinear prediction that cities with many hot days would have violent crime rates lower than or equal to cities with a moderate number of hot days. The tests were nonsignificant ($Fs < 1$).

Interpretational Difficulties

One difficulty in examining the linear-curvilinear hypotheses in many field studies is that crimes (such as murders, rapes, and riots) do not all take place at the hottest time of day. In addition, the affect-aggression models cannot specify how long a time negative affect can last. Presumably, if one gets in a foul mood for a variety of reasons, including being uncomfortably hot, this mood may translate into negative assessments of others that may persist long after the transient (but causal) factors such as temperature are no longer present. Thus the high frequency of violent actions on hot days (as in the Anderson & Anderson, 1984, violent crime studies, or the Carlsmith & Anderson, 1979, riot study) may be either linearly caused by negative affect, malevolent intentions, and aggressive actions; created by the hot temperatures; or curvilinearly caused by aggressive tendencies created by an increase in occurrence of moderate temperatures in the night (on hot days) and during the day.

A recent field study by Kenrick and MacFarlane (1984) provides triangulation evidence that is not amenable to the time-of-day defense of the curvilinear model. The important feature of this study was that aggression and temperature were assessed at the same time of day. These researchers examined the relation between temperature and car horn honking at an experimenter whose car blocked the subject's car at the exit from a residential tract. The major result was that aggression (horn honking) was linearly related to temperature. Furthermore, the effect was more pronounced for subjects in cars with windows rolled down (not air conditioned).

Another defense of the curvilinear position is that the inflection point, where aggression should decrease with further increases in temperature, is seldom reached in the field and then for only limited periods of time in a given hot day. This criticism may be partially valid for the present studies. Certainly, only a small portion of the person-days in the United States have temperatures above 90°F. Again, triangulation from other studies makes this alternative untenable. For example, in Anderson and Anderson's (1984) study of violent crime, one of the target cities was Houston, Texas (Study 2). In Houston, a large portion of the days have very hot temperatures, bad traffic problems, air pollution, and other features known to increase levels of negative affect, presumably beyond the inflection point. Similarly, the Kenrick and MacFarlane (1984) study was conducted in the spring and summer in Phoenix, Arizona, with temperatures well above the theoretical inflection point.

One final defense of the curvilinear hypothesis involves consideration of the broader context in which hot temperatures are experienced. As temperature increases, people may take action to reduce their negative affect. They may get out of the sun, enter air-conditioned buildings, or take cold showers. If the curvilinear model is correct, these actions may reduce negative affect to the most aggressive (midrange) level. Aggressive actions under these conditions would show up on hot days, however, resulting in a misleading linear or monotonic pattern.

Although this alternative explanation seems plausible, there are several reasons to doubt it. First, this position predicts that those who are moderately successful at reducing temperature-induced negative affect should show the largest increase in aggression in hot weather. However, Harries et al. (1984) showed that the hot summer effects on aggressive crime rates are most pronounced in neighborhoods where air conditioning is scarce.

Second, riots typically begin and take place in locales (i.e., outdoors in lower income neighborhoods) where the means to reduce negative affect do not exist. Thus this alternative suggests that the probability of a riot should decrease at hot temperatures. Carlsmith and Anderson (1979), however, showed increases in riot probabilities at high temperatures.

Finally, consider the subjects in the Kenrick and MacFarlane (1984) horn-honking experiment in Phoenix. On hot days, those with air conditioning should have had a moderate level of negative affect while waiting for the experimenter's car to move out of the way and, therefore, should have been maximally aggressive according to the curvilinear model. On cooler days, the air-conditioned subjects should have had low levels of negative affect and low levels of aggression. Thus this alternative curvilinear model predicts a positive relation between temperature and horn honking for those with air conditioning. For those without air conditioning, though, hot days should produce high levels and cooler days should produce moderate levels of negative affect and thus a negative temperature-aggression relation. This is because hot days would be extremely uncomfortable and cooler days (in the spring and summer in Phoenix) would be only mildly uncomfortable. The results, as already mentioned, contradicted this curvilinear model quite strongly; there was a strong positive relation for those without air conditioning and a weak positive relation for those with air conditioning. This is exactly what the linear model predicts.

Of course, all the aforementioned field studies are correlational in nature, making causal statements risky. (Actually, the Kenrick & MacFarlane study is more accurately viewed as a quasi-experiment.) But the widely divergent procedures used in them makes artifactual explanations of the results implausible. Each study had a different set of potential confounds, but each produced the same results. On the whole, it seems reasonable to conclude that the relation between temperature and aggression in natural settings is a positive one, either linear or monotonic.

Theoretical and Practical Implications

Although there is considerable evidence for the hypothesized temperature-aggression relation, the processes underlying this relation are not clear. The best theoretical model at the moment is that uncomfortably hot temperatures produce negative arousal. Negative arousal is fairly general and spills over or gets attached to social objects that are salient, especially those that are generating negative arousal themselves. When the annoyance or anger level gets high enough, aggressive behavior is emitted. This model clearly requires extensive refinement and further testing.

Practical implications for controlling or reducing aggression depend on the underlying processes producing aggression. Obviously there are many aggression factors unrelated to temperature. Just as obviously, there is not much one can do about the weather. However, much of our time is spent in environs that can be air conditioned. Indeed, as noted earlier, Harries et al. (1984) reported data suggesting that some por-

tion of summer violence is due to lack of air conditioning in low-income neighborhoods. I am not suggesting that we should air condition the ghettos; the amount of money involved could probably be spent more effectively on providing the same people with nutritional, educational, and job assistance. But there may be situations in which the most effective use of available resources would be to improve the immediate climate. For instance, in a variety of institutional settings, such as in prisons and factories, violence and productivity problems may be reduced by cooling the environment and modifying other environmental factors that influence aggression (cf. Baron et al., 1985; Charry & Hawkinshire, 1981; Rotton & Frey, 1985).

A second implication derives from the earlier discussion of why the field studies never show the downturn in aggression at very hot temperatures. Recall that one possibility mentioned was that the downturn may occur only if the individual can escape the circumstances giving rise to negative affect by performing some nonaggressive behavior. Removing environmentally induced negative affect (as mentioned earlier) does not eliminate all negative affect, but probably only a small fraction in most cases. Providing ready avenues of escape from the major frustrations may reduce violence in general as well as the negative effects of hot temperatures. The problems associated with unemployment, for instance, are likely a major source of negative arousal that cannot easily be avoided. Job training programs may provide one escape route.

Finally, the temperature-aggression model suggests that people typically misattribute negative arousal arising from uncomfortable temperatures to readily available social targets. That is, we blame other people for upsetting us, even when much of our negative arousal is actually due to temperature. Perhaps making people aware of how much impact hot temperatures have on mood state and on aggressive tendencies will allow them to identify times when this is occurring and to combat the process. Indeed, this reattribution process may be what happens in the laboratory studies that find occasional downturns in aggression at high temperatures.

Studies designed to investigate the utility of these practical implications will also inform us about the validity of the underlying process assumptions. Particularly rich directions for future research would seem to include investigations of the cognitive, attributional, and physiological components of temperature-induced negative affect and aggression.

Social Values

Cultural Values

READING 22

Excerpt from *The Mountain People*

Colin M. Turnbull (1972)

People generally consider their values to be very private aspects of their lives and a matter of individual choice. They also recognize that ethics, morals, and beliefs are shaped by family and perhaps by religious upbringing. Few of us, however, have carefully explored the many ways that our particular social groups shape our perceptions regarding what is important to us in our interactions with each other, as well as in our lives overall. Throughout this section, we explore how some of our values are developed and expressed as a consequence of the presence of others, either in terms of the influence of society as a whole or the presence of specific individual others.

We begin that exploration by considering an extreme case. It is sometimes easier to see our own values when contrasted with values that we do not share. Looking across culture, we find the Ik (pronounced "eke") of Uganda, a people with a culture that was initially very different from ours, and who have since experienced extreme survival stress. Turnbull's important study of the Ik highlights the capacity for human behavior to be diverse and changeable. One might take the Hobbesian view that humans are inherently self-interested, or a situational perspective, which recognizes the impact of extreme long-term stresses on human behavior. Turnbull (personal communication, February, 1989) describes his view as functional. He believes "...that we all have the capability of responding as the Ik did, in that (context) or some other context. Equally, we have a potential for what we consider 'civilized' or 'humane' behavior—and the potential will also be related to a possible plurality of contexts." From our perspective on social values, this case suggests that many values are group derived, and can change dramatically when groups meet with massive situational change.

Abstract

Anthropologist Colin M. Turnbull, author of The Forest People *and* The Lonely Africans, *went to study the Ik of Uganda, who he believed were still primarily hunters, in order to compare them with other hunting-and-gathering societies he had studied in totally different environments. He was surprised to discover that they were no longer hunters but primarily farmers, well on their way to starvation and something worse in a drought-stricken land.*

In what follows, there will be much to shock, and the reader will be tempted to say, "how primitive, how savage, how disgusting," and, above all, "how inhuman." The first judgments are typical of the kind of ethno- and egocentricism from which we can never quite escape. But "how inhuman" is of a different order and supposes that there are certain values inherent in humanity itself, from which the people described here seem to depart in a most drastic manner. In living the experience, however, and perhaps in reading it, one finds that it is oneself one is looking at and questioning; it is a voyage in quest of the basic human and a discovery of his potential for inhumanity, a potential that lies within us all.

Just before World War II the Ik tribe had been encouraged to settle in northern Uganda, in the mountainous northeast corner bordering on Kenya to the east and Sudan to the north. Until then they had roamed in nomadic bands, as hunters and gatherers, through a vast region in all three countries. The Kidepo Valley below Mount Morungole was their major hunting territory. After they were confined to a part of their former area, Kidepo was made a national park and they were forbidden to hunt or gather there.

The concept of family in a nomadic society is a broad one; what really counts most in everyday life is community of residence, and those who live close to each other are likely to see each other as effectively related, whether there is any kinship bond or not. Full brothers, on the other hand, who live in different parts of the camp may have little concern for each other.

It is not possible, then, to think of the family as a simple, basic unit. A child is brought up to regard any adult living in the same camp as a parent, and age-mate as a brother or sister. The Ik had this essentially social attitude toward kinship, and it readily lent itself to the rapid and disastrous changes that took place following the restriction of their movement and hunting activities. The family simply ceased to exist.

It is a mistake to think of small-scale societies as "primitive" or "simple." Hunters and gatherers, most of all, appear simple and straightforward in terms of their social organization, yet that is far from true. If we can learn about the nature of society from a study of small-scale societies, we can also learn about human relationships. The smaller the society, the less emphasis there is on the formal system and the more there is on interpersonal and intergroup relations. Security is seen in terms of these relationships, and so is survival. The result, which appears so deceptively simple, is that hunters frequently display those characteristics that we find so admirable in man: kindness, generosity, consideration, affection, honesty, hospitality, compassion, charity. For them, in their tiny, close-knit society, these are necessities for survival. In our society anyone possessing even half these qualities would find it hard to survive, yet we think these virtues are inherent in man. I took it for granted that the Ik would possess these same qualities. But they were as unfriendly, uncharitable, inhospitable and generally mean as any people can be. For those positive qualities we value so highly are no longer functional for them; even more than in our own society they spell ruin and disaster. It seems that, far from being basic human qualities, they are luxuries we can afford in times of plenty or are mere mechanisms for survival and security. Given

the situation in which the Ik found themselves, man has no time for such luxuries, and a much more basic man appears, using more basic survival tactics.

Turnbull had to wait in Kaabong, a remote administration outpost, for permission from the Uganda government to continue to Pirre, the Ik water hole and police post. While there he began to learn the Ik language and became used to their constant demands for food and tobacco. An official in Kaabong gave him, as a "gift," 20 Ik workers to build a house and a road up to it. When they arrived at Pirre, however, wages for the workers were negotiated by wily Atum, "the senior of all the Ik on Morungole."

The police seemed as glad to see me as I was to see them. They hungrily asked for news of Kaabong, as though it were the hub of the universe. They had a borehole and pump for water, to which they said I was welcome, since the water holes used by the Ik were not fit for drinking or even for washing. The police were not able to tell me much about the Ik, because every time they went to visit an Ik village, there was nobody there. Only in times of real hunger did they see much of the Ik, and then only enough to know that they were hungry.

The next morning I rose early, but even though it was barely daylight, by the time I had washed and dressed, the Ik were already outside. They were sitting silently, staring at the Land Rover. As impassive as they seemed, there was an air of expectancy, and I was reminded that these were, after all, hunters, and the likelihood was that I was their morning's prey. So I left the Land Rover curtains closed and as silently as possible prepared a frugal breakfast.

Atum was waiting for me. He said that he had told all the Ik that Iciebam [friend of the Ik] had arrived to live with them and that I had given the workers a "holiday" so they could greet me. They were waiting in the villages. They were very hungry, he added, and many were dying. That was probably one of the few true statements he ever made, and I never even considered believing it.

There were seven villages in all. Village Number One was built on a steep slope, and even the houses tilted at a crazy angle. Atum rapped on the outer stockade with his cane and shouted a greeting, but there was no response. This was Giriko's village, he said, and he was one of my workers.

"But I thought you told them to go back to their villages," I said.

"Yes, but you gave them a holiday, so they are probably in their fields," answered Atum, looking me straight in the eye.

At Village Number Two there was indisputably someone inside, for I could hear loud singing. The singing stopped, a pair of hands gripped the stockade and a craggy head rose into view, giving me an undeniably welcoming smile. This was Lokelea. When I asked him what he had been singing about, he answered, "Because I'm hungry."

Village Number Three, the smallest of all, was empty. Village Number Four had only 8 huts, as against the 12 or so in Lokelea's village and the 18 in Giriko's. The outer stockade was broken in one section, and we walked right in. We ducked through a low opening and entered a compound in which a woman was making pottery. She kept on at her work but gave us a cheery welcome and laughed her head off when I tried to speak in Icietot. She willingly showed me details of her work and did not seem unduly surprised at my interest. She said that everyone else had left for the fields except old Nangoli, who, on hearing her name mentioned, appeared at a hole in the stockade shutting off the next compound. Nangoli mumbled toothlessly at Losike, who told Atum to pour her some water.

As we climbed up to his own village, Number Five, Atum said that Losike never gave anything away. Later I remembered that gift of water to Nangoli. At the time I did not stop to think that in this country a gift of water could be a gift of life.

Atum's village had nearly 50 houses, each within its compound within the stout outer stockade. Atum did not invite me in.

A hundred yards away stood Village Number Six. Kauar, one of the workers, was sitting on a rocky slab just outside the village. He had a smile like Losike's, open and warm, and he said he had been waiting for me all morning. He offered us water and showed me his own small compound and that of his mother.

Coming up from Village Number Seven, at quite a respectable speed, was a blind man. This was Logwara, emaciated but alive and remarkably active. He had heard us and had come to greet me, he said, but he added the inevitable demand for tobacco in the same breath. We sat down in the open sunlight. For a brief moment I felt at peace.

After a short time Atum said we should start back and called over his shoulder to his village. A muffled sound came from within, and he said, "That's my wife, she is very sick—and hungry." I offered to go and see her, but he shook his head. Back at the Land Rover I gave Atum some food and some aspirin, not knowing what else to give him to help his wife.

I was awakened well before dawn by the lowing of cattle. I made an extra pot of tea and let Atum distribute it, and then we divided the workers into two teams. Kauar was to head the team building the house, and Lokelatom, Losike's husband, was to take charge of the road workers.

While the Ik were working, their heads kept turning as though they were expecting something to happen. Every now and again one would stand up and peer into the distance and then take off into the bush for an hour or so. On one such occasion, after the person had been gone two hours, the others started drifting off. By then I knew them better; I looked for a wisp of smoke and followed it to where the road team was cooking a goat. Smoke was a giveaway, though, so they economized on cooking and ate most food nearly raw. It is a curious hangover from what must have once have been a moral code that Ik will offer food if surprised in the act of eating, though they now go to enormous pains not to be so surprised.

I was always up before dawn, but by the time I got up to the villages they were always deserted. One morning I followed the little *oror* [gulley] up from *oror a pirre'i* [Ravine of Pirre] while it was still quite dark, and I met Lomeja on his way down. He took me on my first illicit hunt in Kidepo. He told me that if he got anything he would share it with me and with anyone else who managed to join us but that he certainly would not take anything back to his family. "Each one of them is out seeing what he can get for himself, and do you think they will bring any back for me?"

Lomeja was one of the very few Ik who seemed glad to volunteer information. Unlike many of the others, he did not get up and leave as I approached. Apart from him, I spent most of my time, those days, with Losike, the potter. She told me that Nangoli, the old lady in the adjoining compound, and her husband, Amuarkuar, were rather peculiar. They helped each other get food and water, and they brought it back to their compound to eat together.

I still do not know how much real hunger there was at that time, for most of the younger people seemed fairly well fed, and the few skinny old people seemed healthy and active. But my laboriously extracted genealogies showed that there were quite a number of old people still alive and allegedly in these villages, though they were never to be seen. Then Atum's wife died.

Atum told me nothing about it but kept up his demands for food and medicine. After a while the beady-eyed Lomongin told me that Atum was selling the medicine I was giving him for his wife. I was not unduly surprised and merely remarked that that was too bad for his wife. "Oh no," said Lomongin, "she has been dead for weeks."

It must have been then that I began to notice other things that I suppose I had chosen to ignore before. Only a very few of the Ik helped me with the language. Others would understand when it suited them and would pretend they did not understand when they did not want to listen. I began to be forced into a similar isolationist attitude myself, and although I cannot say I enjoyed it, it did make life much easier. I even began to enjoy, in a peculiar way, the company of the silent Ik. And the more I accepted it, the less often people got up and left as I approached. On one occasion I sat on the *di* [sitting place] by Atum's rain tree for three days with a group of Ik, and for three days not one word was exchanged.

The work teams were more lively, but only while working. Kauar always played and joked with the children when they came back from foraging. He used to volunteer to make the two-day walk into Kaabong and the even more tiring two-day climb back to get mail for me or to buy a few things for others. He always asked if he had made the trip more quickly than the last time.

Then one day Kauar went to Kaabong and did not come back. He was found on the last peak of the trail, cold and dead. Those who found him took the things he had been carrying and pushed his body into the bush. I still see his open, laughing face, see him giving precious tidbits to the children, comforting some child who was crying, and watching me read the letters he carried so lovingly for me. And I still think of him probably running up that viciously steep mountainside so he could break his time record and falling dead in his pathetic prime because he was starving.

Once I settled down into my new home, I was able to work more effectively. Having recovered at least some of my anthropological detachment, when I heard the telltale rustling of someone at my stockade, I merely threw a stone. If when out walking I stumbled during a difficult descent and the Ik shrieked with laughter, I no longer even noticed it.

Anyone falling down was good for a laugh, but I never saw anyone actually trip anyone else. The adults were content to let things happen and then enjoy them; it was probably conservation of energy. The children, however, sought their pleasures with vigor. The best game of all, at this time, was teasing poor little Adupa. She was not so little—in fact she should have been an adult, for she was nearly 13 years old—but Adupa was a little mad. Or you might say she was the only sane one, depending on your point of view. Adupa did not jump on other people's play houses, and she lavished enormous care on hers and would curl up inside it. That made it all the more jump-on-able. The other children beat her viciously.

Children are not allowed to sleep in the house after they are "put out," which is at about three years old, four at the latest. From then on they sleep in the open courtyard, taking what shelter they can against the stockade. They may ask for permission to sit in the doorway of their parents' house but may not lie down or sleep there. "The same thing applies to old people," said Atum, "if they can't build a house of their own and, of course, *if* their children let them stay in their compounds."

I saw a few old people, most of whom had taken over abandoned huts. For the first time I realized that there really was starvation and saw why I had never known it before: it was confined to the aged. Down in Giriko's village the old ritual priest, Lolim, confidentially told me that he was sheltering an old man who had been refused shelter by his son. But Lolim did not have enough food for himself, let alone his guest; could I... I liked old Lolim, so, not believing that Lolim had a visitor at all, I brought him a double ration that evening. There was a rustling in the back of the hut, and Lolim helped ancient Lomeraniang to the entrance. They shook with delight at the sight of the food.

When the two old men had finished eating, I left; I found a hungry-looking and disapproving little crowd clustered outside. They muttered to each other about wasting food. From then on I brought food daily, but in a very short time Lomeraniang was dead, and his son refused to come down from the village above to bury him. Lolim scratched a hole and covered the body with a pile of stones he carried himself, one by one.

Hunger was indeed more severe than I knew, and, after the old people, the children were the next to go. It was all quite impersonal—even to me, in most cases, since I had been immunized by the Ik themselves against sorrow on their behalf. But Adupa was an exception. Her madness was such that she did not know just how vicious humans could be. Even worse, she thought that parents were for loving, for giving as well as receiving. Her parents were not given to fantasies. When she came for shelter, they drove her out; and when she came because she was hungry, they laughed that Icien laugh, as if she had made them happy.

Adupa's reactions became slower and slower. When she managed to find food—fruit peels, skins, bit of bone, half-eaten berries—she held it in her hand and looked at it with wonder and delight. Her playmates caught on quickly; they put tidbits in her way and watched her simple drawn little face wrinkle in a smile. Then as she raised her hand to her mouth, they set on her with cries of excitement, fun and laughter, beating her savagely over the head. But that is not how she died. I took to feeding her, which is probably the cruelest thing I could have done, a gross selfishness on my part to try to salve my own rapidly disappearing conscience. I had to protect her, physically, as I fed her. But the others would beat her anyway, and Adupa cried, not because of the pain in her body but because of the pain she felt at the great, vast, empty wasteland where love should have been.

It was *that* that killed her. She demanded that her parents love her. Finally they took her in, and Adupa was happy and stopped crying. She stopped crying forever because her parents went away and closed the door tight behind them, so tight that weak little Adupa could never have moved it.

The Ik seem to tell us that the family is not such a fundamental unit as we usually suppose, that it is not essential to social life. In the crisis of survival facing the Ik, the family was one of the first institutions to go, and the Ik as a society have survived.

The other quality of life that we hold to be necessary for survival—love—the Ik dismiss as idiotic and highly dangerous. But we need to see more of the Ik before their absolute lovelessness becomes truly apparent.

In this curious society there is one common value to which all Ik hold tenaciously. It is *ngag,* "food." That is the one standard by which they measure right and wrong, goodness and badness. The very word for "good" is defined in terms of food. "Goodness" is "the possession of food," or the "*individual* possession of food." If you try to discover their concept of a "good man," you get the truly Icien answer: one who has a full stomach.

We should not be surprised, then, when the mother throws her child out at three years old. At that age a series of *rites de passage* begins. In this environment a child has no chance of survival on his own until he is about 13, so children form age bands. The junior band consists of children between three and seven, the senior of eight- to twelve-year-olds. Within the band each child seeks another close to him in age for defense against the older children. These friendships are temporary, however, and inevitably there comes a time when each turns on the one that up to then had been the closest to him; that is the *rite de passage,* the destruction of the fragile bond called friendship. When this has happened three or four times, the child is ready for the world.

The weakest are soon thinned out, and the strongest survive to achieve leadership of the band. Such a leader is eventually driven out, turned against by his fellow band members. Then the process starts all over again; he joins the senior age band as its most junior member.

The final *rite de passage* is into adulthood, at the age of 12 or 13. By then the candidate has learned the wisdom of acting on his own, for his own good, while acknowledging that on occasion it is profitable to associate temporarily with others.

One year in four the Ik can count on a complete drought. About this time it began to be apparent that there were going to be two consecutive years of drought and famine. Men as well as women took to gathering what wild fruits and berries they could find, digging up roots, cutting grass that was going to seed, threshing and eating the seed.

Old Nangoli went to the other side of Kidepo, where food and water were more plentiful. But she had to leave her husband, Amuarkuar, behind. One day he appeared at my *odok* and asked for water. I gave him some and was going to get him food when Atum came storming over and argued with me about wasting water. In the midst of the dispute Amuarkuar quietly left. He wandered over to a rocky outcrop and lay down there to rest. Nearby was a small bundle of grass that evidently he had cut and had been dragging painfully to the ruins of his village to make a rough shelter. The grass was his supreme effort to keep a home going until Nangoli returned. When I went over to him, he looked up and smiled and said that my water tasted good. He lay back and went to sleep with a smile on his face. That is how Amuarkuar died, happily.

There are measures that can be taken for survival involving the classical institutions of gift and sacrifice. These are weapons, sharp and aggressive. The object is to build up a series of obligations so that in times of crisis you have a number of debts you can recall; with luck one of them may be repaid. To this end, in the circumstances of Ik life, considerable sacrifice would be justified, so you have the odd phenomenon of these otherwise singularly self-interested people going out of their way to "help" each other. Their help may very well be resented in the extreme, but is done in such a way that it cannot be refused, for it has already been given. Someone may hoe another's field in his absence or rebuild his stockade or join in the building of a house.

The danger in this system was that the debtor might not be around when collection was called for and, by the same token, neither might the creditor. The future was too uncertain for this to be anything but one additional survival measure, though some developed it to a fine technique.

There seemed to be increasingly little among the Ik that could by any stretch of the imagination be called social life, let alone social organization. The family does not hold itself together; economic interest is centered on as many stomachs as there are people; and cooperation is merely a device for furthering an interest that is consciously selfish. We often do the same thing in our so-called "altruistic" practices, but we tell ourselves it is for the good of others. The Ik have dispensed with the myth of altruism. Though they have no centralized leadership or means of physical coercion, they do hold together with remarkable tenacity.

In our world, where the family has also lost much of its value as a social unit and where religious belief no longer binds us into communities, we maintain order only through coercive power that is ready to uphold a rigid law and through an equally rigid penal system. The Ik, however, have learned to do without coercion, either spiritual or physical. It seems that they have come to a recognition of what they accept as man's basic selfishness, of his natural determination to survive as an individual before all else. This they consider to be man's basic right, and they allow others to pursue that right without recrimination.

In large-scale societies such as our own, where members are individual beings rather than social beings, we rely on law for order. The absence of both a common law and a common belief would surely result in lack of any community of behavior; yet Ik society is not anarchical. One might well expect religion, then, to play a powerful role in Icien life, providing a source of unity.

The Ik, as may be expected, do not run true to form. When I arrived, there were still three ritual priests alive. From them and from the few other old people, I learned something of the Ik's belief and practice as they had been before their world was so terribly changed. There had been

a powerful unity of belief in Didigwari—a sky god—and a body of ritual practice reinforcing secular behavior that was truly social.

Didigwari himself is too remote to be of much practical significance to the Ik. He created them and abandoned them and retreated into his domain somewhere in the sky. He never came down to earth, but the *abang* [ancestors] have all known life on earth; it is only against them that one can sin and only to them that one can turn for help, through the ritual priest.

While Morungole has no legends attached to it by the Ik, it nonetheless figures in their ideology and is in some ways regarded by them as sacred. I had noticed this by the almost reverential way in which they looked at it—none of the shrewd cunning and cold appraisal with which they regarded the rest of the world. When they talked about it, there was a different quality to their voices. They seemed incapable of talking about Morungole in any other way, which is probably why they talked about it so very seldom. Even that weasel Lomongin became gentle the only time he talked about it to me. He said, "If Atum and I were there, we would not argue. It is a good place." I asked if he meant that it was full of food. He said yes. "Then why do Ik never go there?" "They do go there." "But if hunting is good there, why not live there?" "We don't hunt there, we just go there." "Why?" "I told you, it is a good place." If I did not understand him, that was my fault; for once he was doing his best to communicate something to me. With others it was the same. All agreed that it was "a good place." One added, "That is the Place of God."

Lolim, the oldest and greatest of the ritual priests, was also the last. He was not much in demand any longer, but he was still held in awe, which means kept at a distance. Whenever he approached a *di,* people cleared a space for him, as far away from themselves as possible. The Ik rarely called on his services, for they had little to pay him with, and he had equally little to offer them. The main things they did try to get out of him were certain forms of medicine, both herbal and magical.

Lolim said that he had inherited his power from his father. His father had taught him well but could not give him the power to hear the *abang*—that had to come from the *abang* themselves. He had wanted his oldest son to inherit and had taught him everything he could. But his son, Longoli, was bad, and the *abang* refused to talk to him. They talked instead to his oldest daughter, bald Nangoli. But there soon came the time when all the Ik needed was food in their stomachs, and Lolim could not supply that. The time came when Lolim was too weak to go out and collect the medicines he needed. His children all refused to go except Nangoli, and then she was jailed for gathering in Kidepo Park.

Lolim became ill and had to be protected while eating the food I gave him. Then the children began openly ridiculing him and teasing him, dancing in front of him and kneeling down so that he would trip over them. His grandson used to creep up behind him and with a pair of hard sticks drum a lively tattoo on the old man's bald head.

I fed him whenever I could, but often he did not want more than a bite. Once I found him rolled up in his protective ball, crying. He had had nothing to eat for four days and no water for two. He had asked his children, who all told him not to come near them.

The next day I saw him leaving Atum's village, where his son Longoli lived. Longoli swore that he had been giving his father food and was looking after him. Lolim was not shuffling away; it was almost a run, the run of a drunken man, staggering from side to side. I called to him, but he made no reply, just a kind of long, continuous and horrible moan. He had been to Longoli to beg him to let him into his compound because he knew he was going to die in a few hours, Longoli calmly told me afterward. Obviously Longoli could not do a thing like that: a man of Lolim's importance would have called for an enormous funeral feast. So he refused. Lolim

begged Longoli then to open up Nangoli's *asak* for him so that he could die in *her* compound. But Longoli drove him out, and he died alone.

Atum pulled some stones over the body where it had fallen into a kind of hollow. I saw that the body must have lain parallel with the *oror*. Atum answered without waiting for the question: "He was lying looking up at Mount Meraniang."

Insofar as ritual survived at all, it could hardly be said to be religious, for it did little or nothing to bind Icien society together. But the question still remained: Did this lack of social behavior and communal ritual or religious expression mean that there was no community of belief?

Belief may manifest itself, at either the individual or the communal level, in what we call morality, when we behave according to certain principles supported by our belief even when it seems against our personal interest. When we call ourselves moral, however, we tend to ignore that ultimately our morality benefits us even as individuals, insofar as we are social individuals and live in a society. In the absence of belief, law takes over and morality has little role. If there was such a thing as an Icien morality, I had not yet perceived it, though traces of a moral past remained. But it still remained a possibility, as did the existence of an unspoken, unmanifest belief that might yet reveal itself and provide a basis for the reintegration of society. I was somewhat encouraged in this hope by the unexpected flight of old Nangoli, widow of Amuarkuar.

When Nangoli returned and found her husband dead, she did an odd thing: she grieved. She tore down what was left of their home, uprooted the stockade, tore up whatever was growing in her little field. Then she fled with a few belongings.

Some weeks later I heard that she and her children had gone over to the Sudan and built a village there. This migration was so unusual that I decided to see whether this runaway village was different.

Lojieri led the way, and Atum came along. One long day's trek got us there. Lojieri pulled part of the brush fence aside, and we went in and wandered around. He and Atum looked inside all the huts, and Lojieri helped himself to tobacco from one and water from another. Surprises were coming thick and fast. That households should be left open and untended with such wealth inside...That there should have been such wealth, for as well as tobacco and jars of water there were baskets of food, and meat was drying on racks. There were half a dozen or so compounds, but they were separated from each other only by a short line of sticks and brush. It was a village, and these were homes, the first and last I was to see.

The dusk had already fallen, and Nangoli came in with her children and grandchildren. They had heard us and came in with warm welcomes. There was no hunger here, and in a very short time each kitchen hearth had a pot of food cooking. Then we sat around the central fire and talked until late, and it was another universe.

There was no talk of "how much better it is here than there"; talk revolved around what had happened on the hunt that day. Loron was lying on the ground in front of the fire as his mother made gentle fun of him. His wife, Kinimei, whom I had never seen even speak to him at Pirre, put a bowl of fresh-cooked berries and fruit in front of him. It was all like a nightmare rather than a fantasy, for it made the reality of Pirre seem all the more frightening.

The unpleasantness of returning was somewhat alleviated by Atum's suffering on the way up the stony trail. Several times he slipped, which made Lojieri and me laugh. It was a pleasure to move rapidly ahead and leave Atum gasping behind so that we could be sitting up on the *di* when he finally appeared and could laugh at his discomfort.

The days of drought wore on into weeks and months and, like everyone else, I became rather bored with sickness and death. I survived rather as did the young adults, by diligent attention to my own needs while ignoring those of others.

More and more it was only the young who could go far from the village as hunger became

starvation. Famine relief had been initiated down at Kasile, and those fit enough to make the trip set off. When they came back, the contrast between them and the others was that between life and death. Villages were villages of the death and dying, and there was little difference between the two. People crawled rather than walked. After a few feet some would lie down to rest, but they could not be sure of ever being able to sit up again, so they mostly stayed upright until they reached their destination. They were going nowhere, these semianimate bags of skin and bone; they just wanted to be with others, and they stopped whenever they met. Perhaps it was the most important demonstration of sociality I ever saw among the Ik. Once they met, they neither spoke nor did anything together.

Early one morning, before dawn, the village moved. In the midst of a hive of activity were the aged and crippled, soon to be abandoned, in danger of being trampled but seemingly unaware of it. Lolim's widow, Lo'ono, whom I had never seen before, also had been abandoned and had tried to make her way down the mountainside. But she was totally blind and had tripped and rolled to the bottom of the *oror a pirre'i;* there she lay on her back, her legs and arms thrashing feebly, while a little crowd laughed.

At this time a colleague was with me. He kept the others away while I ran to get medicine and food and water, for Lo'ono was obviously near dead from hunger and thirst as well as from the fall. We treated her and fed her and asked her to come back with us. But she asked us to point her in the direction of her son's new village. I said I did not think she would get much of a welcome there, and she replied that she knew it but wanted to be near him when she died. So we gave her more food, put her stick in her hand and pointed her the right way. She suddenly cried. She was crying, she said, because we had reminded her that there had been a time when people had helped each other, when people had been kind and good. Still crying, she set off.

The Ik up to this point had been tolerant of my activities, but all this was too much. They said that what we were doing was wrong. Food and medicine were for the living, not the dead. I thought of Lo'ono. And I thought of other old people who had joined in the merriment when they had been teased or had a precious morsel of food taken from their mouths. They knew that it was silly of them to expect to go on living, and, having watched others, they knew that the spectacle really was quite funny. So they joined in the laughter. Perhaps if we had left Lo'ono, she would have died laughing. But we prolonged her misery for no more than a few brief days. Even worse, we reminded her of when things had been different, of days when children had cared for parents and parents for children. She was already dead, and we made her unhappy as well. At the time I was sure we were right, doing the only "human" thing. In a way we *were*—we were making life more comfortable for ourselves. But now I wonder if the Ik way was not right, if I too should not have laughed as Lo'ono flapped about, then left her to die.

Ngorok was a man at 12. Lomer, his older brother, at 15 was showing signs of strain; when he was carrying a load, his face took on a curious expression of pain that was no physical pain. Giriko, at 25 was 40, Atum at 40 was 65, and the very oldest, perhaps a bare 50, were centenarians. And I, at 40, was younger than any of them, for I still enjoyed life, which they had learned was not "adult" when they were 3. But they retained their will to survive and so offered grudging respect to those who had survived for long.

Even in the teasing of the old there was a glimmer of hope. It denoted a certain intimacy that did not exist between adjacent generations. This is quite common in small-scale societies. The very old and the very young look at each other as representing the future and the past. To the child, the aged represent a world that existed before their own birth and the unknown world to come.

And now that all the old are dead, what is left? Every Ik who is old today was thrown out at three and has survived, and in consequence has thrown his own children out and knows that they will not help him in his old age any more than he helped his parents. The system has turned one full cycle and is now self-perpetuating; it has eradicated what we know as "humanity" and has turned the world into a chilly void where man does not seem to care even for himself, but survives. Yet into this hideous world Nangoli and her family quietly returned because they could not bear to be alone.

For the moment abandoning the very old and the very young, the Ik as a whole must be searched for one last lingering trace of humanity. They appear to have disposed of virtually all the qualities that we normally think of as differentiating us from other primates, yet they survive without seeming to be greatly different from ourselves in terms of behavior. Their behavior is more extreme, for we do not start throwing our children out until kindergarten. We have shifted responsibility from family to state; the Ik have shifted it to the individual.

It has been claimed that human beings are capable of love and, indeed, are dependent upon it for survival and sanity. The Ik offer us an opportunity for testing this cherished notion that love is essential to survival. If it is, the Ik should have it.

Love in human relationships implies mutuality, a willingness to sacrifice the self that springs from a consciousness of identity. This seems to bring us back to the Ik, for it implies that love is self-oriented, that even the supreme sacrifice of one's life is no more than selfishness, for the victim feels amply rewarded by the pleasure he feels in making the sacrifice. The Ik, however, do not value emotion above survival, and they are without love.

But I kept looking, for it was the one thing that could fill the void their survival tactics had created; and if love was not there in some form, it meant that for humanity love is not a necessity at all, but a luxury or an illusion. And if it was not among the Ik, it meant that mankind can lose it.

since we have already become individualized and desocialized, we say that extermination will not come in our time, which shows about as much sense of family devotion as one might expect from the Ik.

Even supposing that we can avert nuclear holocaust or the almost universal famine that may be expected if population keeps expanding and pollution remains unchecked, what will be the cost if not the same already paid by the Ik? They too were driven by the need to survive, and they succeeded at the cost of their humanity. We are already beginning to pay the same price, but we not only still have the choice (though we may not have the will or courage to make it), we also have the intellectual and technological ability to avert an Icien end. Any change as radical as will be necessary is not likely to bring material benefits to the present generation, but only then will there be a future.

The Ik teach us that our much vaunted human values are not inherent in humanity at all but are associated only with a particular form of survival called society and that all, even society itself, are luxuries that can be dispensed with. That does not make them any less wonderful, and if man has any greatness, it is surely in his ability to maintain these values, even shortening an already pitifully short life rather than sacrifice his humanity. But that too involves choice, and the Ik teach us that man can lose the will to make it. That is the point at which there is an end to truth, to goodness and to beauty, an end to the struggle for their achievement, which gives life to the individual and strength and meaning to society. The Ik have relinquished all luxury in the name of individual survival, and they live on as a people without life, without passion, beyond humanity. We pursue those trivial, idiotic technological encumbrances, and all the time we are losing our potential for social rather than individual survival, for hating as well as loving, losing perhaps our last chance to enjoy life with all the passion that is our nature.

Living with Television: The Dynamics of the Cultivation Process

George Gerbner, Larry Gross, Michael Morgan, and Nancy Signorielli (1986)

Gerbner, Gross, Morgan, and Signorielli explore how we as a society construct our own values and perpetuate them through television. Watching television has taken precedence over leisure activities such as reading, sewing, gardening, and other family- and community-oriented activities that occupied previous generations in our society. That fact alone is a value choice.

Gerbner and his colleagues discuss how television cultivates, or socializes, values. It also creates a common shared perspective about the world. What we as a society watch on television might affect our world views, whether we select our own programs or whether they are selected for us (i.e., by the networks). Gerbner et al. highlight the dynamic, interactive nature of television messages; they suggest that these messages both shape and are shaped by the public, who, in turn, both influence and are influenced by the media. Testing such broad claims, however, is difficult. Like most field research, these studies face problems associated with controlling extraneous variables, setting up appropriate designs, and finding appropriate control groups (McGuire, 1985). Because the issues and implications discussed are important, we must be cautious and evaluate the data in light of possible confounds. Gerbner et al. are sensitive to these issues, and they discuss some of the difficulties they encounter in their research. Other perceived effects of television are discussed in reviews by Liebert and Sprafkin (1988) and Oskamp (1988).

The longer we live with television, the more invisible it becomes. As the number of people who have never lived without television continues to grow, the medium is increasingly taken for granted as an appliance, a piece of furniture, a storyteller, a member of the family. Ever fewer parents and even grandparents can explain to children what it was like to grow up before television.

Television is the source of the most broadly shared images and messages in history. Although new technologies transform business and professional communications, the public and much of the research community continue to be concerned with over-the-air television, and for good reasons. Saturation and viewing time, incredibly high for decades, continue to increase. The mass ritual that is television shows no signs of weakening its hold over the common symbolic environment into which our children are born and in which we all live out our lives. For most viewers, new types of delivery systems (e.g., cable, satellite, and cassette) signal even further penetration and integration of established viewing patterns into everyday life.

And yet, far too little is known and even less is agreed upon about the dynamic role of television in our lives. The reasons for this lack of consensus include institutional resistance (high economic stakes and political interests might be affected), the relative youth of the field, the inherent clumsiness of research methods and measures, and the "hit-and-run" proclivities and sporadic funding of those who seek to understand television's overall impact. In contrast, we have been fortunate to obtain research grant support from a variety of public sources over a long period of time. We have thus been able, since 1968, to follow a fairly consistent line of theory and research on the implications of television. Our research project, called *cultural indicators*, has accumulated large amounts of data with which to develop and refine our theoretical approach and the research strategy we call *cultivation analysis* (see Gerbner, Gross, Morgan, & Signorielli, 1980). In this chapter, we summarize and illustrate our theory of the dynamics of the cultivation process.

TELEVISION IN SOCIETY

Television is a centralized system of storytelling. It is part and parcel of our daily lives. Its drama, commercials, news, and other programs bring a relatively coherent world of common images and messages into every home.

Television cultivates from infancy the very predispositions and preferences that used to be acquired from other primary sources. Transcending historic barriers of literacy and mobility, television has become the primary common source of socialization and everyday information (mostly in the form of entertainment) of an otherwise heterogeneous population. The repetitive pattern of television's mass-produced messages and images forms the mainstream of a common symbolic environment.

Many of those who now live with television have never before been part of a shared national culture. Television provides, perhaps for the first time since preindustrial religion, a daily ritual of highly compelling and informative content that forms a strong cultural link between elites and the rest of the population. The heart of the analogy of television and religion, and the similarity of their social functions, lies in the continual repetition of patterns (myths, ideologies, "facts," relationships, etc.), which serve to define the world and legitimize the social order.

The stories of the dramatic world need not present credible accounts of what things are in order to perform the more critical function of demonstrating how things work. The illumination of the invisible relationships of life and society has always been the principal function of storytelling. Television today serves that function, telling most of the stories to most of the people most of the time.

This superimposition of a relatively homogeneous process upon a relatively diversified print and film context is a central cultural feature of our age. Television differs from other media in its centralized mass production and ritualistic use of a coherent set of images and messages produced for total populations. Therefore, exposure to the total pattern rather than only to specific genres or programs is what accounts for the historically new and distinct consequences of living with television, namely, the cultivation of shared conceptions of reality among otherwise diverse publics.

We do not deny or minimize the importance of specific programs, selective attention and perception, specifically targeted communications, individual and group differences, and research on effects defined in terms of short-run individual attitude and behavior change. But exclusive concentration on those aspects and terms of traditional effects research risks losing sight of what is basically new and significant about television as the common storyteller of our age.

Compared to other media, television provides a relatively restricted set of choices for a virtually unrestricted variety of interests and publics. Most of its programs are by commercial necessity designed to be watched by nearly everyone in a relatively nonselective fashion. Surveys show that amount of viewing follows the style of life of the viewer and is relatively insensitive to programming. The audience is always the group available at a certain time of the day, the week, and the season, regardless of the programs. Most viewers watch by the clock and either do not know what they will watch when they turn on the set or follow established routines rather than choose each program as they would choose a book, a movie, or an article. The number and variety of choices available when most viewers are available to watch are also limited by the fact that many programs designed for the same broad audience tend to be similar in their basic makeup and appeal.

According to the 1984 Nielsen Report, the television set in the typical home is in use for about 7 hrs a day, and actual viewing by persons older than 2 years averages over 4 hrs a day. With that much viewing, there can be little selectivity. And the more people watch, the less selective they can and tend to be. Most regular and heavy viewers watch more of everything. Researchers who attribute findings to news viewing or preference for action programs and the like overlook the fact that most of those who watch more news or

action programs watch more of all types of programs and that, in any case, many different types of programs manifest the same basic features.

Therefore, from the point of view of the cultivation of relatively stable and common images, the pattern that counts is that of the total pattern of programming to which total communities are regularly exposed over long periods of time. That is the pattern of settings, casting, social typing, actions, and related outcomes that cuts across most program types and defines the world of television, a world in which many viewers live so much of their lives that they cannot avoid absorbing or dealing with its recurrent patterns, probably many times each day.

Thus the patterns central to cultivation analysis are those central to the world of television. They pervade most if not all programs. What matters most for the study of television is not so much what this or that viewer may prefer as what virtually no regular viewer can escape. Therefore, the focus of cultivation analysis is not on what this or that campaign may achieve but on what all campaigns are up against: a widening circle of standardized conceptions superimposed upon a more selectively used print culture and appearing to be increasingly resistant to change.

THE SHIFT FROM EFFECTS TO CULTIVATION RESEARCH

The vast bulk of scientific inquiry about television's social impact can be seen as directly descended from the theoretical models and the methodological procedures of marketing and attitude change research. Large amounts of time, energy, and money have been spent in attempts to determine how to change people's attitudes or behaviors. By and large, however, this conceptualization of effect as immediate change among individuals has not produced research that helps us understand the distinctive features of television: massive, long-term, and common exposure of large and heterogeneous publics to centrally produced, mass-distributed, and repetitive systems of stories.

Traditional effects research perspectives are based on evaluating specific informational, educational, political, or marketing efforts in terms of selective exposure and immediately measurable differences between those exposed and others. Scholars steeped in those traditions find it difficult to accept the emphasis of cultivation analysis upon total immersion rather than selective viewing and upon the spread of stable similarities of outlook rather than of remaining sources of cultural differentiation and change. Similarly, we are all imbued with the perspectives of print culture and its ideals of freedom, diversity, and an active electorate producing as well as selecting information and entertainment from the point of view of a healthy variety of competing and conflicting interests. Therefore, many also question the emphasis of cultivation analysis upon the passive viewer being programmed from birth and the dissolution of authentic publics that this emphasis implies. These scholars and analysts argue that other circumstances do intervene and can affect or even neutralize the cultivation process, that many, even if not most, viewers do watch selectively, and that those program selections do make a difference.

We do not dispute these contentions. As we describe subsequently, we account for them in our analytic strategies. But we believe, again, that concentrating on individual differences and immediate change misses the main point of television: the absorption of divergent currents into a stable and common mainstream.

Others have, of course, suggested that mass media may involve functions and processes other than overt change. Lazarsfeld and Merton (1948) argued that the primary impact of exposure to mass communication is likely to be not change but maintenance of the status quo. Similar notions have been expressed by Glynn (1956) and Bogart (1956). Our own studies in institutional process analysis show that media content and functions reflect institutional organization, interest, and control (Gerbner 1969b, 1972). Television's goal of greatest audience appeal at least cost demands

that most of its messages follow conventional social morality (cf. Weigel & Jessor, 1973).

Culture cultivates the social relationships of a society. The mainstream defines its dominant current. We focus on the implications of accumulated exposure to the most general system of messages, images, and values that underly and cut across the widest variety of programs. These are the continuities that most effects studies overlook.

If, as we argue, the messages are so stable, the medium is so ubiquitous, and accumulated total exposure is what counts, then almost everyone should be affected. Even light viewers live in the same cultural environment as most others, and what they do not get through the tube can be acquired indirectly from others who do watch television. It is clear, then, that the cards are stacked against finding evidence of effects. Therefore, the discovery of a systematic pattern of even small but pervasive differences between light and heavy viewers may indicate far-reaching consequences.

A slight but pervasive (e.g., generational) shift in the cultivation of common perspectives may alter the cultural climate and upset the balance of social and political decision making without necessarily changing observable behavior. A single percentage point difference in ratings is worth millions of dollars in advertising revenue, as the networks know only too well. It takes but a few degrees shift in the average temperature to have an ice age. A range of 3% to 15% margins (typical of our cultivation differentials) in a large and otherwise stable field often signals a landslide, a market takeover, or an epidemic, and it certainly tips the scale of any closely balanced choice or decision. Cultivation theory is based on the persistent and pervasive pull of the television mainstream on a great variety of currents and countercurrents.

If that theory is correct, it is the current system of television, and not our methodology, that challenges theories of self-government predicated on print-based assumptions of ideologically diverse, distinct, and selective publics conscious of their own divergent interests. Thus, the decision to focus on what most viewers share is more than a shift of research emphasis. It is an attempt to develop a methodology appropriate to the distinct and central cultural dynamics of the age of television. This requires a set of theoretical and methodological assumptions and techniques different from those of traditional media effects research. Through the cultural indicators project, we have begun to develop such an alternative approach.

CULTURAL INDICATORS

The cultural indicators approach involves a three-pronged research strategy (for a more detailed description, see Gerbner, 1973). The first prong, called *institutional process analysis,* is designed to investigate the formation of policies directing the massive flow of media messages. Because of its direct policy orientation, this research is the most difficult to fund and, therefore, the least developed (for some examples, see Gerbner, 1969b, 1972). More directly relevant to our present focus are the other two prongs called *message system analysis* and *cultivation analysis.* Both relate to and help develop a conception of the dynamics of the cultivation process.

In the second prong, we record week-long samples of network television drama each year and subject these systems of messages to rigorous and detailed content analysis in order to reliably delineate selected features of the television world. We consider these the potential lessons television cultivates and use them as a source of questions for the cultivation analysis.

In the third prong, we examine the responses given to these questions (phrased to refer to the real world) among those with varying amounts of exposure to the world of television. (Nonviewers are too few and demographically too scattered for serious research purposes.) We want to determine whether those who spend more of their time with television are more likely to answer these questions in ways that reflect the potential lessons of the television world (give the "television answer") than are those who watch less television but are otherwise comparable (in terms of important de-

mographic characteristics) to the heavy viewers. We have used the concept of cultivation to describe the contributions television viewing makes to viewer conceptions of social reality. Cultivation differential is the margin of difference in conceptions of reality between light and heavy viewers in the same demographic subgroups.

CULTIVATION: A MULTIDIRECTIONAL PROCESS

Our use of the term *cultivation* for television's contribution to conceptions of social reality is not simply a fancier word for effects. Nor does it necessarily imply a one-way, monolithic process. The effects of a pervasive medium upon the composition and structure of the symbolic environment are subtle, complex, and intermingled with other influences. This perspective, therefore, assumes an interaction between the medium and its publics.

The elements of cultivation do not originate with television or appear out of a void. Layers of demographic, social, personal, and cultural contexts also determine the shape, scope, and degree of the contribution television is likely to make. Yet, the meanings of those contexts and factors are in themselves aspects of the cultivation process. That is, although a viewer's sex, age, or class may make a difference, television helps define what it means, for example, to be an adolescent female member of a given social class. The interaction is a continuous process (as is cultivation) taking place at every stage, from cradle to grave.

Thus, television neither simply creates nor reflects images, opinions, and beliefs. Rather, it is an integral aspect of a dynamic process. Institutional needs and objectives influence the creation and distribution of mass-produced messages which create, fit into, exploit, and sustain the needs, values, and ideologies of mass publics. These publics, in turn, acquire distinct identities as publics partly through exposure to the ongoing flow of messages.

The question of which came first is misleading and irrelevant. People are born into a symbolic environment with television as its mainstream. Children begin viewing several years before they begin reading, and well before they can even talk. Television viewing is both a shaper and a stable part of certain life styles and outlooks. It links the individual to a larger if synthetic world, a world of television's own making. Most of those with certain social and psychological characteristics, dispositions, and world views—and fewer alternatives as attractive and compelling as television—use it as their major vehicle of cultural participation. The content shapes and promotes their continued attention. To the extent that television dominates their sources of information, continued exposure to its messages is likely to reiterate, confirm, and nourish (i.e., cultivate) their values and perspectives.

The point is that cultivation is not conceived as a unidirectional process but rather more like a gravitational process. The angle and direction of the "pull" depends on where groups of viewers and their styles of life are in reference to the center of gravity, the "mainstream" of the world of television. Each group may strain in a different direction, but all groups are affected by the same central current. Cultivation is thus part of a continual, dynamic, ongoing process of interaction among messages and contexts. This holds even though (and in a sense, especially because) the hallmark of the process is either relative stability or slow change.

As successive generations grow up with television's version of the world, the former and traditional distinctions become blurred. Cultivation thus implies the steady entrenchment of mainstream orientations in most cases and the systematic but almost imperceptible modification of previous orientations in others; in other words, affirmation for the believers *and* indoctrination for deviants. That is the process we call *mainstreaming*.

The observable manifestations of the process vary as a function of the environmental context and other attributes of the viewer. In order to explain these variations, however, it is necessary to describe the central components of the symbolic environment composed by television. We return to the concept of mainstreaming after a brief consideration of the values, ideology, demography, and action structure of the television mainstream itself.

THE WORLD OF TELEVISION

Message system analysis is a tool for making systematic, reliable, and cumulative observations about television content. We use message system analysis not to determine what any individual viewer (or group of viewers) might see, but to assess the most representative, stable, and recurrent aggregate patterns of messages to which total communities are exposed over long periods of time. The analysis is based on the premise that although findings about media content cannot be taken at face value as evidence of impact, representative and reliable observations of content (rather than selective and idiosyncratic impressions) are critical prerequisites to a valid consideration of media influence. In other words, a relatively few unambiguous, dominant, and common content patterns provide the basis for interaction and shared assumptions, meanings, and definitions (though not necessarily agreement) among large and heterogeneous mass publics. Message system analysis records those patterns and establishes the bases for cultivation analysis. We have been conducting annual analyses of prime time and weekend daytime network television drama since 1969.[1]

The world of prime time is animated by vivid and intimate portrayals of over 300 major dramatic characters a week, mostly stock types, and their weekly rounds of dramatic activities. Conventional and normal though that world may appear, it is in

---

[1] By 1984, 2,105 programs (1,204 prime time and 901 weekend daytime), 6,055 major characters, and 19,116 minor characters had been analyzed.

fact far from the reality of anything but consumer values and the ideology of social power.

Men outnumber women by at least 3:1 who are younger (but age faster) than the men they meet. Young people (under 18) comprise one-third and older people (over 65) one-fifth of their true proportion in the population. Figure 1 shows the difference between the age distribution in the television world and reality. Similarly, blacks on television represent three-fourths, and Hispanics one-third of their share of the U.S. population, and a disproportionate number are minor rather than major characters.

The point is not that culture should duplicate real-life statistics. It is rather that the direction and thrust of cultural amplification or neglect provide a clue to the treatment of social types, groups, and values, and yield suggestions for cultivation analysis. For example, the prominent and stable overrepresentation of well-to-do white men in the prime of life dominates prime time and indicates a relatively restrictive view of women's and minorities' opportunities and rights. As Figure 1 suggests, the general demography of the television world bears greater resemblance to the facts of consumer income than to the U.S. census.

The myth of the middle class as the all-American norm pervades the world of television. Nearly 7 out of 10 television characters appear in the "middle-middle" of a five-way classification system. Most of them are professionals and managers. Blue collar and service work occupies 67% of all Americans but only 25% of television characters.

In the world of prime time, the state acts mostly to fend off threats to law and order in a mean and dangerous world. Enforcing the law of that world takes nearly three times as many characters as the number of all blue-collar and service workers. The typical viewer of an average week's prime time programs encounters seemingly realistic and intimate (but usually false) representations of the life and work of 30 police officers, 7 lawyers, and 3 judges, but only 1 engineer or scientist and very few blue-collar workers. Again, nearly everybody appears to be comfortably managing on an average income of the mythical norm of middle class.

But threats abound. Crime in prime time is at least 10 times as rampant as in the real world. An average of 5 to 6 acts of overt physical violence per hour menace over half of all major characters. However, pain, suffering, and med-

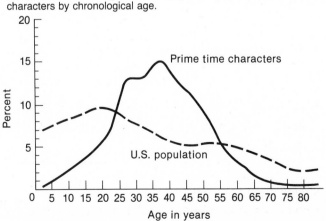

FIGURE 1 Percentages of U.S. population and all prime-time TV characters by chronological age.

ical help rarely follow this mayhem. Symbolic violence demonstrates power, not therapy; it shows who can get away with what against whom. The dominant white men in the prime of life are more likely to be victimizers than victims. Conversely, old, young, and minority women, and young boys, are more likely to be victims rather than victimizers in violent conflicts. The analysis of content data as a message system rather than as isolated incidents of violence or sex, for example, makes it possible to view these acts in context as representing social relationships and the distribution (as well as symbolic enforcement) of the structure of power according to television.

The stability and consistency of basic patterns over the years is one of their most striking (but not surprising) features. A central cultural arm of society could hardly avoid reflecting (and cultivating) some of its basic structural characteristics, as well as more specific institutional positions and interests. Television has obviously changed on many levels (e.g., there have been ebbs and flows in the popularity and distribution of various genres, new production values, visible but token minority representation, and many short-lived trends and fads), but these changes are superficial. The underlying values, demography, ideology, and power relationships have manifested only minor fluctuations with virtually no significant deviations over time, despite the actual social changes which have occurred. The remarkable pattern of uniformity, durability, and resilience of the aggregate messages of prime time network drama explains its cultivation of both stable concepts and the resistance to change.

MODES OF CULTIVATION ANALYSIS

Our tracking and documentation of the shape and contours of the television world have led to several analytical strategies concerning the cultivation potential of television. These include analyses of the extent to which television teaches various facts about the world, of extrapolations from those facts to more general images and orientations, and of the incorporation of the lessons into viewers' personal assumptions and expectations.

Each of these involves somewhat different processes and relies on the specific findings of message system analysis to varying degrees. The content findings form the conceptual basis for the questions we ask respondents. The margins of difference ("cultivation differentials") between demographically matched light and heavy viewers' response patterns define the extent of cultivation. Where possible or appropriate, we use large surveys that were conducted for other purposes, with the accompanying advantages and limitations of secondary analysis. In any case, the questions do not mention television, and the respondents' awareness or perceptions of the source of their information are irrelevant for our purposes. Any resulting relationship between amount of viewing and the tendency to respond to these questions according to television's portrayals (with other things held constant) illuminates television's contribution to viewers' conceptions of social reality.

The cases of clear-cut divergence between symbolic reality and objective reality provide convenient tests of the extent to which television's versions of the facts are incorporated or absorbed into what heavy viewers take for granted about the world. For example, television drama tends to sharply underrepresent older people. While those over 65 constitute the fastest growing segment of the real-world population, heavy viewers are more likely to feel that the elderly are a "vanishing breed"—that compared to 20 years ago, they are fewer in number, they are in worse health, and they don't live as long—all contrary to fact (Gerbner, Gross, Signorielli, & Morgan, 1980).

As another example, consider how likely television characters are to encounter violence compared to the rest of us. Well over half of all major characters on television are involved each week in some kind of violent action. Although

FBI statistics have clear limitations, they indicate that in any 1 year less than 1% of people in the U.S. are victims of criminal violence. Accordingly, we have found considerable support for the proposition that heavy exposure to the world of television cultivates exaggerated perceptions of the number of people involved in violence in any given week (Gerbner et al., 1979; Gerbner, Gross, Morgan, & Signorielli, 1980), as well as numerous other inaccurate beliefs about crime and law enforcement.

The facts (which are evidently learned quite well) are likely to become the basis for a broader world view, thus making television a significant source of general values, ideologies, and perspectives as well as specific assumptions, beliefs, and images. This extrapolation beyond the specific facts derived from message system analysis can be seen as second-order cultivation analysis. Hawkins and Pingree (1982) call this the cultivation of "value systems."

One example is what we have called the "mean world" syndrome. Our message data say little directly about either the selfishness or altruism of people, and there are certainly no real-world statistics about the extent to which people can be trusted. Yet, we have found that one lesson viewers derive from heavy exposure to the violence-saturated world of television is that in such a mean and dangerous world, most people "cannot be trusted" and that most people are "just looking out for themselves" (Gerbner, Gross, Morgan, & Signorielli, 1980). We have also found that the differential ratios of symbolic victimization among women and minorities on television cultivate different levels of insecurity among their real-life counterparts, a "hierarchy of fears" that confirms and tends to perpetuate their dependent status (Morgan, 1983).

Another example of extrapolated assumptions relates to the image of women. The dominant majority status of men on television does not mean that heavy viewers ignore daily experience and underestimate the number of women in society. But it does mean that most heavy viewers absorb the implicit assumptions that women have more limited abilities and interests than men. Most groups of heavy viewers, with other characteristics held constant, score higher on our sexism scale.

Other second-order extrapolations from content patterns have also led to fruitful discoveries of more explicit political importance. For example, we have argued that as television seeks large and heterogeneous audiences, its messages are designed to disturb as few as possible. Therefore, they tend to balance opposing perspectives and to steer a middle course along the supposedly nonideological mainstream. We have found that heavy viewers are significantly and substantially more likely to label themselves as being "moderate" rather than either "liberal" or "conservative" (see Gerbner, Gross, Morgan, & Signorielli, 1982; 1984).

Finally, we have observed a complex relationship between the cultivation of general orientations or assumptions about facts of life and more specific personal expectations. For example, television may cultivate exaggerated notions of the prevalence of violence and risk out in the world, but the cultivation of expectations of personal victimization depends on the neighborhood of the viewer (see Gerbner, Gross, Morgan, & Signorielli, 1981a). Different groups may hold the same assumptions about the facts but relate to them in different ways, depending on their own situations.

Thus, the cultivation of a general conception of social reality (e.g., about women's place or violence in the world) may lead to a certain position on public issues or to some marketing decision, but it need not result in other behavior consonant with that conception. The latter (e.g., career expectation, likelihood of victimization) may be deflected by demographic or personal situations or other currents in the television mainstream. Our focus has generally been on those basic perspectives and conceptions that bear the strongest relationships to common expectations and the formation of public policy.

THE NATURE OF CULTIVATION

Since the early 1970s, the range of topics we have subjected to cultivation analysis has greatly expanded. On issue after issue we found that the assumptions, beliefs, and values of heavy viewers differ systematically from those of comparable groups of light viewers. The differences tend to reflect both the dominant patterns of life in the television world and the characteristics of different groups of light and heavy viewers.

Sometimes we found that these differences hold across-the-board, meaning that those who watch more television are more likely—in all or most subgroups—to give what we call "television answers" to our questions. But in most cases, the patterns were more complex. As we looked into the cultivation process in more and more aspects of life and society, from health-related beliefs to political orientations and occupational images (and much more), we found that television viewing usually relates in different but consistent ways to different groups' life situations and world views.

We have found that personal interaction makes a difference. Adolescents whose parents are more involved in their viewing show sharply smaller relationships between amount of viewing and perceiving the world in terms of television's portrayals (Gross & Morgan, 1985). Children who are more integrated into cohesive peer groups are less receptive to cultivation (Rothschild, 1984). In contrast, adolescents who watch cable programming show significantly stronger cultivation patterns (Morgan & Rothschild, 1983). The implication is that cultivation is both dependent on and a manifestation of the extent to which mediated imagery dominates the viewers' sources of information. Personal interaction and affiliation reduce cultivation; cable television (presumably by providing even more of the same) increases it.

Personal, day-to-day, direct experience also plays a role. We have found that the relationship between amount of viewing and fear of crime is strongest among those who have good reason to be afraid. When one's everyday environment is congruent with and reinforces television's messages, the result is a phenomenon we call *resonance*. For example, the cultivation of insecurity is most pronounced among those who live in high crime urban areas (Doob & Macdonald, 1979; Gerbner, Gross, Morgan, & Signorielli, 1980). In these cases, everyday reality and television provide a double dose of messages that resonate and amplify cultivation.

Demographic correspondence between viewers and television characters also predicts the extent and nature of cultivation. Our message system analyses have revealed consistent differences in the relative likelihood of different demographic groups to be portrayed as victims or as perpetrators of violence (known as *risk ratios*). Relationships of amount of viewing and the tendency to hold exaggerated perceptions of violence are much more pronounced within the real-world demographic subgroups whose fictional counterparts are most victimized (Morgan, 1983). The symbolic power hierarchy of relative victimization is thus reflected in differential cultivation patterns.

MAINSTREAMING

We have seen that a wide variety of factors produce systematic and theoretically meaningful variations in cultivation. We have named the most general and important of these patterns *mainstreaming*.

The mainstream can be thought of as a relative commonality of outlooks and values that exposure to features and dynamics of the television world tends to cultivate. By mainstreaming we mean the expression of that commonality by heavy viewers in those demographic groups whose light viewers hold divergent views. In other words, differences found in the responses of different groups of viewers, differences that can be associated with other cultural, social, and political characteristics of these groups, may be diminished or even absent from the responses of heavy viewers in the same groups.

Mainstreaming represents the theoretical elaboration and empirical verification of our assertion that television cultivates common perspectives. Mainstreaming means that television viewing may absorb or override differences in perspectives and behavior that stem from other social, cultural, and demographic influences. It represents a homogenization of divergent views and a convergence of disparate viewers. Mainstreaming makes television the true 20th-century melting pot of the American people.

The mainstreaming potential of television stems from the way the institution is organized, the competition to attract audiences from all regions and classes, and the consistency of its messages (see, e.g., Hirsch, 1979; Seldes, 1957). In every area we have examined, mainstreaming is the strongest and most consistent explanation for differences in the strength and direction of television's contributions to viewer conceptions.

SUMMARY

In summary, our theory of the cultivation process is an attempt to understand and explain the dynamics of television as a distinctive feature of our age. It is not a substitute for, but a complement to, traditional approaches to media effects research concerned with processes more applicable to other media. Designed primarily for television and focusing on its pervasive and recurrent patterns of representation and viewing, cultivation analysis concentrates on the enduring and common consequences of growing up and living with television: the cultivation of stable, resistant, and widely shared assumptions, images, and conceptions reflecting the institutional characteristics and interests of the medium itself. Our explorations of this process in many ways and contexts have been enriched and confirmed by studies of a growing number of independent investigators in the United States and abroad and have led to the development of some theoretical models for further testing and elaboration.

We believe that television has become the common symbolic environment that interacts with most of the things we think and do. Therefore, understanding its dynamics can help develop and maintain a sense of alternatives and independence essential for self-direction and self-government in the television age.

X: A Fabulous Child's Story

Lois Gould (1972)

Gould examines an intriguing issue, the importance of bringing up a child in accordance with appropriate gender roles. Although many people give lip service to the idea of raising children in nonsexist ways, in fact, most parents expect or require gender-role-appropriate behavior in their children. This hypothetical case is more a fantasy than a thought experiment, but it highlights, nonetheless, two important considerations. First, it points out some of the difficulties in actually trying to raise children who are not traditional in their gender-role behaviors, and second, it shows some of the difficulties of defying commonly held beliefs. Living in society has some costs, and these are most notable when applying a distinctive and different set of values. We predict that this story would not have such a happy ending in true life. We also find that our students intellectually admire Baby X's parents, yet very few of them plan to try to follow in their footsteps in the least. Exactly how important is it for *you* to raise either gender-role oriented or nontraditional (androgynous) children, and how far might you go in providing a different type of upbringing?

Once upon a time, a baby named X was born. This baby was named X so that nobody could tell whether it was a boy or a girl. Its parents could tell, of course, but they couldn't tell anybody else. They couldn't even tell Baby X, at first.

You see, it was all part of a very important Secret Scientific Xperiment, known officially as Project Baby X. The smartest scientists had set up this Xperiment at a cost of Xactly 23 billion dollars and 72 cents, which might seem like a lot for just one baby, even a very important Xperimental baby. But when you remember the prices of things like strained carrots and stuffed bunnies, and popcorn for the movies and booster shots for camp, let alone 28 shiny quarters from the tooth fairy, you begin to see how it adds up.

Also, long before Baby X was born, all those scientists had to be paid to work out the details of the Xperiment, and to write the *Official Instruction Manual* for Baby X's parents and, most important of all, to find the right set of parents to bring up Baby X. These parents had to be selected very carefully. Thousands of volunteers had to take thousands of tests and answer thousands of tricky questions. Almost everybody failed because, it turned out, almost everybody really wanted either a baby boy or a baby girl, and not Baby X at all. Also, almost everybody was afraid that a Baby X would be a lot more trouble than a boy or a girl. (They were probably right, the scientists admitted, but Baby X needed parents who wouldn't *mind* the Xtra trouble.)

There were families with grandparents named Milton and Agatha, who didn't see why the baby couldn't be named Milton or Agatha instead of X, even if it *was* an X. There were families with aunts who insisted on knitting tiny dresses and uncles who insisted on sending tiny baseball mitts. Worst of all, there were families that already had other children who couldn't be trusted to keep the secret. Certainly not if they knew the secret was worth 23 billion dollars and 72 cents—and all you had to do was take one little peek at Baby X in the bathtub to know if it was a boy or a girl.

But, finally, the scientists found the Joneses, who really wanted to raise an X more than any other kind of baby—no matter how much trouble it would be. Ms. and Mr. Jones had to promise they would take equal turns caring for X, and feeding it, and singing it lullabies. And they had to promise never to hire any baby-sitters. The government scientists knew perfectly well that a baby-sitter would probably peek at X in the bathtub, too.

The day the Joneses brought their baby home, lots of friends and relatives came over to see it. None of them knew about the secret Xperiment, though. So the first thing they asked was what kind of a baby X was. When the Joneses smiled and said, "It's an X!" nobody knew what to say. They couldn't say, "Look at her cute little dimples!" And they couldn't say, "Look at his husky little biceps!" And they couldn't even say just plain "kitchycoo." In fact, they all thought the Joneses were playing some kind of rude joke.

But, of course, the Joneses were not joking. "It's an X" was absolutely all they would say. And that made the friends and relatives very angry. The relatives all felt embarrassed about having an X in the family. "People will think there's something wrong with it!" some of them whispered. "There *is* something wrong with it!" others whispered back.

"Nonsense!" the Joneses told them all cheerfully. "What could possibly be wrong with this perfectly adorable X?"

Nobody could answer that, except Baby X, who had just finished its bottle. Baby X's answer was a loud, satisfied burp.

Clearly, nothing at all was wrong. Nevertheless, none of the relatives felt comfortable about buying a present for a Baby X. The cousins who sent the baby a tiny football helmet would not come and visit any more. And the neighbors who sent a pink-flowered romper suit pulled their shades down when the Joneses passed their house.

The *Official Instruction Manual* had warned the new parents that this would happen, so they didn't fret about it. Besides, they were too busy with baby X and the hundreds of different Xercises for treating it properly.

Ms. and Mr. Jones had to be Xtra careful about how they played with little X. They knew that if they kept bouncing it up in the air and saying how *strong* and *active* it was, they'd be treating it more like a boy than an X. But if all they did was cuddle it and kiss it and tell it how *sweet* and *dainty* it was, they'd be treating it more like a girl than an X.

On page 1,654 of the *Official Instruction Manual,* the scientists prescribed: "plenty of bouncing and plenty of cuddling, *both.* X ought to be strong and sweet and active. Forget about *dainty* altogether."

Meanwhile, the Joneses were worrying about other problems. Toys, for instance. And clothes. On his first shopping trip, Mr. Jones told the store clerk, "I need some clothes and toys for my new baby." The clerk smiled and said, "Well, now, is it a boy or a girl?" "It's an X," Mr. Jones said, smiling back. But the clerk got all red in the face and said huffily, "In *that* case, I'm afraid I can't help you, sir." So Mr. Jones wandered helplessly up and down the aisles trying to find what X needed. But everything in the store was piled up in sections marked "Boys" or "Girls." There were "Boys' Pajamas" and "Girls' Underwear" and "Boys' Fire Engines" and "Girls' Housekeeping Sets." Mr. Jones went home without buying anything for X. That night he and Ms. Jones consulted page 2,326 of the *Official Instruction Manual.* "Buy plenty of everything!" it said firmly.

So they bought plenty of sturdy blue pajamas in the Boys' Department and cheerful flowered underwear in the Girls' Department. And they bought all kinds of toys. A boy doll that made pee-pee and cried, "Pa-pa." And a girl doll that talked in three languages and said, "I am the Pres-i-dent of Gen-er-al Mo-tors." They also bought a storybook about a brave princess who rescued a handsome prince from his ivory tower, and another one about a sister and brother who grew up to be a baseball star and a ballet star, and you had to guess which was which.

The head scientists of Project Baby X checked all their purchases and told them to keep up the good work. They also reminded the Joneses to see page 4,629 of the *Manual,* where it said, "Never make Baby X feel *embarrassed* or *ashamed* about what it wants to play with. And if X gets dirty climbing rocks, never say 'Nice little Xes don't get dirty climbing rocks.'"

Likewise, it said, "If X falls down and cries, never say 'Brave little Xes don't cry.' Because, of course, nice little Xes *do* get dirty, and brave little Xes *do* cry. No matter how dirty X gets, or how hard it cries, don't worry. It's all part of the Xperiment."

Whenever the Joneses pushed Baby X's stroller in the park, smiling strangers would come over and coo: "Is that a boy or a girl?" The Joneses would smile back and say, "It's an X." The strangers would stop smiling then, and often snarl something nasty—as if the Joneses had snarled at *them.*

By the time X grew big enough to play with other children, the Joneses' troubles had grown bigger, too. Once a little girl grabbed X's shovel in the sandbox, and zonked X on the head with it. "Now, now, Tracy," the little girl's mother began to scold, "little girls mustn't hit little—" and she turned to ask X, "Are you a little boy or a little girl, dear?"

Mr. Jones, who was sitting near the sandbox, held his breath and crossed his fingers.

X smiled politely at the lady, even though X's head had never been zonked so hard in its life. "I'm a little X," X replied.

"You're a *what?*" the lady exclaimed angrily. "You're a little b-r-a-t, you mean!"

"But little girls mustn't hit little Xes, either!" said X, retrieving the shovel with another polite smile. "What good does hitting do, anyway?"

X's father, who was still holding his breath, finally let it out, uncrossed his fingers, and grinned back at X.

And at their next secret Project Baby X meeting, the scientists grinned, too. Baby X was doing fine.

But then it was time for X to start school. The Joneses were really worried about this, because school was even more full of rules for boys and girls, and there were no rules for Xes. The teacher would tell boys to form one line, and girls to form another line. There would be boys' games and girls' games, and boys' secrets and girls' secrets. The school library would have a list of recommended books for girls, and a different list of recommended books for boys. There would even be a bathroom marked BOYS and another one marked GIRLS. Pretty soon boys and girls would hardly talk to each other. What would happen to poor little X?

The Joneses spent weeks consulting their *Instruction Manual* (there were 249½ pages of advice under "First Day of School"), and attending urgent special conferences with the smart scientists of Project Baby X.

The scientists had to make sure that X's mother had taught X how to throw and catch a ball properly, and that X's father had been sure to teach X what to serve at a doll's tea party. X had to know how to shoot marbles and how to jump rope and, most of all, what to say when the Other Children asked whether X was a Boy or a Girl.

Finally, X was ready. The Joneses helped X button on a nice new pair of red-and-white checked overalls, and sharpened six pencils for X's nice new pencilbox, and marked X's name clearly on all the books in its nice new bookbag. X brushed its teeth and combed its hair, which just about covered its ears, and remembered to put a napkin in its lunchbox.

The Joneses had asked X's teacher if the class could line up alphabetically, instead of forming separate lines for boys and girls. And they had asked if X could use the principal's bathroom, because it wasn't marked anything except BATH ROOM. X's teacher promised to take care of all those problems. But nobody could help X with the biggest problem of all—Other Children.

Nobody in X's class had ever known an X before. What would they think? How would X make friends?

You couldn't tell what X was by studying its clothes—overalls don't even button right-to-left, like girls' clothes, or left-to-right, like boys' clothes. And you couldn't guess whether X had a girl's short haircut or a boy's long haircut. And it was very hard to tell by the games X liked to play. Either X played ball very well for a girl, or else X played house very well for a boy.

Some of the children tried to find out by asking X tricky questions, like "Who's your favorite sports star?" That was easy. X had two favorite sports stars: a girl jockey named Robyn Smith and a boy archery champion named Robin Hood. Then they asked, "What's your favorite TV program?" And that was even easier. X's favorite TV program was "Lassie," which stars a girl dog played by a boy dog.

When X said that its favorite toy was a doll, everyone decided that X must be a girl. But then X said that the doll was really a robot, and that X had computerized it, and that it was programmed to bake fudge brownies and then clean up the kitchen. After X told them that, the other children gave up guessing what X was. All they knew was they'd sure like to see X's doll.

After school, X wanted to play with the other children. "How about shooting some baskets in the gym?" X asked the girls. But all they did was make faces and giggle behind X's back.

"How about weaving some baskets in the arts and crafts room?" X asked the boys. But they all made faces and giggled behind X's back, too.

That night, Ms. and Mr. Jones asked X how things had gone at school. X told them sadly that the lessons were okay, but otherwise school was a terrible place for an X. It seemed as if Other Children would never want an X for a friend.

Once more, the Joneses reached for their *Instruction Manual.* Under "Other Children," they found the following message: "What did you Xpect? *Other Children* have to obey all the silly boy-girl rules, because their parents taught them to. Lucky X—you don't have to stick to the rules at all! All you have to do is be yourself. P.S. We're not saying it'll be easy.''

X liked being itself. But X cried a lot that night, partly because it felt afraid. So X's father held X tight, and cuddled it, and couldn't help crying a little, too. And X's mother cheered them both up by reading an Xciting story about an enchanted prince called Sleeping Handsome, who woke up when Princess Charming kissed him.

The next morning, they all felt much better, and little X went back to school with a brave smile and a clean pair of red-and-white checked overalls.

There was a seven-letter-word spelling bee in class that day. And a seven-lap boys' relay race in the gym. And a seven-layer-cake baking contest in the girls' kitchen corner. X won the spelling bee. X also won the relay race. And X almost won the baking contest, except it forgot to light the oven. Which only proves that nobody's perfect.

One of the Other Children noticed something else, too. He said: ''Winning or losing doesn't seem to count to X. X seems to have fun being good at boys' skills *and* girls' skills.''

''Come to think of it,'' said another one of the Other Children, ''maybe X is having twice as much fun as we are!''

So after school that day, the girl who beat X at the baking contest gave X a big slice of her prizewinning cake. And the boy X beat in the relay race asked X to race him home.

From then on, some really funny things began to happen. Susie, who sat next to X in class, suddenly refused to wear pink dresses to school any more. She insisted on wearing red-and-white checked overalls—just like X's. Overalls, she told her parents, were much better for climbing monkey bars.

Then Jim, the class football nut, started wheeling his little sister's doll carriage around the football field. He'd put on his entire football uniform, except for the helmet. Then he'd put the helmet *in* the carriage, lovingly tucked under an old set of shoulder pads. Then he'd start jogging around the field, pushing the carriage and singing ''Rockabye Baby'' to his football helmet. He told his family that X did the same thing, so it must be okay. After all, X was now the team's star quarterback.

Susie's parents were horrified by her behavior, and Jim's parents were worried sick about his. But the worst came when the twins, Joe and Peggy, decided to share everything with each other. Peggy used Joe's hockey skates, and his microscope, and took half his newspaper route. Joe used Peggy's needlepoint kit, and her cookbooks, and took two of her three baby-sitting jobs. Peggy started running the lawn mower, and Joe started running the vacuum cleaner.

Their parents weren't one bit pleased with Peggy's wonderful biology experiments, or with Joe's terrific needlepoint pillows. They didn't care that Peggy mowed the lawn better, and that Joe vacuumed the carpet better. In fact, they were furious. It's all that little X's fault, they agreed. Just because X doesn't know what it is, or what it's supposed to be, it wants to get everybody *else* mixed up, too!

Peggy and Joe were forbidden to play with X any more. So was Susie, and then Jim, and then *all* the Other Children. But it was too late; the Other Children stayed mixed up and happy and free, and refused to go back to the way they'd been before X.

Finally, Joe and Peggy's parents decided to call an emergency meeting of the school's Parents' Association, to discuss ''The X Problem.'' They sent a report to the principal stating that X was a ''disruptive influence.'' They demanded immediate action. The Joneses, they said, should be *forced* to tell whether X was a boy or a girl. And then X should be *forced* to behave like whichever it was. If the Joneses refused to tell, the Parents' Association said, then X must take an Xamination. The school psychiatrist must Xamine it physically and mentally, and issue a full report. If X's test showed it was a boy, it would have to obey all the boys' rules. If it proved to be a girl, X would have to obey all the girls' rules.

And if X turned out to be some kind of mixed-up misfit, then X should be Xpelled from the school. Immediately!

The principal was very upset. Disruptive influence? Mixed-up misfit? But X was an Xcellent student. All the teachers said it was a delight to have X in their classes. X was president of the student council. X had won first prize in the talent show, and second prize in the art show, and honorable mention in the science fair, and six athletic events on field day, including the potato race.

Nevertheless, insisted the Parents' Association, X is a Problem Child. X is the Biggest Problem Child we have ever seen!

So the principal reluctantly notified X's parents that numerous complaints about X's behavior had come to the school's attention. And that after the psychiatrist's Xamination, the school would decide what to do about X.

The Joneses reported this at once to the scientists, who referred them to page 85,759 of the *Instruction Manual.* "Sooner or later," it said, "X will have to be Xamined by a psychiatrist. This may be the only way any of us will know for sure whether X is mixed up—or whether everyone else is."

The night before X was to be Xamined, the Joneses tried not to let X see how worried they were. "What if—?" Mr. Jones would say. And Ms. Jones would reply, "No use worrying." Then a few minutes later, Ms. Jones would say, "What if—?" and Mr. Jones would reply, "No use worrying."

X just smiled at them both, and hugged them hard and didn't say much of anything. X was thinking, What if—? And then X thought: No use worrying.

At Xactly 9 o'clock the next day, X reported to the school psychiatrist's office. The principal, along with a committee from the Parents' Association, X's teacher, X's classmates, and Ms. and Mr. Jones, waited in the hall outside. Nobody knew the details of the tests X was to be given, but everybody knew they'd be *very* hard, and that they'd

reveal Xactly what everyone wanted to know about X, but were afraid to ask.

It was terribly quiet in the hall. Almost spooky. Once in a while, they would hear a strange noise inside the room. There were buzzes. And a beep or two. And several bells. An occasional light would flash under the door. The Joneses thought it was a white light, but the principal thought it was blue. Two or three children swore it was either yellow or green. And the Parents' Committee missed it completely.

Through it all, you could hear the psychiatrist's low voice, asking hundreds of questions, and X's higher voice, answering hundreds of answers.

The whole thing took so long that everyone knew it must be the most complete Xamination anyone had ever had to take. Poor X, the Joneses thought. Serves X right, the Parents' Committee thought. I wouldn't like to be in X's overalls right now, the children thought.

At last, the door opened. Everyone crowded around to hear the results. X didn't look any different; in fact, X was smiling. But the psychiatrist looked terrible. He looked as if he was crying! "What happened?" everyone began shouting. Had X done something disgraceful? "I wouldn't be a bit surprised!" muttered Peggy and Joe's parents. "Did X flunk the *whole* test?" cried Susie's parents. "Or just the most important part?" yelled Jim's parents.

"Oh, dear," sighed Mr. Jones.

"Oh, dear," sighed Ms. Jones.

"Sssh," ssshed the principal. "The psychiatrist is trying to speak."

Wiping his eyes and clearing his throat, the psychiatrist began, in a hoarse whisper. "In my opinion," he whispered—you could tell he must be very upset—"in my opinion, young X here—"

"Yes? Yes?" shouted a parent impatiently.

"Sssh!" ssshed the principal.

"Young *Sssh* here, I mean young X," said the doctor, frowning, "is just about—"

"Just about *what?* Let's have it!" shouted another parent.

"...just about the *least* mixed-up child I've ever Xamined!" said the psychiatrist.

"Yay for X!" yelled one of the children. And then the others began yelling, too. Clapping and cheering and jumping up and down.

"*SSSH!*" SSShed the principal, but nobody did.

The Parents' Committee was angry and bewildered. How *could* X have passed the whole Xamination? Didn't X have an *identity* problem? Wasn't X mixed up at *all?* Wasn't X *any* kind of a misfit? How could it *not* be, when it didn't even *know* what it was? And why was the psychiatrist crying?

Actually, he had stopped crying and was smiling politely through his tears. "Don't you see?" he said. "I'm crying because it's wonderful! X has absolutely no identity problem! X isn't one bit mixed up! As for being a misfit— ridiculous! X knows perfectly well what it is! Don't you, X?" The doctor winked. X winked back.

"But what *is* X?" shrieked Peggy and Joe's parents. "*We* still want to know what it is!"

"Ah, yes," said the doctor, winking again. "Well, don't worry. You'll all know one of these days. And you won't need me to tell you."

"What? What does he mean?" some of the parents grumbled suspiciously.

Susie and Peggy and Joe all answered at once.

"He means that by the time X's sex matters, it won't be a secret any more!"

With that, the doctor began to push through the crowd toward X's parents. "How do you do," he said, somewhat stiffly. And then he reached out to hug them both. "If I ever have an X of my own," he whispered, "I sure hope you'll lend me your instruction manual."

Needless to say, the Joneses were very happy. The Project Baby X scientists were rather pleased, too. So were Susie, Jim, Peggy, Joe, and all the Other Children. The Parents' Association wasn't, but they had promised to accept the psychiatrist's report, and not make any more trouble. They even invited Ms. and Mr. Jones to become honorary members, which they did.

Later that day, all X's friends put on their red-and-white checked overalls and went over to see X. They found X in the back yard, playing with a very tiny baby that none of them had ever seen before. The baby was wearing very tiny red-and-white checked overalls.

"How do you like our new baby?" X asked the Other Children proudly.

"It's got cute dimples," said Jim.

"It's got husky biceps, too," said Susie.

"What kind of baby is it?" asked Joe and Peggy.

X frowned at them. "Can't you tell?" Then X broke into a big, mischievous grin. *"It's a Y!"*

Stereotyping and Prejudice

Excerpt from *The Nature of Prejudice*

Gordon W. Allport (1954)

One of the foundations of the social values that exist in the United States is embodied in the credo: "All men are created equal." Although hampered by the nonconscious ideology that "all men" meant "white males only," our country's founders were moving toward the principle of equality that is at the root of democracy. Yet many people in our society have not been and are not presently being treated in an egalitarian fashion.

The effects of inequitable treatment are many, from economic and job disadvantages to poor health and health care. An early and continuing focus for psychologists has been the influence of inequality on self-esteem. In 1947, Kenneth and Mamie Clark investigated the development of racial identity and self-esteem among American black children. Their startling result was that black children preferred white dolls over black dolls when given a choice between two dolls of each color. This research was so important that it was cited in the 1954 Supreme Court's *Brown v. Board of Education* decision mandating school desegregation. More recent (and controversial) evidence (Powell-Hopson & Hopson, 1988) argues that the civil rights advances and the rhetoric of racial pride from the 1960s and beyond has had little influence on children's preference. Powell-Hopson and Hopson replicated the Clark and Clark study utilizing Cabbage Patch dolls that were identical to each other except for color. They found that black children's preference for white dolls was remarkably similar to those of the black children tested 45 years earlier.

That we live in a nation still struggling with its values and treatment of minorities, be they blacks, women, American Indians, etc., is no surprise to anyone. Despite progress in civil rights, prejudice and discrimination continue to exist. Social psychology has a tradition of attempting to analyze the source of such behavior as well as trying to provide solutions that might ultimately lead to egalitarian treatment of all peoples.

The first reading in this section is excerpted from Allport's classic, *The Nature of Prejudice*. It has an abundance of hypotheses about prejudice. Allport discusses "erroneous generalization," a cognitive catch-all phrase that serves as a precursor for many cognitive concepts investigated today. Ingroup and outgroup influences are discussed as well as labeling and categorization. He describes erroneous generalization and hostility as "natural and common capacities of the mind." Later, Allport distinguishes capacities from instincts (see also Reading 19, on instincts). He argues that whereas instincts demand some expression, a capacity is more similar to a predisposition, which may never be developed or displayed. Allport realizes that if prejudice is due only to instinct, then not much can change. If, however, prejudice is due to other influences, such as historical, motivational, or cognitive factors, then there is much that can be done. Allport is pragmatic as well as hopeful about the ability of social psychologists to ameliorate social conditions.

Recognizing the multicausality of prejudice, Allport later identifies six causes of prejudice, all of which must be considered as important components. Although his descriptions and stories about racial and ethnic differences may seem surprising to our modern ears, Allport was a leader in advocating complete equality by race and religion. Perhaps our surprise is a good sign and shows how far we have actually come, as well as reminding us how far we still have to go in achieving the egalitarian society that Allport hoped social psychology could assist in bringing about.

THE NORMALITY OF PREJUDGMENT

Why do human beings slip so easily into ethnic prejudice? They do so because the two essential ingredients that we have discussed—*erroneous generalization* and *hostility*—are natural and common capacities of the human mind. For the time being we shall leave hostility and its related problems out of account. Let us consider only those basic conditions of human living and thinking that lead naturally to the formation of erroneous and categorical prejudgment—and which therefore deposit us on the very threshold of ethnic and group antagonism.

The reader is warned that the full story of prejudice cannot be told in this—or in any other—single chapter of this book. Each chapter, taken by itself, is one-sided. This is the inevitable defect of any *analytical* treatment of the subject.

The Separation of Human Groups

Everywhere on earth we find a condition of separateness among groups. People mate with their own kind. They eat, play, reside in homogeneous clusters. They visit with their own kind, and prefer to worship together. Much of this automatic cohesion is due to nothing more than convenience. There is no need to turn to out-groups for companionship. With plenty of people at hand to choose from, why create for ourselves the trouble of adjusting to new languages, new foods, new cultures, or to people of a different educational level?

Thus most of the business of life can go on with less effort if we stick together with our own kind. Foreigners are a strain. So too are people of a higher or lower social and economic class than our own. We don't play bridge with the janitor. Why? Perhaps he prefers poker; almost certainly he would not grasp the type of jests and chatter that we and our friends enjoy; there would be a certain awkwardness in blending our differing manners. It is not that we have class prejudice, but only that we find comfort and ease in our own class. And normally there are plenty of people of our own class, or race, or religion to play, live, and eat with, and to marry.

It is not always the dominant majority that forces minority groups to remain separate. They often prefer to keep their identity, so that they need not strain to speak a foreign language or to watch their manners. Like the old grads at a college reunion, they can "let down" with those who share their traditions and presuppositions.

One enlightening study shows that high school students representing American minorities display even greater ethnocentrism than do native white Americans. Negro, Chinese, and Japanese young people, for example, are much more insistent upon choosing their friends, their work companions, and their "dates" from their own group than are white students. It is true that they do not select "leaders" from their own group, but prefer the non-Jewish white majority. But while agreeing that class leaders should come from the dominant group, they then seek the greater comfort of confining their intimate relations to their own kind.

The initial fact, therefore, is that human groups tend to stay apart. We need not ascribe this tendency to a gregarious instinct, to a "consciousness of kind," or to prejudice. The fact is adequately explained by the principles of ease, least effort, congeniality, and pride in one's own culture.

Once this separatism exists, however, the ground is laid for all sorts of psychological elaboration. People who stay separate have few channels of communication. They easily exaggerate the degree of difference between groups, and readily misunderstand the grounds for it. And, perhaps most important of all, the separateness may lead to genuine conflicts of interests, as well as to many imaginary conflicts.

The Process of Categorization

The human mind must think with the aid of categories (the term is equivalent here to *generalizations*). Once formed, categories are the basis for normal prejudgment. We cannot possibly avoid this process. Orderly living depends upon it.

We may say that the process of categorization has five important characteristics.

(1). *It forms large classes and clusters for guiding our daily adjustments.* We spend most of our waking life calling upon preformed categories for this purpose. When the sky darkens and the barometer falls we prejudge that rain will fall. We adjust to this cluster of happenings by taking along an umbrella. When an angry looking dog charges down the street, we categorize him as a "mad dog" and avoid him. When we go to a physician with an ailment we expect him to behave in a certain way toward us. On these, and countless other occasions, we "type" a single event, place it within a familiar rubric, and act accordingly. Sometimes we are mistaken: the event does not fit the category. It does not rain; the dog is not mad; the physician behaves unprofessionally. Yet our behavior was rational. It was based on high probability. Though we used the wrong category, we did the best we could.

What all this means is that our experience in life tends to form itself into clusters (concepts, categories), and while we may call on the right cluster at the wrong time, or the wrong cluster at the right time, still the process in question dominates our entire mental life. A million events befall us every day. We cannot handle so many events. If we think of them at all, we type them.

Open-mindedness is considered to be a virtue. But, strictly speaking, it cannot occur. A new experience *must* be redacted into old categories. We cannot handle each event freshly in its own right. If we did so, of what use would past experience be? Bertrand Russell, the philosopher, has summed up the matter in a phrase, "a mind perpetually open will be a mind perpetually vacant."

(2). *Categorization assimilates as much as it can to the cluster.* There is a curious inertia in our thinking. We like to solve problems easily. We can do so best if we can fit them rapidly into a satisfactory category and use this category as a means of prejudging the solution. The story is told of the pharmacist's mate in the Navy who had only two categories into which he fitted every ailment that came to his attention on sick call: if you can *see* it put iodine on it; if you *can't,* give the patient a dose of salts. Life was simple for this pharmacist's mate; he ran his whole professional life with the aid of only two categories.

The point may be stated in this way: the mind tends to categorize environmental events in the "grossest" manner compatible with the need for action. If the pharmacist's mate in our story were called to task for his overcrude practice of medicine, he might then mend his ways and learn to employ more discriminated categories. But so long as we can "get away" with coarse overgeneralizations we tend to do so. (Why? Well, it takes less effort, and effort, except in the area of our most intense interests, is disagreeable.)

The bearing of this tendency on our problem is clear. It costs the Anglo employer less effort to guide his daily behavior by the generalization "Mexicans are lazy," than to individualize his workmen and learn the real reasons for their conduct. If I can lump thirteen million of my fellow citizens under a simple formula, "Negroes are stupid, dirty, and inferior," I simplify my life enormously. I simply avoid them one and all. What could be easier?

(3). *The category enables us quickly to identify a related object.* Every event has certain marks that serve as a cue to bring the category of prejudgment into action. When we see a red-breasted bird, we say to ourselves "robin." When we see a crazily swaying automobile, we think, "drunken driver," and act accordingly. A person with dark brown skin will activate whatever concept of Negro is dominant in our mind. If the dominant category is one composed of negative attitudes and beliefs we will automatically avoid him, or adopt whichever habit of rejection is most available to us.

Thus categories have a close and immediate tie with what we see, how we judge, and what we do. In fact, their whole purpose seems to be to facilitate perception and conduct—in other words, to make our adjustment to life speedy, smooth, and consistent. This principle holds even though we often make mistakes in fitting events to categories and thus get ourselves into trouble.

(4). *The category saturates all that it contains with the same ideational and emotional flavor.* Some categories are almost purely intellectual. Such categories we call concepts. *Tree* is a concept made up of our experience with hundreds of kinds of trees and with thousands of individual trees, and yet it has essentially one ideational meaning. But many of our concepts (even *tree*) have in addition to a "meaning" also a characteristic "feeling." We not only know what *tree* is but we *like* trees. And so it is with ethnic categories. Not only do we know what Chinese, Mexican, Londoner mean, but we may have a feeling tone of favor or disfavor accompanying the concept.

(5). *Categories may be more or less rational.* We have said that generally a category starts to grow up from a "kernel of truth." A rational category does so, and enlarges and solidifies itself through the increment of relevant experience. Scientific laws are examples of rational categories. They are backed up by experience. Every event to which they pertain turns out in a certain way. Even if the laws are not 100 percent perfect, we consider them rational if they have a high probability of predicting a happening.

Some of our ethnic categories are quite rational. It is probable a Negro will have dark skin (though this is not always true). It is probable

that a Frenchman will speak French better than German (though here, too, are exceptions). But is it true that the Negro will be superstitious, or that the Frenchman will be morally lax?

To make a rational prejudgment of members of a group requires considerable knowledge of the characteristics of the group. It is unlikely that anyone has sound evidence that Scots are more penurious than Norwegians, or that Orientals are more wily than Caucasians, yet these beliefs grow as readily as do more rational beliefs.

In a certain Guatemalan community there is fierce hatred of the Jews. No resident has ever seen a Jew. How did the Jew-is-to-be-hated category grow up? In the first place, the community was strongly Catholic. Teachers had told the residents that the Jews were Christ-killers. It also so happened that in the local culture was an old pagan myth about a devil who killed a god. Thus two powerfully emotional ideas converged and created a hostile prejudgment of Jews.

We have said that irrational categories are formed as easily as rational categories. Probably they are formed *more* easily, for intense emotional feelings have a property of acting like sponges. Ideas, engulfed by an overpowering emotion, are more likely to conform to the emotion than to objective evidence.

There is a story of an Oxford student who once remarked, "I despise all Americans, but have never met one I didn't like." In this case the categorization went against even his firsthand experience. Holding to a prejudgment when we know better is one of the strangest features of prejudice. Theologians tell us that in prejudgments based on ignorance there is no question of sin; but that in prejudgments held in deliberate disregard of evidence, sin is involved.

When Categories Conflict with Evidence

For our purposes it is important to understand what happens when categories conflict with evidence. It is a striking fact that in most instances categories are stubborn and resist change. After all, we have fashioned our generalizations as we have because they have worked fairly well. Why change them to accommodate every new bit of evidence? If we are accustomed to one make of automobile and are satisfied, why admit the merits of another make? To do so would only disturb our satisfactory set of habits.

We selectively admit new evidence to a category if it confirms us in our previous belief. A Scotsman who is penurious delights us because he vindicates our prejudgment. It is pleasant to say, "I told you so." But if we find evidence that is contradictory to our preconception, we are likely to grow resistant.

There is a common mental device that permits people to hold to prejudgments even in the face of much contradictory evidence. It is the device of admitting exceptions. "There are nice Negroes but..." or "Some of my best friends are Jews but...." This is a disarming device. By excluding a few favored cases, the negative rubric is kept intact for all other cases. In short, contrary evidence is not admitted and allowed to modify the generalizatiion; rather it is perfunctorily acknowledged but excluded.

Let us call this the "re-fencing" device. When a fact cannot fit into a mental field, the exception is acknowledged, but the field is hastily fenced in again and not allowed to remain dangerously open.

A curious instance of re-fencing takes place in many discussions concerning the Negro. When a person with a strong anti-Negro bias is confronted with evidence favorable to the Negro he frequently pops up with the well-known matrimonial question: "Would you want your sister to marry a Negro?" This re-fencing is adroit. As soon as the interlocutor says, "No," or hesitates in his reply, the biased person can say in effect, "See, there just *is* something different and impossible about the Negro," or, "I was right all along—for the Negro has an objectionable essence in his nature."

There are two conditions under which a person will not strive to re-fence his mental field in such a way as to maintain the generalization. The first of these is the somewhat rare condition of *habitual open-mindedness*. There are people who seem to go through life with relatively little of the rubricizing tendency. They are suspicious of all labels, of categories, of sweeping statements. They habitually insist on knowing the evidence for each and every broad generalization. Realizing the complexity and variety in human nature, they are especially chary of ethnic generalizations. If they hold to any at all it is in a highly tentative way, and every contrary experience is allowed to modify the pre-existing ethnic concept.

The other occasion that makes for modification of concepts is plain *self-interest*. A person may learn from bitter failure that his categories are erroneous and must be revised. For example, he may not have known the right classification for edible mushrooms and thus find himself poisoned by toadstools. He will not make the same mistake again: his category will be corrected. Or he may think that Italians are primitive, ignorant, and loud until he falls in love with an Italian girl of a cultured family. Then he finds it greatly to his self-interest to modify his previous generalization and act thereafter on the more correct assumption that there are many, many kinds of Italians.

Personal Values as Categories

We have been arguing that rubics are essential to mental life, and that their operation results inevitably in prejudgments which in turn may shade into prejudice.

The most important categories a man has are his own personal set of values. He lives by and for his values. Seldom does he think about them or weigh them; rather he feels, affirms, and defends them. So important are the value categories that evidence and reason are ordinarily forced to conform to them. A farmer in a dusty area of the country listened to a visitor complain against the dust-bowl character of the region. The farmer evaded this attack on the place he loved by saying, "You know I like the dust; it sort of purifies the air." His reasoning was poor, but it served to defend his values.

As partisans of our own way of life we cannot help thinking in a partisan manner. Only a small portion of our reasoning is what psychologists have called "directed thinking," that is, controlled exclusively by outer evidence and focused upon the solution of objective problems. Whenever feeling, sentiment, values enter we are prone to engage in "free," "wishful," or "fantasy" thinking. Such partisan thinking is entirely natural, for our job in this world is to live in an integrated way as value-seekers. Prejudgments stemming from these values enable us to do so.

Personal Values and Prejudice

It is obvious, then, that the very act of affirming our way of life often leads us to the brink of prejudice. The philosopher Spinoza has defined what he calls "love-prejudice." It consists, he says, "in feeling about anyone through love more than is right." The lover overgeneralizes the virtues of his beloved. Her every act is seen as perfect. The partisan of a church, a club, a nation may also feel about these objects "through love more than is right."

Now there is a good reason to believe that this love-prejudice is far more basic to human life than is its opposite, hate-prejudice (which Spinoza says "consists in feeling about anyone through hate less than is right"). One must first overestimate the things one loves before one can underestimate their contraries. Fences are built primarily for the protection of what we cherish.

Positive attachments are essential to life. The young child could not exist without his dependent relationship on a nurturant person. He must love and identify himself with someone or something before he can learn what to hate. Young children must have family and friendship circles before they can define the "out-groups" which are a menace to them.

Why is it that we hear so little about love-prejudice—the tendency to overgeneralize our categories of attachment and affection? One reason is that prejudices of this sort create no social problem. If I am grossly partisan toward my own children, no one will object—unless at the same time it leads me, as it sometimes does, to manifest antagonism toward the neighbor's children. When a person is defending a categorical value of his own, he may do so at the expense of other people's interests or safety. If so, then we note his hate-prejudice, not realizing that it springs from a reciprocal love-prejudice underneath.

A student in Massachusetts, an avowed apostle of tolerance—so he thought—wrote, "The Negro question will never be solved until those dumb white Southerners get something through their ivory skulls." The student's positive values were idealistic. But ironically enough, his militant "tolerance" brought about a prejudiced condemnation of a portion of the population which he perceived as a threat to his tolerance-value.

Somewhat similar is the case of the lady who said, "Of course I have no prejudice. I had a dear old colored mammy for a nurse. Having grown up in the South and having lived here all my life I understand the problem. The Negroes are much happier if they are just allowed to stay in their place. Northern troublemakers just don't understand the Negro." This lady in her little speech was (psychologically speaking) defending her own privileges, her position, and her cosy way of life. It was not so much that she disliked Negroes or northerners, but she loved the status quo.

It is convenient to believe, if one can, that all of one category is good, all of the other evil. A popular workman in a factory was offered a job in the office by the management of the company. A union official said to him, "Don't take a management job or you'll become a bastard like all the rest of them." Only two classes existed in this official's mind: the workmen and the "bastards."

These instances argue that negative prejudice is a reflex of one's own system of values. We prize our own mode of existence and correspondingly underprize (or actively attack) what seems to us to threaten it. The thought has been expressed by Sigmund Freud: "In the undisguised antipathies and aversion which people feel towards strangers with whom they have to do, we recognize the expression of self-love, of narcissism."

The process is especially clear in time of war. When an enemy threatens all or nearly all of our positive values we stiffen our resistance and exaggerate the merits of our cause. We feel—and this is an instance of overgeneralization—that we are wholly right. (If we did not believe this we could not marshal all our energies for our defense.) And if we are wholly right then the enemy must be wholly wrong. Since he is wholly wrong, we should not hesitate to exterminate him. But even in this wartime example it is clear that our basic love-prejudice is primary and that the hate-prejudice is a derivative phenomenon.

Summary

This chapter has argued that man has a propensity to prejudice. This propensity lies in his normal and natural tendency to form generalizations, concepts, categories, whose content represents an oversimplification of his world of experience. His rational categories keep close to first-hand experience, but he is able to form irrational categories just as readily. In these even a kernel of truth may be lacking, for they can be composed wholly of hearsay evidence, emotional projections, and fantasy.

One type of categorization that predisposes us especially to make unwarranted prejudgments is our personal values. These values, the basis of all human existence, lead easily to love-prejudices. Hate-prejudices are secondary developments, but they may, and often do, arise as a reflex of positive values.

In order to understand better the nature of love-prejudice, which at bottom is responsible

for hate-prejudice, we turn our attention next to the formation of in-group loyalties.

THEORIES OF PREJUDICE

The time has come for us to seek an over-all theoretical orientation to the problem of prejudice.

What do we mean when we speak of a "theory" of prejudice? Do we imply that the theory in question is offered as a complete and sovereign explanation for all human prejudice? Seldom is this the case, even though when we read enthusiastic exponents of the Marxian view, or of the scapegoat theory, or of some other, we sometimes gain the impression that the author feels that he has buttoned up the subject completely. Yet as a rule most "theories" are advanced by their authors to call attention to some one important casual factor, without implying that no other factors are operating. Usually an author selects for emphasis one of the six approaches in our diagram; he then develops his ideas concerning certain forces that operate within this approach to create prejudice.

Our own approach to the problem is eclectic. There seems to be value in all of the six main approaches, and some truth in virtually all of the resulting theories. It is not possible at the present time to reduce them to a single theory of human action.

It will help the reader to note that causal influences lying toward the right side of Fig. 1 tend to be more immediate in time and more specifiable in operation. A person acts with prejudice in the first instance because he perceives the object of prejudice in a certain way. But he perceives it in a certain way partly because his personality is what it is. And his personality is what it is chiefly because of the way he was socialized (training in family, school, neighborhood). The existing social situation is also a factor in his socialization and may also be a determinant of his perceptions. Behind these forces lie other valid but more remote causal influences. They involve

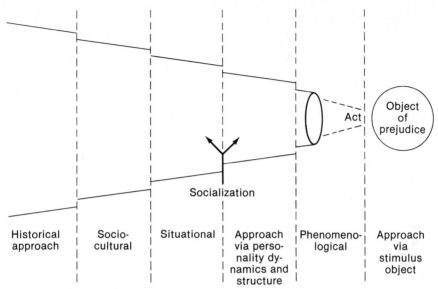

FIGURE 1   Theoretical and methodological approaches to the study of the causes of prejudice. (From G. W. Allport, Prejudice: A problem in psychological and social causation. *Journal of Social Issues,* Supplement Series, No. 4, 1950.)

the structure of society in which one lives, long-standing economic and cultural traditions, as well as national and historical influences of long duration. While these factors seem so remote as to be alien to the immediate psychological analysis of prejudiced acts, they are, nonetheless, important causal influences.

Let us look now more closely at some of the characteristic features of each of the six major approaches indicated in Fig. 1.

Historical Emphasis

Impressed by the long history that lies behind each and every present-day ethnic conflict, historians insist that only the total background of a conflict can lead to its understanding. Anti-Negro prejudice in America, for example, is a historical matter, having its roots in slavery, in carpetbagging, and in the failure of reconstruction in the South following the Civil War.

Commenting on recent efforts to establish a purely psychological view of the subject, one historian objects:

Such studies are enlightening only within narrow limits. For personality is itself conditioned by social forces; in the last analysis, the search for understanding must reach into the broad social context within which personality is shaped.

While admitting the force of this criticism, we may point out that while history provides "the broad social context" it cannot tell why within this context one personality develops prejudice and another does not. And this is precisely the question that the psychologist most wants to answer. Here, then, is an instance of an unprofitable quarrel. Both specialists are indispensable, for they are seeking to answer not identical, but complementary, questions.

Historical studies are markedly diverse in type. Some, but not all, stress the importance of economic determinants. An example of this treatment is the *exploitation theory* of prejudice held by Marxists and others. A brief summary of its argument is given by Cox.

Race prejudice is a social attitude propagated among the public by an exploiting class for the purpose of stigmatizing some group as inferior so that the exploitation of either the group itself or its resources may both be justified.

This author goes on to argue that race prejudice rose to unprecedented heights in the nineteenth century when European imperial expansion called for some justification. Therefore, poets (Kipling), racial theorists (Chamberlain), and statesmen proclaimed colonial peoples to be "inferior," "requiring protection," a "lower form of evolution," a "burden" to be borne altruistically. All this pious concern and condescension masked the financial advantage that came from exploitation. Segregation developed as a device for preventing sympathy and sentiments of equality. Sexual and social taboos placed on the colonial peoples prevented them from developing expectations of equality and freedom of choice.

Many considerations make this theory attractive. It explains the rationalizations for economic exploitation that are frequently heard: the Orientals only "need" a handful of rice a day to live on; the Negro shouldn't receive high wages, for he will spend them unwisely trying to rise above his racial station; the Mexicans are so primitive that they would only drink and gamble away their money if they had it; so too the American Indian.

While there is obvious truth in the exploitation theory it is weak in many particulars. It fails to explain why there is not equal prejudice against all exploited people. Many of the immigrant groups coming to America have been exploited without suffering from prejudice to the extent that Negroes and Jews have suffered. Nor is it clear that Jews are, in fact, victims of economic exploitation. The Quakers and Mormons were at one time severely persecuted in America, but certainly not primarily for economic reasons.

Nor is it correct to consider bigotry against even the Negro in America as wholly an economic phenomenon, though it is here that Cox's argument is strongest. While it seems obvious that many white people derive advantage from underpaying Negro workers and rationalizing the injustice through theories concerning their "animal nature," still the story is more complex. White employees in factories, or white tenant farmers, are similarly exploited, but no ritual of discrimination has developed against them. In sociological studies of certain Southern communities, for example, it turns out that on an objective scale of "class," Negroes are no lower than the whites. Their cabins are no smaller, their income is no less, their household facilities are the same. Yet their position socially and psychologically is lower.

We conclude, therefore, that the Marxist theory of prejudice is far too simple, even though it points a sure finger at *one* of the factors involved in prejudice, viz., rationalized self-interest of the upper classes.

The contributions of history to the understanding of prejudice are by no means confined to the economic interpretation. The rise of Hitler in Germany together with his genocide policies cannot be understood except by tracing an ominous sequence of events historically.

Whether this fateful progression can be explained fully by history without the help of psychology is not here the question. We insist only that any pattern of prejudice existing in any part of the world receives marked illumination when it is examined from the historical point of view.

Sociocultural Emphasis

The following chapters will deal with some of the multitude of sociocultural factors that help explain group conflict and prejudice. Sociologists and anthropologists place principal weight on this type of theorizing. Like the historian, they are impressed by the total social context in which prejudiced attitudes develop. Within this social context some writers emphasize the traditions that lead to conflict; some the relative upward mobility in out-groups and in-groups; some the density of the populations concerned; some the type of contacts that exist between groups.

For the present, let us cite one example from theories in this class—the phenomenon known as *urbanization* and its possible relation to ethnic prejudice. The case is argued somewhat as follows.

Although people desire peaceful and affiliative relations with others, this striving has been badly blocked by the mechanical culture of our day—especially by the culture of our cities that arouses so much insecurity and uncertainity in men's minds. In the city personal contacts are diminished. Literally or figuratively the assembly line rules us. Central government replaces local and more intimate forms of government. Advertising controls our standards of living and our desires. Giant corporations fill the landscape with monstrous factories, regulating our employment, income, and safety. No longer do personal thrift, private effort, face-to-face adjustments count for much. Fear of the Juggernaut settles upon us. Big city life expresses to us what is inhuman, impersonal, dangerous. We fear and hate our subservience to it.

What has this urban insecurity to do with prejudice? For one thing, as mass-men we follow the conventions of the times. The snob-appeals of advertising affect us deeply. We want more goods, more luxury, more status. The standards forced upon us by advertisers call for contempt of people who are poor, who do not reach the level of material existence that is prescribed. Hence we look down upon groups economically below us—upon Negroes, immigrants and rustics. (Here we note echoes of the Marxian view.)

But while we yield to the materialistic urban values, we also hate the city that engenders them. We hate the domination of finance and shady politics. We despise the traits that develop in response to urban pressures. We dislike those who are sneaky, dishonest, self-

ish, too clever, too ambitious, vulgar, noisy and on the fringe of old-fashioned virtues. These urban traits have been personified in the Jew. "The Jews are hated today," writes Arnold Rose, "primarily because they serve as a symbol of city life." They are symbols especially of that monster, all-dominant, much feared City of New York. The city has emasculated us. We will therefore hate the symbol of the city—the Jew.

The merit of this theory is that it has a logic that applies both to anti-Semitism and to feelings of condescension toward other minorities who have not "made the grade." It would have some difficulty, however, in explaining why Japanese-American farmers were so vehemently feared and hated during World War II. It would also be forced to concede that "city hatred" is as intense among rural dwellers as among urbanites, for ethnic prejudice is certainly as acute in the country as in the town.

Blending a historical and a sociocultural emphasis, we have the *community* pattern theory of prejudice. Here the stress is upon the basic ethnocentrism of every group.

In Europe there is an intricate network of historic hostilities. A given city, especially in the eastern sectors, might at various times have been "owned" by Russia, Lithuania, Poland, Sweden, the Ukraine. Descendants of all these assorted conquerors might stil reside in the city and with some justification regard all other claimants as pretenders or intruders. A veritable checkerboard of prejudice results. Even should the settlers of disputed territories migrate, say to America, the traditional hostilities may move with them. But unless there is a strong community pattern in the New World as well as in the Old, ancient animosities are likely to die out. Many, perhaps most, immigrants want to start a new life, and have chosen a new community pattern where (to their mind) there is an atmosphere of freedom, equal opportunity, and a sense of dignity available to all.

Situational Emphasis

If we subtract the historical background from the sociocultural approach we have left a *situational emphasis*. That is to say, emphasis upon the past patterns gives way to emphasis upon current forces. Several theories of prejudice are of this order. One might, for example, speak of an *atmosphere* theory. A child grows up surrounded by immediate influences and very soon reflects them all. Lillian Smith, in *Killers of the Dream*, propounds such a theory. The Southern child obviously has no knowledge of historical events, of exploitation, or of urban values as such. All he knows is that he must *conform* to the complex and inconsistent teaching that he receives. His prejudice is thus merely a mirror image of what he now sees around him.

An instance of the subtle impact of atmosphere in shaping attitudes is implied in the following incident.

> An inspector of education in a Bristish African colony wondered why so little progress was made in learning English in a certain native school. Visiting the classroom, he asked the native teacher to put on a demonstration of his method of teaching English. The teacher complied, first making, however, the following preface to the lesson in the vernacular which he did not know the inspector understood: "Come now, children, put away your things, and let us wrestle for an hour with the enemy's language."

Other situational theories may stress the present *employment situation*: and see hostility primarily in terms of prevailing economic competition. Or they may regard prejudice primarily as a phenomenon of upward and downward *social mobility*. Situational theories also may stress the importance of *types of contact* between groups, or the relative *density* of groups. These situational theories are so important that they will be examined separately in subsequent chapters.

Psychodynamic Emphasis

If man is by nature quarrelsome or hostile we must expect conflict to flourish. Theories that stress causation in human nature are inevitably psychological in type in contrast to the historical, economic, sociological, or cultural points of view mentioned above.

In good standing is the *frustration* theory of prejudice. It is a psychological theory rooted in the "nature of man." It can readily admit that affiliative needs seem as basic, or more basic, than protest and hatred, and at the same time hold that when positive and friendly advances toward the environment are thwarted, ugly consequences result.

We can clarify the theory by citing the vehement prejudice of a World War II veteran:

> When asked about possible unemployment and a future depression he replied:
> We'd better not have it. Chicago'll blow wide open. On South Park the niggers are gettin' so smart. We'll have a race riot that'll make Detroit look like a Sunday School picnic. So many are bitter about the part the Negro played in the war. They got all the soft jobs—the quartermasters, engineers. They're no good for anything else. The white got his ass shot off. They're pretty bitter. If both whites and niggers get laid off, that'll be bad. I'm gonna eat. I know how to use a gun.

This case clearly shows the role of frustration in causing, or intensifying, prejudice. Deprivation and frustration lead to hostile impluses, which if not controlled are likely to discharge against ethnic minorities. With emotional provocation, a person's view of his social world becomes constricted and distorted. He sees personal demons (minorities) at work because his normal directed thinking is blocked by the intensity of his feelings. He cannot analyze the evil; he can only personify it.

The frustration theory is sometimes known as the *scapegoat* theory. All formulations of this theory assume that anger once engendered may be displaced upon a (logically irrelevant) victim.

It has been pointed out that the chief weakness of this theory is that it fails to tell upon what victim the hostility will be discharged. It also fails to explain why in many personalities no such displacement takes place, however great the frustration. But these complications we shall consider later.

Another type of "nature of man" theory emphasizes the *character structure* of the individual person. Only certain types of people develop prejudice as an important feature in their lives. These seem to be insecure and anxious personalities who take the authoritarian and exclusionist way of life rather than the relaxed and trusting democratic way.

Like the frustration theory, the character structure theory has much evidence to back it up . These two theories are not, however, all-sufficient, but require supplementation from other theories we are here surveying.

Phenomenological Emphasis

A person's conduct proceeds immediately from his view of the situation confronting him. His response to the world conforms to his definition of the world. He attacks members of one group because he perceives them as repulsive, annoying, or threatening; members of another he derides because to him they are crude, dirty, and stupid. Both visibility and verbal labels, as we have seen, help define the object in perception so that it can be readily identified. Again, as we have seen, historical and cultural forces, and the person's entire character structure, may lie behind his hypotheses and perceptions. Writers who approach the study of prejudice from the phenomenological point of view assume the convergence of all these factors into a final common focus. What the man finally believes and perceives is the important thing. Obviously, the stereotype plays a prominent part in sharpening the perception prior to action.

The phenomenal level, as we have said, is the immediate level of causation, but it is well to combine this approach with others. If we do not do so we are likely to lose sight of the equally important determinants that are to be found in the underlying dynamics of personality as well as in the situational, cultural, and historical contexts of life.

Emphasis on Earned Reputation

Finally we come once again to the problem of the *stimulus object* itself. There may be bona fide differences between groups that provoke dislike and hostility. Enough has been said, however, to show that these differences are much *less* than they are imagined to be. In most cases a reputation is not earned but is gratuitously thrust upon a group.

It would be impossible to find any social scientist today who would subscribe completely to the *earned reputation* theory. At the same time, some warn against assuming that every minority group is always blameless. There may be ethnic or national traits that *are* menacing, and that therefore invite realistic hostility. Or, still more likely, hostility may feed partly on realistic estimates of the stimulus (the true nature of groups) and partly on the many unrealistic factors that comprise prejudice. Some writers, therefore, advocate an *interaction theory*. Hostile attitudes are *in part* determined by the nature of the stimulus (earned reputation) and *in part* by considerations essentially irrelevant to the stimulus (e.g., scapegoating, conforming to tradition, stereotypes, guilt projection, etc.).

There is certainly no objection to such an interaction theory provided proper weight is given to each of the two sets of factors. It says little more than "Let's allow for the simultaneous operation of all scientifically established causes of hostile attitudes, not forgetting to include relevant features of the stimulus object itself." Taken in this broad sense, there can be no possible objection to the theory.

Final Word

By far the best view to take toward this multiplicity of approaches is to admit them all. Each has something to teach us. None possesses a monopoly of insight, nor is any one safe as a solitary guide. We may lay it down as a general law applying to all social phenomena that *multiple causation* is invariably at work and nowhere is the law more clearly applicable than to prejudice.

The Aversive Form of Racism

Samuel L. Gaertner and John F. Dovidio (1986)

Gaertner and Dovidio argue that racism is alive and well, though much more subtle in its present-day form than was the more overt racism of the past. In a chapter that was awarded the Gordon Allport Intergroup Relations Prize in 1985, Gaertner and Dovidio demonstrate how insidious racism can be; even well-intentioned people may unconsciously harbor and perpetuate such views. Thus, people who find racism aversive and therefore try to avoid engaging in discriminatory behavior will still succumb to racist beliefs and behavior. Gaertner and Dovidio suggest that this is due to certain types of cognitive biases in information processing and negative socialization experiences regarding members of the groups. In a society that continues to debate such issues as affirmative action, equal opportunity, and desegregation, their research takes on added significance.

Given that we seem to have "new forms" of prejudice and discrimination, the next question seems to be, What can we do now to create an egalitarian society? The tradition that Allport, Lewin, and others began, of ameliorating societal problems by applying social psychological knowledge, continues today. What social psychological principles can *you* identify that might be useful in this process? Further, how might social psychologists team up with attorneys and educators to effect change (e.g., Cohen, 1984; *Furman v. Georgia,* 1972; Miller & Brewer, 1986; Slavin, 1985, 1986)?

INTRODUCTION

The results of several recent surveys indicate that white America's racial attitudes have become substantially more tolerant and liberal over the past few decades (Campbell, 1971; Greeley & Sheatsley, 1971; *Newsweek,* 1979, Taylor, Sheatsley, & Greeley, 1978). Other evidence, however, suggests that although the old-fashioned, "red-necked" form of bigotry is less prevalent, prejudice continues to exist in more subtle, more indirect, and less overtly negative forms (Crosby, Bromley, & Saxe, 1980; Gaertner, 1976; Gaertner & Dovidio, 1981; Katz, 1981; McConahay & Hough, 1976; Sears & Allen, 1984). The present chapter, like that of Katz, Wackenhut, and Hass (1986), proposes that the fundamental nature of white America's current attitudes toward blacks is complex and conflicted. Consistent with this assumption, Katz and his colleagues have accumulated evidence supporting Myrdal's (1944) conclusions that the attitudes of many whites toward blacks and other minorities are neither uniformly negative nor totally favorable, but rather are ambivalent.

The aversive racism perspective assumes that given the historically racist American culture and human cognitive mechanisms for processing categorical information, racist feelings and beliefs among white Americans are generally the rule rather than the exception. We use the term *aversive racism* (also see Kovel, 1970) to describe the type of racial attitude that we believe characterizes many white Americans who possess strong egalitarian values. In contrast to aversive racism is the more traditional, dominative form of racism (Kovel, 1970). The *dominative racist*, who exhibits the more "red-necked" form of discrimination, is the "type who acts out bigoted beliefs—he represents the open flame of racial hatred" (Kovel, 1970, p. 54). Aversive racists, in comparison, sympathize with the victims of past injustice; support public policies that, in principle, promote racial equality and ameliorate the consequences of racism; identify more generally with a liberal political agenda; regard themselves as nonprejudiced and nondiscriminatory; but, almost unavoidably, possess negative feelings and beliefs about blacks. Because of the importance of the egalitarian value system to aversive racists' self-concept, these negative feelings and associated beliefs are typically excluded from awareness. When a situation or event threatens to make the negative portion of their attitude salient, aversive racists are motivated to repudiate or dissociate these feelings from their self-image, and they vigorously try to avoid acting wrongly on the basis of these feelings. In these situations, aversive racists may overreact and amplify their positive behavior in ways that would reaffirm their egalitarian convictions and their apparently nonracist attitudes. In other situations, however, the underlying negative portions of their attitudes are expressed, but in subtle, rationalizable ways.

In terms of etiology, aversive racism is conceived to be an adaptation resulting from an assimilation of an egalitarian value system with (1) feelings and beliefs derived from historical and contemporary culturally racist contexts, and (2) impressions derived from human cognitive mechanisms that contribute to the development of stereotypes and prejudice (see Hamilton, 1981). The aversive racism perspective assumes that cognitive biases in information processing and the historically racist culture of the United States lead most white Americans to develop beliefs and feelings that result in antipathy toward blacks and other minorities. Because of traditional cultural values, however, most whites also have convictions concerning fairness, justice, and racial equality. The existence both of almost unavoidable racial biases and the desire to be egalitarian forms the basis of the ambivalence that aversive racists experience. While we believe that the prevalence of the old-fashioned red-neck form of racism may have declined since the 1930s, we also believe that it would be a mistake to assume that this old-fashioned form is no longer a significant social force in the United States. Indeed, not all racists are ambivalent.

The negative affect that aversive racists have for blacks is not hostility or hate. Instead, this negativity involves discomfort, uneasiness, disgust, and sometimes fear, which tend to motivate avoidance rather than intentionally destructive behaviors. There are a variety of different sources that we believe contribute to the negative content of the aversive racist's attitude. This negativity may be partially due to the affective connotations of blackness and whiteness per se. *White* is considered good and active, whereas *black* is considered bad and passive (Williams, 1964; Williams, Tucker, & Dunham, 1971). Differences in the physical appearance of blacks and whites may also provide bases for differential responses. From an anthropological perspective, Margaret Mead proposes that although people must "be taught to hate, the appreciation and fear of difference is everywhere" (Mead & Baldwin, 1971, p. 28). From a psychological perspective, biasing effects of mere categorization into an ingroup and an outgroup have been empirically demonstrated and are thoroughly reviewed by Brewer (1979) and more recently by Stephan (1985). People behave more positively toward ingroup than toward outgroup members (e.g., Billig & Tajfel, 1973); they also evaluate ingroup members more favorably and associate more desirable personal and physical characteristics to ingroup than to outgroup members (e.g., Doise, Csepeli, Dann, Gouge, Larsen, & Ostell, 1972). Furthermore, greater belief similarity is attributed to members of the ingroup than to members of the outgroup (Stein, Hardyck, & Smith, 1965). Assumptions of belief similarity or dissimilarity can, in turn, mediate interracial attraction (Rokeach & Mezei, 1966). Also, because our society provides greater opportunity for intraracial than interracial contact, the "mere exposure effect'' (Zajonc, 1968)—that familiarity promotes liking—could contribute to whites' more positive attitudes toward whites than toward blacks.

In addition, motivational factors can operate on these and other bases to promote and maintain racial biases. At the individual level, needs for self-esteem and superior status are frequently hypothesized to be among the major causes and perpetuators of prejudice and racial discrimination (Allport, 1954; Ashmore & Del Boca, 1976; Harding, Proshansky, Kutner, & Chein, 1969; Tajfel & Turner, 1979). At the societal level, economic competition that threatens to alter the traditionally subordinate status of blacks relative to whites fosters discrimination of whites against blacks (Wilson, 1980). The theory of internal colonization (Hechter, 1975), for example, proposes that the powerful majority group is motivated to ensure its advantages by initiating policies that perpetuate the existing stratification system. Given that traditional social structures have given privileges to whites, practices that threaten deprivation of that advantaged status, particularly when they involve the preferential treatment of blacks, may create negative affect even among people who in principle support ameliorative programs such as affirmative action.

The attempt to maintain a nonprejudiced self-image can, in itself, also increase disaffection for blacks because interracial interactions become characterized by anxiety or uneasiness. Rather than being relaxed and spontaneous, aversive racists may have to guard vigilantly against even an unwitting transgression that could be attributed by themselves or by others to racial antipathy. Thus interracial interactions may arouse negative affect that can become associated directly with blacks.

Social and cultural factors also contribute to aversive racists' negative feelings toward blacks. Black culture in the United States emphasizes values that are not always consistent with the tenets of white culture's Protestant ethic (see Jones & Block, 1984). Thus, belief or value dissimilarity also fosters disaffection. Furthermore, the context of

socialization directly influences feelings and beliefs about racial differences. In the United States, traditional cultural stereotypes characterize blacks as lazy, ignorant, and superstitious; they portray whites, in contrast, as ambitious, intelligent, and industrious (Karlins, Coffman, & Walters, 1969). In our culture, blacks are frequently associated with poverty, crime, illegitimacy, and welfare. For example, in the 1950s and 1960s blacks on television "had minor roles and were rarely portrayed as powerful or prestigious" (Liebert, Sprafkin, & Davidson, 1982, p. 161). Even in the 1970s, when blacks were no longer generally characterized less favorably in the media than were whites, blacks were more likely to appear on television as poor, employed in service occupations, and involved in murders and other criminal activities (U.S. Commission on Civil Rights, 1977, 1979). These portrayals of blacks in the media and the culture more generally which associate blacks with roles and values that have negative connotations for whites may contribute to the development of negative affect toward blacks.

From a sociological perspective, the structure of society tends to perpetuate prejudice and discrimination. Specifically, the institutional racism framework proposes that, through the process of internal colonization, beliefs about relative status and power become embedded in social roles and norms (see Feagin & Feagin, 1978). These beliefs, in turn, help to maintain the social, educational, political, and economic advantages that whites have over blacks. Whites currently have advantages relative to blacks in most important aspects of American life: infant mortality, standard of living, educational achievement, socioeconomic status, and life expectancy.

Thus, even if people genuinely attempt to reject the socially less desirable stereotypes and characterizations of blacks, it may be difficult for even the most well-intentioned white persons to escape the development of negative beliefs concerning blacks and to avoid feelings of superiority and relative good fortune over the fact that they are white rather than black and are culturally advantaged rather than disadvantaged (also see Ryan, 1971). These impressions, however, are not rooted in the traditional, old-fashioned bigoted belief that white superiority results from innate racial differences. Instead, these impressions of superiority, and accompanying feelings of sympathy, reflect historical and contemporary realities, which aversive racists believe result from racist traditions and practices. Nevertheless, the issue of white superiority characterizes whites' perceptions of the relationship between blacks and whites and may continue to play a role in the forces of oppression.

While we have identified many cognitive, motivational, and sociocultural factors that can contribute to the formation and maintenance of prejudice, the list is by no means exhaustive. Many other processes (e.g., illusory correlation, polarization and schema complexity) are discussed in other chapters in the present volume and are well documented in the literature. Nevertheless, in a nation founded on the principle that ''all men [sic] are created equal,'' there are strong forces that promote racial equality. Norms of fairness and equality have had great social, political, and moral impact on the history of the United States. The prevalence of these egalitarian norms has been clearly documented in experimental (e.g., Sigall & Page, 1971) and survey (e.g., Schuman & Harding, 1964) research. And, of course, because of the civil rights legislation of the 1960s, it is no longer merely immoral to discriminate against blacks; it is also illegal. Thus, due to contradictory influences that operate on the levels of both the individual and the culture, most whites in the United States experience an ''American dilemma'' (Myrdal, 1944). This chapter, then, is about people who have developed a value system that maintains it is wrong to discriminate against a person because of his or her race, who reject the content of racial stereotypes, who attempt to dissociate negative feelings and beliefs about blacks from their self-concepts, but who nonetheless cannot entirely escape cultural and cognitive forces.

AVERSIVE RACISM: DERIVATION OF HYPOTHESES AND EMPIRICAL TESTS

Our formulation of aversive racism enables the derivation of predictions concerning when egalitarian values and negative racial attitudes will each be observable. Because aversive racists are very concerned about their egalitarian self-images, they are strongly motivated in interracial contexts to avoid acting in recognizably unfavorable or normatively inappropriate ways. Indeed, if the fear of acting inappropriately in interracial contexts is a salient concern of many whites, then racial discrimination would be most likely to occur when normative structure within the situation is weak, ambiguous, or conflicting. Under these conditions, the concepts of right and wrong are less applicable, and the more negative components of aversive racists' attitudes may be more clearly observable. Here, blacks may be treated unfavorably or in a manner that disadvantages them, yet whites can be spared the recognition that they behaved inappropriately. When the normative structure of a situation is salient, however, racial discrimination would not then be expected. That is, in situations in which norms prescribing appropriate behavior are clear and unambiguous, blacks would not be treated less favorably than would whites because wrongdoing would be obvious and would more clearly challenge the nonprejudiced self-image. Nevertheless, even when normative guidelines are clear, aversive racists may unwittingly search for ostensibly nonracial factors that could justify a negative response to blacks. These nonracial factors, and not race, are then used to rationalize unfavorable actions. Negative racial attitudes can therefore be expressed indirectly, while whites perceive themselves as nondiscriminating and nonprejudiced.

Interracial Behavior: The Influence of Normative Structure

Because of the conflict and ambivalence that aversive racists experience, we hypothesize that negative racial affect is expressed subtly and indirectly in interactions involving blacks. Thus racial discrimination among aversive racists may typically go unrecognized because it usually occurs in situations in which there is a lack of normative structure defining appropriate action or under circumstances that allow an unfavorable response to be rationalized by attributing its cause to some factor other than race. When norms indicating appropriate behavior are clear, and rationalization is not possible, deviations from these guidelines during interactions with blacks could readily be attributed to racial bias; here, we hypothesize that aversive racists would be unlikely to discriminate against blacks. Given the high salience of race and racially symbolic issues on questionnaires designed to measure racial prejudice, as well as aversive racists' vigilance and sensitivity to these issues, effective questionnaire measures of aversive racism, in our opinion, would be difficult if not impossible to develop.

Instead, our strategy for assessing the usefulness of including aversive racism within a typology of racial attitudes relies heavily on the degree of discriminatory behavior observed in specially constructed situations of varying normative structure. In some of this research, we preselected subjects from among the highest and lowest prejudice-scoring undergraduates, based on an 11-item scale, which was composed of traditional and modern racism items and correlated highly with portions of Woodmansee and Cook's (1967) inventory. Because even the highest prejudice-scoring students on a university campus are usually not dominative racists, we did not expect to obtain main effects or interactions involving prejudice scores.

The evidence that we have accumulated in support of the aversive racism framework draws heavily from experiments addressing the willingness of whites to act prosocially toward black and white people in need of assistance. We have used prosocial behavior as a dependent measure in our work for both practical and theoretical reasons. Pragmatically, helping behavior provides an index that is sensitive to both race (e.g.,

Crosby et al., 1980) and attraction (see Piliavin, Dovidio, Gaertner, & Clark, 1981). Theoretically, the Kerner Commission's investigation of the causes of civil disorders suggests that white America's responsibility for racial unrest may reside largely in its inability to recognize and understand institutional racism and in its lack of positive response to the needs of minorities. Thus, the culpability of whites may currently lie primarily in their reluctance to help those who are oppressed by institutional racism. Resistance to affirmative action, for example, may partially be attributable to an unwillingness to personally bear the costs associated with helping blacks and other historically disadvantaged minorities.

The first study, which initiated our interest in aversive racism, was a field experiment that examined the likelihood of black and white persons eliciting prosocial behavior from Liberal and Conservative Party members residing in Brooklyn, New York (Gaertner, 1973). Using a method devised earlier by Gaertner and Bickman (1971), Liberal and Conservative households received apparent wrong-number telephone calls that quickly developed into requests for assistance. The callers, who were clearly identifiable from their dialects as being black or white, explained that their car was disabled and that they were attempting to reach a service garage from a public phone along the parkway. The callers further claimed that they had no more change to make another call and asked the subject to help by calling the garage. If the subject refused to help or hung up after the caller explained that he or she had no more change, a "not helping" response was recorded. If the subject hung up prior to learning that the motorist had no more change, the response was considered to be a "premature hang-up." Based on previous findings relating political ideology to authoritarianism, ethnocentrism, and racial prejudice, the major prediction was easily and directly derived: The extent to which black callers would be helped less frequently than white callers would be greater among Conservative than among Liberal Party members.

The results, excluding consideration of premature hang-up responses, indicated that Conservatives were significantly less helpful to blacks than to whites (65% vs. 92%), whereas Liberals helped blacks and whites about equally (75% vs. 85%). In terms of helping, therefore, Liberals seemed relatively well-intentioned. Surprisingly, though, Liberals hung up prematurely more frequently on blacks than on whites (19% vs. 3%), whereas Conservatives did not discriminate in this way (8% vs. 5%). Liberals discriminated against the black male in particular in this regard. That is, Liberals hung up prematurely on black and white male callers 28% and 10% of the time, respectively.

While this study was in progress, other Liberal and Conservative Party members were interviewed about what they believed that they would do if they received a wrong-number call from a black or a white motorist. In virtually every case, participants indicated that they would help and that they would do so without regard to the person's race. These people genuinely seemed to believe that race would not influence their behavior under such circumstances. Nevertheless, the finding that Liberals did not discriminate against blacks once they recognized that help was needed but hung up prematurely more frequently on blacks than on whites suggested the importance of normative structure on the interracial behavior of liberal, well-intentioned people.

Specifically, when social responsibility norms, norms that people should help others who are in need (Berkowitz & Daniels, 1963), were made salient by the plight of the victim or by a full description of the motorist's need, Liberals did not discriminate against blacks. Failure to offer assistance to a black person once the necessity for help has been recognized would violate prescriptions for appropriate behavior and could be attributed to racial antipathy. Discrimination did occur, though, before the motorist's need became clear and when it was not inappropriate to terminate the conversation with a wrong-number caller. That is, at the point where the caller simply explained that he or she reached the wrong number, there were no guidelines for appropriate action; after explaining that the caller reached the wrong number, the question of hanging up or continuing the conversation has no prescribed answer. Because we did not have control over whether or not subjects heard the entire plea for help from the motorist or hung up prematurely, it is of course possible that there were other reasons besides normative structure that could explain the pattern of results. In subsequent research, therefore, we systematically manipulated the salience of normative guidelines.

As a further test of the role of normative structure on the interracial behavior of whites, another experiment (Frey & Gaertner, 1986) varied the clarity of normative structure regarding the appropriateness of delivering assistance to black and white partners on an experimental anagram task. As suggested by the results of the Liberal-Conservative study, we expected that whites would be less helpful to blacks than to whites only in situations in which the failure to help would not violate normative guidelines. When normative guidelines indicate that the failure to help would be clearly inappropriate, it was predicted that discrimination against blacks would be unlikely to occur because not helping a black person would be less rationalizable and would more likely be attributed to bigoted intent.

Normative appropriateness for helping was varied by manipulating the causal locus (internal vs. external) of the recipient's need and the source of the request for help (recipient vs. observer). With respect to the locus of need, Schopler and Matthews (1965) suggest that someone who is dependent because of moral weakness or personal choice does not raise the salience of social responsibility norms relative to victims of unavoidable circumstances. Considering the source of the request for aid, Enzle and Harvey (1977) concluded that, because a request for help from a third party influences a potential benefactor's normative beliefs about the appropriateness of helping, more help is given when a request for assistance is issued by a disinterested third party than by the potential recipient.

In our experiment, the need of the potential recipient, who was a black or a white fellow student working on an experimental task, was either self-induced by a failure to work hard (internal cause) or due to the unusual difficulty of the assignment (external cause). Female subjects subsequently received a request for aid that originated either from the potential recipient or from a third-party observer. They then had an opportunity to help by providing the other student with Scrabble letters to complete a task and bonus points to earn a prize. The dependent measures were whether or not the subject helped, the number of letters given, the utility value of these letters, and the number of bonus points awarded. Because either the external locus of need or the third-party request for assistance could increase the salience of social responsibility norms, the aversive racism framework expected that black recipients would be helped less than whites only in the condition in which the recipient did not work hard and personally made the request for assistance.

The results supported our prediction. They indicated that subjects helped blacks significantly less than they helped whites only in the internal need-recipient request condition. When the locus of need was external (i.e., due to task difficulty), or the request originated from a third party, or both, there was no significant effect of race on helping. Thus when social responsibility norms were salient, racial bias in helping did not exist. Only when the deservingness of the victim was questionable, rendering the failure to help more justifiable and rationalizable, were blacks disadvantaged relative to whites. Consistent with our framework, the normative structure of the situation played a critical role in determining the prosocial behavior of whites toward blacks.

Interracial Behavior: The Salience of Nonracial Factors

Another proposition of the aversive racist perspective is that even when normative guidelines are relatively clear, aversive racists are sensitive to nonracial factors that can justify, rationalize, or legitimize behavior that more generally disadvantages blacks relative to whites. In particular, we propose an indirect attitudinal process that operates differentially as a function of another person's race to enhance the salience and potency of *non-race-related* elements in a situation that would justify or rationalize a negative response even if a white person were involved (Gaertner & Dovidio, 1977).

Because of the increased salience of these nonracial factors in interracial situations, whites may discriminate against blacks and still perceive themselves as being nonprejudiced and egalitarian: They can attribute the reasons for their behavior to factors other than race. For example, children have been bused for a variety of reasons to public and private schools for many years without substantial vocal opposition from parents. When busing became a tool to implement desegregation, however, there was strong opposition. This protest often was not about desegregation per se but about the nonracial element—busing. Thus, people may discriminate against blacks while maintaining a nondiscriminating self-concept.

In another experiment, we investigated the influence of the hypothesized indirect attitudinal process in a situation in which an individual's decision to help or not to help could have significant, immediate consequences for a person in need of emergency assistance. In this experiment (Gaertner & Dovidio, 1977), high- and low-prejudice-scoring college women heard an unambiguous emergency involving a black or a white female victim. Subjects were led to believe that they were participating in an extrasensory perception (ESP) experiment in which they would try to receive telepathic messages from a sender who was located in a cubicle across the hallway and whom they could hear through an intercom system. Ostensibly to determine the relationship between physiological reactions and ESP receptivity, subjects were wired with biotelemetry equipment that monitored their heartrates. The race of the sender, who would later become the victim of the emergency, was manipulated by her dialect and also by the picture on her ID card, which was exchanged with the subject at the beginning of the study. Half of the participants in the experiment were informed that they would be the only receiver, whereas the others were told that there were two other receivers, each located in a separate cubicle across the hallway from the sender. Additional ID cards indicated that the other receivers (who were not actually present) were white and female. After several trials of the ESP task passed uneventfully, the sender interrupted the procedure and explained that a stack of chairs piled up to the ceiling of her cubicle looked as if they were about to fall. In a few moments the emergency occurred. The sound of chairs crashing to the floor was accompanied by the victim's screams: "They're falling on me!"

The presence of other bystanders was introduced in this study to provide a non-race-related factor that could allow a bystander to justify or rationalize a failure to intervene. In Darley and Latané's (1968) classic experiment, it was discovered that the mere belief that other bystanders are capable of helping affects the likelihood that a bystander will intervene. When a person is alone, all of the responsibility for helping is focused on this one bystander. Under these conditions, the probability of this bystander intervening is quite high. As the number of bystanders is increased, though, each bystander becomes more likely to believe that one of the other bystanders will intervene or already has intervened, and each bystander's share of the responsibility for helping is decreased. Consequently, the likelihood that each person will intervene is reduced.

We predicted that the belief that other bystanders are present would have a greater inhibiting effect on the subject's response when the emergency involved a black victim than when it involved a white victim. Failure to help a black person in this situation could be justified or rationalized by the belief that the victim is being helped by someone else. Bystanders believing themselves to be the sole witness, however, were not expected to discriminate against black victims relative to white victims because any search for non-race-related factors to rationalize a failure to intervene would not be as successful as when subjects believed that other people were available to help. When alone, the failure to help a black victim could be more readily attributed to bigoted intent. Even relatively high-prejudice-scoring college students were expected to help without regard for the victim's race when they were the sole bystander. Although many of these relatively high-prejudice-scoring people (compared to other college students) may have awareness of their negative racial feelings, we believe that they would not regard themselves as particularly bigoted, and certainly not bigoted enough to be unresponsive to an emergency solely because of the victim's race.

As predicted, the results revealed a significant interaction involving the victim's race and whether or not bystanders thought that other people were available to intervene. Bystanders who thought that they were the only witness helped black victims somewhat more often than they helped white victims (94% vs. 81%). Subjects aware of the presence of other bystanders, however, helped black victims much less frequently than they helped white victims (38% vs. 75%). No main effects or interactions involving subjects' prejudice scores were obtained. Thus, the opportunity to diffuse responsibility for intervening, an apparently nonracial factor, had greater salience and potency among both low- and high-prejudice-scoring subjects when the victim was black than when she was white.

This experiment indicated that the presence of other bystanders—a nonracial element in an emergency involving a black or white victim—differentially influenced the reactions of both low- and high-prejudice-scoring subjects. This pattern of results supports the hypothesis that when a racially biased response can be rationalized or attributed to factors other than race even well-intentioned people will discriminate, probably un-intentionally, against blacks in a situation of deep consequence to the victim. Yet, the subtlety by which motivational factors alter the cognitive and emotional experience of the situation permits the continued maintenance of a nondiscriminating image among these people.

Belief Systems within Contemporary Racial Attitudes: Attributions and Associations

The implication of aversive racism for contemporary racial attitudes is rather straightforward. We hypothesize that because most whites want to see themselves as fair, just, and egalitarian, they will not directly express their prejudice against blacks. Expressing negative attitudes or endorsing overtly prejudiced statements would obviously challenge a person's egalitarian self-image. Thus, we propose that prejudice and stereotyped belief systems, like discrimination, still exist but that the contemporary forms are more subtle and less overtly negative than their more traditional ancestors.

On the basis of our assumptions about the type of ambivalence that aversive racists experience, we have conducted several experiments to determine the content of contemporary stereotypes among college students. In contrast to previous research (e.g., Woodmansee & Cook, 1967) that directly assessed attitudes toward blacks and assumed a favorable-unfavorable continuum of feelings, we have attempted to measure independently both negative *and* positive beliefs and feelings about blacks *relative* to whites.

With the assumption that a stereotype is a collection of associations that link a target group to a set of descriptive characteristics, Gaertner and McLaughlin (1983, Studies 1 and 2) engaged high- and low-prejudice-scoring white subjects in a task patterned after Meyer and Schvaneveldt's (1971, 1976) lexical decision procedure. This procedure yields a measure of associative strength between

two words, based on the time that it takes subjects to decide if two strings of letters are both words. Meyer and Schvaneveldt (1971, 1976) report that highly associated word pairs (e.g., Doctor-Nurse) produce faster reaction times than do unassociated word pairs (e.g., Doctor-Butter).

In our research, the words "blacks" and "whites" were paired with negative (lazy, stupid, welfare) and positive (ambitious, smart, clean) words. It was hypothesized that if white people's characterizations of whites are more positive than are their characterizations of blacks, then subjects would be expected to make more rapid decisions about positive characteristics when they are paired with *whites* than when they are paired with *blacks*. Furthermore, if contemporary stereotypes are actually antiblack, then *blacks* paired with negative attributes would yield faster reaction times than would *whites* paired with these same words. This lexical decision task offers a less reactive approach than do adjective checklists to the study of stereotyping. Subjects are not directly asked to endorse the appropriateness of a specific word-pair combination, but only to indicate whether or not members of the pair are both words.

The results demonstrate the predicted interaction between the evaluative nature of the stereotype-related word and the racial category word. White subjects responded reliably faster when positive traits were paired with *whites* than when they were paired with *blacks*. Both high- and low-prejudice-scoring subjects, however, responded as quickly to *whites* paired with negative attributes as to *blacks* paired with negative attributes. A second experiment that substituted the word *negroes* for *blacks* replicated this pattern of results. These findings, then, are quite consistent with the results of our rating scale studies. Specifically, the data indicate that white college students, irrespective of prejudice score, differentially associate positive, but not negative, stereotypic characteristics to whites and blacks.

Our reaction-time experiments provide consistent evidence across two different experimental procedures, subject populations, and sets of characteristics that contemporary stereotypes involve differential association of positively valued characteristics to whites but not negatively valued traits to blacks. How does this pattern translate into expressed racial attitudes? We performed additional self-report studies that addressed this question.

One of our rating scale experiments (Gaertner & McLaughlin, 1983, Study 3) provided separate groups of white subjects with six-point semantic differential-type rating scales in which either two positive (e.g., Smart-Not Stupid) or two negative (e.g., Unambitious-Lazy) traditionally stereotypic items were presented as anchors. Each of the negative scales represented a negative-to-less-negative dimension, and each of the positive scales reflected a positive-to-less-positive dimension. Using either the positive or the negative rating scales, subjects were asked to complete the phrase, "Blacks relative to whites are _____ ." Then subjects, using the same scales, were asked to complete the phrase, "Whites relative to blacks are _____ ." It was expected that if negative attributes are not differentially ascribed to blacks and whites, then ratings on the scales with negative traits as anchors would be quite similar when subjects responded to "black relative to whites" as when they responded to "whites relative to blacks." Furthermore, if positive traits are differentially ascribed to the racial groups, then the ratings of "whites relative to blacks" should be closer to the more positive end of the scale than with the ratings of "blacks relative to whites." This pattern is precisely what occurred. Blacks were not evaluated as more lazy, stupid, or dirty than were whites on the negative trait scales. Whites, however, were regarded as more ambitious, smart, and clean relative to blacks on the positive trait scales.

White college students, at least those from primarily northern populations, do not readily express antiblack sentiments and do not appear to have strong antiblack associations. They do, however, exhibit a racially based ingroup bias. Our subjects consistently rated whites more favorably than blacks, and they had stronger positive associations with whites than with blacks. Thus, even though our subject samples appear to be quite liberal and egalitarian on traditional prejudice scales (Dovidio,Tannenbaum, & Ellyson, 1984), racial bias is still evident in their responses. Consistent with our assumptions about racism among well-intentioned people, prejudice is expressed indirectly and in a way that is not recognizably antiblack.

DISCUSSION

In general, the results of several different types of experiments conducted since 1970 have produced consistent support for our aversive racism framework. Specifically, the behavioral findings (presented in the first two subsections) and the findings concerning subjects' associations and beliefs (presented in the third subsection) yield similar conclusions: Prejudiced thinking and discrimination still exist, but the contemporary forms are more subtle, more indirect, and less overtly negative than are more traditional forms. Furthermore, the contemporary form of prejudice is expressed in ways that protect and perpetuate a nonprejudiced, nondiscriminating self-image.

In terms of interracial behavior, the presence or absence of norms governing appropriate behavior is a critical factor mediating the expression of prejudice. When norms are clear, bias is unlikely to occur; when norms are ambiguous or conflicting, discrimination is often exhibited. Regarding the expression of racial attitudes and stereotypes, people do not appear to associate negative traits more strongly with blacks than with whites, an act that would likely appear bigoted. Whites do, however, consistently ascribe more positive characteristics to whites than to blacks. In addition, even when norms are clear, whites continue to be more sensitive to ostensibly nonracial factors that could permit them to rationalize a negative response toward blacks. Specifically, we propose that in situations involving blacks, an indirect attitudinal process operates to increase the salience and potency of factors that can substitute for the issue of race in justifying negative behavior. These nonracial factors may be related to characteristics of the situation (e.g., the presence of other bystanders who could share responsibility for helping) or may refer to personal or cultural values (e.g., perceptions of equity or justice). We do not mean, however, that contemporary white Americans are hypocritical; rather, they are victims of cultural forces and cognitive processes that continue to promote prejudice and racism.

We believe that aversive racism, although it represents a subtle form of racism, is a particularly insidious type. One reason that old-fashioned racism has shown a significant decline in recent years may be that, because it is direct and obvious, it may be susceptible to conventional techniques of attitude change and to social and legal pressures. It is unlikely, however, that aversive racism can be alleviated by such direct methods. Attempts to educate people to accept egalitarian ideals would have little impact on aversive racists; aversive racists already believe that they are egalitarian, nonprejudiced, and nondiscriminating. In fact, whenever aversive racists consciously monitor their behavior in interracial situations, they react in ways that consistently reinforce their egalitarian self-images. Techniques directed at revealing the negative components of aversive racists' attitudes would probably only produce reverse discrimination (Dutton & Lake, 1973) or a token reaction (Dutton & Lennox, 1974) that would permit aversive racists to deny their antiblack feelings. Introducing clear, salient norms into interracial situations would be an effective way of controlling discrimination, but it would probably not have long-term, generalizable consequences. Because

of the salient external justification for their actions, aversive racists would not necessarily internalize the principles involved in their interracial behavior. Thus, like a virus that mutates into new forms, old-fashioned prejudice seems to have evolved into a new type that is, at least temporarily, resistant to traditional attitude-change remedies that emphasize the evils of prejudice as a means of eliminating racism.

READING 27

Aging Labels: The Decline of Control and the Fall of Self-Esteem

Judith Rodin and Ellen Langer (1980)

Racial intolerance is not the only instance of prejudice in our society. What are your images of the aging process and the elderly? Have you ever thought what it would be like to be "old"? Usually, we assume a slowing or loss of function with aging; we expect that speed in walking, thinking, and responding will gradually slow down. Then hearing and/or sight will diminish as well, and memory will begin to slip. The ads for bladder control undergarments aimed at the elderly increase our negative expectations.

American stereotypes of aging are grim. Many elderly report, however, that the physical aspects of aging are not as frustrating as the negative assumptions and treatment they receive from a society that has so little respect or time for the elderly. Rodin and Langer suggest that our stereotypes of aging and our responses to the aged (as a consequence of our stereotypes) are an important aspect of what makes aging difficult in American society. They also utilize some of Allport's ideas for reducing prejudice, for example, greater and more equal contact, perceived similarity, and an improved media image.

By the year 2000, it is estimated that over 15 percent of the population, 30 million people, will be 65 or over. Although aging affords status to people in some countries, in the United States and other industrialized nations the elderly often suffer a loss of status, reduction in personal contacts and income, and a social climate that views aging with fearfulness and distaste. Even in some earlier civilizations aging was viewed as a negative process. For example, the Nambikwara Indians have a single word that means 'young and beautiful' and another that means 'old and ugly' (de Beauvoir, 1972). Since in the United States less than 5 percent of all people over 65 actually require custodial care (Berezin, 1972; Brotman, 1974), it may be asserted that at least 95 percent of the aged do not conform to the stereotype of the helpless and sick old person. Nevertheless, such stereotypes exist (cf. Butler, 1970). Indeed, a number of studies examining such diverse cultural influences as children's and adolescent's literature (Blue, 1978; Peterson & Karnes, 1976), contemporary fiction and poetry (Sohngen, 1977; Sohngen & Smith, 1978), and popular jokes (Davis, 1977; Richman, 1977), all found at least some negative stereotypes of the elderly.

In this paper, we describe several studies that investigated the social psychological correlates of aging. Our goal was to understand how negative labeling and stigmatization of the elderly might contribute to behavior that actually confirmed prevalent stereotypes of old age and led to lowered self-esteem and diminished feelings of control. Given that stereotypes and social labels are in a sense simply summaries of cultural expectations, such expectations might be assumed to affect all members of the culture, including those about whom the labels are held. If one's self-image and behavior come to portray these negative stereotypes (cf. Kelley, 1967; Rosenthal, 1971; Snyder & Swann, 1978), self-esteem should decline. As self-esteem decreases, belief in one's ability to exercise control over the environment also declines (Rodin, 1980).

Aging individuals may therefore overestimate decrements in their capacities that may be experienced as discrepant with their evaluative standards for competent behavior (Bandura, 1971), and the effects of this awareness may be more debilitating than the change itself (Langer, 1979b). When, in addition, there actually is a reduction of the number and kinds of potential options for control of the environment, as is the case for the elderly, this self-view is reconfirmed.

If these deleterious causal relationships can in fact be demonstrated, the underlying mechanisms determined, and the effects reversed, we expect that there would follow a restoration of both a more positive self-concept and a greater sense of control for the aged, as well as less age-stereotyped behavior. A simplified diagrammatic illustration of this process appears below.

The next section examines some of the research bearing on these questions.

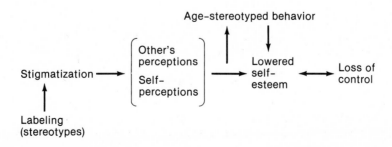

EFFECTS OF NEGATIVE LABELS

Some Background

Working in a different domain, Langer and Abelson (1974) have demonstrated that manipulating expectations by labeling a person influenced how that person was subsequently perceived. In their study, therapists were shown a single videotape of a man in an interview who discussed his recent job experiences, and were asked to evaluate him on several dimensions. Prior to viewing the tape, half the therapists were told the interviewee was a "patient," and half were told he was a "job applicant." When wearing the patient label, his behavior was viewed as pathological but when he was labeled "job applicant," the same behavior was considered well-adjusted. The Langer and Abelson study showed the effects of negative labels on the observer's perception of the target person. Subsequent effects on the target may be inferred.

Studies by Langer and Benevento (1978) explicitly demonstrated negative effects on the target as a function of certain kinds of labels. Here baseline measures were taken as subjects successfully performed a task. They then performed a second task in pairs, under one of three labeling conditions: labeled as "assistant" or as "boss," or no label. Finally, subjects individually returned to the original task. Despite their initial success at the first task, and the fact that the labels they wore applied to their role in performing a different kind of task, subjects who were labeled "assistant" now performed the first task only half as well as they had originally. Thus, a label may be viewed as summarizing a set of expectations that then determines the kinds of interaction that the therapist ("boss") and the interviewee ("assistant") would have, and feeds back into the interviewee's (assistant's) view of self, affecting own subsequent performance.

Negative Stereotypes Toward Old Age

If our society has developed labels that create certain sets of negative expectations with regard to aging, it is likely that people will act in a manner that is consistent with these labels. To the extent that a particular stereotype is actually believed, elderly persons may also begin to act in a manner that is consistent with that stereotype. Expectations based on the label senility, for example, may have a great impact on the way old people and those approaching old age view themselves.

Every time a mistake is made or a thought is forgotten, older people may question whether their mental capacities are diminishing. If people are worrying about their failing memory while in a situation where new learning could take place (e.g., learning the name of a new acquaintance), they might indeed "forget" what they had just learned. However, the problem would have been in the conditions surrounding the learning (distraction) and not a problem of memory at all. But how could the elderly come to this more benign conclusion in the face of the salient stereotypes that exist with respect to their cognitive capacities? Any such fears the elderly have about themselves are exacerbated by the dearth of appropriate role models who could serve as counter examples of what life after seventy might be like. Thus, it is critical to determine what negative stereotypes exist about the elderly, what behaviors they produce, and the extent to which older people also accept these views.

Langer and Mulvey (1980) conducted a study to determine what specific behaviors are most commonly cited as characteristic of older people. Since they expected senility to be prominent among them (cf. Butler, 1970), they also asked whether there is a single conception of senility or whether these views change as a result of age? And most important, they questioned whether being old is seen as akin to being senile.

In this study, questionnaires were used to assess beliefs about the behavior of old age, and to determine whether information and attitudes about senile behavior vary as a function of age and familiarity with the elderly. Subjects were 75 adults, twenty-five between the ages of 25 and

40, twenty-five between the ages of 45 and 60, and twenty-five over the age of 70.

Following an introduction describing the purpose of the interview, several social demographic factors (e.g., size of family, education and income) were assessed. None of these factors significantly affected the results. As part of the interview, respondents were then asked to list those behaviors they believed to be characteristic of people in three different age groups: 35–45, 65–75, and 75 and older. They were asked to go back over all the behaviors they had listed and indicate which if any, they believed to be indications of senility. Next, they read descriptions of various events and were asked to describe what a senile person was likely to do in each situation. For example, "A senile person walks into a store and picks up a loaf of bread. He or she then _____ ." Finally, respondents were asked to indicate the likelihood that they themselves will become senile.

Responses were rated by judges who were unaware of both the population that the respondent represented and the experimental hypotheses. Categories of behaviors were tallied, and the descriptive passages were rated along the dimensions of negative-positive and active-passive, as well as on intelligence-related, memory-related, social-related, and personality-related dimensions.

The young and middle age samples perceived old people as involved primarily in non-social behaviors and passive activities, and as possessing negative psychological characteristics to a much greater extent than positive ones. The old sample perceived just the opposite, placing significantly greater emphasis on social activities and positive psychological characteristics. Similarly, the younger population was more likely than their older counterparts to view the elderly as sickly. While the reactions of the elderly to general behavior seem more positive, we will see in the next study that when age-stereotyped behaviors are involved, their reactions become even more negative than those of younger adults.

For elderly, middle-aged and young respondents alike, there appeared to be a stereotype of the elderly adult that included a fairly well-defined conception of senility. All age group samples viewed senility in very negative terms and labeled it as a condition of physical deterioration evidenced by memory loss, mental incompetence, loss of contact with reality, and helplessness. In addition, and most interesting, was the finding that over 65 percent of the younger group felt certain that they would not become senile, while only 10 percent of the elderly group expressed this sentiment. Thus, it appears that the fear of senility is very real for elderly people, even though according to medical criteria only 4 percent of persons over 65 years old suffer from a severe form of senility, and only another 10 percent of this population suffer from a milder version (Katzman & Carasu, 1975).

The approach used in this study was also intended to develop a list of behaviors associated with senility and to assess attitudes towards these behaviors. One factor limiting the validity of its results, however, is that responses to questions with value-laden content are always difficult to interpret. In an attempt to give what is felt to be the socially desirable answer, people very often respond as they think they should respond even if the response is at odds with the way they actually think or feel (Crowne & Marlowe, 1955). This is especially true when people are asked to express negative attitudes.

Consequently, we designed a second study to determine the extent to which different subject populations spontaneously apply the label "senility" to those behaviors most frequently listed by subjects in the first experiment, and to assess the consequences of those labels for other attitudes.

Forty female high school students, 40 middle-age women, and 40 older women were recruited for a study on person perception. To reduce differences among the age groups due to socioeconomic status and religion, the adults were the mothers and grandmothers of the students, who were randomly selected from a local high school. Each of the three groups of subjects was randomly assigned to one of two experimental conditions described below.

The three members of each family, tested individually, were shown three video-taped scenes involving dyadic interactions that they were asked to rate. Two of the scenes were the same for all subjects: one was of a young child and mother pleasantly interacting, and one was of two friends quarreling. These served as filler items. The experimental question was tested in the third scene, which for half the subjects in each age group depicted an interview where the target person, the interviewee, appeared forgetful by asking the interviewer to repeat something he said earlier on three separate occasions. This was the behavior most frequently cited in Study 1 as indicative of senility. The third scene for the remaining subjects also depicted an interview, but here the target person responded to the interviewer's questions without engaging in forgetful behavior.

Each group was further subdivided so that for half of the subjects in each group above, the person engaging in the senility-related or non-related behavior appeared to be about 35 years old, and for the other half, about 75 years old. These manipulations also provided an opportunity to assess the generality of the negative labeling process. Specifically, we were interested in learning whether even non-age related behaviors of the elderly were likely to be labeled as evidence of senility and whether any of these behaviors, regardless of the label, were seen as more negative in older than younger persons.

To summarize, the study was a $3 \times 2 \times 2$ design where age of subject (approximately 18 years old, 40 years old, and 65 years old), behavior of target (senility-related or non-related), and age of target (young or old) were the independent variables. The relevant measures were responses to a questionnaire that followed each scene. The items were designed to determine whether the behavior of elderly persons was spontaneously labeled as senile and/or whether their behavior was generally evaluated more negatively. Subjects were asked to rate, for example, how much they liked the target person, how alert they thought she was, and how stable she appeared to be, on a series of 10-point scales. Open-ended questions asked for description of the people and interactions in the video-taped sequences.

We found a main effect for age of the target person for both measures. Regardless of the subjects' age, they were more likely to label the older target as "senile" than the young target person, which is hardly surprising. However, subjects also evaluated the same behaviors more negatively in the older target person than in the younger. We also found that the older, not the younger, respondents tended to evaluate the forgetful elderly target most negatively, suggesting that the older one gets, the more frightened one is of being or becoming senile or showing other presumably age-related negative traits. This fear is likely to motivate older people to distance themselves, psychologically, from old people with difficulties such as forgetfulness, by evaluating them as negatively as possible, and thereby making them seem different from themselves. Taking this finding, together with the data from the Langer and Mulvey study, it appears that older people are more positive towards the elderly overall than are younger people, but are also more negative than young people about the negative features of old age.

In general, this study also suggests that old age per se carries with it enough negative expectations so that a behavior that is seen as normal in a young person may be seized upon when engaged in by an elderly person as confirmation of the stereotype, and cloud the perception of the rest of the (target) individual's behavior.

EFFECTS OF AGE-RELEVANT LABELS ON BEHAVIOR

In the next study, we considered the extent to which professionals, who may deal with the elderly, use age as a cue for interpreting behavior, and whether the labels they assign then affect their behavior. Miller, Lowenstein and Winston (1976) have reported very negative attitudes among physicians working with the aged ill. In this study, Caplovitz and Rodin (1980) provided psychotherapists with information describing the pathological behavior of seven different individuals, randomly ordered in a questionnaire. These questionnaires were given to psychologists and psychiatrists asking them to provide a DSM-II diagnosis, describe briefly the course of treatment plan, and describe the site of treatment (e.g., hospital, community mental health center, out-patient). Identical behaviors were described to all therapists, the only difference being that for half the subjects, six of the cases gave a young age as part of the case history. For the other half of the subjects, the target person was described as in his or her sixties or seventies. As a control, the seventh case described a middle-aged person and was identical for all subjects.

The experiment showed a greater propensity to diagnose the same psychotic behavior as organically based when the individual was old rather than young. When the pathology was less serious, both older and younger target persons received the diagnosis of depression about equally often, but the treatment prescribed for the two age groups varied in many cases. Not surprisingly, more longterm therapy was prescribed for younger than older targets. However, in addition, less use of drug therapy and more community-based and group treatments were suggested for the young individuals. The same case history for an older individual elicited treatment diagnoses that were often drug-related and more demanding of acute institutionalization. Thus, it is apparent that age does influence both diagnosis and recommendations for treatment of elderly persons. We are not implying that age does not provide some useful diagnostic or treatment information, but simply that it may be accounting for too much of the variance in these decisions.

Having demonstrated some features of the nature and extent of labeling processes regarding the elderly, we next wished to consider how these labels and negative stereotypes might affect actual interactions involving older people. In the following study we investigated the effects of expectations regarding the elderly on the demands that a younger person was willing to make on an older person.

Subjects were asked to participate in a study on interviewing methods and were told that our goal was to determine the effectiveness of open-ended questions in learning about personality. Subjects were drawn from a population of middle-aged adults and were randomly assigned to one of two conditions. They were given biographical information leading them to expect to interact with, and interview, either a person 42 years old or a person 71 years old. Each group was further subdivided and given additional expectations regarding the interviewee's competence: they were told that the person was either typical for her age, below average for her age, or above average for her age in mental alertness. All subjects were given a questionnaire, which presumably was to guide their subsequent interview, and were asked to look it over and check off those questions they intended to ask. The questions covered several areas and were of varying difficulty.

Older targets were given, on the average, easier questions than younger targets, regardless of their competence level. Furthermore, preliminary analyses also suggest that the interviewee's competence was a more important determinant of question selection for the younger target than for the older. The questions were more difficult for the young respondent presumed to be competent; this was less true for the older target.

The studies described thus far have tried to determine whether or not some negative stereotypes regarding aging exist. They do indeed appear to be salient and prevalent. For example, while only a small proportion of elderly people actually are senile (Katzman & Carasu, 1975), attributions of senility were extensive. While 95 percent of elderly adults are not in need of custodial care (Berezin,

1972; Brotman, 1974), younger people assume that the typical elderly adult is sick. The studies discussed thus far also were designed to assess deleterious effects of negative labels. The results point to the kind (or lack) of treatment older people might get from health practitioners, and to the kind (or lack) of demands that society at large might make on them, which may work to lower self-esteem and actually bring about performance decrements. It should be kept in mind that negative stereotyping is detrimental for all people. However, we believe that it is particularly harmful for the aged because they are a highly vulnerable population due to increased incidence of significant life changes and environmental strains (Rodin, 1980). The following studies were designed to begin to specify why these stereotypes, reflecting an overestimate of the population frequency or intensity of the characteristics being rated, exist.

Reasons for the Occurrence of Negative Labels

One might first want to consider why certain negative stereotypes of the elderly persist in the absence of large numbers of helpless elderly people. One explanation lies in the work on the use of the availability and representativeness heuristics in judging frequency (Kahneman & Tversky, 1973; Tversky & Kahneman, 1973). This work suggests that the more easily instances come to mind, the more frequent they are judged to be. Consider this in conjunction with the likelihood that older people who are physically fit are often mistaken for younger adults, leaving the extremes of the aged population as the most salient members of the class. (Of course, the error of mistaking old-looking young people for older adults would lead to the same conclusion.) Images of these elderly people would then be called to mind most readily when one thinks of old age, resulting in inappropriate conclusions about late adulthood.

Factors other than availability-based errors also contribute to the maintenance of negative stereotypes. Langer, Taylor, Fiske, and Chanowitz

(1976) have shown that persons from relatively unfamiliar groups make others uncomfortable and are often avoided, and that such negative reactions are the result of a conflict that these persons arouse in others. On the one hand, people are motivated to stare at unfamiliar or novel stimuli in an attempt to understand them; while on the other hand, there are strong proscriptive norms that prohibit engaging in that very behavior when the novel stimulus is another person. The conflict is resolved by avoiding that person. This has been demonstrated to be true when the novel stimuli are people with physical handicaps or pregnant women. Specifically, the hypothesis tested was that sanctioned visual access to a novel stimulus person, prior to an interaction with that person, would result in subject behavior similar to that which follows sanctioned visual access to a "normal" adult. This hypothesis received strong support in the Langer et al. (1976) studies.

Most of the settings where younger adults and children spend their time are not places likely to have a great number of older persons present; for example, sports activities and work sites. This may make older persons relatively novel stimuli when they are present, for example, at restaurants. We could deduce, therefore, that negative feelings and avoidance would be likely on those occasions. By removing the conflict that novel-stimulus persons create, avoidance should be reduced. Thus, we reasoned that at least some of the bias against the elderly may be decreased by making them less novel.

If the old are avoided, and this avoidance has in other contexts been shown to be reduced by allowing someone simply to watch the person, it seems worthwhile to broaden the scope of our inquiry in two ways:

1. by studying the impact of avoidance on the elderly's self-concept and behavior;
2. by studying the effects of increased exposure to effective elderly persons on the behavior of both elderly and nonelderly populations.

We have already begun a study to determine how avoidance by others affects one's self-concept and behavior. It has been suggested in the literature on aging that dissociation is produced by a nonaccepting culture. Strauss (1963), for example, maintains that those elderly persons who perceive the environment as one that devalues them tend, as a result, to withdraw from involvement in their surroundings and instead engage in more solitary activities. While this argument is compelling, virtually all data reported in this area are correlational, making it difficult to separate cause from effect. Do people retreat because they are rejected, or do they appear to be rejected merely because they have voluntarily retreated, as disengagement theory suggests (Cumming, Dean, Newell, & McCaffrey, 1960)?

In a study on avoidance and self-concept, we have been developing an experimental model of the rejection process using a nonelderly population to determine whether rejection can produce the social withdrawal and disengagement-like behavior frequently seen in the aged. Clearly, persons who are already old do not provide the appropriate sample with which to test the causal factors of this process, because it is assumed that they are currently displaying the effects. We therefore are testing younger subjects who are either avoided or not avoided. It is expected that being avoided will lead to negative feelings and withdrawal. To reverse these effects, in half the cases subjects are encouraged to attribute this result to some aspect of the situation. It is expected that attribution to the situation, rather than to oneself, will lessen the impact of social avoidance.

Attribution About Aging

We have observed that chronological age per se is not sufficient to provide a person with the self-definition of ''old,'' although obviously there is some relationship between chronological age and self-perception. Rather, a series of events or experiences forces acceptance, although reluc-

tantly, of the fact that one is old, and often these events have avoidance and/or the loss of control at their core. Once this occurs, it may be that older people then evaluate themselves on the basis of feelings and behaviors that they attribute to aging rather than to the environment and circumstance.

Negative attributional processes deriving from feeling avoided and from reduced feelings of control can create at least two different types of problems for older people that may lower their number of coping attempts and thus detrimentally affect their health (see Rodin, 1978, for a longer discussion of the effects of attributions on health in general). First, there is a tendency to over-attribute most of their negative physical symptoms to aging per se, especially to the presumed physical decline with which aging is associated. Biological attributions may incorrectly focus the person away from situational and social factors such as the loss of a loved one or feeling unsafe; these are stress-inducing in part because they are associated with a loss of control. Recent work has shown that even among healthy college students, loss of control is related to increased experience of symptoms (Pennebaker & Skelton, 1978). Second, when events are attributed to the aging process, they are seen as inevitable; and remedial steps that could be extremely beneficial may not be undertaken.

The negative self-concept of elderly persons would further increase the likelihood that they will make damaging self, rather than situational, attributions when they perceive, whether veridically or not, that they are being avoided, or when they experience reduced feelings of control. Interventions might then be developed to redirect these attributions. We have already conducted some work on this question, looking more generally at the consequences of attributional processes and the possibility of changing them.

We interviewed people in the week that followed their entering a nursing home, and selected the 80 percent who made explicit negative attributions to physical decline associated with aging as either causing or contributing greatly to some of their problems. We took a variety of premeasures including interviews, health measures, and observations of level of participation. There were three randomly assigned groups: one group was untreated; one group was simply given information trying to argue against physical decline in aging as being the real source of their problems (using material taken from doctors' reports and journal articles); and the third group was given environmental explanations (or at least age-environment interactional attributions) as being the source of their problems.

As an example of some environmental attributions that were used, subjects in the latter group were told that the floors in the nursing home are very slippery because they are tiled in order to keep them clean. Even young people slip on them. By this means, we tried to reduce the attribution that slipping was due to weak knees or poor movement that resulted from their age. As another example, they were reminded that they were awakened at 5:30 in the morning, which would make most people tired by evening. Again, we tried to minimize the likelihood that they would attribute their weariness to aging per se. Thus, we simply attempted to refocus their explanations for their own feelings and behavior onto plausible factors in the environment that could have been producing some of the physical symptoms they were likely to be experiencing.

As a result of the reattribution intervention, patients showed greatly improved behavior, including an increase in active participation and sociability relative to groups simply given information or to untreated controls. There were also benefits in the area of general health and indices of stress. Thus, debilitating and often excessive attribution to physical states associated with aging and decline can be refocused, with beneficial effects, onto more easily changed aspects of the environment.

In another study (Langer, Rodin, Beck, Weinman, & Spitzer, 1979) we demonstrated that attributions about whether the same task was a memory test, or was a new activity being introduced into the nursing home, dramatically influenced subjects' subsequent performance. Those expecting to be tested performed significantly less well than those expecting to try out a new "activity."

Reversing Memory "Loss"

Over-attribution to aging rather than to environmental sources, coupled with the negative labeling process described above, work together to decrease self-esteem and diminish performance. Often this results in a lack of motivation to engage in a variety of behaviors, rather than an inability to do so. Over time, and with disuse, the abilities themselves may also decline.

Taking loss of memory as an example, we speculated that some component of memory loss may be due to the operation of these social psychological factors, which produce symptoms of forgetfulness and confusion that have nothing to do with aging per se. We reasoned that, in some older individuals, apparently diminished memory could be reversed by increasing motivation for thinking and remembering.

In two studies, we attempted to motivate elderly nursing home residents to adhere to a recommended course of action over time that asked them to think about and remember a variety of events (Langer et al., 1979). In the first study, we tried to increase motivation to remember by providing the opportunity for reciprocal self-disclosure between the subject and an interviewer who recommended the particular course of cognitive activity. Janis and Rodin (1979) have hypothesized that establishing referent power (French & Raven, 1959) is an important way to increase motivation and promote commitment. Persons have referent power for those who perceive them as benevolent and accepting. Eliciting and sometimes reciprocating self-disclosure is one factor that is critical in helping a person to establish referent power (Rodin & Janis, 1979). In the second study we tried to increase motivation to use one's memory by setting up a contingency in which greater cognitive effort resulted in greater tangible reward (chips that could be traded for gifts). In both studies, the recommended course of action involved remembering a series of questions and probing the environment and one's long-term memory for information relevant to their answers. Both studies had "no treatment" controls as well as a control group treated in all ways identical to experimental subjects except that, in the first study, *low* reciprocal self-disclosure was elicited and, in the second study, the rewards were *not contingent* upon performance.

In both studies, experimental subjects showed a significant improvement on standard short-term memory tests including probe and pattern recall, as well as improvement on nurses' ratings of alertness, mental activity and social adjustment, relative to controls. Thus, we found that restructuring the environment to make it more demanding, and then motivating elderly people to increase their cognitive activity, leads to improvements in memory that are generalizable. It is critical to note that the experimental treatments provided no explicit training for the memory tests that constituted the dependent variables of greatest interest. While we did not measure self-esteem directly, we found that experimental subjects were rated as happier and more involved following the intervention, and we may infer that they were feeling better about themselves.

Thus, it appears that the consequences of major changes associated with aging, overattribution to physical decline associated with aging, and the effects of negative stereotypes regarding aging, can be reversed by appropriate environmental manipulations. We predict that this will be true for many factors other than apparent memory loss, which have been adduced to be inevitable consequences of aging for most persons (see Langer, 1979a, for a discussion of the environmental determinants of aging). Our earliest work in this area showed that when even relatively debilitated nursing home residents were given the opportunity to make decisions and to feel increased responsibility, thus potentially reducing their negative self-labeling, they became more involved, active and self-initiating, as well as considerably happier, and they showed dramatic health-related benefits (Langer & Rodin, 1976; Rodin & Langer, 1977). Thus, reversals are even possible in nursing home environments, which foster a sense of dependency and loss of control (see Wack & Rodin, 1978, for a full discussion of the reasons for creation and effects of nursing homes).

CONCLUSIONS

Although there have been papers suggesting that aging is correlated with negative labels (e.g., Butler, 1970), for the most part these notions have not been examined under controlled experimental conditions, nor have the antecedent variables been elucidated. In this paper, we described our studies examining the relationship between aging and cognitive social psychological factors with specific references to labeling, control and self-concept. In this research, we investigated if and how the aged are negatively stereotyped, and the consequences of negative labels associated with aging. We demonstrated how such labels and attributions may, in turn, affect the self-concept and behavior of the elderly, and lead to decrements in perceived control. We then investigated how changing labels, and giving control experiences, can serve to reinstate motivation in some elderly individuals, thereby promoting more self-benefiting behavior. However, we also believe that making these changes at the individual level is only a short-term solution.

Social change is a complex process that does not lend itself to easy analysis. Nevertheless, it seems that every successful movement has at least included the following elements: (1) There is a public protest when media or important professional groups are intentionally or unintentionally (usually the latter) insulting. (2) The social stereotype of the affected group becomes so well-known that it becomes a public joke and an emblem of bigotry. Comic villians like Archie Bunker bring home the message. (3) There is exposure of the person for whom acceptance is sought. The first black was seen on a television commercial in New York City in the late sixties. Now it is routine. The exposure seems to shift first from merely including the person in situations from which they were previously omitted, for example, an office setting, to gradually presenting them in a positive light, and then making them the focal heroes or heroines (Wooley & Wooley, 1977).

The elderly have not yet been this fortunate. In the mid 1970's, one of the three major networks pilot-tested a situation comedy in which two elderly people lived together, rather than marrying, in order to keep earning maximal social security benefits. Their relationship to their shocked, conservative children and to the outside world formed the basis for the satire. It was funny, endearing and very human. But the project was abandoned; neither commercial sponsors nor the test market were ready. Perhaps the turn of the decade will prove a more opportune time to reverse cultural biases against this population.

However, we must end with two important caveats. First, the solicitousness and increased care that this type of consciousness-raising may bring could result in even greater debilitation for the elderly (Langer & Benevento, 1978; Langer & Rodin, 1976; Rodin, 1980; Rodin & Langer, 1977). What is needed is not simply attention or pampering, which foster dependency, but rather increased opportunities for esteem-building and self-control. Second, this line of reasoning argues strongly for social change that provides opportunities for real control, not simply strategies that increase perceived control while options for actual control remain unavailable. If older persons are led to expect more control over their destinies, which they then find themselves unable to exercise, they are most likely to blame themselves. Once again, this could produce great debilitation and even death, given the strong association between chronic stress, induced by a lack of control, and ill health among the elderly (Rodin, 1980).

Gender Issues

Social Devices for Impelling Women to Bear and Rear Children

Leta S. Hollingsworth (1916)

This article by Hollingsworth was an astonishing paper for its time and is still a considerably strong statement today. Examining societal attitudes toward and claims about women, Hollingsworth analyzes how society shapes and controls the desires and behaviors of women.

Hollingsworth builds on Ross's (1904) list of social means of control. The seven categories she describes (personal ideals, the media (public opinion), law, religion, education, concealing information, and the wonderful class called "bugaboos") are non-independent and overlapping, yet they derive their strength from differing aspects of societal structure. Many of these continue to be powerful mechanisms of persuasion and control in today's society. We have already discussed briefly how society perpetuates the importance of following gender roles in the story of "X" (Reading 24). Can you think of other examples of broad values about men or women that are perpetuated by these seven (or other) social means of control?

"Again, the breeding function of the family would be better discharged if public opinion and religion conspired, as they have until recently, to crush the aspirations of woman for a life of her own. But the gain would not be worth the price."—E. A. Ross, Social Control *(1904).*

In this quotation from Ross we have suggested to us an exceedingly important and interesting phase of social control, namely, the control by those in social power over those individuals who alone can bring forth the human young, and thus perpetuate society. It is necessary that at the very outset of this discussion we should consent to clear our minds of the sentimental conception of motherhood and to look at facts. Sumner states these facts as well as they have ever been stated, in his consideration of the natural burdens of society. He says:

> Children add to the weight of the struggle for existence of their parents. The relation of parent to child is one of sacrifice. The interests of parents and children are antagonistic. The fact that there are or may be compensations does not affect the primary relation between the two. It may well be believed that, if procreation had not been put under the dominion of a great passion, it would have been caused to cease by the burdens it entails.

This is especially true in the case of the mothers.

The fact is that child-bearing is in many respects analogous to the work of soldiers: it is necessary for tribal or national existence; it means great sacrifice of personal advantage; it involves danger and suffering, and, in a certain percentage of cases, the actual loss of life. Thus we should expect that there would be a continuous social effort to insure the group-interest in respect to population, just as there is a continuous social effort to insure the defense of the nation in time of war. It is clear, indeed, that the social devices employed to get children born, and to get soldiers slain, are in many respects similar.

But once the young are brought into the world they still must be reared, if society's ends are to be served, and here again the need for and exercise of social control may be seen. Since the period of helpless infancy is very prolonged in the human species, and since the care of infants is an onerous and exacting labor, it would be natural for all persons not biologically attached to infants to use all possible devices for fastening the whole burden of infant-tending upon those who are so attached. We should expect this to happen, and we shall see, in fact, that there has been consistent social effort to establish as a

291

norm the woman whose vocational proclivities are completely and "naturally" satisfied by child-bearing and child-rearing, with the related domestic activities.

There is, to be sure, a strong and fervid insistence on the "maternal instinct," which is popularly supposed to characterize all women equally, and to furnish them with an all-consuming desire for parenthood, regardless of the personal pain, sacrifice, and disadvantage involved. In the absence of all verifiable data, however, it is only common-sense to guard against accepting as a fact of human nature a doctrine which we might well expect to find in use as a means of social control. Since we possess no scientific data at all on this phase of human psychology, the most reasonable assumption is that if it were possible to obtain a quantitative measurement of maternal instinct, we should find this trait distributed among women, just as we have found all other traits distributed which have yielded to quantitative measurement. It is most reasonable to assume that we should obtain a curve of distribution, varying from an extreme where individuals have a zero or negative interest in caring for infants, through a mode where there is a moderate amount of impulse to such duties, to an extreme where the only vocational or personal interest lies in maternal activities.

The facts, shorn of sentiment, then, are: (1) The bearing and rearing of children is necessary for tribal or national existence and aggrandizement. (2) The bearing and rearing of children is painful, dangerous to life, and involves long years of exacting labor and self-sacrifice. (3) There is no verifiable evidence to show that a maternal instinct exists in women of such all-consuming strength and fervor as to impel them voluntarily to seek the pain, danger, and exacting labor involved in maintaining a high birth rate.

We should expect, therefore, that those in control of society would invent and employ devices for impelling women to maintain a birth rate sufficient to insure enough increase in the population to offset the wastage of war and disease. It is the purpose of this paper to cite specific illustrations to show just how the various social institutions have been brought to bear on women to this end. Ross has classified the means which society takes and has taken to secure order, and insure that individuals will act in such a way as to promote the interests of the group, *as those interests are conceived by those who form "the radiant points of social control."* These means, according to the analysis of Ross, are public opinion, law, belief, social suggestion, education, custom, social religion, personal ideals (the type), art, personality, enlightenment, illusion, and social valuation. Let us see how some of these means have been applied in the control of women.

Personal Ideals (The Type)

The first means of control to which I wish to call attention in the present connection is that which Ross calls "personal ideals." It is pointed out that "a developed society presents itself as a system of unlike individuals, strenuously pursuing their personal ends." Now, for each person there is a "certain zone of requirement," and since "altruism is quite incompetent to hold each unswervingly to the particular activities and forbearances belonging to his place in the social system," the development of such allegiance must be—

> effected by means of types or patterns, which society induces its members to adopt as their guiding ideals.... To this end are elaborated various patterns of conduct and of character, which may be termed social types. These types may become in the course of time personal ideals, each for that category of persons for which it is intended.

For women, obviously enough, the first and most primitive "zone of requirement" is and has been to produce and rear families large enough to admit of national warfare being carried on, and of colonization.

Thus has been evolved the social type of the "womanly woman," "the normal woman," the chief criterion of normality being a willingness to engage enthusiastically in maternal and allied activities. All those classes and professions which form "the radiant points of social control" unite upon this criterion. Men of science announce it with calm assurance (though failing to say on what kind or amount of scientific data they base their remarks). For instance, McDougall writes:

The highest stage is reached by those species in which each female produces at birth but one or two young, and protects them so efficiently that most of the young born reach maturity; the maintenance of the species thus becomes in the main the work of the parental instinct. In such species the protection and cherishing of the young is the constant and all-absorbing occupation of the mother, to which she devotes all her energies, and in the course of which she will at any time undergo privation, pain, and death. The instinct (maternal instinct) becomes more powerful than any other, and can override any other, even fear itself.

Professor Jastrow writes:

...*charm* is the technique of the maiden, and *sacrifice* the passion of the mother. One set of feminine interests expresses more distinctly the issues of courtship and attraction; the other of qualities of motherhood and devotion.

The medical profession insistently proclaims desire for numerous children as the criterion of normality for women, scornfully branding those so ill-advised as to deny such desires as "abnormal." As one example among thousands of such attempts at social control let me quote the following, which appeared in a New York newspaper on November 29, 1915:

Only abnormal women want no babies. Trenchant criticism of modern life was made by Dr. Max G. Schlapp, internationally known as a neurologist. Dr. Schlapp addressed his remarks to the congregation of the Park Avenue M. E. Church. He said, "The birth rate is falling off. Rich people are the ones who have no children, and the poor have the greatest number of offspring. Any woman who does

not desire offspring is abnormal. We have a large number, particularly among the women, who do not want children. Our social society is becoming intensely unstable."

And this from *The New York Times,* September 5, 1915:

Normally woman lives through her children; man lives through his work.

Scores of such implicit attempts to determine and present the type or norm meet us on every hand. This norm has the sanction of authority, being announced by men of greatest prestige in the community. No one wishes to be regarded by her fellow-creatures as "abnormal" or "decayed." The stream of suggestions playing from all points inevitably has its influence, so that it is or was, until recently, well-nigh impossible to find a married woman who would admit any conflicting interests equal or paramount to the interest of caring for children. There is a universal refusal to admit that the maternal instinct, like every other trait of human nature, might be distributed according to the probability curve.

Public Opinion

Let us turn next to public opinion as a means of control over women in relation to the birth rate. In speaking of public opinion Ross says:

Haman is at the mercy of Mordecai. Rarely can one regard his deed as fair when others find it foul, or count himself a hero when the world deems him a wretch....For the mass of men the blame and the praise of the community are the very lords of life.

If we inquire now what are the organs or media of expression of public opinion we shall see how it is brought to bear on women. The newspapers are perhaps the chief agents, in modern times, in the formation of public opinion, and their columns abound in interviews with the eminent, deploring the decay of the population. Magazines print articles based on statistics of depopulation, appealing to the patriotism of women. In the year just passed fifty-five articles on the birth rate have chanced to come to the notice of the present writer. Fifty-four were written by men, including editors, statesmen, educators, ex-presidents, etc. Only one was written by a woman. The following quotation is illustrative of the trend of all of them:

M. Emil Reymond has made this melancholy announcement in the Senate: "We are living in an age when women have pronounced upon themselves a judgment that is dangerous in the highest degree to the development of the population. . . . We have the right to do what we will with the life that is in us, say they."

Thus the desire for the development of interests and aptitudes other than the maternal is stigmatized as "dangerous," "melancholy," "degrading," "abnormal," "indicative of decay." On the other hand, excessive maternity receives many cheap but effective rewards. For example, the Jesuit priests hold special meetings to laud maternity. The German Kaiser announces that he will now be godfather to seventh, eighth, and ninth sons, even if daughters intervene. The ex-President has written a letter of congratulation to the mother of nine.

Law

Since its beginning as a human institution law has been a powerful instrument for the control of women. The subjection of women was originally an irrational consequence of sex differences in reproductive function. It was not *intended* by either men or women, but simply resulted from the natural physiological handicaps of women, and the attempts of humanity to adapt itself to physiological nature through the crude methods of trial and error. When law was formulated, this subjection was defined, and thus furthered. It would take too long to cite all the legal provisions that contribute, indirectly to keep women from developing individualistic interests and capacities. Among the most important indirect forces in law which affect women to keep them child-bearers and child-rearers only are those provisions that tend to re-

strain them from possessing and controlling property. Such provisions have made of women a comparatively possessionless class, and have thus deprived them of the fundamentals of power. While affirming the essential nature of woman to be satisfied with maternity and with maternal duties only, society has always taken every precaution to close the avenues to ways of escape therefrom.

Two legal provisions which bear directly on women to compel them to keep up the birth rate may be mentioned here. The first of these is the provision whereby sterility in the wife may be made a cause of divorce. This would be a powerful inducement to women who loved their husbands to bear children if they could. The second provision is that which forbids the communication of the data of science in the matter of the means of birth control. The American laws are very drastic on this point. Recently in New York City a man was sentenced to prison for violating this law.

The more advanced democratic nations have ceased to practice military conscription. They no longer conscript their men to bear arms, depending on the volunteer army. But they conscript their women to bear children by legally prohibiting the publication or communication of the knowledge which would make child-bearing voluntary.

Child-rearing is also legally insured by those provisions which forbid and punish abortion, infanticide, and infant desertion. There could be no better proof of the insufficiency of maternal instinct as a guaranty of population than the drastic laws which we have against birth control, abortion, infanticide, and infant desertion.

Belief

Belief, "which controls the hidden portions of life," has been used powerfully in the interests of population. Orthodox women, for example, regard family limitation as a sin, punishable in the hereafter. Few explicit exhortations concerning the birth rate are discoverable in the various ''Words'' of God. The belief that family limitation will be punished in the hereafter seems to have been evolved mainly by priests out of the slender materials of a few quotations from Holy Writ, such as ''God said unto them, 'Multiply and replenish the earth,''' and from the scriptural allusion to children as the gifts of God. Being gifts from God, it follows that they may not be refused except at the peril of incurring God's displeasure.

Education

The education of women has always, until the end of the nineteenth century, been limited to such matters as would become a creature who could and should have no aspirations for a life of her own. We find the proper education for girls outlined in the writings of such educators as Rousseau, Fénelon, St. Jerome, and in Godey's *Lady's Book*. Not only have the ''social guardians'' used education as a negative means of control, by failing to provide any real enlightenment for women, but education has been made a positive instrument for control. This was accomplished by drilling into the young and unformed mind, while yet it was too immature to reason independently, such facts and notions as would give the girl a conception of herself only as future wife and mother. Rousseau, for instance, demanded freedom and individual liberty of development for everybody except Sophia, who was to be deliberately trained up as a means to an end. In the latter half of the nineteenth century when the hard battle for the real enlightenment of women was being fought, one of the most frequently recurring objections to admitting women to knowledge was that ''the population would suffer,'' ''the essential nature of woman would be changed,'' ''the family would decay,'' and ''the birth rate would fall.'' Those in control of society yielded up the old prescribed education of women only after a stubborn struggle, realizing that with the passing of the old training an important means of social control was slipping out of their hands.

Art

A very long paper might be written to describe the various uses to which art has been put in holding up the ideal of motherhood. The mother, with children at her breast, is the favorite theme of artists. The galleries of Europe are hung full of Madonnas of every age and degree. Poetry abounds in allusions to the sacredness and charm of motherhood, depicting the yearning of the adult for his mother's knee. Fiction is replete with happy and adoring mothers. Thousands of songs are written and sung concerning the ideal relation which exists between mother and child. In pursuing the mother-child theme through art one would not be led to suspect that society finds it necessary to make laws against contraception, infanticide, abortion, and infant desertion. Art holds up to view only the compensations of motherhood, leaving the other half of the theme in obscurity, and thus acting as a subtle ally of population.

Illusion

This is the last of Ross's categories to which I wish to refer. Ross says:

> In the taming of men there must be provided coil after coil to entangle the unruly one. Mankind must use snares as well as leading-strings, will-o-the-wisps as well as lanterns. The truth by all means, if it will promote obedience, but in any case obedience! We shall examine not creeds now, but the films, veils, hidden mirrors, and half lights by which men are duped as to that which lies nearest them, their own experience. This time we shall see men led captive, not by dogmas concerning a world beyond experience, but by artfully fostered misconceptions of the pains, satisfactions, and values lying under their very noses.

One of the most effective ways of creating the desired illusion about any matter is by concealing and tabooing the mention of all the painful and disagreeable circumstances connected with it. Thus there is a very stern social taboo on conversation about the processes of birth. The utmost care is taken to conceal the agonies and risks of child-birth from the young. Announcement is rarely made of the true cause of deaths from child-birth. The statistics of maternal mortality have been neglected by departments of health, and the few compilations which have been made have not achieved any wide publicity or popular discussion. Says Katharine Anthony, in her recent book on *Feminism in Germany and Scandinavia* (1915):

> There is no evidence that the death rate of women from child-birth has caused the governing classes many sleepless nights.

Anthony gives some statistics from Prussia (where the figures have been calculated), showing that

> between 1891 and 1900 11 per cent of the deaths of all women between the ages of twenty-five and forty years occurred in child-birth.... During forty years of peace Germany lost 400,000 mothers' lives, that is, ten times what she lost in soldiers' lives in the campaign of 1870 and 1871.

Such facts would be of wide public interest, especially to women, yet there is no tendency at all to spread them broadcast or to make propaganda of them. Public attention is constantly being called to the statistics of infant mortality, but the statistics of maternal mortality are neglected and suppressed.

The pains, the dangers, and risks of child-bearing are tabooed as subjects of conversation. The drudgery, the monotonous labor, and other disagreeable features of child-rearing are minimized by "the social guardians." On the other hand, the joys and compensations of motherhood are magnified and presented to consciousness on every hand. Thus the tendency is to create an illusion whereby motherhood will appear to consist of compensations only, and thus come to be desired by those for whom the illusion is intended.

There is one further class of devices for controlling women that does not seem to fit any of the categories mentioned by Ross. I refer to threats of evil consequence to those who refrain from child-bearing. This class of social devices I shall call "bugaboos." Medical men have done much to help population (and at the same time to increase obstetrical practice!) by inventing bugaboos. For example, it is frequently stated by medical men, and is quite generally believed by women, that if first child-birth is delayed until the age of thirty years the pains and dangers of the process will be very gravely increased, and that therefore women will find it advantageous to begin bearing children early in life. It is added that the younger the woman begins to bear the less suffering will be experienced. One looks in vain, however, for any objective evidence that such is the case. The statements appear to be founded on no array of facts whatever, and until they are so founded they lie under the suspicion of being merely devices for social control.

One also reads that women who bear children live longer on the average than those who do not, which is taken to mean that child-bearing has a favorable influence on longevity. It may well be that women who bear many children live longer than those who do not, but the only implication probably is that those women who could not endure the strain of repeated births died young, and thus naturally did not have many children. The facts may indeed be as above stated, and yet child-bearing may be distinctly prejudicial to longevity.

A third bugaboo is that if a child is reared alone, without brothers and sisters, he will grow up selfish, egoistic, and an undesirable citizen. Figures are, however, so far lacking to show the disastrous consequences of being an only child.

From these brief instances it seems very clear that "the social guardians" have not really believed that maternal instinct is alone a sufficient guaranty of population. They have made use of all possible social devices to insure not only child-bearing, but child-rearing. Belief, law, public opinion, illusion, education, art, and bugaboos have all been used to re-enforce maternal instinct. We shall never know just how much maternal instinct alone will do for population until all the forces and influences exemplified above have become inoperative. As soon as women become fully conscious of the fact that they have been and are controlled by these devices the latter will become useless, and we shall get a truer measure of maternal feeling.

> One who learns why society is urging him into the straight and narrow way will resist its pressure. One who sees clearly how he is controlled will thenceforth be emancipated. To betray the secrets of ascendancy is to forearm the individual in his struggle with society.

The time is coming, and is indeed almost at hand, when all the most intelligent women of the community, who are the most desirable child-bearers, will become conscious of the methods of social control. The type of normality will be questioned; the laws will be repealed and changed; enlightenment will prevail; belief will be seen to rest upon dogmas; illusion will fade away and give place to clearness of view; the bugaboos will lose their power to frighten. How will "the social guardians" induce women to bear a surplus population when all these cheap, effective methods no longer work?

The natural desire for children may, and probably will, always guarantee a stationary population, even if child-bearing should become a voluntary matter. But if a surplus population is desired for national aggrandizement, it would seem that there will remain but one effective social device whereby this can be secured, namely, *adequate compensation,* either in money or in fame. If it were possible to become rich or famous by bearing numerous fine children, many a woman would no doubt be eager to bring up eight or ten, though if acting at the dictation of maternal instinct only, she would have brought up but one or two. When the cheap devices no longer work, we shall expect expensive devices to replace them, if the same result is still desired by the governors of society.

If these matters could be clearly raised to consciousness, so that this aspect of human life could be managed rationally, instead of irrationally as at present, the social gain would be enormous—assuming always that the increased happiness and usefulness of women would, in general, be regarded as social gain.

READING 29

The Rape Culture

Dianne Herman (1984)

Herman's chapter highlights how our social values perpetuate rape through our images of masculinity. There has been much discussion about the relationship between pornography and rape in the past few years, and some fine research on this topic has been done (see, for instance, Donnerstein & Berkowitz, 1981; Linz, Donnerstein, & Penrod, 1988; Zillmann & Bryant, 1982, 1984; and the many articles in Malamuth & Donnerstein, 1984). Herman suggests that two very important relationships that have not been studied sufficiently are the relationships between rape and the construction of masculinity in our society, and between rape and our cultural acceptance of violence. (See also Readings 20–22.)

Though some of the statistics reported may have already changed somewhat by the time you read this selection, the issues are unfortunately the same. A recent, carefully conducted study of 6,159 students from 32 representative colleges and universities (Koss, Gidycz, and Wisniewski, 1987), found that "27.5% of college women reported experiencing and 7.7% of college men reported perpetrating an act that met legal definitions of rape, which includes attempts" (p. 168). That is a lot of people. Further, this rape victimization rate is ten to fifteen times greater than rates reported by the United States Government's 1984 National Crime Survey. Even using the lower rate admitted by these college men produces rates that are two to three times greater than those from the National Crime Survey. These rates must cause us to pause.

That there are so few personality characteristics associated with rapists suggests that there must be something in the situation that allows or drives aggression against women. That there are so few behavioral correlates associated with the women who are raped also suggests something beyond the particular individuals involved. Herman suggests that it is the broader value of masculinity that is the culprit. How might we test this hypothesis, and if supported, effect change in our society?

When Susan Griffin wrote, "I have never been free of the fear of rape," she touched a responsive chord in most women. Every woman knows the fear of being alone at home late at night or the terror that strikes her when she receives an obscene phone call. She knows also of the "mini-rapes"—the pinch in the crowded bus, the wolf whistle from a passing car, the stare of a man looking at her bust during a conversation. Griffin has argued, "Rape is a kind of terrorism which severely limits the freedom of women and makes women dependent on men."

Women live their lives according to a rape schedule.

> There is what might be called a universal curfew on women in this country. Whenever a woman walks alone at night, whenever she hitchhikes, she is aware that she is violating well-established rules of conduct and, as a result, that she faces the possibility of rape. If in one of these situations she *is* raped, the man will almost always escape prosecution and the woman will be made to feel responsible because she was somehow "asking for it."

One solution to this problem is suggested by Golda Meir. When a cabinet meeting discussed the number of assaults at night on women, one minister suggested that the women stay home after dark. Meir replied, "But it's the men who are attacking the women. If there's to be a curfew, let the men stay home, not the women." Golda Meir's suggestion wouldn't strike us as funny or odd if we did not assume that women must bear the responsibility for men's sexual aggression.

Underlying this view of rape is a traditional concept of male and female sexuality, one that assumes that males are sexually aggressive and females are sexually passive. Those sharing these assumptions conclude that rape is a natural act that arises out of a situation in which men are unrestrained by convention or threat of punishment. Thus the only way to stop rape is to prevent the opportunity for it to happen by insisting that women avoid "dangerous" situations or by providing a deterrent through stiff penalties. An example of this mentality is Judge Archie Simonson's 1977 explanation when he released on probation a fifteen-year-old boy who raped a girl in a high school stairwell. "This community is well-known to be sexually permissive," he said. "Should we punish a fifteen- or sixteen-year-old boy who reacts to it normally?" (Simonson's comment provoked a successful recall campaign by his Madison, Wisconsin, constituents. He was replaced by a female lawyer who won the judgeship with the support of local feminist groups.)

Most studies on rape take as a given the aggressive nature of male sexuality. Hans von Hentig wrote in the early fifties that the incidence of rape reflects a demographic imbalance, where there are too many males compared to females in the population. Yet studies sympathetic to his basic premise have found no relationship between rape and a lack of females for male sexual outlet. Along the same lines, proposals have been offered to make prostitution legal in the hope that the incidence of rape will decrease. However, as researchers point out, "Three cities that had allowed open prostitution actually experienced a decline in rape and other sexual assaults after prostitution was prohibited." Because rape is held to be a natural behavior, there have been few attempts to understand the cultural conditions that give rise to this crime.

Animals in their natural habitat do not rape, and many societies have existed where rape was not known. According to Margaret Mead in *Sex and*

Temperament, the Arapesh do not have "any conception of the male nature that might make rape understandable to them." Among the Arapesh, men and women are both expected to act with gentleness and concern. Thus there is no reason to maintain the assumption that rape is a natural act.

Anthropological studies like those of Margaret Mead have demonstrated that sexual attitudes and practices are learned, not instinctual. In this country people are raised to believe that men are sexually active and aggressive and women are sexually passive and submissive. Since it is assumed that men cannot control their desires, every young woman is taught that she must be the responsible party in any sexual encounter. In such a society men and women are trained to believe that the sexual act involves domination. Normal heterosexual relations are pictured as consisting of an aggressive male forcing himself on a female who seems to fear sex but unconsciously wants to be overpowered.

Because of the aggressive/passive, dominant/submissive, me-Tarzan/you-Jane nature of the relationship between the sexes in our culture, there is a close association between violence and sexuality. Words that are slang sexual terms, for example, frequently accompany assaultive behavior or gestures. "Fuck you" is meant as a brutal attack in verbal terms. In the popular culture, "James Bond alternately whips out his revolver and his cock, and though there is no known connection between the skills of a gun-fighter and love-making, pacifism seems suspiciously effeminate." The imagery of sexual relations between males and females in books, songs, advertising, and films is frequently that of a sadomasochistic relationship thinly veiled by a romantic facade. Thus it is very difficult in our society to differentiate rape from "normal" heterosexual relations. Indeed, our culture can be characterized as a rape culture because the image of heterosexual intercourse is based on a rape model of sexuality.

If healthy heterosexuality were characterized by loving, warm, and reciprocally satisfying actions, then rape could be defined as sex without consent, therefore involving either domination or violence. Instead, rape is legally defined as sexual intercourse by a male with a female, *other than his wife,* without the consent of the woman and effected by force, duress, intimidation, or deception as to the nature of the act. The spousal exemption in the law, which still remains in effect in thirty-three of the fifty states, means that a husband cannot be guilty of raping his wife, even if he forces intercourse against her will. The implication of this loophole is that *violent, unwanted* sex does not necessarily define rape. Instead, rape is *illegal* sex—that is, sexual assault by a man who has no legal rights over the woman. In other words, in the law's eyes violence in legal sexual intercourse is permissible, but sexual relations with a woman who is not one's property is not. The statutory rape laws support this contention very well. In this instance, rape is simply intercourse outside marriage with a minor, who is considered too young to render legal consent (as a minor, her property—her body—is still controlled by others).

From their inception, rape laws have been established not to protect women, but to protect women's property value for men.

> Society's view of rape was purely a matter of economics—of assets and liabilities. When a married woman was raped, her husband was wronged, not her. If she was unmarried, her father suffered since his investment depreciated. It was the monetary value of a woman which determined the gravity of the crime. Because she had no personal rights under the law, her own emotions simply didn't matter.

Because rape meant that precious merchandise was irreparably damaged, the severity of the punishment was dependent on whether the victim was a virgin. In some virgin rapes, biblical law ordered that the rapist marry the victim since she was now devalued property. The social status of the victim was also important, as a woman of higher social status was more valuable.

While these laws are no longer present in the same form, attitudes and customs have remained much the same. For example, "shotgun weddings" are still with us, and rape is far more likely to be prosecuted if the woman is a virgin of the middle or upper class who is attacked by a lower-class male. Gary LaFree recently examined the effect of race in the handling of 881 sexual assaults in a large midwestern city, and he found that black males who assaulted white women received more serious charges, longer sentences, and more severe punishment in terms of executed sentences and incarceration in the state penitentiary. On the other hand, rape is least prosecuted if the victim is black. The rape of poor, black women is not an offense against men of power. But as Eldridge Cleaver has explained, the black male who sexually assaults a white woman is seen as a vengeful castrator, deserving of the most severe punishment.

In a society in which a man's worth is measured by his ability to be aggressive, the rapist is demonstrating that he is more masculine than a man who cannot protect, hold on to, and control his woman. "In raping another man's woman, a man may aggrandize his own manhood and concurrently reduce that of another man." Rape is therefore an offense that one man commits against another. Many men perceive a sexual assault against a woman with whom they have been intimate as an attack against themselves. One husband whose wife was raped said, for example, "It's a matter of territorial imperative. I fantasized ways of getting back at him, like shoving a shot-gun down his throat and pulling the trigger until it quit clicking." Another husband admitted, "I wanted to kill that bastard. I wanted to destroy him for what he'd done to me." The overwhelming desire for revenge reflects two strong needs: revenge would not only allow men to express their anger at being humiliated but also serve to restore their self-esteem in socially prescribed ways (acting in a "manly," aggressive fashion).

The husband whose wife has been sexually violated not only may question his masculinity but also may feel that his wife participated in some way in her own victimization or enjoyed the experience. His self-esteem is thus lowered by his wife's presumed complicity as well as by the rapist's act.

Husbands who blame their wives may view the rape as marital infidelity. Victims have reported that their husband's inability to "adjust" to the fact that the rape had occurred was the cause of their divorce. Studies have shown a considerable difference in the way that men and women, in general, perceive the victim's causal role in the crime of rape. One group of researchers stated that "typically, males expressed greater agreement with the notion of a rape victim being responsible or in some way precipitating her victimization. Women, on the other hand, were apparently less willing to subscribe to such notions and perceived the rape victim to be less personally responsible."

One of the most surprising findings of studies on rape is that the rapist is normal in personality, appearance, intelligence, behavior, and sexual drive. According to Amir, the only significant psychological difference between the rapist and the normal, well-adjusted male appears to be the greater tendency of the former to express rage and violence. But this finding probably tends to overemphasize the aggressive personality characteristics of rapists, since generally only imprisoned rapists have been studied. Those few rapists who are sentenced to prison tend to be the more obviously violent offenders. In fact, studies by some researchers have found one type of rapist who is fairly meek and mild-mannered. What is clear is that the rapist is not an exotic freak. Rather, rape evolves out of a situation in which "normal" males feel a need to prove themselves to be "men" by displaying dominance over females.

In our society men demonstrate their competence as people by being "masculine." Part of this definition of masculinity involves a contempt for anything feminine or for females in general. Reported rapes, in fact, are frequently associated with some form of ridicule and sexual humiliation, such as urination on the victim, anal intercourse, fellatio, and ejaculation in the victim's face and hair. Insertion into the woman's vagina of broomsticks, bottles, and other phallic objects is not an uncommon coup de grace. The overvaluing of toughness expresses itself in a disregard for anything associated with fragility. In the rapist's view, his assertion of maleness is automatically tied to a violent repudiation of anything feminine.

Nothing supports more convincingly the premise that rape in our society is the act of a male attempting to assert his masculinity than the studies that have been conducted on homosexual rapes in prisons. Interestingly, researchers have discovered that aggressors in prison rape cases usually have little or no prior history of homosexual behavior. They do not consider themselves homosexuals, and neither do the other inmates. Rather, they equate their actions with those of an aggressive, heterosexual male. They are often called "jockers" or "wolves" by other inmates, terms that characterize them as males. One researcher commented with some astonishment:

> We were struck by the fact that the typical sexual aggressor does not consider himself to be a homosexual, or even to have engaged in homosexual acts. This seems to be based upon his startlingly primitive view of sexual relationships, one that defines as male whichever partner is aggressive and as homosexual whichever partner is passive.

While the other inmates and the aggressors consider their behavior normal under circumstances of heterosexual deprivation, Davis has noted that sexual release is not the primary motivation of the rapist. Rather the motive appears to be the need of some males in prison to exercise control and domination over others.

> A primary goal of the sexual aggressor, it is clear, is the conquest and degradation of his victim. We repeatedly found that aggressors used such language as "Fight or fuck," "We're gonna make a girl out of you."

The attempt to control other men, and in fact to transform them into women (passive, sexual objects), demonstrates to the rapist himself and to others of the prison population that he is in fact a "real man." Genet wrote, "A male that fucks another male is a double-male." Being removed from the heterosexual world, the prison rapist needs to affirm his identity as a male by being dominant over less "masculine" men. "A man who has become accustomed to validating his masculinity through regular interaction with members of the opposite sex may suddenly find his ego-image in grave jeopardy once a prison sentence consigns him to an all-male world." Imprisonment knocks out whatever props the rapist may have established to prove his masculinity. Only the demonstration of sexual and physical prowess can stave off feelings of emasculation in the limited environment of the prison.

Many prison rapists display little, if any, concern for the attitudes or feelings of their partners. One study reported that a group of seventeen men raped one inmate over the course of four hours. Another prisoner was raped repeatedly even after he was bleeding from his rectum, had become ill, and had vomited. But the callousness of the rapist's attitude toward his victim is required by the prison culture. For, in the narrow view of sexuality subscribed to by most inmates, one is either a "woman" or a "man." If any member of the prison population displays emotion or vulnerability, he is likely to be tagged a "woman" and is therefore open to sexual attack. It is for this reason that many inmates refuse to aid the victim and may actually take part in a gang-bang themselves. In a world where one is either dominant and a rapist or submissive and a victim, the pressures to be the former are so great that many men find themselves forced to be the sexual violators of others.

The rapist's attraction to dominance and violence stems from his interpretation of sexuality—"man ravishes, woman submits." Many rapists believe that women enjoy sadomasochistic sex. One group of authors has said of the rape offender:

He sees her struggle and protestation not as a refusal but as part of her own sexual excitement. "Women like to get roughed up, they enjoy a good fight." This belief is maintained even when the victim is literally fighting for her life and the offender has to brutally injure her to force her to submit to intercourse.

In one instance where a sixty-three-year-old woman was robbed and raped at gunpoint by a twenty-four-year-old man, her assailant threw her a kiss and said before running away, "I bet I made your day." Some offenders have been incredulous when arrested, complaining that they may have been a little rough but that the women enjoyed their advances.

One of the most overlooked aspects of rape is that it is frequently a group phenomenon. In Amir's study, 43 percent of the cases involved two or more offenders. Out of a total of 646 cases, 370 were single rapes, 105 were pair rapes, and 171 were group rapes. The rapist in a group rape is not only expressing his hostility toward women and asserting his masculinity to himself but also proving his manhood to others. Group rapes are usually characterized by a considerable amount of violence, "even though this is one situation in which no brutality, no threat even, would be necessary to subdue the victim." The measure of masculinity is not just the ability to have sexual intercourse with a female but also the ability to exert control over her, and control is equated with dominance. "Through the forcing of the victim to sexual relations the rapist expresses, proves, tests, and gains his image of masculinity, which involves sexual as well as social dominance over women." In addition, acts of sexual humiliation are more common in group rapes. The group most likely to be offenders in either pair or group rapes are youths in the ten-to-fourteen age bracket.

In general, rapists tend to be very young. Amir found offenders were most likely to be between fifteen and nineteen years old. According to the *Uniform Crime Reports,* published by the FBI, the age group of males between sixteen and twenty-four has the greatest concentration of arrests for forcible rape. Of the men charged with this crime in 1981, 52 percent were under twenty-five, with 27 percent of the arrestees being in the eighteen-to-twenty-two age group. On reflection this should come as no surprise, for adolescence is the time when most males probably feel the most doubts about their masculinity and the consequent need to affirm it. Brownmiller captures this insight in a personal reflection:

> They are desperately trying to learn the way to be successful men. When I have stood, almost mesmerized, on my Fourteenth Street subway platform and watched a gang of youths methodically assault a gum machine for its pennies—in escalation of a dare—I could only think *That could be my body.*

Perhaps this need of some men to prove their masculinity to themselves and to others explains why rape is so common in war. The U.S. military has generally eulogized the values of masculinity and emphasized aggressiveness: the Marines built their image on their ability to form "men" out of adolescent youths. For those who lead armies, stressing that soldiers are "real men" is a perfect mechanism by which to keep in line those who might otherwise question the validity of a military conquest. Cowardice in the face of the enemy is equated with femininity. At the same time, however, the real dangers of combat cause many men to question their masculinity. Such situations are ripe for rape.

> In 1966, an American patrol held a 19-year-old Vietnamese girl captive for several days, taking turns raping her and finally murdering her. The sergeant planned the crime in advance, telling the soldiers during the mission's briefing that the girl would improve their "morale." When one soldier refused to take part in the rape, the sergeant called him "queer" and "chicken," another testified later that he joined in the assault to avoid such insults.

While violence is particularly associated with rape, it is not absent from ordinary heterosexual relations. In Kirkpatrick and Kanin's study of male sexual aggression in dating and courtship relations in the late 1950s, first-semester college women were asked to report forceful sexual attempts they considered offensive. Behavior considered repugnant to the women included forced necking, forced petting above and below the waist, attempted intercourse, and rape. Of the 291 responding women, 56 percent reported themselves offended at least once during the academic year at some level of erotic intimacy. A large proportion of these were serious sexual assaults.

> The experiences of being offended were not altogether associated with trivial situations as shown by the fact that 20.9% were offended by forceful attempts to intercourse and 6.2% by "aggressively forceful attempts at sexual intercourse in the course of which menacing threats or coercive infliction of physical pain were employed."

Those women most likely to experience forced petting or intercourse were regular dates, "pinned" or engaged to their attackers. *Ms.* magazine recently reported on a series of studies on college campuses confirming that, even given new and more liberal attitudes about premarital sex and women's liberation, date rape and other forms of acquaintance rape may be reaching epidemic proportions in higher education. In some cases women have even been assaulted by men ostensibly acting as protective escorts to prevent rape. *Cosmopolitan* magazine found in its September 1980 survey that, of the more than 106,000 women who responded, 24 percent stated that they had been raped at least once: 51 percent of those had been raped by friends, 37 percent by strangers, 18 percent by relatives, and 3 percent by husbands.

Studies such as these, in which women report anonymously to researchers instead of to legal authorities, seem to indicate that rape is a crime commonly committed by an assailant who is known to the victim. Even in cases where women do report to police, victim and offender are frequently acquainted. In a 1972 study undertaken by the National League of Cities, it was found that victim-offender relationships differed from city to city but that generally between 33 percent and 48 percent of victims reporting knew their attacker.

Indeed, one of the most common myths attached to the crime of rape is the notion that the rapist is a stranger to his victim. When the word *rape* is mentioned, most people conjure up images of a woman alone walking late at night in a bad section of a large city. She is being followed by a tall, dark (black?) male who overtakes her, throws her in an alley, and rapes her. Perhaps the only accurate parts of this image are that rape is much more likely to occur in urban areas and at night.

The myth that rape is committed only by a stranger serves to keep many women from reporting an unpleasant sexual episode with a man known to them—or even defining such an incident as attempted rape. It also serves to keep the men involved from construing their actions to be those of a rapist.

> The male learns the same basic mythology of rape as the woman. He is aware of the notion that rape can only be committed by a stranger. This definition can serve as a justification since it precludes the possibility that he can be called a rapist after an encounter with a woman who knew his name.

The fact that victim and offender are acquainted in such a high percentage of reported cases has sometimes been interpreted to mean that large numbers of rapes are precipitated by the victim. Amir classified rape cases as victim-precipitated when

> the victims actually—or so it was interpreted by the offender—agreed to sexual relations but retracted before the actual act or did not resist strongly enough when the suggestion was made by the offenders. The term applies also to cases in which the victim enters vulnerable situations charged with sexuality, especially when she uses what could be taken as an invitation to sexual relations.

Despite such a broad definition, Amir found that only 19 percent of all rapes in his study were victim-precipitated. Some of the factors characteristic of these types of rapes were the victim's "bad" reputation; the fact that the victim met the offender in a bar, at a picnic, or at a party; or the involvement of the victim and the offender in a "primary relationship," excluding relatives.

It is difficult to imagine, however, that offenders could misinterpret the sexual signals they thought they were receiving given the finding that the closer the relationship between the participants in rape, the greater is the use of physical force. In fact, in Amir's study, neighbors and acquaintances were the most likely to engage in brutal rape. Amir was forced to conclude that rape involving people who know each other is not the result of a sexual encounter in which a woman "teases" a man.

> In general, the analysis of the interpersonal relations between victim and offender lent support to those who reject the myth of the offender who attacks victims unknown to him. But equally rejected is the notion that rape is generally an affair between, or a result of intimate relations between victim and rapist.

Once it is understood that rape occurs quite commonly between people who are acquainted, other findings about this crime start to make sense. Most studies, for example, report that about half of all rapes occur in the victim's or rapist's home. Another 15 percent occur in automobiles. Car rapes are especially likely to involve participants who are intimate.

In addition, the rapist and his victim are generally of the same race and age: 90 percent of all reported rapes are intraracial, not interracial, occurrences. One reason the myth dies hard that black men rape white women is because these cases frequently receive the most publicity. In a study of rape in Philadelphia, it was discovered that the two major newspapers, when they reported on rape cases, mentioned mainly inter-racial offenses. Intraracial rapes were only occasionally mentioned.

The myth also survives that most rapes are spontaneous. However, statistics compiled from reported rapes show that the overwhelming majority are planned. In one study, 71 percent of all reported rapes were prearranged, and another 11 percent were partially planned. Only 18 percent were impulsive acts. Planning is most common in cases of group rape, but, even when the rapist is acting alone a majority of the rapes involve some manipulations on the part of the offender to place his victim in a vulnerable situation that he can exploit.

It is often assumed that the rapist had no prior intent to commit rape but was overcome by the sexual provocations of his victim. The conventional scenario is one of a man who is sexually aroused by a seductive woman. But the image of the rape victim as seductive and enticing is also at odds with reality. Rapes have been committed on females as young as six months and as old as ninety-three years. Most victims tend to be very young. In Amir's study, 20 percent were between ten and fourteen; another 25 percent were between fifteen and nineteen. According to data compiled in 1974 by Women Organized Against Rape, 41 percent of rape victims seen in hospital emergency rooms in Philadelphia were sixteen or younger. The category with the highest frequency of victims was the range between thirteen and sixteen years old.

Most convicted rapists tend to project the blame on others, particularly the victim. Schultz found that the sex offender is twice as likely to insist on his innocence as the general offender. "In two-thirds of the cases one hears, 'I'm here on a phoney beef,' or 'I might have been a little rough with her but she was asking for it,' or 'I might have done it but I was too drunk to remember.'" They also rationalize the act by labeling their victims "bad" women.

The amazing thing is that the offender's view of the situation and of his victim is not very far removed from the view held by society in general. Just as the rapist blames his victim, so do the police, prosecutors, judges, juries, friends, and relatives.

Women have often complained that their veracity is in question when they report charges of rape. The first public agency with which a woman makes contact when she reports a rape is usually the police department, and it has often been less than sympathetic to rape complaints. Some officers have actually asked victims questions such as, "How many orgasms did you have?" and "Didn't I pick you up last week for prostitution?" A 1971 California police textbook, *Patrol Procedure,* begins its discussion on sexual assaults with the statement, "Forcible rape is one of the most falsely reported crimes."

The police have considerable discretion in determining whether a crime has been committed. In 1976, according to the FBI, 19 percent of all forcible rapes reported to the police were unfounded. *Unfounding* simply means that the police decide not to advise prosecution.

A study conducted in 1966 of the procedures used by the Philadelphia Police Department in unfounding rape cases discovered that one of the major factors for the unfounding of a case was the moral appraisal of the victim by the police. For example, if the woman had been drinking, police in most instances dismissed her charges. Police were also most likely to unfound cases involving black participants and least likely to do so when victim and offender were both white. In a more recent study in a large midwestern city, involving an analysis of 905 sexual assault complaints over a six-year period, it was found that police practices have become less discriminatory. But when police felt the victim had been guilty of "misconduct," they still were reluctant to pursue charges.

According to many studies, one of the most frequent causes of unfounding rape is a prior relationship between the participants. In the Philadelphia study, 43 percent of all date rapes were

unfounded. The police, according to the researcher, seemed to be more concerned that the victim had "assumed the risk" than they were with the fact that she had not given consent to intercourse.

Another common reason police unfound cases is the apparent lack of force in the rape situation. The extent of injuries seems to be even more important in the decision to unfound than whether the offender had a weapon. There is no requirement that a businessman must either forcibly resist when mugged or forfeit protection under the law. But proof of rape, both to the police and in court, is often in the form of resistance, and resistance is substantiated by the extent of injuries suffered by the victim. Yet local police departments frequently advise women not to resist if faced with the possibility of rape.

> In a confusion partially of their own making, local police precincts point out contradictory messages: they "unfound" a rape case because, by the rule of their own male logic, the woman did not show normal resistance; they report on an especially brutal rape case and announce to the press that the multiple stab wounds were the work of an assailant who was enraged because the woman resisted.

In other words the victim is told that if she was raped it was because she did not resist enough. But if she fights back and is raped and otherwise assaulted, police blame her again for bringing about her own injuries because of her resistance.

The number of unfounded rapes is probably underestimated because of police practices. Police may turn away a complaint and not file an incident report at all. Or rape complaints may be categorized as "investigations of persons"— a catchall for incidents requiring an investigation report but for which there is insufficient information for classification into other crime categories. If further investigation confirms police doubts and the case is closed, then the incident is not recorded as an unfounded rape complaint. Because of these police practices, one author estimates that the FBI's 19 percent unfounding rate is far too low and that the true figure is probably at least 50 percent. Other investigators who have interviewed police personnel have found from their comments that the police believe 80 percent to 90 percent of the rapes reported to them are not really rapes. In addition, the Philadelphia study found that the prosecutor's office was even less likely than the police to believe that the victim had been forced against her will to have intercourse.

In reported rape cases where police *do* believe the victim, only about half of the rape offenders are actually arrested. Even if the police catch up with an accused rapist, however, he is unlikely to be convicted. In 1976, for example, of all adult men arrested in rape cases, only 67 percent were prosecuted for rape, and of these, 49 percent were acquitted or had the charges dismissed, while another 9 percent were found guilty of lesser offenses. Even though they constitute a large proportion of offenders, juveniles were even more likely to be treated leniently by the courts, with only 20 percent of those arrested being officially charged with forcible rape. In some jurisdictions, the conviction rate, based on arrests, is only 3 percent.

Using FBI statistics, LeGrand calculated that

a man who rapes a woman who reports the rape to police has roughly seven chances out of eight of walking away without any conviction. Assuming only one woman in five reports the rape, his chances increase to 39 out of 40. If these figures take into account the high percentage of those who receive probation or suspended sentences, his chances of escaping incarceration are in the vicinity of 98 to 99 out of 100. Forcible rape has a lower conviction rate than any other crime listed in the *Uniform Crime Reports.*

Most individuals convicted of rape serve a sentence of no longer than four years, except when the victim is white and the offender is black. Of the 455 men executed for rape from 1930 to 1967,

405 were black. Black males, however, do not uniformly receive the most severe punishment. If their victims are black females, they are likely to receive the most lenient sentences. According to a study of rape convictions in Baltimore in 1967: "Of the four categories of rapist and victim in a racial mix, blacks received the stiffest sentences for raping white women and the mildest sentences for raping black women."

There is a bias in the criminal justice system against rape complaints that seems to be based on the fear that women frequently accuse innocent men of rape. This position is sometimes stated explicitly, for example, in this comment in the *University of Pennsylvania Law Review:*

Women often falsely accuse men of sexual attacks to extort money, to force marriage, to satisfy a childish desire for notoriety, or to attain personal revenge. Their motives include hatred, a sense of shame after consenting to illicit intercourse, especially when pregnancy results, and delusion.

Many states still allow judges to include in the jury charge a version of the "Hale instructions": "Rape is an accusation easily made and hard to be proved, and harder to be defended by the party accused, though never so innocent."

These kinds of attitudes, however, are not limited to the legal profession. The general public believes that "a woman with her skirt up can run faster than a man with his pants down," and medical experts argue that "rape cannot be perpetrated *by one man* alone on an adult woman of good health and vigor." The famous sexologist Alfred Kinsey has stated that the only difference between a rape and a good time depends on whether the girl's parents were awake when she finally got home.

The claim that women easily make false accusations of rape is refuted even by the FBI. According to the *Uniform Crime Report,* "Even with the advent of rape crisis centers and an improved awareness by police dealing with rape victims, forcible rape, a violent crime against the person, is still recognized as one of the most underreported of all Index crimes." Medea and Thompson discovered that 70 percent of the women in their sample did not report the crime. A number of studies have estimated that only 20 percent of all forcible rapes are reported to authorities.

The disbelief of judges, juries, police, and prosecutors that a rape victim faces is compounded by the distrust she encounters from family and friends when she admits she has been raped. Responses of parents, relatives, friends, and spouses are either anger at the victim for being foolish enough to get raped or anger at the rapist for the humiliation and shame that family members will suffer as a result of the attack.

Burgess and Holmstrom recorded three responses from parents of child victims of rape:

1. Blaming the assailant—"If we ever find out who did it, there won't be enough left to pick him up if I see him."
2. Blaming the child—"We have her on punishment for one month. She can't go out and see any of her friends. Only one friend she can telephone and no friends permitted in the house. This is because of what happened."
3. Blaming themselves—"My wife is not well and says she is going to commit suicide. She says she is not good as a mother and wants to kill herself. What should I do?"

Facing disbelief on every side, victims do blame themselves. In fact, much of the psychological discomfort suffered by women who have been raped stems from their belief that they were in part responsible for their own sexual violation. Women frequently ask themselves why they let it happen. "There is a strong desire for the victim to try and think of how she could undo what has happened. She reports going over in her mind how she might have escaped from the assailant, how she might have handled the situation differently." For many women the aftermath of the rape is worse than the physical pain of the actual rape. They are plagued by feelings

of guilt, shame, loss of self-esteem, and humiliation. Many rapes go unreported because victims have been unjustifiably convinced that they were guilty of precipitating the attack. This is even more probable in cases where the victim knows the offender. Some women have confessed that it was only when they were involved in more healthy relationships that they realized that their initial introduction into sex was rape.

The attitude of victims of rape can be characterized more as despair than as resentment or anger. They have been taught to assume the responsibility for male sexuality—and many have. When they are raped, they feel that they have failed and that they are at fault. Medea and Thompson have argued that many female rape victims feel like sentinels who fell asleep while on guard duty.

> The male is the aggressor, the soldier laying siege to the castle; the woman is the guardian of the gate, and defender of the sacred treasure. If the male forces his way in with a battering ram and captures the treasure, he has succeeded in his purpose. There is no cause for guilt or remorse. The woman, on the other hand, has failed in her purpose. She has allowed the treasure to be taken and feels herself to be at fault. She suffers from feelings of guilt, besides the feelings of violation, humiliation and defeat.

In a rape culture, even the victims believe that men are naturally sexual aggressors. Their response to the rape is to blame themselves for not taking proper precautions rather than to demand a change in the behavior of men.

As long as sex in our society is construed as a dirty, low, and violent act involving domination of a male over a female, rape will remain a common occurrence. The erotization of male dominance means that whenever women are in a subordinate position to men the likelihood for sexual assault is great. We are beginning to see that rape is not the only way in which women are sexually victimized, and that other forms of sexual exploitation of women are rampant in our society. Feminists have raised our consciousness about rape by developing rape crisis centers and other programs to assist victims and their families, reforming laws and challenging politicians, training professionals in medicine and the criminal justice system, and educating women and the general public on the subject. They are also enlightening us about pornography; sexual harassment on the job and in higher education; sexual exploitation in doctor, dentist, and therapist relations with patients; and sexual assault in the family, such as incest and rape in marriage.

Rape is the logical outcome if men act according to the "masculine mystique" and women act according to the "feminine mystique." But rape does not have to occur. Its presence is an indication of how widely held are traditional views of appropriate male and female behavior and how strongly enforced they are. Our society is a rape culture because it fosters and encourages rape by teaching males and females that it is natural and normal for sexual relations to involve aggressive behavior on the part of males. To see an end to rape, people must be able to envision a relationship between the sexes that involves sharing, warmth, and equality and to bring about a social system in which those values are fostered.

some very real issues are underlying them.* Are men and women *that* different? What are the magnitude and direction of differences? And for which behaviors during which situations?

Of all the differences that exist between people in our society, perhaps none is as important in determining what your own personal world is like as whether you are male or female. It is not surprising then that social psychologists have been interested in research on gender issues. In this reading, Deaux describes the three major approaches found in the burgeoning literature on sex and gender. And she highlights the complexity of human behavior in the tradition of Lewin (1935; Reading 3), who first proposed the importance of studying the person-situation interaction. Deaux goes further, however, by identifying specific aspects of the active and dynamic process by which gender and related behavior is individually and socially constructed within social interaction. She also suggests directions for future research.

In recent work, Deaux and Major (1987; 1990) have followed that advice, developing a complex, comprehensive model that examines the influence of gender within the dynamic sociocultural context. Two claims of the model are (1) that gender-based behavior is constructed within dyadic interaction, which itself changes over time and situation, and (2) that this process of social instruction is an active process in which individuals make concurrent choices about their own behavior and the behavior of others.

READING 30

From Individual Differences to Social Categories: Analysis of a Decade's Research on Gender

Kay Deaux (1984)

"Why can't a woman be more like a man?" "Men, you can't live with them, and you can't live without them." While these and similar ideas make for great Broadway songs and plots for movies,

Recent research on sex and gender is analyzed in terms of three major approaches: (a) sex as a subject variable; (b) individual differences in masculinity, femininity, and androgyny; and (c) sex as a social category. Main effect differences of subject sex are found to be surprisingly small in most cases, and the status of androgyny is uncertain, limiting the potential of the first two approaches. The impact of sex as a social category is considerable, but

---

*Editors' note: Speaking of values, we can learn a tremendous amount about our cultural beliefs by studying popular songs. For example, can you imagine Eliza Doolittle singing "Why can't a man be more like a woman?" And what kind of battle mentality is invoked in the second quote?

more detailed research is needed. Further advances in understanding gender will depend on more process-oriented approaches that will take into account both subject and social category factors.

During the past decade, research related to sex and gender has accelerated. Imposing some structure on this proliferating literature is a necessary task. The analysis presented here emphasizes three distinct approaches. The first is consideration of sex as a subject variable (Grady, 1979, 1981; Unger, 1979). This is perhaps the most traditional approach and attempts to determine how men and women are different in any of a multitudinous number of behaviors, traits, and capabilities. In a second and more recent approach, the emphasis remains on individual subject differences, but differences of a psychological rather than demographic nature. Exemplifying this approach is the abundant literature on masculinity, femininity, and the immensely popular but theoretically uncertain concept of androgyny. The third approach takes a somewhat different perspective. Rather than looking for differences between women and men, or between individuals differing in masculinity and femininity, this approach concerns responses made to the categories of male and female, and the variables that may affect perceptions of gender.

Although discussions of gender often cross these boundaries freely, the three approaches are fundamentally different in their assumptions and implications. Awareness of these distinctions is a necessary prerequisite to the advancement of theory. Given the abundance of recent literature, this review is necessarily selective, and in general the perspective is that of a social psychologist. For each of the three approaches, selected research will be presented to illustrate the major issues and controversies. An assessmen of each area will be made, and suggestions will be offered for future research.

INDIVIDUAL DIFFERENCES

Sex as a Subject Variable

Maccoby and Jacklin's 1974 book, *The Psychology of Sex Differences,* provides a classic statement of the approach to sex as a subject variable. In this ambitious work, the authors attempted to survey all of the available literature on sex differences in a wide variety of areas, including cognitive functions, temperment, and social behavior. As the authors state, "Our objective is to sift the evidence to determine which of the many beliefs about sex differences have a solid basis in fact and which do not" (Maccoby & Jacklin, 1974, p. vii). On the basis of their review of more than 1,400 published studies, these authors concluded that very few sex differences have been substantiated.[1] They argued that the evidence supported only four clear differences between males and females. Three of these differences are in the areas of cognitive and intellectual skills: male superiority in mathematical and visual-spatial abilities, and female superiority in verbal abilities. Only in one area of social behavior—aggression—were sex differences believed to be supported, in this case showing that males are more aggressive than females. Although Maccoby and Jacklin pointed to only four areas in which clear sex differences appear, they acknowledged that many other areas had received insufficient investigation to establish either the presence or absence of sex differences. Much of the research during the 1970s attempted to correct this deficit. Thus, to note only a small sample of areas that received attention, investigators have considered possible sex differences in conformity, aggression, prosocial behavior, reward allocation, nonverbal behavior, and love—in short, in nearly every area of social behavior that psy-

---

[1] These conclusions have not gone unchallenged, however. For one critique, see Block (1976).

chologists had previously explored without a specific interest in sex.

Research on causal attributions for performance can serve as an example of the analysis of sex differences. The fertile theoretical soil of Fritz Heider (1958) has been hoed by many investigators in the past 25 years. Within the specific area of performance attribution, Bernard Weiner and his colleagues (Weiner et al., 1971) are best known for their development of a model for categorizing the explanations that people offer for their success and failure. In its simplest form, this model emphasizes two dimensions: temporary-stable and internal-external.

In a direct test of sex differences in causal attribution patterns, Deaux and Farris (1977) asked male and female subjects to explain successful performance on an anagram task. Although the task itself is sex-neutral, instructions were varied to make it appear that the task was typically performed better by either males or females. Differences between men and women occurred primarily when the task was labeled masculine. In that case men expected to do better, evaluated their performance more favorably (despite no differences in actual performance), and claimed more ability and less luck. In contrast, when the task was labeled feminine, there were few differences in how the sexes evaluated their performance, the only exception being a tendency for women to continue to invoke luck to a greater degree.

From this perspective, it becomes particularly important to look at the nature of the task as a critical factor in influencing expectations. As noted earlier, the sex linkage of the task is one influential aspect. When the task was labeled feminine, the Deaux and Farris study found no differences in expectations and few differences in attributions. Other investigators, such as Lenney (1977, 1981), have also explored the conditions under which sex differences in expectations will be absent.

The same form of analysis applies to the understanding of preferences for luck and skill ac-

tivities. Once again, these choices can be best understood in the context of expectancies for performance: Both women and men will choose that activity for which their expectancy of success is higher. In the Deaux, White, and Farris (1975) study, the use of an electronic dart game revealed the expectancies for males to be higher than females when skill instructions were given. Yet if the task is in some way male-linked, the observed preferences may not indicate a general sex difference in choices of luck or skill, but rather an apparent sex difference that depends on specific situational features. In fact, a recent study by Karabenick, Sweeney, and Penrose (1983) has shown the latter interpretation to be the true one. When these investigators varied luck and skill activities, including social skills and knowledge of infants as well as dart game performance, women showed a preference for skill rather than luck in the more female-linked activities. Consistent with these preferences was evidence that women's expectations for performance on female-linked skill activities exceeded those for chance.

Thus, an important qualification to findings of sex differences has been uncovered during the past decade. Many observed sex differences are not durable main effects, but rather are influenced by task characteristics, resulting in frequent interactions between sex of subject and sex-linkage of task. Although argued in the context of attribution research, this principle is far more general in its application, applying to a wide variety of social settings. To cite just a few additional examples, studies of helping behavior, reward allocation, and conformity have all found evidence of the influence of task characteristics on the direction and size of sex differences. (See Deaux, 1977; Major & Deaux, 1982, for a more extensive discussion of some of these areas.) Consequently, it behooves the investigator to pay particular attention to the selection of tasks: Some tasks may not be neutral arenas for a test of possible sex differences, but rather influential sources of those differences.

Several review papers, each dealing with an extensive body of literature in some circumscribed area of social behavior, have revealed a second important limitation to the traditional sex-of-subject approach. To cite just a few examples, there have been Eagly's analyses of the social influence literature (Eagly, 1978; Eagly & Carli, 1981); Hall's review of sex differences in nonverbal decoding (Hall, 1978); and analyses of the aggression literature by J. S. Hyde (1982) and by Frodi, Macaulay, and Thome (1977). Without going into detail on each of these contributions, at least three general conclusions can be drawn. First, reliable sex differences can be observed in some areas that were not included on Maccoby and Jacklin's list of four. For example, women are more likely to conform in group-pressure settings and are more susceptible to attempts to persuade. Women are also superior in decoding nonverbal messages.

A second conclusion provides an important qualification of the first. Although these main effects are established, they are often qualified by interactions. Thus, Eagly and Carli found that women conform significantly more in face-to-face interaction but not reliably so in situations that lack surveillance. The Eagly and Carli analysis also revealed disturbing evidence of interactions with sex of author: Authors are more likely to report behaviors that are socially desirable for members of their own sex. Thus, male authors are more likely to report evidence of female conformity or male independence; female authorship is associated with finding greater female superiority in nonverbal decoding.

Situational factors also emerged as important qualifications in the Frodi et al. (1977) analysis of aggression. Contrary to the conclusions of Maccoby and Jacklin that sex differences are consistently in evidence in aggressive behavior, Frodi and her colleagues found much more limited evidence for sex differences. Further, they reported numerous situational factors that appear to elicit or minimize differences between women and men. For example, sex of the instigator or the victim, arousal of anxiety or guilt, and certain types of external aggressive cues are related to observed sex differences in aggressive behavior.

Perhaps the more important message from these reviews, however, is the relative weakness of subject sex as a determinant of behavior, even when reliable main effects are found. Through meta-analytic procedures, many of the review authors have been able to estimate the percentage of variance accounted for by sex. Their results are important in the caution that they suggest. In Eagly and Carli's review of social influence, sex differences in influenceability accounted for approximately 1% of the variance. Similarly, Hall (1978) reported that less than 4% of the variance in nonverbal decoding was explained by sex. J. S. Hyde's (1982) recent assessment of the aggression literature found a median variance estimate of 5%. Analysis of the attribution data also suggests only a limited portion of variance due to sex of subject (Frieze, Whitley, Hanusa, & McHugh, 1982; Sohn, 1982). Finally, Hyde (1981) recently analyzed those studies reported by Maccoby and Jacklin to substantiate sex differences in verbal, quantitative, and visual-spatial ability. She found that sex accounted for approximately 1% of variance in verbal ability, 1% in quantitative ability, and 4.5% of visual-spatial ability. Thus, although additional evidence remains to be gathered, 5% may approximate the upper boundary for the explanatory power of subject-sex main effects in specific social and cognitive behaviors.

To summarize this line of research, sex-of-subject differences are less pervasive than many have thought. Main effects of sex are frequently qualified by situational interactions, and the selection of tasks plays a critical role in eliciting or suppressing differences. Furthermore, the amount of variance accounted for by sex, even when main effects are reliable, is typically quite small. Thus, when any particular behavior is considered, differences between males and females may be of relatively little consequence. Approaching sex as a subject variable, although a popular pursuit with a long history, may not be the most productive route for understanding gender, at least in its simplest form.

Yet we cannot dismiss this approach so readily without some additional considerations. The majority of sex-difference analyses have focused on a specific behavior, often observed in the laboratory with a selected subject population. Such settings may put more stress on what a subject *can* do than on what she or he *will* do given free choice in a more natural environment. Further, as Eagly (1983) has observed, the pressures of the laboratory experiment may emphasize the subject role to the exclusion of more complex sex-related roles that may be prevalent in the field. Consequently, we cannot deny the potential relevance of sex of subject without more careful consideration of patterns of choice and bahavior in settings less constrained than the laboratory. Further, as will be discussed later, the influence of stereotypes and expectations of others can exert differential influence on males and females, and thus may elicit sex-related patterns of behavior in some situations.

Masculinity, Femininity, and Androgyny

Psychologists have long recognized the limitations of sex as a psychological variable. Among other problems, it is descriptive rather than conceptual and dischotomous rather than continuous (Deaux, 1977). As such, it serves as only a gross marker in predicting individual differences in behavior.

Early in the history of research related to gender, psychologists developed a variety of instruments that would assess masculinity-femininity as a continuous psychological variable, ranging from high masculinity at one end of the dimension to high femininity at the other end. In 1973, Constantinople presented an influential critique of these early measures, carefully assessing three of the assumptions on which such scales were founded. In brief, Constantinople (1973) questioned whether masculinity and femininity are

best represented as bipolar opposites, whether the concept is undimensional, and whether it is best defined in terms of sex differences in item responses. She concluded that none of these assumptions were justified.

Although earlier writers such as Jung and Bakan had discussed the independence of masculine and feminine patterns, or agency and communion in Bakan's (1966) terms, the empirical attention to this distinction mushroomed in the 1970s, with the development of a number of scales to assess masculinity and femininity as separate and orthogonal constructs. The best-known of these measures are the Bem Sex Role Inventory (BSRI), developed by Sandra Bem (1974), and the Personal Attributes Questionnaire (PAQ), developed by Janet Spence and Robert Helmreich (Spence, Helmreich, & Stapp, 1974). Other measures with similar intent have been offered by Berzins (Berzins, Welling, & Wetter, 1978), Heilbrun (1976), and others.

The attributes included under the androgyny umbrella are considerable. As originally stated by Bem, androgynous people should be more flexible in their behavior, be able to perform masculine tasks as well as the more traditionally masculine sex-typed persons, and be able to perform feminine tasks as well as traditionally feminine sex-typed persons. (Biological sex was considered irrelevant to these predictions.) At a theoretical level, Bem's conception of androgyny and the BSRI is broad. It assumes that various components of sex-related behavior, such as traits, role behaviors, and interpersonal styles, are all part of a single domain.

Equally responsible for the considerable attention gained by androgyny both within and without the scientific community is the openly sociopolitical context that Bem established. Not only was androgyny to be a particular conceptual focus, it was also proclaimed as a value. Thus it was good and wise and liberal to be androgynous, and mental health was proposed to be synonymous with androgynous scores. Androgyny soon became a code word for an egalitarian, gender-free society, and disciples have advocated androgynous therapy, androgynous curricula for school children, and androgynous criteria for professional positions. The value of such attempts can be debated; it is certainly clear that they go far beyond what the scientific data base would allow.

Not surprisingly, a backlash to androgyny has developed in the 1980s. Writers of various political persuasions have debated the value of androgyny, ranging from questions as to whether the androgynous person is a product of an over-individualized Western perspective and a poor alternative to traditional male-female roles (Sampson, 1977) to criticism of the theory's continued reliance on traditional notions of masculinity and femininity, thus reifying the distinction that it proposed to blur (Lott, 1981).

At the same time, a number of investigators have begun to engage in more careful scientific analyses, attempting to weigh the existent evidence and logically examine the proposed theoretical structure. Perhaps the central issue concerns the meaning of the scale itself and what it measures. As noted, Bem's conception of this measure is broad, assuming unidimensional concepts of masculinity and femininity that relate to most gender-related behaviors. In contrast, many investigators, led by Spence and Helmreich (1978), have argued for a narrower interpretation. From this alternative viewpoint, the typi-

cal scales in this area assess two reasonably limited domains of behavior. The so-called "masculinity" scale is primarily a measure of instrumentality, and the "femininity" scale is primarily a measure of expressiveness.[2] As such, they should allow good prediction to behaviors that are highly weighted in favor of instrumental and expressive traits, respectively, but should not necessarily be predictive to other domains of gender-related behavior. There is an increasing amount of evidence for this narrower position. Spence and Helmreich (1980) have recently reviewed some of the literature and find only limited relationships between masculinity/femininity as assessed by the PAQ or the BSRI and other sex-role attitudes and behaviors.

A second and related issue concerns the unique predictability of androgyny (defined as a combination of masculinity and femininity) versus the main effect contributions of the masculinity (instrumental) and femininity (expressive) scales alone. A recent review by Taylor and Hall (1982) presents persuasive evidence for the latter position. In a comprehensive analysis of the

---

[2]Typically, males score higher than females on the masculinity (instrumentality) scale, and females score higher than males on the femininity (expressiveness) scale. Although these differences are statistically significant in most cases, they are generally small in magnitude, and the distributions show considerable overlap. Thus, as in the research described earlier, sex-of-subject effects are limited but not inconsequential.

TABLE 1				
SUMMARY OF DIRECTION OF MAIN EFFECTS IN ANDROGYNY RESEARCH				
	Masculinity effect (%)		**Femininity effect (%)**	
Measure	**Positive**	**Negative**	**Positive**	**Negative**
Male-typed dependent measures	93	7	56	44
Female-typed dependent measures	47	53	80	20
Non-sex-typed healthy measures	91	9	79	21

Note: This table is adapted from data presented in "Psychological Androgyny: Theories, Methods, and Conclusions" by M. C. Taylor and J. A. Hall, 1982, *Psychological Bulletin*, 92, pp. 347–366. Copyright 1982 by the American Psychological Association, Inc. Adapted by permission.

published literature, these authors found that the masculinity scale relates positively to the majority of behaviors that fall within an instrumental domain (see Table 1). Similarly, the femininity scale relates positively to the majority of behaviors in the expressive domain. Essentially, these results demonstrate the construct validity of the scales as measures of instrumentality and expressiveness. In contrast, measures of psychological health promise to go beyond construct validation and offer a test of some of the basic assumptions of androgyny theorizing. As shown in the third row of the table, both masculinity and femininity are associated with high scores on variables such as self-esteem and adjustment. The effect of masculinity is greater, however, as indicated by these percentages and by additional analyses using standardized coefficients. More importantly, the Taylor and Hall analysis indicates that the contributions of masculinity and femininity are essentially additive and that the interaction of the two scales does not offer greater predictability, thus arguing against androgyny as a concept with emergent properties.

Similar evidence for the importance of main effects versus interactions is seen in a recent report by Markus, Crane, Bernstein, and Siladi (1982) investigating the operation of self-schema related to sex. Their results suggest that each dimension separately predicts responses to schema-related material, but there is little evidence for a unique state of androgyny that predicts responses over and above these main effects.

The brief history of androgyny research shows parallels with earlier investigations of personality and the controversy as to whether personality can in fact predict behavior. Unfortunately, the androgyny research in many respects seems to confirm Santayana's warning to those who do not know history. The concept itself has not been examined thoroughly, and in the interim it has been asked to bear too much conceptual baggage. In turn, use of this global concept to predict a wide variety of often tangentially related, single-act behaviors has often met with failure.

In summary, approaching issues of gender via measures of masculinity, femininity, and androgyny has been an active arena. Although the promise may have outstripped the product, the product is not without value. Understanding more about individual differences in expressive and instrumental traits and analyzing situations more carefully are valuable outcomes. They do not, however, provide an ultimate answer for issues of roles and gender.

SEX AS A SOCIAL CATEGORY

From the third perspective, sex is viewed as a social category, as a cue or a type of information on which observers base judgments and individuals choose actions. Here the focus is not on how men and women actually differ, but how people *think* that they differ.

Some of the earliest research in the past decade's flurry of work on gender concerned the differential judgments that people make of males and females. In the heavily cited Goldberg (1968) study, for example, women who were asked to judge the quality of professional articles and the skill of their authors showed a bias toward male authors when all information except sex of author was equivalent. Although this particular finding has not always been replicated (see Wallston & O'Leary, 1981, for a review), it marked the initial foray into an area that has generated considerable data.

In a similar study, Deaux and Taynor (1973) asked college students to judge the qualifications of either a male or female student who was being considered for a program of study abroad. Again, subjects showed bias in their judgment of the sexes, although the direction of bias was contingent on the outcome. Successful males were rated more positively than successful females; in the case of failure, males were judged more harshly than females. Such findings are reminiscent of Margaret Mead's observation that although women are "unsexed" by success, men are "unsexed" by failure.

Demonstrations that the performances of males and females are judged differently were followed by a closer examination of the judgment process. Hansen and O'Leary (1983), for example, found that observers often explain variations in women's behavior by personal causes, while looking to environmental influences for variations in men's behavior.

Other work during the 1970s considered the ways in which causal attributions are made to explain the success and failure of males and females. Using the same logic that characterized the work on self-attributions, Deaux and Emswiller (1974) predicted that the explanations given for the performance of a male and a female would differ even if the level of performance were identical. In this experiment subjects were asked to account for the successful performance of either a male or a female who performed well on an object-identification task. In addition to sex of the performer, the sex linkage of the task was varied as well by depicting the objects as either mechanical tools or household utensils. Judgments of performance were made on a scale anchored by skill as an explanation at one end and by luck as an explanation at the other end.

As shown in Figure 1, judgments differed significantly when the task was a male-linked one. Whereas a male was believed to have done well because of his ability, the female's performance was attributed to a greater extent to luck. Interestingly, performance on a female-linked task showed no difference in judgment. Although relatively less ability was attributed to the male and relatively more ability to the female (compared to explanations given on the male task), the difference between the two was not significant and the expected reversal did not occur. Thus, this study demonstrated not only that sex of actor is an important cue in judgment, but that sex-linked tasks are also influential.

The issues involved with task are interesting ones, and underline some of the problems involved in studying issues of gender. It is clear

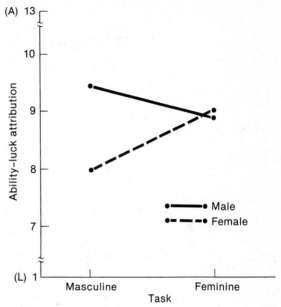

Figure 1 Ability-luck attributions as a function of sex of task and performer.

on the basis of several studies that tasks defined as feminine are inevitably judged as simpler than tasks defined as masculine. If one uses naturally defined male and female tasks, there is, of course, little control over the dimensions of difference. Traditionally female jobs are often considered less difficult, but this does not necessarily indicate bias in judgments—perhaps those jobs are inherently easier, or perhaps not. In an applied context, such questions have been raised concerning the classification of jobs in the *Occupational Titles Handbook,* where many jobs traditionally held by women are given lower ratings than seemingly equivalent or less demanding male jobs. To cite just one example from this admittedly controversial area, the job of *home health aide* is rated lower than is the job of *newspaper carrier* (Briggs, 1974). Yet even when one uses experimental techniques to control the situation, as by using the identical task and simply providing false information on the alleged superiority of one sex over the other, people will often judge the female task to be easier.

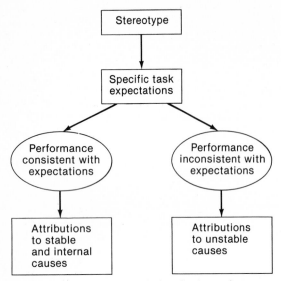

Figure 2 Expectancy model of attributions: observers.

Causal attributions that observers make for male and female performance are linked to the initial expectations that they have for those performances, paralleling the pattern of actor attributions. Differential expectations lead to differential attributions even when outcome is held constant: attributions to stable and internal causes when there is a fit between expectancy and performance, and attribution to unstable causes when there is a discrepancy (Weiner et al., 1971). These expectations for specific tasks can be understood in terms of the more general stereotypes held of women and men (see Figure 2).

In the case of the attributional literature, there is some evidence that general attitudes toward women and men are indeed correlated with attributions. Garland and Price (1977) correlated the attitudes of subjects toward women as managers (using a scale developed by Peters, Terborg, and Taynor, 1974) with the attributions these same subjects made for the successful or unsuccessful performance of a female manager. Subjects whose general attitudes toward women were most positive were also more likely to attribute the individual woman's success to ability or effort; subjects who were most negative were more likely to invoke luck or task ease as an explanation.

The realization that expectations, and in turn attributions, can be linked to basic beliefs about women and men calls for a closer look at the nature of such stereotypes. Although the recognition that there are gender stereotypes is longstanding, surprisingly little work has been done to define those stereotypes very precisely (cf. Ruble & Ruble, 1982). The most widely cited work in this area is that of Broverman and her colleagues (Broverman, Vogel, Broverman, Clarkson, & Rosenkrantz, 1972), in which students were asked to endorse a set of traits as characteristic of males or females. This work found that there were two basic clusters of traits, warmth-expressiveness and competence, that could be associated with women and men, respectively. In more recent work, Spence, Helmreich, & Stapp (1975) have derived two similar factors of instrumentality and expressiveness.

Both of these approaches rely exclusively on personality traits to define gender stereotypes. Yet the popular conception of stereotypes includes a much broader range of characteristics, including physical appearance, role behaviors, and occupations (Ashmore & Del Boca, 1979). Recent work is aimed at exploring this more multidimensional conception of gender stereotypes (Deaux & Lewis, 1983).

Two assumptions underlie this approach. First, it is assumed that there are a number of separate and identifiable components of gender stereotypes. Specific components being considered are traits, role behaviors, physical appearance, occupations, and sexual orientation. It is an empirical question as to how closely related these components are. Referring to research on the relationship among sex-related characteristics as subject variables, one finds that similar types of characteristics are only moderately correlated with one another in young adults (Spence & Helmreich, 1980). Thus, a person high in instrumentality is not necessarily one who engages frequently in male role behaviors or who has liberal attitudes toward women's rights. Similarly, it is possible that the various components of gender stereotypes are also related only weakly under normal circumstances.

A second assumption concerns the question of relative versus absolute differences. It is clear that one's choice of method can predetermine the answer to this question. For example, the early work on ethnic stereotypes using a checklist procedure necessarily yielded an absolute view of ethnic stereotypes. In contrast, research by Broverman and by Spence and Helmreich allows relative judgments, leading to the conclusion that men are seen as *more* instrumental than women, rather than as instrumental *instead of* expressive. A more refined analysis of the relative position can be obtained through the use of probabilistic methods (cf. McCauley & Stitt, 1978; McCauley, Stitt, & Segal, 1980).

The validity of these two assumptions can be assessed by consideration of some recent data (Deaux & Lewis, 1983). Subjects were asked to estimate the probability that the average man or woman has a particular trait, engages in a particular role behavior, or holds a particular job or occupation. Multiple items were used, and items were summed within each component; these component scores were in turn correlated with one another. In general, these correlations were significant but only moderate (.3 to .5) in size. These data suggest that there is a definite relationship among sex-related characteristics and that subjects are not making judgments on one dimension independent of their judgments on other dimensions. At the same time, the correlations are far from perfect. Even in the case of the largest correlation, only around 25% of the variance was accounted for, suggesting that judgments of masculine and feminine attributes are not unidimensional.

The question of the relative versus absolute assignment of characteristics to men and women is considered in Table 2, which presents a sample of the traits, role behaviors, and physical character-

---

TABLE 2

STEREOTYPES OF MALES AND FEMALES: PROBABILITY JUDGMENTS

Characteristic	Judgment[a]	
	Men	Women
Trait		
Independent	.78	.58
Competitive	.82	.64
Warm	.66	.77
Emotional	.56	.84
Role behaviors		
Financial provider	.83	.47
Takes initiative with opposite sex	.82	.54
Takes care of children	.50	.85
Cooks meals	.42	.83
Physical characteristics		
Muscular	.64	.36
Deep voice	.73	.30
Graceful	.45	.68
Small-boned	.39	.62

[a]Probability that the average person of either sex would possess a characteristic.

---

istics for which judgments have been obtained (Deaux & Lewis, 1983). In each case, the judgments made about males and females differ significantly at the .001 level. Yet the pattern is clearly not one of the all-or-none variety. For example, there is not absolute certainty on the part of subjects that men are independent, competitive, muscular, or that they serve as financial providers. And in many cases, subjects believe that there is a reasonable probability that women have the same qualities. Thus these data suggest that although stereotypes do in fact assume differences between males and females, the concepts are not mutually exclusive.

In focusing on male and female stereotypes, it is important to consider the extent to which information about sex will contribute to other judgments. As Locksley and her colleagues (Locksley, Borgida, Brekke, & Hepburn, 1980) have suggested, information about sex may pale in the face of other, more diagnostic, information. A similar theme is reflected in recent work by Eagly and Wood (1982). In analyzing the link between sex and status in perceptions of social influence, these authors have found that because *female* implies lower status, people will assume that the woman is more readily influenced. However, when specific status information is supplied, sex loses its prominence as a determinant of judgments.

Further consideration of this issue is provided by Deaux and Lewis (1984). In a set of three studies, subjects were provided either with a sex label or with specific information about the role behaviors of an individual. They were then asked to make judgments about other aspects of the person. In nearly every case, the percentage of variance accounted for by role behaviors was greater than the amount accounted for by sex. Thus, information about a target may be more influential than sex identity *if* that other information is available and salient. In the absence of such information, however, stereotyped conceptions prevail. Furthermore, when people are given information about one aspect of a person's character, the data suggest that sex-related components coalesce more strongly. The introduction of information about masculine role behaviors leads to inferences about the person's possession of masculine traits, masculine physical characteristics, and male-dominated occupations, suggesting that the concept of stereotyping cannot be easily dismissed.

There is considerable evidence that sex serves as a social category, influencing judgments, explanations for performance, and expectations for behavior. Although its influence is not immutable, and indeed can be minimized by more specific diagnostic information, sex must be considered an important factor in the process of social cognition (Grady, 1977).

ASSESSMENT AND OUTLOOK

To summarize the research adopting one of the three approaches described here, the following statements can be made.

1. The variance accounted for by main effects of sex is quite limited on any specific task. Consideration of sex by task interactions may provide some additional explanatory power.
2. The unique contribution of androgyny, in the sense of a construct with emergent properties, has yet to be demonstrated. Individual dimensions of masculinity and femininity predict behavior in instrumental and expressive domains, respectively, but probably are not very useful in accounting for the wider range of sex-related behaviors.
3. Gender stereotypes are pervasive. Although additional work is needed to understand the precise content and structure of these stereotypes, there is ample evidence that they exist and that they relate to a variety of judgments and evaluations of males and females.

Yet an understanding of the role of gender in our society cannot rest on stereotypes alone, despite their seeming ubiquitousness. To fully deal with the ways in which gender is influential, one must ultimately deal with the *processes* involved. Indeed, if one had to note a limitation common to each of the approaches described above, it would be the static nature of the assumptions— that sex-related phenomena are best approached either through biological categories, via stable traits, or in terms of relatively stable stereotypic conceptions.

In contrast to these static assumptions, I would argue that attention should be directed toward more active interaction sequences, toward the processes through which gender information is presented and acted upon (see Sherif, 1982, for a related discussion). Although the outlines of such a process orientation are still sketchy, two directions can be tentatively charted. A first direction is to consider more carefully the choices that men and women make, as opposed to the capabilities that they show in a particular domain. A second direction is to explore the process of interaction and sequences of expectancy confirmation. In both cases, consideration of gender categories can be brought to bear on the more traditional sex-of-subject literature.

Male and Female Choices

Evidence that men and women differ little in their performance on any particular task often seems to fly in the face of conventional wisdom. Looking around, one can surely see evidence of different patterns of behavior by women and men. For example, although women are increasingly entering the labor force, far fewer women than men are employed. Women and men who are employed are found in typically different occupations. Similarly, although more men are becoming involved in home and family care, there are large statistical differences in the participation rates of the sexes in these activities. Men are still more likely to fix cars, women are still more likely to sew, and so forth.

However, when one looks for differences between women and men engaged in a specific activity, relatively few are found. As discussed earlier, in laboratory studies main effects are often limited in size. From a field perspective, one can compare selected groups of women and men who are engaged in similar tasks and find few differences. Thus, consideration of the attribution patterns of the male and female managers, for example, found differences much smaller than those obtained in the laboratory (Deaux, 1979). Recent work on blue-collar workers in the steel industry has found almost no evidence of sex differences: Men and women were alike in their self-evaluations, their aspirations, and their likes and dislikes about the work situation (Deaux & Ullman, 1983). A review of leadership studies reports a similar absence of differences between practicing male and female leaders (Hollander, 1985).

These seeming contradictions can be reconciled only if the element of choice is recognized and incorporated into our understanding of gender. Stereotypes and discriminatory behavior of course play a role in this process, encouraging some choices and discouraging others. Individual differences (including, perhaps, instrumentality and expressiveness) may also influence the choices that a particular individual makes. Choices are not made in a vacuum, and such pervasive norms and dispositions cannot be ignored. In the context of such influences, however, other determinants of the choices must be considered.

It has been suggested that many behavioral differences between women and men are the result of conscious self-presentational strategies (Deaux, 1977). According to this line of argument, the behavioral repertoires of men and women are basically the same. However, from this available repository, males and females may select different actions—either of a long-term nature, such as occupation or family role, or of a short-term nature in a particular situation, as in a choice to be aggressive or conciliatory. In other words, enacted differences may derive from similar potentials.

An understanding of this self-presentation process is still embryonic. Certain situations seem more likely to invoke differing self-presentational strategies (Deaux, 1977). For example, situations that are more interactive in nature are more likely to show sex differences than will less social, more individualistic tasks. Thus sex differences are common in dyadic interaction studies, for example, and are infrequent in investigations of impression formation, cognitive balance, or attitude structure. Similarly, women and men do not differ when they are asked to allocate rewards to other people, but differences do emerge when allocations are to be divided between a partner and the self (Major & Deaux, 1982). Zanna and his colleagues (von Baeyer, Sherk, & Zanna, 1981; Zanna & Pack, 1975) have shown that women will readily alter their presentational manner, presenting themselves in a more or less stereotypically feminine manner, depending on their beliefs about their male partner's views on women.

These still fragmentary findings suggest the need for a fuller understanding of the role of behavioral choice in explaining the function of gender.

Expectancy Confirmation Sequences

A process understanding of gender cannot rest on the behavioral choices of women and men alone. The second element that must be considered is the interaction between the individual male or female and others in his or her environment, interactions that may influence subsequent choices. As has been noted, there is considerable evidence for the existence of stereotypes. The eye of the beholder does not affect perceptions alone, but can affect behavior as well. Darley and Fazio (1980) have recently reviewed the evidence for self-fulfilling prophecies and have detailed the steps by which expectancies are confirmed in social interaction. This process, although broader in application than gender, offers some important insights into the issues of gender.

As Darley and Fazio outline the process, a perceiver may hold a particular expectancy for the target's (in this case, the man's or woman's) behavior, and may act on that expectancy. The target person will then interpret that behavior and act on his or her interpretation. In turn, both the perceiver and the target may in the future choose actions based on their interpretation of the situation.

In the case of sex, to the extent that the perceiver's expectancies are stereotypic, a sequence may be instigated in which people eventually play out their stereotypes. The validity of this general sequence has been shown in research by Snyder and his colleagues (Snyder & Swann, 1978; Snyder, Tanke, & Berscheid, 1977); its specific application to gender stereotypes has been shown in a study by Skrypnek and Snyder (1982). In the Skrypnek and Snyder study, pairs of male and female subjects were asked to divide the labor in selecting among pairs of activities, some of which were male-linked and others of which were female-linked. In some cases, the male was told his partner was a male; in other cases he believed her to be female (which she always was). When the male subject believed his partner to be a female, he selected more stereotypically masculine activities for himself and allotted her more stereotypically feminine tasks than when he believed his partner to be male. More significantly, when subsequently given the initiative to choose, the female partner herself was more prone to choose feminine tasks when her partner believed that she was female than when he believed she was male (although she was blind to the expectations of her partner).

This pattern of differences highlights the critical role of other people and their expectancies as a potential influence on behavior. Pursuing such a line of thinking in relation to sex offers other benefits as well. Although sex is one of the more salient categories of social interaction, it is not the only one. Race, for example, is another important category that may have similar effects. Understanding the role that these social categories play should provide insights into the general process of social interaction. Thus, an initial focus on gender may provide the ground for more comprehensive theory about the interplay among cognition, action, and the general communication process.

Research on sex-related issues has hardly been quiescent during the past decade. Considerable activity has led to genuine insights into the influence of sex as a subject variable, the contribution of individual difference traits, and the pervasiveness of gender stereotypes. Further advances will require not more of the same, but rather a conceptual shift. Views of gender as a static category must give way, or at least be accompanied by, theories that treat sex-related phenomena as a process—a process that is influenced by individual choices, molded by situational pressures, and ultimately understandable only in the context of social interaction.

Social Control

Subtle Influences

Social Determinants of Bystander Intervention in Emergencies

Bibb Latané and John M. Darley (1970)

People desire at least some control over their lives, and most of us want at least some control over other people's lives as well. Further, as social beings, humans do exert social influence on one another, sometimes subtly and without conscious intent, other times clearly and intentionally. A type of influence that is so subtle that people are unaware that they are a part of it, much less aware that they are being affected by it, is the number of people around them. Yet Latané and Darley clearly show in this article how powerful the presence of individuals is in influencing our behavior. With these studies, Latané and Darley launched the "bystander apathy" research area, and also provoked greater interest in helping behavior. Stimulated by the tragic murder of Kitty Genovese in 1964 (during which 38 people heard her screams for help but failed to come to her aid, or even call the police), this line of research is a classic example of social psychological attempts to make sense of timely social phenomena.

Fifteen years after the advent of bystander apathy research, Krebs and Miller (1985) developed a conceptual scheme that describes the multiple influences on altruism. At the broadest level, they consider how biological capacities and cultural prescriptions affect helping behavior. At the middle level, they examine personality and situational influences, and at the most proximal level, they assess the cognitive and affective processes within the individual as influencing altruistic behavior. Although Latané and Darley focus only on one situational influence, you can see how significant it is in affecting prosocial behavior. Almost all of us have personal anecdotes about how we failed to act in groups when we felt we should have, or how difficult it was to overcome fear of embarrassment or indecision when we did act. You may also wish to consider, using Krebs and Miller's model, how other levels of influence have affected your own prosocial inclinations to act.

Almost 100 years ago, Charles Darwin wrote: "As man is a social animal, it is almost certain that he would...from an inherited tendency be willing to defend, in concert with others, his fellow-men; and be ready to aid them in any way, which did not too greatly interfere with his own welfare or his own strong desires" (*The Descent of Man*). Today, although many psychologists would quarrel with Darwin's assertion that altruism is inherited, most would agree that men will go to the aid of others even when there is no visible gain for themselves. At least, most would have agreed until a March night in 1964. That night, Kitty Genovese was set upon by a maniac as she returned home from work at 3:00 AM. Thirty-eight of her neighbors in Kew Gardens came to their windows when she cried out in terror; but none came to her assistance, even though her stalker took over half an hour to murder her. No one even so much as called the police.

Since we started our research on bystander response to emergencies, we have heard about dozens of such incidents. We have also heard many explanations: "I would assign this to the effect of the megalopolis in which we live, which makes closeness very difficult and leads to the alienation of the individual from the group," contributed a psychoanalyst. "A disaster syndrome," explained a sociologist, "that shook the sense of safety and sureness of the individuals involved and caused psychological withdrawal from the event by ignoring it." "Apathy," others claim. "Indifference." "The gratification of unconscious sadistic impulses." "Lack of concern for our fellow men." "The Cold Society." These explanations and many more have been applied to the surprising failure of bystanders to intervene in emergencies—failures which suggest that we no longer care about the fate of our neighbors.

But can this be so? We think not. Although it is unquestionably true that the witnesses in the incidents above did nothing to save the victim, "apathy," "indifference," and "unconcern" are not entirely accurate descriptions of their reactions. The 38 witnesses of Kitty Genovese's murder did not merely look at the scene once and then ignore it. Instead they continued to stare out of their windows at what was going on. Caught, fascinated, distressed, unwilling to act but unable to turn away, their behavior was neither helpful nor heroic; but it was not indifferent or apathetic either.

Actually, it was like crowd behavior in many other emergency situations; car accidents, drownings, fires, and attempted suicides all attract substantial numbers of people who watch the drama in helpless fascination without getting directly involved in the action. Are these people alienated and indifferent? Are the rest of us? Obviously not. It seems only yesterday we were being called overconforming. But why, then, do we not act?

Paradoxically, the key to understanding these failures of intervention may be found exactly in the fact that so surprises us about them: so many bystanders fail to intervene. If we think of 38, or 11, or 100 individuals, each looking at an emergency and callously deciding to pass by, we are horrified. But if we realize that each bystander is picking up cues about what is happening and how to react to it from the other bystanders, understanding begins to emerge. There are several ways in which a crowd of onlookers can make each individual member of that crowd less likely to act.

DEFINING THE SITUATION

Most emergencies are, or at least begin as, ambiguous events. A quarrel in the street may erupt into violence or it may be simply a family argument. A man staggering about may be suffering a coronary, or an onset of diabetes, or he simply may be drunk. Smoke pouring from a building may signal a fire, but on the other hand, it may be simply steam or airconditioner vapor. Before a bystander is likely to take action in such ambiguous situations, he must first define the event as an emergency and decide that intervention is the proper course of action.

In the course of making these decisions, it is likely that an individual bystander will be considerably influenced by the decisions he perceives other bystanders to be taking. If everyone else in a group of onlookers seems to regard an event as nonserious and the proper course of action as nonintervention, this consensus may strongly affect the perceptions of any single individual and inhibit his potential intervention.

The definitions that other people held may be discovered by discussing the situation with them, but they may also be inferred from their facial expressions or behavior. A whistling man with his hands in his pockets obviously does not believe he is in the midst of a crisis. A bystander who does not respond to smoke obviously does not attribute it to fire. An individual, seeing the inaction of others, will judge the situation as less serious then he would if alone.

But why should the others be inactive? Probably because they are aware that other people are also watching them. The others are an audience to their own reactions. Among American males, it is considered desirable to appear poised and collected in times of stress. Being exposed to the public view may constrain the actions and expressions of emotion of any individual as he tries to avoid possible ridicule and embarrassment. Even though he may be truly concerned and upset about the plight of a victim, until he decides what to do, he may maintain a calm demeanor.

If each member of a group is, at the same time, trying to appear calm and also looking around at the other members to gauge their reactions, all members may be led (or misled) by each other to define the situation as less critical than they would if alone. Until someone acts, each person sees only other nonresponding bystanders and is likely to be influenced not to act himself. A state of "pluralistic ignorance" may develop.

It has often been recognized that a crowd can cause contagion of panic, leading each person in the crowd to overreact to an emergency to the detriment of everyone's welfare. What we suggest here is that a crowd can also force inaction on its members. It can suggest by its passive behavior that an event is not to be reacted to as an emergency, and it can make any individual uncomfortably aware of what a fool he will look for behaving as if it is.

Where There's Smoke, There's (Sometimes) Fire[1]

In this experiment we presented an emergency to individuals either alone or in groups of three. It was our expectation that the constraints on behavior in public combined with social influence processes would lessen the likelihood that members of three-person groups would act to cope with the emergency.

College students were invited to an interview to discuss "some of the problems involved in life at an urban university." As they sat in a small room waiting to be called for the interview and filling out a preliminary questionnaire, they faced an ambiguous but potentially dangerous situation. A stream of smoke began to puff into the room through a wall vent.

Some subjects were exposed to this potentially critical situation while alone. In a second condition, three naive subjects were tested together. Since subjects arrived at slightly different times, and since they each had individual questionnaires to work on, they did not introduce themselves to each other or attempt anything but the most rudimentary conversation.

As soon as the subjects had completed two pages of their questionnaires, the experimenter began to introduce the smoke through a small

---

[1]A more complete account of this experiment is provided in Latané and Darley (1968).

vent in the wall. The "smoke," copied from the famous Camel cigarette sign in Times Square, formed a moderately fine-textured but clearly visible stream of whitish smoke. It continued to jet into the room in irregular puffs, and by the end of the experimental period, it obscured vision.

All behavior and conversation were observed and coded from behind a oneway window (largely disguised on the subject's side by a large sign giving preliminary instructions). When and if the subject left the experimental room and reported the smoke, he was told that the situation "would be taken care of." If the subject had not reported the smoke within 6 minutes from the time he first noticed it, the experiment was terminated.

The typical subject, when tested alone, behaved very reasonably. Usually, shortly after the smoke appeared, he would glance up from his questionnaire, notice the smoke, show a slight but distinct startle reaction, and then undergo a brief period of indecision, perhaps returning briefly to his questionnaire before again staring at the smoke. Soon, most subjects would get up from their chairs, walk over to the vent and investigate it closely, sniffing the smoke, waving their hands in it, feeling its temperature, etc. The usual Alone subject would hesitate again, but finally would walk out of the room, look around outside, and, finding somebody there, calmly report the presence of the smoke. No subject showed any sign of panic, most simply said: "There's something strange going on in there, there seems to be some sort of smoke coming through the wall . . . ." The median subject in the Alone condition had reported the smoke within 2 minutes of first noticing it. Three-quarters of the 24 people run in this condition reported the smoke before the experimental period was terminated.

Because there are three subjects present and available to report the smoke in the Three Naive Bystanders condition as compared to only one subject at a time in the Alone condition, a simple comparison between the two conditions is not appropriate. We cannot compare speeds in the Alone condition with the average speed of the three sub-jects in a group because, once one subject in a group had reported the smoke, the pressures on the other two disappeared. They could feel legit-imately that the emergency had been handled and that any action on their part would be redundant and potentially confusing. Therefore, we used the speed of the first subject in a group to report the smoke as our dependent variable. However, since there were three times as many people available to respond in this condition as in the Alone con-dition, we would expect an increased likelihood that at least one person would report the smoke by chance alone. Therefore, we mathematically created "groups" of three scores from the Alone condition to serve as a baseline.[2]

In contrast to the complexity of this proce-dure, the results were quite simple. Subjects in the three-person-group condition were markedly inhibited from reporting the smoke. Since 75% of the Alone subjects reported the smoke, we would expect over 98% of the three-person groups to include at least one reporter. In fact, in only 38% of the eight groups in this condition did even one person report ($p < .01$). Of the 24 people run in these eight groups, only one per-son reported the smoke within the first 4 min-utes before the room got noticeably unpleasant. Only three people reported the smoke within the entire experimental period. Social inhibition of reporting was so strong that the smoke was re-ported faster when only one person saw it than when groups of three were present ($p < .01$).

Subjects who had reported the smoke were relatively consistent in later describing their re-actions to it. They thought the smoke looked somewhat "strange." They were not sure ex-actly what it was or whether it was dangerous, but they felt it was unusual enough to justify some

examination. "I wasn't sure whether it was a fire, but it looked like something was wrong." "I thought it might be steam, but it seemed like a good idea to check it out."

Subjects who had not reported the smoke were also unsure about exactly what it was, but they uniformly said that they had rejected the idea that it was a fire. Instead, they hit upon an astonishing variety of alternative explanations, all sharing the common characteristic of interpreting the smoke as a nondangerous event. Many thought the smoke was either steam or airconditioning vapors, sev-eral thought it was smog, purposely introduced to stimulate an urban environment, and two actually suggested that the smoke was a "truth gas" fil-tered into the room to induce them to answer the questionnaire accurately! Predictably, some de-cided that "it must be some sort of experiment" and stoically endured the discomfort of the room rather than overreact.

The results of this study clearly support the prediction. Groups of three naive subjects were less likely to report the smoke than solitary by-standers. Our predictions were confirmed—but this does not necessarily mean that our expla-nation of these results is the correct one. As a matter of fact, several alternative explanations center around the fact that the smoke repre-sented a possible danger to the subject himself as well as to others in the building. For instance, it is possible that the subjects in groups saw them-selves as engaged in a game of "chicken" in which the first person to report would admit his cowardliness. Or it may have been that the pres-ence of others made subjects feel safer, and thus reduced their need to report.

To rule out such explanations, a second ex-periment was designed to see whether similar group inhibition effects could be observed in sit-uations where there is no danger to the individ-ual himself for not acting. In this study, male Columbia University undergraduates waited ei-ther alone or with a stranger to participate in a market research study. As they waited they heard a woman fall and apparently injure herself

---

[2] The formula for calculating the expected proportion of the groups in which at least one person will have acted by a given time is $1 - (1 - p)^n$ where p is the proportion of single individuals who acted by that time and n is the num-ber of persons in the group.

in the room next door. Whether they tried to help and how long they took to do so were the main dependent variables of the study.

The Fallen Woman[3]

Subjects were telephoned and offered $2 to participate in a survey of game and puzzle preferences conducted at Columbia by the Consumer Testing Bureau (CTB), a market research organization. When they arrived, they were met at the door by an attractive young woman and taken to the testing room. On the way, they passed the CTB office, and through its open door they were able to see a desk and bookcase piled high with papers and filing cabinets. They entered the adjacent testing room, which contained a table and chairs and a variety of games, and they were given questionnaires to fill out. The representative told subjects that she would be working next door in her office for about 10 minutes while they were completing the questionnaire and left by opening the collapsible curtain which divided the two rooms. She made sure that subjects were aware that the curtain was unlocked and easily opened and that it provided a means of entry to her office. The representative stayed in her office, shuffling papers, opening drawers, and making enough noise to remind the subjects of her presence. Four minutes after leaving the testing area, she turned on a high fidelity stereophonic tape recorder.

The Emergency If the subject listened carefully, he heard the representative climb up on a chair to reach for a stack of papers on the bookcase. Even if he were not listening carefully, he heard a loud crash and a scream as the chair collapsed and she fell to the floor. "Oh, my God, my foot...I...I...can't move...it. Oh...my ankle," the representative moaned. "I...can't get this...thing...off me." She cried and moaned for about a minute longer, but the cries gradually got

more subdued and controlled. Finally she muttered something about getting outside, knocked over the chair as she pulled herself up and thumped to the door, closing it behind her as she left. The entire incident took 130 seconds.

The main dependent variable of the study, of course, was whether the subjects took action to help the victim and how long it took them to do so. There were actually several modes of intervention possible: a subject could open the screen dividing the two rooms, leave the testing room and enter the CTB office by the door, find someone else, or most simply, call out to see if the representative needed help. In one condition, each subject was in the testing room alone while he filled out the questionnaire and heard the fall. In the second condition, strangers were placed in the testing room in pairs. Each subject in the pair was unacquainted with the other before entering the room and they were not introduced.

Across all experimental groups, the majority of subjects who intervened did so by pulling back the room divider and coming into the CTB office (61%). Few subjects came the round-about way through the door to offer their assistance (14%), and a surprisingly small number (24%) chose the easy solution of calling out to offer help. No one tried to find someone else to whom to report the accident.

Since 70% of Alone subjects intervened, we should expect that at least one person in 91% of all two-person groups would offer help if members of a pair had no influence upon each other. In fact, members did influence each other. In only 40% of the groups did even one person offer help to the injured woman. Only eight subjects of the 40 who were run in this condition intervened. This response rate is significantly below the hypothetical baseline ($p < .001$). Social inhibition of helping was so strong that the victim was actually helped more quickly when only one person heard her distress than when two did ($p < .01$).

When we talked to subjects after the experiment, those who intervened usually claimed that they did so either because the fall sounded very

---

[3] This experiment is more fully described in Latané and Rodin (1969).

serious or because they were uncertain what had occurred and felt they should investigate. Many talked about intervention as the "right thing to do" and asserted they would help again in any situation.

Many of the noninterveners also claimed that they were unsure what had happened (59%), but had decided that it was not too serious (46%). A number of subjects reported that they thought other people would or could help (25%), and three said they refrained out of concern for the victim—they did not want to embarrass her. Whether to accept these explanations as reasons or rationalizations is moot—they certainly do not explain the differences among conditions. The important thing to note is that noninterveners did not seem to feel that they had behaved callously or immorally. Their behavior was generally consistent with their interpretation of the situation. Subjects almost uniformly claimed that in a "real" emergency they would be among the first to help the victim.

These results strongly replicate the findings of the Smoke study. In both experiments, subjects were less likely to take action if they were in the presence of others than if they were alone. This congruence of findings from different experimental settings supports the validity and generality of the phenomenon; it also helps rule out a variety of alternative explanations suitable to either situation alone. For example, the possibility that smoke may have represented a threat to the subject's personal safety and that subjects in groups may have had a greater concern to appear "brave" than single subjects does not apply to the present experiment. In the present experiment, nonintervention cannot signify bravery. Comparison of the two experiments also suggests that the absolute number of nonresponsive bystanders may not be a critical factor in producing social inhibition of intervention; pairs of strangers in the present study inhibited each other as much as did trios in the former study.

Other studies we have done show that group inhibition effects hold in real life as well as in the laboratory, and for members of the general pop-ulation as well as college students. The results of these experiments clearly support the line of theoretical argument advanced earlier. When bystanders to an emergency can see the reactions of other people, and when other people can see their own reactions, each individual may, through a process of social influence, be led to interpret the situation as less serious than he would if he were alone, and consequently be less likely to take action.

These studies, however, tell us little about the case that stimulated our interest in bystander intervention: the Kitty Genovese murder. Although the 38 witnesses to that event were aware, through seeing lights and silhouettes in other windows, that others watched, they could not see what others were doing and thus be influenced by their reactions. In the privacy of their own apartments, they could not be clearly seen by others, and thus inhibited by their presence. The social influence process we have described above could not operate. Nevertheless, we think that the presence of other bystanders may still have affected each individual's reponse.

DIFFUSION OF RESPONSIBILITY

In addition to affecting the interpretations that he places on a situation, the presence of other people can also alter the rewards and costs facing an individual bystander. Perhaps most importantly, the presence of other people can reduce the cost of not acting. If only one bystander is present at an emergency, he carries all of the responsibility for dealing with it; he will feel all of the guilt for not acting; he will bear all of any blame others may level for nonintervention. If others are present, the onus of responsibility is diffused, and the individual may be more likely to resolve his conflict between intervening and not intervening in favor of the latter alternative.

When only one bystander is present at an emergency, if help is to come it must be from him. Although he may choose to ignore them out of concern for his personal safety, or desire "not to get involved," any pressures to intervene focus uniquely on him. When there are several observers present, however, the pressures to intervene do not focus on any one of the observers; instead, the responsibility for intervention is shared among all the onlookers and is not unique to any one. As a result, each may be less likely to help.

Potential blame may also be diffused. However much we wish to think that an individual's moral behavior is divorced from considerations of personal punishment or reward, there is both theory and evidence to the contrary. It is perfectly reasonable to assume that under circumstances of group responsibility for a punishable act, the punishment or blame that accrues to any one individual is often slight or nonexistent.

Finally, if others are known to be present, but their behavior cannot be closely observed, any one bystander may assume that one of the other observers is already taking action to end the emergency. If so, his own intervention would only be redundant—perhaps harmfully or confusingly so. Thus, given the presence of other onlookers whose behavior cannot be observed, any given bystander can rationalize his own inaction by convincing himself that "somebody else must be doing something."

These considerations suggest that even when bystanders to an emergency cannot see or be influenced by each other, the more bystanders who are present, the less likely any one bystander would be to intervene and provide aid. To test this suggestion, it would be necessary to create an emergency situation in which each subject is blocked from communicating with others to prevent his getting information about their behavior during the emergency.

A Fit to Be Tried[4]

A college student arrived in the laboratory, and was ushered into an individual room from which

[4]Further details of this experiment can be found in Darley and Latané (1968).

a communication system would enable him to talk to other participants (who were actually figments of the tape recorder). Over the intercom, the subject was told that the experimenter was concerned with the kinds of personal problems faced by normal college students in a high-pressure, urban environment, and that he would be asked to participate in a discussion about these problems. To avoid embarrassment about discussing personal problems with strangers, the experimenter said, several precautions would be taken. First, subjects would remain anonymous, which was why they had been placed in individual rooms rather than face-to-face. Second, the experimenter would not listen to the initial discussion himself, but would only get the subject's reactions later by questionnaire.

The plan for the discussion was that each person would talk in turn for 2 minutes, presenting his problems to the group. Next, each person in turn would comment on what others had said, and finally there would be a free discussion. A mechanical switching device regulated the discussion, switching on only one microphone at a time.

The Emergency The discussion started with the future victim speaking first. He said he found it difficult to get adjusted to New York and to his studies. Very hesitantly and with obvious embarrassment, he mentioned that he was prone to seizures, particularly when studying hard or taking exams. The other people, including the one real subject, took their turns and discussed similar problems (minus the proneness to seizures). The naive subject talked last in the series, after the last prerecorded voice.

When it was again the victim's turn to talk, he made a few relatively calm comments, and then, growing increasingly loud and incoherent, he continued:

> I er I think I I need er if if could er er somebody er er er er er er er give me a little er give me a little help here because I er I'm er h-h-having a a a a real problem er right now and I er if somebody could help

me out it would er er s-s-sure be sure be good...because er there er er a cause I er I uh I've got a a one of the er sie...er er things coming on and and I could really er use some help so if somebody would er give me a little h-help uh er-er-er-er-er c-could somebody er er help er uh uh uh (choking sounds)...I'm gonna die er er I'm...gonna die er help er er seizure (chokes, then quiet).

The major independent variable of the study was the number of people the subject believed also heard the fit. The subject was led to believe that the discussion group was one of three sizes: a two-person group consisting of himself and the victim; a three-person group consisting of himself, the victim and the other person; or a six-person group consisting of himself, the victim, and four other persons.

The major dependent variable of the experiment was the time elapsed from the start of the victim's seizure until the subject left his experimental cubicle. When the subject left his room, he saw the experimental assistant seated at the end of the hall, and invariably went to the assistant to report the seizure. If 5 minutes elapsed without the subject's having emerged from his room, the experiment was terminated.

Ninety-five percent of all the subjects who ever responded did so within the first half of the time available to them. No subject who had not reported within 3 minutes after the fit ever did so. This suggests that even had the experiment been allowed to run for a considerably longer period of time, few additional subjects would have responded.

Eighty-five percent of the subjects who thought they alone knew of the victim's plight reported the seizure before the victim was cut off; only 31% of those who thought four other bystanders were present did so. Every one of the subjects in the two-person condition, but only 62% of the subjects in the six-person condition ever reported the emergency. To do a more detailed analysis of the results, each subject's time score was transformed into a "speed" score by taking the reciprocal of the response time in sec-

onds and multiplying by 100. Analysis of variance of these speed scores indicates that the effect of group size was highly significant ($p < .01$), and all three groups differed significantly one from another ($p < .05$).

Subjects, whether or not they intervened, believed the fit to be genuine and serious. "My God, he's having a fit," many subjects said to themselves (and we overheard via their microphones). Others gasped or simply said, "Oh." Several of the male subjects swore. One subject said to herself, "It's just my kind of luck, something has to happen to me!" Several subjects spoke aloud of their confusion about what course of action to take: "Oh, God, what should I do?"

When those subjects who intervened stepped out of their rooms, they found the experimental assistant down the hall. With some uncertainty but without panic, they reported the situation. "Hey, I think Number 1 is very sick. He's having a fit or something." After ostensibly checking on the situation, the experimenter returned to report that "everything is under control." The subjects accepted these assurances with obvious relief.

Subjects who failed to report the emergency showed few signs of the apathy and indifference thought to characterize "unresponsive bystanders." When the experimenter entered her room to terminate the situation, the subject often asked if the victim was all right. "Is he being taken care of?" "He's all right, isn't he?" Many of these subjects showed physical signs of nervousness; they often had trembling hands and sweating palms. If anything, they seemed more emotionally aroused than did the subjects who reported the emergency.

Why, then, didn't they respond? It is not our impression that they had decided not to respond. Rather, they were still in a state of indecision and conflict concerning whether to respond or not. The emotional behavior of these nonresponding subjects was a sign of their continuing conflict, a conflict that other subjects resolved by responding.

The fit created a conflict situation of the avoidance-avoidance type. On the one hand, subjects worried about the guilt and shame they would feel if they did not help the person in distress. On the other hand, they were concerned not to make fools of themselves by overreacting, not to ruin the ongoing experiment by leaving their intercoms, and not to destroy the anonymous nature of the situation, which the experimenter had earlier stressed as important. For subjects in the two-person condition, the obvious distress of the victim and his need for help were so important that their conflict was easily resolved. For the subjects who knew that there were other bystanders present, the cost of not helping was reduced and the conflict they were in was more acute. Caught between the two negative alternatives of letting the victim continue to suffer or rushing, perhaps foolishly, to help, the nonresponding bystanders vacillated between them rather than choosing not to respond. This distinction may be academic for the victim, since he got no help in either case, but it is an extremely important one for understanding the causes of bystanders' failures to help.

Although subjects experienced stress and conflict during the emergency, their general reactions to it were highly positive. On a questionnaire administered after the experimenter had discussed the nature and purpose of the experiment, every single subject found the experiment either "interesting" or "very interesting" and was willing to participate in similar experiments in the future. All subjects felt that they understood what the experiment was all about and indicated that they thought the deceptions were necessary and justified. All but one felt they were better informed about the nature of psychological research in general.

CONCLUSION

We have suggested two distinct processes which might lead people to be less likely to intervene in an emergency if there are other people present than if they are alone. On the one hand, we suggested that the presence of other people may affect the interpretations each bystander puts on an ambiguous emergency situation. If other people are present at an emergency, each bystander will be guided by their apparent reactions in formulating his own impressions. Unfortunately, their apparent reactions may not be a good indication of their true feelings. It is possible for a state of "pluralistic ignorance" to develop, in which each bystander is led by the apparent lack of concern of the others to interpret the situation as being less serious than he would if alone. To the extent that he does not feel the situation is an emergency, he will be unlikely to take any helpful action.

Even if an individual does decide that an emergency is actually in process and that something ought to be done, he still is faced with the choice of whether he himself will intervene. Here again, the presence of other people may influence him—by reducing the costs associated with nonintervention. If a number of people witness the same event, the responsibility for action is diffused, and each may feel less necessity to help.

"There's safety in numbers," according to an old adage, and modern city dwellers seem to believe it. They shun deserted streets, empty subway cars, and lonely dark walks in dark parks, preferring instead to go where others are or to stay at home. When faced with stress, most individuals seem less afraid when they are in the presence of others than when they are alone.

A feeling so widely shared should have some basis in reality. Is there safety in numbers? If so, why? Two reasons are often suggested: individuals are less likely to find themselves in trouble if there are others about, and even if they do find themselves in trouble, others are likely to help them deal with it. While it is certainly true that a victim is unlikely to receive help if nobody knows of his plight, the experiments above cast doubt on the suggestion that he will be more likely to receive help if more people are present. In fact, the opposite seems to be true. A victim may be more likely to get help, or an emergency be reported, the fewer the people who are available to take action.

Although the results of these studies may shake our faith in "safety in numbers," they also may help us begin to understand a number of frightening incidents where crowds have heard but not answered a call for help. Newspapers have tagged these incidents with the label, "apathy." We have become indifferent, they say, callous to the fate of suffering of others. Our society has become "dehumanized" as it has become urbanized. These glib phrases may contain some truth, since startling cases such as the Genovese murder often seem to occur in our large cities, but such terms may also be misleading. Our studies suggest a different conclusion. They suggest that situational factors, specifically factors involving the immediate social environment, may be of greater importance in determining an individual's reaction to an emergency than such vague cultural or personality concepts as "apathy" or "alienation due to urbanization." They suggest that the failure to intervene may be better understood by knowing the relationship among bystanders rather than that between a bystander and the victim.

READING 32

Social Perception and Interpersonal Behavior: On the Self-Fulfilling Nature of Social Stereotypes

Mark L. Snyder, Elizabeth Decker Tanke, and Ellen Berscheid (1977)

The subtle influence now known as *self-fulfilling prophecy* or *behavioral confirmation* was identified many decades ago, and is best described by W. I. Thomas: "If men define situations as real, they are real in their consequences" (Merton, 1948). Actual research on this phenomenon was first conducted by Rosenthal in the 1960s. One famous study investigated the influence of teachers' beliefs of children's ability (Rosenthal and Jacobson, 1968). Teachers received their students' scores on a test predicting "intellectual blossoming." These scores were fictitious, however, and were randomly assigned to the children. Although many of the teachers just glanced at the test scores and did not keep them on file, by the end of the year the "intellectual blossomers" actually did experience greater intellectual spurts than did the other children in the same classrooms. This study and many others since 1968 suggest that teachers may subtly and nonconsciously create behavior in their students that fulfills their expectations.* You should also remember that students may also do this with their teachers! Rosenthal and colleagues (Rosenthal, 1973; Harris & Rosenthal, 1986) also identify specific mediators that teachers may use in acting upon their positive expectancies and in encouraging students' academic success. These include: accepting students' input; acknowledging, shaping, or developing their ideas; creating a warmer and nonnegative socioemotional climate for learning; and attempting to teach more material overall and/or more difficult material.

In the following reading, Snyder, Tanke, and Berscheid extend these findings to interpersonal behavior in college students. In their study, male college students conversed over an intercom system with female college students whom they believed to be either attractive or unattractive. As predicted, female college students' conversations were influenced by male students' perceptions of the female's attractiveness, even though these perceptions were manipulated by the experimenters.

---

*Editors' note: Many people have questioned the ethics of this research. Rosenthal and Jacobson (1968) provide a good defense of their study. Briefly, children's intelligence scores in the control group also went up, possibly as a function of participating in a study (the Hawthorne Effect). Thus, the children overall benefited from the study occurring in their school. Also, the results suggest that self-fulfilling prophecies have been a persistent phenomenon in many classrooms for many years. Identification of this effect has and will be beneficial to generations of children as teachers struggle to communicate only their positive expectations to their students.

Two points are important here. First, in terms of social control, one can see how subtle the influence of others can be. The women in this study had no idea why their conversations were going so well (or so poorly), but changed those conversations were, based on the college men's perceptions of the women. Because the study includes only the voice channel for communication (participants never did see each other), expectancies were communicated only by paralinguistic and verbal means. The judges' ratings measured more global impressions of the subjects, but these tapes could also be analyzed to identify which specific nonverbal and verbal behaviors changed as a function of the male interactants' attractive or unattractive perceptions of the female participants. You might try to predict which behaviors would be most important in being interpersonally successful.

Second, this study affirms the importance of physical attractiveness in interpersonal situations. Whereas many people claim that they are unaffected by others' external appearance, and that they "don't judge a book by its cover," it appears that, in fact, people do make such judgments, and alter their behavior based on these judgments rather often (see Reading 16). In the Social Values section, we discuss our unconscious acceptance of many socially accepted values. The intrinsic importance of physical attractiveness appears to be one such value. Should attractiveness be that important? The cosmetics industry certainly believes so. Is this a cultural trap from which there is no escape?

Abstract

This research concerns the self-fulfilling influences of social stereotypes on dyadic social interaction. Conceptual analysis of the cognitive and behavioral consequences of stereotyping suggests that a perceiver's actions based upon stereotype-generated attributions about a specific target individual may cause the behavior of that individual to confirm the perceiver's initially erroneous attributions. A paradigmatic investigation of the behavioral confirmation of stereotypes involving physical attractiveness (e.g., "beautiful people are good people") is presented. Male "perceivers" interacted with female "targets" whom they believed (as a result of an experimental manipulation) to be physically attractive or physically unattractive. Tape recordings of each participant's conversational behavior were analyzed by naive observer judges for evidence of behavioral confirmation. These analyses revealed that targets who were perceived (unknown to them) to be physically attractive came to behave in a friendly, likeable, and sociable manner in comparison with targets whose perceivers regarded them as unattractive. It is suggested that theories in cognitive social psychology attend to the ways in which perceivers create the information that they process in addition to the ways that they process that information.

Thoughts are but dreams
Till their effects be tried

—William Shakespeare
The Rape of Lucrece

Cognitive social psychology is concerned with the process by which individuals gain knowledge about behavior and events that they encounter in social interaction, and how they use this knowledge to guide their actions. From this perspective, people are "constructive thinkers" searching for the causes of behavior, drawing inferences about people and their circumstances, and acting upon this knowledge.

Most empirical work in this domain—largely stimulated and guided by the attribution theories (e.g., Heider, 1958; Jones & Davis, 1965; Kelley, 1973)—has focused on the processing of information, the "machinery" of social cognition. Some outcomes of this research have been the specification of how individuals identify the causes of an actor's behavior, how individuals make inferences about the traits and dispositions of the actor, and how individuals make predictions about the actor's future behavior (for reviews, see Harvey, Ickes, & Kidd, 1976; Jones et al., 1972; Ross, 1977).

It is noteworthy that comparatively little theoretical and empirical attention has been directed to the other fundamental question within the cognitive social psychologist's mandate: What are the cognitive and behavioral consequences of our impressions of other people? From our vantage point, current-day attribution theorists leave the individual "lost in thought," with no machinery that links thought to action. It is to this concern that we address ourselves, both theoretically and empirically, in the context of social sterotypes.

Social stereotypes are a special case of interpersonal perception. Stereotypes are usually simple, overgeneralized, and widely accepted (e.g., Karlins, Coffman, & Walters, 1969). But stereotypes are often inaccurate. It is simply not true that all Germans are industrious or that all women are dependent and conforming. Nonetheless, many social stereotypes concern highly visible and distinctive personal characteristics; for example, sex and race. These pieces of information are usually the first to be noticed in social interaction and can gain high priority for channeling subsequent information processing and even social interaction. Social stereotypes are thus an ideal testing ground for considering the cognitive and behavioral consequences of person perception.

Numerous factors may help sustain our stereotypes and prevent disconfirmation of "erroneous" stereotype-based initial impressions of specific others. First, social stereotypes may influence information processing in ways that serve to bolster and strengthen these stereotypes.

COGNITIVE BOLSTERING OF SOCIAL STEREOTYPES

As information processors, humans readily fall victim to the cognitive process described centuries ago by Francis Bacon (1620/1902):

> The human understanding, when any proposition has been once laid down...forces everything else to add fresh support and confirmation...it is the peculiar and perpetual error of the human understanding to be more moved and excited by affirmatives than negatives (pp. 23–24).

Empirical research has demonstrated several such biases in information processing. We may overestimate the frequency of occurrence of confirming or paradigmatic examples of our stereotypes simply because such instances are more easily noticed, more easily brought to mind, and more easily retrieved from memory (cf. Hamilton & Gifford, 1976). Evidence that confirms our stereotyped intuitions about human nature may be, in a word, more cognitively "available" (Tversky & Kahneman, 1973) than nonconfirming evidence.

Moreover, we may fill in the gaps in our evidence base with information consistent with our preconceived notions of what evidence should support our beliefs. For example, Chapman and Chapman (1967, 1969) have demonstrated that both college students and professional clinicians perceive positive associations between particular Rorschach responses and homosexuality in males, even though these associations are demonstrably absent in real life. These "signs" are simply those that comprise common cultural stereotypes of gay males.

Furthermore, once a stereotype has been adopted, a wide variety of evidence can be interpreted readily as supportive of that stereotype, including events that could support equally well an opposite interpretation. As Merton (1948) has suggested, in-group virtues ("We are thrifty") may become out-group vices ("They are cheap") in our attempts to maintain negative stereotypes about disliked out-groups. (For empirical demonstrations of this bias, see Regan, Straus, & Fazio, 1974; Rosenhan, 1973; Zadny & Gerard, 1974).

Finally, selective recall and reinterpretation of information from an individual's past history may be exploited to support a current stereotype-based inference (cf. Loftus & Palmer, 1974). Thus, having decided that Jim is stingy (as are all members of his group), it may be all too easy to remember a variety of behaviors and incidents that are insufficient one at a time to support an attribution of stinginess, but that taken together do warrant and support such an inference.

BEHAVIORAL CONFIRMATION OF SOCIAL STEREOTYPES

The cognitive bolstering process discussed above may provide the perceiver with an "evidence base" that gives compelling cognitive reality to any traits that he or she may have erroneously attributed to a target individual initially. This reality is, of course, entirely cognitive: It is in the eye and mind of the beholder. But stereotype-based attributions may serve as grounds for predictions about the target's future behavior and may guide and influence the perceiver's interactions with the target. This process itself may generate behaviors on the part of the target that erroneously confirm the predictions and validate the attributions of the perceiver. How others treat us is, in large measure, a reflection of our treatment of them (cf. Bandura, 1977; Mischel, 1968; Raush, 1965). Thus, when we use our social perceptions as guides for regulating our interactions with others, we may constrain their behavioral options (cf. Kelley & Stahelski, 1970).

Consider this hypothetical, but illustrative, scenario: Michael tells Jim that Chris is a cool and aloof person. Jim meets Chris and notices expressions of coolness and aloofness. Jim proceeds to overestimate the extent to which Chris' self-presentation reflects a cool and aloof disposition and underestimates the extent to which this posture was engendered by his own cool and aloof behavior toward Chris, that had in turn been generated by his own prior beliefs about Chris. Little does Jim know that Tom, who had heard that Chris was warm and friendly, found that his impressions of Chris were confirmed during their interaction. In each case, the end result of the process of "interaction guided by perceptions" has been the target person's *behavioral confirmation* of the perceiver's initial impressions of him.

This scenario makes salient key aspects of the process of behavioral confirmation in social interaction. The perceiver (either Jim or Tom) is not aware that his original perception of the target individual (Chris) is inaccurate. Nor is the perceiver aware of the causal role that his own behavior (here, the enactment of a cool or warm expressive style) plays in generating the behavioral evidence that erroneously confirms his expectations. Unbeknownst to the perceiver, the reality that he confidently perceives to exist in the social world has, in fact, been actively constructed by his own transactions with and operations upon the social world.

In our empirical research, we proposed to demonstrate that stereotypes may create their own social reality by channeling social interaction in ways that cause the stereotyped individual to behaviorally confirm the perceiver's stereotype. Moreover, we sought to demonstrate behavioral confirmation in a social interaction context designed to mirror as faithfully as possible the spontaneous generation of impressions in everyday social interaction and the subsequent channeling influences of these perceptions on dyadic interaction.

One widely held stereotype in this culture involves physical attractiveness. Considerable evidence suggests that attractive persons are assumed to possess more socially desirable personality traits and are expected to lead better lives than their unattractive counterparts (Berscheid & Walster, 1974). Attractive persons are perceived to have virtually every character trait that is socially desirable to the perceiver: "Physically attractive people, for example, were perceived to be more sexually warm and responsive, sensitive, kind, interesting, strong, poised, modest, sociable, and outgoing than persons of lesser physical attractiveness" (Berscheid & Walster, 1974, p. 169). This powerful stereotype holds for male and female perceivers and for male and female stimulus persons.

What of the validity of the physical attractiveness stereotype? Are the physically attractive actually more likable, friendly, and confident than the unattractive? Physically attractive young adults are more often and more eagerly sought out for social dates

(Dermer, 1973; Krebs & Adinolphi, 1975; Walster, Aronson, Abrahams, & Rottman, 1966). Even as early as nursery school age, physical attractiveness appears to channel social interaction: The physically attractive are chosen and the unattractive are rejected in sociometric choices (Dion & Berscheid, 1974; Kleck, Richardson, & Ronald, 1974).

Differential amount of interaction with the attractive and unattractive clearly helps the stereotype persevere, for it limits the chances for learning whether the two types of individuals differ in the traits associated with the stereotype. But the point we wish to focus upon here is that the stereotype may also channel interaction so that it behaviorally confirms itself. Individuals may have different styles of interaction for those whom they perceive to be physically attractive and for those whom they consider unattractive. These differences in interaction style may in turn elicit and nurture behaviors from the target person that are in accord with the stereotype. That is, the physically attractive may actually come to behave in a friendly, likable, sociable manner—not because they necessarily possess these dispositions, but because the behavior of others elicits and maintains behaviors taken to be manifestations of such traits.

Accordingly, we sought to demonstrate the behavioral confirmation of the physical attractiveness stereotype in dyadic social interaction. In order to do so, pairs of previously unacquainted individuals (designated, for our purposes, as a perceiver and a target) interacted in a getting-acquainted situation that had been constructed to allow us to control the information that one member of the dyad (the male perceiver) received about the physical attractiveness of the other individual (the female target). To measure the extent to which the actual behavior of the target matched the perceiver's stereotype, naive observer judges, who were unaware of the actual or perceived physical attractiveness of either participant, listened to and evaluated tape recordings of the interaction.

METHOD

Participants

Fifty-one male and 51 female undergraduates at the University of Minnesota participated, for extra course credit, in a study of "the processes by which people become acquainted with each other." Participants were scheduled in pairs of previously unacquainted males and females.

The Interaction Between Perceiver and Target

To insure that participants would not see each other before their interactions, they arrived at separate experimental rooms on separate corridors. The experimenter informed each participant that she was studying acquaintance processes in social relationships. Specifically, she was investigating the differences between those initial interactions that involve nonverbal communication and those, such as telephone conversations, that do not. Thus, she explained, the participant would engage in a telephone conversation with another student in introductory psychology.

Before the conversation began, each participant provided written permission for it to be tape recorded. In addition, both dyad members completed brief questionnaires concerning such information as academic major in college and high school of graduation. These questionnaires, it was explained, would provide the partners with some information about each other with which to start the conversation.

Activating the Perceiver's Stereotype The getting-acquainted interaction permitted control of the information that each male perceiver received about the physical attractiveness of his female target. When male perceivers learned about the biographical information questionnaires, they also learned that each person would receive a snapshot of the other member of the dyad, because "other people in the experiment have told us they feel more comfortable when they have a mental picture of the person they're talking to.'' The experimenter then used a Polaroid camera to photograph the male. No mention of any snapshots was made to female participants.

When each male perceiver received his partner's biographical information form, it arrived in a folder containing a Polaroid snapshot, ostensibly of his partner. Although the biographical information had indeed been provided by his partner, the photograph was not. It was one of eight photographs that had been prepared in advance.

Twenty females students from several local colleges assisted (in return for $5) in the preparation of stimulus materials by allowing us to take Polaroid snapshots of them. Each photographic subject wore casual dress, each was smiling, and each agreed (in writing) to allow us to use her photograph. Twenty college-age men then rated the attractiveness of each picture on a 10-point scale. We then chose the four pictures that had received the highest attractiveness ratings ($M = 8.10$) and the four photos that had received the lowest ratings ($M = 2.56$). There was virtually no overlap in ratings of the two sets of pictures.

Male perceivers were assigned randomly to one of two conditions of perceived physical attractiveness of their targets. Males in the attractive target condition received folders containing their partners' biographical information form and one of the four attractive photographs. Males in the unattractive target condition received folders containing their partners' biographical information form and one of the four unattractive photographs. Female targets knew nothing of the photographs possessed by their male interaction partners, nor did they receive snapshops of their partners.

The Perceiver's Stereotype-Based Attributions
Before initiating his getting-acquainted conversation, each male perceiver rated his initial impressions of his partner on an Impression Formation Questionnaire. The questionnaire was constructed by supplementing the 27 trait adjec-

tives used by Dion, Berscheid, and Walster (1972) in their original investigation of the physical attractiveness stereotype with the following items: intelligence, physical attractiveness, social adeptness, friendliness, enthusiasm, trustworthiness, and successfulness. We were thus able to assess the extent to which perceivers' initial impressions of their partners reflected general stereotypes linking physical attractiveness and personality characteristics.

The Getting-Acquainted Conversation Each dyad then engaged in a 10-minute unstructured conversation by means of microphones and headphones connected through a Sony TC-570 stereophonic tape recorder that recorded each participant's voice on a separate channel of the tape.

After the conversation, male perceivers completed the Impression Formation Questionnaires to record final impressions of their partners. Female targets expressed self-perceptions in terms of the items of the Impression Formation Questionnaire. Each female target also indicated, on 10-point scales, how much she had enjoyed the conversation, how comfortable she had felt while talking to her partner, how accurate a picture of herself she felt that her partner had formed as a result of the conversation, how typical her partner's behavior had been of the way she usually was treated by men, her perception of her own physical attractiveness, and her estimate of her partner's perception of her physical attractiveness. All participants were then thoroughly and carefully debriefed and thanked for their contribution to the study.

Assessing Behavioral Confirmation

To assess the extent to which the actions of the target women provided behavioral confirmation for the stereotypes of the men perceivers, 8 male and 4 female introductory psychology students rated the tape recordings of the getting-acquainted conversations. These observer judges were unaware of the experimental hypotheses and knew nothing of the actual or perceived physical attractiveness of the individuals on the tapes. They listened, in random order, to two 4-minute segments (one each from the beginning and end) of each conversation. They heard *only* the track of the tapes containing the target women's voices and rated each woman on the 34 bipolar scales of the Impression Formation Questionnaire as well as on 14 additional 10-point scales; for example, "How animated and enthusiastic is this person?", "How intimate or personal is this person's conversation?", and "How much is she enjoying herself?" Another group of observer judges (3 males and 6 females) performed a similar assessment of the male perceivers' behavior based upon only the track of the tapes that contained the males' voices.

RESULTS

To chart the process of behavioral confirmation of social stereotypes in dyadic social interaction, we examined the effects of our manipulation of the target women's apparent physical attractiveness on (a) the male perceivers' initial impressions of them and (b) the women's behavioral self-presentation during the interaction, as measured by the observer judges' ratings of the tape recordings.

The Perceivers' Stereotype

Did our male perceivers form initial impressions of their specific target women on the basis of general stereotypes that associate physical attractiveness and desirable personalities? To answer this question, we examined the male perceivers' initial ratings on the Impression Formation Questionnaire. Recall that these impressions were recorded *after* the perceivers had seen their partners' photographs, but *before* the getting-acquainted conversation. Indeed, it appears that our male perceivers did fashion their initial impressions of their female partners on the basis of stereotyped beliefs about physical attractiveness, multivariate $F(34, 3) = 10.19$, $p < .04$. As dictated by the physical

attractiveness stereotype, men who anticipated physically attractive partners expected to interact with comparatively sociable, poised, humorous, and socially adept women; by contrast, men faced with the prospect of getting acquainted with relatively unattractive partners fashioned images of rather unsociable, awkward, serious, and socially inept women, all $Fs(1, 36) > 5.85$, $p < .025$.

Behavioral Confirmation

Not only did our perceivers fashion their images of their discussion partners on the basis of their stereotyped intuitions about beauty and goodness of character, but these impressions initiated a chain of events that resulted in the behavioral confirmation of these initially erroneous inferences. Our analyses of the observer judges' ratings of the women's behavior were guided by our knowledge of the structure of the men's initial impressions of their target women's personality. Specifically, we expected to find evidence of behavioral confirmation only for those traits that had defined the perceivers' stereotypes. For example, male perceivers did not attribute differential amounts of sensitivity or intelligence to partners of differing apparent physical attractiveness. Accordingly, we would not expect that our observer judges would "hear" different amounts of intelligence or sensitivity in the tapes. By contrast, male perceivers did expect attractive and unattractive targets to differ in sociability. Here we would expect that observer judges would detect differences in sociability between conditions when listening to the women's contributions to the conversations, and thus we would have evidence of behavioral confirmation.

To assess the extent to which the women's behavior, as rated by the observer judges, provided behavioral confirmation for the male perceivers' stereotypes, we identified, by means of a discriminant analysis (Tatsuoka, 1971), those 21 trait items of the Impression Formation Questionnaire for which the mean initial ratings of the men in the attractive target and unattractive target conditions differed by more than 1.4 standard deviations.[1] This set of "stereotype traits" (e.g., sociable, poised, sexually warm, outgoing) defines the differing perceptions of the personality characteristics of target women in the two experimental conditions.

We then entered these 21 stereotype traits and the 14 additional dependent measures into a multivariate analysis of variance. This analysis revealed that our observer judges did indeed view women who had been assigned to the attractive target condition quite differently than women in the unattractive target condition, $Fm(35, 2) = 40.003$, $p < .025$. What had initially been reality in the minds of the men had now become reality in the behavior of the women with whom they had interacted—a behavioral reality discernible even by naive observer judges, who had access *only* to tape recordings of the women's contributions to the conversations.

When a multivariate analysis of variance is performed on multiple correlated dependent measures, the null hypothesis states that the vector of means is equal across conditions. When the null hypothesis is rejected, the nature of the difference between groups must then be inferred from inspection of group differences on the individual dependent measures. In this case, the differences between the behavior of the women in the attractive target and the unattractive target conditions were in the same direction as the male perceivers' initial stereotyped impressions for fully 17 of the 21 measures of behavioral confirmation. The binomial probability that at least 17 of these adjectives would be in the predicted direction by chance alone is a scant .003. By contrast, when we examined the 13 trait pairs that our discriminant analysis had indicated did *not* define the male perceivers' stereotype, a sharply different pattern emerged. Here,

we would not expect any systematic relationship between the male perceivers' stereotyped initial impressions and the female targets' actual behavior in the getting acquainted conversations. In fact, for only 8 of these 13 measures is the difference between the behavior of the women in the attractive target condition in the same direction as the men's stereotyped initial impressions. This configuration is, of course, hardly different from the pattern expected by chance alone if there were no differences between the groups (exact binomial $p = .29$). Clearly, then, behavioral confirmation manifested itself only for those attributes that had defined the male perceivers' stereotype; that is, only in those domains where the men believed that there did exist links between physical attractiveness and personal attributes did the women come to behave differently as a consequence of the level of physical attractiveness that we had experimentally assigned to them.

Moreover, our understanding of the nature of the difference between the attractive target and the unattractive target conditions identified by our multivariate analysis of variance and our confidence in this demonstration of behavioral confirmation are bolstered by the consistent pattern of behavioral differences on the 14 additional related dependent measures. Our raters assigned to the female targets in the attractive target condition higher ratings on *every* question related to favorableness of self-presentation. Thus, for example, those who were thought by their perceivers to be physically attractive appeared to the observer judges to manifest greater confidence, greater animation, greater enjoyment of the conversation, and greater liking for their partners than those women who interacted with men who perceived them as physically unattractive.

In Search of Mediators of Behavioral Confirmation

We next attempted to chart the process of behavioral confirmation. Specifically, we searched for evidence of the behavioral implications of the

---

[1]After the 21st trait dimension, the differences between the experimental conditions drop off sharply. For example, the next adjective pair down the line has a difference of 1.19 standard deviations, and the one after that has a difference of 1.02 standard deviations.

perceivers' stereotypes. Did the male perceivers present themselves differently to target women whom they assumed to be physically attractive or unattractive? Because we had 50 dependent measures of the observer judges' ratings of the males—12 more than the number of observations (male perceivers)—a multivariate analysis of variance is inappropriate. However, in 21 cases, univariate analyses of variance did indicate differences between conditions (all ps $< .05$). Men who interacted with women whom they believed to be physically attractive appeared (to the observer judges) more sociable, sexually warm, interesting, independent, sexually permisssive, bold, outgoing, humorous, obvious, and socially adept than their counterparts in the unattractive target condition. Moreover, these men were seen as more attractive, more confident, and more animated in their conversation than their counterparts. Further, they were considered by the observer judges to be more comfortable, to enjoy themselves more, to like their partners more, to take the initiative more often, to use their voices more effectively, to see their women partners as more attractive and, finally, to be seen as more attractive by their partners than men in the unattractive target condition.

It appears, then, that differences in the level of sociability manifested and expressed by the male perceivers may have been a key factor in bringing out reciprocating patterns of expression in the target women. One reason that target women who had been labeled as attractive may have reciprocated these sociable overtures is that they regarded their partners' images of them as more accurate, $F(1, 28) = 6.75$, $p < .02$, and their interaction style to be more typical of the way men generally treated them, $F(1, 28) = 4.79$, $p < .04$, than did women in the unattractive target condition. These individuals, perhaps, rejected their partners' treatment of them as unrepresentative and defensively adopted more cool and aloof postures to cope with their situations.

DISCUSSION

Of what consequence are our social stereotypes? Our research suggests that stereotypes can and do channel dyadic interaction so as to create their own social reality. In our demonstration, pairs of individuals got acquainted with each other in a situation that allowed us to control the information that one member of the dyad (the perceiver) received about the physical attractiveness of the other person (the target). Our perceivers, in anticipation of interaction, fashioned erroneous images of their specific partners that reflected their general stereotypes about physical attractiveness. Moreover, our perceivers had very different patterns and styles of interaction for those whom they perceived to be physically attractive and unattractive. These differences in self-presentation and interaction style, in turn, elicited and nurtured behaviors of the target that were consistent with the perceivers' initial stereotypes. Targets who were perceived (unbeknownst to them) to be physically attractive actually came to behave in a friendly, likable, and sociable manner. The perceivers' attributions about their targets based upon their stereotyped intuitions about the world had initiated a process that produced behavioral confirmation of those attributions. The initially erroneous attributions of the perceivers had become real: The stereotype had truly functioned as a self-fulfilling prophecy (Merton, 1948).[2]

We regard our investigation as a particularly compelling demonstration of behavioral confir-

---

[2] Our research on behavioral confirmation in social interaction is a clear "cousin" of other demonstrations that perceivers' expectations may influence other individuals' behavior. Thus, Rosenthal (1974) and his colleagues have conducted an extensive program of laboratory and field investigations of the effects of experimenters' and teachers' expectations on the behavior of subjects in psychological laboratories and students in classrooms. Experimenters and teachers led to expect particular patterns of performance from their subjects and pupils act in ways that selectively influence or shape those performances to confirm initial expectations (e.g., Rosenthal, 1974).

mation in social interaction. For if there is any social-psychological process that ought to exist in "stronger" form in everyday interaction than in the psychological laboratory, it is behavioral confirmation. In the context of years of social interaction in which perceivers have reacted to their actual physical attractiveness, our 10-minute getting-acquainted conversations over a telephone must seem minimal indeed. Nonetheless, the impact was sufficient to permit outside observers who had access only to one person's side of a conversation to detect manifestations of behavioral confirmation.

Might not other important and widespread social stereotypes—particularly those concerning sex, race, social class, and ethnicity—also channel social interaction so as to create their own social reality? For example, will the common stereotype that women are more conforming and less independent than men (cf. Broverman, Vogel, Broverman, Clarkson, & Rosenkrantz, 1972) influence interaction so that (within a procedural paradigm similar to ours) targets believed to be female will actually conform more, be more dependent, and be more successfully manipulated than interaction partners believed to be male? At least one empirical investigation has pointed to the possible self-fulfilling nature of apparent sex differences in self-presentation (Zanna & Pack, 1975).

Any self-fulfilling influences of social stereotypes may have compelling and pervasive societal consequences. Social observers have for decades commented on the ways in which stigmatized social groups and outsiders may fall "victim" to self-fulfilling cultural stereotypes (e.g., Becker, 1963; Goffman, 1963; Merton, 1948; Mydral, 1944; Tannenbaum, 1938). Consider Scott's (1969) observations about the blind:

> When, for example, sighted people continually insist that a blind man is helpless because he is blind, their subsequent treatment of him may preclude his even exercising the kinds of skills that would enable him to be independent. It is in this sense that stereotypic beliefs are self-actualized (p. 9).

And all too often it is the "victims" who are blamed for their own plight (cf. Ryan, 1971) rather than the social expectations that have constrained their behavioral options.

Of what import is the behavioral confirmation process for our theoretical understanding of the nature of social perception? Although our empirical research has focused on social stereotypes that are widely accepted and broadly generalized, our notions of behavioral confirmation may apply equally well to idiosyncratic social perceptions spontaneously formed about specific individuals in the course of every day social interaction. In this sense, social psychologists have been wise to devote intense effort to understanding the processes by which impressions of others are formed. Social perceptions are important precisely because of their impact on social interaction. Yet, at the same time, research and theory in social perception (mostly displayed under the banner of attribution theory) that have focused on the manner in which individuals process information provided them to form impressions of others may underestimate the extent to which information received in actual social interaction is a product of the perceiver's own actions toward the target individual. More careful attention must clearly be paid to the ways in which perceivers *create* or *construct* the information that they process in addition to the ways in which they *process* that information. Events in the social world may be as much the *effects* of our perceptions of those events as they are the *causes* of those perceptions.

From this perspective, it becomes easier to appreciate the perceiver's stubborn tendency to fashion images of others largely in trait terms (e.g., Jones & Nisbett, 1972), despite the poverty of evidence for the pervasive cross-situational consistencies in social behavior that the existence of "true" traits would demand (e.g., Mischel, 1968). This tendency, dubbed by Ross (1977) as the "fundamental attribution error," may be a self-erasing error. For even though any target individual's behavior may lack, overall, the trait-defining properties of cross-situational consistency, the actions of the perceiver himself may produce consistency in the samples of behavior available to that perceiver. Our impressions of others may cause those others to behave in consistent trait-like fashion for us. In that sense, our trait-based impressions of others are veridical, even though the same individual may behave or be led to behave in a fashion perfectly consistent with opposite attributions by other perceivers with quite different impressions of that individual. Such may be the power of the behavioral confirmation process.

A Social Psychological Analysis of Physician-Patient Rapport: Toward a Science of the Art of Medicine

M. Robin DiMatteo (1979)

The interpersonal expectancy (behavioral confirmation) literature (see Reading 32) argues that social control can be persuasive even when subtle. It can affect children's achievement in school and the positiveness of social interactions. It can influence performance on job interviews (Word, Zanna, & Cooper, 1974) and judges' communications in jury trials (Blanck, Rosenthal, & Cordell, 1985). Research on the socioemotional aspects of the physician-patient relationship suggests that patients' physical health can also be altered by the quality of the interpersonal relationship between the physician and the patient. DiMatteo's review of the literature indicates that patient compliance with doctor's orders can be significantly increased by doctor concern for and empathy toward the patient. How physicians can better develop such subtle control for the sake of the patient's well-being is also discussed. Other questions that are increasingly important as health issues and that need to be addressed in future research involve (a) patients' means of developing their own sense of control in the doctor-patient

relationship and (b) the relationship between a patient's sense of control and actual health outcomes.

Control is often thought of in a negative sense, and people may strongly resist the influence attempts of others, such as is evident in the literature on "psychological reactance." It is important to remember, however, that control can have positive effects, e.g., for children's success in school, for friendly and sociable conversations, and for successful acceleration of healing.

Abstract

The interpersonal relationship between physician and patient involves a highly charged affective component. As a result, patients' satisfaction with medical care, their compliance with treatment regimens, and the outcome of treatment tend to be substantially related to their physicians' ability to satisfy their socio-emotional needs in the health care encounter. This critical aspect of health care is termed "rapport." While it is not yet clear exactly how rapport with patients can be achieved, evidence reviewed here suggests that a physician's ability to establish rapport with patients is at least partially dependent upon his or her communication skills, especially the ability to decode and encode nonverbal messages of affect. Implications for teaching physicians the elements of empathic communication are discussed.

Nearly every society has defined specific roles and status for the ill and their healers, and for many years the rights and duties of the individuals who occupy these roles have been examined by sociologists and anthropologists (King, 1962). In modern American society, the primary healing role is given to the physician. This professional role ranks highly in prestige and power, and demands technical competence, emotional neutrality, and a commitment to serving people (Parsons, 1951). Likewise, the sick person occupies a social role. Parsons (1958) has delineated the benefits to and obligations of the individual who is ill. He or she is relieved of normal social responsibilities, and is expected both to seek medical help and to profess a desire to get well. When the physician and patient are brought together on the health care stage, their interaction is not a mere enactment of script or a simple learned scenario. The interpersonal nature of the physician-patient relationship involves a highly charged affective component. This intensity results from the physician's access to the patient's body and intimate details of the patient's life, as well as from the considerable emotional dependency of people who are ill. The treatment of illness is partly a process of social influence (King, 1962; Fox, 1959; Bloom, 1963; Wilson and Bloom, 1972). The physician and patient bring to their interaction their characteristics, backgrounds and past experiences, and their personal attitudes, beliefs, and values. Albert Schweitzer said of this interaction: "It is our duty to remember at all times and anew that medicine is not only a science, but also the art of letting our own individuality interact with the individuality of the patient" (Strauss, 1968, p. 361).

During the past few decades, medicine has made more significant strides in the diagnosis and treatment of disease than in all the years of its long history. Medicine has begun performing treatment miracles and is now one of America's largest industries, accounting for about 9% of the gross national product (Hamburg and Brown, 1978). Yet, as Eisenberg (1977) has noted, "It is...curious that dissatisfaction with medicine in America is at its most vociferous just at a time when doctors have at their disposal the most powerful medical technology the world has yet seen. The 'old fashioned' general practitioner, with few drugs that really worked and not much surgery to recommend, is for some reason looking good to many people—in retrospect, at least" (p. 235). Eisenberg has gone on to explain that... "Present-day disenchantment with physicians, at a time when they can do more than ever in history to halt and repair the ravages of serious illness, probably reflects the perception by people that they are not being cared for.... The patient wants time, sympathetic attention, and concern for himself as a person" (Eisenberg, 1977, p. 238).

A solution to these complaints is not likely to emerge naturally in today's health care system, for in order to maintain and further develop the technical excellence of modern medicine, medical students are selected primarily for their scientific abilities. Very little attention is paid to the depth of their interpersonal skills. In addition, present day medical training emphasizes the scientific aspects of patient care, with little recognition of what has been termed the "Art of Medicine." Many modern physicians have developed a very narrow view of what is "scientific" and have come to believe that medicine is a much more specific science than it actually is. They seem to ignore ancient and modern evidence that patients' responses to their physicians are no less real than their responses to drugs and other treatments, and that patients benefit (or suffer) not only from the medications they are given but also from their physicians' behavior toward them (Eisenberg, 1977; Engel, 1977).

Compassion and an effective bedside manner were almost all that physicians had to offer their patients throughout much of the history of medicine. Thus, the early physicians emphasized the significance of the physician's manner and interpersonal sensitivity to patients. In the fourth century B.C. (1923 Translations) Hippocrates wrote of the physician-patient relationship: "The patient, though conscious that his condition is perilous, may recover his health simply through his contentment with the goodness of the physician." Hippocrates wrote of the ways in which the physician must communicate this goodness. "On entering [the sick person's room, the physician must] bear in mind [his] manner of sitting, reserve, arrangement of dress, decisive utterance, brevity of speech, composure, bedside manners, care, replies to objections, calm self-control...his manner must be serious and humane; without stopping to be jocular or failing to be just, he must avoid excessive austerity; he must always be in control of himself." In a similar vein, Sir William Osler advocated that

"The practice of medicine is an art, not a trade; a calling, not a business; a calling in which your heart will be exercised equally with your head" (Osler, 1904). Frederick Shattuck, a prominent 20th century American physician, wrote in 1907 of what he perceived as a potentially serious gap between the developing science of medicine and what he knew as the art of medicine. He emphasized that disease is one phenomenon but the *diseased person* is another. The physician must have sympathy and empathy for his or her patient as well as gentleness and cheerfulness. He warned that concern for the newly developing scientific aspects of medicine should never replace compassionate medical care and treatment of the patient as a person both because of humanitarian concerns and because medical care without compassion may be ineffective.

In spite of this warning, however, as the body of technical medical knowledge grew there developed a sharp division between the physical care of the patient as science and the emotional care of the patient as interpersonal art. In 1963, Bloom proposed that the physician-patient relationship must now be seen as being composed of two independent dimensions: the "instrumental dimension," which emphasizes the purely technical aspects of the physician's treatment of the patient, and the "expressive dimension" which emphasizes the affective or socio-emotional components of the relationship.

The major purpose of this paper is to review evidence that these two components of the physician-patient relationship should still, as in the earlier days of medicine, be inseparable, and that focusing on one to the exclusion of the other results in ineffective medical care. However, with the help of sound basic and applied social psychological research, physicians can combine the two dimensions for more humane, more effective, and possibly more efficient (and, hence, less expensive) medical care delivery.

THE SIGNIFICANCE OF THE SOCIO-EMOTIONAL DIMENSION IN PATIENT CARE

It is obvious that the practice of medicine in modern times in a manner that emphasizes compassion and ignores technical expertise is quackery. It is not so obvious that the technical treatment of patients without attention to the socio-emotional dimension of the physician-patient relationship may result in equally serious problems. In recent years, a considerable amount of social psychological research has begun to examine the importance of the socio-emotional side of the physician-patient relationship. A brief review of this literature points to the overwhelming influence of this dimension on patient satisfaction with medical care, patient cooperation with medical regimens, and the actual outcome of treatment.

Patient Cooperation

A major unsolved problem in medicine today is patients' lack of cooperation (often called noncompliance) with medical regimens (Gillum and Barsky, 1974). Davis (1966) estimated that at least one-third of all patients fail to cooperate with doctors' orders. Studies have reported rates of noncooperation ranging from 15 to 93 percent. Research evidence suggests that a very important factor may be the failure of the physician to communicate effectively to the patient the correct information about the prescribed treatment (see Stone, 1979, for a detailed review of this informational aspect of communication). The evidence also suggests the necessity of affective communication—a kindness and concern that communicates to the patient that he or she is cared for as a person.

The socio-emotional dimension of the physician-patient relationship can significantly affect patient cooperation. In a study by Francis, Korsch, and Morris (1969), for example, lack of cooperation was related to the pediatrician's lack of sensitivity to, and subsequent failure to meet, the mother's expectations for her visit.

Similarly, patients most likely to fail to keep appointments in an out-patient referral clinic tend to be those who feel that they have no doctor with whom they can talk (Alpert, 1964). Davis (1968a, 1968b) analyzed verbal communication from tape-recordings of doctor-patient interactions and determined the degree of patient cooperation by questioning patients and physicians and by content-analyzing medical records. Failure to cooperate was found to be high when the doctor behaved in an antagonistic manner. If the physician collected information from the patient and ignored the patient's need for feedback, the patient tended to be uncooperative. When the physician concentrated solely on an analysis of the patient's medical situation (ignoring the psychological), and on the expression of the physician's own opinions, lack of cooperation was also a likely outcome. On the other hand, if tension built up in the interaction was released through joking or laughing, the probability of patient cooperation with medical regimens was increased.

Other studies have shown that in a psychiatric intake interview, the reported anger of the psychiatric resident correlates negatively with the walk-in applicant's cooperation with recommendations for return to a second diagnostic interview (Salzman, Shader, Scott, and Binstock, 1970). The cooperation of alcoholic patients with prescribed treatment regimens has been shown to be related to the communicated affect of their physicians toward alcoholics in general (Milmoe, Rosenthal, Blane, Chafetz, and Wolf, 1967).

In summary, then, it appears from correlational data that the socio-emotional dimension of the physician-patient interaction bears an important relationship to patients' cooperation with medical advice. The existing evidence tends to suggest that a patient's willingness to accept and follow the prescribed treatment regimen might be increased if the physician is sensitive to the patient's needs as a person, communicates caring, and develops rapport with the patient. (See Rodin and Janis, 1979, for an analysis of the development and conse-

quences of a possible mediating mechanism in this relationship—the physician's referent power.)

The Outcome of Treatment

There is evidence that the quality of the interpersonal relationship between the physician and patient can significantly influence the outcome of treatments that may appear to depend solely upon technical factors. In one of the few experimental studies of this kind, Egbert, Battit, Welch, and Bartlett (1964) demonstrated the importance of effective anesthesiologist-patient communication. Surgical patients were randomly divided into two groups. Half of these patients were visited pre-operatively by their anesthesiologist and told about the post-operative pain they would experience and how to relax their muscles in order to reduce the pain. The other patients were told nothing about post-operative pain. After the first post-operative day the group of patients given the special visit and information required a significantly lower dosage of narcotics and their surgeons (blind to each patient's experimental condition) discharged experimental group patients from the hospital an average of 2.7 days earlier than those in the control group. While this result may have been due to any number of factors such as information, familiarity with the anesthesiologist before surgery, some unknown component of the one-to-one contact, or the patients' actual compliance with muscle relaxation techniques, the results did demonstrate that the physician's efforts to reach out to the patient with reassurance and information can influence the outcome of a technical procedure such as surgery.

Pain and illness are accompanied by a significant amount of anxiety, which can have important health-related consequences. For example, a patient's level of anxiety and fear before surgery can affect post-operative recovery (Janis, 1958; Langer, Janis, and Wolfer, 1975). Confidence in the physician and the reduction of patient anxiety have been found to be inextricably intertwined. Confidence in the physician's technical expertise is significantly influenced by the patient's perception of the physician's affective behavior (Ben-Sira, 1976). Patients tend to judge the competence of their physicians in part by the degree of emotional support they receive. Confidence in their physicians, in turn, lowers the anxiety of patients, thus increasing the chance of more rapid recovery.

There is some evidence that the physician's interpersonal behavior toward the acutely ill patient can influence the patient's observable physiological condition. Järvinen (1955) found a significant increase in the number of sudden deaths among coronary patients during or shortly after ward rounds conducted by the medical staff. Ward rounds are nearly always conducted as a formal procedure with little regard for the patient as a person, but rather with attention to the patient as a "case." Järvinen suggested that this formal behavior on the part of the physicians serves to increase the fear and anxiety of patients to the point where it can reach a dangerously high level. Indeed, human interaction in a frightening, upsetting, or negative emotional context, has been found to have major effects on the cardiac rhythm and the electrical impulses of the hearts of cardiac patients (Lynch, Thomas, Mills, Malinow, and Katcher, 1974). This recognition of the physician's possible influence on the physiological condition of his or her patient highlights the importance of attending to effective bedside manner in medical practice.

Patient Satisfaction

Another important consequence of an effective socio-emotional relationship between physician and patient is the patient's own satisfaction with the care he or she receives. A number of studies reveal that patients clearly desire a good rapport and clear communication with their physicians, and that when they receive it, they are less likely to turn from the medical profession to quacks and charlatans or to bring medical malpractice suits against their physicians.

Koos (1955) surveyed a random sample of one thousand urban families, stratified on economic level, regarding their satisfaction with medical care. The greatest criticism of a majority of the respondents (64%) was about the nature of the physician-patient relationship they experienced. Similarly, a majority of Friedson's (1961) survey respondents felt that good medical care requires an interest in the patient as a person. More recently, Doyle and Ware (1977) found that physician conduct toward the patient was the strongest influence on satisfaction with medical care. Korsch, Gozzi, and Francis (1968) identified specific characteristics of physician-patient verbal interaction that contribute to patient satisfaction and dissatisfaction with medical care. Eight hundred patient visits to a pediatric walk-in clinic were studied by analysis of (a) a tape-recording of the doctor-patient (mother) interaction, and (b) a follow-up interview with the patient. Communication barriers such as the doctor's lack of warmth and friendliness, failure to take account of the patient's concerns and expectations from the medical visit, lack of a clear-cut explanation concerning diagnosis and causation of illness, and use of medical jargon, were all significant contributors to patient dissatisfaction.

Many patients change primary care physicians because they are dissatisfied with the interpersonal treatment they receive. In an extensive survey reported in 1953, Gray and Cartwright found that a considerable number of adults in the United Kingdom's National Health Service changed physicians because of "inadequate treatment and attention." Patients terminated the physician-patient relationship if the doctor was too busy to talk with them or appeared to be uninterested in them as people. In a more recent survey in the United States, Kasteler, Kane, Olsen, and Thetford (1976) found that patient's dislike of the doctor as a person, their dissatisfaction with the amount of time spent with them, and their perception of their physician's seeming lack of interest in them, significantly increased doctor-shopping behavior.

Thus, physicians' inability to satisfy their patients with meaningful affective behavior can contribute to the economic and human costs associated with health care delivery, such as extensive lack of patient cooperation with medical advice, seeking of nonmedical healers by seriously ill patients, extensive doctor-shopping, and an increasing incidence of malpractice litigation. Because of their potential for minimizing or eliminating these costs, programs to train physicians in the interpersonal aspects of the healing process should be developed without delay. The interpersonal aspects of patient care must balance and blend with the extensive, sophisticated training in the technological aspects of patient care. Both the recognition and implementation of this vital part of the physician's training is long overdue.

DEFINING THE AFFECTIVE COMPONENT OF THE PHYSICIAN-PATIENT RELATIONSHIP

In order that physicians may be taught to develop and nurture more effective socio-emotional relationships with their patients, researchers must be able to define clearly what this socio-emotional component consists of. There is strong evidence that the ability to establish rapport with patients tends to be uncorrelated with measures of intellectual performance such as Grade Point Average in the pre-medical years and the Medical College Admission Test (Flom, 1971; Gough, Hall, and Harris, 1963, 1964; Richards, Taylor and Price, 1962). Some personality measures have been found to correlate with a physician's ability to relate to patients on a socio-emotional level (Gough, Hall, and Harris, 1964; Flom, 1971; Howell, 1966). The results of these studies of personality measures are rather weak and equivocal, however, and they are further limited because criterion measures of the inter-

personal success of the physicians in these studies were only ratings by other physicians, not the actual expressed satisfaction of their patients. The weakness in the criterion measures and the equivocality of the findings to date, point to the importance of further research on components of physicians' affective care of patients.

The inability to identify, empirically, predictors of rapport is paralleled by weak theoretical specification of its components. Chafetz (1970), Kaufman (1970), and Headlee (1973) have proposed that rapport requires good manners, respect and compassion. It is simply a matter of common etiquette to reassure patients that they are more than just cases, that they are people whose welfare is important to the physician. The components that these authors suggest are far from simply defined. Moreover, they are far from simply enacted. How does one define "good manners," for example? What behaviors insure the communication of "respect" and "compassion" and "reassurance"? These are complex aspects of human social interaction not necessarily understood by intuition alone. Rather, these complex behaviors involve subtleties and nuances in the interplay of verbal and nonverbal messages. Clarion calls for physicians to develop "pleasing bedside manner" and to "understand" and "empathize with" their patients constitute unproductive rhetoric. Granted, the physician's motivation is a crucial component in these matters. But the physician's role requires continuous patient contact. Probably few highly introverted, anti-social individuals choose primary care as their life's profession. Indeed, studies of the job satisfaction of physicians in primary patient care reveal that effective communication with patients, and the deep and lasting human relationships that are developed in taking care of people, are the most satisfying aspects of the role of the primary care physician (Ford, Liske, Ort, and Denton, 1967).

Most physicians, then, probably have at least some degree of motivation to engage in effective interpersonal communication with their patients. Some may even be familiar with and persuaded by social scientific investigations of the influence of the affective/socio-emotional components of patient care on compliance, satisfaction, and the outcome of treatment. But due to a serious lack of readily available information and effective techniques for analyzing and improving affective communication with patients, these physicians' desires are often frustrated. Recent efforts by basic and applied social psychological researchers represent some noteworthy first steps toward the understanding of the socio-emotional component of the patient-practitioner relationship. One encouraging line of research involves the investigation of the physician's nonverbal communication skill as a component of successful affective relationships with patients. Closely related is the research on "empathy" in the helper-helpee relationship.

In the psychological literature, empathy is used to refer to an individual's ability to relate to another person—to put oneself in the place of the other person. According to Truax and Carkhuff (1967), "Accurate empathy involves both the therapist's *sensitivity to current feelings* and his *verbal facility to communicate this understanding* in a language attuned to the client's current feeling" (p. 46). Later in their development of the construct of accurate empathy, Traux and Carkhuff expanded their definition to include the nonverbal components of communication. The therapist who is at the highest stage of empathy is "completely attuned to the client's shifting emotional content; he senses each of the client's feelings and reflects them in his words and voice" (p. 56). McGowan and Schmidt (1962) noted that "what we say as counselors is not as important as how we say it" (p. 322). As early as Hippocrates' time it was recognized that the physician's ability to *detect* and to *respond* to a patient's nonverbally expressed needs and anx-

ieties could significantly influence the course of the patient's recovery (Hippocrates, 1923 edition; Shattuck, 1907).

Physicians' Detection of Patient Affect

Nonverbal communication in the physician-patient interaction may be a crucial socio-emotional component for a number of reasons (Friedman, 1979). Of special interest to empathy is the idea that people may "leak" their true feelings through body as well as facial cues (Ekman and Friesen, 1969, 1974). Hence, it is probable that a physician can enhance his or her communication with patients (and thereby improve the socio-emotional aspects of interaction with patients) if the physician can develop skill at reading body-movement cues. By recognizing cues of dissatisfaction and negative affect in the body language of patients, the physician can, for example, become aware of the patient's distress, and deal with it before the patient terminates the relationship, attenuates treatment effects by lack of cooperation, or retaliates with malpractice litigation. By accurately reading the nonverbal cues of the patient which accompany his or her verbal expression of understanding of a treatment regimen, the physician may be able to identify signs of confusion or discomfort which indicate the patient's lack of understanding or possible unwillingness to follow the prescription.

Recent studies by Rosenthal, Hall, DiMatteo, Rogers, and Archer (1979) have produced evidence supporting these suggestions in one kind of therapeutic relationship. These investigations measured nonverbal sensitivity with the PONS test, a film test providing quantitative indices of a respondent's abilities to decode accurately the nonverbal communication of affect in another person's facial expressions, body movements and postures, and voice tone. The studies involved counselors and psychotherapists and persons in training for those professions. Within each of six samples, there was a tendency for individuals rated high (by their

supervisors) in therapeutic skills and effectiveness to be more sensitive to nonverbal information, particularly about body movement and
postural cues to emotion.

In a series of recent studies by the author and
associates, the criterion measure of physician
rapport with patients consisting of ratings of satisfaction *by patients* was examined in relation to
physicians' sensitivity to nonverbal communication (DiMatteo, Friedman, and Taranta, 1979).
In two studies, a total of 64 medical house officers (physicians receiving residency training in
internal medicine) at an urban community teaching hospital were administered the PONS test,
and an average of six of each house officer's patients were interviewed about their satisfaction
with the physician's interpersonal treatment of
them. In both studies, ratings of the physicians
by their patients were significantly positively correlated with the physicians' accuracy in decoding emotion expressed through body posture and
movement on the PONS test. These studies provide some evidence that a physician's ability to
decode nonverbal cues may be an important component of his or her empathy in dealing with
patients.

Physicians' Communication of Affect to Patients

The physician's ability to communicate caring
and concern to patients through verbal and nonverbal channels may be an essential addition to
technical expertise in the effective delivery of
medical care, for without the communication of
positive affect, patients may have little confidence in their physicians (Ben-Sira, 1976). Patients' perceptions of the caring and concern,
warmth, and positive feeling of their physicians
can strongly influence their desire to continue
the relationship (DiMatteo, Prince, and Taranta,
1979) and their tendency to comply with physicians' orders (Francis, Korsch, and Morris, 1969).
In the communication of empathy, nonverbal
cues have been found to be extremely important,

possibly even more important than the verbal message itself (Haase and Tepper, 1972).

Friedman, DiMatteo, and Taranta (1980) report two studies conducted with medical house
officers that measured directly their nonverbal
expressiveness, and examined its relationship to
patient satisfaction. In the two studies, a total of
forty-seven medical residents were audiotaped
and/or filmed while expressing (to a person who
was simulating a patient) a number of verbally
neutral sentences communicating various emotions. These emotions were Happiness, Sadness,
Anger, and Surprise. These audiotapes and films
were then edited and played back to large groups
of raters or judges. The judges were asked to
guess which emotion was being "sent" in each
communication. The proportion of judges who
correctly labelled the communication (for example, labelled the emotion Happiness when the
physician was in fact trying to communicate Happiness) was taken as a measure of the physician's
ability successfully to communicate the emotion
to others. If a high percentage of the judges
guessed correctly what the physician was
"sending," or encoding, then the physician was
a successful sender; if few understood his or her
communications, the physicians' nonverbal encoding skills were scored as poor. Patients' ratings of the physician's interpersonal behavior
were collected, and these ratings were found to
be moderately correlated with the "sending
skill" scores. The results of both studies indicated that a physician's ability to communicate
emotions through nonverbal channels of facial
expression and voice tone was related to his or
her patients' satisfaction with the interpersonal
aspects of care.

These findings are consistent with social-
psychological theories of social influence. For
example, the patient may look to the physician
for cues as to how he or she should respond to
the medical situation and to what the patient
should attribute emotional arousal. If the patient's anxiety is high regarding aspects of the
treatment or details of the diagnosis, the physi-

cian can do much to communicate to the patient that the appropriate response should be calm and hopeful rather than a response fraught with panic, fear or hopelessness (see Friedman, 1979). A friendly physician who can communicate warmth and bring the receiver of a persuasive communication to like him or her will be more successful in changing attitudes (such as increasing compliance) than will someone who is not liked by the receiver of the message (see Rodin and Janis, 1979).

These notions are also closely aligned to Carl Rogers' (1957) specifications for effective counselling and psychotherapy: (a) the communication of warmth and unconditional positive regard to the client, (b) an understanding of the client's feelings and a communication of that understanding, and (c) the communication of genuineness and sincerity. The latter has been operationally defined by researchers on nonverbal communication, such as Friedman (1979), in terms of consistency between verbal and nonverbal cues. The physician's nonverbal sensitivity and expressiveness, therefore, appear to be linked both theoretically and empirically, to patient satisfaction with medical treatment. Social psychologists are making headway toward more precise definitions of physician-patient rapport and the socioemotional aspects of patient care.

Teaching Nonverbal Skills

Recent research suggests some avenues for developing training programs for nonverbal behavior skills for physicians and other health care professionals. There is some direct evidence for the possibility of increasing an individual's nonverbal sensitivity (the ability to decode accurately another's nonverbal cues) from two studies. In one study using videotapes, DiMatteo and Hall (1979) found a high positive correlation between college student subjects' sensitivity to a particular nonverbal channel (face or body) and their tendency to attend to that channel more than to others. Per-

sons who preferred to attend to and receive information from the face or body channel instead of from other channels also tended to be more sensitive to communications from, respectively, the face or body channels. This result might imply that (at least when video communications are involved) paying added attention to a particular channel increases one's accuracy at reading that channel. Other interpretations are plausible, though, and these correlational findings should be considered with caution. However, they do provide some evidence that it may be possible to train an individual to become more sensitive to particular channels of nonverbal communication.

In another study, a randomized experiment by Rosenthal, et al. (1979), a group of 25 mental health professionals were given direct training in reading nonverbal cues and the effects of this training were assessed. These twenty-five clinical staff members of a mental health center (social workers, counselors, nurses, paraprofessionals, psychologists and psychiatrists) took the PONS test after having been "exposed" or "not exposed" to a short-term training program designed to increase nonverbal sensitivity. The training and control groups were determined by random assignment. For the group that received the training, the 90 minute program included the following techniques: (a) a brief lecture on the importance of nonverbal communication in clinical settings; (b) a demonstration of voice alteration techniques which filtered out verbal content, to help focus on the communication of affect through tone-of-voice; (c) practice in judging the affects represented in the voices of a male adult, a female adult and a female child (all content filtered and content standard speech); (d) practice in listening for slight differences in the emphasis given various words of instructions read by a psychological experimenter; (e) practice in judging the affect represented in adult male and adult female faces shown in slides; and (f) practice in judging the affect communicated in the facial expressions and body movements and postures of an adult female shown in a series of brief videotape segments. The results of this pilot research demonstrated that while the difference between the trained group and the control group was of borderline statistical significance ($p < .09$), the effect was of promising magnitude (.58 standard deviation in total nonverbal sensitivity score). Thus, there was a trend in this small sample for clinicians trained in reading nonverbal cues to perform better on a post-test of nonverbal communication than comparable individuals in the same profession who received no training. These preliminary results are encouraging and point to the possibility that nonverbal sensitivity can be taught to physicians using some of the techniques outlined here.

While some studies show that nonverbal sensitivity can be taught, there is no research examining directly whether one can improve one's nonverbal expressiveness using similar techniques. The success of acting courses may provide some indirect evidence for this, however. Perhaps one reason for the lack of formal research on the development of teaching techniques in the nonverbal communication of such behaviors as caring and understanding is the only very recent specification of what "caring" and "understanding" might mean in nonverbal terms. That is, only very recently have researchers been able to specify the specific facial, body, and voice tone cues which comprise the affective dimension in the helping role. The enactment of certain gestures can cause a person to be perceived as either warm or cold, empathic or nonempathic. Certain affiliative nonverbal behaviors such as smiles, head nods, gestures with the hands, eye contact and a 20 degree forward lean by a counselor, for example, tend to increase perceptions by clients of that counselor's attractiveness and warmth (LaCrosse, 1975). Closed arm positions seem to indicate coldness, rejection and inaccessibility while moderately open arm positions tend to indicate warmth and ac-

ceptance (Spiegel and Machotka, 1974; Smith-Hanen, 1977). If nonverbal components of empathic communication can be specified, perhaps skill in the components can be taught to physicians in an effort to improve their communication of caring and understanding in interactions with patients.

A large number of medical schools and residency programs in the United States already routinely use videotape feedback techniques in an effort to teach physicians interviewing and interactional skills in the physician-patient relationship. The precise components of these feedback training programs are not usually reported, however, and their effectiveness is rarely rigorously evaluated. Perhaps the most well known and best documented efforts to train medical personnel in interactional skills are those of Norman Kagan. Kagan's (1974) technique is called Interpersonal Process Recall. It is essentially a program to teach "empathy," loosely defined in a counselling framework. It involves approximately 40 hours of classroom and individual instruction during which individuals are trained to be sensitive to various affective communications of others, to label their own and others' feelings correctly, and to communicate this understanding to others. The training actually consists of a variety of techniques which are used in combinations that fit the wishes and needs of the instructors. For example, the student may be asked to watch a movie with a series of staged vignettes, then asked to describe what the person in each vignette is feeling, and then given some feedback about the situation. The student might also be videotaped while watching the vignettes. When the videotape is played back, the student is encouraged to recall the various emotional reactions he or she had to the taped vignettes and to acknowledge and explore those feelings. Sometimes the student is asked to interact with another (who is an actor or actress instructed to guide the interaction along certain predetermined lines). The interaction is videotaped and the student's behaviors are played back and analyzed in detail.

Some of these techniques have been applied to the teaching of medical students in courses designed to improve their interviewing skills. For example, Werner and Schneider (1974) used the IPR technique to increase medical students' attention to and awareness of the nature of patients' statements and the nature of their own responses, so that the students might develop a natural and comfortable flow in interviewing of patients. Eighty-seven members of a first-year medical school class were videotaped as they interacted with and interviewed an actor or actress whose job it was to simulate a patient with a certain problem. The videotapes were played back for the students, and critical analyses of the behaviors in each videotape were undertaken by instructors and students. This attempt at teaching the socio-emotional aspect of patient care represented an innovation in the training of medical students. But methodological weaknesses prevented effective evaluation of Werner and Schneider's procedure as a training program.

The recent evidence in favor of nonverbal communication components of physician-patient rapport suggest the importance of social psychological research in improving the socio-emotional aspects of patient care. Such research must be undertaken with a firm theoretical foundation and precise methodological care and sophistication. Far too many poorly developed efforts to teach the "Art of Medicine" have already been reported in the literature. They suffer from difficulties and inadequacies which include: "experiential" approaches that do not utilize existing reliable scientific evidence linking specific overt behaviors to specific inner states; a concentration on the whole communication without a careful analysis of the parts; lack of clarity about what exactly is being taught and the effectiveness of each procedure so that valuable time is not wasted training irrelevant skills or those not amenable to improvement; lack of sound evaluation techniques on which to base decisions regarding the effectiveness of the training procedures (due to inadequate experimental designs, missing con-

trol groups, etc.); "artificial" situations used for training which may limit the extent to which the training is taken seriously and may have little carry-over to actual physician-patient interactions; no examination of the degree to which the effects of training continue to last beyond the period of time immediately after the training when evaluation measures are collected; and no evaluation criteria directly relevant to patient care, such as patient satisfaction, compliance, or the efficiency with which the physician is able to deliver the care. Future research must be designed to overcome these difficulties and to provide for physicians and other health care professionals some effective tools with which to develop empathy and other aspects of the socio-emotional component of patient care.

TOWARD A SCIENCE OF THE ART OF MEDICINE

Health care professionals, especially medical educators, will probably listen carefully to what social scientists have to say (Engel, 1977) about the "art of medicine" if the information is based upon methodologically sound research findings.

There is some sound evidence to suggest that nonverbal communication between the physician and the patient is especially important in the socio-emotional dimension of care. The physician must learn to read the patient's cues to emotion in facial expressions, body movements, and voice tone and must learn to use these same nonverbal channels in communicating with his or her patients. Social psychology has made great strides in this area of human behavior in recent years. Many principles of nonverbal communication have already been rigorously derived and tested. These principles, as well as many other axioms of human interaction, are now ready to be taught to physicians, and the success of this instruction is now ready to be evaluated rigorously.

The successful development of scientifically based training programs in the Art of Medicine holds, perhaps, the most significant promise of transforming an habitual, stereotyped scenario acted out by physician and patient into a fruitful interpersonal encounter. The improved quality of this interchange might be expected to have a significant positive impact on patients emotional responses to treatment, and hence increase the actual effectiveness of this treatment. Enhanced affective communication in the physician-patient relationship might significantly increase patients' satisfaction with their care, and hence decrease the incidence of anger-induced rejection of the physician, and/or patient retaliation with malpractice litigation. Finally, physicians' increased responsiveness to patients' emotional reactions and needs, as well as physicians' enhanced abilities to communicate warmth, caring, and concern might significantly increase patients'' understanding and acceptance of, as well as their motivation to cooperate with, prescribed treatment regimens. Investments in the development of training programs in the Art of Medicine might well produce immediate gains in the efficiency and effectiveness with which health care is delivered, and the cost-effectiveness of such programs might well become immediately evident. This is likely, however, only if these programs are firmly grounded in a rigorous science of human behavior and social interaction.

Conformity, Obedience, and Persuasion

Effects of Group Pressure upon the Modification and Distortion of Judgments

Solomon E. Asch (1958)

The first influential study on conformity was conducted by Sherif (1935), who used the autokinetic effect as an ambiguous stimulus: a stationary light in an otherwise dark room appears to move. Sherif found that subjects' reports of perceived movement were significantly influenced by the reports of movement made by others present in the room. Asch, in the study reported here, chose unambiguous stimuli instead. The choice of stimuli might suggest a difference in the researchers' basic goals of finding conformity (Sherif) versus not finding it (Asch). Despite the obviousness of the right answers in the Asch paradigm, however, a high degree of conformity was still obtained.

A later study by Crutchfield (1955) replicated and expanded Asch's work on conformity using a variety of ambiguous *and* unambiguous stimuli. Again a high degree of conformity was observed, and Crutchfield began exploring which personality factors were associated with conformity.

Interestingly, Crutchfield is often identified with the hypothesis that females conform more than do males, although he actually found greater conformity in females relative to males in only one study. This is an example of a very good reason to read the original research and not to rely on second-hand distillations by others. The latest meta-analyses of sex differences in conformity suggest that women are slightly more influenceable than men in persuasion, group pressure, and other conformity studies, although the differences are small indeed, explaining only about 1 percent of the variability in those studies. The size of the difference depends on the type of study, the outcome measures, and, interestingly, the author's sex (Becker, 1986; Eagly, 1983; Eagly & Carli, 1981.)

We shall here describe in summary form the conception and first findings of a program of investigation into the conditions of independence and submission to group pressure.

Our immediate object was to study the social and personal conditions that induce individuals to resist or to yield to group pressures when the latter are perceived to be *contrary to fact*. The issues which this problem raises are of obvious consequence for society; it can be of decisive importance whether or not a group will, under certain conditions, submit to existing pressures. Equally direct are the consequences for individuals and our understanding of them, since it is a decisive fact about a person whether he possesses the freedom to act independently, or whether he characteristically submits to group pressures.

The problem under investigation requires the direct observation of certain basic processes in the interaction between individuals, and between individuals and groups. To clarify these seems necessary if we are to make fundamental advances in the understanding of the formation and reorganization of attitudes, of the functioning of public opinion, and of the operation of propaganda. Today we do not possess an adequate theory of these central psycho-social processes. Empirical investigation has been predominantly controlled by general propositions concerning group influence which have as a rule been assumed but not tested. With few exceptions investigation has relied upon descriptive formulations concerning the operation of suggestion and prestige the inadequacy of which is becoming increasingly obvious, and upon schematic applications of stimulus-response theory.

Basic to the current approach has been the axiom that group pressures characteristically induce psychological changes *arbitrarily*, in far-reaching disregard of the material properties of the given conditions. This mode of thinking has almost exclusively stressed the slavish submission of individuals to group forces, has neglected to inquire into their possibilities for independence and for productive relations with the human environment, and has virtually denied the capacity of men under certain conditions to rise above group passion and prejudice. It was our aim to contribute to a clarification of these questions, important both for theory and for their human implications, by means of direct observation of the effects of groups upon the decisions and evaluations of individuals.

THE EXPERIMENT AND FIRST RESULTS

To this end we developed an experimental technique which has served as the basis for the present series of studies. We employed the procedure of placing an individual in a relation of radical conflict with all the other members of a group, of measuring its effect upon him in quantitative terms, and of describing its psychological consequences. A group of eight individuals was instructed to judge a series of simple, clearly structured perceptual relations—to match the length of a given line with one of three unequal lines. Each member of the group announced his judgments publicly. In the midst of this monotonous "test" one individual found himself suddenly contradicted by the entire group, and this contradiction was repeated again and again in the course of the experiment. The group in question had, with the exception of one member, previously met with the experimenter and received

instructions to respond at certain points with wrong—and unanimous—judgments. The errors of the majority were large (ranging between $\frac{1}{2}''$ and $1\frac{3}{4}''$) and of an order not encountered under control conditions. The outstanding person—the critical subject—whom we had placed in the position of a *minority of one* in the midst of a *unanimous majority*—was the object of investigation. He faced, possibly for the first time in his life, a situation in which a group unanimously contradicted the evidence of his senses.

This procedure was the starting point of the investigation and the point of departure for the study of further problems. Its main features were the following: (1) The critical subject was submitted to two contradictory and irreconcilable forces—the evidence of his own experience of a clearly perceived relation, and the unanimous evidence of a group of equals. (2) Both forces were part of the immediate situation; the majority was concretely present, surrounding the subject physically. (3) The critical subject, who was requested together with all others to state his judgments publicily, was obliged to declare himself and to take a definite stand *vis-à-vis* the group. (4) The situation possessed a self-contained character. The critical subject could not avoid or evade the dilemma by reference to conditions external to the experimental situation. (It may be mentioned at this point that the forces generated by the given conditions acted so quickly upon the critical subjects that instances of suspicion were infrequent.)

The technique employed permitted a simple quantitative measure of the "majority effect" in terms of the frequency of errors in the direction of the distorted estimates of the majority. At the same time we were concerned to obtain evidence of the ways in which the subjects perceived the group, to establish whether they became doubtful, whether they were tempted to join the majority. Most important, it was our object to establish the grounds of the subject's independence or yielding—whether, for example, the yielding subject was aware of the effect of the majority upon him, whether he abandoned his judgment deliberately or compulsively. To this end we constructed a comprehensive set of questions which served as the basis of an individual interview immediately following the experimental period. Toward the conclusion of the interview each subject was informed fully of the purpose of the experiment, of his role and of that of the majority. The reactions to the disclosure of the purpose of the experiment became in fact an integral part of the procedure. The information derived from the interview became an indispensable source of evidence and insight into the psychological structure of the experimental situation and, in particular, of the nature of the individual differences. It should be added that it is not justified or advisable to allow the subject to leave without giving him a full explanation of the experimental conditions. The experimenter has a responsibility to the subject to clarify his doubts and to state the reasons for placing him in the experimental situation. When this is done most subjects react with interest, and some express gratification at having lived through a striking situation which has some bearing on them personally and on wider human issues.

Both the members of the majority and the critical subjects were male college students. There were twelve critical trials on which the responses of the majority responded incorrectly. The quantitative results are clear and unambiguous.

1. There was a marked movement toward the majority. One third of all the estimates in the critical group were errors identical with or in the direction of the distorted estimates of the majority. The significance of this finding becomes clear in the light of the virtual absence of errors in the control group, the members of which recorded their estimates in writing. The relevant data of the critical and control groups are summarized in Table 1.
2. At the same time the effect of the majority was far from complete. The preponderance of estimates in the critical group (68 percent)

TABLE 1

DISTRIBUTION OF ERRORS IN EXPERIMENTAL AND CONTROL GROUPS

Number of critical errors	Critical group* (N = 50) F	Control group (N = 37) F
0	13	35
1	4	1
2	5	1
3	6	
4	3	
5	4	
6	1	
7	2	
8	5	
9	3	
10	3	
11	1	
12	0	
Total	50	37
Mean	3.84	0.08

*All errors in the critical group were in the direction of the majority estimates.

was correct despite the pressure of the majority.

3. We found evidence of extreme individual differences. There were in the critical group subjects who remained independent without exception, and there were those who went nearly all the time with the majority. (The maximum possible number of errors was 12, while the actual range of errors was 0–11.) One fourth of the critical subjects was completely independent; at the other extreme, one third of the group displaced the estimates toward the majority in one half or more of the trials.

The differences between the critical subjects in their reactions to the given conditions were equally striking. There were subjects who remained completely confident throughout. At the other extreme were those who became disoriented, doubt-ridden, and experienced a powerful impulse not to appear different from the majority.

For purposes of illustration we include a brief description of one independent and one yielding subject.

Independent After a few trials he appeared puzzled, hesitant. He announced all disagreeing answers in the form of "Three, sir; two, sir''; not so with the unanimous answers on the neutral trials. At Trial 4 he answered immediately after the first member of the group, shook his head, blinked, and whispered to his neighbor: "Can't help it, that's one." His later answers came in a whispered voice, accompanied by a deprecating smile. At one point he grinned embarrassedly, and whispered explosively to his neighbor: "I always disagree—darn it!" During the questioning, this subject's constant refrain was: "I called them as I saw them, sir." He insisted that his estimates were right without, however, committing himself as to whether the others were wrong, remarking that "that's the way I see them and that's the way they see them." If he had to make a practical decision under similar circumstances, he declared, "I would follow my own view, though part of my reason would tell me that I might be wrong." Immediately following the experiment the majority engaged this subject in a brief discussion. When they pressed him to say whether the entire group was wrong and he alone right, he turned upon them defiantly, exclaiming: "You're *probably* right, but you *may* be wrong!" To the disclosure of the experiment this subject reacted with the statement that he felt "exultant and relieved," adding, "I do not deny that at times I had the feeling: 'to heck with it, I'll go along with the rest.'"

Yielding This subject went with the majority in 11 out of 12 trials. He appeared nervous and somewhat confused, but he did not attempt to evade discussion; on the contrary, he was helpful and tried to answer to the best of his ability. He opened the discussion with the statement:

"If I'd been first I probably would have responded differently," this was his way of stating that he had adopted the majority estimates. The primary factor in his case was loss of confidence. He perceived the majority as a decided group, acting without hesitation: "If they had been doubtful I probably would have changed, but they answered with such confidence." Certain of his errors, he explained, were due to the doubtful nature of the comparisons; in such instances he went with the majority. When the object of the experiment was explained, the subject volunteered: "I suspected about the middle—but tried to push it out of my mind." It is of interest that his suspicion did not restore his confidence or diminish the power of the majority. Equally striking is his report that he assumed the experiment to involve an "illusion" to which the others, but not he, were subject. This assumption too did not help to free him; on the contrary, he acted as if his divergence from the majority was a sign of defect. The principal impression this subject produced was of one so caught up by immediate difficulties that he lost clear reasons for his actions, and could make no reasonable decisions.

A FIRST ANALYSIS OF INDIVIDUAL DIFFERENCES

On the basis of the interview data described earlier, we undertook to differentiate and describe the major forms of reaction to the experimental situation, which we shall now briefly summarize.

Among the *independent* subjects we distinguished the following main categories:

(1). Independence based on *confidence* in one's perception and experience. The most striking characteristic of these subjects is the vigor with which they withstand the group opposition. Though they are sensitive to the group, and experience the conflict, they show a resilience in coping with it, which is expressed in their continuing reliance on their perception and the effectiveness with which they shake off the oppressive group opposition.

(2). Quite different are those subjects who are independent and *withdrawn*. These do not react in a spontaneously emotional way, but rather on the basis of explicit principles concerning the necessity of being an individual.

(3). A third group of independent subjects manifests considerable tension and doubt, but adhere to their judgment on the basis of a felt necessity to deal adequately with the task.

The following were the main categories of reaction among the *yielding* subjects, or those who went with the majority during one half or more of the trials.

(1). *Distortion of perception* under the stress of group pressure. In this category belong a very few subjects who yield completely, but are not aware that their estimates have been displaced or distorted by the majority. These subjects report that they came to perceive the majority estimates as correct.

(2). *Distortion of judgment*. Most submitting subjects belong to this category. The factor of greatest importance in this group is a decision the subjects reach that their perceptions are inaccurate, and that those of the majority are correct. These subjects suffer from primary doubt and lack of confidence; on this basis they feel a strong tendency to join the majority.

(3). *Distortion of action*. The subjects in this group do not suffer a modification of perception nor do they conclude that they are wrong. They yield because of an overmastering need not to appear different from or inferior to others, because of an inability to tolerate the appearance of defectiveness in the eyes of the group. These subjects suppress their observations and voice the majority position with awareness of what they are doing.

The results are sufficient to establish that independence and yielding are not psychologically homogeneous, that submission to group pressure and freedom from pressure can be the result of different psychological conditions. It should also be noted that the categories described above, being based exclusively on the subjects' reactions to the experimental conditions, are descriptive, not presuming to explain why a given individual responded in one way rather than another. The further exploration of the basis for the individual differences is a separate task.

EXPERIMENTAL VARIATIONS

The results described are clearly a joint function of two broadly different sets of conditions. They are determined first by the specific external conditions, by the particular character of the relation between social evidence and one's own experience. Second, the presence of pronounced individual differences points to the important role of personal factors, or factors connected with the individual's character structure. We reasoned that there are group conditions which would produce independence in all subjects, and that there probably are group conditions which would induce intensified yielding in many, though not in all. Secondly, we deemed it reasonable to assume that behavior under the experimental social pressure is significantly related to certain characteristics of the individual. The present account will be limited to the effect of the surrounding conditions upon independence and submission. To this end we followed the procedure of experimental variation, systematically altering the quality of social evidence by means of systematic variation of the group conditions and of the task.

The Effect of Nonunanimous Majorities

Evidence obtained from the basic experiment suggested that the condition of being exposed *alone* to the opposition of a "compact majority" may have played a decisive role in determining the course and strength of the effects observed. Accordingly we undertook to investigate in a series of successive variations the effects of *nonunanimous* majorities. The technical problem of altering the uniformity of a majority is, in terms of our procedure, relatively simple. In most instances we merely directed one or more members of the instructed group to deviate from the majority in prescribed ways. It is obvious that we cannot hope to compare the performance of the same individual in two situations on the assumption that they remain independent of one another; at best we can investigate the effect of an earlier upon a later experimental condition. The comparison of different experimental situations therefore requires the use of different but comparable groups of critical subjects. This is the procedure we have followed. In the variations to be described we have maintained the conditions of the basic experiment (e.g., the sex of the subjects, the size of the majority, the content of the task, and so on) save for the specific factor that was varied. The following were some of the variations studied:

(1). *The presence of a "true partner."* (*a*) In the midst of the majority were *two* naïve, critical subjects. The subjects were separated spatially, being seated in the fourth and eighth positions, respectively. Each therefore heard his judgments confirmed by one other person (provided the other person remained independent), one prior to, the other after announcing his own judgment. In addition, each experienced a break in the unanimity of the majority. There were six pairs of critical subjects. (*b*) In a further variation the "partner" to the critical subject was a member of the group who had been instructed to respond correctly throughout. This procedure permits the exact control of the partner's responses. The partner was always seated in the fourth position; he therefore announced his estimates in each case before the critical subject.

The results clearly demonstrate that a disturbance of the unanimity of the majority markedly increased the independence of the critical subjects. The frequency of promajority errors dropped to 10.4 percent of the total number of estimates in variation (*a*), and to 5.5 percent in variation (*b*). These results are to be compared with the frequency of yielding to the unanimous majorities in the basic experiment, which was 32 percent of the total number of estimates. It is clear that the presence in the field of *one other* individual who responded correctly was sufficient to deplete the power of the majority, and in some cases to destroy it. This finding is all the more striking in the light of other variations which demonstrate the effect of even small minorities provided they are unanimous. Indeed, we have been able to show that a unanimous majority of 3 is, under the given conditions, far more effective than a majority of 8 containing 1 dissenter. That critical subjects will under these conditions free themselves of a majority of 7 and join forces with one other person in the minority is, we believe, a result significant for theory. It points to a fundamental psychological difference between the condition of being alone and having a minimum of human support. It further demonstrates that the effects obtained are not the result of a summation of influences proceeding from each member of the group; it is necessary to conceive the results as being relationally determined.

(2). *Withdrawal of a "true partner."* What will be the effect of providing the critical subject with a partner who responds correctly and then withdrawing him? The critical subject started with a partner who responded correctly. The partner was a member of the majority who had been instructed to respond correctly and to "desert" to the majority in the middle of the experiment. This procedure permits the observation of the same subjects in the course of the transition from one condition to another. The withdrawal of the partner produced a powerful and unexpected result. We had assumed that the critical subject, having gone through the experience of opposing the majority with a minimum of support, would maintain his independence when alone. Contrary to this expectation, we found that the experience of having had and then lost a partner restored the majority effect to its full force, the proportion of errors rising to 28.5 percent of all judgments, in contrast to the preceding level of 5.5 percent. Further experimentation is needed to establish whether the critical subjects were responding to the sheer fact of being alone, or to the fact that the partner abandoned them.

(3). *Late arrival of a "true partner."* The critical subject started as a minority of 1 in the midst of a unanimous majority. Toward the conclusion of the experiment one member of the majority "broke" away and began announcing correct estimates. This procedure, which reverses the order of conditions of the preceding experiment, permits the observation of the transition from being alone to being a member of a pair against a majority. It is obvious that those critical subjects who were independent when alone would continue to be so when joined by a partner. The variation is therefore of significance primarily for those subjects who yielded during the first phase of the experiment. The appearance of the late partner exerts a freeing effect, reducing the level of yielding to 8.7 percent. Those who had previously yielded also became markedly more independent, but not completely so, continuing to yield more than previously independent subjects. The reports of the subjects do not cast much light on the factors responsible for the result. It is our impression that some subjects, having once committed themselves to yielding, find it difficult to change their direction completely. To do so is tantamount to a public admission that they had not acted rightly. They therefore follow to an extent the precarious course they had chosen in order to maintain an outward semblance of consistency and conviction.

(4). *The presence of a "compromise partner."* The majority was consistently extremist, always matching the standard with the most unequal line. One instructed subject (who, as in the other variations, preceded the critical subject) also responded incorrectly, but his estimates were always intermediate between the truth and the majority position. The critical subject therefore faced an extremist majority whose unanimity was broken by one more moderately erring person. Under these conditions the frequency of errors was reduced but not significantly. However, the lack of unanimity determined in a striking consistent way the *direction* of the errors. The preponderance of the errors, 75.7 percent of the total, was moderate, whereas in a parallel experiment in which the majority was unanimously extremist (i.e., with the "compromise" partner excluded), the incidence of moderate errors was 42 percent of the total. As might be expected, in a unanimously moderate majority, the errors of the critical subjects were without exception moderate.

The Role of Majority Size

To gain further understanding of the majority effect, we varied the size of the majority in several different variations. The majorities, which were in each case unanimous, consisted of 2, 3, 4, 8, and 10–15 persons, respectively. In addition, we studied the limiting case in which the critical subject was opposed by one instructed subject. Table 2 contains the mean and the range of errors under each condition.

With the opposition reduced to 1, the majority effect all but disappeared. When the opposition proceeded from a group of 2, it produced a measurable though small distortion, the errors being 12.8 percent of the total number of estimates. The effect appeared in full force with a

TABLE 2							
ERRORS OF CRITICAL SUBJECTS WITH UNANIMOUS MAJORITIES OF DIFFERENT SIZE							
Size of majority	Control	1	2	3	4	8	10–15
N	37	10	15	10	10	50	12
Mean number of errors	0.08	0.33	1.53	4.0	4.20	3.84	3.75
Range of errors	0–2	0–1	0–5	1–12	0–11	0–11	0–10

majority of 3. Larger majorities did not produce effects greater than a majority of 3.

The effect of a majority is often silent, revealing little of its operation to the subject, and often hiding it from the experimenter. To examine the range of effects it is capable of inducing, decisive variations of conditions are necessary. An indication of one effect is furnished by the following variation in which the conditions of the basic experiment were simply reversed. Here the majority, consisting of a group of 16, was naïve; in the midst of it we placed a single individual who responded wrongly according to instructions. Under these conditions the members of the naïve majority reacted to the lone dissenter with amusement. Contagious laughter spread through the group at the droll minority of 1. Of significance is the fact that the members lacked awareness that they drew their strength from the majority, and that their reactions would change radically if they faced the dissenter individually. These observations demonstrate the role of social support as a source of power and stability, in contrast to the preceding investigations which stressed the effects of social opposition. Both aspects must be explicitly considered in a unified formulation of the effects of group conditions on the formation and change of judgments.

The Role of the Stimulus-Situation

It is obviously not possible to divorce the quality and course of the group forces which act upon the individual from the specific stimulus-conditions. Of necessity the structure of the situation molds the group forces and determines

their direction as well as their strength. Indeed, this was the reason that we took pains in the investigations described above to center the issue between the individual and the group around an elementary matter of fact. And there can be no doubt that the resulting reactions were directly a function of the contradiction between the observed relations and the majority position. These general considerations are sufficient to establish the need to vary the stimulus-conditions and to observe their effect on the resulting group forces.

Accordingly we have studied the effect of increasing and decreasing the discrepancy between the correct relation and the position of the majority, going beyond the basic experiment which contained discrepancies of a relatively moderate order. Our technique permits the easy variation of this factor, since we can vary at will the deviation of the majority from the correct relation. At this point we can only summarize the trend of the results which is entirely clear. The degree of independence increases with the distance of the majority from correctness. However, even glaring discrepancies (of the order of 3–6″) did not produce independence in all. While independence increases with the magnitude of contradiction, a certain proportion of individuals continues to yield under extreme conditions.

We have also varied systematically the structural clarity of the task, employing judgments based on mental standards. In agreement with other investigators, we find that the majority effect grows stronger as the situation diminishes in clarity. Concurrently, however, the disturbance of the subjects and the conflict-quality of the situation decrease markedly. We consider it of significance that the majority achieves its most pronounced effect when it acts most painlessly.

SUMMARY

We have investigated the effects upon individuals of majority opinion when the latter were seen to be in a direction contrary to fact. By means of a simple technique we produced a radical divergence between a majority and a minority, and observed the ways in which individuals coped with the resulting difficulty. Despite the stress of the given conditions, a substantial proportion of individuals retained their independence throughout. At the same time a substantial minority yielded, modifying their judgments in accordance with the majority. Independence and yielding are a joint function of the following major factors: (1) The character of the stimulus situation. Variations in structural clarity have a decisive effect: with diminishing clarity of the stimulus-conditions the majority effect increases. (2) The character of the group forces. Individuals are highly sensitive to the structural qualities of group opposition. In particular, we demonstrated the great importance of the factor of unanimity. Also, the majority effect is a function of the size of group opposition. (3) The character of the individual. There were wide and, indeed, striking differences among individuals within the same experimental situation.

READING 35

Behavioral Study of Obedience

Stanley Milgram (1963)

In 1950, Adorno, Frenkel-Brunswik, Levinson, and Sanford published *The Authoritarian Personality,* a scientific investigation attempting to explain how human beings could participate in such atrocities as occurred in Nazi Germany during World War II. Adorno and his colleagues used a personality explanation which generated a great deal of research on the authoritarian personality. They found that authoritarians endorse conventional values and behaviors, and they respect and obey authority. Authoritarians also support severe punishment of minor transgressions, and they reject personal weaknesses in others while denying and repressing recognition of weakness in themselves or their parents.

Authoritarianism was a comforting hypothesis because individuals could say to themselves, "I'm not an authoritarian so I know that *I* could never have committed such evil deeds." Since authoritarianism seems to be socialized during childhood, societies might also be able to effect change in creating less authoritarian generations.

Milgram's landmark study, with its strong situational explanation, removes that comfortable self-protection for most individuals. In fact, 65 percent of the subjects in Milgram's first experiment obeyed the experimenter's requests and delivered shock at the highest level on the shock generator, at which point the victim appeared to be dead, or at least unconscious.

Milgram reports another 17 studies in his highly readable book, *Obedience to Authority* (1974). Most of these experiments probe ways in which the situation influences the subjects' level of obedience, including variations in the proximity of the victim and of the authority figure, the status implicit in the institution where the research is conducted, characteristics of the victim, and group obedience. These factors and others that promote obedience have recently been organized into eleven principles of obedience (Padgett, 1987).

Milgram also examined women's obedience and found that men's and women's levels of obedience were extremely similar. Personality differences between obedient and disobedient subjects were also examined. Despite persistent efforts by the researchers, the only personality characteristic that was found to predict obedience was authoritarianism (Elms, 1972). Also, subjects' actual levels of obedience were not related to their own paper and pencil predictions of their obedience in ten different circumstances. Thus, Milgram's studies of obedient behavior strongly suggest the power of the situation. Authoritarian personality may predict obedience somewhat, but the situational constraints are powerful and must be considered in any analysis of the degree to which people will obey requests made by a "legitimate" authority.

Abstract

This article describes a procedure for the study of destructive obedience in the laboratory. It consists of ordering a naive S to administer increasingly more severe punishment to a victim in the context of a learning experiment. Punishment is administered by means of a shock generator with 30 graded switches ranging from Slight to Danger: Severe Shock. The victim is a confederate of the E. The primary dependent variable is the maximum shock the S is willing to administer before he refuses to continue further. 26 Ss obeyed the experimental commands fully, and administered the highest shock on the generator. 14 Ss broke off the experiment at some point after the victim protested and refused to provide further answers. The procedure created extreme levels of nervous tension in some Ss. Profuse sweating, trembling, and stuttering were typical expressions of this emotional disturbance. One unexpected sign of tension—yet to be explained—was the regular occurrence of nervous laughter, which in some Ss developed into uncontrollable seizures. The variety of interesting behavioral dynamics observed in the experiment, the reality of the situation for the S, and the possibility of parametric variation within the framework of the procedure, point to the fruitfulness of further study.

Obedience is as basic an element in the structure of social life as one can point to. Some system of authority is a requirement of all communal living, and it is only the man dwelling in isolation who is not forced to respond, through defiance or submission, to the commands of others. Obedience, as a determinant of behavior, is of particular relevance to our time. It has been reliably established that from 1933–45 millions of innocent persons were systematically slaughtered on command. Gas chambers were built, death camps were guarded, daily quotas of corpses were produced with the same efficiency as the manufacture of appliances. These inhumane policies may have originated in the mind of a single person, but they could only be carried out on a massive scale if a very large number of persons obeyed orders.

Obedience is the psychological mechanism that links individual action to political purpose. It is the dispositional cement that binds men to systems of authority. Facts of recent history and observation in daily life suggest that for many persons obedience may be a deeply ingrained behavior tendency, indeed, a prepotent impulse overriding training in ethics, sympathy, and moral conduct. C. P. Snow (1961) points to its importance when he writes:

> When you think of the long and gloomy history of man, you will find more hideous crimes have been committed in the name of obedience than have ever been committed in the name of rebellion. If you doubt that, read William Shirer's "Rise and Fall of the Third Reich." The German Officer Corps were brought up in the most rigorous code of obedience...in the name of obedience they were party to, and assisted in, the most wicked large scale actions in the history of the world [p. 24].

While the particular form of obedience dealt with in the present study has its antecedents in these episodes, it must not be thought all obedience entails acts of aggression against others. Obedience serves numerous productive functions. Indeed, the very life of society is predicated on its existence. Obedience may be ennobling and educative and refer to acts of charity and kindness, as well as to destruction.

General Procedure

A procedure was devised which seems useful as a tool for studying obedience (Milgram, 1961). It consists of ordering a naive subject to administer electric shock to a victim. A simulated shock generator is used, with 30 clearly marked voltage levels that range from 15 to 450 volts. The instrument bears verbal designations that range from Slight Shock to Danger: Severe Shock. The responses of the victim, who is a trained confederate of the experimenter, are standardized. The orders to administer shocks are given to the naive subject in the context of a "learning experiment" ostensibly set up to study the effects of punishment on memory. As the experiment proceeds the naive subject is commanded to administer increasingly more intense shocks to the victim, even to the point of reaching the level marked Danger: Severe Shock. Internal resistances become stronger, and at a certain point the subject refuses to go on with the experiment. Behavior prior to this rupture is considered "obedience," in that the subject complies with the commands of the experimenter. The point of rupture is the act of disobedience. A quantitative value is assigned to the subject's performance based on the maximum intensity shock he is willing to administer before he refuses to participate further. Thus for any particular subject and for any particular experimental condition the degree of obedience may be specified with a numerical value. The crux of the study is to systematically vary the factors believed to alter the degree of obedience to the experimental commands.

The technique allows important variables to be manipulated at several points in the experiment. One may vary aspects of the source of command, content and form of command, instrumentalities for its execution, target object, general social setting, etc. The problem, therefore, is not one of designing increasingly more numerous experimental conditions, but of selecting those that best illuminate the *process* of obedience from the sociopsychological standpoint.

Related Studies

The inquiry bears an important relation to philosophic analysis of obedience and authority (Arendt, 1958; Friedrich, 1958; Weber, 1947), an early experimental study of obedience by Frank (1944), studies in "authoritarianism" (Adorno,

Frenkel-Brunswik, Levinson, & Sanford, 1950; Rokeach, 1961), and a recent series of analytic and empirical studies in social power (Cartwright, 1959). It owes much to the long concern with *suggestion* in social psychology, both in its normal forms (e.g., Binet, 1900) and in its clinical manifestations (Charcot, 1881). But it derives, in the first instance, from direct observation of a social fact; the individual who is commanded by a legitimate authority ordinarily obeys. Obedience comes easily and often. It is a ubiquitous and indispensable feature of social life.

METHOD

Subjects

The subjects were 40 males between the ages of 20 and 50, drawn from New Haven and the surrounding communities. Subjects were obtained by a newspaper advertisement and direct mail solicitation. Those who responded to the appeal believed they were to participate in a study of memory and learning at Yale University. A wide range of occupations is represented in the sample. Typical subjects were postal clerks, high school teachers, salesman, engineers, and laborers. Subjects ranged in educational level from one who had not finished elementary school, to those who had doctorate and other professional degrees. They were paid $4.50 for their participation in the experiment. However, subjects were told that payment was simply for coming to the laboratory, and that the money was theirs no matter what happened after they arrived. Table 1 shows the proportion of age and occupational types assigned to the experimental condition.

Personnel and Locale

The experiment was conducted on the grounds of Yale University in the elegant interaction laboratory. (This detail is relevant to the perceived legitimacy of the experiment. In further variations, the experiment was dissociated from the univer-

TABLE 1

DISTRIBUTION OF AGE AND OCCUPATIONAL TYPES IN THE EXPERIMENT

Occupations	20–29 years n	30–39 years n	40–50 years n	Percentage of total (occupations)
Workers, skilled and unskilled	4	5	6	37.5
Sales, business, and white-collar	3	6	7	40.0
Professional	1	5	3	22.5
Percentage of total (Age)	20	40	40	

Note: Total *N* = 40.

sity, with consequences for performance.) The role of experimenter was played by a 31-year-old high school teacher of biology. His manner was impassive, and his appearance somewhat stern throughout the experiment. He was dressed in a gray technician's coat. The victim was played by a 47-year-old accountant, trained for the role; he was of Irish-American stock, whom most observers found mild-mannered and likable.

Procedure

One naive subject and one victim (an accomplice) performed in each experiment. A pretext had to be devised that would justify the administration of electric shock by the naive subject. This was effectively accomplished by the cover story. After a general introduction on the presumed relation between punishment and learning, subjects were told:

> But actually, we know *very little* about the effect of punishment on learning, because almost no truly scientific studies have been made of it in human beings.
>
> For instance, we don't know how *much* punishment is best for learning—and we don't know how much difference it makes as to who is giving the punishment, whether an adult learns best from a younger or an older person than himself—or many things of that sort.

So in this study we are bringing together a number of adults of different occupations and ages. And we're asking some of them to be teachers and some of them to be learners.

We want to find out just what effect different people have on each other as teachers and learners, and also what effect *punishment* will have on learning in this situation.

Therefore, I'm going to ask one of you to be the teacher here tonight and the other one to be the learner.

Does either of you have a preference?

Subjects then drew slips of paper from a hat to determine who would be the teacher and who would be the learner in the experiment. The drawing was rigged so that the naive subject was always the teacher and the accomplice always the learner. (Both slips contained the word "Teacher.") Immediately after the drawing, the teacher and learner were taken to an adjacent room and the learner was strapped into an "electric chair" apparatus.

The experimenter explained that the straps were to prevent excessive movement while the learner was being shocked. The effect was to make it impossible for him to escape from the situation. An electrode was attached to the learner's wrist, and electrode paste was applied "to avoid blisters and burns." Subjects were told that the electrode was attached to the shock generator in the adjoining room.

In order to improve credibility the experimenter declared, in response to a question by the learner: "Although the shocks can be extremely painful, they cause no permanent tissue damage."

Learning Task   The lesson administered by the subject was a paired-associate learning task. The subject read a series of word pairs to the learner, and then read the first word of the pair along with four terms. The learner was to indicate which of the four terms had originally been paired with the first word. He communicated his answer by pressing one of four switches in front of him, which in turn lit up one of four numbered quadrants in an answer-box located atop the shock generator.

Shock Generator The instrument panel consists of 30 lever switches set in a horizontal line. Each switch is clearly labeled with a voltage designation that ranges from 15 to 450 volts. There is a 15-volt increment from one switch to the next going from left to right. In addition, the following verbal designations are clearly indicated for groups of four switches going from left to right: Slight Shock, Moderate Shock, Strong Shock, Very Strong Shock, Intense Shock, Extreme Intensity Shock, Danger: Severe Shock. (Two switches after this last designation are simply marked XXX.)

Upon depressing a switch: a pilot light corresponding to each switch is illuminated in bright red; an electric buzzing is heard; an electric blue light, labeled "voltage energizer," flashes; the dial on the voltage meter swings to the right; various relay clicks are sounded.

The upper left-hand corner of the generator is labeled Shock Generator, Type ZLB, Dyson Instrument Company, Waltham, Mass. Output 15 Volts–450 Volts.

Details of the instrument were carefully handled to insure an appearance of authenticity. The panel was engraved by precision industrial engravers, and all components were of high quality. No subject in the experiment suspected that the instrument was merely a simulated shock generator.[1]

---

[1] A related technique, making use of a shock generator, was reported by Buss (1961) for the study of aggression in the laboratory. Despite the considerable similarity of technical detail in the experimental procedures, both investigators proceeded in ignorance of the other's work. Milgram provided plans and photographs of his shock generator, experimental procedure, and first results in a report to the National Science Foundation in January 1961. This report received only limited circulation. Buss reported his procedure 6 months later, but to a wider audience. Subsequently, technical information and reports were exchanged.

Sample Shock Each naive subject is given a sample shock on the shock generator, prior to beginning his run as teacher. This shock is always 45 volts, and is applied by pressing the third switch of the generator. The shock is applied to the wrist of the naive subject, and has its source in a 45-volt battery wired into the generator. This further convinces the subject of the authenticity of the generator.

Shock Instructions The subject is told to administer a shock to the learner each time he gives a wrong response. Moreover—and this is the key command—the subject is instructed to "move one level higher on the shock generator each time the learner flashes a wrong answer." He is also instructed to announce the voltage level before administering a shock. This serves to continually remind subjects of the increasing intensity of shocks administered to the learner.

Preliminary and Regular Run Pretests revealed that the procedure of reading words and administering shocks requires some practice before it can be handled smoothly. Therefore, immediately preceding the regular run, the teacher is given a preliminary series of 10 words to read to the learner. There are 3 neutral words in the practice series (i.e., words that the learner answers correctly), so that shocks are administered for 7 of the words, with the maximum shock at 105 volts (moderate shock). Almost all subjects master the procedure by the time the preliminary run is over.

Subjects are then presented with a second list, and are told that the procedure is the same as for the first list; the experimenter adds, however:

> When you get to the bottom of the list, repeat it over again, and continue giving shocks, until the learner has learned all the pairs correctly.

The experimenter instructs the subject to

> start from 15 volts and increase the shock level one step each time the learner gives a wrong answer.

Feedback from the Victim In all conditions the learner gives a predetermined set of responses to the word pair test, based on a schedule of approximately three wrong answers to one correct answer. In the present experimental condition no vocal response or other sign of protest is heard from the learner until Shock Level 300 is reached. When the 300-volt shock is administered, the learner pounds on the wall of the room in which he is bound to the electric chair. The pounding can be heard by the subject. From this point on, the learner's answers no longer appear on the four-way panel.

At this juncture, subjects ordinarily turn to the experimenter for guidance. The experimenter instructs the subject to treat the absence of a response as a wrong answer, and to shock the subject according to the usual schedule. He advises the subjects to allow 5–10 seconds before considering no response as a wrong answer, and to increase the shock level one step each time the learner fails to respond correctly. The learner's pounding is repeated after the 315-volt shock is administered; afterwards he is not heard from, nor do his answers reappear on the four-way signal box.

Experimenter Feedback At various points in the experiment the subject may turn to the experimenter for advice on whether he should continue to administer shocks. Or he may indicate that he does not wish to go on. It was important to standardize the experimenter's responses to these inquiries and reactions.

If the subject indicated his unwillingness to go on, the experimenter responded with a sequence of "prods," using as many as necessary to bring the subject into line.

Prod 1: Please continue *or* Please go on.

Prod 2: The experiment requires that you continue.

Prod 3: It is absolutely essential that you continue.

Prod 4: You have no other choice, you *must* go on.

The prods were always made in sequence: Only if Prod 1 had been unsuccessful, could Prod 2 be used. If the subject refused to obey the experimenter after Prod 4, the experiment was terminated. The experimenter's tone of voice was at all times firm, but not impolite. The sequence was begun anew on each occasion that the subject balked or showed reluctance to follow orders.

Special prods. If the subject asked if the learner was liable to suffer permanent physical injury, the experimenter said:

> Although the shocks may be painful, there is no permanent tissue damage, so please go on. [Followed by Prods 2, 3, and 4 if necessary.]

If the subject said that the learner did not want to go on, the experimenter replied:

> Whether the learner likes it or not, you must go on until he has learned all the word pairs correctly. So please go on. [Followed by Prods 2, 3, and 4, if necessary.]

Dependent Measures

The primary dependent measure for any subject is the maximum shock he administers before he refuses to go any further. In principle this may vary from 0 (for a subject who refuses to administer even the first shock) to 30 (for a subject who administers the highest shock on the generator). A subject who breaks off the experiment at any point prior to administering the thirtieth shock level is termed a *defiant* subject. One who complies with experimental commands fully, and proceeds to administer all shock levels commanded, is termed an *obedient* subject.

Further Records With few exceptions, experimental sessions were recorded on magnetic tape. Occasional photographs were taken through one-way mirrors. Notes were kept on any unusual behavior occurring during the course of the experiments. On occasion, additional observers were directed to write objective descriptions of the subjects' behavior. The latency and duration of shocks were measured by accurate timing devices.

Interview and Dehoax Following the experiment, subjects were interviewed; open-ended questions, projective measures, and attitude scales were employed. After the interview, procedures were undertaken to assure that the subject would leave the laboratory in a state of well being. A friendly reconciliation was arranged between the subject and the victim, and an effort was made to reduce any tensions that arose as a result of the experiment.

RESULTS

Preliminary Notions

Before giving an account of the experimental results, it is instructive to consider how persons predict others will perform when commanded to administer powerful shocks to another person. Fourteen Yale seniors, all psychology majors, were provided with a detailed description of the experimental situation. They were asked to reflect carefully on it, and to predict the behavior of 100 hypothetical subjects. More specifically, they were instructed to plot the distribution of obedience of "100 Americans of diverse occupations, and ranging in age from 20 to 50 years," who were placed in the experimental situation.

There was considerable agreement among the respondents on the expected behavior of hypothetical subjects. All respondents predicted that only an insignificant minority would go through to the end of the shock series. (The estimates ranged from 0 to 3%; i.e., the most "pessimistic" member of the class predicted that of 100 persons, 3 would continue through to the most potent shock available on the shock generator—450 volts.) The class mean was 1.2%. The question was also posed informally to colleagues of the author, and the most general feeling was

that few if any subjects would go beyond the designation Very Strong Shock.

Result of Experiment I

Subjects Accept Situation With few exceptions subjects were convinced of the reality of the experimental situation, that they were administering shocks to another person, and the most potent shocks were extremely painful. In the post-experimental interview subjects were asked: "How painful to the learner were the last few shocks that you administered to him?" Subjects were instructed to indicate their answers on a printed 14-point scale ranging from "Not at all painful" to "Extremely painful." The modal response was 14 (Extremely painful) with the mean at 13.42.

Signs of Extreme Tension Many subjects showed signs of nervousness in the experimental situation, and especially upon administering the more powerful shocks. In a large number of cases the degree of tension reached extremes that are rarely seen in sociopsychological laboratory studies. Subjects were observed to sweat, tremble, stutter, bite their lips, groan, and dig their fingernails into their flesh. These were characteristic rather than exceptional responses to the experiment.

One sign of tension was the regular occurrence of nervous laughing fits. Fourteen of the 40 subjects showed definite signs of nervous laughter and smiling. The laughter seemed entirely out of place, even bizarre. Full-blown, uncontrollable seizures were observed for 3 subjects. On one occasion we observed a seizure so violently convulsive that it was necessary to call a halt to the experiment. The subject, a 46-year-old encyclopedia salesman, was seriously embarrassed by his untoward and uncontrollable behavior. In the post-experimental interviews, subjects took pains to point out that they were not sadistic types, and that the laughter did not mean they enjoyed shocking the victim.

Distribution of Scores It had been conjectured that persons would not, in general, agree to administer shocks beyond the level designated as Very Strong Shock. The distribution of maximum shocks for this experiment is shown in Table 2. The obtained distribution of scores deviates radically from the prediction.

Upon command of the experimenter, each of the 40 subjects went beyond the expected breakoff point. No subject stopped prior to administering Shock Level 20. (At this level—300 volts—the victim kicks on the wall and no longer provides answers to the teacher's multiple-choice questions.)

Of the 40 subjects, 5 refused to obey the experimental commands beyond the 300-volt level. Four more subjects administered one further shock, and then refused to go on. Two broke off at the 330-volt level, and 1 each at 345, 360, and 375 volts. Thus a total of 14 subjects defied the experimenter. It is instructive to reprint their remarks at the point of defiance, as transcribed from the tape recordings:

[0124] I think he's trying to communicate, he's knocking....Well it's not fair to shock the guy...these are terrific volts. I don't think this is very humane....Oh, I can't go on with this; no, this isn't right. It's a hell of an experiment. The guy is suffering in there. No, I don't want to go on. This is crazy. [Subject refused to administer more shocks.]

[0123] He's banging in there. I'm gonna chicken out. I'd like to continue, but I can't do that to a man....I'm sorry I can't do that to a man. I'll hurt his heart. You take your check....No really, I couldn't do it.

These subjects were frequently in a highly agitated and even angered state. Sometimes, verbal protest was at a minimum, and the subject simply got up from his chair in front of the shock generator, and indicated that he wished to leave the laboratory.

TABLE 2

DISTRIBUTION OF BREAKOFF POINTS

Verbal designation and voltage indication	Number of subjects for whom this was maximum shock
Slight Shock	
15	0
30	0
45	0
60	0
Moderate Shock	
75	0
90	0
105	0
120	0
Strong Shock	
135	0
150	0
165	0
180	0
Very Strong Shock	
195	0
210	0
225	0
240	0
Intense Shock	
255	0
270	0
285	0
300	5
Extreme Intensity Shock	
315	4
330	2
345	1
360	1
Danger: Severe Shock	
375	1
390	0
405	0
420	0
XXX	
435	0
450	26

Of the 40 subjects, 26 obeyed the orders of the experimenter to the end, proceeding to punish the victim until they reached the most potent shock available on the shock generator. At that point, the experimenter called a halt to the session. (The maximum shock is labeled

450 volts, and is two steps beyond the designation: Danger: Severe Shock.) Although obedient subjects continued to administer shocks, they often did so under extreme stress. Some expressed reluctance to administer shocks beyond the 300-volt level, and displayed fears similar to those who defied the experimenter; yet they obeyed.

After the maximum shocks had been delivered, and the experimenter called a halt to the proceedings, many obedient subjects heaved sighs of relief, mopped their brows, rubbed their fingers over their eyes, or nervously fumbled cigarettes. Some shook their heads, apparently in regret. Some subjects had remained calm throughout the experiment, and displayed only minimal signs of tension from beginning to end.

DISCUSSION

The experiment yielded two findings that were surprising. The first finding concerns the sheer strength of obedient tendencies manifested in this situation. Subjects have learned from childhood that it is a fundamental breach of moral conduct to hurt another person against his will. Yet, 26 subjects abandon this tenet in following the instructions of an authority who has no special powers to enforce his commands. To disobey would bring no material loss to the subject; no punishment would ensue. It is clear from the remarks and outward behavior of many participants that in punishing the victim they are often acting against their own values. Subjects often expressed deep disapproval of shocking a man in the face of his objections, and others denounced it as stupid and senseless. Yet the majority complied with the experimental commands. This outcome was surprising from two perspectives: first, from the standpoint of predictions made in the questionnaire described earlier. (Here, however, it is possible that the remoteness of the respondents from the actual situation, and the difficulty of conveying to them the concrete details of the experiment, could ac-

count for the serious underestimation of obedience.) But the results were also unexpected to persons who observed the experiment in progress, through one-way mirrors. Observers often uttered expressions of disbelief upon seeing a subject administer more powerful shocks to the victim. These persons had a full acquaintance with the details of the situation, and yet systematically underestimated the amount of obedience that subjects would display.

The second unanticipated effect was the extraordinary tension generated by the procedures. One might suppose that a subject would simply break off or continue as his conscience dictated. Yet, this is very far from what happened. There were striking reactions of tension and emotional strain. One observer related:

> I observed a mature and initially poised businessman enter the laboratory smiling and confident. Within 20 minutes he was reduced to a twitching, stuttering wreck, who was rapidly approaching a point of nervous collapse. He constantly pulled on his earlobe, and twisted his hands. At one point he pushed his fist into his forehead and muttered: "Oh God, let's stop it." And yet he continued to respond to every word of the experimenter, and obeyed to the end.

Any understanding of the phenomenon of obedience must rest on an analysis of the particular conditions in which it occurs. The following features of the experiment go some distance in explaining the high amount of obedience observed in the situation.

1. The experiment is sponsored by and takes place on the grounds of an institution of unimpeachable reputation, Yale University. It may be reasonably presumed that the personnel are competent and reputable. The importance of this background authority is now being studied by conducting a series of experiments outside of New Haven, and without any visible ties to the university.

2. The experiment is, on the face of it, designed to attain a worthy purpose—advancement of

knowledge about learning and memory. Obedience occurs not as an end in itself, but as an instrumental element in a situation that the subject construes as significant and meaningful. He may not be able to see its full significance, but he may properly assume that the experimenter does.

3. The subject perceives that the victim has voluntarily submitted to the authority system of the experimenter. He is not (at first) an unwilling captive impressed for involuntary service. He has taken the trouble to come to the laboratory presumably to aid the experimental research. That he later becomes an involuntary subject does not alter the fact that, initially, he consented to participate without qualification. Thus he has in some degree incurred an obligation toward the experimenter.

4. The subject, too, has entered the experiment voluntarily, and perceives himself under obligation to aid the experimenter. He has made a commitment, and to disrupt the experiment is a repudiation of this initial promise of aid.

5. Certain features of the procedure strengthen the subject's sense of obligation to the experimenter. For one, he has been paid for coming to the laboratory. In part this is canceled out by the experimenter's statement that:

Of course, as in all experiments, the money is yours simply for coming to the laboratory. From this point on, no matter what happens, the money is yours.[2]

6. From the subject's standpoint, the fact that he is the teacher and the other man the learner is purely a chance consequence (it is determined by drawing lots) and he, the subject, ran the same risk as the other man in being assigned the role of learner. Since the assignment of positions in the experiment was achieved by fair means, the learner is deprived of any basis of complaint on this count. (A similar situation obtains in Army units, in which—in the absence of volunteers—a particularly dangerous mission may be assigned by drawing lots, and the unlucky soldier is expected to bear his misfortune with sportsmanship.)

7. There is, at best, ambiguity with regard to the prerogatives of a psychologist and the corresponding rights of his subject. There is a vagueness of expectation concerning what a psychologist may require of his subject, and when he is overstepping acceptable limits. Moreover, the experiment occurs in a closed setting, and thus provides no opportunity for the subject to remove these ambiguities by discussion with others. There are few standards that seem directly applicable to the situation, which is a novel one for most subjects.

8. The subjects are assured that the shocks administered to the subject are "painful but not dangerous." Thus they assume that the discomfort caused the victim is momentary, while the scientific gains resulting from the experiment are enduring.

9. Through Shock Level 20 the victim continues to provide answers on the signal box. The subject may construe this as a sign that the victim is still willing to "play the game." It is only after Shock Level 20 that the victim repudiates the rules completely, refusing to answer further.

These features help to explain the high amount of obedience obtained in this experiment. Many of the arguments raised need not remain matters of speculation, but can be reduced to testable proportions to be confirmed or disproved by further experiments.[3]

The following features of the experiment concern the nature of the conflict which the subject faces.

---

[2]Forty-three subjects, undergraduates at Yale University, were run in the experiment without payment. The results are very similar to those obtained with paid subjects.

[3]A series of recently completed experiments employing the obedience paradigm is reported in Milgram (1964).

10. The subject is placed in a position in which he must respond to the competing demands of two persons: the experimenter and the victim. The conflict must be resolved by meeting the demands of one or the other; satisfaction of the victim and the experimenter are mutually exclusive. Moreover, the resolution must take the form of a highly visible action, that of continuing to shock the victim or breaking off the experiment. Thus the subject is forced into a public conflict that does not permit any completely satisfactory solution.

11. While the demands of the experimenter carry the weight of scientific authority, the demands of the victim spring from his personal experience of pain and suffering. The two claims need not be regarded as equally pressing and legitimate. The experimenter seeks an abstract scientific datum; the victim cries out for relief from physical suffering caused by the subject's actions.

12. The experiment gives the subject little time for reflection. The conflict comes on rapidly. It is only minutes after the subject has been seated before the shock generator that the victim begins his protests. Moreover, the subject perceives that he has gone through but two-thirds of the shock levels at the time the subject's first protests are heard. Thus he understands that the conflict will have a persistent aspect to it, and may well become more intense as increasingly more powerful shocks are required. The rapidity with which the conflict descends on the subject, and his realization that it is predictably recurrent may well be sources of tension to him.

13. At a more general level, the conflict stems from the opposition of two deeply ingrained behavior dispositions: first, the disposition not to harm other people, and second, the tendency to obey those whom we perceive to be legitimate authorities.

READING 36

Central and Peripheral Routes to Advertising Effectiveness: The Moderating Role of Involvement

Richard E. Petty, John T. Cacioppo, and David Schumann (1983)

Almost as soon as people began to study attitudes, they began to study how to change them (see Readings 4, 6, 28). We now have an illustrious tradition in attitude change research, with its heyday in the 1950s (e.g., Hovland, 1951; Hovland, Janis, & Kelley, 1953; Hovland, Lumsdaine, & Sheffield, 1949). These researchers focused on four major variables: the communicator, the recipient of the message, the message itself, and the manner in which the message is communicated. After some time, the lack of theoretical advancement in this area, along with results that were increasingly resistant to the theoretical structures currently available, lead researchers to move on to more fertile topics.

Petty and Cacioppo turned to this fallow area in the late 1970s, developing a deceptively simple model with which to reorganize the research in attitude change. This model has already been applied to a variety of types of persuasion, including public relations, voting behavior, and counseling. In the reading that follows, Petty, Cacioppo, and Schumann describe the central and peripheral routes to persuasion, and test this model within the context of advertising effectiveness.

Abstract

Undergraduates expressed their attitudes about a product after being exposed to a magazine ad under conditions of either high or low product involvement. The ad contained either strong or weak arguments for the product and featured either prominent sports celebrities or average citizens as endorsers. The manipulation of argument quality had a greater impact on attitudes under high than low involvement, but the manipulation of product endorser had a greater impact under low than high involvement. These results are consistent with the view that there are two relatively distinct routes to persuasion.

Over the past three decades, a large number of studies have examined how consumers' evaluations of issues, candidates, and products are affected by media advertisements. Research on the methods by which consumers' attitudes are formed and changed has accelerated at a pace such that Kassarjian and Kassarjian were led to the conclusion that "attitudes clearly have become the central focus of consumer behavior research" (1979, p. 3). Not only are there a large number of empirical studies on consumer attitude formation and change, but there are also a large number of different theories of persuasion vying for the attention of the discipline (see Engel and Blackwell 1982; Kassarjian 1982).

In our recent reviews of the many approaches to attitude change employed in social and consumer psychology, we have suggested that—even though the different theories of persuasion possess different terminologies, postulates, underlying motives, and particular "effects" that they specialize in explaining—these theories emphasize one of two distinct routes to attitude change (Petty and Cacioppo 1981, 1983). One, called the *central route*, views attitude change as resulting from a person's diligent consideration of information that s/he feels is central to the true merits of a particular attitudinal position. The theoretical approaches following this route emphasize factors such as (1) the cognitive justification of attitude discrepant behavior (Cummings and Venkatesan 1976; Festinger 1957); (2) the comprehension, learning, and retention of issue- or product-relevant information (Bettman 1979; Hovland, Janis, and Kelley 1953; McGuire 1976); (3) the nature of a person's idiosyncratic cognitive responses to external communications (Cacioppo and Petty 1980a; Greenwald 1968; Petty, Ostrom, and Brock 1981; Wright 1980); and (4) the manner in which a person combines and integrates

issue- or product-relevant beliefs into an overall evaluative reaction (Ajzen and Fishbein 1980; Lutz and Bettman 1977; Troutman and Shanteau 1976). Attitude changes induced via the central route are postulated to be relatively enduring and predictive of behavior (Cialdini, Petty, and Cacioppo 1981; Petty and Cacioppo 1980).

A second group of theoretical approaches to persuasion emphasizes a more *peripheral route* to attitude change. Attitude changes that occur via the peripheral route do not occur because an individual has personally considered the pros and cons of the issue, but because the attitude issue or object is associated with positive or negative cues—or because the person makes a simple inference about the merits of the advocated position based on various simple cues in the persuasion context. For example, rather than diligently considering the issue-relevant arguments, a person may accept an advocacy simply because it was presented during a pleasant lunch or because the source is an expert. Similarly, a person may reject an advocacy simply because the position presented appears to be too extreme. These cues (e.g., good food, expert sources, extreme positions) and inferences (e.g., "If an expert says it, it must be true") may shape attitudes or allow a person to decide what attitudinal position to adopt without the need for engaging in any extensive thought about issue- or product-relevant arguments. The theoretical approaches following the peripheral route emphasize factors such as (1) whether a simple attitudinal inference can be made based on observing one's own behavior (Bem 1972; Scott 1978); (2) whether the advocacy falls within one's latitude of acceptance or rejection (Newman and Dolich 1979; Sherif, Sherif, and Nebergall 1965); (3) whether some transient situational utility is associated with adopting a particular attitude (Schlenker 1978, 1980); and (4) whether an advocated position or product is classically conditioned to basic but issue-irrelevant cues, such as food and pain (Janis, Kaye, and Kirschner 1965; Sternthal and Craig 1974), or is associated with secondary cues, such as pleasant pictures and attractive endorsers (Kelman 1961;

Mitchell and Olson 1981; Mowen 1980). Attitude changes induced under the peripheral route are postulated to be relatively temporary and unpredictive of behavior.

Unfortunately, none of the unique theories of persuasion has yet provided a comprehensive view of attitude change. For example, cognitive response theory—an approach that falls under the central route—assumes that people are usually interested in thinking about and elaborating incoming information, or in self-generating issue- or product-relevant thoughts (Brock and Shavitt 1983). Yet, as Miller and his colleagues have noted, "It may be irrational to scrutinize the plethora of counterattitudinal messages received daily. To the extent that one possesses only a limited amount of information processing time and capacity, such scrutiny would disengage the thought process from the exigencies of daily life." (Miller, Maruyama, Beaber, and Vallone 1976, p. 623). Haines (1974), in fact, has proposed a principle of information-processing parsimony according to which consumers seek to process as little data as necessary in order to make decisions.

The accumulated research on persuasion clearly indicates that neither the central nor the peripheral approach alone can account for the diversity of attitude-change results observed. Thus, a general framework for understanding attitude change must consider that in some situations people are avid seekers and manipulators of information, and in others they are best described as "cognitive misers" who eschew any difficult intellectual activity (Burnkrant 1976; McGuire 1969). An important question for consumer researchers then is: when will consumers actively seek and process product-relevant information, and when will they be more cursory in their analysis of ads? Recent research in consumer behavior and social psychology has focused on the concept of "involvement" as an important moderator of the amount and type of information processing elicited by a persuasive communication (see Burnkrant and Sawyer 1983; Petty and Cacioppo 1981, 1983). One major goal of the experiment reported in this paper was to test the hypothesis that under "high involvement" attitudes in response to an advertisement would be affected via the central route, but that under "low involvement" attitudes would be affected via the peripheral route.

INVOLVEMENT AND ATTITUDE CHANGE

Methods of Studying Involvement

Although there are many specific definitions of involvement within both social and consumer psychology, there is considerable agreement that high involvement messages have greater personal relevance and consequences or elicit more personal connections than low involvement messages (Engel and Blackwell 1982; Krugman 1965; Petty and Cacioppo 1979; Sherif and Hovland 1961). Various strategies have been employed in studying involvement. For example, both social (Hovland et al. 1957) and consumer (Newman and Dolich 1979) researchers have investigated existing groups that differed in the extent to which an issue or product was personally important, or have employed designs allowing subjects to assign themselves to high and low involvement groups. These correlational methods may be high in external validity, but they confound involvement with all other existing differences between the high and low involvement groups (attitude extremity, amount of prior information, and so on), and thus compromise internal validity (Kiesler, Collins, and Miller 1969). Other social (Rhine and Severance 1970) and consumer (Lastovicka and Gardner 1979) researchers have defined involvement in terms of the specific issue or product under consideration. This procedure, of course, confounds involvement with aspects of the issue or product that may be irrelevant to its personal importance. Finally, some researchers have studied involvement by varying the medium of message presentation. Interestingly, some investigators have argued that television is a more involving medium than print (Worchel, Andreoli, and Eason 1975), whereas others have argued just the opposite (Krugman 1967).

A preferred procedure for studying involvement would be to hold recipient, message, and medium characteristics constant and randomly assign participants to high and low involvement groups. Apsler and Sears (1968) employed an ingenious method to manipulate involvement: some participants were led to believe that a persuasive proposal had personal implications for them (an advocated change in university regulations would take effect while the student participants were still in school), while others were led to believe that it did not (i.e., the change would not take effect until after the students had graduated). A variation of this procedure was developed by Wright (1973, 1974) to manipulate involvement in an advertising study. Participants in the high involvement group were told that they would subsequently be asked to evaluate the product in an advertisement they were about to see, and were given some additional background information. Participants in the low involvement group did not expect to evaluate the product and were given no background information. The background information provided to the high involvement subjects explained the relevance of their product decisions to "their families, their own time and effort, and their personal finances" (Wright 1973, p. 56). However, it is somewhat unclear to what extent this background information made certain product-relevant arguments salient or suggested appropriate dimensions of product evaluation for high but not low involvement subjects.

In the present experiment, participants in both the high and low involvement groups were told that they would be evaluating advertisements for products, but subjects in the high involvement group were led to believe that the experimental advertised product would soon be available in their local area, and that after viewing a variety of advertisements they would be allowed to choose one brand from the experimental product category to take home as a gift. Low involvement participants were led to believe that the experimental advertised product would not be available in their local area in the near future, and that after viewing the ads they would be allowed to take home one brand from a category of products other than the experimental category.

Theories of Involvement

In addition to the methodological differences that have plagued the involvement concept, another area of disagreement concerns the effects on persuasion that involvement is expected to have. Perhaps the dominant notion in social psychology stems from the Sherifs' social judgment theory (Sherif et al. 1965). Their notion is that on any given issue, highly involved persons exhibit more negative evaluations of a communication because high involvement is associated with an extended "latitude of rejection." Thus, incoming messages on involving topics are thought to have an enhanced probability of being rejected because they are more likely to fall within the unacceptable range of a person's implicit attitude continuum. Krugman (1965) has proposed an alternative view that has achieved considerable recognition among consumer researchers. According to this view, increasing involvement does not increase resistance to persuasion, but instead shifts the sequence of communication impact. Krugman argues that under high involvement, a communication is likely to affect cognitions, then attitudes, and then behaviors, whereas under low involvement, a communication is more likely to affect cognitions, then behaviors, then attitudes (see also Ray et al. 1973).

As noted earlier, a focal goal of this study is to assess the viability of a third view of the effects of involvement on consumer response to advertisements. This view stems from our Elaboration Likelihood Model (ELM) of attitude change (Petty and Cacioppo 1981). The basic tenet of the ELM is that different methods of inducing persuasion may work best depending on whether the elaboration likelihood of the communication situation (i.e., the probability of message- or issue-relevant thought occurring) is high or low. When the elaboration likelihood is high, the central route to persuasion should be particularly effective, but when the elaboration likelihood is low, the peripheral route should be better. The ELM contends that as an issue or product increases in personal relevance or consequences, it becomes more important and adaptive to forming a reasoned and veridical opinion. Thus, people are more motivated to devote the cognitive effort required to evaluate the true merits of an issue or product when involvement is high rather than low. If increased involvement increases one's propensity to think about the true merits of an issue or product, then manipulations that require extensive issue- or product-relevant thought in order to be effective should have a greater impact under high rather than low involvement conditions. On the other hand, manipulations that allow a person to evaluate an issue or product without engaging in extensive issue- or product-relevant thinking should have a greater impact under low rather than high involvement.

Research in social psychology has supported the view that different variables affect persuasion under high and low involvement conditions. For example, the quality of the arguments contained in a message has had a greater impact on persuasion under conditions of high rather than low involvement (Petty and Cacioppo 1979; Petty, Cacioppo, and Heesacker 1981). On the other hand, peripheral cues such as the expertise or attractiveness of a message source (Chaiken 1980; Petty, Cacioppo, and Goldman 1981; Rhine and Severance 1970) have had a greater impact on persuasion under conditions of low rather than high involvement. In sum, under high involvement conditions people appear to exert the cognitive effort required to evaluate the issue-relevant arguments presented, and their attitudes are a function of this information-processing activity (central route). Under low involvement conditions, attitudes appear to be affected by simple acceptance and rejection cues in the persuasion context and are less affected by argument quality (peripheral route). Although the accumulated research in social psychology is quite consistent with the ELM, it is not yet clear whether or not the ELM predictions would hold when in-

volvement concerns a product (such as toothpaste) rather than an issue (such as capital punishment), and when the persuasive message is an advertisement rather than a speech or editorial.

Central and Peripheral Routes to Advertising Effectiveness

One important implication of the ELM for advertising messages is that different kinds of appeals may be most effective for different audiences. For example, a person who is about to purchase a new refrigerator (high involvement) may scrutinize the product-relevant information presented in an advertisement. If this information is perceived to be cogent and persuasive, favorable attitudes will result, but if this information is weak and specious, unfavorable attitudes will result (central route). On the other hand, a person who is not considering purchasing a new refrigerator at the moment (low involvement) will not expend the effort required to think about the product-relevant arguments in the ad, but may instead focus on the attractiveness, credibility, or prestige of the product's endorser (peripheral route). Some evidence in consumer psychology is consistent with this reasoning. For example, Wright (1973, 1974) exposed people to an advertisement for a soybean product under high and low involvement conditions (see earlier description) and measured the number of source comments (derogations) and message comments (counterarguments) generated after exposure. Although Wright (1974) predicted that involvement would increase both kinds of comments, he found that more message comments were made under high rather than low involvement, but that more source comments were made under low involvement conditions. This finding, of course, is consistent with the ELM.

In an initial attempt to provide a specific test of the utility of the ELM for understanding the effectiveness of advertising messages (Petty and Cacioppo 1980), we conducted a study in which three variables were manipulated: (1) the personal relevance of a shampoo ad (high involvement subjects were led to believe that the product would be available in their local area, whereas low involvement subjects were not); (2) the quality of the arguments contained in the ad; and (3) the physical attractiveness of the endorsers of the shampoo. Consistent with the ELM predictions, the quality of the arguments contained in the advertisement had a greater impact on attitudes when the product was of high rather than low relevance. Contrary to expectations, however, the attractiveness of the endorsers was equally important under both the high and low involvement conditions. In retrospect, in addition to serving as a peripheral cue under low involvement, the physical appearance of the product endorsers (especially their hair) may have served as persuasive visual testimony for the product's effectiveness. Thus, under high involvement conditions, the physical attractiveness of the endorsers may have served as a cogent product-relevant argument.

The present study was a conceptual replication of previous work (Petty and Cacioppo 1980), except that we employed a peripheral cue that could not be construed as a product-relevant argument. In the current study, participants were randomly assigned to high and low involvement conditions and viewed one of four different ads for a fictitious new product, "Edge disposable razors." The ad was presented in magazine format and was embedded in an advertising booklet along with 11 other ads. Two features of the Edge ad were manipulated: the quality of the arguments in support of Edge (strong or weak), and the celebrity status of the featured endorsers of Edge (celebrity or average citizen). It is important to note that preliminary testing revealed that for most people, the celebrity status of the endorsers was irrelevant to an evaluation of the true merits of a disposable razor, but that because the celebrity endorsers were liked more than the average citizens, they could still serve as a positive peripheral cue.

We had two major hypotheses. First, we expected the quality of the arguments presented in the ad to have a greater impact on product attitudes under high rather than low involvement con-

ditions. Second, we expected the celebrity status of the product endorsers to have a greater impact on product attitudes under low rather than high involvement conditions. If these hypotheses were supported, it would provide the first evidence that the Elaboration Likelihood Model can contribute to understanding the effects of involvement on attitudinal responses to advertisements.

METHOD

Subjects and Design

A total of 160 male and female undergraduates at the University of Missouri—Columbia participated in the experiment to earn credit in an introductory psychology course; 20 subjects were randomly assigned to each of the cells in a 2 (involvement: high or low) $\times$ 2 (argument quality: strong or weak) $\times$ 2 (cue: celebrity or noncelebrity status) factorial design. Subjects participated in groups of three to 15 in a very large classroom. The subjects were isolated from each other so that they could complete the experiment independently, and subjects in a single session participated in different experimental conditions. In fact, if enough subjects were present it was possible to conduct all eight experimental conditions simultaneously. This procedure avoided confounding session with experimental condition.

Procedure

Two booklets were prepared for the study. The first contained the advertising stimuli and the second contained the dependent measures. The first page of the advertising booklet explained that the study concerned the evaluation of magazine and newspaper ads and that the psychology department was cooperating with the journalism school in this endeavor. The first page also contained part of the involvement manipulation (see below). It was explained that each ad in the booklet was preceded by an introductory statement that told a little about the advertisement that followed (e.g., "The _____ company of Paris, France has just opened an American office in New York City. This élite men's clothing company originally sold clothing only in Europe, but is now in the process of attempting to enter the American market. The ad on the next page is one that they will be testing soon in Tampa, Florida before running the ads in other major cities that will eventually carry their products"). The instructions told subjects to continue through the booklet at their own pace and to raise their hands when finished. The ad booklet contained 10 real magazine ads for both relatively familiar (e.g., Aquafresh toothpaste) and unfamiliar (e.g., Riopan antacid) products, and two bogus ads. The sixth ad in each booklet was the crucial fictitious ad for Edge razors (the nature of the other bogus ad was varied but is irrelevant to the present study). When subjects had completed perusing their ad booklets, they were given a questionnaire booklet to complete. Upon completion of the questionnaire, the subjects were thoroughly debriefed, thanked for their participation, and dismissed.

Independent Variables

Involvement   Involvement was embedded in two places in the ad booklet. First, the cover page offered subjects a free gift for participation in the experiment. Subjects were either informed that they would be allowed to choose a particular brand of disposable razor (high involvement with the fictitious Edge ad) or that they would be allowed to choose a brand of toothpaste (low involvement with Edge). A toothpaste ad did appear in the ad booklet, but it was the same ad for all subjects. To bolster the involvement manipulation, the page that introduced the Edge ad also differed in the high and low involvement conditions. High involvement subjects were told that the advertisement and product would soon be test-marketed in medium-sized cities throughout the Midwest, including their own city (Columbia, Missouri); low involvement sub-

jects were told that the advertisement and product were being test-marketed only on the East Coast. Thus high involvement subjects were not only led to believe that they would soon have to make a decision about the product class, they were also led to believe that the product would be available in their area in the near future. Low involvement subjects, on the other hand, did not expect to make a decision about razors (but did expect to make one about toothpaste), and were led to believe that Edge razors would not be available for purchase in their area in the foreseeable future.

Argument Quality   A variety of arguments for disposable razors were pretested for potency on a sample of undergraduates. In the strong arguments ad, the razor was characterized as "scientifically designed," and the following five statements were made about the product:

- New advanced honing method creates unsurpassed sharpness
- Special chemically formulated coating eliminates nicks and cuts and prevents rusting
- Handle is tapered and ribbed to prevent slipping
- In direct comparison tests, the Edge blade gave twice as many close shaves as its nearest competitor
- Unique angle placement of the blade provides the smoothest shave possible

In the weak arguments version of the ad, the razor was characterized as "designed for beauty," and the following five statements were made about the product:

- Floats in water with a minimum of rust
- Comes in various sizes, shapes, and colors
- Designed with the bathroom in mind
- In direct comparison tests, the Edge blade gave no more nicks or cuts than its competition
- Can only be used once but will be memorable

Peripheral Cue   In the "famous endorser" conditions, the headline accompanying the advertisement read "Professional Athletes Agree: Un-

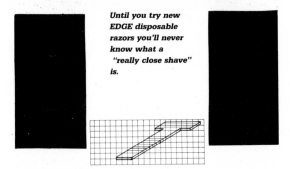

FIGURE A Example mock ads. (Note: Left panel shows celebrity endorser ad for Edge razors employing the strong arguments. Right panel shows average citizen endorser ad for Edge razors employing the weak arguments. Pictures of celebrities and citizens have been blacked out to preserve propriety and anonymity.)

til you try new Edge disposable razors you'll never know what a really close shave is.'' In addition, the ad featured the pictures of two well-known, well-liked golf (male) and tennis (female) celebrities. In the ''nonfamous endorser'' conditions, the headline read ''Bakersfield, California Agrees: _____ ,'' and the ad featured pictures of average looking people who were unfamiliar to the subjects. The average citizens in the ad were middle-aged and characterized as coming from California to minimize perceptions of similarity to the subjects (Missouri college students). Figure A depicts two of the four Edge ads used in the present study.

Dependent Measures

On the first page of the dependent variable booklet, subjects were asked to try to list all of the product categories for which they saw advertisements, and to try to recall the brand name of the product in that category. On the next page, subjects were given descriptions of the 12 product categories and were asked to select the correct brand name from among seven choices provided. Although we had no specific hypotheses about brand recall and recognition, these measures were included because of their practical importance and for purposes of comparison with the attitude data.

Next, subjects responded to some questions about one of the legitimate ads in the booklet; this was followed by the crucial questions about Edge razors. The questions about Edge were placed relatively early in the booklet to avoid subject fatigue and boredom and to maximize the effectiveness of the manipulations. Subjects were first asked to rate, on a four-point scale, how likely it would be that they would purchase Edge disposable razors ''the next time you needed a product of this nature.'' The descriptions for each scale value were: 1 = ''I definitely would not buy it,'' 2 = ''I might or might not buy it,'' 3 = ''I would probably buy it,'' and 4 = ''I would definitely buy it.'' Following this measure of purchase intentions, subjects were asked to rate their overall impression of the product on three nine-point semantic differential scales anchored at -4 and $+4$ (bad–good, unsatisfactory–satisfactory, and unfavorable–favorable). Since the intercorrelations among these measures were very high (average $r = 0.86$), responses were averaged to assess a general positive or negative attitude toward the product.

Following some additional questions that were consistent with the cover story, subjects were instructed to list the thoughts that crossed their minds as they examined the ad for Edge disposable razors. These thoughts were subsequently scored on several dimensions by trained judges. Since subjects listed very few thoughts about the product ($M = 1.18$) and since the manipulations failed to affect this measure, it will not be discussed further. This "cognitive response" measure would probably have been more sensitive if it had been administered immediately after exposure to the Edge ad rather than after exposure to all 12 ads, but in the present study this would have compromised the cover story (for an extended discussion of the reliability, validity, and sensitivity of the thought-listing measure in persuasion research, see Cacioppo and Petty 1981).

After listing their thoughts, several questions were asked to check on the experimental manipulations, and subjects were asked to try to list as many of the attributes mentioned in the ad about Edge razors as they could recall. Following the questions about Edge were several questions about some of the other products and ads in the booklet. As a check on the involvement manipulation, the very last question in the booklet asked subjects to recall the free gift they had been told to expect.

RESULTS

Manipulation Checks

In response to the last question in the dependent variable booklet asking subjects what gift they had been told to expect, 92.5 percent of the subjects in the high involvement conditions correctly recalled that they were to select a brand of disposable razor. In the low involvement conditions, none of the subjects indicated a razor and 78 percent correctly recalled that they were to select a brand of toothpaste. Thus, subjects presumably realized what product they were soon to make a decision about as they examined the ad booklet.

To assess the effectiveness of the endorser manipulation, two questions were asked. First, subjects were asked if they recognized the people in the ad for the disposable razor. When the famous athletes were employed, 94 percent indicated "yes," whereas when the average citizens were employed, 96 percent indicated "no." In addition, subjects were asked to rate the extent to which they liked the people depicted in the ad on an 11-point scale, where 1 indicated "liked very little" and 11 indicated "liked very much." An analysis of this measure revealed that the famous endorsers were liked more ($M = 6.06$) than the average citizens ($M = 3.64$: $F(1, 143) = 40.81$, $p < 0.0001$); on average, women reported liking the endorsers more ($M = 5.32$) than did men ($M = 4.44$; $F(1, 143) = 5.25$, $p < 0.03$).

As a check on the argument-persuasiveness manipulation, two questions were asked. The first required respondents to "rate the reasons as described in the advertisement for using EDGE" on an 11-point scale anchored by "unpersuasive" and "persuasive"; the second question asked them to rate the reasons on an 11-point scale anchored by "weak reasons" and "strong reasons." On the first measure, subjects exposed to the strong arguments rated them as significantly more persuasive ($M = 5.46$) than did subjects exposed to the weak arguments ($M = 4.03$; $F(1, 139) = 12.97$, $p < 0.0004$). Additionally, a main effect for gender was found such that women rated the arguments as more persuasive ($M = 5.26$) than did men ($M = 4.28$; $F(1, 139) = 5.25$, $p < 0.02$). Finally, an

Arguments × Gender interaction emerged ($F(1, 139) = 5.43, p < 0.02$), indicating that the tendency for females to find the arguments more persuasive than males was greater for the strong than for the weak arguments. On the second manipulation check measure, subjects rated the strong arguments as "stronger" ($M = 5.58$) than the weak ones ($M = 4.13$; $F(1, 138) = 14.31$, $p < 0.002$). Again, an Arguments × Gender interaction occurred, indicating that females especially tended to rate the strong arguments more highly than did males. In short, all of the variables were manipulated successfully. The tendency for females to be more positive in their ratings of both endorsers and the arguments in the ads is generally consistent with previous psychological research portraying women as more concerned with social harmony than men (Eagly 1978). Importantly, these sex differences did not lead to any significant gender effects on the crucial measures of attitude and purchase intention.

Attitudes and Purchase Intentions

Table 1 presents the means and standard deviations for each cell on the attitude index. A number of interesting main effects emerged. First, involved subjects were somewhat more skeptical of the product ($M = 0.31$) than were less involved subjects ($M = 0.99$; $F(1, 148) = 6.64$, $p < 0.01$). Second, subjects liked the product significantly more when the ad contained cogent arguments ($M = 1.65$) than when the arguments were specious ($M = -0.35$; $F(1, 148) = 57.81$, $p < 0.0001$). Third, subjects tended to like the product more when it was endorsed by the famous athletes ($M = 0.86$) than by the average citizens of Bakersfield, California ($M = 0.41$; $F(1, 148) = 2.91, p < 0.09$).

Each of these main effects must be qualified and interpreted in light of two important two-way interactions. First, an Involvement × Endorser interaction ($F(1, 148) = 5.94$, $p < 0.02$) revealed that the nature of the product endorser had a significant impact on product attitudes only under low involvement ($F(1, 148) = 5.96$, $p < 0.02$), but not under high involvement ($F < 1$; see top panel of Figure B). On the other hand, an Involvement × Arguments interaction ($F(1, 148 = 18.47, p < 0.0001$) revealed that although argument quality had an impact on product attitudes under both low involvement ($F(1, 148) = 5.40$, $p < 0.02$) and high involvement ($F(1, 148) = 71.36$, $p < 0.0001$), the impact of argument quality on attitudes was significantly greater under high rather than low involvement (see bottom panel of Figure B). Neither the Endorser × Arguments nor the three-way in-

TABLE 1

MEANS AND STANDARD DEVIATIONS FOR EACH EXPERIMENTAL CELL ON THE ATTITUDE INDEX

	Low involvement		High involvement	
	Weak arguments	Strong arguments	Weak arguments	Strong arguments
Citizen endorser	−.12 (1.81)	.98 (1.52)	−1.10 (1.66)	1.98 (1.25)
Celebrity endorser	1.21 (2.28)	1.85 (1.59)	−1.36 (1.65)	1.80 (1.07)

Note: Attitude scores represent the average rating of the product on three nine-point semantic differential scales anchored at −4 and +4 (bad–good, unsatisfactory–satisfactory, and unfavorable–favorable). Standard deviations are in parentheses.

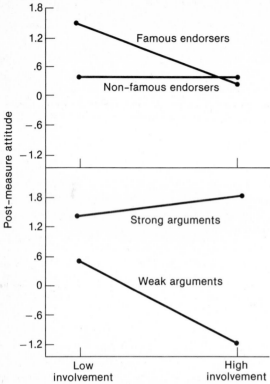

FIGURE B Product attitudes. (Note: Top panel shows interactive effect of involvement and endorser status on attitudes toward Edge razors. Bottom panel shows interactive effect of involvement and argument quality on attitudes toward Edge razors.)

portant determinant of purchase intentions under high rather than low involvement.

The correlation between attitudes and purchase intentions for low involvement subjects was 0.36; and for high involvement subjects it was 0.59. Although both correlations are significantly different from zero ($ps < 0.001$), it is interesting to note that the low involvement correlation is considerably smaller than the high involvement correlation ($p < 0.07$). The fact that the argument quality manipulation affected behavioral intentions while the endorser manipulation did not (although it did affect attitudes)— and the fact that attitudes were better predictors of behavioral intentions under high rather than low involvement—provide some support for the ELM view that attitudes formed via the central route will be more predictive of behavior than attitudes formed via the peripheral route.

Recall and Recognition Measures

Subjects were asked to list all of the products for which they saw ads and all of the brand names they encountered. Following this, all subjects were told that they had seen an advertisement for a disposable razor and were asked to select the correct brand name from a list of seven (Gillette, Wilkinson, Schick, Edge, Bic, Schaffer, and Remington). The proportion of subjects showing correct recall or recognition was calculated for each cell. These proportions were then subjected to an arcsin transformation (Winer 1971) and analyzed by the procedure recommended by Langer and Abelson (1972).

The involvement manipulation had a significant impact on free recall of the product category, with more high involvement subjects (81 percent) recalling the product category than low involvement subjects (64 percent; $Z = 2.4$, $p < 0.02$). Additionally, exposure to the famous endorser increased recall of the product category under low involvement conditions (from 52 percent to 75 percent; $Z = 2.14$, $p < 0.03$), but had

teraction approached significance ($F = 0.14$ and 0.54, respectively).

Two significant effects emerged from the question asking subjects to rate their likelihood of purchasing Edge disposable razors the next time they needed a product of this nature. Subjects said that they would be more likely to buy the product when the arguments presented were strong ($M = 2.23$) rather than weak ($M = 1.68$; $F(1, 152) = 25.37$, $p < 0.0001$). Additionally, an Involvement × Arguments interaction emerged ($F(1, 152) = 4.25$, $p < 0.04$). This interaction paralleled that obtained on the attitude measure and indicated that argument quality was a more im-no effect on product category recall under high involvement (80 versus 82 percent).

Involvement affected free recall of the brand name of the product, increasing it from 42 percent in the low involvement conditions to 60 percent in the high involvement conditions ($Z = 2.28$, $p < 0.01$). There was also an effect for gender on this measure, with males showing greater brand name recall (61 percent) than females (39 percent; $Z = 2.78$, $p < 0.007$). The endorser manipulation had a marginally significant effect on brand name recall, with the famous endorsers tending to enhance recall over average citizens from 43 to 58 percent ($Z = 1.89$, $p < 0.06$).

On the measure of brand name recognition, an interaction pattern emerged. Under low involvement, the use of famous endorsers reduced brand name recognition from 85 to 70 percent, but under high involvement, the use of famous endorsers improved brand name recognition from 77 to 87 percent ($Z = 1.96$, $p < 0.05$).

To summarize the recall and recognition data thus far, it appears that increasing involvement with the product enhanced recall not only of the product category, but also of the brand name of the specific product advertised. The effects of the endorser manipulation were more complex and depended on the level of involvement. In general, under low involvement a positive endorser led to increased recall of the product category but reduced brand name recognition. Thus, people may be more likely to notice the products in low involvement ads when they feature prominent personalities, but because of the enhanced attention accorded the people in the ads and the general lack of interest in assessing the merits of the product (due to low involvement), reductions in brand recognition may occur. This finding is similar to the results of studies on the use of sexually oriented material in ads for low involvement products—the sexual material enhances recognition of the ad, but not the brand name of the product (e.g., Chestnut, LaChance, and Lubitz 1977; Steadman 1969). Under high involvement, however, the use of prominent personalities enhanced brand name recognition. When people are more interested in the product category, they may be more motivated to assess what brand the liked personalities are endorsing. The manipulation of argument quality had no effect on recall of the product category, brand name recall, or brand name recognition.

A final recall measure assessed how many of the specific arguments for Edge razors the subjects could spontaneously recall after they had examined the entire ad booklet. Overall, subjects were able to correctly reproduce only 1.75 of the five arguments presented. This was not affected by any of the experimental manipulations.

Clearly, the manipulations produced a very different pattern of effects on the recall and recognition measures than on the attitude and purchase intention measures. In addition, the recall and recognition measures were uncorrelated with attitudes or intentions toward Edge razors. This finding is consistent with a growing body of research indicating that simple recall or recognition of information presented about an attitude object is not predictive of attitude formation and change (e.g., Cacioppo and Petty 1979; Greenwald 1968; Insko, Lind, and LaTour 1976).

The present data also argue against using measures of brand name recall or recognition as the sole indicants of advertising effectiveness. For example, in the present study, enhancing involvement led to a significant improvement in brand name recall, but increasing involvement led to a decrement in attitude toward the brand when the arguments presented were weak.

DISCUSSION

As we noted earlier, previous research on attitude formation and change has tended to characterize the persuasion process as resulting either from a thoughtful (though not necessarily rational) consideration of issue-relevant arguments and product-relevant attributes (central route), or from associating the attitude object with various positive and negative cues and operating with simple decision rules (peripheral route). Over the past decade, investigators in both social psychology and consumer behavior have tended to emphasize the former process over the latter. Consider the recent comments of Fishbein and Ajzen (1981, p. 359):

> The general neglect of the information contained in a message . . . is probably the most serious problem in communication and persuasion research. We are convinced that the persuasiveness of a communication can be increased much more easily and dramatically by paying careful attention to its content . . . than by manipulation of credibility, attractiveness . . . or any of the other myriad factors that have caught the fancy of investigators in the area of communication and persuasion.

The present study suggests that, although the informational content of an advertisement may be the most important determinant of product attitudes under some circumstances, in other circumstances such noncontent manipulations as the celebrity status (likeability) or credibility of the product endorsers may be even more important. Specifically, we have shown that when an advertisement concerned a product of low involvement, the celebrity status of the product endorsers was a very potent determinant of attitudes about the product. When the advertisement concerned a product of high involvement, however, the celebrity status of the product endorsers had no effect on attitudes, but the cogency of the information about the product contained in the ad was a powerful determinant of product evaluations. These data clearly suggest that it would be inappropriate for social and consumer researchers to overemphasize the influence of issue-relevant arguments or product-relevant attributes and ignore the role of peripheral cues. Each type of attitudinal influence occurs in some instances, and the level of personal involvement with an issue or product appears to be one determinant of which type of persuasion occurs.

According to the Elaboration Likelihood Model, personal relevance is thought to be only one determinant of the route to persuasion. Personal relevance is thought to increase a person's motivation for engaging in a diligent consideration of the issue- or product-relevant information presented in order to form a veridical opinion. Just as different situations may induce different motivations to think, different people may typically employ different styles of information processing, and some people will enjoy thinking more than others (Cacioppo and Petty 1982). However, a diligent consideration of issue- or product-relevant information requires not only the motivation to think, but also the ability to process the information. Thus situational variables (e.g., distraction; Petty, Wells, and Brock 1976) and individual difference variables (e.g., prior knowledge; Cacioppo and Petty 1980b) may also be important moderators of the route to persuasion. In the present study, subjects' ability to think about the product was held at a high level across experimental conditions—that is, the messages were easy to understand, the presentation was self-paced, and so on. Thus the primary determinant of the route to persuasion was motivational in nature.

It is important to note that although our "peripheral" manipulation was a source variable presented visually and our "central" manipulation was a message variable presented verbally, neither the source/message nor the visual/verbal dichotomy is isomorphic with the central/peripheral one. Thus a source variable may induce persuasion via the central route, and a message variable may serve as a peripheral cue. For example, in one study described previously (Petty and Cacioppo 1980), we observed that a physically attractive message endorser might serve as a cogent product-relevant argument for a beauty product. In another study (Petty and Cacioppo, 1983), we found that the mere number of message arguments presented may activate a simple decision rule (the more the better) under low involvement, but not under high involvement, where argument quality is more important than number. Similarly, a "central" manipulation may be presented visually—e.g., depicting a kitten in an advertisement for facial tissue to convey the product-relevant attribute "softness" (Mitchell and Olson 1981)—and a "peripheral" manipulation may be presented verbally—e.g., providing a verbal description of a message source as an expert or as likeable (Chaiken 1980; Petty, Cacioppo, and Goldman 1981). The critical feature of the central route to persuasion is that an attitude change is based on a diligent consideration of information that a person feels is central to the true merits of an issue or product. This information may be conveyed visually, verbally, or in source or message characteristics. In the peripheral route, attitudes change because of the presence of simple positive or negative cues, or because of the invocation of simple decision rules which obviate the need for thinking about issue-relevant arguments. Stimuli that serve as peripheral cues or that invoke simple decision rules may be presented visually or verbally, or may be part of source or message characteristics.

In the present study, the overall pattern of results on the attitude and purchase intention measures is more consistent with the Elaboration Likelihood Model formulation than with the Sherif, Sherif, and Nebergall (1965) social judgment model or with Krugman's (1965, 1967) sequence model of involvement. Although increasing involvement did produce a main effect on the attitude measure (more resistance to the product under high rather than low involvement), as anticipated by social judgment theory, the more complicated interactions of endorser and argument quality with involvement cannot be accounted for by the theory. Thus the social judgment theory view that it is more difficult to change attitudes under high involvement is, at best, only partially correct, and is unable to account for the complete pattern of attitude data. The attitude and behavioral data are generally inconsistent with Krugman's sequence formulation. Krugman suggested that under high involvement, attitude change preceded behavior change, but that under low involvement, behavior change

preceded attitude change. This reasoning would suggest that on immediate measures, attitudinal effects should be easier to detect than behavioral effects under high involvement, while behavioral effects should be easier to detect than attitudinal effects under low involvement. In the present study, both attitudinal and behavioral (intention) effects were observed under high involvement, which is consistent with both models. Under low involvement, however, effects were obtained on the measure of attitude but not on the measure of behavioral intentions. This finding is inconsistent with Krugman's formulation, which expects stronger behavioral effects under low involvement than under high involvement, but it is consistent with the ELM, which postulates a greater correspondence between attitudes and behaviors under high involvement (central route) than under low involvement (peripheral route).

In sum, the present study has provided support for the view that different features of an advertisement may be more or less effective, depending upon a person's involvement with it. Under conditions of low involvement, peripheral cues are more important than issue-relevant argumentation, but under high involvement, the opposite is true. The realization that independent variables may have different effects, depending on the level of personal relevance of a message, may provide some insight into the conflicting pattern of results that is said to characterize much attitude research. It may well be that attitude effects can be arranged on a continuum, depending on the elaboration likelihood of the particular persuasion situation. This continuum would be anchored at one end by the peripheral route and at the other end by the central route to persuasion. Furthermore, these two routes may be characterized by quite different antecedents and consequents. If so, future work could be aimed at uncovering the various moderators of the route to persuasion and at tracking the various consequents of the two different routes.

Group Behavior

Deindividuation and Valence of Cues: Effects of Prosocial and Antisocial Behavior

Robert D. Johnson and Leslie L. Downing (1979)

This study on deindividuation pits two competing hypotheses against each other. The earliest studies on deindividuation (Festinger, Pepitone, & Newcomb, 1952; Singer, Brush, & Lublin, 1965; Zimbardo, 1970) hypothesize that deindividuation leads to antisocial behavior. Gergen, Gergen, and Barton (1973), however, hypothesize that deindividuation leads to greater sensitivity to external cues, which may influence individuals to be either more *antisocial* or more *prosocial*. Gergen et al. agree that the subjects in Zimbardo's (1970) study who wore deindividuating costumes became less self-aware and more disinhibited, but that the direction of their actual behavior was evoked by the "Ku Klux Klannishness" of their costumes. This important methodological point has substantial theoretical implications; we should always be on the lookout for the nonobvious or hidden implications in the operational definitions of our psychological constructs.

Zimbardo and most researchers consider that deindividuation includes at least some degree of anonymity. But deindividuation also includes diffusion of responsibility, group versus individual awareness, and lack of evaluation apprehension. Johnson and Downing help to clarify these ingredients in deindividuation and propose a two-step process involved in leading to antisocial or prosocial action. Future research will hopefully continue the process of clarification.

Abstract

Deindividuation has been shown to relate to increases in antisocial behavior. Typical manipulations, however, have confounded deindividuation with the presence of negatively valenced cues, such cues being inherent in the costumes or situations used to produce deindividuation. The present study manipulated deindividuation and valence of costume cues in a 2 × 2 factorial design. Zimbardo's theory of deindividuation suggests that deindividuation should disinhibit antisocial behavior, independent of cue valence, and should reduce any influence due to cues. Gergen, however, suggests that cues may have increasing influence, given deindividuation, and that deindividuation may increase prosocial behavior, given positive cues, and increase antisocial behavior, given negative cues. Results supported Gergen's position. Given options to increase or decrease shock level received by a stranger, no main effect was found for deindividuation. There was a main effect for costume cues, and an interaction of cues with deindividuation, with deindividuation facilitating a significant increase in prosocial responses in the presence of positive cues and a nonsignificant increase in antisocial responses in the presence of negative cues. Also cues interacted with trial blocks, prosocial behavior increasing with positive cues and antisocial behavior increasing with negative cues over trial blocks.

The construct deindividuation was first systematically investigated by Festinger, Pepitone, and Newcomb (1952). In their view, one consequence of an individual's involvement and identification with a group is a reduction of individual responsibility for individual behavior. They believed that deindividuation was a phenomenon on which groups would differ and that degree of deindividuation in a group could be indexed by the rate of failure of individuals to identify correctly the group members who had contributed different behaviors. It was expected that previously inhibited behaviors (i.e., saying negative things about one's parents) would be disinhibited as a result of deindividuation. As predicted, groups scoring highest on deindividuation did say more negative things about their parents. This was, however, a correlational study in which the direction of causality between deindividuation and disinhibition is unclear. Later studies (Singer, Brush, & Lublin, 1965; Zimbardo, 1970) using lab coats and hoods to obscure the identifiability of individuals, have shown that such a manipulation increases disinhibition of socially undesirable behaviors (i.e., speaking obscene words and administering electrical shock to anotherperson).

Theoretical Issues

Exactly which behaviors will be disinhibited in a given situation is not yet clear. Nor is it clear how situational cues affect the type or amount of disinhibition that occurs. Two major positions on these issues have been advanced.

Zimbardo's View   In Zimbardo's theory of deindividuation (1970), anonymity, along with other input variables, produces a state of the organism, *deindividuation,* that in turn produces a general disinhibition of previously inhibited behavior. Negative comments about parents, college women's use of obscene words, and subjecting others to pain are all behaviors inhibited by prior experience, possibly by expectation of punishment. Deindividuation disinhibits such behaviors by means of a general weakening of inhibitory mechanisms. Which behaviors will be disinhibited depends upon which ones have been inhibited. Inhibited behaviors, once initiated, will tend to increase in frequency and intensity because they are intrinsically reinforcing. According to this theory, because the real source of the behavior is its intrinsically self-rewarding nature, deindividuation should lead to decreasing influence of external cues.

These hypotheses were subjected to an experimental test using what is perhaps the best-known deindividuation paradigm (Zimbardo,

1970). Groups of subjects were individuated (with identifying name tags) or deindividuated (with lab coats and hoods obscuring their identity) and were then given a sanctioned opportunity to administer electrical shocks to another person. Zimbardo has interpreted the increased duration of shocks given by deindividuated subjects to be a result of the deindividuating experience disinhibiting aggressive behavior.

As predicted, individuated subjects decreased shock over trials for a "nice" target person and increased shock for an "obnoxious" target, whereas deindividuated subjects increased shock for both targets. Also, shock duration and negativity of ratings of the target person were significantly correlated for individuated subjects, $r = .67$, but not for deindividuated subjects, $r = .10$. Contrary to prediction, however, the deindividuated subjects' average shock duration was higher for the "obnoxious" than for the "nice" target, whereas during the first half of the trials, individuated subjects actually shocked the "nice" target more than the "obnoxious" one. Deindividuated subjects thus seemed at least initially more "appropriately" responsive to target characteristics than were individuated subjects. Thus evidence for Zimbardo's prediction of reduced influence of situational cues, given deindividuation, is at best equivocal.

Gergen's View   The prediction that antisocial behavior is most likely to be disinhibited by deindividuation was questioned by Gergen, Gergen, and Barton (1973). In their study, darkness- and anonymity-induced deindividuation led not to increased aggression but to increases in touching, caressing, and other affectionate behaviors. These workers advanced the notion that either prosocial or antisocial behavior could be enhanced by deindividuation, depending upon valence of situational cues. In this view, the darkness manipulation may have been more suggestive of intimacy than of aggression, hence anonymity-induced deindividuation increased the frequency of intimacy behaviors.

Experimental Confounds

A more important question is whether the disinhibition observed in prior research was in fact due to deindividuation and not to some unintentionally manipulated variable. One such variable relates to the cue value of the deindividuating costumes, which may be reminiscent of Ku Klux Klan outfits or perhaps of some Halloween ghouls, either of which might be considered cues eliciting aggression (Berkowitz, 1974). It is noteworthy that even without differential identifiability, Berkowitz and his colleagues have demonstrated increased duration of shocks to a target person due to the presence of cues previously associated with aggression (Berkowitz, 1974). A similar line of reasoning could serve as an alternative explanation for differential levels of the use of profanity in the Singer et al. (1965) study. Old clothes (deindividuated condition) may have provided cues for lowered restraints against obscene language, whereas dressy clothes (individuated condition) may have provided cues to a number of learned associations of verbal restraint and propriety. Finally, the dark chamber used by Gergen et al. (1973) to deindividuate subjects may have provided cues (e.g., darkness, the awareness of the presence of others through the sense of smell, the sounds of breathing, and the sense of touch, even if at first accidental) suggestive of intimacy and thus facilitating intimate behavior. In this study, however, a control condition indicated that darkness cues did not disinhibit intimacy if subjects were not anonymous.

The major question addressed by the present study is whether the direction of behavior change induced by nonidentifiability is influenced by the valence of situational cues. Given an influence of cues, Zimbardo's (1970) theory would predict that nonidentifiability will disinhibit aggressive behavior and that any effect of cues should be less than the effect for identifiable subjects. On the other hand, the reasoning of Gergen et al. (1973) predicts that nonidentifiability will lead to increases in antisocial behavior if antisocial cues are present and to increases in prosocial behavior if prosocial cues are present. A third possibility is that anonymity per se has no effect, but that prior demonstrations of anonymity effects actually resulted from confounded differences in situational cues.

METHOD

Subjects

Sixty female subjects were recruited from introductory psychology, sociology, and child development courses to participate in a study described as concerned with changes in group evaluations of a stranger. Most subjects were given extra credit in their course as an incentive to participate.

Procedure

Subjects were randomly assigned, 15 to each of four conditions, in a 2 × 2 factorial design that manipulated individuation (identifiable) versus deindividuation (nonidentifiable) and prosocial versus antisocial cues. Each subject was informed by phone, at the time she was recruited, that the experiment was to be run in groups of four, and that it was therefore very important for her to appear on time. Upon arrival, subjects were informed that each student had been asked to report to a different room in order to preclude interaction with others prior to the experiment. It was also explained that Polaroid pictures of the other group members would be used to establish the essential feeling of being part of a group and that disguises would be worn in the pictures to obscure individual difference characteristics that might be influential. In fact, although as many as four subjects were run in each session, each subject was treated completely independently of the others, and all subjects at any one time were in different treatment conditions. No subject had any contact with any other subject during the experimental session.

It was explained to each subject that the paid nonstudent male volunteer whom they would be evaluating was taking part in a verbal learning experiment and that it was important for them to become involved with the stranger. Involvement was to be established by their participation in selecting the level of shock that this person received for failure to respond correctly in the learning task. Subjects were instructed that it was an exploratory study on the effect of arousal on learning and that the experimenters did not know what effect different shock levels would have. Following each error the learner would be given a shock the base level of which could be increased or decreased by the responses of the subjects. The actual shock level received following an error would be the base level adjusted by the average adjustment selected by the four group members. Each subject would select high, moderate, or slight increases ($+3$, $+2$, $+1$) or decreases (-3, -2, -1) in the shock to be administered. It was explained that following each trial the subject would see on her console the shock selections of the other three subjects plus her own, that these would be averaged to determine the level of shock increase or decrease to be administered on that trial, and that no record would be kept of individual responses but only of the group average for each trial. Thus all subjects' responses, regardless of condition, were to be nonidentifiable to the experimenter and to any others who might see the data. The "learning task" ended when the subject had made 15 errors. The number of correct responses made prior to the 15th error was the measure of successful learning that subjects were to try to facilitate by their shock selections.

Cue Manipulation   The costume manipulation of cues was produced by having each subject wear either a robe resembling those of the Ku Klux Klan or a nurse's uniform. The ostensible purpose of the costumes was to obscure individual differences. The nature of the specific costume given to each subject was presented as an accident of convenience (i.e., "I'm not much of a seamstress; this thing came out looking kind of Ku Klux Klannish." or "I was fortunate the hospital *recovery room* let me borrow these nurses' gowns to use in the study.") A Polaroid picture was taken of each subject in her costume, and pictures of others in the group, in similar costumes, were attached to the subjects' consoles. Each subject was told that copies of her picture had been placed on the consoles of others in the group.

Deindividuation Manipulation   In the individuation condition, consoles were labeled so that each subject could identify the shock level set by each person in the group and the person by whom it was set. Also, large name tags were attached to the costumes of the individuals in the Polaroid pictures. In the deindividuation condition, pictures of others in costume were attached to subject consoles, but no name tags were worn, and subjects were provided with no means of identifying the person who made any given response.

To facilitate subjects' involvement with the target, they were allowed to see and hear the "learner" being interviewed. His behavior in the interview was designed to be obnoxious and distasteful to the subjects. A negative target was used in order to minimize the inhibitions against shocking another person, thus allowing for variability on this response dimension. In fact, subjects proved not to be too inhibited to use the shock increase option, yet the target was not so negative as to preclude use of the shock decrease option.

Following the interview, subjects filled out a preliminary evaluation of the confederate. Learning trials were then begun, errors being indicated by the lights on the subjects' consoles, signaling to them to select $+3$, $+2$, or $+1$ levels of increase or -1, -2, or -3 levels of decrease in intensity of the shock the confederate was to receive. After all subjects in the group had responded, feedback of the choices of others was displayed and shock was supposedly administered. Feedback was preprogrammed to average 0 across each of three blocks of trials. Following the learning task, subjects were asked to fill out a postexperimental questionnaire, after which they were probed for suspicion, debriefed, asked not to divulge the deceptions to others, and dismissed.

RESULTS

Evaluation of the Stranger

Five bipolar scales for evaluating the stranger were administered immediately following the interview, prior to the learning task. The experimental conditions did not significantly differ from each other, the means for each condition being on the *insincere, dishonest, cold, phony,* and *unkind* side of the midpoint. It appears that the confederate was perceived to be obnoxious, as planned, in all conditions.

Manipulation Checks

Perception of Cues   Four bipolar scales on the postexperimental questionnaire were used to assess subjects' perception of costume cues. As intended, the Ku Klux Klan costumes were rated as significantly more tough, harmful, unkind, and cold than were the nurses' costumes, $p < .01$, for each scale. Composite totals of responses to these four scales indicated that the Ku Klux Klan costumes were perceived as significantly more negative than the nurses' costumes, $F(1, 56) = 24.95$, $p < .01$. This difference reflects the negative ratings of the Ku Klux Klan costumes, $M = 5.59$, versus the slightly positive ratings of the nurses' costumes, $M = 3.71$ on a 1 (extremely compassionate) to 7 (extremely aggressive) scale.

Perceived Sense of Deindividuation   As expected, deindividuated subjects, compared to individuated subjects, indicated on the postexperimental questionnaire that it would be more

difficult to identify shock selections of other individuals in their group, $F(1, 6) = 15.84$, $p < .01$, and that it would be more difficult to distinguish members of their group from nongroup members following the experiment, $F(1, 56) = 19.55$, $p < .01$. These measures suggest that in fact deindividuation was manipulated as intended.

Shock Selections

The primary dependent variable, shock selection, was analyzed by a $2 \times 2 \times 3$ analysis of variance, individuation versus deindividuation, and prosocial versus antisocial cues between subjects and trial blocks within subjects. This analysis revealed a significant main effect for cues, $F(1, 56) = 46.28$, $p < .01$, with shock decrease the mean response for prosocial cues and shock increase the mean response for antisocial cues. The main effect for individuation versus deindividuation was not significant, $F(1, 56) = 2.92$, but there was a significant Cues $\times$ Deindividuation interaction, $F(1, 56) = 8.21$, $p < .01$. The interaction (see Table 1) is a result of an increasing effect of cues on behavior in deindividuated versus individuated conditions.

A Newman-Keuls test revealed that each condition was significantly different from each other condition, each at the $p < .01$ level, except the sim-

TABLE 1

MEAN SHOCK SELECTION AS A FUNCTION OF CUE AND DEINDIVIDUATION CONDITIONS

	Condition	
Cue	Individuated	Deindividuated
Prosocial	$-.35_a$	-1.47_b
Antisocial	$.76_c$	$.95_c$

Note: Possible range of scores was from -3 (the prosocial choice of maximally reducing shock level) to $+3$ (the antisocial choice of maximally increasing shock level). Means without a common subscript were significantly different from each other ($p < .01$).

ple effect of deindividuation within antisocial cues. This comparison is essentially a conceptual replication of Zimbardo (1970). It was directionally consistent with that effect but only achieved $p < .15$ even by a one-tailed simple t test.

No significant main effect occurred for trial blocks, $F(2, 112) = 1.31$, or for the interaction of trial blocks with deindividuation, $F(2, 112) = 1.85$. There was, however, a significant Trial Blocks × Cues interaction, $F(2, 112) = 19.78$, $p < .01$, resulting from the tendency for shock levels to increase in the antisocial cues condition and to decrease in the prosocial cues condition, from the first to the second of three blocks.

DISCUSSION

The experimental manipulations appear to have been effective. The prosocial costumes, though closer to neutral than had been intended, were rated as significantly less negative than the antisocial costumes. The manipulation of deindividuation was assessed by self-reports of ability to identify behaviors of specific group members (cf. Festinger et al., 1952) and perceived anonymity of group members (cf. Zimbardo, 1970). Both measures demonstrated that deindividuation was manipulated as intended.

Of primary interest in this research were the effects of cues and of deindividuation on shock selection. In the presence of Ku Klux Klan costume cues, subjects were likely to increase shock levels, whereas in the presence of prosocial cues, subjects were likely to decrease shock levels. This finding by itself suggests alternative interpretations of the Singer et al. (1965) study and the Zimbardo (1970) study presented in this paper's introduction. In those studies costume cues were completely confounded with the manipulations of deindividuation. It is entirely possible that the increased antisocial behavior observed in those studies (i.e., frequency of obscene words and duration of electrical shocks) was a function of the costume cue manipulation alone and de-

pended less on anonymity than has been widely believed.

In contrast to the previous research, the present study allows us to look at the effects of deindividuation independent of costume cues. According to Zimbardo, (a) deindividuation should have resulted in more aggressive, antisocial behavior for both costume variations, and (b) any effect of cues should have been attenuated as a function of deindividuation. According to Gergen et al. (1973), however, cues should interact with deindividuation, deindividuation leading to more antisocial behavior in the presence of antisocial cues and to more prosocial behavior in the presence of prosocial cues. The interaction obtained in the present study (see Table 1) is consistent with Gergen's position.

Theoretical Implications

Antecedents of Deindividuation   Conceptually, most theorists (cf. Zimbardo, 1970) have viewed deindividuation as a state of the organism that can be induced by a variety of input variables, including but not limited to anonymity. Experimentally, however, deindividuation has nearly always been manipulated by varying some aspect of identifiability. This is true of the research discussed in the introduction and is true of the present research. More recently (cf. Diener, 1979), deindividuation has been manipulated by means of complexes of input variables including a sense of group unity, group cohesiveness, group responsibility, and even kinesthetic feedback from physical activity. These inputs may in fact induce a sense of anonymity, but very likely they have additional influences beyond those related to identifiability.

The State of Deindividuation   Confirmation of the relationship between anonymity and disinhibition is not sufficient to support the construct of deindividuation as a mediating state of the organism, and attempts to validate the construct have been largely unsupportive (Diener et al.,

1975; Diener, 1979). Anonymity-induced disinhibition may not require a reduction in the subjective sense of individuation but in many instances could reflect a simple reduction in perceived negative sanctions, hence a disinhibition of behavior previously suppressed by such sanctions. Possibly environmental cues, like demand characteristics, influence the subjects' interpretation of the types of prior sanction that have been lifted.

Individuation and Objective Self-Awareness
Conceptually, a strong parallel seems to exist between Zimbardo's (1970) constructs of individuation versus deindividuation and the Duval and Wicklund (1972) constructs of objective versus subjective self-awareness. For example, both individuation and objective self-awareness imply focusing of attention inward, toward the self. Recent research has shown that a typical manipulation of objective self-awareness does in fact lead to an increased sense of individuation (Ickes, Layden, & Barnes, 1978). Also Diener (1979) has demonstrated a reduction in self-awareness resulting from a broad-based group involvement manipulation of deindividuation but has found this to be not equivalent to lack of self-awareness induced in a nonsocial way. This does not imply that anonymity will not yield a lack of self-awareness comparable to that of typical objective self-awareness manipulations, for Diener's manipulations of deindividuation included much more than anonymity.

Objective Self-Awareness and Situational Cues
The state of objective self-awareness has been shown to increase the influence of internalized standards for correct or appropriate behavior (Carver, 1975; Scheier, Fenigstein, & Buss, 1974). Conversely, one might expect objective self-awareness to reduce the influence of external, situational cues. If anonymity-induced deindividuation is comparable to reduced objective self-awareness, the anonymity should increase the relative influence of external cues. Basically,

we are suggesting that reduced objective self-awareness, anonymity-induced deindividuation, and probably group involvement-induced deindividuation all lead to an outwardly focused attention with increased salience of and influence due to concurrent situational factors such as the cue manipulation in the present study. Also, individuation and objective self-awareness should focus attention inward, increasing the salience of and influence due to internalized standards for behavior (cf. Carver, 1975).

Under some circumstances, internalized standards may themselves be altered by concurrent stimulus information (cf. Carver, 1974), in which case the influence of such external stimuli may be increased by objective self-awareness. Consequently, statements as to whether anonymity will lead to increased or decreased influence of external cues may need to be qualified to take into account how or whether those cues affect a change in internalized standards for behavior.

READING 38

Social Contagion of Binge Eating

Christian S. Crandall (1988)

In one sense, eating is a biological necessity. We eat in order to survive, but everyone knows that there is much more to eating and not eating. What we eat, when we eat, where we eat, and with whom we eat are based to a great extent on our culture. Also, expectations about the desirable size of our bodies vary from culture to culture and even across time within a given culture. Billions of dollars are spent each year on weight control in our society (DeJong & Kleck, 1986). The overwhelming majority of these expenditures are made by women and are made in order to lose weight. Anorexia and bulimia, eating disorders that affect females disproportionately more than males, are currently important medical, psychological, and social problems.

How much we eat has to do with the food itself, obviously, but also other variables such as how hungry we are; our beliefs about food; food's religious, motivational, and psychic meanings; how anxious we are; how we feel about ourselves and our weight; and our relationships with other people. Crandall investigates the latter, and identifies significant group effects in women's eating patterns. This article and several others suggest that eating and not eating are associated with femininity in females. Females convey different messages to others by their eating behaviors, and use different eating patterns to help create or restore positive images to themselves or others (see also Mori, Chaiken, & Pliner, 1987).

Our discussion so far has largely focused on the sociocultural approach to eating and eating disorders. Crandall, however, develops a social psychological account of binge eating that builds on classic group norm research. This fascinating study chronicles how eating patterns of college sorority members change over time, and how these changes are associated with group social influence as well as self-esteem and weight. This social influence model can be applied to other behaviors besides attitudes about tenant organization (Festinger, Schachter, & Back, 1950) or binge eating. Can you think of another set of attitudes or behaviors for which you might predict that social norms would override personal factors? Also, how is responsiveness to group norm influence similar to and/or different from conformity as discussed by Asch (Reading 34)?

Abstract

A social psychological account of the acquisition of binge eating, analogous to the classic social psychological work, "Social Pressures in Informal Groups" (Festinger, Schachter, & Back, 1950), is suggested and tested in two college sororities. In these sororities, clear evidence of group norms about appropriate binge-eating behavior was found; in one sorority, the more one binged, the more popular one was. In the other, popularity was associated with binging the right amount: Those who binged too much or too little were less popular than those who binged at the mean. Evidence of social pressures to binge eat were found as well. By the end of the academic year, a sorority member's binge eating could be predicted from the binge-eating level of her friends (average r = .31). As friendship groups grew more cohesive, a sorority member's binge eating grew more and more like that of her friends (average r = .35). The parsimony of a social psychological account of the acquisition of binge eating behavior is shown. I argue that there is no great mystery to how bulimia has become such a serious problem for today's women. Binge eating seems to be an acquired pattern of behavior, perhaps through modeling, and appears to be learned much like any other set of behaviors. Like other behaviors, it is under substantial social control.

Bulimia is rapidly becoming *the* women's psychological disease of our time, rivaling depression in its prevalence. It is receiving a great deal of attention in both the scientific community (Gandour, 1984; Schlesier-Stropp, 1984; Striegel-Moore, Silberstein, & Rodin, 1986) and the popular press (Boskind-Lodahl & Sirlin, 1977). Bulimia is an eating pattern characterized by periodic episodes of uncontrolled binge eating alternating with periods of fasting, strict dieting, or purging via vomiting, diuretics, or laxatives. The uncontrolled eating is usually accompanied by negative affect, a sense of loss of control, and guilt. Nearly all of those affected are women (Gandour, 1984).

The evidence is that bulimia is indeed quite prevalent; estimates suggest 4-15% of college women have serious problems with bulimia (Halmi, Falk, & Schwartz, 1981; Sinoway, Raupp, & Newman, 1985; Strangler & Printz, 1980). By contrast, there is little evidence to suggest that bulimia afflicted any more than a handful of people prior to the late 1960s and early 1970s (Rosenzweig & Spruill, 1986).

The sudden and dramatic appearance of bulimia as a set of clinical symptoms has prompted a great deal of psychological and psychiatric theorizing about the roots of the syndrome. Surprisingly little is known about the causes of bulimia. Bulimics seem to be virtually indistinguishable from nonbulimic controls on a surprising number of variables, such as height, weight (Gandour, 1984), sex role orientation (Srikameswaran, Leichner, & Harper, 1984), and even ego involvement with food and eating (Crandall, 1987). There have been three general classes of explanations put forward: a sociohistorical/cultural approach, a clinical/psychiatric approach, and an epidemiological/risk factors approach.

SOCIOCULTURAL APPROACH

Sociocultural theorists argue that changing norms in our society, especially those toward thinness for women, have created a cult of dieting (Dwyer, Feldman, & Mayer, 1970; Orbach, 1978). For example, Garner, Garfinkel, Schwartz, and Thompson (1980) have shown that body sizes of the winners of the Miss America Pageant and the Playboy centerfolds have been steadily decreasing over the past 20 years. Apparently, now more than ever, thin is in.

Women have internalized the message that they should care a great deal about how they look and at the same time internalize a thinness norm that is virtually unattainable for most of them (Rodin, Silberstein, & Striegel-Moore, 1984). Initial and subsequent attempts to reach this social rather than biological norm (i.e., dieting) are disruptive to the body's natural balance (Nisbett, 1972), making weight reduction extremely difficult (Bennett & Gurin, 1982; Garrow, 1978). At the same time, because there is a heavy psychological investment in dieting, the success or failure of behaviors related to weight loss attempts are very self-relevant, and strongly affectively tinged.

There is undoubtedly a sociocultural component to bulimia, because severe binge eating accompanied by an emotional roller coaster among women is a new problem, but social history certainly does not contain a complete account of the phenomenon. Thinness norms have come and gone in the past few centuries, and social roles have gone through dramatic changes as well, both apparently without concomitant increases in bulimia. During the Roaring Twenties, for example, although the flappers were as thin as plastic drinking straws, there is no indication that bulimia was a problem then (Bennett & Gurin, 1982). (The exact data to establish this are very difficult to collect; see Rosenzweig & Spruill, 1986, for one attempt.)

More important, however, is that these social pressures operate on all women in the middle-class subculture. Thus, the most difficult problem for the sociocultural perspective is that it fails to specify who is at risk for bulimia and who is not at risk. Although thinness norms and the fear of fatness are everywhere in our society, not all women are in trouble with dieting, binging, and body image. Why beauty norms for thinness work their destruction on only a relative minority of the population is a question that this perspective has a great deal of difficulty in answering.

CLINICAL/PSYCHIATRIC APPROACH

A wide variety of researchers and clinicians have proposed models of bulimia based on existing psychiatric/clinical models, for example, impulsiveness (Dunn & Ondercin, 1981), feelings of inadequacy or low self-efficacy (Garfinkel & Garner, 1982), borderline personality disorder (Radant, 1986), or parents' psychological health and family structure (Strober, Morell, Burroughs, Salkin, & Jacobs, 1985). One approach claims that bulimia is simply a variant of major affective disorder (Pope & Hudson, 1984).

The clinical approach provides an answer to the "Why this person?" question, which the sociocultural perspective does not: Women experiencing psychological distress are at risk. However, a serious problem for the clinical perspective is the vagueness with which it specifies predisposing factors. The personality and family predisposing factors that have been linked to bulimia can separate bulimics from the normal population, but they cannot successfully discriminate bulimics from other globally defined kinds of psychological disorders such as depression (Cantwell, 1985). Also, it is not clear how feelings of inadequacy or low self-efficacy, for example, should lead to problems with binge eating. In their 240-page book, Pope and Hudson (1984) made a reasonable case for the role of depression in bulimia, but they fail to say anything about why depression should lead to problems with binge eating in particular, or whether depression is a cause or a consequence of the disorder.

Most important, problems such as feelings of inadequacy and impulsiveness have been around for some time, long before bulimia became a major health problem. Unless one is willing to argue that such things as clinical levels of inadequacy or impulsiveness are exhibiting a huge growth, it is hard to claim that they are the cause of bulimia. The crucial issues are, why should such things as depression, impulsiveness, or inadequacy be linked to binge eating, and why now?

EPIDEMIOLOGICAL/RISK FACTORS APPROACH

An epidemiological approach to bulimia focuses on the various factors that can be expected to predict bulimia (Johnson, Lewis, & Hagman, 1984). It is a statistical approach: What are the independent variables one can use to predict the dependent variable of bulimia?

Rodin and her colleagues (Rodin et al., 1984; Striegel-Moore et al., 1986) have reviewed an impressive amount of literature relating to binge eating and bulimia and have outlined the various factors that put a person at risk for bulimia. The list is long and diverse, including body image, affective instability, family factors, hormones, sex roles, stress, exercise, genetic factors, coping skills, developmental factors, and so forth. It seems certain that a number of the factors on this list can be used to predict bulimia, using as they do factors from the entire range of theoretical perspectives.

Though practical, the approach is not parsimonious; the focus for this group of theorists has been on inclusion rather than exclusion. The result has been a large compendium of likely risk factors for bulimia. It is both descriptive and predictive, but the process of acquiring bulimic behavior remains obscure.

A useful tool at this point would be an account of bulimia that is both plausible and parsimonious. It should be plausible in that it fits the known facts about bulimia, and it should be parsimonious in that the phenomenon is not overexplained by many concomitant, nonindependent forces. An appropriate theory should define the people at risk for the disorder as well as those not at risk. A good theory should also describe the process of acquiring the symptoms themselves.

None of the existing theories can do all of these things. Although the sociocultural approach can define who is at risk, it neither effectively defines who is not at risk nor how bulimics acquire the binge-eating behavior. The clinical perspective is well suited to defining who is at risk and who is not at risk but has not carefully spelled out how it is that the symptoms are acquired. The epidemiological approach, like the clinical approach, is better suited to defining risk factors than to describing processes of symptom acquisition. I wish to propose a model that is well suited to describing the symptom acquisition process, based on social psychological processes.

SOCIAL PSYCHOLOGICAL FACTORS

There is good reason to think that social processes are implicated in various ways with respect to bulimia and binge eating. Anecdotal evidence suggests that bulimia tends to run in social groups, such as cheerleading squads (Squire, 1983), athletic teams (Crago, Yates, Beutler, & Arizmendi, 1985), and dance camps (Garner & Garfinkel, 1980). There is also indication that the onset of eating disorders follows entrance into the group (e.g., Crago et al., 1985), suggesting that social pressure might be involved.

There is a great deal of speculation about social psychological factors of bulimia by clinicians and the popular press. In *The Slender Balance*, Squire (1983) tells the story of a cheerleader, Laura, who

> explains matter-of-factly "everyone on the [cheerleading] squad binges and vomits. That's how I learned."...Laura considers her behavior frightening and awful, except in one context: before cheerleading a game. "Everybody does it then, so it doesn't seem like the same thing" (p. 48).

One of the most interesting and yet underexamined processes in bulimia is the acquisition of bulimic behavior, particularly binge eating. The few studies that have looked at this problem have focused almost exclusively on particular social groups, for example, dance camps (Garner & Garfinkel, 1980) and athletic teams (Crago et al., 1985).

This focus is not an accident. I wish to argue that social groups are at the very heart of the issue of symptom acquisition. Symptoms are spread from one member to another in these groups, and group membership is at the heart of the transmission. Groups that are most likely to transmit the symptoms of bulimia, most notably binge eating, are groups that are made up almost entirely of women of the same age. This includes dance camps and athletic teams as well as sororities, all-women dormitories, or workplaces comprising mostly women.

Social groups are important to us. They serve to tell us who we are (McGuire & Padawer-Singer, 1976), what to think (Cantril, 1941), and how to behave (Sherif, 1936). The more we value the social group, the more we are willing to be influenced by it.

> The power of a group may be measured by the attractiveness of the group for its members. If a person wants to stay in a group, he will be susceptible to influences coming from the group, and he will be willing to conform to the rules which the group sets up (Festinger, Schachter, & Back, 1950, p. 91).

Members of the same social group tend to be relatively uniform in the attitudes and behaviors that are important to the group (Festinger, 1954). When a particular individual deviates from the group, social pressures are brought to bear to bring the prodigal back into the fold via direct communication, emotional support, or disapproval. Ultimately, the deviate is rejected if he or she fails to conform (Schachter, 1951).

I wish to argue that social pressures in friendship groups are important mechanisms by which binge eating is acquired and spread. Social groups such as athletic teams, cheerleading squads, dormitories, and sororities develop social norms about what is appropriate behavior for their members. If eating, dieting, and losing weight are important to the members, then norms will arise in the group defining how much, when, and with whom. Deviation from these norms will result in rejection from the group, as evidenced by a reduction in the person's popularity (Schachter, 1951). Thus, not only is there likely to be modeling of the behaviors and attitudes associated with bulimia, but there are likely to be sanctions for counternormative behavior.

People are very motivated to imitate or model attitudes or behaviors that are important, characteristic, or definitional to the social group. The more important the social group, and the more central a behavior is to the group, the greater the pressure toward uniformity and the more likely that members of the group will imitate each others' behavior (Festinger, 1950). Friends should become more like each other as they spend time together and grow closer. If binge eating is an important or meaningful behavior to a social group, then over time within groups, people's binge-eating patterns should grow more similar.

SOCIAL PRESSURES IN INFORMAL GROUPS

A classic investigation of the effects of social norms on group life is the study of *Social Pressures in Informal Groups* by Festinger et al. (1950). Their study provides a template to examine how social influence affects binge eating. Festinger et al. were interested in how social norms about attitudes toward a tenant organization were related to popularity and communication patterns within a housing project. Two housing arrangements were studied, Westgate and Westgate West, which were adjoining but physically and architecturally distinct. In Westgate, social groups were defined by courts of grouped houses, ranging from 7 to 13 homes. In Westgate West, social groups were apartment buildings with ten apartments in each.

In Westgate, Festinger et al. (1950) found that the different groups had different norms about the attitudes to take toward the tenant organization; some courts were strongly in favor of the organization, and some were strongly against it. When the court's prevailing attitude toward the tenant organization was positive, those who had negative attitudes toward the organization were less well liked, and when the court's prevailing attitude was negative, those who had a positive attitude were less popular than others.

In Westgate West, the normative pattern was different. Tenants of all of the apartment buildings had primarily favorable attitudes toward the tenant organization. (Westgate West was occupied after the tenant organization had already been established, so that the more controversial aspects of the organization were less salient to the occupants of Westgate West). There was no correlation between attitude and popularity in Westgate West; those who did not share the generally positive attitude toward the organization did not suffer in terms of popularity. Festinger et al. (1950) interpreted this to mean that, although the overarching group norm was a positive attitude, local group norms were neither salient nor particularly strong.

Festinger et al. (1950) studied existing social groups at one point in time (although the comparison between Westgate and Westgate West is implicitly temporal). But social groups have a dynamic life cycle: Groups form, exert pressures on their members, go up and down in cohesion and uniformity, and eventually disband (Moreland & Levine, 1982). Groups usually do not form with ready-made cohesion; when groups are new, one should not expect pressures toward uniformity to have taken effect. It is only after some amount of time that individuals should become more like the other group members. As more information is shared among members, and as the groups become more cohesive, similarity among group members on binge eating should increase.

Festinger et al. (1950) also reasoned that as group pressures increase in strength, characteristics of the person should decrease in importance. They argued that the amount of time one expected to stay in the housing project should be correlated with how much one is concerned with the quality of life there, and so one's expected length of stay would normally be associated with a positive attitude toward the organization. This was true for the Westgate West complex, where norms were weak. However, at Westgate, in the presence of strong local norms about the tenant organization, anticipated length of stay was uncorrelated with attitude.

With respect to binge eating, however, social pressures are not likely to remove completely the importance of personal characteristics, because, in addition to social psychological factors, other psychobiological and psychiatrically relevant variables are likely to affect the behavior. A variety of factors might be important (Striegel-Moore et al., 1986). A woman's weight puts her at risk; the heavier she is, the more likely she is to feel pressure to diet, which puts her at at risk for binge eating (Polivy & Herman, 1985). Her general psychological health is also likely to be a factor, the poorer her mental health, the more likely she is to acquire binging. Furthermore, the lower her self-esteem, the more likely she is to be open to social influence (Janis, 1954).

One social group that is ideally suited for studying such questions as they apply to binge eating is the college sorority. There is anecdotal evidence that sororities are breeding grounds for eating disorders (Squire, 1983), so that one is likely to find a range of binging severity in such a group. Second, women in a sorority are, on average, very interested in physical appearance, weight, and body shape (Rose, 1985), which is a risk factor for bulimia (Johnson et al., 1984; Streigel-Moore et al., 1986).

But most important, sorority membership is a very powerful source of social influence. Much of a sorority woman's social and academic life revolves around the living group, in addition to the more mundane aspects of life, such as sleeping, eating, laundry, and so forth.

From the point of view of social impact theory (Latané & Wolf, 1981), a sorority will have a dramatic impact on its members' lives. It is large enough to generate a strong consensus, the strength of the group is high due to its high degree of attractiveness to members, and the continuing closeness of other members in the sorority ensures the immediacy of their impact.

Finally, a sorority has the distinct advantage of being a well-defined social group with clearly discernible boundaries. With such a social group, one can obtain a fairly clear picture of the social influence patterns in a substantial portion of these women's lives.

If social pressures in friendship groups play a role in the acquisition of binge eating, a variety of research questions present themselves. To what extent are there group norms about binge eating? What role does binging play in determining social acceptance or rejection? To what extent are there social pressures toward uniformity in binge eating? Do women come to have binge eating behavior that resembles that of their friends over time? These questions were looked at in two consecutive studies of 163 women living in sororities.

METHOD

Overview

Two different sororities were investigated during two different academic years. In Study 1, one sorority was studied in the spring only. In Study 2, two sororities were studied in both the fall and spring. Subjects responded to questions of three general sorts: social ties, personal factors, and binge eating. Social ties were measured by having subjects list their friends within the sorority; this served as information to distinguish subgroups or cliques, as well as popularity. Personal factors were used to some extent to help define those women most at risk for binge eating. These included, among other things, self-esteem as a rough measure of a woman's general psychological health, and height and weight.

In Study 1, Sorority Alpha was contacted. The sorority members filled out questionnaires anonymously, 3 weeks before the summer break. In Study 2, both Sorority Alpha and a second house, Sorority Beta, filled out a modified version of the questionnaire. They filled out the questionnaires both in the fall, shortly after "rush" (when new members are selected by the sorority to move in during the following year) and again the spring (as in Study 1). Because social influence takes some time to operate, it was expected that there would be relatively little evidence of social pressures operating in the fall data collection, after only 6 weeks of contact. In the spring, however, after 7 months of steady and intense contact, ample opportunity for pressures toward uniformity to operate was expected. This two-wave design of Study 2 also allowed for comparison over time. If social pressures were operating, then the individual sorority member's levels of binge eating should change over time, and these changes should be predicted by those social influences. In the presence of social influence, whether it is active social pressure or simply modeling, friends should grow more alike.

<table>
<tr><td colspan="6" align="center">**TABLE 1**</td></tr>
</table>

DEMOGRAPHIC DESCRIPTION AND DESIGN OVERVIEW

Variable	Sorority alpha			Sorority beta	
	Spring$_1$	Fall$_2$	Spring$_2$	Fall$_2$	Spring$_2$
Sorority size	46	52	44	66	61
% response rate	100	98	82	100	92
Mean age (years)	19.8	19.5	19.7	20.4	20.6
Weight (kg)					
M	55.8	54.3	55.8	58.2	58.6
SD	5.8	6.3	6.4	6.9	6.5
Body-mass index					
M	21.0	20.6	21.0	20.9	21.3
SD	1.6	1.7	1.9	2.0	2.7
BES scores					
M	13.9	13.7	11.5	11.8	10.1
SD	6.1	6.9	5.8	8.2	7.1
Height (m)					
M	1.63	1.62	1.62	1.69	1.68
SD	0.05	0.06	0.06	0.06	0.07
% fathers with graduate or professional degrees	54	58	—	43	—
% mothers with graduate or professional degree	22	32	—	23	—

Note: Subjects were measured in the spring and fall. Subscripts on seasons indicate either Study 1 or Study 2. Dashes indicate that parents' educational data were not collected for the second wave of Study 2. BES = Binge Eating Scale.

Subjects were active members of two different college sororities (all female). The sororities were both popular and highly sought-after houses at the campus of a large state university. The sororities were paid $150 for each wave of the study.

Subjects were given questionnaires, characterized as "a study of community and sorority life." The questionnaires were given out only to those women actually residing in the sorority house (made up of mostly sophomores and juniors). The pledge class (new recruits) and inactives (mostly seniors living outside the house and relatively removed from sorority life) were not included in these analyses. Responses to the questionnaire were completely anonymous. A code sheet was prepared by a member of the sorority's executive council; code numbers were used instead of names to investigate the social networks within the sororities.

Design

In Study 1, women from Sorority Alpha filled out a nine-page questionnaire in the spring ($n = 46$), a few weeks before the sorority closed down for the end of the term. In Study 2, members of both Sorority Alpha ($n = 51$) and Sorority Beta ($n = 66$) filled out questionnaires of seven pages in the fall and five pages in the spring, at the same time of year as in Study 1.[1]

---

[1]There is, of course, no one who is in both Sorority Alpha and Sorority Beta. However, there is some degree of overlap (40%) within Sorority Alpha over the two studies.

Subjects A general description of the subjects can be found in Table 1. Height, weight, and age were included in all forms of the questionnaire. Parents' educational status, as a proxy for social class, was included in Study 2 only on the fall questionnaire. The body-mass index found in Table 1 is a measure of overweight, or "fatness" (Sjostrom, 1978), and is calculated by the formula: weight (kg)/height^2(m). The body-mass index correlates highly ($>$ .90) with other common measures of overweight, such as the ponderal index and deviation from the Metropolitan Life Insurance tabled norms for height and weight.

Questionnaire

The three versions of the questionnaire from the three waves differed slightly from each other, but there was a central, invariant core to all of them. (Across sororities all questionnaires were identical at any given time. Only the core questions are discussed in this article.)

Binge Eating Bulimia was measured by the Binge Eating Scale (BES; Gormally, Black, Daston, & Rardin, 1982). The 16-item BES was designed to assess the criteria for bulimia defined by the *Diagnostic and Statistical Manual (DSM-III)* of the American Psychiatric Association (1980), but has the advantage of providing a continuous measure rather than a classification of bulimic versus not bulimic. All of the *DSM-III* aspects of bulimia were measured: binge eating, purging (either by vomiting or by restrictive dieting), the emotional consequences of binging, inconspicuous eating during a binge, and so forth. Previous research at the same university has found the BES to have a one-factor solution; all items load substantially on the first factor. It has a 2-month test-retest reliability of .84. Further validation materials are available (Gormally, 1984; Gormally et al., 1982).

How severe was binge eating in the sororities? Only a handful of the nearly 160 different

subjects had high enough scores on the BES to be worthy of professional attention; almost all of the binge eating described here is at subclinical levels. However, binge eating was significantly higher in the sororities than subjects in two all-women dormitories ($n = 86$) measured at the same time as Study 1, $t(131) = 2.47$, $p < .01$. Women with low BES scores reported that they were able to stop eating when they wanted to; they did not feel they had trouble controlling eating urges, and did not think a great deal about food. Women with high BES scores reported frequent uncontrollable eating urges, they spent a lot of time trying not to eat any more food, and had days where they could not seem to think about anything else but food. Women with moderate BES scores reported a compulsion to eat "every so often"; they spent some of their time trying to control eating urges and had brief periods of total occupation with thoughts of food.

Social Networks To uncover the pattern of social ties within the houses, respondents were asked to list their "ten best friends (within the house), in order." Popularity was defined as the number of times one was chosen by other people on their lists of friends. These data were also used to form friendship clusters or cliques, via cluster analyses. Membership in clusters was nonoverlapping; no woman was assigned membership in more than one social group.

The cluster analysis were performed on a square n by n matrix of friendship choices (the "top ten"). In this matrix, rows represented a subject's friendship choices, and columns represented subjects being chosen. Choices were weighed from 10 (*top choice*) to 1 (*10th choice*), and then divided by the weighted sum of all of the choices, $n(n + 1)/2$, so that the weighted choices summed to unity for each set. The diagonal of the matrix, which represents self-choice (all zeros, as no one chose herself from her list of friends), was replaced with ones. The result of this is that being chosen by others in the friendship groups was more important to cluster assignment than sharing choices of other people in common. Thus, friends who chose each other and had similar patterns of friendship choices were put into the same cliques by the cluster analysis. Euclidean distances were used as a measure of similarity, and an average linkage criterion was used to join cases to clusters. Using different measures of similarity, different linkage criteria, a different weighting of the variables, or different values along the diagonal had little effect on the solutions. Separate cluster analyses were performed for each sorority at each time period, so that friendship cliques were determined for each wave of the study. These analyses resulted in an average of 10.0 (SD = 2.9) friendship clusters in each sorority at each time period, with an average of 5.1 (SD = 2.3) persons in each cluster.

Festinger et al.'s (1950) study differs from ours in that they were fortunate enough to have relatively equal-sized groups of individuals, whose members were randomly assigned to membership. In this study, groups were uncovered on the basis of friendship choices rather than being independent of them. The drawback to this is that friendship clusters were almost uniformly cohesive, based as they were on the similarity of their friendship choices. No friendship cluster contains a true isolate. Because groups were based in large part on reciprocated friendship choices (mutual popularity), finding group members particularly low in within-group popularity was relatively difficult.

Self-Esteem   As a brief global measure of psychological health, a six-item version of the Rosenberg Self-Esteem Scale (RSE; Rosenberg, 1965) was included. Among college students at the same university, the RSE correlated with the Eysenck Neuroticism Scale at $r = -.55$, with the Beck Depression Inventory at $r = -.62$, and with the Spielberger Trait Anxiety Scale at $r = -.69$ Self-esteem is also likely to be an important factor in that those low in self-esteem

are more likely to be open to the influence of their peers, compared with those high in self-esteem (Janis, 1954).

RESULTS

Social Norms

The first issue for understanding how social norms work is to uncover their existence and patterns. To look for social norms, we traced the patterns of popularity within each of the social groups. If there are indeed norms about binge eating within a group, then deviation from those norms should be associated with a reduction in popularity. The less conforming to a binge eating norm one is, the more one is likely to be sanctioned through a reduction in popularity.

By the same token, whatever the most popular people do in any group is defined as normative. If the norm for binge eating is at the mean level of binging in the sorority, with absolute deviations from the mean representing deviations from the norm, then distance from the mean represents social deviance. In Sorority Alpha, this measure of social deviance correlated with popularity at $-.30$ in Study 1, and $-.25$ in Study 2, for spring. In this sorority, the highest levels of popularity were among moderate bingers; binging both too little as well as too much were associated with reductions in popularity. These data are summarized in Table 2.

In Sorority Beta, a different pattern emerged. Surprisingly, in this group there was apparently a social norm that promoted binge eating; the more a woman binged, the more popular she was (rs = .28 for fall and .32 for spring). (The actual data peak in popularity was empirically determined to be not at the top of the binging severity distribution, but about 1.3 SDs above the mean, or about 1.2 SDs below the highest end.) Thus, there was evidence for social norms in support of some level of binge eating in both Sorority Alpha and Sorority Beta. The norms appeared to be somewhat different. In Sorority Alpha, a

TABLE 2					

PATTERNS OF POPULARITY AND BINGE EATING

	Sorority alpha			Sorority beta	
Variable	Spring$_1$	Fall$_2$	Spring$_2$	Fall$_2$	Spring$_2$
Popularity and deviation from mean of binging	−.30†	.12	−.25	−.02	−.12
Popularity and binging	−.02	−.04	−.06	.28†	.32†
Prestige of group and group's normative binge level (aggregate)	−.80††	.33	−.53	.61†	.60†
Popularity within-group and within-group level of binge eating	−.10	.16	−.04	.22*	.36††

Note: Correlations are based on *n*s of 46, 51, 36, 66, and 55, respectively. Correlations between prestige and group's normative binge level were calculated with groups as the unit of analysis; the numbers of groups were 7, 9, 8, 12, and 14, respectively. Subscripts on seasons indicate either Study 1 or Study 2.
*$p < .05$, one-tailed. †$p < .05$, two-tailed. ††$p < .01$, two-tailed.

moderate level was associated with greater popularity. In Sorority Beta more binge eating was associated with more popularity.

It is somewhat surprising to find in Sorority Beta that more binging and more popularity went hand-in-hand. It is possible that the popularity of binge eaters was inflated if those women who binged the most in Sorority Beta all chose each other exclusively, whereas the women who did not binge as much spread their choices out among bingers and nonbingers alike. On the other hand, if a higher degree of binge eating was actually associated with greater popularity, then groups with high levels of binging should have been more prestigious within the entire sorority. To test this, average levels of binge eating in the cliques were calculated and correlated with a measure of group prestige: the percentage of out-group members who chose people within that group (i.e., the average amount of times in-group members were chosen by the out-group). This calculation is presented in the third line of Table 2. The prediction was borne out; the groups that binged the most were the most prestigious in Sorority Beta. The companion effect is also shown for Sorority Alpha. The more deviant the group

was from the mean level of binge eating, the more it suffered from a reduction in prestige.

Not only were high-binging groups more popular in Sorority Beta, but also within social groups, those who binged more were better liked. In the bottom row of Table 2, the correlations between within-group popularity[2] and level of binging (adjusted for each group mean) are described; again, Sorority Beta demonstrated a norm in support of greater binge eating.

Festinger et al. (1950) found that, within groups, those who deviated from the local group norm were less popular than those who followed the norm. This suggests that, within friendship clusters, the more a woman deviates from her group mean, the less popular she should be. The patterns of correlations between within-group

---

[2]Within-group popularity is based on the percentage of people within a person's group choosing her. Because smaller clusters are likely to have more reciprocal choices just by chance (a group of two is sure to have 100% reciprocation), each person's percentage choice was divided by the group's average percentage within choice. Each group's mean thus becomes 1.00; numbers above that indicate higher within-group popularity, numbers below it, lower popularity.

popularity and within-group deviance did not support this prediction, however; in the spring they ranged from −.15 to .16, and averaged .03 (all ps were ns). The inability to find the effect was largely due to the manner in which social groups were defined in this study. Because mutual choice and reciprocity were used in the cluster analysis, no social groups could have had true isolates, and thus the variability among group members was likely to be greatly attenuated.

Pressures toward Uniformity

In the presence of social norms in a valued social group there will be pressures toward uniformity. If a woman's friends are binge eaters, then the likelihood that she is also a binge eater increases. This is the crux of the social psychological account of the acquisition of bulimic behavior, and it is represented as the contagion coefficient in the top line of Table 3.

The contagion coefficient is a calculation based on the social networks analysis previously described. Subjects were sorted into social friendship clusters (cliques) by means of a cluster analysis. The contagion coefficient is the Pearson r between a woman's binge-eating level and the average binge-eating level of her closest friends in the sorority (statistically, this is the correlation between her own BES score and the average BES score of her cluster-mates, not including the target subject). The contagion coefficient is a behavior-to-behavior model of influence; it asks the question, To what extent is a woman's binge eating like that of her friends?

The answer, apparent from Table 3, is "considerably." In the fall, after only 6 weeks of interaction within the friendship cliques, there was no indication that friends were more like each other than any other sorority member (rs = .00 and −.15, for Alpha and Beta, respectively). However, after 7 months of interaction, friends had become more uniform (rs ranged from .21 to .40).

It is important to note that the expected value for the contagion coefficient under the null hypothesis is not in fact .00, because when a woman is removed from the population, the mean of that population, and hence the expected value of the sample of friends, is shifted slightly in the opposite direction. To ascertain exactly what size correlation to expect by chance, a Monte Carlo study based on 200 randomly generated data sets was performed for each of the sororities. These analyses yielded, under the null hypothesis, expected contagion coefficients of −.09 for Soror-

	Sorority alpha			Sorority beta	
Variable	Spring$_1$	Fall$_2$	Spring$_2$	Fall$_2$	Spring$_2$
Contagion coefficient	.30†	.00	.21*	−.15	.40††
% choices made in-group	81.6	87.2	89.4†	82.3	85.4††
Deviation from friends in fall with how binging changed over time	—		−.36†		−.34††

TABLE 3

PRESSURE TOWARD UNIFORMITY IN SOCIAL GROUPS

Note: Correlations are based on ns of 46, 51, 36, 66, and 55, respectively. Subscripts on seasons indicate either Study 1 or Study 2.
*different from −.08 at $p < .05$, one-tailed. †$p < .05$, two-tailed. ††$p < .01$, two-tailed.

ity Alpha in Study 1, $-.08$ for Sorority Alpha in Study 2, and $-.07$ for Sorority Beta.

The time difference is probably due to two effects. First, social influence probably would require more than 6 weeks to have an appreciable effect on a woman's binge eating. Second, the more cohesive the group, the more influence it should have over its members.

The second row of Table 3 indicates that, in fact, cohesion increased over time. "Percentage choices made within group" is the total number of in-group choices made, divided by the total number of in-group choices possible. Because the subjects made 10 friendship choices, and the average cluster size was 5.1 members (and the members did not choose themselves), 41% of all possible choices could have been made to the in-group. Across all studies, of the possible 4.1 choices, approximately 3.5, or 85% of possible choices, were made in-group. In spite of the relatively high cohesion even in the fall, cohesion did increase over time (daggers represent the significance levels of pairwise t tests). Thus, it is likely that time and increased cohesion worked together to bring friends' binging levels into agreement.

In fact, at the entire group level, there was a decrease in variability on binge eating over the course of the year. The standard deviation shrank from 6.9 to 5.8 in Sorority Alpha, and from 8.2 to 7.1 in Sorority Beta (see Table 1). This difference across both sororities was significant at $p < .05$ (tests of equality of variances, one-tailed).

Apparently, at both the group level (whole sorority) as well as the friendship level (within clusters), friends became more similar over time. The central question to ask at this point is, Do we have evidence here of social pressure, or is this evidence of assortative friendships (birds of a feather flock together)? Is the behavior-to-behavior correlation found in Table 3 evidence of contagion or of assortment? If sorority members were making friends on the basis of how much they binged, then a similar pattern of

within-group results would obtain in the absence of any actual social pressures or movement toward uniformity. Several converging lines of evidence suggest that this is a pattern of social influence and not merely differential assortment.

Evidence of Social Influence

First, if the phenomenon observed is merely assortment, then personality-type variables other than binge eating should also correlate among friends. This, however, does not seem to be the case; for example, self-esteem (RSE) correlates were .01, .00, and .04 in the spring for Alpha 1, Alpha 2, and Beta, respectively. Such problems, however, are best handled by data collected over time, and Study 2 provided us with just these sorts of data.

If binge eaters were simply reassorting to be with "birds of a feather," the social cliques uncovered in the spring (which differed significantly on binging) should have differed from each other in their past binging level as well; their fall BES scores should have been significantly different by cluster. However, in neither Sorority Alpha nor Sorority Beta were these differences significant. In fact, friendship choices were quite stable. Because friendship patterns are not continuous but nominal variables, a class measure of association, the *contingency coefficient,* was used to describe stability of friendship patterns. From fall to spring, choices were stable, with contingency coefficients of .87 and .94 in Alpha and Beta, respectively.

If the contagion coefficient were due merely to self-selection into similar groups, then one would expect this correlation to be significant in the fall. Six weeks is probably enough time to learn something about one another's eating habits; however, there is no evidence of contagion in the fall, indicating that 6 weeks was not enough time for social influence to take place.

If one allows the necessary passage of time and the increased group cohesion that accompanies it, then we would expect that pressures toward uniformity should, across the two waves, pressure women to become more like their immediate social groups. To test this, we calculated the distance a woman was from her friends at Time 1 by subtracting her binge-eating level from the average binge-eating level of her friends. This number was then correlated with how her binging level moved over the academic year. If there were social pressures toward uniform levels of binging, then the distance a woman was from her friends at Time 1 should have correlated negatively with the change in her binging level. If she binged much less than her friends, she should have increased her binging level; if she binged much more, she should have decreased.

This is exactly what happened. The bottom row of Table 3 describes these correlations. In both sororities Alpha and Beta, women became more like their friends over time. The less each woman was like her friends in the fall, the more she moved toward them over the academic year. Thus, the contagion coefficient seems to be, in sum, a measure of social influence.

One possible interpretation of this finding is that it is regression toward the mean. Certainly, regression toward the mean is likely to take place. But what is the size of correlations that we would expect to find based merely on chance, and are these correlations significantly larger? To test this, a Monte Carlo study based on the same parameters, but using 325 randomly generated data sets, generated expected correlations of $-.079$ for Sorority Alpha and $-.091$ for Sorority Beta, significantly smaller than the correlations found in Table 3 (both $ps < .05$, two-tailed).

Festinger et al. (1950) found that in Westgate, social norms overrode personal factors, so that the potential value of the tenants organization to a person was entirely independent of his or her attitude toward it. This does not seem to be the case in the present study. Because the personal factors are essentially risk factors in the epidemiological model, standardized regressions on

binge eating by risk factors were computed. Both psychological health, as measured by the RSE, and degree of fatness, as measured by the body-mass index, were independently predictive of binge eating in almost all groups at all times (see Table 4). Even as social pressures grew over the course of the year, the correlations between binge eating and the risk factors of fatness and low self-esteem remained relatively stable (no beta weights were significantly different from each other between fall and spring).

TABLE 4

RISK FACTORS FOR BINGE EATING IN STUDIES 1 AND 2 EXPRESSED AS STANDARDIZED BETA WEIGHTS

Sorority and wave	Body-mass index	Self-esteem
Alpha		
Spring$_1$	.28*	$-.46$***
Alpha		
Fall$_2$	.41***	$-.37$**
Spring$_2$	.42**	$-.50$***
Beta		
Fall$_2$	.37***	$-.37$***
Spring$_2$	.20	$-.46$***

Note: Beta weights are based on ns of 46, 51, 36, 66, and 55, for each row, respectively. Subscripts on seasons indicate either Study 1 or Study 2.
*$p < .05$. **$p < .01$. ***$p < .005$.

TABLE 5

SOCIAL INFLUENCE, BODY MASS, AND SELF-ESTEEM: THE SOCIAL CONTAGION MODEL OF BINGE EATING

Study	Adjusted R	Adjusted R^2
Sorority Alpha		
Study 1	.51*	.26
Study 2	.57*	.32
Sorority Beta		
Study 2	.48*	.23

Note: Multiple correlations are based on ns of 46, 36, and 55 for each row, respectively. The regression model includes social influence, self-esteem, and the body-mass index as predictors, and are based on spring data.
*$p < .005$.

To demonstrate the simplicity of this account of the acquisition of the behavior of binge eating, Table 5 shows the regressions within each sorority of an overall regression testing the social contagion model of binge eating. Using only the RSE as a measure of general psychological well-being, the average binging level of a woman's friends, and her body-mass index, one can predict a woman's binge-eating score with a multiple correlation of .48 to .57. Although this is a fairly parsimonious account of binge eating, it nonetheless appears to be fairly useful for explaining patterns of binge eating in these sororities.

DISCUSSION

To demonstrate social norms, popularity patterns were traced with respect to binge eating. In Sorority Alpha, deviations from the normative level of binge eating were associated with reductions in popularity. In Sorority Beta, a different normative pattern emerged; the more a woman binged, the more popular she was.

To demonstrate behavior-to-behavior influence on binge eating, sorority members' binge-eating levels were correlated with the binge-eating levels of their friends. This correlation was found in the spring for both sororities. This finding was most likely due to social influence rather than assortment, based on data including the stability of friendship ties, the lack of friend-to-friend correlation of self-esteem and other person variables, and the lack of difference among spring groups in their prior fall binging levels. Most important, however, is the correlation which directly indicates social influence: Women became more like their friends over time.

I have suggested that when a woman experiences distress, she is open to social influence. When the influence she is receiving in terms of social information and approval is in support of binging, she is more likely to become a binge eater. Some sort of interaction between social influence and susceptiblity is necessary to explain the problem of binge eating. For example, there is no reason to expect that the significant negative correlations between binge eating and self-esteem reflect a fact of nature. Prior to the sociocultural development of binge eating as a symptom related to psychological distress, binge eating and self-esteem had to be uncorrelated; there was such a low incidence of problem binging prior to the early 1970s that little variability existed in binge eating (Rosenzweig & Spruill, 1986). It is only in the presence of models for and information about binge eating that low self-esteem is likely to lead to binge eating. Because both of these sororities had prescriptive norms about binge eating, the appropriate social group with which to compare the self-esteem to binge-eating correlation—no backdrop of social norms—could not be included here. If it is true that an interaction between social influence and susceptibility is necessary, then individuals who are susceptible to influence (e.g., are low in self-esteem), but are not in groups where there are norms about binge eating, should not binge eat any more than average.

A Social Psychological Integration

The social influence account of binge eating provides a parsimonious bridge among the three accounts of bulimia discussed in the introduction. From the sociocultural perspective, one can discern which kinds of influence are likely to be found among social groups. Currently, one kind of influence is toward binge eating, and a college sorority is likely to reflect current concerns of this sort. From the clinical perspective, one can discern who is at risk for this social influence. In fact, many of the personality characteristics that clinicians have uncovered can be characterized as indicators of susceptibility to social influence: low self-esteem, depression, impulsivity, poor family environment, poorly developed sense of self, etc. For the epidemiological perspective, the social influence model provides a mechanism

4by which we can describe how symptoms are acquired and spread.

The social influence model works together with the other three approaches to meet the necessary theoretical criteria specified in the introduction. Who is and who is not at risk for binge eating is a function of both the immediate social influence and one's susceptibility to that influence. Influence and susceptibility will be affected by group cohesion, consensus on norms, and the attractiveness of the group as well as the individuals' general susceptibility to influence based on depression, self-esteem, and so forth.

The sorority milieu is likely to be a breeding ground for eating disorders (Squire, 1983); it is a powerful setting for translating cultural influence into direct social influence. The extreme social importance of body size and shape for this population most likely serves to increase the risk of beginning dieting and hence binge eating. It is likely that in other social groups where physical attractiveness and body shape are not weighed so heavily, the sorts of findings reported here would be greatly attenuated or even nonexistent.

It is important to note that a social influence model of binge eating explicitly predicts this possibility. If the group norm is entirely against dieting and binging but rather for vegetarianism, for example, the correlation between psychological distress and binging should approach zero. Instead, the correlation between distress and vegetarianism should be high. For this reason, the size and direction of correlations should differ between groups, depending on what the norms are for handling personal distress (e.g., Garner & Garfinkel, 1980). The content portion of the social influence model (in this case, binge eating) is a relatively open slot. Distress may be handled in a number of ways, and social pressures could as easily result in smoking, delinquency, heavy drinking, loss of virginity, drug use, or depression (Jessor & Jessor, 1977; Orford, 1985). It may be in this way that bulimia has replaced depressive symptoms as a primary

pathway of expressing psychological distress among younger women. If cultural norms move away from the current overconcern with dieting and thinness, then bulimia and binge eating will disappear with them. The expression of psychological distress will continue to follow cultural norms, wherever they may wander.

These results indicate that a social psychological analysis of eating disorders is warranted and likely to bear fruit. The spread of one important symptom of bulimia—binge eating—through a population is likely to be the result of social influence. Further research in this social psychological vein is necessary to delineate the interrelationship of the variables in the model. The role and development of social norms about binge eating and their importance to friendship ties, the nature of the transfer of behavior from friend to friend, and, especially, whether and how social pressures are applied among friends, are important issues that now face us. What is necessary are longitudinal studies of women at risk for binge eating and bulimia that are begun prior to the development of disordered eating habits. This may mean beginning longitudinal studies as early as junior high school, or even before.

The question remains, what form does social influence take in these sororities? A variety of possibilities exist. It may be that the women are directly teaching each other appropriate binging levels, although several informants indicated that they felt this was unlikely. It may be a case of leadership, where the most popular women set the tone for the rest of the sorority. This would be consistent with an account based on simple imitation or modeling: The high status members' level of binging is transmitted via imitation to the rest of the group. Or members of social groups may be coerced into conforming to a clique's standard. Presumably, the coercion could be based on the giving or withholding of popularity. However, the exact process of acquisition cannot be determined in this study.

Nonetheless, these data do appear to fit the model of behavioral contagion proposed by

Wheeler (1966). Wheeler, following Redl (1949), proposed that in cases where a behavior has both some sort of prior restraint to it (as excessive binge eating certainly does) and at the same time has some other strong impulse or urge toward fulfillment of a need, the presence of a model acting out the conflictual behavior increases the likelihood of the behavior being performed (Wheeler, 1966). In a sense, the avoidance gradient in an approach-avoidance conflict is lowered, making approach more likely. The social norms of the sorority, in combination with the presence of models, are likely to make the costs associated with binge eating appear less severe and increase the likelihood of higher levels of binge eating. In this way, observation of binge eating, motivated (or released) in part by social pressures based on popularity, may account for how binge eating as a behavior is acquired and expressed.

A general model of the social influence patterns in psychological distress could be derived from the social psychological model proposed here. It would involve changing the content of the social influence but not its pattern. In general, the pattern of influence is likely to follow the outline described by Kerckhoff and Back (1968) in their study of contagion in a North Carolina garment factory. Whichever symptom is being spread, it still should appear among people experiencing distress, it should spread out along sociometric and communication networks, and the norms about the behavior should change toward acceptance as the behavior becomes more widespread. Thus, the social influence model could apply to as diverse phenomena as the hysterical fainting found in Freud's day, depression, or bulimia. All one would need to change in the model is the type of data made socially available in terms of social norms and modeling of the behavior, and one can predict fainting, rashes, vomiting, depression, or binge eating.

Indeed, the social influence processes described here look strikingly like those described by Newcomb (1943) in his famous Bennington study. A strong social norm in favor of left-wing politics emerged at Bennington College, first among the faculty, and increasingly with age, the students. New students who did not follow the norm, that is, did not espouse left-wing politics, were sanctioned with a reduction in popularity. Newcomb (1943) argued that the process of social influence and attitude change was not specific to political attitudes, but could generalize to almost any expressible attitude or set of behaviors, and these results with respect to binge eating seem to bear out his claim.

An important task remains. Peer influence may account for how behaviors such as binge eating or alcohol use begin (Orford, 1985), but an account of the sort outlined here does not describe how these behaviors can escalate into full-blown bulimia or alcoholism. Although some social factors have been studied, the role of social influence in this process as yet remains far too unexamined.

READING 39

Social Loafing and Social Facilitation

Stephen G. Harkins (1987)

We chose this Harkins article as our final reading for several reasons. First, social facilitation is the original and hence the oldest research issue in social psychology. You were introduced to this topic in Triplett's 1898 article (Reading 2). In comparison, Harkins presents two of the most recent studies on social facilitation. In a sense, we have come full circle, but at a higher level. Hopefully, these studies will demonstrate how social psychology has improved our understanding of group processes over the century.

Second, social facilitation is a good example of a research area that was productive, but for which interest subsided and then blossomed again (see also Reading 36). The advice given to individuals about mental sets is also useful for a research area as a whole: If you can not make headway in solving a problem, put it away for a while and return to it later with a fresh look. In this case, after a series of studies found social interference rather than facilitation on a variety of tasks and among a variety of animals, this research area was "put away" for a while. Then, several decades later, Zajonc (1965) reorganized the ideas and data in this area by suggesting that: (a) the "mere presence" of others leads to physiological arousal, (b) arousal increases the likelihood of the most dominant response, and therefore (c) the "mere presence" of others increases the likelihood of the most dominant response. The presence of coactors or an audience leads to facilitation when the dominant response is the correct behavior (as with very easy or well-learned responses), but leads to interference when the dominant response is not correct (as with very difficult or poorly learned responses). Although there are now several variations on this theme, Zajonc's theoretical restructuring of the problem renewed interest in the concept of social facilitation.

Harkins continues the examination of this issue by adding another level of analysis. He examines social facilitation and social loafing, a related phenomenon, as part of a larger two-factor design that examines combinations of the *presence of others* (alone versus coaction) as one factor and *evaluation* (present or absent) as the other. The results from the two studies described in Harkins' article suggest the promise of this research and the continued revitalization of the oldest of social psychological concerns.

Abstract

Social facilitation and social loafing have been treated as separate lines of research in the social psychological literature. However, it is argued in the present paper that these two paradigms are closely related: in fact, they are complementary. Viewed from this perspective, the experimental conditions that have been included in loafing and facilitation research fall into three cells of a 2 (Alone vs. Coaction) × 2 (Evaluation vs. No Evaluation) factorial design. In the cur-

rent research, the complete 2 × 2 design was run in two experiments. In both experiments, consistent with the findings of previous loafing research, with number held constant, participants whose outputs could be evaluated outperformed participants whose outputs could not be, but, inconsistent with descriptions of the loafing effect (e.g., B. Latané, K. Williams, & S. Harkins, 1979, Journal of Personality and Social Psychology, 37, 823–832), with evaluation potential held constant, pairs outperfomed singles. These data suggest that both social facilitation and social loafing can be accommodated in the same design. It is argued that combining the paradigms in this way refines our understanding of both phenomena.

In the first published experiment in social psychology, Triplett (1898) found that children reeled more fishing line when working alongside another child similarly occupied than when reeling alone. Some 15 years later, Ringelmann (1913, summarized by Kravitz & Martin, 1986) reported that students working together pulled on a rope with *less* force than was expected on the basis of their individual outputs. Reeling line and pulling rope are both very simple tasks. Yet on one, working together led to better performance than working alone, while on the other, the opposite effect was obtained. These two experiments represent the initial efforts in what have come to be considered two separate lines of research, social facilitation and social loafing. The fact that these two phenomena fall into separate research domains may account for the fact that nothing has been made of the apparently contradictory nature of the findings. However, we will argue that these findings are intimately related, and are not contradictory. In fact, the two research paradigms are complementary.

Actually, these experiments were seen at one time as falling in the same domain. In an early review, Dashiell (1935) included Ringelmann's study in a section entitled "The effects of coworkers upon the individual's work" along with other experiments on social facilitation (e.g., Allport, 1920). Given the inconsistencies that already characterized the research in this area, the discrepancy between the findings of Triplett and Ringelmann must not have appeared noteworthy. As Dashiell (1935) wrote: "Looking backward over this section it appears that results with tests on the effect of the presence of other workers alongside are not in agreement on all points. Very generally there seems to emerge a recognition of contrasted kinds of influence from coworkers, facilitating and inhibiting" (p. 1115). Matters had not progressed by the 1950s when Solomon Asch (1952) noted that so-called explanations for the effects of the presence of others on performance represented restatements of the results, explaining nothing. After several decades of research, there was no convincing refutation of Asch's suspicion, and interest in the area waned.

In 1965, Zajonc suggested a resolution to the muddle. He hypothesized that the "mere presence" of others leads to increased drive, which enhances the tendency to emit dominant responses. If the dominant response is correct, facilitation is obtained. If incorrect, performance is debilitated. Of course, on simple or well-learned tasks, the dominant response is likely to be the correct one, leading to facilitated performance, as in Triplett's case. However, on complex or not well-learned tasks, the dominant response is likely to be incorrect, leading to debilitated performance. Zajonc's (1965) review suggested that this analysis made sense of a large body of research.

But what of Ringelmann's finding? The task was quite simple and people worked together, yet, there was no facilitation effect. Ringelmann's research was not included in Zajonc's review, apparently because, by now, it was considered to be part of the group process literature. In Zajonc's (1966) text, social facilitation effects were presented in a chapter entitled "Coaction," while Ringelmann's findings appeared in the "Group Performance" chapter, and why not? In Triplett's study, "working together" meant working individually, side by side, on the

same task. Ringelmann's students actually "worked together," pulling on the same rope. In the latter case, as Zajonc (1966) noted, the participants had to coordinate their efforts to achieve their full potential. If the participants reached their peak pulls at slightly different times, or if they pulled along slightly different axes, coordination loss would occur, leading to suboptimal performance. As Steiner (1972) has shown, the performance decrements exhibited by Ringelmann's students were directly proportional to the number of coordination links among the participants. The potential for coordination loss is clearly a consequence of working with others. Therefore, it makes sense to consider the Ringelmann effect as a "Group Process," while Triplett's study and the subsequent research are placed in the domain of "Coaction" (i.e., the effects of the presence of others working independently on the same task). Following this classification scheme, Forsyth (1983) presented coaction research in a section of his book entitled "Performance when others are present," while social loafing was presented in "Performance in interacting groups." In most social psychology textbooks, these two phenomena appear in separate sections and no consideration is given to their relationship.

Subsequent research, however, has shown that coordination loss alone is insufficient to account for Ringelmann's findings, and that working together can lead to less output even when there is *no* opportunity for coordination loss. Ingham, Levinger, Graves, and Peckham (1974), after replicating Ringelmann's rope-pulling experiment, arranged things in a second experiment so that, on certain trials, participants were given the impression that they were pulling with others, when they actually pulled alone. This arrangement provided no opportunity for coordination loss. On these pseudogroup trials, participants put out less effort than when they thought they were pulling alone. This reduction in effort has been termed *social loafing* (Latané, Williams, & Harkins, 1979), and this effect has been demonstrated for both sexes on tasks requiring both physical effort (clapping, Harkins, Latané, & Williams, 1980; pumping air, Kerr & Bruun, 1981; shouting, Latané et al., 1979) and cognitive effort (reacting to proposals, Brickner, Harkins, & Ostrom, 1986; brainstorming[1] and vigilance, Harkins & Petty, 1982; solving mazes, Jackson & Williams, 1985; evaluating essays, Petty, Harkins, Williams, & Latané, 1977).

Applying Steiner's (1972) typology, some of these tasks were "maximizing" (requiring the participant to put out as much effort as possible, such as rope-pulling, shouting, pumping air, and brainstorming), while others were "optimizing" (requiring the participant to achieve some criterion performance, such as evaluating essays, vigilance, and solving mazes). On all of these tasks, "groups" failed to achieve even the potential suggested by their individual performances, though the possibility of coordination loss was eliminated, either by using pseudo-groups (e.g., Ingham et al., 1974; Latané et al., 1979), or by using tasks on which individual performances added, with no possibility of coordination loss (e.g., vigilance and brainstorming, Harkins & Petty, 1982; solving mazes, Jackson & Williams, 1985).

Thus, while the potential for coordination loss may have consigned Ringelmann's findings to the group domain, this difference between the paradigms is not sufficient to account for the contradictory findings. In fact, a close examination of the two experimental paradigms reveals many more similarities than differences.

In the prototypic coaction experiment, the outputs of the coacting participants are individually identifiable, and these outputs are compared to the output of a single participant performing the same task. The usual finding in social facilitation research is that working together leads to enhanced performance on simple tasks and debilitated performance on complex ones. As noted previously, Zajonc (1965) offered a drive interpretation of this phenomenon. Over the next decade, this drive account was seen as the most parsimonious theoretical explanation for facilitation effects (e.g., Geen & Gange, 1977), although there was controversy over whether it was the mere presence of the others that increased drive (Zajonc, 1965, 1980), or the fact that these others were associated with evaluation and/or competition (Cottrell, 1972).

However, in a review of the facilitation literature since 1977, Geen (1980) concluded that "today such a confident assertion of the primacy of the drive theoretical approach is not warranted." "Instead several sophisticated alternatives have found considerable support in experimental studies." Geen (1980) organized these theoretical approaches into three broad classes. One class of theories incorporated those approaches that continue to rely on the notion that the presence of others increases drive (e.g., distraction/conflict, Baron, 1986; evaluation apprehension, Cottrell, 1972; social monitoring, Guerin & Innes, 1982; compresence, Zajonc, 1980). The second class of theories included those approaches that suggest that "the presence of others creates either explicit or implicit demands on the person to behave in some way" (Geen, 1980) (e.g., self-presentation, Bond, 1982; self-awareness, Carver & Scheier, 1981), while the third class consisted of Baron's (1986) information processing view of distraction/conflict, which proposes that the presence of others affects focus of attention and information processing.

---

[1]It should be noted that the instructions given in the "brainstorming" experiment are not typical brainstorming instructions. Participants in loafing studies were *not* asked to be "free wheeling (i.e., to produce wild and zany ideas)" (Maginn & Harris, 1980, p. 221). Instead, the participants were asked to generate as many uses as possible, and not to be concerned about the quality of the uses, which could be ordinary or unusual. Given these instructions, participants in previous research (e.g., Harkins & Petty, 1982) have shown the typical loafing effect; participants whose outputs were individually identifiable generated more uses than participants whose outputs were pooled.

Although there are a number of theories that attempt to account for facilitation effects, and "none appears to command the high ground as drive theory did in the 1960s and 1970s" (Geen, 1980), each of these theories focuses on the effects of one or both of the same two features of the facilitation paradigm: the mere presence of others, and/or the potential for evaluation that these others represent. The "number" theories argue that: the mere presence of others leads to the feeling of uncertainty which leads to increased drive (Zajonc, 1980); the presence of others leads to uncertainty and increased drive, when the behavior of these others cannot be monitored (Guerin & Innes, 1982); the simple presence of others may be distracting enough to trigger attentional conflict and increased drive (Baron, 1986); or the simple presence of others may be distracting enough to create an attentional overload affecting focus of attention (Baron, 1986). The "evaluation" theories argue that: the presence of others can come to be associated with evaluation and/or competition, and the resulting evaluation apprehension leads to increased drive (Cottrell, 1972); the possibility of evaluation leads to distraction which increases drive (Baron, 1986); the potential for evaluation makes one self-aware which leads to greater attention to how performance matches some standard (Carver & Scheier, 1981); the prospect of evaluation leads to concerns about self-presentation (Bond, 1982); or the potential for evaluation affects focus of attention (Baron, 1986). Thus, each of these explanations represents an attempt to account for the effects of number and/or evaluation.

Social loafing has been described as the finding that participants working together put out less effort than participants working alone (e.g., Latané et al., 1979). "Working together" in loafing experiments means that the outputs of the participants are pooled. That is, the outputs of the participants are summed, and the "group's" performance is represented by this sum. The Latané et al. (1979) description suggests that the

performances of the participants in this "loafing" condition are compared to the performances of participants working *by themselves*. However, in virtually all of these studies, the number of participants has been held constant. In the within-subjects loafing designs (e.g., Harkins et al., 1980; Ingham et al., 1974; Latané et al., 1979; Williams, Harkins, & Latané, 1981), a fixed number of participants performed individually and in various sized groups. Thus, in these experiments, the trials on which participants were asked to perform individually were like social facilitation trials in which participants performed sequentially rather than simultaneously.

In the between-subjects loafing designs (e.g., Brickner et al., 1986; Harkins & Jackson, 1985; Harkins & Petty, 1982), groups of participants, whose outputs were individually identifiable, performed the task simultaneously (e.g., vigilance, brainstorming) exactly as in facilitation research. Thus, in the prototypic loafing experiment, the performances of a set of participants whose outputs are pooled are compared to the performances of a set of participants whose outputs are individually identifiable.

The Latané et al. (1979) description of the loafing effect suggests that loafing is a "group versus individual" effect. However, our analysis suggests that loafing would be more appropriately viewed as an evaluation effect. In fact, Latané et al. (1979) suggested that the "information reducing" nature of the "group" trials (Davis, 1969) may have been responsible for the loafing effect. When participants' performances were pooled, individual outputs were lost in the crowd, submerged in the total, and were not individually recoverable by the experimenter. Because participants could receive neither praise nor blame for their performances, they loafed. Consistent with this interpretation, Williams et al. (1981) found that when participants were led to believe that their individual outputs could be monitored even when they performed "together" (i.e., pooled outputs), there was no loafing. Also, when participants were led to believe that interest centered on "group" performance and their individual outputs were to be summed, they loafed as much when they performed individually as when they performed "together." Williams et al. concluded on the basis of these findings that identifiability of individual outputs is an important mediator of social loafing.

However, Williams et al. did not manipulate identifiability alone. The participants all worked on the same task; thus, when their performances were individually identifiable, they could be directly compared to the performances of the other participants. This opportunity for comparison may have led participants to believe that their outputs could be evaluated, and it was this potential for evaluation, not identifiability alone, that motivated performance. To test this possibility, Harkins and Jackson (1985) orthogonally manipulated identifiability and comparability, using a brainstorming task in which participants were asked to generate as many uses as possible for an object. Replicating previous loafing research, when outputs were identifiable, participants generated more uses than when their outputs were pooled. However, this difference emerged *only* when participants believed that their outputs could be evaluated through comparison to their co-workers' performances.

These findings suggest that identifiability alone does not motivate performance. Participants must also feel that their outputs can be compared to those of others. Without this potential for evaluation, participants whose outputs were individually identifiable exerted as little effort as those whose outputs were pooled. These data suggest that people are motivated to work when their outputs can be evaluated. When outputs are pooled, evaluation is not possible and it is this aspect of "working together" that leads to loafing.

Viewed in this way, the experimental conditions that have been included in loafing and facilitation research fall into three cells of a 2 (Alone vs. Coaction) × 2 (Evaluation vs. No Evaluation) factorial design. Coaction in this context is defined as more than one person working on the same task during the same period of time.

The manner in which the individual scores are to be treated is left unspecified (e.g., individual evaluation, summed). In this 2 × 2 design, facilitation studies are characterized by the comparison of the performances of coactors whose outputs can be evaluated (Coaction/Evaluation) to the performances of single participants whose outputs can also be evaluated (Alone/Evaluation). In virtually all loafing research, the performances of participants in a Coaction/Evaluation cell have been compared to the performances of coacting participants whose outputs were pooled (Coaction/No Evaluation). The fourth cell, Alone/No Evaluation, has been run in *no* extant coaction study using either the facilitation or loafing paradigms. We propose that this combined design incorporates the processes that account for both facilitation and loafing effects, and addresses weaknesses present in each paradigm taken alone.

For example, Markus (1981) argued that those studies in which the mere presence hypothesis has not been confirmed "are studies in which there has not been a clear 'alone' condition as a comparison baseline" (p. 259). Consistent with the notion that experimenters have not been sufficiently aware of this problem, Bond and Titus (1983), in a review of social facilitation research, wrote: "In 96 of 241 studies, the experimenter was in the room with the 'alone' subject, and in 52 of these studies this 'alone' subject could see the experimenter!" (p. 271). Guerin (1986) reviewed 287 social facilitation studies and found only 11 published experiments that met his criteria for a test of the mere presence hypothesis. However, it could be argued that even Guerin's criteria, which included removing the experimenter from the room, were not strict enough for a reasonable test. Markus (1978) noted: "In virtually all experiments with humans, the subject in the alone condition is not 'phenomenologically' alone even when the experimenter is physically removed and out of sight. That is, he is quite aware of the experimenter and knows that his performance is being recorded, presumably for some present or future evaluation'' (p. 391). What difference does it make whether the experimenter is out of the room, if she or he has immediate access to a record of the participants' performances?

In all but one of the 11 published studies that Guerin cited as representing the best tests of the mere presence hypothesis, the experimenter had access to the participants' scores immediately after completion of the task. The sole exception was the Markus (1978) study in which the mere presence manipulation consisted of an attentive or inattentive audience which was present when the participants donned and doffed familiar and unfamiliar clothing. Apparently, there are no human coaction studies that incorporate appropriate tests of the mere presence hypothesis.

In the combined design we have described, the abilities of potential sources of evaluation, including the experimenter, to evaluate individual performances are minimized in the ''No Evaluation'' conditions. Thus, the addition of the conditions suggested by loafing research may offer a closer approximation to the conditions necessary for a test of the effects of mere presence on coaction, using tasks like those commonly employed in facilitation research.

In the loafing studies that we have described, the number of people present has been held constant. In only one loafing experiment has the performance of a person actually working alone been compared to the performances of people working together (Kerr & Bruun, 1981), and in this experiment, the number of people present and the manipulation of evaluation were confounded. That is, in the alone condition, a single person's outputs could be evaluated by the experimenter through comparison of his/her performance with the performances of the preceding and subsequent participants, while in the together conditions, there were at least two participants whose outputs were pooled and, therefore, could not be evaluated. Did participants in the alone condition put out more effort than the ''pooled'' participants because they were working alone or be-

cause their outputs could be evaluated? The description of the loafing effect points to the former possibility (e.g., Latané et al., 1979); however, the latter possibility is supported by the findings of Williams et al. (1981) and Harkins and Jackson (1985). The unified design clarifies the relationship between number and evaluation by orthogonally manipulating these variables.

EXPERIMENT 1

To test this unified paradigm, the complete 2×2 design was run in two experiments. In the first experiment, participants, run alone or in pairs, were asked to generate as many uses for an object as they could. Crossed with the number manipulation, one-half of the participants were told that everyone in the experiment was generating uses for the same object (*Evaluation*), while the other half were told that each of the participants would be generating uses for a different object (*No Evaluation*).

To replicate previous social facilitation research, participants in the *Coaction/Evaluation* condition should put out greater effort than *Alone/Evaluation* participants. To replicate previous social loafing research, *Coaction/Evaluation* participants should exert greater effort than *Coaction/No Evaluation* participants. If mere presence has an effect in this paradigm, *Coaction/No Evaluation* participants should put out greater effort than participants in the *Alone/No Evaluation* condition. This pattern of results would yield two main effects, suggesting that both ''evaluation'' and ''number'' affect performance. If mere presence has minimal effects, performance in the *Alone/No Evaluation* condition should be equivalent to performance in the *Coaction/No Evaluation* condition, yielding an Evaluation $\times$ Number interaction.

In making the case that loafing and facilitation effects can be accommodated in the same framework, we argued that pooling the participants' outputs leads them to reduce their efforts because it minimizes the possibility of evaluation. To provide additional support for this notion, a *Coaction/Pooled Output* condition was added to the design of the experiment. To replicate the findings of previous loafing research, *Coaction/Evaluation* participants should put out greater effort than *Coaction/Pooled Output* participants, who should perform at the same level as *Coaction/No Evaluation* participants.

Method

Subjects The subjects were 96 males and females who participated in the experiment as a means of earning partial course credit. The basic design was a 2 (Alone vs. Coaction (Pair)) × 2 (Evaluation vs. No Evaluation) with 12 participants run in each of the single conditions and 12 pairs in each of the pair conditions. An additional 12 pairs were run in a loafing replication condition in which the pair's outputs were pooled.

Procedure Upon arrival, the singles or pairs were seated at a semi-circular table with partitions that prevented the pairs from seeing one another, and were given instruction sheets that informed them that we were studying the performance of individuals and groups on a task called brainstorming. They would be given the name of an object and their task would be to generate as many uses as they could for the object. They were also told that we were interested in the number of uses that could be generated for a range of objects. Since some objects were easy and some difficult to generate uses for, the number of uses they generated would be comparable only to the number generated by others working on the same object.

In the *Evaluation* condition, participants were told that in this experiment we were looking at the number of uses that could be generated for one particular object, and so, everyone would be generating uses for the *same* object. The participants were asked to take 1 of 20 small envelopes. To the inside of the envelopes were paperclipped slips on which was written the name

of the object for which they were to generate uses. They were reminded that it did not matter which envelope they took since everyone was generating uses for the same object. In each envelope there were also a number of slips of paper on which the uses were to be written.

In the *No Evaluation* conditions each participant was told that she or he was the only participant who would be presented with this particular object. They were also asked to take one of the 20 envelopes, but were told that each envelope contained a slip on which the name of a different object had been written.

The experimenter then invited the participants to remove the clipped object slip and to read it. In all cases, the participants were asked to generate uses for a knife. They were then asked to dump the blank slips in their envelopes on the table in front of them, to take one slip, to fold it three times, and to slide it down the tube in front of them that extended into a box. The top of the box was then removed and the participants were shown either a single bin (Singles) or a pair of bins (Pairs) into which their use slips would fall.

The participants were asked to write one use per slip, to fold each slip three times, and to slide it down their tube. All of the participants were asked to generate as many uses as they could and to not be concerned about the quality of their reactions. The uses could be ordinary or unusual. They were to simply try to generate as many uses as possible. They were given 12 min to generate their uses, a length of time that previous research (Harkins & Petty, 1982) would suggest provided more than enough time for them to generate as many uses as they could. The experimenter then closed a sound attenuated partition for the 12-min use listing period. After this period, the participants were asked to respond to a set of ancillary measures, were debriefed, and then dismissed.

An additional 12 pairs were run in a loafing replication cell in which pairs were asked to generate uses for the same object but the slips of each pair were deposited in a common bin. Thus, in this condition *No Evaluation* was accomplished through pooling. These participants also responded to the ancillary measures.

Results

The scores for each pair were averaged resulting in 12 observations per cell. The basic data were analyzed in 2 (Alone vs. Coaction) $\times$ 2 (Evaluation vs. No Evaluation) ANOVAs, and Dunnett's test (Kirk, 1982) was used to make comparisons involving the loafing replication cell (Coaction/Pooled output).

Uses   Analysis of the primary dependent variable, the number of uses, revealed two main effects. *Evaluation* participants generated more uses ($M = 20.66$) than *No Evaluation* participants ($M = 16.25$), $F(1, 44) = 16.6$, $p < .01$, and *Coactors* generated more uses per person ($M = 20.45$) than *Singles* ($M = 16.45$), $F(1, 44) = 13.6$, $p < .01$. The interaction was not reliable ($p > .20$).

Replicating the social loafing effect, participants in the *Coaction/Evaluation* condition generated more uses ($M = 22.58$) than participants in the *Coaction/Pooled Output* condition ($M = 19.00$, $p < .05$). The number of uses generated by *Coaction/Pooled Output* participants ($M = 19.00$) was not reliably different from the number generated by participants in the *Coaction/No Evaluation* condition ($M = 18.33$, $p > .20$).

Ancillary Measures   Among the ancillary measures participants were asked to rate the extent to which they believed that the experimenter could determine exactly how many uses they individually generated. Of course, all of the participants in the basic 2 $\times$ 2 design should have believed that the experimenter could tell exactly how many uses they individually generated. Analysis of these data revealed no reliable differences ($ps > .20$). However, in the *Coaction/Pooled Output,* or loafing condition, the participants should have felt that the experimenter was less able to determine exactly how many uses they individually generated than

participants in either the *Coaction/No Evaluation* or the *Coaction/Evaluation* conditions. After all, in both of the latter two conditions the number of uses generated by each person could be counted. Consistent with this analysis, the *Coaction/Pooled Output* participants felt that the experimenter was less able to determine the number of uses generated by each person ($M = 5.08$ on an 11-point scale) than participants in the *Coaction/Evaluation* ($M = 7.83$) or *Coaction/No Evaluation* conditions ($M = 7.58$, $ps < .05$).

Participants were also asked to rate the extent to which they believed that their performance in this experiment could be directly compared to the performances of others. Participants in the *Evaluation* conditions were told that all participants were generating uses for the same object. Thus, they would be expected to report that their performances could be compared to those of others to a greater extent than participants in the *No Evaluation* conditions, who were told that they had different objects for which to generate uses, and they did (M evaluation $= 7.58$, M no evaluation $= 5.58$), $F(1, 44) = 16.1$, $p < .05$. When asked about comparability of performance, *Coaction/Pooled Output* participants reported that they believed that their performances could be compared to the performances of others in the experiment to the same extent ($M = 5.91$) as participants in the *Coaction/No Evaluation* condition ($M = 6.00$, $p > .20$), and believed that their performances could be compared less than participants in the *Coaction/Evaluation* condition ($M = 7.67$, $p < .05$).

Discussion

Coaction/Pooled Output participants generated fewer uses than *Coaction/Evaluation* participants, a replication of the loafing effect. Consistent with the notion that the potential for evaluation is central to the loafing effect, *Coaction/No Evaluation* participants generated the same number of uses as the participants in the *Coaction/Pooled Output* conditions, and reliably fewer than those in the

Coaction/Evaluation condition. The ancillary measures were also supportive of this analysis. Participants in the loafing replication condition could not be evaluated because their outputs were pooled. The different object manipulation was intended to achieve the same end, and, consistent with this expectation, participants in these two conditions reported that their outputs could *not* be evaluated to the same extent, both reliably less than participants in the *Coaction/Evaluation* condition.

In the basic 2 × 2 design, two main effects were obtained. With evaluation held constant, coactors outperformed singles. With number held constant, participants whose outputs could be evaluated outperformed participants whose outputs could not be. This pattern of results suggests that both the potential for evaluation and mere presence affected performance.

The logic underlying the same object/different object manipulation, that was used in Experiment 1, suggests that two conditions must be met for evaluation to be possible. The participants' individual outputs must be identifiable, and there must be some standard against which these outputs can be compared. In the typical loafing paradigm, participants generate uses for the same object, but, because their outputs are pooled, individual efforts cannot be evaluated. When participants have different objects, even though their outputs are identifiable, there is no standard for comparison. Results for the ancillary measures in the present research were consistent with this analysis. Also, the identical same object/different object manipulation was used by Harkins and Jackson (1985), who also found that participants whose outputs were identifiable, but not comparable (different objects), generated as few uses as participants who generated uses for the same object, but whose outputs were pooled.

However, Harkins and Petty (1982) have used a similar manipulation and reported a different outcome. Participants whose uses were to be pooled were told that they would either be generating uses for the same object or for different objects. In these pooled conditions, Harkins and Petty (1982) found

that different-object participants generated *more* uses than same-object participants, the opposite of what was found by Harkins and Jackson (1985) and in the present research. Though these experiments are superficially similar, there were a number of methodological differences that could account for this discrepancy. For example, in the Harkins and Petty (1982) research, participants in the different-object condition were told "you alone are responsible for generating uses for the object that you will be given" (p. 1226), while participants in Harkins and Jackson (1985) and the current research were not. Participants in the Harkins and Jackson (1985) research and the present work were told that some of the objects were easy and some difficult to generate uses for, and, as a result, the number of uses they generated would be comparable only to the number generated by others working on the same object, while the participants in the Harkins and Petty (1982) were not.

EXPERIMENT 2

To assess the reliability of the findings of Experiment 1, the effects of number and evaluation potential were examined in a second experiment, using a different method of manipulating evaluation potential. Participants took part as singles or pairs in a vigilance task that required them to report seldomly occurring signals presented on a TV screen. Evaluation was manipulated by leading the participants to believe either that the computer that kept track of their performances was functioning properly (Evaluation) or had malfunctioned (No Evaluation).

In addition to using a different method of manipulating evaluation potential, this vigilance task is "optimizing" (requiring a criterion level of performance, Steiner, 1972), rather than "maximizing" (requiring as much effort as possible, Steiner, 1972) like the brainstorming task used in Experiment 1, so we can see whether these effects generalize to a different type of task. Finally, in Experiment 2 when the computer fails, there is ostensibly *no* record of performance, unlike in the brainstorming task where there was a product (the number of uses), even though comparison was not possible because all of the objects were supposedly different. Thus, this vigilance task goes even farther toward minimizing the possibility of evaluation.

Method

Subjects The subjects (*S*s) were 90 male and female undergraduates who participated as a means of earning partial course credit. The design was a 2 (Alone vs. Coactors) × 2 (Evaluation vs. No Evaluation) factorial with 15 participants run in each of the Single cells and 15 pairs run in each of the Coaction cells.

Procedure As the experimenter (*E*) was taking the participants to the laboratory, all of them were told that this research was only in its initial stages and all of the bugs had yet to be worked out. Upon arrival, participants were seated at a semi-circular table with partitions that prevented the pairs from seeing one another. Participants then read the following instructions that were presented on a TV monitor:

> We are interested in studying the performance of groups and individuals on vigilance tasks. The vigilance task requires you to watch for a dot to flash on a TV screen. When you see the dot you are to signal by pressing a button. You will be watching one-fourth of the TV screen. In this session, you will be watching the upper lefthand quadrant of the screen.
>
> We are interested in your performance on this task. Over the course of the experiment we will be keeping track of the number of signals you detect. Please try to detect as many signals as you can, while minimizing the number of times you falsely report the presence of a signal.

All participants then took part in a one-minute practice trial during which three signals were presented. The 12-in. TV screen was divided into 4 equal areas by computer-generated graphics, and the *S*s were reminded that they were to watch the upper lefthand quadrant. The signals, which flashed for 1/30th of a second and were each composed of one graphics block, occurred at randomly determined locations in this block and during this practice trial were presented at 15-sec intervals. After the first signal, the display was interrupted by the message "Response Recording Error." The *E* then went through a slightly opened partition into the other half of the room, saying that the response recorder had been malfunctioning. The *E* then returned and asked the *S*s to try again. In the *Evaluation* condition, the *S*s responded to the two remaining signals and no error message appeared. The *S*s were then presented individual hit and false alarm feedback for the two signals they had seen. They were also told that because the experiment was just beginning, the *E* was interested in the *S*s' perceptions regarding the task, and so, at the end of the experiment they would be given a questionnaire which would require them to rate their experience along several dimensions.

In the *No Evaluation* condition, response to the second signal resulted in the same error message, and the *E* told these *S*s that the response recorder would be disabled, but even so, the last signal would be presented to which they should also respond. At the end of the practice session, the feedback showed "0" hits and "0" false alarms for the *S*s. The *E* then told them that the response recorder was malfunctioning, so their performances could not be recorded, but the *E* would like for them to perform the task anyway. Because the experiment was just beginning, the *E* was interested in the *S*s' perceptions concerning the task, and at the end of the experiment, the *S*s would be given a questionnaire which would require them to rate their experience along several dimensions. Only if they took part in the vigilance task would they be able to answer these questions accurately, and so, the *S*s were to try as hard as they could.

All *S*s were then told that if any other error messages appeared on the screen they should go the *E*'s office down the hall to report it.

Otherwise the computer would inform them when the task was over at which time they would be asked some questions about the experiment.

The *E* then closed the room partition and left the room for the 14-min duration of the task. During the 14 min, 14 signals were presented. For each session, the location of the signals within the quadrant was randomly determined, but the timing of the signals across the 14 min was the same for all sessions. After the viewing task ended, the *E* returned, the *S*s responded to the questionnaire, were debriefed, and then dismissed.

Results

The scores for each pair were averaged resulting in 15 observations in each of the cells comprising the 2 (Coactors vs. Alone) × 2 (Evaluation vs. No Evaluation). For analysis, the two types of errors (misses and false alarms) were summed because, consistent with previous research (Harkins & Petty, 1982), a preliminary analysis revealed that these measures were positively related.

Analysis of the error index (misses and false alarms) revealed two main effects. *Evaluation* participants made fewer errors *(M = 2.40)* than *No Evaluation* participants *(M = 7.48)*, $F(1, 56) = 35.5$, $p < .01$, and *Coactors* made fewer errors *(M = 3.95)* than *Singles, (M = 5.93)*, $F(1, 56) = 5.4$, $p < .05$. The interaction was not reliable $(p > .20)$.

Among the ancillary measures, participants were asked to rate the extent to which the *E* could tell exactly how well they individually performed. Participants in the *Evaluation* condition reported that the *E* could tell to a greater extent how they performed. Participants in the *Evaluation* condition reported that the *E* could tell to a greater extent how they performed *(M = 8.26* on an 11-point scale) than *No Evaluation* participants *(M = 4.21)*, $F(1, 56) = 23.12$, $p < .01$.

Discussion

The findings from these experiments refine our understanding of both loafing and facilitation. In both experiments, using very different tasks, main effects were obtained for number and evaluation. Coactors outperformed participants working alone, not the reverse as was suggested by the *description* of the loafing effect (e.g., Latané et al., 1979). Consistent with the *findings* of previous loafing research (e.g., Harkins & Jackson, 1985; Latané et al., 1979; Williams et al., 1981), participants whose outputs could be evaluated outperformed participants whose outputs could not be.

The two main effects are consistent with the argument that both mere presence and evaluation played a role in motivating performance. Of course, it is probably not possible to eliminate all concerns about the possibility of evaluation when participants know that they are taking part in an experiment. However, by minimizing the apparent opportunities for evaluation by the experimenter, the present experiments approached this goal more closely than previous coaction experiments in which no attempt was made to eliminate this source of evaluation. Though mere presence and evaluation apprehension have often been pitted against each other as rival explanations for facilitation effects, Markus (1981) pointed out that both factors could contribute to facilitation effects. In these experiments, both did, and in an additive fashion.

This analysis suggests that there is no discrepancy between the findings of loafing and facilitation research. In fact, the findings from these paradigms are complementary. In social facilitation research, when participants coact, their outputs can be compared and they work harder than participants working alone. In social loafing research, when participants coact, their outputs cannot be evaluated, and they put out less effort than participants whose outputs can be compared. In both cases, evaluation is central. In social facilitation, working together enhances evaluation potential; in social loafing, working together reduces it.

The Latané et al. original definition of loafing could be taken to be generic. That is, any motivation loss in groups could be called "social loafing." For example, Kerr (1983) found evidence of reduced effort that he termed "free rider" and "sucker" effects when disjunctive and conjunctive scoring schemes were used in groups. These findings would appear to fall under the rubric "social loafing," because participants working together put out less effort than those working individually. However, in these experiments, the participants' individual outputs were *always* identifiable. Hence, it is quite unlikely that these findings could be attributed to the effects of evaluation. The current analysis argues in favor of a restricted definition of loafing that focuses on the fact that "working together" leads to reduced effort because there is no opportunity for evaluation.

Our analysis has been limited to the simple, well-learned tasks that have been used in most loafing research. On tasks like rope-pulling, shouting, pumping air, and vigilance, greater effort leads to better performance. However, when *complex* tasks are used in facilitation research (e.g., Martens & Landers, 1972; Seta, Paulus, & Schkade, 1976), greater effort leads to poorer performace. This suggests that if, instead of the simple tasks typically used in loafing research, a complex task were used, participants in the Coaction/No Evaluation (loafing) condition should perform *better* than participants in the Coaction/Evaluation condition, and this outcome is exactly what was found by Jackson and Williams (1985). Participants in a Coaction/Evaluation condition performed better on simple mazes than participants whose outputs were pooled (Coaction/No Evaluation), a loafing effect, but when the mazes were complex, the pattern was reversed. Participants whose outputs were pooled performed better than participants whose individual outputs could be compared. Thus, it appears that this approach can account for performance on both simple and complex tasks.

The potential for evaluation plays a central role in this account of loafing and facilitation effects, but evaluation by whom? In loafing research the role of the experimenter as evaluator has been emphasized. For example, Harkins et al. (1980) wrote: "The results (social loafing) are easily explained by a minimizing strategy where participants are motivated to work only as hard as necessary to gain credit for good performance or to avoid blame for a bad one. Whenever the experimenter was unable to monitor individual outputs directly, performers sloughed off" (p. 464). However, the experimenter is only one of three potential sources of evaluation. When outputs are pooled, participants may also feel that they cannot evaluate their own output, nor can this output be evaluated by their fellow participants.

Social facilitation researchers have referred to each of these potential sources of evaluation in their *accounts* of coaction effects (e.g., coactor evaluation, Klinger, 1969; self-evaluation, Sanders, Baron & Moore, 1978; experimenter evaluation, Seta, Paulus, & Schkade, 1976). Despite the fact that each of these sources has been incorporated into these accounts of coaction effects, there is no compelling evidence that these accounts have captured the motivational structure of the experiments they were meant to describe. For example, though Sanders et al. (1978) allude to self-evaluation in their interpretation, when the participant could evaluate himself or herself, the coactors could also evaluate the participant, and at this time, the evaluation potential of the experimenter was likely to have been particularly salient. In many of these facilitation experiments, it is not clear what the participants were told or inferred about evaluation potential. The haphazard manipulation of evaluation potential may account for Bond and Titus (1983) finding that evaluation potential had no systematic effects in social facilitation research.

Thus, the most that can be said at this point is that the potential for evaluation plays an important role in motivating performance in this "rudimentary social arrangement" (Cottrell, 1972). By using the minimal evaluation conditions suggested by loafing research as a starting point, the motivational structure of this "rudimentary social arrangement" can be examined systematically, leading to a better understanding of both loafing and facilitation effects.

In this analysis, we have focused on the role that evaluation plays in producing facilitation and loafing effects. We are not proposing that effects stemming from manipulations of evaluation potential account for all, or even most, motivation losses in groups. Any number of other variables may affect performance in group settings (e.g., dispensability of member effort, Kerr, 1983). Rather, we are arguing that evaluation potential plays a central role in producing the reduction in effort that has been termed social loafing, and the enhancement in effort that has been termed social facilitation. Even when our attention is limited to the loafing paradigm, it is clear that other factors motivate performance, regardless of the potential for evaluation. For example, creativity (Bartis, Szymanski, & Harkins, 1986), personal involvement (Brickner et al., 1986), partner effort (Jackson & Harkins, 1985), and group cohesion (Williams, 1981) have all been shown to eliminate the loafing effect even though the potential for evaluation by each of the sources was minimized. In future work, it will be necessary to determine how these other factors interact with the potential for evaluation to motivate performance in these settings.

REFERENCES

(Numbers in brackets [ ] following reference refer to reading number [1 through 39] or reading introduction number [RI-1 through RI-39].)

Abbey, A. (1987). Misperceptions of friendly behavior as sexual interest: A survey of naturally occurring incidents. *Psychology of Women Quarterly, 22,* 173–194. [RI-17]

Abbey, A., Cozzarelli, C., McLaughlin, K., & Harnish, R. J. (1987). The effects of clothing and dyad sex composition on perceptions of sexual intent: Do women and men evaluate these cues differently? *Journal of Applied Social Psychology, 17,* 108–126. [RI-17]

Abbey, A., & Melby, C. (1986). The effects of nonverbal cues on gender differences in perceptions of sexual intent. *Sex Roles, 15,* 283–298. [RI-17]

Abelson, R. P. (1976). Script processing in attitude formation and decision making. In J. S. Carroll & J. W. Payne (Eds.), *Cognition and social behavior.* Hillsdale, NJ: Erlbaum. [36]

Ach, N. (1905). *Ueber die Willenstätigkeit und das Denken.* Göttingen: Vanderhoeck & Ruprecht. [4]

Adorno, T. W., Frenkel-Brunswik, E., Levinson, D., & Sanford, R. N. (1950). *The authoritarian personality.* New York: Harper. [35], [RI-35]

Ajzen, I., & Fishbein, M. (1969). The prediction of behavioral intentions in a choice situation. *Journal of Experimental Social Psychology, 5,* 400–416. [5]

Ajzen, I., & Fishbein, M. (1970). The prediction of behavior from attitudinal and normative variables. *Journal of Experimental Social Psychology, 6,* 466–487. [5]

Ajzen, I., & Fishbein, M. (1972). Attitudes and normative beliefs as factors influencing behavioral intentions. *Journal of Personality and Social Psychology, 21,* 1–9. [5]

Ajzen, I., & Fishbein, M. (1973). Attitudinal and normative variables as predictors of specific behaviors. *Journal of Personality and Social Psychology, 27,* 41–57. [5], [RI-5]

Ajzen, I., & Fishbein, M. (1977). Attitude-behavior relations: A theoretical analysis and review of empirical research. *Psychological Bulletin, 84,* 888–918. [RI-5]

Ajzen, I., & Fishbein, M. (1980). *Understanding attitudes and predicting social behavior.* Englewood Cliffs, NJ: Prentice-Hall. [36]

Allport, F. H. (1920). The influence of the group upon association and thought. *Journal of Experimental Social Psychology, 3,* 159–182. [39]

Allport, F. H. (1924). *Social psychology.* Boston: Houghton Mifflin. [4]

Allport, F. H. (1932). Psychology in relation to social and political problems. In P. S. Achilles (Ed.), *Psychology at work.* New York: Whittlesey House. [4]

Allport, F. H. (1933). *Institutional behavior.* Chapel Hill: University of North Carolina Press. [4]

Allport, F. H. (1934). The J-curve hypothesis of conforming behavior. *Journal of Social Psychology, 5,* 141–183. [4]

Allport, F. H., & 34 cosigners (1953). The effects of segregation and the consequences of desegregation.: A social science statement. *Minnesota Law Review, 37,* 429–440. [26]

Allport, G. W. (1929). The composition of political attitudes. *American Journal of Sociology, 35,* 220–238. [4]

Allport, G. W. (1932). Review of P. M. Symond's Diagnosing personality and conduct. *Journal of Social Psychology, 3,* 391–398. [4]

Allport, G. W. (1935). Attitudes. In C. Murchison (Ed.), *Handbook of social psychology.* Worcester, MA: Clark University Press. [RI-4]

Allport, G. W. (1951). Prejudice: A problem in psychological causation. In T. Parsons & E. Shils (Eds.), *Toward a theory of social action* (Part 4, Chapter 1). Cambridge: Harvard University Press. [25]

Allport, G. W. (1954). *The nature of prejudice.* Cambridge, MA: Addison-Wesley. [26]

Allport, G. W. (1955). *Becoming: Basic considerations for a psychology of personality.* New Haven: Yale University Press. [9]

Allport, G. W., & Vernon, P. E. (1931). The field of personality. *Psychological Bulletin, 27,* 677–730. [4]

Allport, G. W., & Vernon, P. E. (1933). *Studies in expressive movement.* New York: Macmillan. [4]

Alpert, J. J. (1964). Broken appointments. *Pediatrics, 34,* 127–132. [33]

Alpert, R., & Haber, R. (1960). Anxiety in academic achievement situations. *Journal of Abnormal and Social Psychology, 61,* 207–215. [8]

American Psychiatric Association. (1980). *Diagnostic and statistical manual of mental disorders* (3rd ed.). Washington, DC: Author. [38]

American Psychological Association. (1983). *Publication manual of the American Psychological Association* (3rd ed.). Washington, DC: Author. [1]

Amir, M. (1967). Forcible rape. *Federal Probation, 31.* [29]

Amir, M. (1971). *Patterns in forcible rape.* Chicago: University of Chicago Press. [17], [29]

Anastasi, A. (1968). *Psychological testing.* New York: Macmillan. [8]

Anderson, C. A., & Anderson, D. C. (1984). Ambient temperature and violent crime: Tests of the linear and curvilinear hypotheses. *Journal of Personality and Social Psychology, 46,* 91–97. [21]

Anderson, H. H. (1939). Domination and social integration in the behavior of kindergarten children and teachers. *Genetic Psychology Monographs, 21,* 287–385. [3]

Anderson, J. R., & Ross, B. H. (1980). Evidence against a semantic-episodic distinction. *Journal of Experimental Psychology: Human Learning and Memory, 6,* 441–465. [12]

Anderson, S. M. (1984). Self-knowledge and social inference: II. The diagnosticity of cognitive/affective and behavioral data. *Journal of Personality and Social Psychology, 46,* 369–406. [9]

Anderson, S. M., & Ross, L. (1984). Self-knowledge and social inference: I. The impact of cognitive/affective and behavioral data. *Journal of Personality and Social Psychology, 46,* 280–293. [9]

Anthony, K. (1915). *Feminism in Germany and Scandinavia.* New York: Holt. [28]

Apsler, R., & Sears, D. O. (1968). Warning, personal involvement, and attitude change. *Journal of Personality and Social Psychology, 9,* 162–166. [36]

Arendt, H. (1958). What was authority? In C. J. Friedrich (Ed.), *Authority* (pp. 81–112). Cambridge, MA: Harvard University Press. [35]

Arnold, M. B. (1980). *Emotion and personality* (2 vols.). New York: Columbia University Press. [15]

Asch, S. E. (1946). Forming impressions of personality. *Journal of Abnormal and Social Psychology, 41,* 258–290. [12]

Asch, S. E. (1952). *Social psychology.* New York: Holt, Rinehart & Winston. [48]

Ashley-Montagu, M. F. (1950). *On being human.* New York: Henry Schumann. [25]

Ashmore, R. D., & Del Boca, F. K. (1976). Psychological approaches to understanding intergroup conflict. In P. Katz (Ed.), *Toward the elim-ination of racism* (pp. 73–123). New York: Pergamon Press. [26]

Ashmore, R. D., & Del Boca, F. K. (1979). Sex stereotypes and implicit personality theory: Toward a cognitive-social psychological conceptualization. *Sex Roles, 5,* 219–248. [30]

Averill, J. R. (1968). Grief: Its nature and significance. *Psychological Bulletin, 70,* 721–748. [15]

Averill, J. R. (1974). An analysis of psychophysiological symbolism and its influence on theories of emotion. *Journal for the Theory of Social Behavior, 4,* 147–190. [15]

Averill, J. R. (1975). A semantic atlas of emotional concepts. *JSAS Catalogue of Selected Documents in Psychology, 5,* 330. (Ms. No. 421) [15]

Averill, J. R. (1976). Emotion and anxiety: Sociocultural, biological, and psychological determinants. In M. Zuckerman & C. D. Spielberger (Eds.), *Emotion and anxiety: New concepts, methods and applications.* New York: LEA-Wiley. [15]

Averill, J. R. (1979a). Anger. In H. Howe & R. Dienstbier (Eds.), *Nebraska Symposium on Motivation*: 1978. Lincoln: University of Nebraska Press. [15]

Averill, J. R. (1979b). The functions of grief. In C. Izard (Ed.), *Emotions in personality and psychopathology.* New York: Plenum. [15]

Averill, J. R. (1980). On the paucity of human emotions. In K. Blankstein, P. Pliner, & J. Polivy (Eds.), *Advances in the study of communication and affect,* Vol. 6: *Assessment and modification of emotional behavior.* New York: Plenum. [15]

Averill, J. R., & Boothroyd, R. (1977). On falling in love in conformance with the romantic ideal. *Motivation and Emotion, 1,* 235–247. [15]

Ax, A. F. (1953). Physiological differentiation of emotional states. *Psychosomatic Medicine, 15,* 433–442. [14]

Bacon, F. (1902). *Novum organum* (J. Devey, Ed.). New York: P. F. Collier & Son. (Original work published 1620.) [32]

Bahrick, H. P. (1969). Measurement of memory by prompted recall. *Journal of Experimental Psychology, 79,* 213–219. [12]

Bahrick, H. P. (1970). Two-phase model for prompted recall. *Psychological Review, 77,* 215–222. [12]

Bain, A. (1868). *Mental science.* New York: Appleton. [4]

Bain, R. (1927–1928). An attitude on attitude research. *American Journal of Sociology, 33,* 940–957. [4]

Bain, R. (1930). Theory and measurement of attitudes and opinions. *Psychological Bulletin, 27,* 357–379. [4]

Bakan, D. (1966). *The duality of human existence.* Chicago: Rand McNally. [30]

Baldwin, J. M. (1897). *Social and ethical interpretations.* New York: MacMillan. [9]

Baldwin, J. M. (1901–1905). *Dictionary of philosophy and psychology* (3 vols.). New York: Macmillan. [4]

Baldwin, J. M. (1906). *Mental development in the child and race* (3rd ed.). New York: Macmillan. [4]

Bandler, R. J., Madaras, G. R., & Bem, D. J. (1968). Self-observation as a source of pain perception. *Journal of Personality and Social Psychology, 9,* 205–209. [6]

Bandura, A. (1960). *Relationship of family patterns to child behavior disorders.* Progress Report, Stanford University, Project No. M-1734, United States Public Health Service. [20]

Bandura, A. (1971). *Social learning theory.* Morristown, NJ: General Learning Press. [27]

Bandura, A. (1977). Self-efficacy: Toward a unifying theory of behavioral change. *Psychological Review, 84,* 191–215. [9]

Bandura, A. (1977). *Social learning theory.* Englewood Cliffs, NJ: Prentice Hall. [32]

Bandura, A., & Huston, A. C. (1961). Identification as a process of incidental learning. *Journal of Abnormal and Social Psychology, 63,* 311–318. [20], [RI-20]

Bandura, A., & Walters, R. H. (1959). *Adolescent aggression.* New York: Ronald. [20]

Bargh, J. A. (1984). Automatic and conscious processing of social information. In R. S. Wyer, Jr., & T. K. Srull (Eds.), *The handbook of social cognition* (Vol. 3, pp. 1–43). Hillsdale, NJ: Erlbaum. [12]

Barker, R., Dembo, T., & Lewin, K. (1941). Studies in topological and vector psychology: II. Frustration and regression. *University of Iowa Studies in Child Welfare, 18,* No. 1. [3]

Baron, R. A. (1972). Aggression as a function of ambient temperature and prior anger arousal. *Journal of Personality and Social Psychology, 21,* 183–189. [21], [RI-21]

Baron, R. A. (1978). Aggression and heat: The "long hot summer" revisited. In A. Baum, J. E. Singer, & S. Valins (Eds.), *Advances in environmental psychology* (pp. 57–84). Hillsdale, NJ: Erlbaum. [21]

Baron, R. A. (1986). Distraction-conflict theory: Progress and problems. In L. Berkowitz (Ed.), *Advances in Experimental Social Psychology* (Vol. 19, pp. 1–40). New York: Academic Press. [39]

Baron, R. A., & Bell, P. A. (1976). Aggression and heat: The influence of ambient temperature, negative affect, and a cooling drink on physical aggression. *Journal of Personality and Social Psychology, 33,* 245–255. [21]

Baron, R. A., & Lawton, S. F. (1972). Environmental influences on aggression: The facilitation of modeling effects by high ambient temperatures. *Psychonomic Science, 26,* 80–82. [21]

Baron, R. A., Russell, G. W., & Arms, R. L. (1985). Negative ions and behavior: Impact on mood, memory, and aggression among Type A and Type B persons. *Journal of Personality and Social Psychology, 48,* 746–754. [21]

Barrett, K. (1982, September). Date rape: A campus epidemic? *Ms., 11,* p. 130. [29]

Barry, K. (1979). *Female sexual slavery.* New York: Avon. [29]

Bartis, S., Szymanski, K., & Harkins, S. (1986). *Evaluation of performance: A two-edged knife.* Manuscript submitted for publication. [39]

Bartlett, F. C. (1932). *Remembering.* Cambridge, England: University Press. [4]

Baum, M. (1972). Love, marriage and the division of labor. In H. P. Dreitzel (Ed.), *Family, marriage and the struggle of the sexes* (pp. 83–106). New York: Macmillan. [18]

Baumeister, R. F. (1982). A self-presentational view of social phenomena. *Psychological Bulletin, 91,* 3–26. [RI-8]

Baumeister, R. F. (1987). How the self became a problem: A psychological review of historical research. *Journal of Personality and Social Psychology, 52,* 163–176. [RI-7]

Beck, A. T. (1967). *Depression: Causes and treatment.* Philadelphia: University of Pennsylvania Press. [9]

Becker, B. J. (1986). Influence again: Another look at studies of gender differences in social influence. In J. S. Hyde & M. Linn (Eds.), *The psychology of gender: Advances through metaanalysis.* Baltimore: Johns Hopkins University Press. [RI-34]

Becker, H. S. (1960). Notes on the concept of commitment. *American Journal of Sociology, 66*, 32–40. [18]

Becker, H. W. (1963). *Outsiders: Studies in the sociology of deviance*. New York: Free Press. [32]

Bell, L. G., Wicklund, R. A., Manko, G., & Larkin, C. (1976). When unexpected behavior is attributed to the environment. *Journal of Research in Personality, 10*, 316–327. [18]

Bell, P. A., Garnand, D. B., & Heath, D. (1984). Effects of ambient temperature and seating arrangement on personal and environmental evaluations. *Journal of General Psychology, 110*, 197–200. [21]

Bem, D. J. (1965). An experimental analysis of self-persuasion. *Journal of Experimental Social Psychology, 1*, 199–218. [6]

Bem, D. J. (1967). Self-perception: An alternative interpretation of cognitive dissonance phenomena. *Psychological Review, 74*, 183–200. [5], [6]

Bem, D. J. (1972). Constructing cross-situational consistencies in behavior: Some thoughts on Alker's critique of Mischel. *Journal of Personality, 40*, 17–26. [8], [RI-6]

Bem, D. J. (1972). Self-perception theory. In L. Berkowitz (Ed.), *Advances in experimental social psychology* (Vol. 6, pp. 1–62). New York: Academic Press. [6], [15], [36], [RI-10]

Bem, S. L. (1974). The measurement of psychological androgyny. *Journal of Consulting and Clinical Psychology, 42*, 155–162. [30]

Bem, S. L. (1977). On the utility of alternative procedures for assessing psychological androgyny. *Journal of Consulting and Clinical Psychology, 45*, 196–205. [30]

Bem, S. L. (1981). Gender schema theory: A cognitive account of sex typing. *Psychological Review, 88*, 354–364. [30]

Bem, S. L., & Bem, D. J. (1970). Case study of a nonconscious ideology: Training the woman to know her place. In D. J. Bem, *Beliefs, attitudes, and human affairs*. Belmont, CA: Wadsworth. [1], [RI-10], [RI-17]

Benedict, R. (1934). *Patterns of culture*. Boston: Houghton Mifflin. [3]

Beneke, T. (1982a). *Men on rape*. New York: St. Martin's Press. [29]

Beneke, T. (1982b, July). Male rage: Four men talk about rape. *Mother Jones*, p. 13. [29]

Bennett, W., & Gurin, J. (1982). *The dieter's dilemma*. New York: Basic Books. [38]

Ben-Sira, Z. (1976). The function of the professional's affective behavior in client satisfaction: A revised approach to social interaction theory. *Journal of Health and Social Behavior, 17*, 3–11. [33]

Benware, C., & Deci, E. L. (1975). Attitude change as a function of the inducement for espousing a proattitudinal communication. *Journal of Experimental Social Psychology, 11*, 271–278. [6]

Berezin, M. (1972). Psychodynamic considerations of aging and the aged: An overview. *American Journal of Psychiatry, 128*, 1483–1491. [27]

Berger, P. L., & Luckmann, T. (1968). *The social construction of reality*. New York: Doubleday. [15]

Berkowitz, L. (1969). The frustration-aggression hypothesis revisited. In L. Berkowitz (Ed.), *Roots of aggression: A re-examination of the frustration-aggression hypothesis*. New York: Atherton. [RI-20]

Berkowitz, L. (1974). Some determinants of impulsive aggression: Role of mediated associations with reinforcements for aggression. *Psychological Review, 81*, 165–176. [15], [37]

Berkowitz, L. (1984). Some effects of thoughts on anti- and prosocial influences of media events: A cognitive-neoassociation analysis. *Psychological Bulletin, 95*, 410–427. [21]

Berkowitz, L., & Daniels, L. R. (1963). Responsibility and dependency. *Journal of Abnormal and Social Psychology, 66*, 429–436. [26]

Bernard, J. (1969). *The sex game*. London: L. Frewin. [17]

Bernard, L. L. (1916–1917). Theory of rural attitudes. *American Journal of Sociology, 22*, 630–649. [4]

Bernard, L. L. (1926). *Introduction to social psychology*. New York: Holt. [4]

Bernard, L. L. (1930). Attitudes, social. In E. R. A. Seligman & A. Johnson (Eds.), *Encyclopedia of the social sciences* (Vol. 2) (pp. 305–306). New York: Macmillan. [4]

Bernberg, R. E. (1952). Socio-psychological factors in industrial morale: The prediction of specific indicators. *Journal of Social Psychology, 36*, 73–82. [5]

Berscheid, E., & Fei, J. (1977). Romantic love and sexual jealousy. In G. Clanton & L. G. Smith (Eds.), *Jealousy* (pp. 101–109). Englewood Cliffs, NJ: Prentice-Hall. [18]

Berscheid, E., Graziano, W., Monson, T., & Dermer, M. (1976). Outcome dependency: Attention, attribution, and attraction. *Journal of Personality and Social Psychology, 34,* 978–989. [12]

Berscheid, E., & Walster, E. (1974). Physical attractiveness. In L. Berkowitz (Ed.), *Advances in experimental social psychology* (Vol. 7). New York: Academic Press. [32]

Berscheid, E., & Walster, E. H. (1978). *Interpersonal attraction* (2nd ed.). Reading, MA: Addison-Wesley. [18]

Berzins, J. I., Welling, M. A., & Wetter, R. E. (1978). A new measure of psychological androgyny based on the Personality Research Form. *Journal of Consulting and Clinical Psychology, 46,* 126–138. [30]

Bettelheim, B., & Janowitz, M. (1950). *The dynamics of prejudice: A psychological and sociological study of veterans.* New York: Harper. [25]

Bettman, J. R. (1979). Memory factors in consumer choice: A review. *Journal of Marketing, 43,* 37–53. [36]

Biddle, W. W. (1931). A psychological definition of propaganda. *Journal of Abnormal and Social Psychology, 26,* 283–295. [4]

Biddle, W. W. (1932). Propaganda and education. *Teachers College Contributions in Education, 521,* 84. [4]

Billig, M., & Tajfel, H. (1973). Social categorization and similarity in intergroup behavior. *European Journal of Social Psychology, 3,* 27–52. [26]

Bilodeau, E. A., & Blick, K. A. (1965). Courses of misrecall over long-term retention intervals as related to strength of pre-experimental habits of word association. *Psychological Reports, 16,* 1173–1192. [12]

Binet, A. (1900). *La suggestibilité.* Paris: Schleicher. [35]

Black, J. D. (Ed.) (1933). *Research in social psychology of rural life* (Bulletin 17). New York: Social Science Research Council. [4]

Blake, R. R. (1958). The other person in the situation. In R. Tagiuri & L. Petrullo (Eds.), *Person perception and interpersonal behavior* (pp. 229–242). Stanford, CA: Stanford University Press. [20]

Blanck, P. D., Rosenthal, R., & Cordell, L. H. (1985). The appearance of justice: Judge's verbal and nonverbal behavior in criminal jury trials. *Stanford Law Review, 38,* 89–164. [RI-33]

Block, J. H. (1976). Debatable conclusions about sex differences. *Contemporary Psychology, 11,* 517–522. [30]

Bloom, S. W. (1963). *The doctor and his patient: A sociological interpretation.* New York: Russell-Sage Foundation. [33]

Blue, G. F. (1978). The aging as portrayed in realistic fiction for children, 1945–1975. *Gerontologist, 18,* 187–192. [27]

Blum, R. H. (1957). *The psychology of malpractice suits.* San Francisco: The California Medical Association. [33]

Blum, R. H. (1960). *The management of the doctor-patient relationship.* New York: McGraw-Hill. [33]

Bogardus, E. S. (1925a). Social distance and its origins. *Journal of Applied Sociology, 9,* 216–226. [4]

Bogardus, E. S. (1925b). Measuring social distances. *Journal of Applied Sociology, 9,* 299–308. [4]

Bogardus, E. S. (1927). Race friendliness and social distances. *Journal of Applied Sociology, 11,* 272–287. [4]

Bogardus, E. S. (1928). Occupational distance. *Sociology and Social Research, 13,* 33–81. [4]

Bogardus, E. S. (1931). *Fundamentals of social psychology* (2nd ed.). New York: Century. [4]

Bogart, L. (1956). *The age of television.* New York: Ungar. [23]

Boldyreff, J. W., & Sorokin, P. A. (1932). An experimental study of the influence of suggestion on the discrimination and the valuation of people. *American Journal of Sociology, 37,* 720–737. [4]

Bond, C. (1982). Social facilitation: A self-presentational view. *Journal of Personality and Social Psychology, 42,* 1042–1050. [39]

Bond, C., & Titus, L. (1983). Social facilitation: A meta-analysis of 241 studies. *Psychological Bulletin, 94,* 265–292. [39]

Bonfadelli, H. (1983). Der Einfluss des Fernsehens auf die Konstruktion der Sozialien Realitat: Befunde aus der Schweiz zur Kultivierungshypothese. *Rundfunk und Fernsehen, 31,* 415–430. [23]

Borden, R. J. (1975). Witnessed aggression: Influence of an observer's sex and values on aggressive responding. *Journal of Personality and Social Psychology, 31,* 567–573. [15]

Boskind-Lodahl, M., & Sirlin, J. (1977, March). The gorging-purging syndrome. *Psychology Today,* pp. 50–52, 82, 85. [38]

Boswell, J. (1934). *The life of Johnson* (Vol. II) (L. F. Powell, Ed.). Oxford: Clarendon Press. (Original work published 1791.) [15]

Bourque, L. B., & Back, K. W. (1971). Language, society, and subjective experience. *Sociometry, 34,* 1–21. [15]

Bowers, W. J. (1968). Normative constraints on deviant behavior in the college context. *Sociometry, 31,* 370–385. [5]

Bradley, G. W. (1978). Self-serving biases in the attribution process: A reexamination of the fact or fiction question. *Journal of Personality and Social Psychology, 36,* 56–71. [17]

Bramel, D. A. (1962). A dissonance theory approach to defensive projection. *Journal of Abnormal and Social Psychology, 64,* 121–129. [11]

Bramel, D. A. (1963). Selection of a target for defensive projection. *Journal of Abnormal and Social Psychology, 66,* 318–324. [11]

Brandt, L. W. (1970). The behaviorist's leap: An inquiry into what attitude researchers measure. *Journal of Social Issues, 52,* 163–166. [5]

Breckler, S. J., & Greenwald, A. G. (1986). Motivational facets of the self. In R. M. Sorrentino & E. T. Higgins (Eds.), *Handbook of motivation and cognition: Foundations of social behavior* (pp. 145–164). New York: Guilford. [9]

Brehm, J. W., & Cohen, A. R. (1962). *Explorations in cognitive dissonance.* New York: Wiley. [18]

Brehm, S. S. (1985). *Intimate relationships.* New York: Random House. [18]

Brewer, M. B. (1979). In-group bias in the minimal intergroup situation: A cognitive-motivational analysis. *Psychological Bulletin, 86,* 307–324. [26]

Brickman, P. (1978). Is it real? In J. H. Harvey, W. J. Ickes, & R. Kidd (Eds.), *New directions in attribution research* (Vol. 2). Hillsdale, NJ: Erlbaum. [17]

Brickman, P., & Janoff-Bulman, R. (1977). Pleasure and pain in social comparison. In J. M. Suls & R. L. K. Miller (Eds.), *Social comparison processes* (pp. 149–186). Washington, DC: Hemisphere. [9]

Brickner, M., Harkins, S., & Ostrom, T. (1986). Personal involvement: Thought provoking implications for social loafing. *Journal of Personality and Social Psychology, 51,* 763–769. [39]

Briggs, N. (1974). *Women in apprenticeship—Why not?* (Manpower Research Monograph No. 33). Washington, DC: U.S. Government Printing Office. [30]

Brislin, R. N., & Olmstead, K. H. (1973). An examination of two models designed to predict behavior from attitude and other verbal measures. *Proceedings of the 81st Annual Convention of the American Psychological Association, 8,* 259–260. [5]

Brislin, R. W., & Lewis, S. A. (1968). Dating and physical attractiveness: A replication. *Psychological Reports, 22,* 976. [16]

Brock, T. C., & Shavitt, S. (1983). Cognitive response analysis in advertising. In L. Percy & A. Woodside (Eds.), *Advertising and consumer psychology.* Lexington, MA: Lexington Books. [36]

Brodyaga, L., Gates, M., Singer, S., Tucker, M., & White, R. (1975). *Rape and its victims: A report for citizens, health facilities, and criminal justice agencies* (National Institute of Law Enforcement and Criminal Justice, Law Enforcement Assistance Administration, U.S. Department of Justice). Washington, DC: U.S. Government Printing Office. [17], [29]

Brotman, H. (1974). The fastest growing minority: The aging. *American Journal of Public Health, 64,* 249–252. [27]

Broverman, I. K., Vogel, S. R., Broverman, D. M., Clarkson, F. E., & Rosenkrantz, P. S. (1972). Sex-role stereotypes: A current appraisal. *Journal of Social Issues, 28,* 59–78. [30], [32]

Brown v. Board of Education, 347 U.S. 483 (1954). [RI-25]

Brown, J. F. (1933). Über die dynamichem Eigenschaften der Realitäts- und Irrealitätsschichten. *Psychologische Forschung, 18,* 1–26. [3]

Brown, J. F. (1936). *Psychology and the social order.* New York: McGraw-Hill. [3]

Brownmiller, S. (1975). *Against our will: Men, women, and rape.* New York: Simon & Schuster. [29]

Bruner, J. (1986). *Actual minds, possible worlds.* New York: Plenum. [9]

Bryant, J., Carveth, R. A., & Brown, D. (1981). Television viewing and anxiety: An experimental examination. *Journal of Communication, 31*(1), 106–119. [23]

Buck, R., Miller, R., & Caul, W. F. (1974). Sex, personality, and physiological variables in the communication of affect via facial expression. *Journal of Personality and Social Psychology, 30,* 587–596. [17]

Buck, R., Savin, V. J., Miller, R., & Caul, W. F. (1972). Nonverbal communication of affect in humans. *Journal of Personality and Social Psychology, 23,* 362–371. [8]

Burgess, A. W., & Holmstrom, L. L. (1974). *Rape: Victims of crisis.* Bowie, MD: Robert J. Brady. [29]

Burke, P. J. (1980). The self: Measurement requirements from an interactionist perspective. *Psychology Quarterly, 43,* 18–29. [9]

Burks, B. S. (1940). Mental and physical developmental patterns of identical twins in relation to organismic growth theory. *Yearbook of National Social Studies Education, 39,* 85–96. [3]

Burnham, W. H. (1924). *The normal mind.* New York: Appleton. [4]

Burnkrant, R. E. (1976). A motivational model of information processing intensity. *Journal of Consumer Research, 3,* 21–30. [36]

Burnkrant, R. E., & Sawyer, A. G. (1983). Effects of involvement and message content on information processing intensity. In R. Harris (Ed.), *Information processing research in advertising.* Hillsdale, NJ: Erlbaum. [36]

Buss, A. (1961). *The psychology of aggression.* New York: Wiley. [35]

Buss, A. H., Booker, A., & Buss, E. (1972). Firing a weapon and aggression. *Journal of Personality and Social Psychology, 22.* 196–202. [15]

Butler, R. (1970). Myths and realities of clinical geriatrics. *Image and Commentary, 12,* 26–29. [27]

Bühler, C. (1939). *The child and his family.* New York: Harper. [3]

Cacioppo, J. T., & Petty, R. E. (1979). Effects of message repetition and position on cognitive responses, recall, and persuasion. *Journal of Personality and Social Psychology, 37,* 97–109. [36]

Cacioppo, J. T., & Petty, R. E. (1980a). Persuasiveness of communications is affected by exposure frequency and message quality: A theoretical and empirical analysis of persisting attitude change. In J. H. Leigh & C. R. Martin (Eds.), *Current issues and research in advertising* (pp. 97–122). Ann Arbor: University of Michigan. [36]

Cacioppo, J. T., & Petty, R. E. (1980b). Sex differences in influenceability: Toward specifying the underlying processes. *Personality and Social Psychology Bulletin, 6,* 651–656. [36]

Cacioppo, J. T., & Petty, R. E. (1981). Social psychological procedures for cognitive response assessment: The thought listing technique. In T. V. Merluzzi, C. R. Glass, & M. Genest (Eds.), *Cog-*

nitive assessment (pp. 309–342). New York: Guilford Press. [36]

Cacioppo, J. T., & Petty, R. E. (1982). The need for cognition. *Journal of Personality and Social Psychology, 42,* 116–131. [36]

Cacioppo, J. T., & Petty, R. E. (1984). The need for cognition: Relationships to social influence and self influence. In R. P. McGlynn, J. E. Maddux, C. D. Stoltenberg, & J. Harvey (Eds.), *Social perception in clinical and counseling psychology.* Lubbock: Texas Tech Press. [36]

Calder, B. J., & Ross, M. (1973). *Attitudes and behavior.* Morristown, NJ: General Learning Press. [5]

Calvin, A., Hanley, C., Hoffman, F., & Clifford, L. (1959). An experimental investigation of the "pull" effect. *Journal of Social Psychology, 49,* 275–283. [11]

Cameron, N. W. (1950). Role concepts in behavior pathology. *American Journal of Sociology, 55,* 464–467. [8]

Cameron, N. W., & Margaret, A. (1951). *Behavior pathology.* Boston: Houghton Mifflin. [11]

Campbell, A. (1971). *White attitudes toward black people.* Ann Arbor, MI: Institute for Social Research. [26]

Campbell, D. J. (1960). Recommendations for APA test standards regarding construct, trait, and discriminant validity. *American Psychologist, 15,* 546–553. [8]

Campbell, D. J., & Fiske, D. W. (1959). Convergent and discriminant validation by the multitrait-multimethod matrix. *Psychological Bulletin, 56,* 81–105. [8]

Cane, D. B., & Gotlib, I. H. (1985). Implicit conceptualizations of depression: Implications for an interpersonal perspective. *Social Cognition, 3,* 341–368. [18]

Cannon, W. B. (1929). *Bodily changes in pain, hunger, fear, and rage.* (2nd ed.). New York: Appleton. [14]

Cantor, N., & Kihlstrom, J. (Eds.) (1986). *Personality and social intelligence.* Englewood Cliffs, NJ: Prentice-Hall. [9]

Cantor, N., & Mischel, W. (1977) Traits as prototypes: Effects on recognition memory. *Journal of Personality and Social Psychology, 35,* 38–48. [18]

Cantor, N., & Mischel, W. (1979). Prototypicality and personality: Effects on free recall and personality impressions. *Journal of Research in Personality, 13,* 187–205. [18]

Cantor, N., Niedenthal, P., & Brower, A. (1985). *Life task problem-solving in the transition to college.* Presented at the Annual Meeting of the Society of Experimental Social Psychology, Evanston, IL. [9]

Cantril, H. (1932). General and specific attitudes. *Psychological Monographs, 42,* 109. [4]

Cantril, H. (1934a). Attitudes in the making. *Understanding the Child, 4,* 13–15. [4]

Cantril, H. (1934b). The social psychology of everyday life. *Psychological Bulletin, 31,* 297–330. [4]

Cantril, H. (1941). *The psychology of social movements.* New York: Wiley. [38]

Cantril, H. (1950). *The "why" of man's experience.* New York: Macmillan. [10]

Cantril, H., & Allport, G. W. (1933). Recent applications of the study of values. *Journal of Abnormal and Social Psychology, 28,* 259–273. [4]

Cantril, H., & Hunt, W. A. (1932). Emotional effects produced by the injection of adrenalin. *American Journal of Psychology, 44,* 300–307. [14]

Cantwell, P. (1985). Understanding bulimia. *Contemporary Psychology, 30,* 196–198. [38]

Caplovitz, L., & Rodin, J. (1980). Unpublished data. Yale University, Department of Psychology, New Haven, CT. [27]

Carlsmith, J. M., & Anderson, C. A. (1979). Ambient temperature and the occurrence of collective violence: A new analysis. *Journal of Personality and Social Psychology, 37,* 337–344. [21]

Carlston, D. E. (1980). Events, inferences, and impression formation. In R. Hastie, T. M. Ostrom, E. B. Ebbesen, R. S. Wyer, Jr., D. L. Hamilton, & D. E. Carlston (Eds.), *Person memory: The cognitive basis of social perception* (pp. 89–119). Hillsdale, NJ: Erlbaum. [12]

Carr, L., & Roberts, S. O. (1965). Correlates of civil rights participation. *Journal of Social Psychology, 67,* 259–267. [5]

Cartwright, S. (Ed.). (1959). *Studies in social power.* Ann Arbor: University of Michigan Institute for Social Research. [35]

Carver, C. S. (1974). Facilitation of physical aggression through objective self-awareness. *Journal of Experimental Social Psychology, 10,* 365–370. [37]

Carver, C. S. (1975). Physical aggression as a function of objective self-awareness and attitudes toward punishment. *Journal of Experimental Social Psychology, 11,* 510–519. [37]

Carver, C. S., & Scheier, M. F. (1981). *Attention and self-regulation: A control theory approach to human behavior.* New York: Springer-Verlag. [9]

Carver, C. S., & Scheier, M. F. (1981). The self-attention-induced feedback loop and social facilitation. *Journal of Experimental Social Psychology, 17,* 545–568. [39]

Cattell, R. B. (1944). Projection and the design of projective tests of personality. *Character and Personality, 12,* 177–194. [11]

Centers, R. (1975). *Sexual attraction and love.* Springfield, IL: Charles C. Thomas. [18]

Chafetz, M. E. (1970). No patient deserves to be patronized. *Medical Insight, 2,* 68–75. [33]

Chaiken, S. (1980). Heuristic versus systematic information processing and the use of source versus message cues in persuasion. *Journal of Personality and Social Psychology, 39,* 752–766. [36]

Chapman, D. W. (1932). Relative effects of determinate and indeterminate Aufgaben. *American Journal of Psychology, 44,* 163–174. [4]

Chapman, L., & Chapman, J. (1967). The genesis of popular but erroneous psychodiagnostic observations. *Journal of Abnormal Psychology, 72,* 193–204. [32]

Chapman, L., & Chapman, J. (1969). Illusory correlations as an obstacle to the use of valid psychodiagnostic signs. *Journal of Abnormal Psychology, 74,* 271–280. [32], [RI-11]

Chappell, D. (1971). Forcible rape: A comparative study of offenses known to police in Boston and Los Angeles. In J. M. Henslin (Ed.), *Studies in the sociology of sex.* New York: Appleton-Century-Crofts. [29]

Charcot, J. M. (1881). *Oeuvres complètes.* Paris: Bureaux du Progrès Médical. [35]

Charry, J. M., & Hawkinshire, F. B. W. (1981). Effects of atmospheric electricity on some substrates of disordered social behavior. *Journal of Personality and Social Psychology, 41,* 185–197. [21]

Chave, E. J. (1928). A new type scale for measuring attitudes. *Relational Education, 23,* 364–369. [4]

Chein, I. (1972). *The science of behavior and the image of man.* New York: Basic Books. [15]

Chen, W. K. C. (1933). The influence of oral propaganda material upon students' attitudes. *Archives of Psychology, 44,* 163–174. [4]

Chestnut, R. W., LaChance, C. C., & Lubitz, A. (1977). The decorative female model: Sexual stimuli and the recognition of advertisements. *Journal of Advertising Research, 6,* 11–14. [36]

Christie, R., & Geis, F. L. (1970) *Studies in Machiavellianism.* New York: Academic Press. [8]

Cialdini, R. B., Petty, R. E., & Cacioppo, J. T. (1981). Attitude and attitude change. *Annual Review of Psychology, 32,* 357–404. [36]

Clark, K. B., & Clark, M. P. (1958). Racial identification and preference in Negro children. In T. M. Newcomb & E. L. Hartley (Eds.), *Readings in social psychology* (pp. 551–560). New York: Holt. [RI-25]

Clarke, H. M. (1911). Conscious attitudes. *American Journal of Psychology, 32,* 214–249. [4]

Cleaver, E. (1968). *Soul on ice.* New York: Dell-Delta/Ramparts. [29]

Cobb, B. (1954). Why do people detour to quacks? *The Psychiatric Bulletin, 3,* 66–69. [33]

Cohen, E. G. (1984). The desegregated school: Problems in status power and interethnic climate. In N. Miller & M. B. Brewer (Eds.), *Groups in contact: The psychology of desegregation* (pp. 77–95). Orlando, FL: Academic Press. [RI-26]

Cohen, J., & Cohen, P. (1975). *Applied multiple regression/correlation analysis for the behavioral sciences.* New York: Wiley. [6], [12], [21]

Cohen, M. L., Garofalo, R., Boucher, R., & Seghorn, T. (1971, Aug.). The psychology of rapists. *Seminars in Psychiatry, 3,* 317. [29]

Coleman, L. M., & Antonucci, T. C. (1983). Impact of work on women at midlife. *Developmental Psychology, 19,* 290–294. [9]

Constaninople, A. (1973). Masculinity-femininity: An exception to a famous dictum? *Psychological Bulletin, 80,* 389–407. [30]

Cook, S. W., & Selltiz, C. A. (1964). A multiple-indicator approach to attitude measurement. *Psychological Bulletin, 62,* 36–55. [5]

Cooley, C. H. (1902). *Human nature and the social order.* New York: Scribner. [9]

Coombs, R. H., & Kenkel, W. F. (1966). Sex differences in dating aspirations and satisfaction with computer-selected partners. *Journal of Marriage and the Family, 28,* 62–66. [16]

Cooper, J., & Fazio, R. H. (1984). A new look at dissonance theory. In L. Berkowitz (Ed.), *Advances in experimental social psychology* (Vol. 17) (pp. 229–266). New York: Academic Press. [RI-6]

Cooper, J., Jones, E. E., & Tuller, S. M. (1972). Attribution, dissonance, and the illusion of uniqueness. *Journal of Experimental Social Psychology, 8,* 45–47. [11]

Cooper, J., & Worchel, S. (1970). Role of undesired consequences in arousing cognitive dissonance. *Journal of Personality and Social Psychology, 16,* 199–206. [6]

Cooper, J., Zanna, M. P., & Taves, P. A. (1975). *On the necessity of arousal for attitude change in the induced compliance paradigm.* Unpublished manuscript, Princeton University. [6]

Costello, C. G. (1976). *Anxiety and depression: The adaptive emotions.* Montreal: McGill-Queen's University Press. [15]

Cottrell, N. (1972). Social facilitation. In C. McClintock (Ed.), *Experimental Social Psychology* (pp. 185–236). New York: Holt, Rinehart & Winston. [39]

Cox, O. C. (1948). *Caste, class, and race.* New York: Doubleday. [25]

Crago, M., Yates, A., Beutler, L. E., & Arizmendi, T. G. (1985). Height-weight ratios among female athletes: Are collegiate athletics the precursor to an anorexic syndrome? *International Journal of Eating Disorders, 4,* 79–87. [38]

Craik, F. G., & Lockhart, R. (1972). Levels of processing: A framework for memory research. *Journal of Verbal Learning and Verbal Behavior, 11,* 671–684. [36]

Crandall, C. S. (1987). Do men and women differ in emotional and ego involvement with food? *Journal of Nutrition Education, 19,* 229–236. [38]

Crespi, I. (1971). What kinds of attitude measures are predictive of behavior? *Public Opinion Quarterly, 35,* 327–334. [5]

Cronbach, L. J. (1951). Coefficient alpha and the internal structure of tests. *Psychometrika, 16,* 297–334. [5]

Cronbach, L. J., & Meehl, P. E. (1955). Construct validity in psychological tests. *Psychological Bulletin, 52,* 281–302. [8]

Crosby, F., Bromley, S., & Saxe, L. (1980). Recent unobtrusive studies of black and white discrimination and prejudice: A literature review. *Psychological Bulletin, 87,* 546–563. [26]

Crowne, D. P., & Marlowe, D. (1964). *The approval motive*. New York: Wiley. [8], [27]

Crutchfield, R. (1955). Conformity and character. *American Psychologist, 10,* 191–198. [RI-34]

Csikszentmihalyi, M. (1975). *Beyond boredom and anxiety*. San Francisco: Jossey-Bass. [9]

Cumming, E., Dean, L., Newell, D., & McCaffrey, I. (1960). Disengagement: A tentative theory of aging. *Sociometry, 23,* 23–35. [27]

Cummings, W., & Venkatesan, M. (1976). Cognitive dissonance and consumer behavior: A review of the evidence. *Journal of Marketing Research, 13,* 303–308. [36]

Cunningham, J. D., & Antill, J. K. (1981). Love in developing romantic relationships. In S. Duck & R. Gilmour (Eds.), *Personal relationships. 2: Developing personal relationships* (pp. 27–51). London: Academic Press. [18]

Cunningham, M. R. (1979). Weather, mood, and helping behavior: Quasi experiments with the sunshine Samaritan. *Journal of Personality and Social Psychology, 37,* 1947–1956. [21]

Dahlgren, K. (1985). The cognitive structure of social categories. *Cognitive Science, 9,* 379–398. [18]

Darley, J. M., & Fazio, R. H. (1980). Expectancy confirmation processes arising in the social interaction sequence. *American Psychologist, 35,* 867–881. [9]

Darley, J. M., Fleming, J. H., Hilton, J. L., & Swann, W. B., Jr. (1986). *Dispelling negative expectancies: The impact of interaction goals and target characteristics on the expectancy confirmation process.* Unpublished manuscript, Princeton University. [9]

Darley, J. M., & Latané, B. (1968). Bystander intervention in emergencies: Diffusion of responsibility. *Journal of Personality and Social Psychology, 8,* 377–383. [26], [31]

Dashiell, J. (1935). Experimental studies of the influence of social situations on the behavior of individual human adults. In C. Murchison (Ed.), *Handbook of social psychology* (pp. 1097–1158). Worcester, MA: Clark University. [39]

Davidson, A. R., & Jaccard, J. J. (1975). Population psychology: A new look at an old problem. *Journal of Personality and Social Psychology, 31,* 1073–1082. [5]

Davis, A. (1975, June). Joanne Little: The dialectics of rape. *Ms., 3,* p. 106. [29]

Davis, A. J. (1970). Sexual assaults in the Philadelphia prison system. In J. A. Gagnon & W. Simon (Eds.), *The sexual scene* (pp. 122–123). Chicago: Aldine. [29]

Davis, J. (1930). A study of one hundred and sixty-three outstanding communist leaders: Studies in quantitative and cultural sociology. *Proceedings of the American Sociological Society, 24,* 42–55. [4]

Davis, J. (1969). *Group performance*. Reading, MA: Addison-Wesley. [39]

Davis, K. E. (1985). Near and dear: Friendship and love compared. *Psychology Today, 19,* 22–30. [RI-18]

Davis, L. J. (1977). Attitudes toward old age and aging as shown by humor. *Gerontologist, 17,* 220–226. [27]

Davis, M. S. (1966). Variations in patients' compliance with doctors' orders: Analyses of congruence between survey responses and results of empirical investigations. *Journal of Medical Education, 41,* 1037–1048. [33]

Davis, M. S. (1968a). Physiologic, psychological, and demographic factors in patient compliance with doctors' orders. *Medical Care, 6,* 115–122. [33]

Davis, M. S. (1968b). Variations in patients' compliance with doctors' advice: An empirical analysis of patterns of communication. *American Journal of Public Health, 58,* 274–288. [33]

Davitz, J. R. (Ed.) (1964). *The communication of emotional meaning*. New York: McGraw-Hill. [8]

de Beauvoir, S. (1972). *The coming of age*. New York: Warner Paperback Library. [27]

Dean, D. G., & Spanier, G. B. (1974). Commitment—an overlooked variable in marital adjustment? *Sociological Focus, 7,* 113–118. [18]

Deaux, K. (1976). Sex: A perspective on the attribution process. In J. H. Harvey, W. J. Ickes, & R. F. Kidd (Eds.), *New Directions in attribution research, Vol. 1* (pp. 335–352). Hillsdale, NJ: Erlbaum. [30]

Deaux, K. (1977). Sex differences. In T. Blass (Ed.), *Personality variables in social behavior* (pp. 357–377). Hillsdale, NJ: Erlbaum. [30]

Deaux, K. (1979). Self-evaluation of male and female managers. *Sex Roles, 5,* 571–580. [30]

Deaux, K., & Emswiller, T. (1974). Explanations for successful performance on sex-linked tasks: What is skill for the male is luck for the female. *Journal of Personality and Social Psychology, 29,* 80–85. [30]

Deaux, K., & Farris, E. (1977). Attributing causes for one's own performance: The effects of sex, norms, and outcome. *Journal of Research in Personality, 32, 629–636.* [30]

Deaux, K., & Lewis, L. L. (1983). Assessment of gender stereotypes: Methodology and components. *Psychological Documents, 13,* 25. (Ms. No. 2583). [30]

Deaux, K., & Major, B. (1987). Putting gender into context: An interactive model of gender behavior. *Psychological Review, 94,* 369–389. [RI-30]

Deaux, K., & Major, B. (1990). A social psychological model of gender. In D. Rhode (Ed.), *Theoretical perspectives on sexual difference.* New Haven, CT: Yale University Press. [RI-30]

Deaux, K., & Taynor, J. (1973). Evaluation of male and female ability: Bias works two ways. *Psychological Reports, 32,* 261–262. [30]

Deaux, K., & Ullman, J. C. (1983). *Woman of steel.* New York: Praeger. [30]

Deaux, K., White, L., & Farris, E. (1975). Skill versus luck: Field and laboratory studies of male and female preferences. *Journal of Personality and Social Psychology, 32,* 629–636. [30]

Deci, E. L. (1971). Effects of externally mediated rewards on intrinsic motivation. *Journal of Personality and Social Psychology, 18,* 105–115. [6]

Deikman, A. J. (1966). Deautomatization and the mystic experience. *Psychiatry, 29,* 324–338. [15]

De Jong, J. P. B. de Josselin. (1952). *Levi-Strauss's theory on kinship and marriage.* Leiden, Holland: Rijksmusuem voor Volkenkunde. [16]

De Jong, W., & Kleck, R. E. (1986). The social psychological effects of overweight. In C. P. Herman, M. P. Zanna, & E. T. Higgins (Eds.), *Physical appearance, stigma, and social behavior: The Ontario Symposium* (Vol. 3). Hillsdale, NJ: Erlbaum. [RI-38]

Dembo, T. (1931). Der Ärger als dynamisches Problem. *Psychologische Forschung, 15,* 1–144. [3]

Dennett, D. (1982). Why do we think what we do about why we think what we do? *Cognition, 12,* 219–237. [9]

Dermer, M. (1973). *When beauty fails.* Unpublished doctoral dissertation, University of Minnesota. [32]

Derry, P. A., Kuiper, N. A. (1981). Schematic processing and self-reference in clinical depression. *Journal of Abnormal Psychology, 90,* 286–297. [9]

Deutsch, M. (1968). Field theory. In G. Lindzey & E. Aronson (Eds.), *Handbook of social psychology* (pp. 412–487) (2nd ed.). Reading, MA: Addison-Wesley. [RI-3]

Deutscher, I. (1966). Words and deeds: Social science and social policy. *Social Problems, 13,* 235–265. [5]

Dewey, J. (1894). The theory of emotion. I: Emotional attitudes. *Psychological Review, 1,* 553–569. [15]

Dewey, J. (1895). The theory of emotion. II: The significance of emotions. *Psychological Review, 2,* 13–32. [15]

Dewey, J. (1917). The need for social psychology. *Psychological Review, 24,* 266–277. [4]

Dewey, J. (1922). *Human nature and conduct.* New York: Holt. [4]

Diener, E. (1979). Deindividuation, self-awareness, and disinhibition. *Journal of Personality and Social Psychology, 37,* 1160–1171. [37]

Diener, E., Dineen, J., Westford, K., Beaman, A. L., & Fraser, S. C. (1975). Effects of altered responsibility, cognitive set, and modeling on physical aggression and deindividuation. *Journal of Personality and Social Psychology, 31,* 328–337. [37]

Dienstbier, R. (1978). Attribution, socialization, and moral decision making. In J. H. Harvey, W. Ickes, & R. F. Kidd (Eds.), *New Directions in Attribution Research* (Vol. 2). Hillsdale, NJ: Erlbaum. [15]

Dillehay, R. C. (1973). On the irrelevance of the classical negative evidence concerning the effect of attitudes on behavior. *American Psychologist, 28,* 887–893. [5]

DiMatteo, M. R., & Hall, J. A. (1979). Nonverbal decoding skill and attention to nonverbal cues: A research note. *Environmental Psychology and Nonverbal Behavior, 3,* 188–192. [33]

DiMatteo, M. R., Prince, L. M., & Taranta, A. (1979). Patients' perceptions of physicians' behavior: Determinants of patient commitment to the therapeutic relationship. *Journal of Community Health, 4,* 280–290. [33]

Dimock, H. S. (1937). *Rediscovering the adolescent.* New York: Association Press. [3]

Dion, K. K., & Berschied, E. (1974). Physical attractiveness and peer perception among children. *Sociometry, 27*(1), 1–12. [32]

Dion, K. K., Berschied, E., & Walster, E. (1972). What is beautiful is good. *Journal of Personality and Social Psychology, 24,* 285–290. [32]

Dion, K. K., & Dion, K. L. (1985). Personality, gender and the phenomonology of romantic love. In P. Shaver (Ed.), *Review of personality and social psychology* (Vol. 6, pp. 209–239). Beverly Hills, CA: Sage. [18], [RI-18]

Dion, K. L., & Dion, K. K. (1976). Love, liking, and trust in heterosexual relationships. *Personality and Social Psychology Bulletin, 2,* 187–190. [18]

Dockeray, D. C. (1932). *General psychology.* New York: Prentice-Hall. [4]

Dodge, R. (1920). The psychology of propaganda. *Relational Education, 15,* 241–252. [4]

Doise, W., Csepeli, G., Dann, H., Gouge, C., Larsen, K., & Ostell, A. (1972). An experimental investigation into the formation of intergroup relations. *European Journal of Social Psychology, 2,* 202–204. [26]

Dollard, J. (1937). *Caste and class in a southern town.* New Haven: Yale University Press. [3]

Dollard, J., Doob, L. W., Miller, N. E., Mowrer, O. H., & Sears, R. R. (1939). *Frustration and aggression.* New Haven: Yale University Press. [RI-20]

Donnerstein, E., & Berkowitz, L. (1981). Victim reactions in aggressive erotic films as a factor in violence against women. *Journal of Personality and Social Psychology, 41,* 710–724. [RI-29]

Doob, A. N., & Macdonald, G. E. (1979). Television viewing and fear of victimization: Is the relationship causal? *Journal of Personality and Social Psychology, 37,* 170–179. [23]

Doob, L. W. (1934). *Psychological factors in propaganda* (unpublished). Cambridge, MA: Harvard University Library. [4]

Doob, L. W. (1947). The behavior of attitudes. *Psychological Review, 54,* 135–156. [5]

Dovidio, J. F. (1984). *Attributions of positive and negative characteristics to blacks and whites.* Unpublished manuscript, Colgate University, Department of Psychology, Hamilton, NY. [26]

Dovidio, J. F., Evans, N., & Tyler, R. (1984). *Racial stereotypes as prototypes.* Unpublished manuscript, Colgate University, Department of Psychology, Hamilton, NY. [26]

Dovidio, J. F., & Gaertner, S. L. (1981). The effects of race, status, and ability on helping behavior. *Social Psychology Quarterly, 44,* 192–203. [26]

Dovidio, J. F., & Gaertner, S. L. (1983a). Race, normative structure, and help-seeking. In B. M. DePaulo, A. Nadler, & J. D. Fisher (Eds.), *New directions in helping, Vol. 2, Help-seeking* (pp. 285–302). New York: Academic Press. [26]

Dovidio, J. F., & Gaertner, S. L. (1983b). The effects of sex, status, and ability on helping be-

havior. *Journal of Applied Social Psychology, 13,* 191–205. [26]

Dovidio, J. F., Tannebaum, S., & Ellyson, S. L. (1984, April). *The irrationality of prejudice: Logical reasoning about blacks and whites.* Paper presented at the annual meeting of the Eastern Psychological Association, Baltimore, MD. [26]

Doyle, B. J., & Ware, J. E. (1977). Physician conduct and other factors that affect consumer satisfaction with medical care. *Journal of Medical Education, 52,* 793–801. [33]

Droba, D. D. (1932). Methods for measuring attitudes. *Psychological Bulletin, 29,* 309–323. [4]

Droba, D. D. (1933). The nature of attitude. *American Journal of Social Psychology, 4,* 444–463. [4]

Droba, D. D. (1934a). Social attitudes. *American Journal of Sociology, 39,* 513–524. [4]

Droba, D. D. (1934b). Political parties and war attitudes. *Journal of Abnormal and Social Psychology, 28,* 468–472. [4]

Duck, S. (1982). A topography of relationship disengagement and dissolution. In S. Duck (Ed.), *Personal relationships. 4: Dissolving personal relationships* (pp. 1–30). London: Academic Press. [18]

Dunlap, K. (1932). *Habits: Their making and unmaking.* New York: Liveright. [4]

Dunn, O. K., & Ondercin, P. (1981). Personality variables related to compulsive eating in college women. *Journal of Clinical Psychology, 37,* 43–49. [38]

Dutton, D. G., & Lake, R. A. (1973). Threat of own prejudice and reverse discrimination in interracial situations. *Journal of Personality and Social Psychology, 28,* 94–100. [26]

Dutton, D. G., & Lennox, V. L. (1974). Effect of prior "token" compliance on subsequent interracial behavior. *Journal of Personality and Social Psychology, 29,* 65–71. [26]

Duval, S., & Wicklund, R. A. (1972). *A theory of objective self-awareness.* New York: Academic Press. [37]

Dwyer, J., Feldman, J. J., & Mayer, J. (1970). The social psychology of dieting. *Journal of Health and Social Behavior, 11,* 269–287. [38]

Eagly, A. H. (1978). Sex differences in influenceability. *Psychological Bulletin, 85,* 86–116. [36]

Eagly, A. H. (1983). Gender and social influence: A social psychological analysis. *American Psychologist, 38,* 971–981. [RI-34]

Eagly, A. H., & Carli, L. L. (1981). Sex of researcher and sex-typed communications as determinants of sex differences in influenceability: A meta-analysis of social influence studies. *Psychological Bulletin, 90*, 1–20. [RI-34]

Eagly, A. H., & Wood, W. (1982). Inferred sex differences in status as a determinant of gender stereotypes about social influence. *Journal of Personality and Social Psychology, 43*, 915–928. [30]

Ebel, R. L. (1951). Estimation of the reliability of ratings. *Psychometrika, 16*, 407–424. [32]

Edlow, D., & Kiesler, C. (1966). Ease of denial and defensive projection. *Journal of Experimental Social Psychology, 2*, 56–69. [11]

Egbert, L. D., Battit, G. E., Welch, C. E., & Bartlett, M. K. (1964). Reduction of postoperative pain by encouragement and instruction of patients: A study of doctor-patient rapport. *New England Journal of Medicine, 270*, 825–827. [33]

Ehrlich, H. J. (1969). Attitudes, behavior and the intervening variables. *American Sociologist, 4*, 29–34. [5]

Einstein, A. (1933). *On the method of theoretical physics.* New York: Oxford University Press. [3]

Eisenberg, L. (1977). The search for care. *Daedalus, 106*, 235–246. [33]

Ekman, P. (1971). Universals and cultural differences in facial expressions of emotion. In J. Cole (Ed.), *Nebraska Symposium on Motivation: 1971.* Lincoln: University of Nebraska Press. [8]

Ekman, P., & Friesen, W. V. (1969). Nonverbal leakage and clues to deception. *Psychiatry, 32*, 88–105. [8], [33]

Ekman, P., & Friesen, W. V. (1972). *Judging deception from the face or body.* Paper presented at the meeting of the Western Psychological Association, Portland, Oregon. [8]

Ekman, P., & Friesen, W. V. (1974). Detecting deception from the body or face. *Journal of Personality and Social Psychology, 29*, 288–298. [8]

Ekman, P., Levenson, R. W., & Friesen, W. V. (1983). Autonomic nervous system activity distinguishes among emotions. *Science, 221*, 1208–1210. [RI-13]

Elder, G. H. (1969). Appearance and education in marriage mobility. *American Sociological Review, 34*, 519–532. [16]

Elms, A. (1972). *Social psychology and social relevance.* Boston: Little, Brown. [RI-35]

Engel, G. L. (1977). The care of the patient: Art or science? *The Johns Hopkins Medical Journal, 140*, 222–232. [33]

Engel, J. F., & Blackwell, R. D. (1982). *Consumer behavior.* Hinsdale, IL: Dryden Press. [36]

Enzle, M. E., & Harvey, M. D. (1977). Effects of third-party requestor's surveillance and recipient awareness of request on helping. *Personality and Social Psychology Bulletin, 3*, 421–424. [26]

Enzle, M. E., & Schopflocher, D. (1978). Instigation of attribution processes by attributional questions. *Personality and Social Psychology Bulletin, 4*, 595–599. [12]

Epstein, S. (1980). The self-concept: A review and the proposal of an integrated theory of personality. In E. Staub (Ed.), *Personality: Basic issues and current research.* Englewood Cliffs, NJ: Prentice-Hall. [9]

Erikson, E. H. (1940). Studies in the interpretation of play: I. Clinical observation of play disruption in young children. *Genetic Psychology Monographs, 22*, 556–671. [3]

Erikson, E. H. (1950). Identification as the basis for a theory of motivation. *American Psychological Review, 26*, 14–21. [9]

Erikson, E. H. (1963). *Childhood and society* (2nd ed.). New York: Norton. [18]

Ewer, B. C. (1929). *Social psychology.* New York: Macmillan. [4]

Fajans, S. (1933). Erfolg, Ausdauer, und Activität beim Saügling und Kleinkind. *Psychologische Forschung, 17*, 368–305. [3]

Faranda, J. A., & Gaertner, S. L. (1979, April). *The effect of inadmissible evidence introduced by the prosecution and the defense, and the defendant's race on the verdicts of high and low authoritarians.* Paper presented at the annual meeting of the Eastern Psychological Association, New York. [26]

Faris, E. (1932). The concept of social attitudes. *Journal of Applied Sociology, 9*, 404–409. [4]

Farley, L. (1978). *Sexual shakedown.* New York: Warner. [29]

Fast, I. (1985). *Event theory: A Piaget-Freud integration.* Hillsdale, NJ: Erlbaum. [9]

Fauls, L. B., & Smith, W. D. (1956). Sex-role learning of five-year olds. *Journal of Genetic Psychology, 89*, 105–117. [20]

Fazio, R. H., Effrein, E. A., & Falender, V. J. (1981). Self-perceptions following social interaction. *Jour-*

nal of Personality and Social Psychology, *41*, 232–242. [9]

Feagin, J. R., & Feagin, L. B. (1978). *Discrimination American style: Institutional racism and sexism.* Englewood Cliffs, NJ: Prentice-Hall. [26]

Fearing, F. (1931). The experimental study of attitude, meaning, and the process antecedent to action by N. Ach and others in the Würzburg laboratory. In S. Rice (Ed.), *Methods in social science.* Chicago: University of Chicago Press. [4]

Feather, N. T., & Simon, J. G. (1973). Fear of success and causal attributions for outcome. *Journal of Personality, 41*, 525–542. [30]

Federal Bureau of Investigation (1981). *Uniform crimes reports for the United States.* Washington, DC: U.S. Government Printing Office. [29]

Fehr, B. (1986). *A prototype analysis of the concepts of love and commitment.* Unpublished doctoral dissertation, University of British Columbia, Vancouver. [18]

Fehr, B., & Russell, J. A. (1984). Concept of emotion viewed from a prototype perspective. *Journal of Experimental Psychology: General, 113*, 464–486. [18]

Fendrich, J. M. (1967). A study of the association among verbal attitudes, commitment, and overt behavior in different experimental situations. *Social Forces, 45*, 347–355. [5]

Féré, C. (1890). Note sur la physiologie de l'attention. *Revue Philosophique, 30*, 393–405. [4]

Festinger, L. (1950). Informal social communication. *Psychological Review, 57*, 271–292. [38]

Festinger, L. (1954). A theory of social comparison processes. *Human Relations, 7*, 114–140. [14], [38]

Festinger, L. (1957). *A theory of cognitive dissonance.* Stanford, CA: Stanford University Press. [6]

Festinger, L., Pepitone, S., & Newcomb, T. (1952). Some consequences of de-individuation in a group. *Journal of Abnormal and Social Psychology, 47*, 382–389. [37], [RI-37]

Festinger, L., Schachter, S., & Back, K. W. (1950). *Social pressures in informal groups.* New York: Harper. [38], [RI-38]

Field, H. E. (1931). The attitudes of prisoners as a factor in rehabilitation. *Annals of the American Academy of Political Science, 157*, 2484. [4]

Fishbein, M. (1966). The relationship between beliefs, attitudes, and behavior. In S. Feldman (Ed.), *Cognitive consistency.* New York: Academic Press. [5]

Fishbein, M. (1967). Attitude and the prediction of behavior. In M. Fishbein (Ed.), *Readings in attitude theory and measurement.* New York: Wiley. [5]

Fishbein, M. (1973). The prediction of behaviors from attitudinal variables. In C. D. Mortensen & K. K. Sereno (Eds.), *Advances in communication research.* New York: Harper & Row. [5]

Fishbein, M., & Ajzen, I. (1974). Attitudes toward objects as predictors of single and multiple behavioral criteria. *Psychological Review, 81*, 59–74. [5]

Fishbein, M. & Ajzen, I. (1981). Acceptance, yielding, and impact: Cognitive processes in persuasion. In R. E. Petty, T. Ostrom, & T. C. Brock (Eds.), *Cognitive responses in persuasion* (pp. 339–359). Hillsdale, NJ: Erlbaum. [36]

Flom, P. K. (1971). Performance in the medical internship. *Dissertation Abstracts International, 32*(2-B), 1188. [33]

Folsom, J. K. (1931). *Social psychology.* New York: Harper. [4]

Footlick, J. K. (1975, Nov. 10). Rape alert. *Newsweek*, p. 71. [29]

Ford, A. B., Liske, R. E., Ort, R. S., & Denton, J. C. (1967). *The doctor's perspective: Physicians view their patients and practice.* Cleveland, OH: Case Western Reserve University Press. [33]

Forgas, J. P., & Dobosz, B. (1980). Dimensions of romantic involvement: Towards a taxonomy of heterosexual relationships. *Social Psychology Quarterly, 43*, 290–300. [18]

Forsyth, D. (1983). *An introduction to group dynamics.* Monterey, CA: Brooks/Cole. [39]

Fox, R. (1971). The cultural animal. In J. F. Eisenberg & W. S. Dillon (Eds.), *Man and beast: Comparative social behavior.* Washington, DC: Smithsonian Institution Press. [15]

Fox, R. C. (1959). *Experiment perilous: Physicians and patients facing the unknown.* Glencoe, IL: The Free Press. [33]

Francis, V., Korsch, B. M., & Morris, M. J. (1969). Gaps in doctor-patient communication: Patients' response to medical advice. *New England Journal of Medicine, 280*, 534–540. [33]

Frank, J. D. (1944). Experimental studies of personal pressure and resistance: II. Methods of overcoming resistance. *Journal of Genetic Psychology, 30*, 43–56. [3]

Frank, L. K. (1938). Cultural control and physiological autonomy. *American Journal of Orthopsychiatry, 8,* 622–626. [3]

French, J. R. P., Jr. (1945). Studies in topological and vector psychology: III. Organized and unorganized groups under fear and frustration. *University of Iowa Studies in Child Welfare, 20.* [3]

French, J. R., & Raven, B. (1959). The bases of social power. In D. Cartwright (Ed.), *Studies in social power.* Ann Arbor, MI: University of Michigan Press. [27]

French, T. (1939). Insight and distortion in dreams. *International Journal of Psychoanalysis, 20,* 287–298. [3]

Freud, A. (1946). *The ego and the mechanisms of defense.* New York: International University Press. [20]

Freud, S. (1903/1959). Fragment of an analysis of a case of hysteria. In A. Strachey & J. Strachey (Eds. and Trans.), *Collected papers* (Vol. 3, pp.13–136). New York: Basic Books. (Original work published 1905.) [8]

Freud, S. (1916). *The interpretation of dreams.* (Trans. by A. A. Brill.) (Rev. ed.) New York: Macmillan. [3]

Freud, S. (1925). *Collected papers.* London: Hogarth. [9]

Freud, S. (1951). *Group psychology and the analysis of the ego* (J. Strachey, Ed. and Trans.) New York: Liveright. (Original work published 1922.) [18]

Frey, D., & Gaertner, S. L. (1986). Helping and avoidance of inappropriate interracial behavior: A strategy that can perpetuate a non-prejudiced self-image. *Journal of Personality and Social Psychology, 50,* 1083–1090. [26]

Frey, K. S., & Ruble, D. N. (1985). What children say when the teacher is not around: Conflicting goals in social comparison and performance assessment in the classroom. *Journal of Personality and Social Psychology, 48,* 550–562. [9]

Frideres, J. S., Warner, L. G., & Albrecht, S. L. (1971). The impact of social constraints on the relationship between attitudes and behavior. *Social Forces, 50,* 102–112. [5]

Friedman, H. S. (1979). Nonverbal communication between patients and medical practitioners. *Journal of Social Issues, 35*(1), 82–99. [33]

Friedman, H. S. (1979). The interactive effects of facial expressions of emotion and verbal messages on perceptions of affective meaning. *Journal of Experimental Social Psychology, 15,* 453–469. [33]

Friedman, H. S., DiMatteo, M. R., & Taranta, A. (1980). A study of the relationship between individual differences in nonverbal expressiveness and factors of personality and social interaction. *Journal of Research in Personality, 14,* 351–364. [18], [33]

Friedrich, C. J. (Ed.). (1958). *Authority.* Cambridge, MA: Harvard University Press. [35]

Friedson, E. (1961). *Patients' views of medical practice.* New York: Russell Sage Foundation. [33]

Frieze, I. H., Fisher, J. R., Hanusa, B. H., McHugh, M. C., & Valle, V. A. (1978). Attributions of the causes of success and failure as internal and external barriers to achievement. In J. L. Sherman & F. L. Denmark (Eds.), *The psychology of women: Future directions in research* (pp. 519–552). New York: Psychological Dimensions. [30]

Frieze, I. H., Whitley, B. E., Jr., Hanusa, B. H., & McHugh, M. C. (1982). Assessing the theoretical models for sex differences in causal attributions for success and failure. *Sex Roles, 8,* 333–343. [30]

Frodi, A. (1975). The effect of exposure to weapons on aggressive behavior from a cross-cultural perspective. *International Journal of Psychology, 10,* 283–292. [15]

Frodi, A., Macaulay, J., & Thome, P. R. (1977). Attitudes toward women in management and attributions for their success and failure in a managerial position. *Psychological Bulletin, 84,* 634–660. [30]

Fromm, E. H. (1956). *The art of loving.* New York: Harper & Row. [18]

Fryer, D. (1931). *The measurement of interests.* New York: Holt. [4]

Furman v. Georgia, 408 U.S. 238 (1972). [RI-26]

Gaertner, S. L. (1973). Helping behavior and discrimination among liberals and conservatives. *Journal of Personality and Social Psychology, 25,* 335–341. [26]

Gaertner, S. L. (1975). The role of racial attitudes in helping behavior. *Journal of Social Psychology, 97,* 95–101. [26]

Gaertner, S. L. (1976). Nonreactive measures in racial attitude research: A focus on "Liberals." In P. Katz (Ed.), *Toward the elimination of racism* (pp. 183–211). New York: Pergamon Press. [26]

Gaertner, S. L., & Bickman, L. (1971). Effects of race on the elicitation of helping behavior. *Journal of Personality and Social Psychology, 20,* 218–222. [26]

Gaertner, S. L., & Dovidio, J. F. (1977). The subtlety of white racism, arousal, and helping behavior. *Journal of Personality and Social Psychology, 35,* 691–707. [26]

Gaertner, S. L., & Dovidio, J. F. (1981). Racism among the well-intended. In E. G. Claussen & J. Bermingham (Eds.), *Pluralism, racism, and public policy: The search for equity* (pp. 208–222). Boston: G. K. Hall. [26]

Gaertner, S. L., Dovidio, J. F., & Johnson, G. (1982). Race of victim, non-responsive bystanders, and helping behavior. *Journal of Social Psychology, 117,* 69–77. [26]

Gaertner, S. L., & McLaughlin, J. P. (1983). Racial stereotypes: Associations and ascriptions of positive and negative characteristics. *Social Psychology Quarterly, 46,* 23–30. [26]

Gandour, M. J. (1984). Bulimia: Clinical description, assessment, etiology, and treatment. *International Journal of Eating Disorders, 3,* 3–38. [38]

Garfinkel, P. E., & Garner, D. M. (1982). *Anorexia nervosa: A multidimensional perspective.* New York: Brunner/Mazel. [38]

Garland, H., & Price, K. H. (1977). Attitudes towards women in management and attributions for their success and failure in a managerial position. *Journal of Applied Psychology, 62,* 29–33. [30]

Garner, D. M., & Garfinkel, P. E. (1980). Sociocultural factors in the development of anorexia nervosa. *Psychological Medicine, 10,* 647–656. [38]

Garner, D. M., Garfinkel, P. E., Schwartz, D., & Thompson, M. (1980). Cultural expectations of thinness in women. *Psychological Reports, 47,* 483–491. [38]

Garrow, J. (1978). The regulation of energy expenditure. In G. A. Bray (Ed.), *Recent advances in obesity research* (Vol. 2). London: Newman. [38]

Geen, R. (1980). Alternative conceptions of social facilitation. In P. B. Paulus (Ed.), *Psychology of group influence.* Hillsdale, NJ: Erlbaum. [39]

Geen, R., & Gange, J. (1977). Drive theory of social facilitation: Twelve years of theory and research. *Psychological Bulletin, 84,* 1267–1288. [39]

Gehlen, F. L. (1977). Toward a revised theory of hysterical contagion. *Journal of Health and Social Behavior, 18,* 27–35. [15]

Gelb, A. (1938). Colour constancy. In W. D. Ellis (Ed.), *Source book of gestalt psychology.* London: Kegan Paul. [3]

Genet, J. (1963). *Our lady of the flowers* (B. Frechtman, Trans.). New York: Grove Press. [29]

Gerbner, G. (1969a). Dimensions of violence in television drama. In R. K. Baker & S. J. Ball (Eds.), *Violence in the media* (Staff Report to the National Commission on the Causes and Prevention of Violence, pp. 311–340). Washington, DC: U.S. Government Printing Office. [23]

Gerbner, G. (1969b). Institutional pressures upon mass communicators. In P. Halmos (Ed.), *The sociology of mass communicators* (Sociological Review Monographs No. 13, pp. 205–248). England: University of Keele. [23]

Gerbner, G. (1969c). Toward "cultural indicators": The analysis of mass mediated message systems. *AV Communication Review, 17*(2), 137–148. [23]

Gerbner, G. (1972). The structure and process of television program content regulation in the U.S. In G. A. Comstock & E. A. Rubinstein (Eds.), *Television and social behavior,* Vol. 1: *Content and control* (pp. 386–414). Washington, DC: U.S. Government Printing Office. [23]

Gerbner, G. (1973). Cultural indicators: The third voice. In G. Gerbner, L. Gross, & H. Melody (Eds.), *Communication technology and social policy* (pp. 555–573). New York: Wiley. [23]

Gerbner, G., & Gross, L. (1976). Living with television: The violence profile. *Journal of Communication, 26*(2), 172–199. [23]

Gerbner, G., Gross, L., Jackson-Beeck, M., Morgan, M., & Signorielli, N. (1979). The demonstration of power: Violence profile no. 10. *Journal of Communication, 29*(3), 177–196. [23]

Gerbner, G., Gross, L., Morgan, M., & Signorielli, N. (1980). The "mainstreaming" of America: Violence profile no. 11. *Journal of Communication, 30*(3), 10–29. [23]

Gerbner, G., Gross, L., Morgan, M., & Signorielli, N. (1981a). Final reply to Hirsch. *Communication Research, 8*(3), 259–280. [23]

Gerbner, G., Gross, L., Morgan, M., & Signorielli, N. (1981b). Health and medicine on television. *The New England Journal of Medicine, 305*(15), 901–904. [23]

Gerbner, G., Gross, L., Morgan, M., & Signorielli, N. (1981c). Scientists on the TV screen. *Society, 18*(4), 41–44. [23]

Gerbner, G., Gross, L., Morgan, M., & Signorielli, N. (1982). Charting the mainstream: Television's contributions to political orientations. *Journal of Communication, 32*(2), 100–127. [23]

Gerbner, G., Gross, L., Morgan, M., & Signorielli, N. (1984). Political correlates of television viewing. *Public Opinion Quarterly, 48,* 283–300. [23]

Gerbner, G., Gross, L., Signorielli, N., & Morgan, M. (1980). Aging with television: Images on television drama and conceptions of social reality. *Journal of Communication, 30*(1), 37–47. [23]

Gerbner, G., Morgan, M., & Signorielli, N. (1982). Programming health portrayals: What viewers see, say, and do. In D. Pearl, L. Bouthilet, & J. Lazar (Eds.), *Television and behavior: Ten years of scientific progress and implications for the 80's* (Vol. II, pp. 291–307.). Washington, DC: U.S. Government Printing Office. [23]

Gergen, K. J. (1965). Interaction goals and personalistic feedback as factors affecting the presentation of self. *Journal of Personality and Social Psychology, 1,* 413–424. [9]

Gergen, K. J. (1968). Personal consistency and the presentation of self. In C. Gordon & K. J. Gergen (Eds.), *The self in social interaction* (Vol. I, pp. 299–308). New York: Wiley. [9]

Gergen, K. J., & Gergen, M. M. (1983). Narrative of the self. In T. R. Sarbin & K. E. Scheibe (Eds.), *Studies in social identity.* New York: Praeger. [9]

Gergen, K. J., Gergen, M. M., & Barton, W. H. (1973). Deviance in the dark. *Psychology Today, 7,* 129–130. [37], [RI-37]

Giddings, F. H. (1896). *The principles of sociology.* New York: Macmillan. [4]

Gillum, R. F., & Barsky, A. J. (1974). Diagnosis and management of patient noncompliance. *Journal of the American Medical Association, 228,* 1563–1567. [33]

Glueck, S., & Glueck, E. T. (1930). *Five hundred criminal careers.* New York: Knopf. [4]

Glueck, S., & Glueck, E. T. (1934). *One thousand juvenile delinquents.* Cambridge, MA: Harvard University Press. [4]

Glynn, E. D. (1956). Television and the American character: A psychiatrist looks at television. In W. Y. Elliot (Ed.), *Television's impact on American culture* (pp.175–182). Lansing: Michigan State University Press. [23]

Goffman, E. (1955). On face work: An analysis of ritual elements in social interaction. *Psychiatry, 18,* 213–221. [8]

Goffman, E. (1959). *The presentation of self in everyday life.* New York: Doubleday Anchor. [15], [RI-8]

Goffman, E. (1963). *Stigma: Notes on the management of spoiled identity.* Englewood Cliffs, NJ: Prentice Hall. [32]

Goldberg, P. (1968). Are women prejudiced against women? *Transaction, 5,* 28–30. [30]

Goldstein, K. (1939). *The organism.* New York: American Book. [15]

Goodchilds, J. D. (1977). *Non-stranger rape: The role of sexual socialization.* Unpublished grant proposal, University of California, Los Angeles. [17]

Goodenough, F. L. (1934). Trends in modern psychology. *Psychological Bulletin, 31,* 81–97. [4]

Goodenough, F. L. (1940). New evidence on environmental influence on intelligence. *Yearbook of National Social Studies Education, 39,* 307–365. [3]

Goodmonson, C., & Glaudin, V. (1971). The relationship of commitment-free behavior and commitment behavior: A study of attitude toward organ transplantation. *Journal of Social Issues, 27,* 171–183. [5]

Gordon, C., & Gergen, K. J. (Eds.), *The self in social interaction,* (Vol. 1). New York: Wiley. [9]

Gormally, J. (1984). The obese binge eater: Diagnosis, etiology and clinical issues. In R. C. Hawkins, W. J. Fremouw, & P. F. Clement (Eds.), *The binge-purge syndrome.* New York: Springer Publishing. [38]

Gormally, J., Black, S., Daston, S., & Rardin, D. (1982). The assessment of binge eating severity among obese persons. *Addictive Behaviors, 7,* 47–55. [38]

Gottschaldt, K. (1926). Über dem Einfluss der Erfahrung auf die Wahrnehmung von Figuren: I. Über den Einfluss gehäufter Einprägung von Figuren auf ihre Sichbarkeit in umfassenden Konfigurationen. *Psychologische Forschung, 8,* 261–318. [3]

Gough, H. G., Hall, W. B., & Harris, R. E. (1963). Admissions procedures as forecasters of performance in medical training. *Journal of Medical Education, 38,* 983–998. [33]

Gough, H. G., Hall, W. B., & Harris, R. E. (1964). Evaluation of performance in medical training. *Journal of Medical Education, 39,* 679–692. [33]

Grady, K. E. (1977). *Sex as a social label: The illusion of sex differences.* Unpublished doctoral dissertation. City University of New York. [30]

Grady, K. E. (1979). Androgyny reconsidered. In J. H. Williams (Ed.), *Psychology of women: Selected readings* (pp. 172–177). New York: Norton. [30]

Grady, K. E. (1981). Sex bias in research design. *Psychology of Women Quarterly, 5,* 628–636. [30]

Gray, P. G., & Cartwright, A. (1953, Dec. 19). Choosing and changing doctors. *The Lancet,* p. 1308. [33]

Greeley, A. M. (1974). *Ecstacy: A way of knowing.* Englewood Cliffs, NJ: Prentice Hall. [15]

Greeley, A. M., & Sheatsley, P. B. (1971). Attitudes toward racial integration. *Scientific American, 225,* 13–19. [26]

Green, D. (1974). Dissonance and self-perception analyses of "forced-compliance": When two theories make competing predictions. *Journal of Personality and Social Psychology, 29,* 819–828. [6]

Greenwald, A. G. (1968). Cognitive learning, cognitive response to persuasion, and attitude change. In A. G. Greenwald, T. C. Brock, & T. Ostrom (Eds.), *Psychological foundations of attitudes* (pp. 147–170). New York: Academic Press. [36]

Greenwald, A. G. (1975). On the inconclusiveness of "crucial" cognitive tests of dissonance vs. self-perception theories. *Journal of Experimental Social Psychology, 11,* 490–499. [6]

Greenwald, A. G. (1980). The totalitarian ego: Fabrication and revision of personal history. *American Psychologist, 35,* 603–618. [9]

Greenwald, A. G. (1982). Ego task analysis: An integration of research on ego-involvement and self-awareness. In A. Hastorf & A. Isen (Eds.), *Cognitive social psychology.* New York: Elsevier. [9]

Greenwald, A. G., & Pratkanis, A. R. (1984). The self. In R. S. Wyer & T. K. Srull (Eds.), *Handbook of social cognition* (Vol. 3). Hillsdale, NJ: Erlbaum. [9]

Griffin, S. (1971, Sept.). Rape: The all-American crime. *Ramparts, 10.* [29]

Griffitt, W. (1970). Environmental effects on interpersonal affective behavior: Ambient effective temperature and attraction. *Journal of Personality and Social Psychology, 15,* 240–244. [21]

Griffitt, W., & Veitch, R. (1971). Hot and crowded: Influences of population density and temperature on interpersonal affective behavior. *Journal of Personality and Social Psychology, 17,* 92–98. [21]

Gross, L. (1984). The cultivation of intolerance: Television, blacks, and gays. In G. Melischek, K. E. Rosengren, & J. Stappers (Eds.), *Cultural indicators: An international symposium* (pp. 345–364). Vienna: Austrian Academy of Sciences. [23]

Gross, L., & Morgan, M. (1985). Television and enculturation. In J. Dominick & J. Fletcher (Eds.), *Broadcasting research methods* (pp. 221–234). Boston: Allyn & Bacon. [23]

Grosser, D., Polansky, N., & Lippitt, R. (1951). A laboratory study of behavior contagion. *Human Relations, 4,* 115–142. [20]

Gruder, C. L. (1977). Choice of comparison persons in evaluating oneself. In J. M. Suls & R. L. K. Miller (Eds.), *Social comparison processes* (pp. 21–41). Washington, DC: Hemisphere. [9]

Guerin, B. (1986). Mere presence effects in humans: A review. *Journal of Experimental Social Psychology, 22,* 38–77. [39]

Guerin, B., & Innes, J. (1982). Social facilitation and social monitoring: A new look at Zajonc's mere presence hypothesis. *British Journal of Social Psychology, 7,* 81–90. [39]

Guntrip, H. (1971). *Psychoanalytic theory, therapy, and the self.* New York: Basic Books. [9]

Haase, R. F., & Tepper, D. T. (1972). Nonverbal components of empathic communication. *Journal of Counseling Psychology, 19,* 417–424. [33]

Haines, G. H. (1974). Process models of consumer decision making. In G. D. Hughes & M. L. Ray (Eds.), *Buyer/consumer information processing* (pp. 89–107). Chapel Hill: University of North Caroline Press. [36]

Hall, A. D., & Fagan, R. E. (1968). Definition of system. In W. B. Buckley (Ed.), *Modern systems research for the behavioral scientist.* Chicago: Aldine. [15]

Hall, E. T. (1966). *The hidden dimension.* Garden City, N.Y.: Doubleday. [8]

Hall, J. A. (1978). Gender effects in decoding nonverbal cues. *Psychological Bulletin, 85,* 845–857. [17]

Halmi, K. A., Falk, J. R., & Schwartz, E. (1981). Binge-eating and vomiting: A survey of a college population. *Psychological Medicine, 11,* 697–706. [38]

Hamburg, D. A., & Brown, S. S. (1978). The science base and social context of health maintenance: An overview. *Science, 200,* 847–849. [33]

Hamilton, D. L. (Ed.). (1981). *Cognitive processes in stereotyping and intergroup behavior.* Hillsdale, NJ: Erlbaum. [26]

Hamilton, D. L., & Gifford, R. K. (1976). Illusory correlation in interpersonal perception: A cognitive basis of stereotypic judgments. *Journal of Experimental Social Psychology, 12,* 392–407. [32]

Hampton, J. A., & Gardiner, M. M. (1983). Measures of internal category structure: A correlational analysis of normative data. *British Journal of Psychology, 74,* 491–516. [18]

Handlin, O. (1948). Prejudice and capitalist exploitation. *Commentary, 6,* 79–85. [25]

Handlin, O. (1951). *The uprooted: The epic story of the great migrations that made the American people.* Boston: Little, Brown. [25]

Hansen, R. D., & O'Leary, V. E. (1983). Actresses and actors: The effect of sex on causal attributions. *Basic and Applied Social Psychology, 4,* 209–230. [30]

Harding, J., Proshansky, H., Kutner, B., & Chein, I. (1969). Prejudice and ethnic relations. In G. Lindzey &. E. Aronson (Eds.), *The handbook of social psychology* (Vol. 5, pp. 1–76) (2nd ed.). Reading, MA: Addison-Wesley. [26]

Harkins, S., & Jackson, J. (1985). The role of evaluation in eliminating social loafing. *Journal of Personality and Social Psychology Bulletin, 11,* 457–465. [39]

Harkins, S., Latané, B. & Williams, K. (1980). Social loafing: Allocating effort or taking it easy? *Journal of Experimental Social Psychology, 16,* 457–465. [39]

Harkins, S., & Petty, R. (1982). Effects of task difficulty and task uniqueness on social loafing. *Journal of Personality and Social Psychology, 43,* 1214–1229. [39]

Harré, R., & Secord, P. S. (1972). *The explanation of social behavior.* London: Basil Blackwell. [15]

Harries, K. D., & Stadler, S. J. (1983) Determinism revisited: Assault and heat stress in Dallas, 1980. *Environment and Behavior, 15,* 235–256. [21]

Harries, K. D., Stadler, S. J., & Zdorkowski, R. T. (1984). Seasonality and assault: Explorations in inter-neighborhood variation, Dallas, 1980. *Annals of the Association of American Geographers, 74,* 590–604. [21]

Harris, M. J., & Rosenthal, R. (1986). Four factors in the mediation of teacher expectancy effects. In R. S. Feldman (Ed.), *The social psychology of education: Current research and theory* (pp. 91–114). New York: Cambridge University Press. [RI-32]

Hart, H. (1933). Changing social attitudes. In *Recent social trends* (Vol. 1, pp. 382–444). New York: McGraw-Hill. [4]

Harter, S. (1983). Developmental perspectives on the self-system. In P. H. Mussen (Ed.), *Carmichael's manual of child psychology* (Vol. 4). New York: Wiley. [9]

Hartshorne, H. & May, M. A. (1928). *Studies in the nature of character.* Vol. 1: *Studies in deceit.* New York: Macmillan. [4]

Hartshorne, H. & May, M. A. (1929). *Studies in the nature of character.* Vol. 2: *Studies in service and self-control.* New York: Macmillan. [3], [4]

Hartshorne, H., May, M. A., & Shuttleworth, F. K. (1930). *Studies in the nature of character.* Vol. 3: *Studies in the organization of character.* New York: Macmillan. [4]

Harvey, J. H., Ickes, W. J., & Kidd, R. F. (1976). *New directions in attribution research.* Hillsdale, NJ: Erlbaum. [32]

Hasher, L., & Zacks, R. T. (1979). Automatic and effortful processes in memory. *Journal of Experimental Psychology: General, 108,* 356–388. [12]

Hatfield, E., & Walster, G. W. (1978). *A new look at love.* Reading, MA: Addison-Wesley. [18]

Hawkins, R. P., & Pingree, S. (1982). Television's influence on social reality. In D. Pearl, L. Bouthilet, & J. Lazar (Eds.), *Television and behavior: Ten years of scientific progress and implications for the 80's* (Vol. II, pp. 224–247.). Washington, DC: U.S. Government Printing Office. [23]

Hayes, S. P., Jr. (1936). The predictive ability of voters. *Journal of Social Psychology, 7,* 183–191. [11]

Headlee, R. (1973). The tacit contract between doctor and patient. *Medical Insight, 5,* 30–37. [33]

Heberlein, T. A., & Black, J. S. (1976). Attitudinal specificity and the prediction of behavior in a field setting. *Journal of Personality and Social Psychology, 33,* 474–479. [5]

Hechter, M. (1975). *Internal colonialism.* Berkeley: University of California Press. [26]

Heider, F. (1944). Social perceptions and phenomenal causality. *Psychological Review, 51,* 358–374. [RI-11]

Heider, F. (1958). *The psychology of interpersonal relations.* New York: Wiley. [11], [32], [RI-11]

Heilbrun, A. B., Jr. (1976). Measurement of masculine and feminine sex role identities as independent dimensions. *Journal of Consulting and Clinical Psychology, 44,* 183–190. [30]

Hendrick, C. A. (1976). *Person perception and rape: An experimental approach.* Unpublished grant proposal, Kent State University. [17]

Hendrick, C. A., & Hendrick, S. (1986). A theory and method of love. *Journal of Personality and Social Psychology, 50,* 392–402. [RI-18]

Heron, A. (1984). Satisfaction and satisfactoriness: Complementary aspects of occupational adjustment. *Occupational Psychology, 28,* 140–153. [5]

Hewett, J. P. (1976). *Self and society: A symbolic interactionist social psychology.* Boston: Allyn and Bacon. [15]

Higgins, E. T. (1983). *A theory of discrepant self-concepts.* Unpublished manuscript, New York University. [9]

Higgins, E. T., & King, G. A. (1981). Accessibility of social constructs: Information processing consequences of individual and contextual variability. In N. Cantor & J. Kihlstrom (Eds.), *Personality and social intelligence* (pp. 69–122). Englewood Cliffs, NJ: Prentice-Hall. [9], [12]

Higgins, E. T., King, G. A., & Mavin, G. H. (1982). Individual construct accessibility and subjective impressions and recall. *Journal of Personality and Social Psychology, 43,* 35–47. [9]

Higgins, E. T., Klein, R., & Strauman, T. (1985). Self-concept discrepancy theory: A psychological model for distinguishing among different aspects of depression and anxiety. *Social Cognition, 3,* 51–76. [9], [RI-9]

Higgins, E. T., Strauman, T., & Klein, R. (1986). Standards and the process of self-evaluation: Multiple affects from multiple stages. In R. M. Sorrentino & E. T. Higgins (Eds.), *Handbook of motivation and cognition: Foundations of social behavior* (pp. 23–63). New York: Guilford. [9]

Hinde, R. A. (1979). *Towards understanding relationships.* London: Academic Press. [18]

Hippocrates. (1923). *Volume II: On Decorum and the Physician* (W. H. S. Jones, Trans.). London: William Heinemann, Ltd. [33]

Hirsch, P. (1979). The role of television and popular culture in contemporary society. In H. Newcomb (Ed.), *Television: The critical view* (2nd ed., pp. 249–279). New York: Oxford University Press. [23]

Hollander, E. P. (1985). Leadership and power. In G. Lindzey & E. Aronson (Eds.), *Handbook of social psychology* (3rd ed.). Reading, MA: Addison-Wesley. [30]

Holliday, S. G., & Chandler, M. (1986). *Wisdom: Explorations in adult competence* (Human Development Monograph No. 17). Basel, Switzerland: Carger Publishing. [18]

Holmes, D. S. (1968). Dimensions of projection. *Psychological Bulletin, 69,* 248–268. [11]

Holt, E. B. (1931). *Animal drive and the learning process.* New York: Holt. [4]

Homa, D. (1984). On the nature of categories. In G. H. Bower (Ed.), *The psychology of learning and motivation* (Vol. 18, pp. 49–94). Orlando, FL: Academic Press. [18]

Homans, G. C. (1941). Anxiety and ritual: The theories of Malinowski and Radcliffe-Brown. *American Anthropologist, 43,* 164–173. [15]

Homburger, E. (1937). Configurations in play: Clinical norms. *Psychoanalytic Quarterly, 6,* 139–214. [3]

Horney, K. (1950). *Neurosis and human growth.* New York: Norton. [9], [RI-9]

Horos, C. V. (1974). *Rape.* New Canaan, CT: Tobey. [29]

Horowitz, E. L. (1936). The development of attitude toward the Negro. *Archives of Psychology New York, 194.* [3]

Horowitz, L. M., deS. French, R., & Anderson, C. A. (1982). The prototype of a lonely person. In L. A. Peplau & D. Perlman (Eds.), *Loneliness: A sourcebook of current theory, research and therapy* (pp. 183–205). New York: Wiley. [18]

House, F. N. (1929). *The range of social theory.* New York: Holt. [4]

Hovland, C. I. (1951). Reconciling conflicting results derived from experimental and survey studies of attitude change. *American Psychologist, 14,* 8–17. [RI-36]

Hovland, C. I., Harvey, O. J., & Sherif, M. (1957). Assimilation and contrast effects in reactions to communication and attitude change. *Journal of Abnormal and Social Psychology, 55,* 244–252. [6]

Hovland, C. I., Janis, I. L., & Kelley, H. H. (1953). *Communication and persuasion.* New Haven, CT: Yale University Press. [36], [RI-36]

Hovland, C. I., Lumsdaine, A. A., & Sheffield, F. D. (1949). *Experiments on mass communication.* Princeton, NJ: Princeton University Press. [RI-36]

Howell, M. A. (1966). Personality factors in medical performance. *Dissertation Abstracts International, 27*(1-B), 303. [33]

Hull, C. L. (1930). Simple trial-and-error learning: A study in psychological theory. *Psychological Review, 37*, 241–256. [3]

Hunt, J. McV., Cole, M. W., & Reis, E. E. (1958). Situational cues distinguishing anger, fear, and sorrow. *American Journal of Psychology, 71*, 136–151. [14]

Hyde, J. S. (1981). How large are cognitive gender differences? A meta-analysis using ω^2 and d. *American Psychologist, 36*, 892–901. [30]

Ichheiser, G. (1949). Sociopsychological and cultural factors in race relations. *American Journal of Sociology, 54*, 395–401. [25]

Ickes, W., Layden, A. L., & Barnes, D. (1978). Objective self-awareness and individuation: An empirical link. *Journal of Personality, 46*, 146–161. [37]

Ingham, A., Levinger, G., Graves, J., & Peckham, V. (1974). The Ringelmann effect: Studies of group size and group performance. *Journal of Experimental Social Psychology, 10*, 371–384. [39]

Ingram, R. E., Smith, T. W., & Brehm, S. S. (1983). Depression and information processing: Self-schemata and the encoding of self-relevant information. *Journal of Personality and Social Psychology, 45*, 412–422. [9]

Insko, C. A., Lind, E. A., & LaTour, S. (1976). Persuasion, recall, and thoughts. *Representative Research in Social Psychology, 7*, 66–78. [36]

Insko, C. A., & Schopler, J. (1967). Triadic consistency: A statement of affective-cognitive-conative consistency. *Psychological Review, 74*, 361–376. [5]

Irwin, O. C. (1930). The amount and nature of activities of newborn infants under constant external stimulating conditions during the first ten days of life. *Genetic Psychology Monographs, 8*, 1–92. [3]

Izard, C. E. (1972). *Patterns of emotions*. New York: Academic Press. [15]

Izard, C. E. (1977). *Human emotions*. New York: Plenum. [15]

Jackson, J., & Harkins, S. (1985). Equity in effort: An explanation of the social loafing effect. *Journal of Personality and Social Psychology, 49*, 1199–1206. [39]

Jackson, J., & Williams, K. (1985). Social loafing on difficult tasks: Working collectively can improve performance. *Journal of Personality and Social Psychology, 49*, 937–942. [39]

James, W. (1890). *The principles of psychology* (2 vols.). New York: Holt. [4], [14], [15], [RI-7]

Janis, I. (1958). *Psychological stress: Psychoanalytic and behavioral studies of surgical patients*. New York: Wiley. [33]

Janis, I., & Field, P. (1973). Sex differences and personality factors related to persuasibility. In C. Hovland & I. Janis (Eds.), *Personality and persuasibility*. New Haven, CT: Yale University Press. [32]

Janis, I., Kaye, D., & Kirschner, P. (1965). Facilitating effects of "eating while reading" on responsiveness to persuasive communication. *Journal of Personality and Social Psychology, 1*, 181–186. [36]

Janis, I., & Rodin, J. (1979). Attitude, control, and decision-making: Social psychology and health care. In G. Stone, N. Adler, & F. Cohen (Eds.), *Health Psychology*. San Francisco: Jossey-Bass. [27]

Janis, I. L. (1954). Personality correlates of susceptibility to persuasion. *Journal of Personality, 22*, 504–518. [38]

Jastrow, J. (1915). *Character and temperament*. New York: Appleton. [28]

Järvinen, K. A. J. (1955). Can ward rounds be a danger to patients with myocardial infarction? *British Medical Journal, 1*, 318–320. [33]

Jensen, D. D. (1970). Polythetic biopsychology: An alternative to behaviorism. In J. H. Reynierse (Ed.), *Current issues in animal learning: A colloquium*. Lincoln: University of Nebraska Press. [15]

Jessor, R., & Jessor, S. (1977). *Problem behavior and psychosocial development: A longitudinal study of youth*. New York: Academic Press. [38]

Johnson, C., Lewis, C., & Hagman, L. (1984). The syndrome of bulimia. *Psychiatric Clinics of America, 7*, 247–274. [38]

Johnson, M. P. (1982). Social and cognitive features of the dissolution of commitment to relationships. In S. Duck (Ed.), *Personal relationships. 4: Dissolving personal relationships* (pp. 51–73). London: Academic Press. [18]

Jones, E., & Davis, K. (1965). From acts to dispositions: The attribution process in person perception. In L. Berkowitz (Ed.), *Advances in experimental social psychology* (Vol. 2). New York: Academic Press. [11]

Jones, E., & Nisbett, R. (1972). The actor and the observer: Divergent perceptions of the cause of behavior. In E. E. Jones, D. E. Kanouse, H. H. Kelley, R.

E. Nisbett, S. Valins, & B. Weiner (Eds.), *Attribution: Perceiving the causes of behavior*. Morristown, NJ: General Learning Press. [11]

Jones, E. E., & Davis, K. E. (1965). From acts to dispositions: The attribution process in person perception. In L. Berkowitz (Ed.), *Advances in experimental social psychology* (Vol. 2, pp. 220–266). New York: Academic Press. [11], [12], [32], [RI-11]

Jones, E. E., & Harris, V. A. (1967). The attribution of attitudes. *Journal of Experimental Social Psychology, 3,* 1–24. [11], [RI-11]

Jones, E. E., Kanouse, D. E., Kelley, H. H., Nisbett, R. E., Valins, S., & Weiner, B. (Eds.) (1972). *Attribution: Perceiving the causes of behavior*. Morristown, NJ: General Learning Press. [11], [32]

Jones, E. E., & Nisbett, R. E. (1972). The actor and the observer: Divergent perceptions of the causes of behavior. In E. Jones, D. Kanouse, H. Kelley, S. Valins, & B. Weiner (Eds), *Attribution: Perceiving the causes of behavior*. Morristown, NJ: General Learning Press. [32]

Jones, J. M., & Block, C. B. (1984). Black cultural perspectives. *The Clinical Psychologist, 37,* 58–62. [26]

Jussim, L. (1986). Self-fulfilling prophesies: A theoretical and integrative review. *Psychological Review, 93,* 429–445. [9]

Kagan, N. I. (1974). Teaching interpersonal relations for the practice of medicine. *Läkartidningen, 71,* 4758–4760. [33]

Kahneman, D. (1973). *Attention and effort*. Englewood Cliffs, NJ: Prentice-Hall. [12]

Kahneman, D., & Tversky, A. (1973). On the psychology of prediction. *Psychological Review, 80,* 237–251. [11], [27]

Kanfer, F. H. (1970). Self-regulation: Research, issues, and speculations. In C. Neuringer & J. L. Michael (Eds.), *Behavior modification in clinical psychology*. New York: Appleton-Century-Crofts. [9]

Kanin, E. J. (1957). Male aggression in dating-courtship relations. *American Journal of Sociology, 63,* 197–204. [17], [29]

Kanin, E. J. (1967). An examination of sexual aggression as a response to sexual frustration. *Journal of Marriage and the Family, 29,* 428–433. [17]

Kanin, E. J. (1969). Selected dyadic aspects of male sex aggression. *Journal of Sex Research, 5,* 12–28. [17]

Kanin, E. J., & Parcell, S. R. (1977). Sexual aggres-

sion: A second look at the offended female. *Archives of Sexual Behavior, 6,* 67–76. [17]

Karabenick, S. A., Sweeney, C., & Penrose, G. (1983). Preferences for skill versus chance-determined activities: The influence of gender and task sex-typing. *Journal of Research in Personality, 17,* 125–142. [30]

Karlins, M., Coffman, T. L., & Walters, G. (1969). On the fading of social stereotypes: Studies in three generations of college students. *Journal of Personality and Social Psychology, 13,* 1–16. [26], [32]

Karpman, B. (1954). *The sexual offender and his offenses*. New York: Julian Press. [29]

Kassarjian, H. H. (1982). Consumer psychology. *Annual Review of Psychology, 33,* 619–649. [36]

Kassarjian, H. H., & Kassarjian, W. M. (1979). Attitudes under low commitment conditions. In J. C. Mahoney & B. Silverman (Eds.), *Attitude research plays for high stakes* (pp. 3–15). Chicago: American Marketing Association. [36]

Kassarjian, W. M. (1962). A study of Riesman's theory of social character. *Sociometry, 25,* 213–230. [8]

Kasteler, J., Kane, R. L., Olsen, D. M., & Thetford, C. (1976). Issues underlying prevalence of "doctor-shopping" behavior. *Journal of Health and Social Behavior, 17,* 328–339. [33]

Katz, D., & Allport, F. H. (1931). *Students' attitudes*. Syracuse, NY: Craftsman Press. [4], [11]

Katz, D., & Braly, K. Racial stereotypes of one hundred college students. *Journal of Abnormal and Social Psychology, 28,* 280–290. [4]

Katz, I. (1981). *Stigma: A social-psychological analysis*. Hillsdale, NJ: Erlbaum. [26]

Katz, S., & Mazur, M. (1979). *Understanding the rape victim: A synthesis of research findings*. New York: Wiley. [17]

Katzman, R., & Carasu, T. B. (1975). Differential diagnosis of dementia. In W. S. Fields (Ed.), *Neurological and sensory disorders in the elderly* (pp. 103–104). Miami: Symposia Specialist Medical Books. [27]

Kaufman, M. R. (1970). Practicing good manners and compassion. *Medical Insight, 2,* 56–61. [33]

Kelley, G. A. (1955). *The psychology of personal constructs* (2 vols.). New York: Norton. [15]

Kelley, H. H. (1967). Attribution theory in social psychology. In D. Levine (Ed.), *Nebraska Symposium on Motivation: 1967* (Vol. 15). Lincoln: University of Nebraska Press. [11], [27], [RI-11]

Kelley, H. H. (1973). The process of causal attribution. *American Psychologist, 28,* 107–128. [11], [32]

Kelley, H. H. (1983). Love and commitment. In H. H. Kelley, E. Berscheid, A. Christensen, J. H. Harvey, T. L. Huston, G. Levinger, E. McClintock, L. A. Peplau, & D. R. Peterson (Eds.), *Close relationships* (pp. 265–314). New York: W. H. Freeman. [18]

Kelley, H. H., & Stahelski, A. J. (1970). The social interaction basis of cooperators' and competitors' beliefs about others. *Journal of Personality and Social Psychology, 16,* 66–91. [11], [32]

Kelley, H. H., Berscheid, E., Christensen, A., Harvey, J. H., Huston, T. L., Levinger, G., McClintock, E., Peplau, L. A., & Peterson, D. R. (1983). Analyzing close relationships. In H. H. Kelley, E. Berscheid, A. Christensen, J. H. Harvey, T. L. Huston, G. Levinger, E. McClintock, L. A. Peplau, & D. R. Peterson (Eds.), *Close relationships* (pp. 20–67). New York: W. H. Freeman. [18]

Kelman, H. C. (1961). Processes of opinion change. *Public Opinion Quarterly, 25,* 57–78. [36]

Kelman, H. C. (1974). Attitudes are alive and well and gainfully employed in the sphere of action. *American Psychologist, 29,* 310–324. [5]

Kenrick, D. T., & MacFarlane, S. W. (1984). Ambient temperature and horn-honking: A field study of the heat/aggression relationship. *Environment and Behavior, 18,* 179–191. [21]

Kerckhoff, A. C., & Back, K. W. (1968). *The june bug: A study of hysterical contagion.* Englewood Cliffs, NJ: Prentice-Hall. [38]

Kerlinger, F. N., & Pedhazur, E. J. (1973). *Multiple regression in behavioral research.* New York: Holt, Rinehart, and Winston. [6]

Kernberg, O. (1977). *Borderline conditions in pathological narcissism.* New York: International University Press. [9]

Kerr, N. (1983). Motivation losses in small groups: A social dilemma analysis. *Journal of Personality and Social Psychology, 45,* 819–828. [39]

Kerr, N., & Bruun, S. (1981). Ringelmann revisited: Alternative explanations for the social loafing effect. *Personality and Social Psychology Bulletin, 7,* 224–231. [39]

Kessler, R. C., & McRae, J. A. (1982). The effect of wives' employment on the mental health of married men and women. *American Sociological Review, 47,* 216–227. [9]

Kiesler, C. A. (1971). *The psychology of commitment.* New York: Academic Press. [18]

Kiesler, C. A., Collins, B. E., & Miller, N. (1969). *Attitude change: A critical analysis of theoretical approaches.* New York: John Wiley. [36]

Kiesler, C. A., Nisbett, R. E., & Zanna, M. P. (1969). On inferring one's belief from one's behavior. *Journal of Personality and Social Psychology, 11,* 321–327. [6]

Kiesler, C. A., & Pallak, M. S. (1976). Arousal properties of dissonance manipulations. *Psychological Bulletin, 83,* 1014–1025. [6]

Kiesler, S., & Baral, R. L. (1966). *The search for a romantic partner: The effects of self-esteem and physical attractiveness on romantic behavior.* Unpublished manuscript. [16]

Kihlstrom, J. F., & Cantor, N. (1984). Mental representations of the self. *Advances in Experimental Social Psychology, 17,* 1–47. [9]

Kilpatrick, F. P. (Ed.) (1952). *Human behavior from the transactional point of view.* Hanover, N.H.: Institute for Associated Research. [10]

King, S. H. (1962). *Perceptions of illness and medical practice.* New York: Russell-Sage Foundation. [33]

Kinsie, P. M. (1950). Sex crimes and the prostitution racket. *Journal of Social Hygiene, 36,* 250–252. [29]

Kirk, R. E. (1968). *Experimental design: Procedures for the behavioral sciences.* Monterey, CA: Brooks/Cole. [12]

Kirk, R. E. (1982). *Experimental design.* Monterey, CA: Brooks/Cole. [39]

Kirkham, G. L. (1971). Homosexuality in prison. In J. M. Henslin (Ed.), *Studies in the sociology of sex.* New York: Appleton-Century-Crofts. [29]

Kirkpatrick, C., & Kanin, E. (1957). Male sex aggression on a university campus. *American Sociological Review, 22,* 52–58. [17], [29]

Kleck, R. E., Richardson, S. A., & Ronald, L. (1974). Physical appearance cues and interpersonal attraction in children. *Child Development, 45,* 305–310. [32]

Klinger, E. (1969). Feedback effects and social facilitation of vigilance performance: Mere coaction versus potential evaluation. *Psychonomic Science, 14,* 161–162. [39]

Klinger, E. (1977). *Meaning and void: Inner experience and the incentives in people's lives.* Minneapolis: University of Minnesota Press. [15]

Koffka, K. (1912). *Zur Analyse der Vorstellungen und ihren Gesetze.* Leipzig: Quelle & Meyer. [4]

Koffka, K. (1928). *The growth of the mind: An introduction to child psychology.* (R. M. Ogden,Trans.) (2nd ed.). New York: Harcourt, Brace. [3]

Köhler, W. (1920). *Die physischen Gestalten in Ruhe und im stationären Zustand.* Braunschweig, Germany: Friedrich Vieweg & Sohn. [3]

Köhler, W. (1929). *Gestalt psychology.* New York: Liveright. [4]

Kolstad, A. (1933). A study of opinions on some international problems. *Teachers College Contributions in Education, 555,* 95. [4]

Komisar, L. (no date). *Violence and the masculine mystique.* Pittsburgh: KNOW. [29]

Koos, E. (1955). "Metropolis"—what city people think of their medical services. *American Journal of Public Health, 45,* 1551–1557. [33]

Korsch, B. M., Gozzi, E. K., & Francis, V. (1968). Gaps in doctor-patient communication. I: Doctor-patient interaction and patient satisfaction. *Pediatrics, 42,* 855–871. [33]

Koss, M. P., Gidycz, C. A., & Wisniewski, N. (1987). The scope of rape: Incidence and prevalence of sexual aggression and victimization in a national sample of higher education students. *Journal of Consulting and Clinical Psychology, 55,* 162–170. [RI-29]

Kounin, J. S. (1939). *Experimental studies of rigidity as a function of age and feeblemindedness.* Unpublished Ph.D. Dissertation, University of Iowa. [3]

Kovel, J. (1970). *White racism: A psychohistory.* New York: Pantheon. [26]

Kravitz, D., & Martin, B. (1986). Ringelmann rediscovered: The original article. *Journal of Personality and Social Psychology, 50,* 936–941. [39]

Krebs, D., & Adinolphi, A. A. (1975). Physical attractiveness, social relations, and personality style. *Journal of Personality and Social Psychology, 31,* 245–253. [32]

Krebs, D. L., & Miller, D. T. (1985). Altruism and aggression. In G. Lindsay & E. Aronson (Eds.), *Handbook of social psychology* (3rd ed.). (Vol. 2, pp. 1–71). New York: Random House. [RI-31]

Krueger, E. T., & Reckless, W. C. (1931). *Social psychology.* New York: Longmans, Green. [4]

Krugman, H. E. (1965). The impact of television advertising: Learning without involvement. *Public Opinion Quarterly, 29,* 349–356. [36]

Krugman, H. E. (1967). The measurement of advertising involvement. *Public Opinion Quarterly, 30,* 583–596. [36]

Kuhl, J. (1984). Volitional aspects of achievement motivation and learned helplessness: Toward a comprehensive theory of action control. *Progress in Experimental Personality Research, 13,* 99–171. [9]

Kuhl, J. (1985). Volitional mediators of cognition-behavior consistency: Self-regulatory processes and action versus state orientation. In J. Kuhl & J. Beckmann (Eds.), *Action control: From cognition to behavior* (pp. 101–128). New York: Springer-Verlag. [9]

Kuiper, N. A., & Derry, P. A. (1981). The self as a cognitive prototype: An application to person perception and depression. In N. Cantor & J. Kihlstrom (Eds.), *Personality and social intelligence* (pp. 215–232). Englewood Cliffs, NJ: Prentice-Hall. [9]

Kuiper, N. A., & Higgins, E. T. (1985). Social cognition and depression. *Social Cognition, 3,* 1–15. [9]

Kuiper, N. A., & MacDonald, M. R. (1982). Self and other perception in mild depressives. *Social Cognition, 1,* 223–239. [9]

Kulp, D. H. Jr. (1933). The form of statements in attitude tests. *Journal of Sociology and Social Research, 18,* 18–25. [4]

Kutner, B., Wilkins, C., & Yarrow, P. R. (1952). Verbal attitudes and overt behavior involving racial prejudice. *Journal of Abnormal and Social Psychology, 47,* 649–652. [5]

LaCrosse, M. B. (1975). Nonverbal behavior and perceived counselor attractiveness and persuasiveness. *Journal of Counseling Psychology, 22,* 563–566. [33]

LaFrance, M., & Mayo, C. (1976). Racial differences in gaze behavior during conversations: Two systematic observational studies. *Journal of Personality and Social Psychology, 33,* 547–552. [17]

LaFrance, M., & Mayo, C. (1978a). Cultural aspects of nonverbal communication. *International Journal of Intercultural Relations, 2,* 71–89. [17]

LaFrance, M., & Mayo, C. (1978b). Gaze direction in interracial dyadic communication. *Ethnicity, 5,* 167–173. [17]

LaFree, G. D. (1980). The effect of sexual stratification by race on official reactions to rape. *American Sociological Review, 45*, 842. [29]

LaFree, G. D. (1981). Official reactions to social problems: Police decisions in sexual assault case. *Social Problems, 28*, 592. [29]

Lakoff, G. (1973). Hedges: A study in meaning criteria and the logic of fuzzy concepts. *Journal of Philosophical Logic, 2*, 458–508. [18]

Landis, C., & Hunt, W. A. (1932). Adrenalin and emotion. *Psychological Review, 39*, 467–485. [14]

Lange, L. (1887). *Ueber Gemuthsbewegungen uebersetzt*. Leipzig: von H. Kurella. [13]

Lange, L. (1888). Neue Experimente über den Vorgang der einfachen Reaction auf Sinneseindrücke. *Philosophie Studies, 4*, 479–510. [4]

Lange, N. (1888). Beiträge zur theorie der sinnlichen Aufmerksamkeit und der activen Apperception. *Philosophie Studies, 4*, 390–422. [4]

Langer, E., Blank, A., & Chanowitz, B. (1978). The mindlessness of ostensibly thoughtful action: The role of "placebic" information in interpersonal attraction. *Journal of Personality and Social Psychology, 36*, 635–642. [36]

Langer, E. J. (1979a). Old age: An artifact? *Biology, behavior, and aging*. Washington, DC: National Research Council publication. [27]

Langer, E. J. (1979b). The illusion of incompetence. In L. Perlmutter & R. Monty (Eds.), *Choice and perceived control*. Hillsdale, NJ: Erlbaum. [27]

Langer, E. J., & Abelson, R. P. (1972). The semantics of asking a favor: How to succeed in getting help without really dying. *Journal of Personality and Social Psychology, 24*, 26–32. [6]

Langer, E. J., & Abelson, R. P. (1974). A patient by any other name. *Journal of Consulting and Clinical Psychology, 42*, 4–9. [27]

Langer, E. J., & Benevento, A. (1978). Self-induced dependence. *Journal of Personality and Social Psychology, 36*, 886–893. [27]

Langer, E. J., Janis, I. L., & Wolfer, J. A. (1975). Reduction of psychological stress in surgical patients. *Journal of Experimental Social Psychology, 11*, 155–165. [33]

Langer, E. J., & Mulvey, A. (1980). Unpublished data. Harvard University, Department of Psychology, Cambridge, MA. [27]

Langer, E. J., & Rodin, J. (1976). The effects of choice and enhanced personal responsibility for the aged: A field experiment in an institutional setting. *Journal of Personality and Social Psychology, 34*, 191–198. [27]

Langer, E. J., Rodin, J., Beck, P., Weinman, C., & Spitzer, L. (1979). Environmental determinants of memory improvement in late adulthood. *Journal of Personality and Social Psychology, 37*, 2003–2013. [27]

Langer, E. J., Taylor, S., Fiske, S., & Chanowitz, B. (1976). Stigma, staring, and discomfort. *Journal of Experimental Social Psychology, 12*, 451–463. [27]

LaPiere, R. T. (1934). Attitudes versus actions. *Social Forces, 13*, 230–237. [5], [RI-5]

Lasker, B. (1929). *Race attitudes in children*. New York: Holt. [4]

Lasswell, T. E., & Lasswell, M. E. (1976). I love you but I'm not in love with you. *Journal of Marriage and Family Counseling, 2*, 211–224. [18]

Lastovicka, J. L., & Gardner, D. M. (1979). Components of involvement. In J. C. Mahoney & B. Silverman (Eds.), *Attitude research plays for high stakes* (pp. 53–73). Chicago: American Marketing Association. [36]

Latané, B., & Darley, J. M. (1968). Group inhibition of bystander intervention. *Journal of Personality and Social Psychology, 10*, 215–221. [31]

Latané, B., & Rodin, J. (1969). A lady in distress: Inhibiting effects of friends and strangers on bystander intervention. *Journal of Experimental Social Psychology, 5*, 189–202. [31]

Latané, B., & Schachter, S. (1962). Adrenalin and avoidance learning. *Journal of Comparative Physiological Psychology, 65*, 369–372. [14]

Latané, B., Williams, K., & Harkins, S. (1979). Many hands make light the work: The causes and consequences of social loafing. *Journal of Personality and Social Psychology, 37*, 823–832. [39]

Latané, B., & Wolf, S. (1981). The social impact of majorities and minorities. *Psychological Review, 88*, 438–454. [38]

Laws, J. L., & Schwartz, P. (1977). *Sexual scripts*. Hinsdale, IL: Dryden Press. [29]

Lazarsfeld, P. F., & Merton, R. K. (1948). Mass communication, popular taste, and organized social action. In L. Bryson (Ed.), *The communication of ideas* (pp. 95–118). New York: Harper. [23]

Lazarus, A. A. (1976). Psychiatric problems precipitated by transcendental meditation. *Psychological Reports, 39*, 601–602. [15]

Lazarus, R. S. (1966). Psychological stress and the coping process. New York: McGraw-Hill. [15]

Lee, J. A. (1977). A typology of styles of loving. *Personality and Social Psychology Bulletin, 3,* 173–182. [18]

Leeper, R. W. (1970). The motivational and perceptual properties of emotions as indicating their fundamental character and role. In M. B. Arnold (Ed.), *Feelings and emotions: The Loyola symposium.* New York: Academic Press. [15]

LeGrand, C. E. (1973). Rape and rape laws: Sexism in society and law. *California Law Review, 61,* 922. [29]

Leik, R. K., & Leik, S. A. (1977). Transition to interpersonal commitment. In R. Hamblin & J. H. Kunkel (Eds.), *Behavioral theory in sociology* (pp. 299–322). New Brunswick, NJ: Transaction Books. [18]

Lemann, T. B., & Solomon, R. L. (1952). Group characteristics as revealed in sociometric patterns and personality ratings. *Sociometry, 15,* 7–90. [11]

Lenauer, M., Sameth, L., & Shaver, P. (1976). Looking back at oneself in time: Another approach to the actor-observer phenomenon. *Perceptual and Motor Skills, 43,* 1283–1287. [12]

Lenney, E. (1977). Women's confidence in achievement settings. *Psychological Bulletin, 84,* 1–13. [30]

Lenney, E. (1981). What's fine for the gander isn't always good for the goose: Sex differences in self-confidence as a function of ability area and comparison with others. *Sex Roles, 7,* 905–924. [30]

Leonard, W. E. (1927). *The locomotive-god.* New York: Century. [4]

Lepper, M. R., Greene, D., & Nisbett, R. E. (1973). Undermining children's intrinsic interest with extrinsic reward: A test of the "overjustification" hypothesis. *Journal of Personality and Social Psychology, 28,* 129–137. [6]

Lester, M. (1984). Self: Sociological portraits. In J. A. Kotarbu & A. Fontana (Eds.), *The existential self in society.* Chicago: University of Chicago Press. [9]

Leventhal, H. A. (1979). A perceptual-motor processing model of emotion. Applications to the study of pain and humor. In P. Pliner, K. R. Blankenstein, & I. M. Spigel (Eds.), *Advances in the study of communication and affect.* Vol. 5: *Perception of emotions in self and others.* New York: Plenum. [15]

Levinger, G. (1980). Toward the analysis of close relationships. *Journal of Experimental Social Psychology, 16,* 510–544. [18]

Levinson, D. J. (1978). *The seasons of a man's life.* New York: Ballentine. [9]

Levitt, E. A. (1964) The relationship between abilities to express emotional meanings vocally and facially. In J. R. Davitz (Ed.), *The communication of emotional meaning.* New York: McGraw-Hill. [8].

Lewin, K. (1931). Environmental forces in child behavior and development. In C. Murchison (Ed.), *A handbook of child psychology* (pp. 94–127). Worcester, MA: Clark University Press. [4]

Lewin, K. (1935). *Dynamic theory of personality.* New York: McGraw-Hill. [3], [RI-30]

Lewin, K. (1936). *Principles of topological personality.* New York: McGraw-Hill. [3]

Lewin, K. (1938). The conceptual representation and measurement of psychological forces. *Contemporary Psychological Theory, 1,* No. 4. [3]

Lewin, K. (1939). Field theory and experiment in social psychology: Concepts and methods. *American Journal of Sociology, 44,* 868–896. [3]

Lewin, K. (1940). Bringing up the child. *Menorah Journal, 28,* 20–45. [3]

Lewin, K., Dembo, T., Festinger, L., & Sears, P. S. (1944). Level of aspiration. In J. McV. Hunt (Ed.), *Personality and the Behavior Disorders.* (Vol. 1, pp. 33–378). New York: Ronald Press. [16]

Lewin, K., Lippitt, R., & White, R. (1939). Patterns of aggressive behavior in experimentally created "social climates." *Journal of Social Psychology, 10,* 271–299. [3]

Liebert, R. M., & Sprafkin, J. N. (1988). *The early window: Effects of television on children and youth* (3rd ed.). New York: Pergaman Press. [RI-23]

Liebert, R. M., Sprafkin, J. N., & Davidson, E. S. (1982). *The early window: Effects of television on children and youth* (2nd ed.). New York: Pergamon Press. [26]

Liebhart, E. H. (1979). Information search and attribution: Cognitive processes mediating the effect of false autonomic feedback. *European Journal of Social Psychology, 9,* 19–37. [36]

Likert, R. (1932–1933). Technique for the measurement of attitudes. *Archives of Psychology, 22,* 55. [4]

Lindquist, E. F. (1956). *Design and analysis of experiments*. Boston: Houghton Mifflin. [20]

Lindsley, D. B. (1951). Emotion. In S. S. Stevens (Ed.), *Handbook of experimental psychology* (pp. 473–516). New York: Wiley. [14]

Linville, P. W. (1982). Affective consequences of complexity regarding the self and others. In M. S. Clarke & S. T. Fiske (Eds.), *Affect and cognition*. Hillsdale, NJ: Erlbaum. [9]

Linz, D., Donnerstein, E., & Penrod, S. (1988). Effects of long-term exposure to violent and sexually degrading depictions of women. *Journal of Personality and Social Psychology, 55*, 758–768. [RI-29]

Lippitt, R. (1939). Field theory and experiment in social psychology: Autocratic and democratic group atmospheres. *American Journal of Sociology, 45*, 26–49. [3]

Lippitt, R., & White, R. (1943). The "social climate" of children's groups. In R. Barker, J. S. Kounin, and B. A. Wright (Eds.), *Child behavior and development*. New York: McGraw-Hill. [3]

Lippmann, W. (1922). *Public opinion*. New York: Harcourt, Brace. [4]

Locksley, A., Borgida, E., Brekke, N., & Hepburn, C. (1980). Sex stereotypes and social judgment. *Journal of Personality and Social Psychology, 39*, 821–831. [30]

Loftus, E., & Palmer, J. (1974). Reconstruction of automobile destruction. *Journal of Verbal Learning and Verbal Behavior, 13*, 585–589. [32]

Logan, F., Olmsted, O. L., Rosner, B. S., Schwartz, R. D., & Stevens, C. M. (1955). *Behavior theory and social science*. New Haven, CT: Yale University Press. [20]

Lott, B. (1981). A feminist critique of androgyny: Toward the elimination of gender attributions for learned behavior. In C. Mayo & N. M. Henley (Eds.), *Gender and nonverbal behavior* (pp. 171–180). New York: Springer. [30]

Loy, J. W., & Andrews, D. S. (1981). They also saw a game: A replication of a case study. *Replications in Social Psychology, 1*(2), 45–59. [RI-10]

Lund, F. H. (1925). The psychology of belief. *Journal of Abnormal and Social Psychology, 20*, 23–81. [4]

Lundberg, A., & Dickson, L. (1952). Selective association among ethnic groups in a high school population. *American Sociological Review, 17*, 23–34. [25]

Lundberg, G. A. (1929). *Social research*. New York: Longmans, Green. [4]

Lutz, R. J., & Bettman, J. R. (1977). Multiattribute models in marketing: A bicentennial review. In A. Woodside, J. Sheth, & P. D. Bennett (Eds.), *Consumer and industrial buying behavior* (pp. 137–150). New York: Elsevier North-Holland. [36]

Lynch, J. J., Thomas, S. A., Mills, M. E., Malinow, K., & Katcher, A. H. (1974). The effects of human contact on cardiac arrhythmia in coronary care patients. *The Journal of Nervous and Mental Disease, 158*, 88–99. [33]

Maccoby, E. E. (1959). Role-taking in childhood and its consequences for social learning. *Child Development, 30*, 239–252. [20]

Maccoby, E. E., & Jacklin, C. N. (1974). *The psychology of sex differences*. Stanford, CA: Stanford University Press. [30]

MacDonald, J. M. (1940). *The behavior of the young child under conditions of insecurity*. Unpublished Ph.D. Dissertation, Harvard University. [3]

Maginn, B., & Harris, R. (1980). Effects of anticipated evaluation on individual brainstorming performance. *Journal of Applied Psychology, 65*, 219–225. [39]

Major, B., & Deaux, K. (1982). Individual differences in justice behavior. In J. Greenberg & R. L. Cohen (Eds.), *Equity and justice in social behavior*. (pp. 43–76). New York: Academic Press. [30]

Malamuth, N. M., & Donnerstein, E. (Eds.) (1984). *Pornography and sexual aggression*, New York: Academic Press. [RI-29]

Malt, B. C., & Smith, E. E. (1982). The role of familiarity in determining typicality. *Memory and Cognition, 10*, 69–75. [18]

Mandler, G. (1975). *Mind and emotion*. New York: Wiley. [15]

Marañon, G. (1924). Contribution à l'étude de l'action émotive de l'adrénaline. *Review Francaise Endocrinal, 2*, 301–325. [14]

Markus, H. (1977). Self-schemata and processing information about the self. *Journal of Personality and Social Psychology, 35*, 63–78. [17]

Markus, H. (1978). The effect of mere presence on social facilitation: An unobtrusive test. *Journal of Experimental Social Psychology, 14*, 389–397. [39]

Markus, H. (1981). The drive for integration: Some comments. *Journal of Experimental Social Psychology, 17*, 257–261. [39]

Markus, H. (1983). Self-knowledge: An expanded view. *Journal of Personality, 51,* 543–565. [9]

Markus, H., Crane, M., Bernstein, S., & Siladi, M. (1982). Self schemas and gender. *Journal of Personality and Social Psychology, 42,* 38–50. [30]

Markus, H., & Nurius, P. (1986). Possible selves. *American Psychologist, 41,* 954–969. [9], [RI-9]

Markus, H., & Sentis, K. (1982). The self in social information processing. In J. Suls (Ed.), *Psychological perspectives of the self* (Vol. 1, pp. 41–70). Hillsdale, NJ: Erlbaum. [9]

Marple, C. H. (1933). The comparative susceptibility of three age levels to the suggestion of group versus expert opinion. *Journal of Social Psychology, 4,* 176–184. [4]

Marquis, D. P. (1931). Can conditioned responses be established in the newborn infant? *Journal of Genetic Psychology, 39,* 479–492. [3]

Martens, R., & Landers, D. (1972). Evaluation potential as a determinant of coaction effects. *Journal of Experimental Social Psychology, 8,* 347–359. [39]

Martindale, C. (1980). Subselves: The internal representation of situational and personal dispositions. In L. Wheeler (Ed.), *Review of Personality and Social Psychology, 1,* 193–218. Beverly Hills, CA: Sage. [9]

Maslow, A. (1954). *Motivation and personality.* New York: Harper. [9]

Massing, P. W. (1949). *Rehearsal for destruction.* New York: Harper. [25]

McArthur, L. A. (1972). The how and what of why: Some determinants and consequences of causal attribution. *Journal of Personality and Social Psychology, 22,* 171–193. [11], [RI-11]

McCaldon, R. J. (1967). Rape. *Canadian Journal of Corrections, 9,* 47. [29]

McCauley, C., & Stitt, C. L. (1978). An individual and quantitative measure of stereotypes. *Journal of Personality and Social Psychology, 36,* 920–940. [30]

McConahay, J. B., & Hough, J. C. (1976). Symbolic racism. *Journal of Social Issues, 32,* 23–45. [26]

McDougall, W. (1908). *Social psychology.* Boston: Luce. [28], [RI-20]

McDougall, W. (1921). *An introduction to social psychology* (14th ed.). Boston: Luce. [4]

McDougall, W. (1926). *Outline of abnormal psychology.* New York: Scribner's. [4]

McDougall, W. (1933). *The energies of men.* New York: Scribner's. [4]

McDougall, W. (1948). *An outline of psychology* (12th ed.). London: Methuen. [15]

McGowen, J. F., & Schmidt, L. D. (1962). *Counseling: Readings in theory and practice.* New York: Holt, Rinehart & Winston. [33]

McGraw, M. B. (1935). *Growth: A study of Johnny and Jimmy.* New York: Appleton-Century. [3]

McGuire, W. J. (1969). The nature of attitudes and attitude change. In G. Lindzey & E. Aronson (Eds.), *Handbook of Social Psychology* (Vol. 3, pp. 136–314). New York: Random House. [36]

McGuire, W. J. (1976). Some internal psychological factors influencing consumer choice. *Journal of Consumer Research, 2,* 302–319. [36]

McGuire, W. J. (1984). Search for the self: Going beyond self-esteem and the reactive self. In R. A. Zucker, A. Aronoff, & I. Rabin (Eds.), *Personality and the prediction of behavior.* New York: Academic. [9]

McGuire, W. J. (1985). Attitudes and attitude change. In G. Lindzey & E. Aronson (Eds.), *Handbook of social psychology* (Vol. 2, pp. 239–346) (3rd ed). New York: Random House. [RI-4], [RI-23]

McGuire, W. J., & McGuire, C. V. (1982). Significant others in the self-space: Sex differences and developmental trends in the social self. In J. Suls (Ed.), *Psychological perspectives of the self* (Vol. 1, pp. 71–96). Hillsdale, NJ: Erlbaum. [9]

McGuire, W. J., & Padawer-Singer, A. (1976). Trait salience in the spontaneous self-concept. *Journal of Personality and Social Psychology, 33,* 743–754. [38]

McQuail, D. (1976). Alternative models of television influence. In R. Brown (Ed.), *Children and television* (pp. 343–360). Beverly Hills, CA: Sage. [23]

Mead, G. H. (1924–1925). Genesis of self and social control. *International Journal of Ethics,* 251–277. [4]

Mead, G. H. (1934). *Mind, self, and society.* Chicago: University of Chicago Press. [9], [15]

Mead, M. (1928). *Coming of age in Samoa.* New York: Morrow. [3]

Mead, M. (1937). *Cooperation and competition among primitive peoples.* New York: McGraw-Hill. [3]

Mead, M. (1968). *Sex and temperament in three primitive societies.* New York: Dell. [29]

Mead, M., & Baldwin, J. (1971). *A rap on race.* New York: J. B. Lippincott. [26]

Mechanic, D. (1968). *Medical sociology: A selective view.* New York: The Free Press. [33]

Medea, A., & Thompson, K. (1974). *Against rape.* New York: Farrar, Strauss & Giroux. [17], [29]

Medin, D. L., Altom, M. W., & Murphy, T. D. (1984). Given versus induced category representations: Use of prototype and exemplar information classification. *Journal of Experimental Psychology: Learning, Memory, and Cognition, 10,* 333–352. [18]

Medin, D. L., & Smith, E. E. (1984). Concepts and concept formation. *Annual Review of Psychology, 35,* 113–138. [18]

Mednick, M. T. S., & Weissman, H. J. (1975). The psychology of women: Selected topics. *Annual Review of Psychology, 26,* 1–18. [30]

Mehrabian, A. (1969). Significance of posture and position in the communication of attitude and status relationship. *Psychological Bulletin, 71,* 359–372. [8]

Merton, R. K. (1948). The self-fulfilling prophecy. *Antioch Review, 8,* 193–210. [32], [RI-32]

Mervis, C. B., & Rosch, E. (1981). Categorization of natural objects. *Annual Review of Psychology, 32,* 89–115. [18]

Meyer, D. E., & Schvaneveldt, R. W. (1971). Facilitation in recognizing pairs of words: Evidence of dependence between retrieval operations. *Journal of Experimental Psychology, 90,* 227–234. [26]

Meyer, D. E., & Schvaneveldt, R. W. (1976). Meaning, memory structure, and mental processes. *Science, 192,* 27–33. [26]

Milgram, S. (1961, Jan. 25). *Dynamics of obedience.* Washington: National Science Foundation. [35]

Milgram, S. (1964). Some conditions of obedience and disobedience to authority. *Human Relations, 18,* 57–76. [35]

Milgram, S. (1974). *Obedience to authority.* New York: Harper & Row. [RI-35]

Miller, D. B., Lowenstein, R., & Winston, R. (1976). Physicians' attitudes toward the ill aged and nursing homes. *Journal of the American Geriatrics Society, 24,* 498–505. [27]

Miller, D. T., & Ross, M. (1975). Self-serving biases in the attribution of causality: Fact or fiction? *Psychological Bulletin, 82,* 213–225. [17], [RI-11]

Miller, N. & Brewer, M. B. (1986). Social categorization theory and team learning procedures. In R. S. Feldman (Ed.), *The social psychology of education: Current research and theory* (pp. 172–198). New York: Cambridge University Press. [RI-26]

Miller, N., Maruyama, G., Beaber, R. J., & Vallone, K. (1976). Speed of speech and persuasion. *Journal of Personality and Social Psychology, 34,* 615–624. [36]

Miller, N. E. (1941). The frustration-aggression hypothesis. *Psychological Review, 48,* 337–342. [21]

Miller, N. E., & Dollard, J. (1941). *Social learning and imitation.* New Haven, CT: Yale University Press. [20]

Milmoe, S., Rosenthal, R., Blane, H. T., Chafetz, M. L., & Wolf, I. (1967). The doctor's voice: Postdictor of successful referral of alcoholic patients. *Journal of Abnormal Psychology, 72,* 78–84. [33]

Minard, R. D. (1952). Race relationships in the Pocahontas coal field. *Journal of Social Issues, 8,* 29–44. [5]

Mischel, W. (1968). *Personality and assessment.* New York: Wiley. [8], [12], [32]

Mitchell, A. A., & Olson, J. C. (1981). Are product attribute beliefs the only mediator of advertising effects on brand attitude? *Journal of Marketing Research, 18,* 318–332. [36]

Money, J. (1980). *Love and love sickness.* Baltimore: Johns Hopkins University Press. [18]

Moore, B. S., Sherrod, D. R., Liu, T. J., & Underwood, B. (1979). The dispositional shift in attribution over time. *Journal of Experimental Social Psychology, 15,* 553–569. [12]

Moore, H. T. (1921). The comparative influence of majority and expert opinion. *American Journal of Psychology, 32,* 16–20. [4]

Moore, H. T. (1925). Innate factors in radicalism and conservatism. *Journal of Abnormal and Social Psychology, 20,* 234–244. [4]

Moos, R. H. (1968). Situational analysis of a therapeutic community milieu. *Journal of Abnormal Psychology, 73,* 49–61. [8]

Moos, R. H. (1969). Sources of variance in responses to questionnaires and in behavior. *Journal of Abnormal Psychology, 74,* 403–412. [8]

Moreland, R. L., & Levine, J. M. (1982). Socialization in small groups: Temporal changes in individual-group relations. In L. Berkowitz (Ed.), *Advances in experimental social psychology* (Vol. 15, pp. 137–189). New York: Academic Press. [38]

Morgan, J. J. B. (1934). *Keeping a sound mind.* New York: Macmillan. [4]

Morgan, M. (1982). Television and adolescents' sex-role stereotypes: A longitudinal study. *Journal of Personality and Social Psychology, 43,* 947–955. [23]

Morgan, M. (1983). Symbolic victimization and real-world fear. *Human Communication Research, 9*(2), 146–157. [23]

Morgan, M. (1984). *Television and the erosion of regional diversity.* Paper presented at the meeting of the International Association for Mass Communications Research, Prague. [23]

Morgan, M., & Gerbner, G. (1982). TV professions and adolescent career choices. In M. Schwarz (Ed.), *TV and teens: Experts look at the issues* (pp. 121–126). Reading, MA: Addison-Wesley. [23]

Morgan, M., & Gross, L. (1982). Television and educational achievement and aspirations. In D. Pearl, L. Bouthilet, & J. Lazar (Eds.), *Television and behavior: Ten years of scientific progress and implications for the 80's* (Vol. II, pp. 78–90). Washington, DC: U.S. Government Printing Office. [23]

Morgan, M., & Rothschild, N. (1983). Impact of the new television technology: Cable TV, peers, and sex-role cultivation in the electronic environment. *Youth and Society, 15*(1), 33–50. [23]

Mori, D., Chaiken, S., & Pliner, P. (1987). "Eating lightly" and the self-presentation of femininity. *Journal of Personality and Social Psychology, 53,* 693–702. [RI-38]

Morse, S., & Gergen, K. J. (1970). Social comparison, self-consistency, and the concept of self. *Journal of Personality and Social Psychology, 16,* 148–156. [9]

Mowen, J. C. (1980). On product endorser effectiveness: A balance model approach. In J. H. Leigh & C. R. Martin (Eds.), *Current issues and research in advertising* (pp. 41–57). Ann Arbor: University of Michigan. [36]

Mowrer, O. H. (1950). Identification: A link between learning theory and psychotherapy. In O. H. Mowrer (Ed.), *Learning theory and personality dynamics* (pp. 69–94). New York: Ronald. [20]

Mullen, B., Atkins, J. L., Champion, D. S., Edwards, C., Hardy, D., Story, J. E., & Vanderklok, M. (1985). The false consensus effect: A meta-analysis of 115 hypothesis tests. *Journal of Experimental Social Psychology, 21,* 262–283. [RI-11]

Müller, G. E., & Pilzecker, A. (1900). Experimentelle Beiträge zur Lehre vom Gedächtniss, *Zeitschrift für Psychologie,* Ergbd. *1.* [4]

Münsterberg, H. (1889). *Beiträge zur experimentellen Psychologie* (Vol. I). Freiburg: Mohr. [4]

Murchison, C. (Ed.). (1935). *Handbook of social psychology.* Worchester, MA: Clark University Press. [RI-4]

Murphy, G., & Murphy, L. B. (1931). *Experimental social psychology.* New York: Harper. [4]

Murphy, L. B. (1937). *Social behavior and child personality: An explorative study of some roots of sympathy.* New York: Columbia University Press. [3]

Murray, H. A. (1933). The effect of fear upon estimates of the maliciousness of other personalities. *Journal of Social Psychology, 4,* 310–339. [11]

Murray, H. A. (1938). *Explorations in personality.* London: Oxford University Press. [3]

Murstein, B. I., & Pryer, R. S. (1959). The concept of projection: A review. *Psychological Bulletin, 56,* 353–374. [11]

Myrdal, G. (1944). *An American dilemma.* New York: Harper & Row. [26], [32]

National Institute of Law Enforcement and Criminal Justice. (1977). *Forcible rape: A national survey of the response by prosecutors* (Vol. 1). Washington, DC: U.S. Government Printing Office. [29]

Nel, E., Helmreich, R., & Aronson, E. (1969). Opinion change in the advocate as a function of the persuasibility of his audience: A clarification of the meaning of dissonance. *Journal of Personality and Social Psychology, 12,* 117–124. [6]

Newcomb, T. M. (1943). *Personality and social change.* New York: Dryden. [38]

Newman, L. M., & Dolich, I. J. (1979). An examination of ego-involvement as a modifier of attitude changes caused from product testing. In W. L. Wilkie (Ed.), *Advances in consumer research* (Vol. 6, pp. 180–183). Ann Arbor, MI: Association for Consumer Research. [36]

Newsweek, February 26, 1979. [26]

New York Times (1967, Sept. 18). Negroes accuse Maryland bench: Double standard is charged in report on rape case, p. 33. [29]

New York Times (1977, May 17). Judge in Wisconsin calls rape by boy "normal" reaction. p. 9. [29]

Nisbett, R. E. (1972). Hunger, obesity and the ventromedial hypothalamus. *Psychological Review, 79,* 433–453. [38]

Nisbett, R. E., & Borgida, E. (1975). Attribution and the psychology of prediction. *Journal of Personality and Social Psychology, 32,* 932–943. [11]

Nisbett, R. E., Borgida, E., Crandall, R., & Reed, H. (1976). Popular induction: Information is not necessarily informative. In J. Carroll & J. Payne (Eds.), *Cognition and social behavior*. Potomac, MD: Erlbaum. [11]

Nisbett, R. E., Caputo, G. C., Legant, P., & Maracek, J. (1973). Behavior as seen by the actor and as seen by the observer. *Journal of Personality and Social Psychology, 27*, 154–164. [11]

Nisbett, R. E., & Ross, L. (1980). *Human inference: Strategies and shortcomings of social judgment*. Englewood Cliffs, NJ: Prentice-Hall. [9]

Nisbett, R. E., & Valins, S. (1971). Perceiving the causes of one's own behavior. In E. E. Jones, D. E. Kanouse, H. H. Kelley, R. E. Nisbett, S. Valins, & B. Weiner, *Attribution: Perceiving the causes of behavior*. Morristown, NJ: General Learning Press. [15]

Nisbett, R. E., & Wilson, T. D. (1977). Telling more than we can know: Verbal reports on mental processes. *Psychological Review, 84*, 229–259. [12], [18]

North, C. C. (1932). *Social problems and social planning*. New York: McGraw-Hill. [4]

Nowlis, V., & Nowlis, H. H. (1956). The description and analysis of mood. *Annals of the New York Academy of Science, 65*, 345–355. [14]

Noyes, R. (1972). The experience of dying. *Psychiatry, 35*, 174–184. [15]

Nunnally, J. C. (1967). *Psychometric theory*. New York: McGraw-Hill. [8]

Nuttin, J. (1984). *Motivation, planning, and action: A relational theory of behavior dynamics*. Hillsdale, NJ: Erlbaum. [9]

Nuttin, J., & Lens, W. (1986). *Future time perspective and motivation*. Hillsdale, NJ: Erlbaum. [9]

Ogden, R. M. (1926). *Psychology and education*. New York: Harcourt, Brace. [4]

Ogilvie, D. M. (1987). The undesired self: A neglected variable in personality research. *Journal of Personality and Social Psychology, 52*, 379–385. [RI-9]

Orbach, S. (1978). *Fat is a feminist issue*. New York: Berkeley Press. [38]

Orford, J. (1985). *Excessive appetites*. London: Wiley. [38]

Oskamp, S. (Ed.) (1988). *Television as a social issue*. Beverley Hills, CA: Sage. [RI-23]

Osler, W. (1904). The master-word in medicine. In *Aequanimitas with other addresses to medical students, nurses, and practitioners of medicine* (pp. 369–371). Philadelphia: Blakiston Co. [33]

Padgett, V. R. (1987). *Predicting violence in totalitarian organizations: An application of 11 powerful principles of obedience from Milgram's experiments on obedience to authority*. Unpublished manuscript, Department of Psychology, Marshall University, Huntington, W. Va. [RI-35]

Palamarek, D. L., & Rule, B. G. (1979). The effects of ambient temperature and insult on the motivation to retaliate or escape. *Motivation and Emotion, 3*, 83–92. [21]

Pallak, M. S., & Kleinhesselink, R. R. (1976). Polarization of attitudes: Belief inference from consonant behavior. *Personality and Social Psychology Bulletin, 2*, 55–58. [6]

Park, R. E. (1924). Experience and race relations. *Journal of Applied Sociology, 9*, 18–24. [4]

Park, R. E., & Burgess, E. W. (1924). *Introduction to the science of sociology*. Chicago: University of Chicago Press. [4]

Parsons, T. (1951). *The social system*. Glencoe, IL: The Free Press. [15], [33]

Parsons, T. (1958). Definitions of health and illness in the light of American values and social structure. In E. G. Jaco (Ed.), *Patients, physicians, and illness* (pp. 165–187). New York: The Free Press. [33]

Parsons, T. (1959). An approach to psychological theory in terms of the theory of action. In S. Koch (Ed.), *Psychology: A study of a science*, Vol. 3: *Formulations of the person and the social context*. New York: McGraw-Hill. [15]

Pennebaker, J. W., & Skelton, J. A. (1978). Psychological parameters of physical symptoms. *Personality and Social Psychology Bulletin, 4*, 524–530. [27]

Perlman, D., & Fehr, B. (1987). The development of intimate relationships. In D. Perlman & S. Duck (Eds.), *Intimate relationships: Development, dynamics, and deterioration* (pp. 13–42). Beverly Hills, CA: Sage. [18]

Peters, L. H., Terborg, J. R., & Taynor, J. (1974). Women as managers scale: A measure of attitudes toward women in management positions. *JSAS Catalogue of Selected Documents in Psychology, 4*, 27. (Ms. No. 585). [30]

Peterson, D. A., & Karnes, E. L. (1976). Older people in adolescent literature. *Gerontologist, 16*, 252–231. [27]

Peterson, R. C., & Thurstone, L. L. (1933). *Motion pictures and the social attitudes of children.* New York: Macmillan. [4]

Petty, R. E., & Cacioppo, J. T. (1979). Issue involvement can increase or decrease persuasion by enhancing message-relevant cognitive responses. *Journal of Personality and Social Psychology, 37,* 1915–1926. [36]

Petty, R. E., & Cacioppo, J. T. (1980). Effects of issue involvement on attitudes in an advertising context. In G. G. Gorn & M. E. Goldberg (Eds.), *Proceedings of the Division 23 Program* (pp. 75–79). Montreal: American Psychological Association. [36]

Petty, R. E., & Cacioppo, J. T. (1981). *Attitudes and persuasion: Classic and contemporary approaches.* Dubuque, IA: William C. Brown. [36]

Petty, R. E., & Cacioppo, J. T. (1983). Central and peripheral routes to persuasion: Application to advertising. In L. Percy & A. Woodside (Eds.), *Advertising and consumer psychology* (pp. 3–23). Lexington, MA: Lexington Books. [36]

Petty, R. E., & Cacioppo, J. T. (1986). *Communication and persuasion: Central and peripheral routes to attitude and age.* New York: Springer-Verlag. [36]

Petty, R. E., & Cacioppo, J. T. (1987). The effects of involvement on responses to argument quality and quantity: Central and peripheral routes to persuasion. *Journal of Personality and Social Psychology, 46,* 69–81. [36]

Petty, R. E., Cacioppo, J. T., & Goldman, R. (1981). Personal involvement as a determinant of argument-based persuasion. *Journal of Personality and Social Psychology, 41,* 847–855. [36]

Petty, R. E., Cacioppo, J. T., & Heesacker, M. (1981). The use of rhetorical questions in persuasion: A cognitive response analysis. *Journal of Personality and Social Psychology, 40,* 432–440. [36]

Petty, R. E., Harkins, S., Williams, K., & Latané, B. (1977). The effects of group size on cognitive effort and evaluation. *Personality and Social Psychology Bulletin, 3,* 579–582. [39]

Petty, R. E., Ostrom, T., & Brock, T. C. (1981). Historical foundations of the cognitive response approach to attitudes and persuasion. In R. E. Petty, T. Ostrom, & T. C. Brock (Eds.), *Cognitive responses in persuasion* (pp. 5–29). Hillsdale, NJ: Erlbaum. [36]

Petty, R. E., Wells, G. L., & Brock, T. C. (1979). Distraction can enhance or reduce yielding to propaganda: Thought disruption versus effort justification. *Journal of Personality and Social Psychology, 34,* 847–884. [36]

Piaget, J. (1932). *The moral judgment of the child.* (M. Gabain, Trans.) New York: Harcourt, Brace; London: Kegan Paul. [3]

Pietromonaco, P. R. (1985). The influence of affect on self-perception. *Social Cognition, 3,* 121–134. [9]

Pietromonaco, P. R., Manis, J., & Markus, H. (1987). The relationship of employment to self-perception and well-being in women: A cognitive analysis. *Sex Roles, 17,* 467–477. [9]

Piliavin, J. A., Dovidio, J. F., Gaertner, S. L., & Clark, R. D. III. (1981). *Emergency intervention.* New York: Academic Press. [26]

Pilkonis, P. A. (1977). The influence of consensus information and prior expectations on dispositional and situational attributions. *Journal of Social Psychology, 101,* 267–279. [11]

Pingree, S., & Hawkins, R. P. (1980). U.S. programs on Australian television: The cultivation effect. *Journal of Communication, 31*(1), 97–105. [23]

Pintner, R. (1933). A comparison of interests, abilities, and attitudes. *Journal of Abnormal and Social Psychology, 27,* 351–357. [4]

Plutchik, R. (1962). *The emotions: Facts, theories and a new model.* New York: Random House. [15]

Pogrebin, L. C. (1974, Nov.). Do women make men violent? *Ms., 3,* p. 55. [29]

Polivy, J., & Herman, C. P. (1985). Dieting and binging: A causal analysis. *American Psychologist, 40,* 193–204. [38]

Pope, H. G., & Hudson, J. I. (1984). *New hope for binge eaters: Advances in the understanding and treatment of bulimia.* New York: Harper & Row. [38]

Posner, M. I., & Snyder, C. R. R. (1975). Attention and cognitive control. In R. L. Solso (Ed.), *Information processing and cognition: The Loyola Symposium* (pp. 55–85). Hillsdale, NJ: Erlbaum. [12]

Postman, L. (1972). A pragmatic view of organization theory. In E. Tulving & W. Donaldson (Eds.), *Organization of memory* (pp. 3–48). New York: Academic Press. [12]

Potter, H. W., & Klein, H. R. (1957). On nursing behavior. *Psychiatry, 20,* 39–46. [5]

Powell-Hopson, D., & Hopson, D. S. (1988). Implications of doll color preferences among black preschool children and white preschool children. *Journal of Black Psychology, 14,* 57–63. [RI-25]

Pratt, K. C. (1933). The neonate. In C. Muchison (Ed.), *A handbook of psychology* (2nd ed., rev.), pp. 163–208. Worcester, MA: Clark University Press. [3]

Pratt, K. C., Nelson, A. K., & Sun, K. H. (1930). The behavior of the newborn infant. *Ohio State University Contributions in Psychology, 10.* 1–24. [4]

Privette, G. (1983). Peak experience, peak performance, and flow: A comparative analysis of positive human experience. *Journal of Personality and Social Psychology, 45,* 1361–1368. [9]

Pryor, J. B., & Kriss, M. (1977). The cognitive dynamics of salience in the attribution process. *Journal of Personality and Social Psychology, 33,* 49–55. [12]

Pyle, W. H. (1928). *The psychology of learning* (rev. ed.). Baltimore: Warwick & York. [4]

Pyszczynski, T. A., & Greenberg, J. (1981). Role of disconfirmed expectancies in the instigation of attributional processing. *Journal of Personality and Social Psychology, 40,* 31–38. [12]

Radant, S. (1986, May). *Bulimia as a subtype of borderline personality disorder: A comparison study.* Paper presented at the meeting of the Western Psychological Association, Seattle, WA. [38]

Raush, H. L. (1965). Interaction sequences. *Journal of Personality and Social Psychology, 2,* 487–499. [32]

Ray, M. L., Sawyer, A. G., Rothschild, M. L., Heeler, R. M., Strong, E. C., & Reed, J. B. (1973). Marketing communication and the hierarchy of effects. In P. Clarke (Ed.), *New models for mass communication research* (Vol. 2, pp. 147–176). Beverly Hills, CA: Sage Publications. [36]

Redl, F. (1949). The phenomenon of contagion and "shock-effect" in group therapy. In K. R. Eissler (Ed.), *Searchlights on delinquency.* New York: International Universities Press. [38]

Reedy, M. N., Birren, J. E., & Schaie, K. W. (1981). Age and sex differences in satisfying love relationships across the adult life span. *Human Development, 24,* 52–66. [18]

Regan, D. T., Straus, E., & Fazio, R. (1974). Liking and the attribution process. *Journal of Experimental Social Psychology, 10,* 385–397. [32]

Regents of the University of California v. Bakke (1978). *U.S. Law Weekly, 46,* 4896. [26]

Reichenbach, H. (1928). *Philosophie der Raum-Zeitlehre.* Leipzig: De Gruyter. [3]

Reisenzein, R. (1983). The Schachter theory of emotion: Two decades later. *Psychological Bulletin, 94,* 239–264. [RI-14]

Remmers, H. H. (Ed.). (1934). Studies in attitudes. *Studies in Higher Education, 26,* 12–36. [4]

Reuter, E. B. (1937). The sociology of adolescence. *American Journal of Sociology, 43,* 414–427. [3]

Reyes, R. M., Thompson, W. C., & Bower, G. H. (1980). Judgmental biases resulting from differing availabilities of arguments. *Journal of Personality and Social Psychology, 39,* 2–12. [12]

Rhine, R., & Severance, L. J. (1970). Ego-involvement, discrepancy, source credibility, and attitude change. *Journal of Personality and Social Psychology, 16,* 175–190. [36]

Rhodewalt, F. (1986). Self-presentation and the phenomenal self: On the stability and malleability of self-conceptions. In R. Baumeister (Ed.), *Private and public selves.* New York: Springer-Verlag. [9]

Rhodewalt, F., & Agustdottir, S. (1986). The effects of self-presentation on the phenomenal self. *Journal of Personality and Social Psychology, 50,* 47–55. [9]

Rice, S. A. (1926–1927). Stereotypes: A source of error in judging human character. *Journal of Personality Research, 5,* 267–276. [4]

Rice, S. A. (1930). Statistical studies of social attitudes and public opinion. *Statistics in social studies.* Philadelphia: University of Pennsylvania Press (pp. 171–192). [4]

Richards, J. M., Jr., Taylor, C. W., & Price, P. B. (1962). The prediction of medical intern performance. *Journal of Applied Psychology, 46,* 142–146. [33]

Richman, J. (1977). The foolishness and wisdom of age: Attitudes toward the elderly as reflected in jokes. *Gerontologist, 17,* 219–229. [27]

Ring, K., & Wallston, K. (1968). A test to measure performance styles in interpersonal relations. *Psychological Reports, 22,* 147–154. [8]

Ringelmann, M. (1913). Recherches sur les moteurs animes: Travail de l'homme. *Annales de l'Institut National Agronomique, 2e serie, 12,* 1–40. [39]

Rodin, J. (1978). Somatophysics and attribution. *Personality and Social Psychology Bulletin, 4,* 531–540. [27]

Rodin, J. (1980). Managing the stress of aging: The role of control and coping. In S. Levine & H. Ursin

3(Eds.), *NATO Conference on Coping and Health.* New York: Academic Press. [27]

Rodin, J., & Janis, I. L. (1979). The social power of health-care practitioners as agents of change. *Journal of Social Issues, 35,* 60–81. [27], [33]

Rodin, J., & Langer, E. (1977). Long-term effects of a control-relevant intervention with the institutionalized aged. *Journal of Personality and Social Psychology, 35,* 897–902. [27]

Rodin, J., Silberstein, L. & Striegel-Moore, R. (1984). Women and weight: A normative discontent. *Nebraska Symposium on Motivation* (Vol. 27, pp. 367–407). Lincoln: University of Nebraska Press. [38]

Rogers, C. R. (1951). *Client-centered therapy.* Boston: Houghton Mifflin. [9]

Rogers, C. R. (1954). The case of Mrs. Oak: A research analysis. In C. R. Rogers & R. F. Dymond (Eds.), *Psychotherapy and behavior change* (pp. 348–359). Chicago: University of Chicago Press. [RI-9]

Rogers, C. R. (1957). The necessary and sufficient conditions of therapeutic personality change. *Journal of Consulting Psychology, 21,* 95–103. [33]

Rogers, T. B. (1981). A model of the self as an aspect of the human information processing system. In N. Cantor & J. Kihlstrom (Eds.), *Personality and social intelligence* (pp. 193–214). Englewood Cliffs, NJ: Prentice-Hall. [9]

Roguin, E. (1931). *Sociologie* (Vol. 1). Lausanne: Charles Pach. [4]

Roguin, E. (1932). *Sociologie* (Vol. 2). Lausanne: Charles Pach. [4]

Rokeach, M. (1961). Authority, authoritarianism, and conformity. In I. A. Berg & B. M. Bass (Eds.), *Conformity and deviation* (pp. 230–257). New York: Harper. [35]

Rokeach, M., & Mezei, L. (1966). Race and shared belief as factors in social choice. *Science, 151,* 167–172. [26]

Rosch, E. (1973). On the internal structure of perceptual and semantic categories. In T. E. Moore (Ed.), *Cognitive development and the acquisition of language* (pp. 111–144). New York: Academic Press. [18]

Rosch, E. (1975a). Cognitive representations of semantic categories. *Journal of Experimental Psychology: General, 104,* 192–233. [18], [26]

Rosch, E. (1975b). Cognitive reference points. *Cognitive Psychology, 7,* 532–547. [26]

Rosch, E. (1977). Human categorization. In N. Warren (Ed.), *Studies in cross-cultural psychology* (Vol. 1, pp. 1–49). London: Academic Press. [18]

Rosch, E. (1978). Principles of categorization. In E. Rosch & B. B. Lloyd (Eds.), *Cognition and categorization* (pp. 27–48). Hillsdale, NJ: Erlbaum. [18]

Rosch, E., & Mervis, C. B. (1975). Family resemblances: Studies in the internal structure of categories. *Cognitive Psychology, 7,* 573–605. [18]

Rose, A. (1948). Anti-semitism's roots in city-hatred. *Commentary, 6,* 374–378. [25]

Rose, A. (1951). Anti-semitism's roots in city-hatred. In A. Rose (Ed.), *Race, prejudice, and discrimination* (Ch. 49). New York; Knopf. [25]

Rose, M. A. (1985). *Rush: The girl's guide to sorority success.* New York: Villard. [38]

Rosenbaum, M. E., & deCharms, R. (1960). Direct and vicarious reduction of hostility. *Journal of Abnormal and Social Psychology, 60,* 105–111. [20]

Rosenberg, M. (1965). *Society and adolescent self-image.* Princeton, NJ: Princeton University Press. [38]

Rosenberg, M. (1979). *Conceiving the self.* New York: Basic Books. [9]

Rosenberg, S., & Gara, M. A. (1985). The multiplicity of personal identity. In P. Shaver (Ed.), *Review of Personality and Social Psychology, 6,* 87–113. Beverly Hills, CA: Sage. [9]

Rosenberg, S., & Jones, R. (1972). A method for investigating and representing a person's implicit theory of personality: Theodore Drieser's view of people. *Journal of Personality and Social Psychology, 22,* 372–386. [18]

Rosenberg, S., & Sedlak, A. (1972). Structural representations of perceived personality traits. In A. K. Romney, R. N. Shepard, & S. Nerlove (Eds.), *Multidimensional scaling: Theory and application in the behavioral sciences* (Vol. 2, pp. 133–162). New York: Seminar Press. [18]

Rosenblatt, P. C. (1977). Needed research on commitment in marriage. In G. Levinger & H. L. Raush (Eds.), *Close relationships* (pp. 73–86). Amherst: University of Massachusetts Press. [18]

Rosenblith, J. F. (1959). Learning by imitation in kindergarten children. *Child Development, 30,* 69–80. [20]

Rosenfeld, D., & Stephan, W. G. (1978). Sex differences in attributions for sex-typed tasks. *Journal of Personality, 46,* 244–259. [30]

Rosenfeld, H. M. (1964). Social choice conceived as a level of aspiration. *Journal of Abnormal and Social Psychology, 68,* 491–499. [16]

Rosenhan, D. L. (1973). On being sane in insane places. *Science, 179,* 250–258. [32]

Rosenthal, R. (1966). *Experimenter effects in behavioral research.* New York: Appleton-Century-Crofts. [RI-32]

Rosenthal, R. (1971). Pygmalion reaffirmed. In J. Elashoff & R. Snow (Eds.), *Pygmalion reconsidered* (pp. 139–155). Worthington, OH: C. A. Jones. [27]

Rosenthal, R. (1974). *On the social psychology of the self-fulfilling prophecy: Further evidence for Pygmalion effects and their mediating mechanisms.* New York: Modular Publications. [32], [RI-32]

Rosenthal, R., Hall, J. A., DiMatteo, M. R., Rogers, P. L., & Archer, D. (1979). *Sensitivity to nonverbal communication: The PONS test.* Baltimore: Johns Hopkins University Press. [17], [33]

Rosenthal, R., & Jacobson, L. (1968). *Pygmalion in the classroom: Teacher expectation and intellectual development.* New York: Holt, Rinehart & Winston. [RI-32]

Rosenzweig, M., & Spruill, J. (1986). Twenty years after Twiggy: A retrospective investigation of bulimic-like behaviors. *International Journal of Eating Disorders, 6,* 24–31. [38]

Ross, E. A. (1904). *Social control.* New York: Macmillan. [28], [RI-28]

Ross, E. A. (1908). *Social psychology.* New York: Macmillan. [4]

Ross, L. (1977). The intuitive psychologist and his shortcomings: Distortions in the attribution process. In L. Berkowitz (Ed.), *Advances in experimental social psychology* (Vol. 10). New York: Academic Press. [32], [RI-11]

Ross, L., & Anderson, C. A. (1982). Shortcomings in the attribution process: On the origins and maintenance of erroneous social assessments. In D. Kahneman, P. Slovic, & A. Tversky (Eds.), *Judgment under uncertainty: Heuristics and biases* (pp. 129–152). Cambridge, England: Cambridge University Press. [12]

Ross, M. (1976). The self-perception of intrinsic motivation. In J. H. Harvey, W. J. Ickes, & R. F. Kidd (Eds.), *New directions in attribution research.* Hillsdale, NJ: Erlbaum. [6]

Ross, M., & Conway, M. (1986). Remembering one's own past: The construction of personal histories. In R. M. Sorrentino & E. T. Higgins (Eds.), *Handbook of motivation and cognition: Foundations of social behavior* (pp. 122–144). New York: Guilford. [9]

Ross, M., & Shulman, R. F. (1973). Increasing the salience of initial attitudes: Dissonance versus self-perception theory. *Journal of Personality and Social Psychology, 28,* 138–144. [6]

Rothschild, N. (1984). Small group affiliation as a mediating factor in the cultivation process. In G. Melischek, K. E. Rosengren, & J. Stappers (Eds.), *Cultural indicators: An international symposium* (pp. 377–388). Vienna: Austrian Academy of Sciences. [23]

Rotton, J., & Frey, J. (1985). Air pollution, weather, and violent crimes: Concomitant time-series analysis of archival data. *Journal of Personality and Social Psychology, 49,* 1207–1220. [21]

Rotton, J., Frey, J., Barry, T., Milligan, M., & Fitzpatrick, M. (1979). The air pollution experience and physical aggression. *Journal of Applied Social Psychology, 9,* 397–412. [21]

Rowan, J. (1983). Person as group. In H. H. Blumberg, A. P. Hare, J. Kent, & M. Davies (Eds.), *Small groups and social interaction* (Vol. 2). London: Wiley. [9]

Rubin, Z. (1970). Measurement of romantic love. *Journal of Personality and Social Psychology, 16,* 265–273. [18]

Rubin, Z. (1973). *Liking and loving: An invitation to social psychology.* New York: Holt, Rinehart, & Winston. [15], [18]

Ruble, D. N., & Ruble, T. L. (1982). Sex stereotypes. In A. G. Miller (Ed.), *In the eye of the beholder: Contemporary issues in stereotyping* (pp. 188–252). New York: Praeger. [30]

Ruckmick, C. A. (1936). *The psychology of feeling and emotion.* New York: McGraw-Hill. [14]

Rusbult, C. E. (1980). Commitment and satisfaction in romantic associations: A test of the investment model. *Journal of Experimental Social Psychology, 16,* 172–186. [18]

Russell, D. E. H. (1975). *The politics of rape.* New York: Stein & Day. [17]

Ryan, W. (1971). *Blaming the victim.* New York: Pantheon. [26], [32]

Salancik, J. R. (1974). Inference of one's attitude from behavior recalled under linguistically manipulated cognitive sets. *Journal of Experimental Social Psychology, 10,* 415–427. [6]

Salovey, P., & Rodin, J. (1985). Cognitions about the self: Connecting feeling states and social behavior. In L. Wheeler (Ed.), *Review of Personality and Social Psychology, 6,* 143–167. Beverly Hills, CA: Sage. [9]

Salzman, C., Shader, R., Scott, D. A., & Binstock, W. (1970). Interviewer anger and patient dropout in a walk-in clinic. *Comprehensive Psychiatry, 11,* 267–273. [33]

Sampson, E. E. (1977). Psychology and the American ideal. *Journal of Personality and Social Psychology, 35,* 767–782. [30]

Sanders, G. S., Baron, R. S., & Moore, D. (1978). Distraction and social comparison as mediators of social facilitation effects. *Journal of Experimental Social Psychology, 14,* 291–303. [39]

Sarbin, T. R., & Coe, W. C. (1972). *Hypnosis: A social psychological analysis of influence communication.* New York: Holt, Rinehart, and Winston. [15]

Schachter, J. (1957). Pain, fear, and anger in hypertensives and normotensives: A psychophysiologic study. *Psychosomatic Medicine, 19,* 17–29. [14]

Schachter, S. (1951). Deviation, rejection, and communication. *Journal of Abnormal and Social Psychology, 46,* 190–207. [38]

Schachter, S. (1959). *The psychology of affiliation.* Stanford, CA: Stanford University Press. [14], [15]

Schachter, S. (1971). *Emotion, obesity, and crime.* New York: Academic Press. [15]

Schachter, S., & Hall, R. (1952). Group-derived restraint and audience persuasion. *Human Relations, 5,* 397–406. [20]

Schachter, S., & Singer, J. (1962). Cognitive, social, and physiological determinants of emotional state. *Psychological Review, 69,* 379–399. [8]

Schachter, S., & Wheeler, L. (1962). Epinephrine, chlorpromazine, and amusement. *Journal of Abnormal and Social Psychology, 65,* 121–128. [14]

Schafer, R. (1971). *A new language for psychoanalysis.* New Haven: Yale University Press. [15]

Schaffer, D. R. (1975). Some effects of consonant and dissonant attitudinal advocacy on initial attitude salience and attitude change. *Journal of Personality and Social Psychology, 32,* 160–168. [6]

Schanck, R. L. (1932). A study of a community and its groups and institutions conceived of as behaviors of individuals. *Psychological Monographs, 195,* 133. [3], [4]

Scheibe, K. E. (1985). Historical perspectives on the presented self. In B. R. Schlenker (Ed.), *The self and social life* (pp. 33–65). New York: McGraw-Hill. [9]

Scheier, M. F., Fenigstein, A., & Buss, A. H. (1974). Self-awareness and physical aggression. *Journal of Experimental Social Psychology, 10,* 264–273. [37]

Schlenker, B. R. (1978). Attitudes as actions: Social identity theory and consumer research. In H. K. Hunt (Ed.), *Advances in consumer research* (Vol. 5, pp. 352–359). Ann Arbor, MI: Association for Consumer Research. [36]

Schlenker, B. R. (1980). *Impression management: The self-concept, social identity, and interpersonal relations.* Monterey, CA: Brooks/Cole. [9], [36]

Schlenker, B. R. (1985a). *The self and social life.* New York: McGraw-Hill. [9]

Schlenker, B. R. (1985b). Identity and self-identification. In B. R. Schlenker (Ed.), *The self and social life* (pp. 65–100). New York: McGraw-Hill. [9]

Schlesier-Stropp, B. (1984). Bulimia: A review of the literature. *Psychological Bulletin, 95,* 247–257. [38]

Schneider, D. J., Hastorf, A. H., & Ellsworth, P. C. (1979). *Person perception.* Reading, MA: Addison-Wesley. [12]

Schneider, W., & Shiffrin, R. M. (1977). Controlled and automatic human information processing: I. Detection, search, and attention. *Psychological Review, 84,* 1–61. [12], [36]

Schoeneman, T. J. (1981). Reports of the sources of self-knowledge. *Journal of Personality, 49,* 284–294. [9]

Schofield, J. W. (1975). Effect of norms, public disclosure, and need for approval on volunteering behavior consistent with attitudes. *Journal of Personality and Social Psychology, 31,* 1126–1133. [5]

Schopler, J., & Matthews, M. (1965). The influence of perceived causal locus of partner's dependence on the use of interpersonal power. *Journal of Personality and Social Psychology, 2,* 247–254. [26]

Schultz, L. (1960). Interviewing the sex offender's victim. *Journal of Criminal Law, Criminology and Police Science, 50,* 451. [29]

Schuman, H., & Harding, J. (1964). Prejudice and the norm of rationality. *Sociometry, 27,* 353–371. [26]

Schutz, A. (1964). On multiple realities. In M. Natunson (Ed.), *Collected papers of Alfred Schutz* (Vol. 1). The Hague: Martinus Nijhoff. [9]

Schutz, A. (1968). On multiple realities. In C. Gordon & K. J. Gergen (Eds.), *The self in social interaction* (Vol. 1). New York: Wiley. [15]

Schwartz, S. H., & Tessler, R. C. (1972). A test of a model for reducing measured attitude-behavior discrepancies. *Journal of Personality and Social Psychology, 24,* 225–236. [5]

Schwendinger, J. R., & Schwendinger, H. (1974). Rape myths: In legal, theoretical, and everyday practice. *Crime and Social Justice, 1,* 19. [29]

Scott, C. A. (1978). Self-perception processes in consumer behavior: Interpreting one's own experiences. In H. K. Hunt (Ed.), *Advances in consumer research* (Vol. 5, pp. 714–720). Ann Arbor, MI: Association for Consumer Research. [36]

Scott, J. P. (1969). The emotional basis of social behavior. *Annals of the New York Academy of Science, 159,* 777–790. [15]

Scott, R. A. (1969). *The making of blind men.* New York: Russell Sage. [32]

Scott, W. A. (1968). Attitude measurement. In G. Lindsay & E. Aronson (Eds.), *Handbook of social psychology* (Vol. 2). Reading, MA: Addison-Wesley. [5]

Sears, D. O., & Allen, H. M., Jr. (1984). The trajectory of local desegregation controversies and 4whites' opposition to busing. In N. Miller & M. B. Brewer (Eds.), *Groups in contact: The psychology of desegregation* (pp. 123–151). New York: Academic Press. [26]

Sears, P. S. (1940). Levels of aspiration in academically successful and unsuccessful children. *Journal of Abnormal and Social Psychology, 35,* 498–536. [3]

Secord, P. F., & Jourard, S. M. (1953). The appraisal of body cathexis; Body cathexis and the self. *Journal of Consulting Psychology, 17,* 343–347. [16]

Segall, A. (1976). The sick role concept: Understanding illness behavior. *Journal of Health and Social Behavior, 17,* 162–169. [15]

Seldes, G. (1957). *The new mass media: Challenge to a free society.* Washington, DC: American Association of University Women. [23]

Seta, J., Paulus, P., & Schkade, J. (1976). Effects of group size and proximity under cooperative and competitive conditions. *Journal of Personality and Social Psychology, 34,* 47–53. [39]

Shattuck, F. C. (1907). The science and art of medicine in some of their aspects. *Boston Medical and Surgical Journal, 157,* 63–67. [33]

Shaver, P. R., & Hazan, C. (1988) A biased view of the study of love. *Journal of Social and Personal Relationships, 5,* 473–501. [RI-18]

Shaver, P. R., Schwartz, J., Kiron, D., & O'Connor, C. (1987). Emotion knowledge: Further exploration of a prototype approach. *Journal of Personality and Social Psychology, 52,* 1061–1086. [18]

Sherif, C. W. (1982). Needed concepts in the study of gender identity. *Psychology of Women Quarterly, 6,* 375–398. [30]

Sherif, C. W., Sherif, M., & Nebergall, R. E. (1965). *Attitude and attitude change: The social judgment-involvement approach.* Philadelphia: Saunders. [6], [36]

Sherif, M. (1935). A study on some social factors in perception. *Archives of Psychology, 27,* No. 187, 1–60. [RI-34]

Sherif, M. (1935). An experimental study of stereotypes. *Journal of Abnormal and Social Psychology, 29,* 371–375. [4]

Sherif, M. (1936). *The psychology of group norms.* New York: Harper. [38]

Sherif, M., & Hovland, C. I. (1961). *Social judgment.* New Haven: Yale University Press. [36]

Sherman, M. (1932). Theories and measurement of attitudes. *Child Development, 3,* 15–28. [4]

Sherman, S. J., Skov, R. B., Herritz, E. F., & Stock, C. B. (1981). The effects of explaining hypothetical future events: From possibility to probability to actuality and beyond. *Journal of Experimental Social Psychology, 17,* 142–158. [9]

Shiffrin, R. M., & Schneider, W. (1977). Controlled and automatic human information processing: II. Perceptual learning, automatic attending, and a general theory. *Psychological Review, 84,* 127–190. [12]

Sigall, H., & Page, R. (1971). Current stereotypes: A little fading, a little faking. *Journal of Personality and Social Psychology, 18,* 247–255. [26]

Signorielli, N. (1979, April). *Television's contribution to sex-role socialization.* Paper presented at the seventh annual Telecommunications Policy Research Conference, Skytop, PA. [23]

Silverman, L. H., & Weinberger, J. (1985). Mommy and I are one. *American Psychologist, 40,* 1296–1308. [9]

Singer, J. E. (1961). *The effects of epinephrine, chlorpromazine, and dibenzyline upon the fright responses of rats under stress and non-stress conditions.* Unpublished doctoral dissertation, University of Minnesota. [14]

Singer, J. E., Brush, C. A., & Lublin, S. C. (1965). Some aspects of deindividuation, identification, and conformity. *Journal of Experimental Social Psychology, 1,* 356–378. [37], [RI-37]

Singer, J. L., & Salovey, P. (1985). *Organized knowledge structures and personality: Schemas, self-schemas, prototypes, and scripts.* Presented at Program on Conscious and Unconscious Mental Processes of the John O. and Katherine A. MacArthur Foundation, Center for the Advanced Study of Behavioral Science, Stanford, CA. [9]

Singer, J. L., & Singer, D. G. (1983). Psychologists look at television: Cognitive, developmental, personality, and social policy implications. *American Psychologist, 38,* 826–834. [23]

Sinoway, C. G., Raupp, C. D., & Newman, J. (1985, Aug.). *Binge eating and bulimia: Comparing incidence and characteristics across universities.* Paper presented at the meeting of the 93rd Annual Convention of the American Psychological Association, Los Angeles, CA. [38]

Sjolstrom, L. (1978). The contribution of fat cells to the determination of body weight. In G. A. Bray (Ed.), *Recent advances in obesity research* (Vol. 2). London: Newman. [38]

Skinner, B. F. (1953). *Science and human behavior.* New York: Macmillan. [20]

Skolnick, A. (1978). *The intimate environment: Exploring marriage and the family* (2nd ed.). Boston: Little, Brown. [18]

Skrypnek, B. J., & Snyder, M. (1982). On the self-perpetuating nature of stereotypes about women and men. *Journal of Experimental Social Psychology, 18,* 277–291. [30]

Slavin, R. E. (1985). Cooperative learning: Applying contact theory in desegregated schools. *Journal of Social Issues, 41,* 45–62. [RI-26]

Slavin, R. E. (1986). Cooperative learning: Engineering social psychology in the classroom. In R. S. Feldman (Ed.), *The social psychology of education: Current research and theory* (pp. 153–171). New York: Cambridge University Press. [RI-26]

Sliosberg, S. (1934). A contribution to the dynamics of substitution in serious and play situations. *Psychologische Forschung, 19,* 122–181. [3]

Smith, A. (1960). The attribution of similarity: The influence of success and failure. *Journal of Abnormal and Social Psychology, 61,* 419–423. [11]

Smith, E. R., & Miller, F. D. (1979). Salience and the cognitive mediation of attribution. *Journal of Personality and Social Psychology, 37,* 2240–2252. [12]

Smith, J. (1930). *Social psychology.* Boston: Badger. [4]

Smith, L. (1949). *Killers of the dream.* New York: Norton. [25].

Smith-Hanen, S. (1977). Effects of nonverbal behaviors on judged levels of counselor warmth and empathy. *Journal of Counseling Psychology, 24,* 87–91. [33]

Snow, C. P. (1961, Feb.). Either-or. *Progressive, 24.* [35]

Snyder, M., & Swann, W. B., Jr. (1978). Hypothesis-testing processes in social interaction. *Journal of Personality and Social Psychology, 36,* 1202–1212. [30]

Snyder, M., Tanke, E. D., & Berscheid, E. (1977). Social perception and interpersonal behavior: On the self-fulfilling nature of social stereotypes. *Journal of Personality and Social Psychology, 35,* 655–666. [30]

Snyder, M. L. (1981). Seek and ye shall find: Testing hypotheses about other people. In E. T. Higgins, C. P. Herman, & M. P. Zanna (Eds.), *Social cognition: The Ontario symposium* (Vol. I, pp. 277–303). Hillsdale, NJ: Erlbaum. [12]

Snyder, M. L. (1982). When believing means doing: Creating links between attitudes and behavior. In M. Zanna, E. T. Higgins, & C. P. Herman (Eds.), *The Ontario symposium, Consistency in social behavior* (Vol. II, pp. 105–130). Hillsdale, NJ: Erlbaum. [9]

Snyder, M. L., & Ebbeson, E. (1972). Dissonance awareness: A test of dissonance theory versus self-perception theory. *Journal of Experimental Social Psychology, 8,* 502–517. [6]

Snyder, M. L., & Gangestad, S. (1985). On the nature of self-monitoring: Matters of assessment, matters of validity. *Journal of Personality and Social Psychology, 51,* 125–139. [RI-8]

Snyder, M. L., Stephan, W. G., & Rosenfield, D. (1976). Egoism and attribution. *Journal of Personality and Social Psychology, 33,* 435–441. [17]

Snyder, M. L., & Swann, W. (1978). Behavioral confirmation in social interaction: From social perception to social psychology. *Journal of Experimental Social Psychology, 14,* 148–162. [27]

Sohn, D. (1982). Sex differences in achievement self attributions: An effect-size analysis. *Sex Roles, 8,* 345–357. [30]

Sohngen, M. (1977). The experiences of old age as depicted in contemporary novels. *Gerontologist, 17,* 70–78. [27]

Sohngen, M., & Smith, R. J. (1978). Images of old age in poetry. *Gerontologist, 18,* 181–186. [27]

Sokal, R. R., & Sneath, P. H. A. (1963). *Principles of numerical taxonomy.* San Francisco: W. H. Freeman. [15]

Solomon, R. C. (1976). *The passions.* Garden City, NY: Doubleday Anchor. [15]

Solomon, R. C. (1981). *Love: Emotion, myth and metaphor.* Garden City, NY: Anchor Press/Doubleday. [18]

Sommer, R. (1969). *Personal space.* Englewood Cliffs, N. J.: Prentice-Hall. [8]

Sorrentino, R. M., & Short, J. A. C. (1986). Uncertainty orientation, motivation, and cognition. In R. M. Sorrentino & E. T. Higgins (Eds.), *Handbook of motivation and cognition: Foundations of social behavior* (pp. 379–403). New York: Guilford. [9]

Spence, J. T., Deaux, K., & Helmreich, R. L. (1985). Sex roles in contemporary American society. In G. Lindzey & E. Aronson (Eds.), *Handbook of social psychology* (3rd ed.). Reading, MA: Addison-Wesley. [30]

Spence, J. T., & Helmreich, R. L. (1978). *Masculinity & femininity: Their psychological dimensions, correlates, and antecedents.* Austin: University of Texas Press. [30]

Spence, J. T., & Helmreich, R. L. (1980). Masculine instrumentality and feminine expressiveness: Their relationships with sex role attitudes and behaviors. *Psychology of Women Quarterly, 5,* 147–163. [30]

Spence, J. T., Helmreich, R. L., & Stapp, J. (1974). The Personal Attributes Questionnaire: A measure of sex role stereotypes and masculinity-femininity. *JSAS Catalogue of Selected Documents in Psychology, 4, 43.* (Ms. No. 617). [30]

Spence, J. T., Helmreich, R. L., & Stapp, J. (1975). Ratings of self and peers on sex role attributes and their relation to self esteem and conceptions of masculinity and femininity. *Journal of Personality and Social Psychology, 32,* 29–39. [30]

Spencer, H. (1862). *First principles.* (Reprinted from 5th London ed.). New York: Burt. [4]

Spiegel, P., & Machotka, P. (1974). *Messages of the body.* New York: The Free Press. [33]

Spiro, M. E. (1965). Religious systems as culturally conditioned defense mechanisms. In M. E. Spiro (Ed.), *Context and meaning in cultural anthropology.* New York: Free Press. [15]

Squire, S. (1983). *The slender balance.* New York: Pinnacle. [38]

Srikameswaran, S., Leichner, P., & Harper, D. (1984). Sex role ideology among women with anorexia nervosa and bulimia. *International Journal of Eating Disorders, 3,* 39–43. [38]

Srull, T. K., & Wyer, R. S. (1979). The role of category accessibility in the interpretation of information about persons: Some determinants and implications. *Journal of Personality and Social Psychology, 37,* 1660–1672. [12]

Staff. (1968). Police discretion and the judgment that a crime has been committed: Rape in Philadelphia. *University of Pennsylvania Law Review, 117,* 318. [29]

Staff. (1980). The rape corroboration requirement: Repeal not reform. *Yale Law Journal, 81,* 1366. [29]

Staff. (1982). The corroboration rule and crimes accompanying a rape. *University of Pennsylvania Law Review, 118,* 461. [29]

Steadman, M. (1969). How sexy illustrations affect brand recall. *Journal of Advertising Research, 9,* 15–19. [36]

Steck, R., Levitan, D., McLane, D., & Kelley, H. H. (1982). Care, need, and conceptions of love. *Journal of Personality and Social Psychology, 43,* 481–491. [18]

Steckelings, W. (1929). *Die Schuldfrage im eigenen Urteil des Rechtbrechers.* Paderborn: Schöningh. [4]

Stein, D. D., Hardyck, J. A., & Smith, M. B. (1965). Race and belief: An open and shut case. *Journal of Personality and Social Psychology, 1,* 281–299. [26]

Steiner, I. (1972). *Group process and productivity.* New York: Academic Press. [39]

Stephan, W. G. (1985). Intergroup relations. In G. Lindzey & E. Aronson (Eds.), *Handbook of social psychology* (pp. 599–658) (3rd ed.). New York: Random House. [26]

Sternberg, R. J. (1986). A triangular theory of love. *Psychological Review, 93,* 119–135. [18], [RI-18]

Sternberg, R. J., & Barnes, M. (Eds.) . (1988). *The psychology of love*. New Haven, CT: Yale University Press. [RI-18]

Sternthal, B., & Craig, C. S. (1974). Fear appeals: Revisited and revised. *Journal of Consumer Research, 1*, 22–34. [36]

Stoddard, G. D., & Wellman, B. L. (1934). *Child psychology*. New York: Macmillan. [3]

Stone, C. L. (1933). The personality factor in vocational guidance. *Journal of Abnormal and Social Psychology, 28*, 274. [4]

Stone, G. (1979). Compliance and the role of the expert. *Journal of Social Issues, 35*(1), 34–59. [33]

Strangler, R. S., & Printz, A. M. (1980). DSM-III: Psychiatric diagnosis in a university population. *American Journal of Psychiatry, 137*, 937–940. [38]

Strauss, D. (1963). The relationship between perception of the environment and the retrenchment syndrome in a geriatric population. *Dissertation Abstracts, 24*, 1975–1976. [27]

Strauss, M. B. (Ed.) . (1968). *Familiar medical quotations*. Boston: Little-Brown. [33]

Striegel-Moore, R. H., Silberstein, L., & Rodin, J. (1986). Toward an understanding of risk factors for bulimia. *American Psychologist, 41*, 246–263. [38]

Strober, M., Morell, W., Burroughs, J., Salkin, B., & Jacobs, C. (1985). A controlled family study of anorexia nervosa. *Journal of Psychiatric Research, 19*, 239–246. [38]

Strong, E. K., Jr. (1927). Vocational interest test. *Educational Records, 8*, 107–121. [4]

Stryker, S. (1980). *Symbolic interactionalism*. Menlo Park, CA: Benjamin/Cummings. [9]

Stryker, S. (1986). Identity theory: Developments and extensions. In K. Yardley & T. Honess (Eds.), *Self and identity*. New York: Wiley. [9]

Sullivan, H. S. (1953). *The interpersonal theory of psychiatry*. New York: Norton. [9], [RI-9]

Suls, J. (Ed.) (1982). *Psychological perspectives of the self* (Vol. 1). Hillsdale, NJ: Erlbaum. [9]

Suls, J., & Greenwald, A. G. (Eds.) (1983). *Psychological perspectives on the self* (Vol. 2). Hillsdale, NJ: Erlbaum. [9]

Suls, J., & Miller, R. L. K. (Eds.) (1977). *Social comparison processes*. Washington, DC: Hemisphere. [9]

Sumner, W. G. (1906). *Folkways*. Boston: Ginn. [28]

Swann, W. B. Jr., & Ely, R. J. (1984). A battle of wills: Self-verification versus behavioral confirmation. *Journal of Experimental Social Psychology, 46*, 1287–1302. [9]

Swann, W. B., & Pittman, T. S. (1975). Salience of initial ratings and attitude change in the "forbidden toy" paradigm. *Personality and Social Psychology Bulletin, 1*, 493–496. [6]

Swensen, C. H., Jr. (1972). The behaviors of love. In A. Otto (Ed.), *Love today* (pp. 86–101). New York: Association Press. [18]

Symonds, P. M. (1927). What is an attitude? *Psychological Bulletin, 24*, 200. [4]

Symonds, P. M. (1928). *The nature of conduct*. New York: Macmillan. [4]

Symonds, P. M. (1931). *Diagnosing personality and conduct*. New York: Century. [4]

Szasz, T. S. (1968). *Law, liberty and psychiatry*. New York: Collier Books. [15]

Tagiuri, R. (1958). Introduction. In R. Tagiuri & L. Petrullo (Eds.), *Person perception and interpersonal behavior*. Stanford, CA: Stanford University Press. [12]

Tajfel, H. (1974). Social identity and intergroup behavior. *Social Science Information, 13*, 65–93. [17]

Tajfel, H. (1978). The psychological structure of intergroup relations. In H. Tajfel (Ed.), *Differentiation between social groups*. New York: Academic Press. [17]

Tajfel, H., & Turner, J. C. (1979). An integrative theory of intergroup conflict. In W. G. Austin & S. Worshel (Eds.), *The social psychology of intergroup relations* (pp. 33–47). Monterey, CA: Brooks/Cole. [26]

Tan, A. S. (1979). TV beauty ads and role expectations of adolescent female viewers. *Journalism Quarterly, 56*(2), 283–288. [23]

Tan, A. S. (1982). Television use and social stereotypes. *Journalism Quarterly, 59*(1), 119–122.[23]

Tannenbaum, F. (1938). *Crime and the community*. Boston: Ginn. [32]

Tatsuoka, M. M. (1971). *Multivariate analysis*. New York: Wiley. [32]

Taylor, D. G., Sheatsley, P. B., & Greeley, A. M. (1978). Attitudes toward racial integration. *Scientific American, 238*, 42–49. [26]

Taylor, M. C., & Hall, J. A. (1982). Psychological androgyny: Theories, methods, and conclusions. *Psychological Bulletin, 92*, 347–366. [30]

Taylor, S. E., & Crocker, J. (1981). Schematic bases of social information processing. In E. T. Higgins,

C. P. Herman, & M. P. Zanna (Eds.), *Social cognition: The Ontario Symposium* (Vol. 1, pp. 89–133). Hillsdale, NJ: Erlbaum. [18]

Taylor, S. E., & Fiske, S. (1978). Salience, attention, and attribution: Top-of-the-head phenomena. In L. Berkowitz (Ed.), *Advances in experimental social psychology* (Vol. 11, pp. 249–288). New York: Academic Press. [12]

Taylor, S. E., Wood, J. V., & Lichtman, R. R. (1983). It could be worse: Selective evaluation as a response to victimization. *Journal of Social Issues, 39,* 19–40. [9]

Tedeschi, J. T., & Norman, N. (1985). Social power, self-presentation, and the self. In B. R. Schlenker (Ed.), *The self and social life* (pp. 293–323). New York: McGraw-Hill. [9]

Terman, L. M. (1919). *The intelligence of school children.* Boston: Houghton Mifflin. [3]

Tesser, A. (1986). Some effects of self-evaluation maintenance on cognition and action. In R. M. Sorrentino & E. T. Higgins (Eds.), *Handbook of motivation and cognition: Foundations of social behavior* (pp. 435–464). New York: Guilford. [9]

Tesser, A., & Campbell, J. (1984). Friendship choice and performance: Self-evaluation maintenance in children. *Journal of Personality and Social Psychology, 46,* 561–574. [9]

Thibault, J. W., & Kelley, H. H. (1959). *The social psychology of groups.* New York: Wiley. [18]

Thoits, P. A. (1983). Multiple identities and psychological well-being: A reformulation and test of the social isolation hypothesis. *American Sociological Review, 48,* 174–187. [9]

Thomas, W. I. (1923). *The unadjusted girl.* Boston: Little, Brown. [4]

Thomas, W. I., & Znaniecki, F. (1918). *The Polish peasant in Europe and America* (Vol. 1). Boston: Badger. [4]

Thomsen, A. (1941). Psychological projection and the election: A simple class experiment. *Journal of Psychology, 11,* 115–117. [11]

Thorton, B., Robbin, M. A., & Johnson, J. A. (1981). Social perception of the rape victim's culpability: The influence of respondent's personal environmental causal attributional tendencies. *Human Relations, 34,* 233. [29]

Thurstone, L. L. (1927–1928). Attitudes can be measured. *American Journal of Sociology, 33,* 529–554. [4]

Thurstone, L. L. (1928). An experimental study of nationality preferences. *Journal of Genetic Psychology, 1,* 405–425. [4]

Thurstone, L. L. (1929). Theory of attitude measurement. *Psychological Review, 36,* 222–241. [4]

Thurstone, L. L. (1931). The measurement of attitude. *Journal of Abnormal and Social Psychology, 26,* 249–269. [5]

Thurstone, L. L. (1932). The measurement of social attitudes. *Journal of Abnormal and Social Psychology, 26,* 249–269. [4]

Thurstone, L. L., & Chave, E. J. (1929). *The measurement of attitudes.* Chicago: University of Chicago Press. [4]

Thurstone, L. L., Chave, E. J., & Else, S. B. (1930). *Various scales for the measurement of attitudes.* Chicago: University of Chicago Press. [4]

Tinsley, H. E. A., & Weiss, D. J. (1975). Interrater reliability and agreement of subjective judgment. *Journal of Counseling Psychology, 22,* 358–376. [32]

Titchener, E. B. (1909). *Experimental psychology of the thought processes.* New York: Macmillan. [4]

Titchener, E. B. (1916). *A textbook of psychology* (new ed.). New York: Macmillan. [4]

Tittle, C. R., & Hill, R. J. (1967a). Attitude measurement and the prediction of behavior: An evaluation of conditions and measurement techniques. *Sociometry, 30,* 199–213. [5]

Tittle, C. R., & Hill, R. J. (1967b). The accuracy of self-reported data and prediction of political activity. *Public Opinion Quarterly, 31,* 103–106. [5]

Tolman, E. C. (1935). Psychology versus immediate experience. *Philosophical Science, 2,* 356–380. [3]

Tomarken, A. J., & Kirschenbaum, D. S. (1982). Self-regulatory failure: Accentuate the positive? *Journal of Personality and Social Psychology, 43,* 584–597. [9]

Tomkins, S. S. (1970). Affect as the primary motivational system. In M. B. Arnold (Ed.), *Feelings and emotions: The Loyola symposium.* New York: Academic Press. [15]

Travers, R. M. W. (1941). A study in judging the opinions of groups. *Archives of Psychology,* No. 266. [11]

Triandis, H. C., Kilty, K., Shanmugan, A. V., Tanaka, Y., & Vassiliou, V. (1972). Cognitive structures and the analysis of values. In H. C. Triandis (Ed.), *The analysis of subjective culture* (pp. 181–261). New York: Wiley. [18]

Triplett, N. (1898). The dynamogenic factors in pacemaking and competition. *American Journal of Psychology, 9,* 507–533. [39]

Trope, Y. (1983). Self-assessment in achievement behavior. In J. Suls & A. G. Greenwald (Eds.). *Psychological perspectives on the self* (Vol. 2, pp. 93–121). Hillsdale, NJ: Erlbaum. [9]

Trope, Y. (1986). Self-enhancement and self-assessment in achievement behavior. In R. M. Sorrentino & E. T. Higgins (Eds.), *Handbook of motivation and cognition: Foundations of social behavior* (pp. 350–378). New York: Guilford. [9]

Troutman, C. M., & Shanteau, J. (1976). Do consumers evaluate products by adding or averaging attribute information. *Journal of Consumer Research, 3,* 101–106. [36]

Truax, C. B., & Carkhuff, R. R. (1967). *Toward effective counseling and psychotherapy.* Chicago: Aldine. [33]

Tulving, E. (1972). Episodic and semantic memory. In E. Tulving & W. Donaldson (Eds.), *Organization of memory* (pp. 381–403). New York: Academic Press. [12]

Tulving, E., & Osler, S. (1968). Effectiveness of retrieval cues in memory for words. *Journal of Experimental Psychology, 77,* 593–601. [12]

Tulving, E., & Pearlstone, Z. (1966). Availability versus accessibility of information in memory for words. *Journal of Verbal Learning and Verbal Behavior, 5,* 381–391. [12]

Tulving, E., & Thomson, D. M. (1973). Encoding specificity and retrieval processes in episodic memory. *Psychological Review, 80,* 352–373. [12]

Tversky, A., & Kahneman, D. (1973). Availability: A heuristic for judging frequency and probability. *Cognitive Psychology, 5,* 207–232. [27], [32]

U.S. Department of Commerce. (1983a). *1971–1980 climatological data: National summary.* Washington, DC: U.S. Government Printing Office. [21]

U.S. Department of Commerce. (1983b). *1980 census of the population: General population characteristics* (PC80-1-C1). Washington, DC: U.S. Government Printing Office. [21]

U.S. Department of Commerce. (1983c). *1980 census of the population: General social and economic characteristics* (PC80-1-B1). Washington, DC: U.S. Government Printing Office. [21]

U.S. Department of Justice. (1981). *1980 uniform crime reports for the United States.* Washington, DC: U.S. Government Printing Office. [21]

U.S. Department of Justice. (1982). *1981 uniform crime reports for the United States.* Washington, DC: U.S. Government Printing Office. [21]

Uhrbrock, R. S. (1933). Attitudes of 4500 factory workers. *Psychological Bulletin, 30,* 733. [4]

Unger, R. K. (1979). *Female and male: Psychological perspectives.* New York: Harper & Row. [30]

Unger, R. K., Draper, R. C., & Pendergrass, M. L. (1986). Personal epistemology and personal experience. *Journal of Social Issues, 42,* 67–79. [RI-10]

United States Commission on Civil Rights. (1977). *Window dressing on the set: Women and minorities in television.* Washington, DC: U.S. Government Printing Office. [26]

United States Commission on Civil Rights. (1979). *Window dressing on the set: An update.* Washington, DC: U.S. Government Printing Office. [26]

Vaccarino, J. M. (1977). Malpractice: The problem in perspective. *Journal of the American Medical Association, 238,* 861–863. [33]

Vetter, G. B. (1930a). The study of social and political opinion. *Journal of Abnormal and Social Psychology, 25,* 26–39. [4]

Vetter, G. B. (1930b). The measurement of social and political attitudes and the related personality factors. *Journal of Abnormal and Social Psychology, 25,* 149–189. [4]

Vetter, G. B., & Green, M. (1932). Personality and group factors in the making of atheists. *Journal of Abnormal and Social Psychology, 27,* 179–194. [4]

Voelker, P. F. (1921). The function of ideal and attitudes in social education. *Teachers College Contributions in Education, 112,* 126. [4]

Volgy, T., & Schwarz, J. E. (1980). Television entertainment programming and sociopolitical attitudes. *Journalism Quarterly, 57*(1), 150–155. [23]

von Baeyer, C. L., Sherk, D. L., & Zanna, M. P. (1981). Impression management in the job interview: When the female applicant meets the male "chauvinist" interviewer. *Personality and Social Psychology Bulletin, 7,* 45–51. [30]

Wack, J., & Rodin, J. (1978). Nursing homes for the aged: The human consequences of legislation-shaped environments. *Journal of Social Issues, 34*(4), 6–21. [27]

Wallace, J. (1966). An abilities conception of personality: Some implications for personality measurement. *American Psychologist, 21,* 132–138. [15]

Wallen, R. (1941). Individual estimates of group attitudes. *Psychological Bulletin, 38,* 539–540. [11]

Wallen, R. (1943). Individuals' estimates of group opinion. *Journal of Social Psychology, 17,* 269–274. [11]

Wallston, B. S., & O'Leary, V. E. (1981). Sex and gender make a difference: The differential perceptions of women and men. *Review of Personality and Social Psychology, 2,* 9–41. [30]

Walster, E. (1970). The effect of self-esteem on liking for dates of various social desirabilities. *Journal of Experimental Social Psychology, 6,* 248–253. [16]

Walster, E., Aronson, V., Abrahams, D., & Rottman, L. (1966). Importance of physical attractiveness in dating behavior. *Journal of Personality and Social Psychology, 4,* 508–516. [16], [32]

Walster, E., & Walster, G. W. (1969). The matching hypothesis. *Journal of Personality and Social Psychology, 6,* 248–253. [16]

Wang, C. K. A. (1932). Suggested criteria for writing attitude statements. *Journal of Social Psychology, 3,* 367–373. [4]

Waring, E. B., Dwyer, F. M., & Junkin, E. (1939). Guidance: The case of Ronald. *Cornell Bulletin for Homemakers, 418,* 1–112. [3]

Warner, L. G., & DeFleur, M. L. (1969). Attitude as an interactional concept: Social constraint and social distance as intervening variables between attitudes and actions. *American Sociological Review, 34,* 153–169. [5]

Warren, H. C. (1922). *Elements of human psychology.* Boston: Houghton Mifflin. [4]

Warren, H. C. (Ed.). (1934). *Dictionary of psychology.* Boston: Houghton Mifflin. [4]

Warren, H. C., & Carmichael, L. (1930). *Elements of human psychology.* Boston: Houghton Mifflin. [4]

Washburn, M. F. (1916). *Movement and mental imagery.* Boston: Houghton Mifflin. [4]

Watson, J. B. (1924). Hereditary modes of response: Emotion. In *Psychology from the standpoint of a behaviorist* (2nd ed.) (pp. 194–230). Philadelphia: Lippincott. [18]

Weber, M. (1947). *The theory of social and economic organization.* Oxford: Oxford University Press. [35]

Weigel, R. H., & Amsterdam, J. T. (1976). The effect of behavior relevant information on attitude-behavior consistency. *Journal of Social Psychology, 98,* 247–251. [5]

Weigel, R. H., & Jessor, R. (1973). Television and adolescent conventionality: An exploratory study. *Public Opinion Quarterly, 37,* 76–90. [23]

Weigel, R. H., Vernon, D. T. A., & Tognacci, L. N. (1974). The specificity of the attitude as a determinant of attitude-behavior congruence. *Journal of Personality and Social Psychology, 30,* 724–728. [5]

Weigert, A. (1983). Identity: Its emergence within sociological psychology. *Symbolic Interaction, 6,* 183–206. [9]

Weimann, G. (1984). Images of life in America: The impact of American T.V. in Israel. *International Journal of Intercultural Relations, 8,* 185–197. [23]

Weiner, B., Frieze, I., Kukla, A., Reed, L., Rest, S., & Rosenbaum, R. M. (1971). *Perceiving the causes of success and failure.* Morristown, NJ: General Learning Press. [30]

Weinstein, A. G. (1972). Predicting behavior from attitudes. *Public Opinion Quarterly, 36,* 355–360. [5]

Weis, K., & Borges, S. S. (1973). Victimology and rape: The case of the legitimate victim. *Issues in Criminology, 8,* 71–115. [17], [29]

Wellman, B. L. (1932–1933). The effect of preschool attendance upon the IQ. *Journal of Experimental Education, 1,* 48–69. [3]

Werner, A., & Schneider, J. M. (1974). Teaching medical students interactional skills. A research-based course in the doctor-patient relationship. *New England Journal of Medicine, 290,* 1232–1237. [33]

Wheeler, L. (1966). Toward a theory of behavioral contagion. *Psychological Review, 73,* 179–192. [38]

Wicker, A. W. (1969). Attitudes versus action: The relationship of verbal and overt behavioral responses to attitude objects. *Journal of Social Issues, 25,* 41–48. [5], [RI-5]

Wicker, A. W., & Pomazal, R. J. (1971). The relationship between attitudes and behavior as a function of specificity of attitude object and presence of significant others during assessment conditions. *Representative Research in Social Psychology, 2,* 26–31. [5]

Wicklund, R. A. (1986). Orientation to the environment versus preoccupation with human potential. In R. M. Sorrentino & E. T. Higgins (Eds.), *Handbook of motivation and cognition: Foundations of social behavior* (pp. 64–95). New York: Guilford. [9]

Wicklund, R. A., Cooper, J., & Linder, D. E. (1967). Effects of expected effort on attitude change prior to exposure. *Journal of Experimental Social Psychology, 4,* 416–428. [6]

Wicklund, R. A., & Gollwitzer, P. M. (1982). *Symbolic self-completion.* Hillsdale, NJ: Erlbaum. [9]

Willerman, L., Turner, R. G., & Peterson, M. (1976). A comparison of the predictive validity of typical and maximal personality measures. *Journal of Research in Personality, 10,* 482–492. [15]

Williams, J. E. (1964). Connotations of color names among Negroes and Caucasians. *Perceptual and Motor Skills, 18,* 721–731. [26]

Williams, J. E., Tucker, R. D., & Dunham, F. Y. (1971). Changes in the connotations of color names among Negroes and Caucasians. *Journal of Personality and Social Psychology, 19,* 222–228. [26]

Williams, K. (1981, May). *The effects of group cohesiveness on social loafing.* Paper presented at the annual meeting of the Midwestern Psychological Association, Detroit, MI. [39]

Williams, K., Harkins, S., & Latané, B. (1981). Identifiability as a deterrent to social loafing: Two cheering experiments. *Journal of Experimental Social Psychology, 40,* 303–311. [39]

Williams, T. M., Zabrack, M. L., & Joy, L. A. (1983). The portrayal of aggression on North American television. *Journal of Applied Social Psychology, 12,* 360–380. [23]

Williamson, R. C. (1966). *Marriage and family relations* (pp. 268–271). New York: Wiley [16]

Wills, T. A. (1983). Social comparison in coping and help-seeking. In B. M. DePaulo, A. Nadler, & J. D. Fisher (Eds.), *New directions in helping,* Vol. 2, *Help-seeking* (pp. 109–141). New York: Academic Press. [26]

Wilson, R. N., & Bloom, S. W. (1972). Patient-practitioner relationships. In H. E. Freeman, S. Levine, & L. G. Reeder (Eds.), *Handbook of medical sociology* (pp. 315–339). Englewood Cliffs, NJ: Prentice-Hall. [33]

Wilson, T. D., & Linville, P. W. (1982). Improving the academic performance of college freshmen: Attribution therapy revisited. *Journal of Personality and Social Psychology, 42,* 367–376. [RI-17]

Wilson, T. D., & Linville, P. W. (1985). Improving the performance of college freshmen with attributional techniques. *Journal of Experimental Social Psychology, 49,* 283–293. [RI-17]

Wilson, W. J. (1980). *The declining significance of race* (2nd ed.). Chicago: University of Chicago Press. [26]

Winer, B. J. (1971). *Statistical principles in experimental design.* New York: McGraw-Hill. [21], [36]

Wish, M., Deutsch, M., & Kaplan, S. J. (1976). Perceived dimensions of interpersonal relationships. *Journal of Personality and Social Psychology, 33,* 409–420. [18]

Wolf, S., & Wolff, H. G. (1947). *Human gastric function.* New York: Oxford University Press. [14]

Wong, P. T. P., & Weiner, B. (1981). When people ask "why" questions, and the heuristics of attributional search. *Journal of Personality and Social Psychology, 40,* 650–663. [12]

Wood, P. L. (1973). The victim in a forcible rape case: A feminist view. *American Criminal Law Review, 7,* 348. [29]

Woodmansee, J. J., & Cook, S. W. (1967). Dimensions of verbal racial attitudes: Their identification and measurement. *Journal of Personality and Social Psychology, 7,* 240–250. [26]

Woodworth, R. S. (1935). *Dynamic psychology.* New York: Columbia University Press. [4]

Woodworth, R. S., & Schlosberg, H. (1958). *Experimental psychology.* New York: Holt. [14]

Wooley, S., & Wooley, O. W. (1977). *Obesity and women, I: A closer look at the facts.* Paper presented at the Second International Congress on Obesity, Washington, DC. [27]

Worchel, S., Andreoli, V., & Eason, J. (1975). Is the medium the message? A study of the effects of media, communicator, and message characteristics on attitude change. *Journal of Applied Social Psychology, 5,* 157–172. [36]

Worchel, S., & Arnold, S. E. (1974). The effect of combined arousal states on attitude change. *Journal of Experimental Social Psychology, 10,* 549–560. [6]

Word, C. O., Zanna, M. P., & Cooper, J. (1974). The nonverbal mediation of self-fulfilling prophecies in interracial interaction. *Journal of Experimental Social Psychology, 10,* 109–120. [RI-33]

Wright, B. A. (1941). An experimentally created conflict expressed in a projective technique. *Psychological Bulletin, 38,* 718. [3]

Wright, B. A. (1942a). Altruism in children and the perceived conduct of others. *Journal of Abnormal and Social Psychology, 37,* 218–233. [3]

Wright, B. A. (1942b). The development of the ideology of altruism and fairness in children. *Psychological Bulletin, 39,* 485–486. [3]

Wright, P. L. (1973). The cognitive processes mediating acceptance of advertising. *Journal of Marketing Research, 10,* 53–62. [36]

Wright, P. L. (1974). Analysing media effects on adverting responses. *Public Opinion Quarterly, 38,* 192–205. [36]

Wright, P. L. (1980). Message-evoked thoughts: Persuasion research using thought verbalizations. *Journal of Consumer Research, 7,* 151–175. [36]

Wrightsman, L. S. (1960). Effects of waiting with others on changes in level of felt anxiety. *Journal of Abnormal and Social Psychology, 61,* 216–222. [14]

Wurf, E. (1986). *The critical role of self in the coping process.* Unpublished manuscript, University of Michigan. [9]

Wurf, E., & Markus, H. (1983). *Cognitive consequences of the negative self.* Presented at the Annual Meeting of the American Psychological Association, Anaheim, CA. [9]

Wylie, R. C. (1974). *The self concept.* Lincoln: University of Nebraska Press. [9]

Young, K. (Ed.) (1931). *Social attitudes.* New York: Holt. [4]

Zadny, J., & Gerard, H. B. (1974). Attributed intentions and informational selectivity. *Journal of Experimental Social Psychology, 10,* 34–52. [32]

Zaidel, S., & Mehrabian, A. (1969). The ability to communicate and infer positive and negative attitudes facially and vocally. *Journal of Experimental Research in Personality, 3,* 233–241. [8]

Zajonc, R. B. (1965). Social facilitation. *Science, 149,* 269–274. [39], [RI-39]

Zajonc, R. B. (1966). *Social psychology: An experimental approach.* Belmont, CA: Wadsworth. [39]

Zajonc, R. B. (1968). Attitudinal effects of mere exposure. *Journal of Personality and Social Psychology, 9,* 1–27. [26]

Zajonc, R. B. (1980). Compresence. In P. Paulus (Ed.), *Psychology of group influence* (pp. 35–60). Hillsdale, NJ: Erlbaum. [39]

Zanna, M. P., & Cooper, J. (1974). Dissonance and the pill: An attribution approach to studying the arousal properties of dissonance. *Journal of Personality and Social Psychology, 29,* 703–709. [6]

Zanna, M. P., & Cooper, J. (1976). Dissonance and the attribution process. In J. H. Harvey, W. J.

Ickes, & R. F. Kidd (Eds.), *New directions in attribution research.* Hillsdale, NJ: Erlbaum. [6]

Zanna, M. P., Higgins, E. T., & Taves, P. A. (1976). Is dissonance phenomenologically aversive? *Journal of Experimental Social Psychology, 12,* 530–538. [6]

Zanna, M. P., & Kiesler, C. A. (1971). Inferring one's belief from one's behavior as a function of belief relevance and consistency of behavior. *Psychonomical Science, 24,* 283–285. [6]

Zanna, M. P., & Pack, S. J. (1975). On the self-fulfilling nature of apparent sex differences in behavior. *Journal of Experimental Social Psychology, 11,* 583–591. [30], [32]

Zawadski, B. (1948). Limitations of the scapegoat theory of prejudice. *Journal of Abnormal and Social Psychology, 43,* 127–141. [25]

Zeligs, R., & Hendrickson, G. (1933). Racial attitudes of two hundred sixth-grade children. *Sociology and Social Research, 18,* 26–36. [4]

Zellman, G. L., Johnson, P. B., Giarrusso, R., & Goodchilds, J. D. (1979). *Adolescent expectations for dating relationships: Consensus and conflict between the sexes.* Proceedings of the Annual Meeting of the American Psychological Association, New York City. [17]

Zillig, M. (1928). Einstellung und Aussage. *Zeitschrift für Psychologie, 106,* 58–106. [4]

Zillmann, D. (1978). Attribution and misattribution of excitatory reactions. In J. Harvey, W. Ickes, & R. Kidd (Eds.), *New directions in attribution research* (Vol. 2, pp. 335–368). Hillsdale, NJ: Erlbaum. [15], [21]

Zillmann, D. & Bryant, J. (1982). Pornography, sexual callousness, and the trivialization of rape. *Journal of Communication,* Autumn, 10–29. [RI-29]

Zillmann, D. & Bryant, J. (1984). Effects of massive exposure to pornography. In N. M. Malamuth & E. Donnerstein (Eds.), *Pornography and sexual aggression,* New York: Academic Press. [RI-29]

Zimbardo, P. (1960). Involvement and communication discrepancy as determinants of opinion conformity. *Journal of Abnormal and Social Psychology, 60,* 86–94. [36]

Zimbardo, P. G. (1970). The human choice: Individuation, reason, and order versus deindividuation, impulse, and chaos. In W. J. Arnold & D. Levine (Eds.), *Nebraska Symposium on Motivation* (Vol. 18. Lincoln: University of Nebraska Press. [37], [RI-37]

Copyrights and Acknowledgment of Permissions (by reading number)

FUNDING CREDITS

Authors whose works are reprinted in this volume listed the following funding credits in their original manuscripts:

Asch: The present investigation was begun in 1943 when the writer was a Fellow of the John Simon Guggenheim Memorial Foundation.

Averill: Preparation of this chapter was supported, in part, by a grant (MH 22299) from the National Institute of Mental Health.

Bandura, Ross, & Ross: This research was supported by National Institute of Mental Health PHS Grant M-4398.

Berscheid, Dion, Walster (Hatfield), & Walster: This research was supported in part by National Science Foundation Grants GS 1897 and GS 1577, by National Institute of Mental Health Grants MH 16661 and MH 16739, and by the Office of Student Affairs, University of Minnesota.

Crandall: Financial support came from an NIMH training grant in health and social behavior to the University of Michigan, the Michigan Alumni Fund, University of Michigan Continuing Education for Women, a Society for the Psychological Study of Social Issues Grant-in-Aid, and NSF Grant SE85-07342 to Richard Nisbett.

Fehr: This research was supported by a Social Sciences and Humanities Research Council of Canada Doctoral Fellowship (#453-85-0206).

Gaertner & Dovidio: This research was supported in part by the Office of Naval Research, Organizational Effectiveness Research Programs (under contract numbers N00014-70-A-003 and N00014-76-C-0062) and in part by the Colgate University Research Council.

Gerbner, Gross, Morgan, & Signorielli: Portions of this research began in 1967–1968 with a study for the National Commission on the Causes and Prevention of Violence. It continued under the sponsorships of the U.S. Surgeon General's Scientific Advisory Committee on Television and Social Behavior, the National Institute of Mental Health, the White House Office of Telecommunications Policy, the American Medical Association, the U.S. Administration on Aging, and the National Science Foundation.

Latané & Darley: This research was supported by National Science Foundation Grants GS 1238, GS 1239, GS 2292, and GS 2293.

Markus & Wurf: This research was supported by an NSF grant to Hazel Markus (BNS-8408057). The second author was supported by a National Science Foundation Graduate Fellowship.

Milgram: This research was supported by National Science Foundation Grant G-17916.

Petty, Cacioppo, & Schumann: This research was supported by the University of Missouri Research Council.

Schachter & Singer: This research was supported by National Institute of Mental Health PHS Grant M-2584.

Snyder: This research was supported in part by National Institute of Mental Health Training Grant MH-12283 in Social Psychology and in part by a Canada Council Doctoral Fellowship.

Snyder, Tanke, & Berscheid: This research was supported in part by National Science Foundation Grants SOC 75-13872 and GS 35157X.

Winter & Uleman: This research was supported in part by National Institute of Mental Health Grant MH08573 to the first author.

AUTHOR CREDITS

Research in social psychology is often a collaborative effort. The talents of advisors, reviewers, statistical analysts, computer specialists, data gatherers, confederates, and student assistants are critical to the successful completion of a research project. Many of the reading authors recognized individuals for various contributions to their research efforts. We include those named below.

Abbey: Camille B. Wortman, Elizabeth Holland Hough. Lisa Schurer, Rich Mazanak, Glenn Cohen.

Anderson: Morgan Slusher, Lynn Arnoult, David Lane, Constantine Tsedikides, Robert A. Baron, Douglas T. Kendrick.

Bandura, Ross, & Ross: Edith Downey, Patricia Rowe.

Crandall: Eugene Brunstein, Hazel Markus, Andre Modigliani, Richard Nisbett, Monica Biernat, Steve Cardoze, Adam Drewnowski, Martin Gold, Norbert Kerr, Adam Lehman, Judith Rodin, Jonathan Shedler, Lisa Silberstein, David Smith.

Deaux: Alice H. Eagly, Laurie L. Lewis, Brenda Major, Janet T. Spence, Barbara Strudler Wallston.

DiMatteo: Carol Eckmann, Howard Friedman, J. Phillip Loge, Angelo Taranta.

Fazio, Zanna, & Cooper: Peter A. Taves, Michael Ross.

Fehr: Dan Perlman, Jennifer Campbell, Lawrence Ward, Ross Broughton, Patricia Fairey, Karen

Dion, Phil Shaver, Robert Sternberg, John Kihlstrom, Harry Reis.

Gaertner & Dovidio: Kristen Anderson, Jeffrey Mann, Richard Tyler.

Hastorf & Cantril: Virginia Zerega, J. L. McCandless, E.S. Horton, Adelbart Ames, Jr.

Johnson & Downing: Abe Tesser, Sid Rosen, Dick Endsley, Dave Schaffer.

Latané & Darley: Keith Gerritz, Lee Ross.

Markus & Wurf: Diane Crane, Deborah Francis.

Milgram: Alan C. Elms, Jon Wayland.

Petty, Cacioppo, & Schumann: Rob Greene, Nancy Stabler, Trez Bayer, Karen King, Brian Kinkade, Edith Meredith, Tim Nash, Todd Nixon.

Ross, Greene, & House: Michael Fleming.

Schachter & Singer: Jean Carlin, Ruth Hase, Bibb Latané, Leonard Weller.

Snyder: Daryl J. Bem, J. Merrill Carlsmith, Lee D. Ross, Phillip G. Zimbardo, John Grether, Tom Price, Chris Ryan, Anne Coffey, Sheridan Crawford, Julie Steinmetz, Mike Cochran, Kris Keller, Richard Quan, Mike Boyle.

Snyder, Tanke, & Berscheid: Marilyn Steere, Craig Daniles, Dwain Boelter, J. Merrill Carlsmith, Thomas Hummel, E. E. Jones, Mark Lepper, Walter Mischel.

Weigel & Newman: Joan R. Weigal, Stuart W. Cook, Richard Jessor.

Winter & Uleman: John J. Winters, John Bargh, Bert Holland, Frederick D. Miller